OXFORD WORLD'S CLASSICS

HELLENISTIC LIVES

PLUTARCH was born about 45 CE, and lived most of his life in the small town of Chaeronea in central Greece, dying some time after 120. In the first decades of the second century CE, when he did much of his writing, the Roman empire was in its most prosperous and peaceful period. Plutarch wrote a large number of dialogues, treatises, and essays covering diverse subjects, such as the oracle at Delphi, vegetarianism, and the nature of love, which are loosely classified as his *Moralia* or *Moral Essays*. Alongside these essays Plutarch created a collection of forty-six biographies of ancient Greek and Roman statesmen, arranged in pairs ('parallel'), a Roman matching a Greek. These *Parallel Lives* were written when he was at the height of his powers, and are his major and enduring achievement. Drawing upon earlier histories, anecdotes, inscriptions, and his own researches and broad acquaintance, he shaped masterful portraits of the most famous figures of the classical world. The value of the *Parallel Lives* as a historical source, questioned in the nineteenth century, has been reaffirmed by recent scholarship.

ROBIN WATERFIELD is a writer, living in Greece. His previous translations for Oxford World's Classics include Plato's *Republic* and five other editions of Plato's dialogues, Aristotle's *Physics*, Demosthenes' *Selected Speeches*, Herodotus' *Histories*, Polybius' *Histories*, Plutarch's *Greek Lives* and *Roman Lives*, two editions of Euripides' plays, Xenophon's *The Expedition of Cyrus*, and *The First Philosophers: The Presocratics and the Sophists*.

ANDREW ERSKINE is Professor of Ancient History at the University of Edinburgh. He is a specialist in Hellenistic history and Roman imperialism, and the author of a number of books, including *The Hellenistic Stoa: Political Thought and Action* (1990, 2011) and *Roman Imperialism* (2009), and the editor of *A Companion to the Hellenistic World* (2003).

OXFORD WORLD'S CLASSICS

For over 100 years Oxford World's Classics have brought readers closer to the world's great literature. Now with over 700 titles—from the 4,000-year-old myths of Mesopotamia to the twentieth century's greatest novels—the series makes available lesser-known as well as celebrated writing.

The pocket-sized hardbacks of the early years contained introductions by Virginia Woolf, T. S. Eliot, Graham Greene, and other literary figures which enriched the experience of reading. Today the series is recognized for its fine scholarship and reliability in texts that span world literature, drama and poetry, religion, philosophy, and politics. Each edition includes perceptive commentary and essential background information to meet the changing needs of readers.

OXFORD WORLD'S CLASSICS

PLUTARCH

Hellenistic Lives

Translated by

ROBIN WATERFIELD

With Introductions and Notes by

ANDREW ERSKINE

UNIVERSITY PRESS

OXFORD
UNIVERSITY PRESS

Great Clarendon Street, Oxford, OX2 6DP
United Kingdom

Oxford University Press is a department of the University of Oxford. It furthers the University's objective of excellence in research, scholarship, and education by publishing worldwide. Oxford is a registered trade mark of Oxford University Press in the UK and in certain other countries

First published as an Oxford World's Classics paperback 2016
Impression: 9

Published in the United States of America by Oxford University Press
198 Madison Avenue, New York, NY 10016, United States of America

British Library Cataloguing in Publication Data
Data available

Library of Congress Control Number: 2015934066

ISBN 978–0–19–966433–7

Printed and bound in Great Britain by Clays Ltd, Elcograf S.p.A.

PREFACE

THE Greek text used as the basis for this translation is the Teubner edition. All deviations from the Teubner text have been marked in the translation with an obelus, which refers the interested reader to a note in the Textual Notes section at the back of the book. An asterisk in the text means that there is a note on that passage in the Explanatory Notes.

The translation of the Life of Alexander that appears in this book is a somewhat revised version of the one that first appeared in the 1998 Oxford World's Classic *Plutarch: Greek Lives*. The notes from that volume, written by Philip Stadter, have been replaced for this volume with notes by Andrew Erskine.

Writing this book has been an enjoyable work of collaboration. We would also like to thank Shane Wallace for his careful reading of sections of the typescript.

CONTENTS

GENERAL INTRODUCTION

IN 331 BCE Alexander the Great defeated the Persian king at Gaugamela in modern Iraq, deep inside the Persian empire. This was a turning-point in the history of the eastern Mediterranean. Persia had ruled a huge territory, from the Aegean Sea to the edges of India, and its formidable presence in the East had shaped Greek thinking on international relations since the two Persian invasions at the beginning of the fifth century. Now a small kingdom in the north of Greece had toppled it and the Persian empire had become a Macedonian empire.

Alexander's astonishing success was built on the foundations laid by his father, Philip II. In 359 Philip had inherited an unstable and vulnerable kingdom, one ill equipped to deal with the hostile forces that surrounded it, but by the time of his death Macedon had been transformed. Far from being at the mercy of its neighbours, it had become the dominant state on the Greek mainland. The army that Philip had created provided Alexander with his main instrument for the defeat of Persia. Philip himself was already in the early stages of a campaign against Persia at the time of his assassination in 336, but it is likely that what he intended was rather different from the campaign carried out by Alexander. Philip probably had the limited objective of liberating the Greek cities of Asia Minor from Persian rule, a long-standing Greek aspiration. It is impossible to know how ambitious Alexander's initial plans were, but the result is clear: a Macedonian empire that stretched from the Balkans to Afghanistan.

But no united empire under the command of a single Macedonian king lay in the future. In 323 Alexander died, leaving no obvious heir and making no provision for the succession. The result was decades of conflict between Macedonian warlords and the consequent fragmentation of the empire (for a brief review of the wars of the Successors see pp. xviii–xxii below). Out of that conflict emerged three main dynasties: the Ptolemies, whose kingdom was centred on Egypt; the Seleucids, who with Syria and Babylonia under their control held the core of the old Persian empire; and the Antigonids, who occupied the throne of Macedon itself and exerted considerable influence over mainland Greece. A fourth dynasty, the Attalids, whose influence was largely limited to Asia Minor, would establish itself in the late third century.

This, however, was no mere change in the political superstructure of the East. Macedonian supremacy brought new Greek foundations and an immigrant Greek population to inhabit them. Most prominent among these new cities was Alexandria in Egypt, founded by Alexander but developed by the Ptolemies. There were also many others, such as Antioch on the Orontes in Syria or Seleuceia on the Tigris, not far from Babylon. Greek cities were even founded as far east as Bactria, a region which lies mostly in modern Afghanistan. As a result, markers of Greek identity and culture, such as the gymnasium and the theatre, can be seen throughout this huge area. Greek influence too was felt in native cities such as Babylon and Jerusalem, although it should not be imagined that influence only went in one direction.

This vast and complex new world is today known as the Hellenistic world, its name suggestive of the diffusion of Greek culture within it, even though scholars disagree about the nature of this cultural interchange and express concern that the name undervalues the contribution of the native populations. The cities of the old Greek world in many ways carried on as before, but both politically and culturally they were affected by the changes that had taken place elsewhere in the Mediterranean.

Politicians from the old cities of Greece had to take account of the interests and whims of powerful kings, who could be based in Macedon, Thrace, or as far away as Egypt. This is evident in the Lives in this volume. When the Achaean politician Aratus, in the mid-third century, wanted to expel the Macedonian garrisons from the Peloponnese, he turned to the more distant Ptolemy, king of Egypt, who was prepared to give financial support because he too wanted to limit Macedonian power. But, threatened by a reinvigorated Sparta, Aratus did a political about-turn and sought help from Macedon. Sparta, on the other hand, faced with the combined forces of Achaea and Macedon, sought help from Egypt. Thus the rivalry between kingdoms was played out in local political conflicts.

The Stoic school of philosophy offers a good example of the greater degree of connectivity at this time, while also showing the continuing cultural importance of Athens. Named after the Painted Stoa in Athens, where its founder taught, the school offered the

Hellenistic world in microcosm. It was founded by Zeno of Citium, a city in Cyprus (modern Larnaca), while leading figures in the school included men from Asia Minor (Cleanthes of Assos and Chrysippus of Soli), the Black Sea (Sphaerus of Borysthenes), and Babylon (Diogenes). The conflict in the Peloponnese, mentioned in the previous paragraph, also found Stoics involved. Persaeus of Citium, a pupil of Zeno, was not only a member of the Macedonian court—he was also said to have been in charge of the Acrocorinth when Aratus expelled its Macedonian garrison. Sphaerus acted as an adviser to the Spartan king Cleomenes in between stints at the Ptolemaic court in Egypt.

These Hellenistic kingdoms were to hold sway over the eastern Mediterranean and beyond for more than a hundred years, until challenged by the rising power of Rome. The first sign that a new and dynamic military state was emerging in the west came in the 270s, when the Epirote king Pyrrhus crossed to Italy to aid the Greek city of Tarentum and discovered a tougher and more resilient enemy than he had expected. Victories over Carthage in the first two Punic Wars (264–241 and 218–201) demonstrated to all that Rome was the dominant power in the West, and sounded a warning to those in the East. It took only ten years at the beginning of the second century for two major Hellenistic dynasties, the Antigonids and the Seleucids, to be defeated by Roman legions. By the middle of the century the Antigonid dynasty, and with it the kingdom of Macedon, had ceased to exist, defeated once again by Roman arms. The two remaining successor kingdoms, the Seleucids and Ptolemies, struggled on into the first century BCE, the one being extinguished by Pompey in the 60s, the other ending more dramatically with the suicide of Cleopatra in 30 BCE, the year frequently designated by scholars as the end not only of the Ptolemaic dynasty but also of the Hellenistic Age.

Plutarch and the Hellenistic Lives

Plutarch came from the small Boeotian city of Chaeronea, whose fame was otherwise limited to its hosting of two significant battles, the importance of which would not have been lost on him. It was here, in 338, that Philip II of Macedon defeated the allied forces of Athens and Thebes to bring southern Greece under his control, and here again, in the early first century BCE, that Sulla overcame Mithradates, to put an end to any hopes that Greece might free itself of Roman rule. Born in the 40s CE to a prominent local family, Plutarch grew up in a world in which Roman power was taken for granted, some two-and-a-half centuries after Roman legions had first come to Greece. The Roman empire by this time embraced the whole Mediterranean, and even extended northwards through Gaul into Britain. Authority lay with the Roman emperor, who, since Augustus in the late first century BCE, had effectively replaced the aristocratic council of the Senate that had overseen Rome's initial expansion.

Plutarch's life and literary work reflect this dual context, distinctively Greek but with the Roman present never far away. In many ways he acted just as his predecessors among the landowning elite of Chaeronea would have done before the rise of Rome. He studied at nearby Athens, held a priesthood at equally nearby Delphi, supervised building work in Chaeronea itself, visited Alexandria, and took part in embassies.[1] But public life also meant engaging with Rome. In his twenties he went as an ambassador to the Roman provincial governor, and later he would go on public business to Rome itself. While there, he tells us, he spent time giving lectures on philosophy that were attended by some of the leading Romans of the day.[2] Indeed, he numbered among his friends several men of consular rank, including Quintus Sosius Senecio, dedicatee of the *Parallel Lives*, and Lucius Mestrius Florus, thanks to whom he gained Roman citizenship and the Roman name Mestrius Plutarchus. The intersection between the Greek and the Roman is evident in a brief inscription from Delphi late in his life that decorated the base of a statue of the Roman emperor Hadrian. In an official role as representative of the Amphictyonic Council that was honouring Hadrian he is 'Mestrius Plutarchus the priest', a mode of reference that presents him in two guises, both public, the Roman citizen and the priest of the historic Greek oracle of Apollo.[3] Yet in his own extensive literary output he never refers to his Roman citizenship, perhaps because it had no

[1] The best account of Plutarch's life in so far as it can be reconstructed is to be found in Part 1 of C. P. Jones, *Plutarch and Rome* (Oxford, 1971), but for Plutarch in his Roman context, see now also P. A. Stadter, *Plutarch and His Roman Readers* (Oxford, 2014), especially Part 1.

[2] Plutarch, *Precepts of Statecraft* 20 (*Moralia* 816d), *Demosthenes* 2, *On Curiosity* 15 (*Moralia* 522d).

[3] W. Dittenberger, *Sylloge Inscriptionum Graecarum*³, no. 829a.

place there, perhaps because it was so common among the elite that there was no need to mention it. His writings brought him increasing celebrity with both Greeks and Romans, but he remained intensely loyal to his hometown and resisted the temptation to move somewhere more glamorous or with a better library. In his *Demosthenes* (2) he wrote: 'the city where I live is small, and I refuse to desert it in case it becomes any smaller'.

Not only did Plutarch write an enormous amount but, unusually, much of it survives, making the study of Plutarch a major academic industry; rarely does a year pass without a conference on some aspect of his work. Indeed, more survives of Plutarch's literary output than of almost any other non-Christian writer from antiquity, yet, even so, this is only about half of what he wrote, if we are to judge from the Lamprias catalogue, a list of his writings that dates from the third or fourth century CE. Plutarch's range is impressive. Although he is now best known for his *Parallel Lives*, he also wrote on many other subjects, which were subsequently collected under the rather deceptive title *Moral Essays* (*Moralia*).

The *Moral Essays*, in fact, make up the greater part of his work, and cover a wide variety of topics. Taken together they are a testament both to Plutarch's extensive interests and his learning. Much of his writing was informed by his philosophical training, which had made him a committed Platonist, so much so that he and his friends would celebrate the birthdays of Socrates and Plato, conveniently occurring on successive days (*Table Talk* 717b). His serious philosophical writing includes a treatment of Plato's *Timaeus* and a polemic against the Stoics, *On Stoic Self-contradictions*. Then there were the more popular works that addressed subjects such as brotherly love, superstition, and the desire for riches, or offered advice on questions as diverse as the control of anger, how to conduct a marriage, and how to distinguish a flatterer from a friend. There were also essays on religion, such as *On Isis and Osiris* and several works on the Delphic oracle, various collections of sayings (*Laconian Sayings*, *The Sayings of Kings and Commanders*), antiquarian studies (*Roman Questions*, *Greek Questions*), and a trenchant analysis of Herodotus (*On the Malice of Herodotus*). There is also the deeply personal, in the form of a moving letter of consolation to his wife after the death of their two-year-old daughter.

The surviving biographies were for the most part contained in the

Parallel Lives, products of the latter part of Plutarch's life, but he also wrote a largely lost set of the lives of Roman emperors and a few stand-alone lives, of which *Aratus*, printed in the present volume, is one. The *Parallel Lives* is a collection of paired biographies, each set taking the bold step of juxtaposing a Greek with a Roman. The first pair, *Epaminondas* and *Scipio*, is lost, but twenty-two of the remainder survive (taking *Agis and Cleomenes/Tiberius and Gaius Gracchus* as a single pair). The very idea of pairing Greeks and Romans in this way says something about the place of Greeks and their history in the Roman empire, implicitly asserting that Greeks, despite their subordination, are the equals of their masters. Modern translations, driven by the demands of the publishing industry and university history courses, generally split the pairs to create separate collections of Greek and Roman Lives. It is important to remember, however, that Plutarch conceived and wrote each pair as a unity. There was usually a prologue signposting key themes in the Lives that followed, and the pair concluded with a comparison (*synkrisis*), the latter often rather heavy-handed in contrast to the subtlety of the Lives themselves. This means that each Life is shaped around the other. In this volume the Lives have for the most part been separated from their partners, although the introduction to each will say what the Life was paired with and the significance of that pairing. There is one exception: we are printing *Philopoemen* and *Flamininus* as a single unit, complete with Plutarch's concluding comparison.

The Lives are immensely readable, full of anecdotes without being gossipy, and written with style and casual learning. A couple of lines of poetry or a philosophical theory will often be introduced by way of illumination. Thus, for example, in the Life of Demetrius (5) the wars between Alexander's Successors are compared to Empedocles' four-element theory, in which Strife stirs up conflict among the elements, especially those in close proximity to each other. Although their subject matter is the lives of great men, they were not intended simply as biographies, as can be inferred from Plutarch's innovative idea of composing them in pairs.

Plutarch's purpose in writing the *Parallel Lives* was to explore the character of his subjects, especially their moral character. Coupling Lives together allowed Plutarch and his readers to make comparisons between the two men and thus observe similarities and differences. This might involve how they responded to similar events or how they shared certain virtues and vices. Plutarch expands on his concern with character in the introduction to the Life of Alexander:

I am not writing history but biography, and the most outstanding exploits do not always have the property of revealing the goodness or badness of the agent; often, in fact, a casual action, the odd phrase, or a jest reveals character better than battles involving the loss of thousands upon thousands of lives, huge troop movements, and whole cities besieged. And so, just as a painter reproduces his subject's likeness by concentrating on the face and the expression of the eyes, by means of which character is revealed, and pays hardly any attention to the rest of the body, I must be allowed to devote more time to those aspects which indicate a person's mind and to use these to portray the life of each of my subjects, while leaving their major exploits and battles to others.

Plutarch may not have been writing history, but at the same time this was a very particular and selective form of biography, its purpose not the narration of a man's life so much as an exploration of his character. In general Plutarch assumes some knowledge of these historical figures on the part of his reader, so it is the way character emerges from the events rather than a full narrative that is important.

Although the Lives may have a moral purpose, they are not moralizing. In a revealing passage in the introduction to the Lives of Demetrius and Antony, Plutarch explains why he has included two men who were anything but models of virtue:

Just as Ismenias of Thebes would get his students to listen to both good and bad pipe-playing, and used to say '*That's* how to play' and '*That's* how not to play', and just as Antigeneidas was convinced that young people would get more pleasure from listening to pipes well played if they also had experience of the opposite, so I think we shall be more ready to observe and imitate the lives of better men if we have before us accounts of the lives of men of reprehensible wickedness.

Readers, therefore, are encouraged to think for themselves about what constitutes virtue and then to imitate it. Plutarch's audience would doubtless have been fairly varied, but this passage suggests that he envisaged young people as making up an important section of that audience, something suggested also by an earlier example in the same Life of Demetrius. Young Spartans, he relates, used to learn about the dangers of alcohol from watching drunken helots.

The historical figures that are the subjects of the Lives tend to be military men, while those who are purely politicians and statesmen are very much the exception—in the present volume there is only Demosthenes. The transformation to Roman rule is marked by the end of independent Greek military activity. This sense of closure is evident in Plutarch's conclusion to his account of Aratus' seizure of the Acrocorinth from the Macedonians in 243:

> Now, the Romans used to express their admiration of Philopoemen by calling him 'the last of the Greeks', in the sense that no great man was born in Greece after him. In my opinion, however, Aratus' capture of Corinth was the last significant Greek achievement, and it was on a par with the greatest of them not just in its boldness, but in the good fortune that attended it. (*Aratus* 24)

This characterization of Philopoemen as 'the last of the Greeks' also appears in the introduction to his own Life, where he is represented as a figure from Greece's old age. Plutarch thus brings the active history of Greece to an end around this time. In his own day, he observed in his *Precepts of Statecraft* (*Moralia* 805a), warfare, the toppling of tyrannies, and the making of alliances were no longer part of the repertoire of the Greek political leader. Instead, the aspiring politician had to seek glory through the law-courts and embassies to the emperor.

Macedon and its king, Alexander, are central to the present volume, since all the Lives contained in it revolve around them to some extent. It begins, therefore, with Alexander and his conquest of the Persian empire. In the Lives that follow we see first the varying responses of the Greeks to Macedon, in the Lives of the Athenians Demosthenes and Phocion, the one resolutely hostile, the other willing to compromise. The next three Lives tell the stories of some of the warlords who followed: Eumenes, a Greek who sought to win a chunk of Alexander's empire for himself; Demetrius Poliorcetes, whose colourful life included a brief occupancy of the Macedonian throne; and his rival, Pyrrhus of Epirus, who was said to have captured the spirit of Alexander and was the first of the Hellenistic kings to fight a war with Rome. Later third-century Greek resistance to (and accommodation with) Macedon is reflected in the biographies of some prominent Peloponnesians, Aratus of Sicyon, a leading figure in the Achaean League, and Agis and Cleomenes, two revolutionary kings of Sparta. The volume concludes with the emergence of Rome as a significant element in Greek affairs, encapsulated in two Lives, that of the Greek Philopoemen, an Achaean politician, and the Roman Titus Quinctius Flamininus, the general who defeated the Macedonian king Philip V at Cynoscephalae in 198.

These Lives are enormously valuable for the Hellenistic historian, because they supplement the rather meagre narrative accounts that survive. Diodorus Siculus devotes books 18–20 of his world history to the years from Alexander's death to 302, but after that his history only exists in a fragmentary form. This is in-depth treatment by Diodorus' standards, but relatively brief if compared to a historian like Polybius. Justin's epitome of Pompeius Trogus' world history continues into the third century, but it is an epitome, so what it offers is selective and sketchy. Both were writing under Roman rule in the later part of the first century BCE. There is no Herodotus, Thucydides, or even Xenophon to provide a continuous and relatively contemporary narrative of events. This is not to say that no historians covered this period in detail. Important contemporary histories were written by men such as Hieronymus of Cardia, Duris of Samos, and Phylarchus, but their work is all now lost, at least until Polybius of Megalopolis in the mid-second century, whose history of the rise of Rome is partially extant. Generally Plutarch is not thought to have drawn on earlier biographies for his Lives but to have gathered the material himself, and it is from these narrative histories that he would have acquired much of it. All the above are named in the Lives along with many other writers (see the Index of Sources). But Plutarch is writing biography, not history and, as is so often the case among biographers, he tends to adopt the perspective of his subjects. This makes for interesting contrasts when he writes about those who shared in the same events, even opposing each other, for example Demosthenes and Phocion with their differing attitudes to democracy and Macedon, Pyrrhus and Demetrius vying for power in Greece, and Aratus and Cleomenes at odds in the Peloponnese.

Despite Plutarch's usefulness for the Hellenistic historian, it is striking that his Lives do not include any of the major monarchs; there are no Lives of Seleucus I or Ptolemy I, innovative creators of two of the great Hellenistic dynasties, nor of later kings such as Antiochus III, who sought to revitalize the Seleucid empire. Rather than looking to the extended Greek world created by Alexander, Plutarch turns to those who have particular relevance to the Greeks of the old world like himself. They include leading figures of mainland Greek cities, such as Aratus of Sicyon, Philopoemen of Megalopolis, and Agis and Cleomenes of Sparta; Eumenes, the only Greek among the Macedonian Successors; and two kings who had a significant impact on the Greek mainland, Pyrrhus of Epirus and Demetrius Poliorcetes. Indeed, the latter's Life reveals almost as much about Athens as it does about Demetrius, with the result that the combined Lives of Demosthenes, Phocion, and Demetrius offer a valuable picture of early Hellenistic Athens and its relations with the Macedonians. After the wars of the Successors other parts of the Hellenistic world enter the Lives tangentially: Demetrius' dealings with his son-in-law Seleucus (*Demetrius* 31–2), Pyrrhus' stay at the court of Ptolemy I (*Pyrrhus* 4), the curious story of Antiochus I's romance with his father's wife (*Demetrius* 38), or Cleomenes of Sparta's last days in Alexandria (*Agis and Cleomenes* 53–9). All this shows that Plutarch knew well the history of this wider world, but that was not what concerned him in the Lives.

After Alexander

The world after Alexander's death is particularly complex, so it seems appropriate to conclude with a brief review of the wars of the Successors and their impact, in order to set the context for the overlapping Lives that deal with this period. The nature of the evidence means that many dates in the Hellenistic period are uncertain and disputed. Even the decade or so following the death of Alexander has generated especially vigorous scholarly debate, paradoxically because the evidence is better and certainty seems so much more within our reach.[4] The chronology adopted in this volume can be found on pp. xxvi–xxx.

Alexander's death in Babylon presented the Macedonians with major problems. They were in charge of the vast former Persian

[4] The chronology for 323–311 is that put forward by T. Boiy, *Between High and Low. A Chronology of the Early Hellenistic Period* (Frankfurt, 2007) and A. Meeus, 'Diodorus and the Chronology of the Third Diadoch War', *Phoenix* 66 (2012), 74–96, conveniently summarized in J. C. Yardley, P. V. Wheatley, and W. Heckel, *Justin: Epitome of the Philippic History of Pompeius Trogus*, vol. 2: *Books 13–15: The Successors to Alexander the Great* (Oxford, 2011) 8–22. It is not, however, accepted by everyone, see E. Anson, *Alexander's Heirs: The Age of the Successors, 323–281 BC* (Chichester, 2014) 58–9, 116–21, 157–62.

empire, but there was no designated heir, and the only available male blood relatives were an unborn child and an adult half-brother who had some form of mental disability. These two would become pawns in the power-game that followed. The post-Alexander world, however, was soon upset by the deaths of three of its main players, first Craterus and Perdiccas, one in battle against Eumenes, the other at the hands of his own soldiers, then Antipater, the governor of Macedon, who died of natural causes. The remainder of Alexander's officers, lesser-ranking for the most part, moved to divide up powers and territories among themselves, inaugurating years of shifting and treacherous alliances. These one-time comrades now sought to entrench themselves across Alexander's former empire—Cassander in Macedon, Lysimachus in neighbouring Thrace, Antigonus in Asia Minor, Seleucus in Babylon, and Ptolemy in Egypt (on each of these see Biographies of Prominent Figures). Military force was one source of legitimacy, but Alexander himself was another. Even dead, he had clout. Ptolemy stole his body and brought it to Egypt, Eumenes claimed to his soldiers that Alexander had visited him in a dream, while the nominal kings, Alexander's infant son and his half-brother, passed from one regent to another until they reached Macedon. Whatever people's real motives, publicly everything was done in the name of Alexander and his heirs.

To be protector of Alexander's realm held short-term benefit, but in the long term the new world order had no place for Alexander's family, except in so far as its members served to promote the legitimacy of these new rulers. Many aspiring dynasts sought to marry Alexander's female relatives, notably his sister Cleopatra, whose influence is evident in the *Eumenes* (chapters 3 and 5), but the very link with Alexander which made them so desirable was also the reason for killing them. Violent deaths awaited his charismatic mother Olympias, his sisters Cleopatra and Cynane, his half-brother Philip Arrhidaeus, and most importantly his son, Alexander IV.

The main contender for Alexander's empire was a man old enough to be his father, Antigonus Monophthalmus (the One-Eyed), ageing, overweight, and a little sensitive about his single eye, the result of a war wound (sensitive enough to execute a man who made an ill-judged joke on the subject). While Alexander had raced through the Persian empire, Antigonus had safeguarded the conquered territory in Asia Minor and crushed any opposition, putting himself in an ideal position for the struggles of the years to follow. By 315 he was master of an empire so extensive that his rivals overcame any reservations they might have had about each other to form a coalition against what was now seen as a major threat to their own security. Antigonus made peace, but swiftly publicized himself as the true friend of Greek freedom and thereby gave the impression that his rivals were somehow the enemies of freedom. 'Liberating' Athens from Cassander and capturing Cyprus from Ptolemy, Antigonus and his son Demetrius took the radical step of assuming the title of king for themselves, staking their claim to be Alexander's true heirs. Elsewhere Ptolemy, Lysimachus, Seleucus, and Cassander watched this revival of Antigonid power with growing concern. The first step was to claim kingship for themselves.

Antigonus and his son may have presented themselves as the liberators of the Greeks, but they were pragmatic about such things. Seeing that the independent island of Rhodes would be a useful acquisition, Demetrius embarked on a lengthy and notorious siege that earned him little positive result except a lasting sobriquet, 'Poliorcetes' or 'the Besieger'. Despite the failure at Rhodes, Antigonid power was reaching dangerous levels. An unsuccessful assault on Egypt and a rather more successful one on Macedon and Greece signalled their ambition and prompted the coalition of the previous decade to re-form. Faced with this coalition, Demetrius was called back from his military and amorous campaigns in Greece to join his father in Asia. Together, in 301, they faced the coalition at Ipsus, a battle that would determine the shape of the Hellenistic world. Some 150,000 men and almost 500 elephants were said to have taken the field. The octogenarian Antigonus died on the battlefield amidst a downpour of javelins, while Demetrius fled, a king without a kingdom. The empire was rapidly carved up by the victors, and there was a flurry of marriage alliances to reflect this new international situation.

While some may have harboured hopes of reuniting Alexander's empire under their own leadership, Ptolemy Soter (the Saviour) early on recognized that separatism was the way forward. Innovative and far-seeing, he secured the defensible territory of Egypt for himself and created the Hellenistic world's most identifiable and memorable kingdom. He did not ignore overseas adventures, but he did not prioritize them. The victory at Ipsus gave him greater influence outside Egypt, extending his network of naval bases and marriage alliances.

Ipsus left Demetrius without a kingdom but not short of resources and influence—he had troops and treasuries in some of the most secure fortresses in the Mediterranean. Now that he was no longer perceived as a threat, his victors were prepared to make overtures to him; Seleucus, for instance, became his son-in-law. His opportunity came in 297, when Cassander and his intended heir fell ill and died. Demetrius saw his chance and seized Macedon, ridding himself of Cassander's remaining sons with ease, killing one and forcing the other out. But this was a king of Macedon who had left his homeland while still a child and been brought up with his father in Asia. Far from behaving like a traditional Macedonian king, he adopted the manners and dress of the absolutist monarchs of the East, behaviour that did much to alienate his subjects. In 288, when his expansionist plans provoked an alliance between his rival kings, his discontented army revolted, forcing him to abandon Macedon to his enemies. Demetrius had achieved the remarkable feat of losing two kingdoms in little more than twelve years.

Seleucus Nicator (the Conqueror) was a major beneficiary of Ipsus. Prior to that he controlled extensive territory from Babylon as far east as the Indus river, but Ipsus brought him access to the Mediterranean coast and made him a significant player in Mediterranean politics. As so often in his kingdom he staked a claim by founding a city, in this case Antioch, in line with his tendency to name his foundations after himself or members of his family, thus asserting his family's claim to the land—Antiochus was the name of both his father and his son. Seleucus' empire in its developed form was huge, disparate, and multicultural. Seleucus appeared in different guises to different peoples, by and large respecting the traditions of each. Significantly, his wife Apama was an Iranian from Bactria, and thus his son and successor Antiochus brought together the conquered and the conqueror. Late in his life Seleucus also married the daughter of Demetrius, Stratonice, whom, in a move symbolic of the succession, he subsequently transferred to his son.

Being the father-in-law of Seleucus did Demetrius little good. Seleucus concluded that he would be less trouble if kept under house arrest on one of his estates, where Demetrius duly followed his natural inclination and drank himself to death. But Seleucus still treated his fellow Macedonian with respect. His ashes were escorted with great decorum by the Seleucid fleet to be handed over in a golden urn to

Demetrius' son, Antigonus Gonatas, who at that time had charge of various of his father's bases in Greece.

By the late 280s Ptolemy, Seleucus, and Lysimachus, all now well into their seventies, were looking to their own succession. All was going smoothly in Egypt and Syria. Ptolemy had begun sharing power with his son Ptolemy II Philadelphus in 285, and died a natural death in 283; a similar power-sharing agreement was operating in Syria. But Lysimachus' kingdom was thrown into turmoil by his decision to execute his son and presumed heir Agathocles, a decision for which his young wife Arsinoe, daughter of Ptolemy I, is sometimes held responsible. Seleucus, old though he may have been, was still energetic and not one to miss an opportunity. He led a major campaign against Lysimachus, defeating and killing him at Corupedium in 281. With a kingdom that now stretched from Thrace to the Indus, he marched on Macedon. Was he claiming Alexander's empire for himself and his son, or was he an old man wanting to see once more the homeland he left fifty years previously? If he did see it, it was brief. Soon after his victory he was assassinated by Ptolemy Ceraunus (the Thunderbolt), a troublesome son of the recently deceased king of Egypt. Back in Syria Antiochus, already joint ruler with his father, took control of the kingdom with relative ease.

Any hopes Ptolemy the Thunderbolt might have had of claiming the Macedonian throne for himself came to an abrupt end when Celtic tribes took advantage of the instability in Macedon to pour southwards. On the way they seized Ptolemy's head and carried it aloft on the end of a pike. The Celts were rapidly mythologized into monsters that Greece needed to be saved from. It was to be Antigonus Gonatas, very much the opposite of his father Demetrius in character, who would defeat the Celts and use the victory to assert his claim to the Macedonian throne, which would be held by his descendants until Roman intervention brought an independent Macedon to an end a century later.

SELECT BIBLIOGRAPHY

Further reading on specific Lives can be found in the introductions to each Life.

Plutarch: General

Aalders, G. J. D., *Plutarch's Political Thought* (Amsterdam, 1982).

Beck, M., *A Companion to Plutarch* (Chichester, 2014).

Beneker, J., *The Passionate Statesman: Eros and Politics in Plutarch's Lives* (Oxford, 2012).

Duff, T., *Plutarch's Lives: Exploring Virtue and Vice* (Oxford, 1999).

Humble, N., *Plutarch's Lives: Parallelism and Purpose* (Swansea, 2010).

Jones, C. P., *Plutarch and Rome* (Oxford, 1971).

Lamberton, R., *Plutarch* (New Haven, 2002).

Mossman, J. (ed.), *Plutarch and his Intellectual World* (London, 1997).

Nikolaidis, A. G. (ed.), *The Unity of Plutarch's Work: 'Moralia' Themes in the 'Lives', Features of the 'Lives' in the 'Moralia'* (Berlin, 2008).

Pelling, C., *Plutarch and History: Eighteen Studies* (London, 2002).

Podlecki, A., and Duane, S., 'A Survey of Work on Plutarch's Greek Lives, 1951–88', *Aufstieg und Niedergang der römischen Welt*, II.33.6 (1992), 4053–127.

Preston, R., 'Roman Answers, Greek Questions: Plutarch and the Construction of Identity', in S. Goldhill (ed.), *Being Greek Under Rome: Cultural Identity, the Second Sophistic and the Development of Empire* (Cambridge, 2001), 86–122.

Roskam, G., and van der Stockt (eds.), *Virtues for the People: Aspects of Plutarchan Ethics* (Leuven, 2011).

Russell, D. A., *Plutarch* (London, 1973).

Scardigli, B. (ed.), *Essays on Plutarch's Lives* (Oxford, 1995).

Stadter, P. A. (ed.), *Plutarch and the Historical Tradition* (London, 1992).

—— *Plutarch and His Roman Readers* (Oxford, 2014).

Swain, S., *Hellenism and Empire: Language, Classicism and Power in the Greek World* (Oxford, 1996), 135–86.

Swain, S., 'Plutarch, Plato, Athens and Rome', in J. Barnes and M. Griffin (eds.), *Philosophia Togata II: Plato and Aristotle at Rome* (Oxford, 1997), 165–87.

Wardman, A., *Plutarch's Lives* (London, 1974).

Plutarch: Translations

Also in the Oxford World's Classics series:

Russell, D. A., *Plutarch: Selected Essays and Dialogues* (Oxford, 1993).

Waterfield, R., and Stadter, P. A., *Plutarch: Greek Lives* (Oxford, 1998), containing *Lycurgus*, *Solon*, *Themistocles*, *Cimon*, *Pericles*, *Nicias*, *Alcibiades*, *Agesilaus*, and *Alexander*.

Waterfield, R., and Stadter, P. A., *Plutarch: Roman Lives* (Oxford, 1999), containing *Cato the Elder*, *Aemilius Paullus*, *The Gracchi*, *Marius*, *Sulla*, *Pompey*, *Caesar*, and *Antony*.

The complete Greek text of the Lives in their original pairs with facing English translation by B. Perrin is in the Loeb Classical Library, 11 vols. (Cambridge, Mass., 1917–51); similarly the *Moralia*, by various translators, 15 vols. (Cambridge, Mass., 1927–76).

Penguin Classics are in the process of bringing out revised editions of the Lives under the general editorship of C. Pelling:

Scott-Kilvert, I., *Plutarch: The Rise and Fall of Athens* (Harmondsworth, 1973).

—— and Duff, T., *Plutarch: The Age of Alexander* (London, 2011).

—— and Pelling, C., *Plutarch: Rome in Crisis* (London, 2010).

—— Tatum, J., and Pelling, C., *Plutarch: The Rise of Rome* (London, 2013).

Talbert, R., *Plutarch on Sparta* (London, 2005).

Warner, R., and Seager, R., *Plutarch: The Fall of the Roman Republic* (London, 2006).

There is a complete set of the Lives with French translations and commentaries published in the Collection Budé by R. Flacelière *et al.* (Paris, 1957–83).

For other translations of selected *Moralia*:

Hadas, M., *Plutarch: Selected Essays on Love, the Family, and the Good Life* (New York, 1957).

Warner, R., and Russell, D. A., *Plutarch: Moral Essays* (Harmondsworth, 1971).

Waterfield, R., and Kidd, I., *Plutarch: Essays* (Harmondsworth, 1992).

Macedon and the Hellenistic World

Anson, E., *Alexander's Heirs: The Age of the Successors, 323–281 BC* (Oxford, 2014).

Austin, M., *The Hellenistic World from Alexander to the Roman Conquest: A Selection of Ancient Sources in Translation* (2nd edn., Cambridge, 2006).

Bagnall, R., and Derow, P., *The Hellenistic Period: Historical Sources in Translation* (Oxford, 2004).

Bosworth, A. B., *The Legacy of Alexander: Politics, Warfare, and Propaganda under the Successors* (Oxford, 2002).

Bugh, G. (ed.), *The Cambridge Companion to the Hellenistic World* (Cambridge, 2006).

Eckstein, A. *Rome Enters the Greek East: From Anarchy to Hierarchy in the Hellenistic Mediterranean, 230–170 BC* (Chichester, 2008).

Errington, R. M., *A History of the Hellenistic World* (Oxford, 2008).

Erskine, A. (ed.), *A Companion to the Hellenistic World* (Oxford, 2003).

Erskine, A., and Llewellyn-Jones, L., *Creating a Hellenistic World* (Swansea, 2011).

Gruen, E., *The Hellenistic World and the Coming of Rome* (Berkeley, 1984).

Habicht, C., *Athens from Alexander to Antony*, trans. by D. L. Schneider (Cambridge, Mass., 1997).

Hammond, M., and Atkinson, J., *Arrian: Alexander the Great: The Anabasis and the Indica*, Oxford World's Classics (Oxford, 2013).

Hammond, N. G. L., and Walbank, F. W., *A History of Macedonia*, vol. 3: *336–167 BC* (Oxford, 1988).

Hornblower, S., *The Greek World 479–323 BC* (4th edn., London, 2011).

Lane Fox, R. (ed.), *Brill's Companion to Ancient Macedon: Studies in the Archaeology and History of Macedon, 650 BC–300 AD* (Leiden, 2011).

Rhodes, P. J., *A History of the Classical Greek World 478–323 BC* (Oxford, 2006).

Roisman, J., and Worthington, I. (eds.), *A Companion to Ancient Macedonia* (Chichester, 2010).

Shipley, G., *The Greek World after Alexander 323–30 BC* (London, 2000).

Walbank, F. W., *The Hellenistic World* (rev. edn., London, 1993).

Waterfield, R., *Dividing the Spoils: The War for Alexander the Great's Empire* (Oxford, 2011).

—— *Taken at the Flood: The Roman Conquest of Greece* (Oxford, 2014).

CHRONOLOGY

359	Accession of Philip II
356	Birth of Alexander
346	Peace of Philocrates
338	Battle of Chaeronea: Macedon defeats Athens and Thebes
337	Establishment of League of Corinth
336	Philip assassinated; accession of Alexander
335	Destruction of Thebes
334	Battle of the Granicus
333	Battle of Issus
331	Foundation of Alexandria in Egypt
	Battle of Gaugamela
330	Burning of Persepolis
	Death of Darius III of Persia
	Execution of Parmenio and Philotas
329–328	Alexander campaigns in Bactria
327	Alexander marries Rhoxane
	Conspiracy of Pages; death of Callisthenes
326	Alexander reaches Indus; defeat of Porus at the Hydaspes river
325	Alexander returns through the Gedrosian desert
324	Mass wedding at Susa
	Mutiny at Opis
	Death of Hephaestion
323	Death of Alexander at Babylon (June)
	Outbreak of Lamian War
	Birth of Alexander IV
322	Battle of Crannon: Antipater and Craterus defeat rebellious Greeks
	Deaths of Aristotle and Demosthenes
320	Death of Craterus in battle against Eumenes

	Perdiccas invades Egypt; murdered by his own officers
	Conference at Triparadeisus; Antipater made regent
319	Death of Antipater; Polyperchon becomes regent
318	Death of Phocion
317	Demetrius of Phalerum takes power in Athens
	Execution of Philip III Arrhidaeus by Olympias
	Battle of Paraetacene
317/16	(Winter) Battle of Gabene and subsequent death of Eumenes
316	Cassander executes Olympias
	Seleucus flees Babylon and takes refuge with Ptolemy
315	Proclamation of Tyre: Antigonus proclaims freedom of the Greeks
312	Battle of Gaza
311	Seleucus recovers Babylon
	Peace between Ptolemy, Lysimachus, Cassander, and Antigonus
310	Murder of Alexander IV and Rhoxane; the end of Argead dynasty
307	Demetrius Poliorcetes captures Athens from Cassander
306	Demetrius defeats Ptolemy off Salamis and captures Cyprus
	Antigonus and Demetrius take title of 'king'
305–304	Demetrius besieges Rhodes
302	Antigonus and Demetrius establish Hellenic League
301	Battle of Ipsus: defeat and death of Antigonus Monophthalmus
298/7	Death of Cassander
295	Ptolemy recaptures Cyprus
294	Demetrius Poliorcetes becomes king of Macedon
	Seleucus I shares rule with Antiochus I
288 or 287	Overthrow of Demetrius as king of Macedon
287	Macedon split between Pyrrhus and Lysimachus
287 or 286	Revolt of Athens from Demetrius
285	Demetrius captured by Seleucus I
283	Deaths of Ptolemy I Soter and Demetrius Poliorcetes
281	Battle of Corupedium: defeat and death of Lysimachus against Seleucus I

	Ptolemy Ceraunus assassinates Seleucus I and becomes king of Macedon
280–275	Pyrrhus in Italy and Sicily
279–278	Celtic invasions of Macedon and Greece; death of Ptolemy Ceraunus
277	Antigonus II Gonatas becomes king of Macedon
274	Pyrrhus invades Macedonia
272	Pyrrhus killed fighting at Argos
267–261	Chremonidean War
264–241	First Punic War: Rome v. Carthage
251	Aratus overthrows tyranny at Sicyon
245	Aratus becomes General of Achaean League for the first time
*c.*244	Agis IV becomes king in Sparta
243	Aratus captures Acrocorinth; Corinth joins Achaean League
241	Execution of Agis in Sparta
240/39	Death of Antigonus Gonatas; Demetrius II becomes king of Macedon
235	Megalopolis joins Achaean League
	Accession of Cleomenes III at Sparta
229	Athens gains independence from Macedon
	Antigonus III Doson succeeds Demetrius II
	Rome fights First Illyrian War
227	Cleomenes III's revolution at Sparta
224	Achaeans make agreement with Antigonus Doson
223	Accession of Antiochus III after assassination of Seleucus III
222	Battle of Sellasia: Cleomenes defeated by Macedonians; flees to Egypt
221	Ptolemy IV Philopator succeeds Ptolemy III Euergetes
	Philip V succeeds Antigonus Doson
220–217	Social War: Philip V and Achaeans against the Aetolians
220/19	Death of Cleomenes III in Egypt
218–202	Second Punic War: Rome against Carthage
217	Battle of Raphia: Antiochus III defeated by Ptolemy IV
	Battle of Lake Trasimene: Hannibal defeats Rome

	Peace of Naupactus
216	Battle of Cannae: Hannibal defeats Rome
215	Treaty between Philip V and Hannibal
214–205	First Macedonian War
213	Death of Aratus
211	Treaty between Aetolia and Rome
207	Nabis becomes king of Sparta
206	Aetolians make peace with Philip V
205	Peace of Phoenice
204	Ptolemy V Epiphanes succeeds Ptolemy IV
202	Battle of Zama: Rome defeats Carthage in North Africa
200–197	Second Macedonian War: Rome against Philip V
198	Consulship of T. Quinctius Flamininus
197	Battle of Cynoscephalae: Flamininus defeats Philip V
	Eumenes II succeeds Attalus I at Pergamum
196	Roman declaration of the freedom of the Greeks at the Isthmian Games
195	Roman war against Nabis
194	Roman army withdraws from Greece
192	Assassination of Nabis; Sparta brought into Achaean League
192–188	War between Rome and Antiochus III
189	Aetolians submit to Rome
	Battle of Magnesia: Romans defeat Antiochus
188	Peace of Apamea
183	Revolt of Messene from Achaean League
182	Death of Philopoemen
180	Philip V executes Demetrius his son
179	Perseus succeeds Philip V in Macedon
174	Death of T. Quinctius Flamininus
171–168	Third Macedonian War: Rome against Perseus
168	Battle of Pydna: Romans defeat Perseus
167	End of Macedonian kingdom; replaced by four republics
146	War between Achaean League and Rome; destruction of Corinth

	Roman destruction of Carthage
133	Attalus III of Pergamum dies, bequeathing his kingdom to Rome
64–62	Pompey reorganizes the East; end of Seleucid kingdom
31	Battle of Actium: Octavian defeats Antony and Cleopatra
30	Deaths of Antony and Cleopatra; end of kingdom of Ptolemies

MAPS

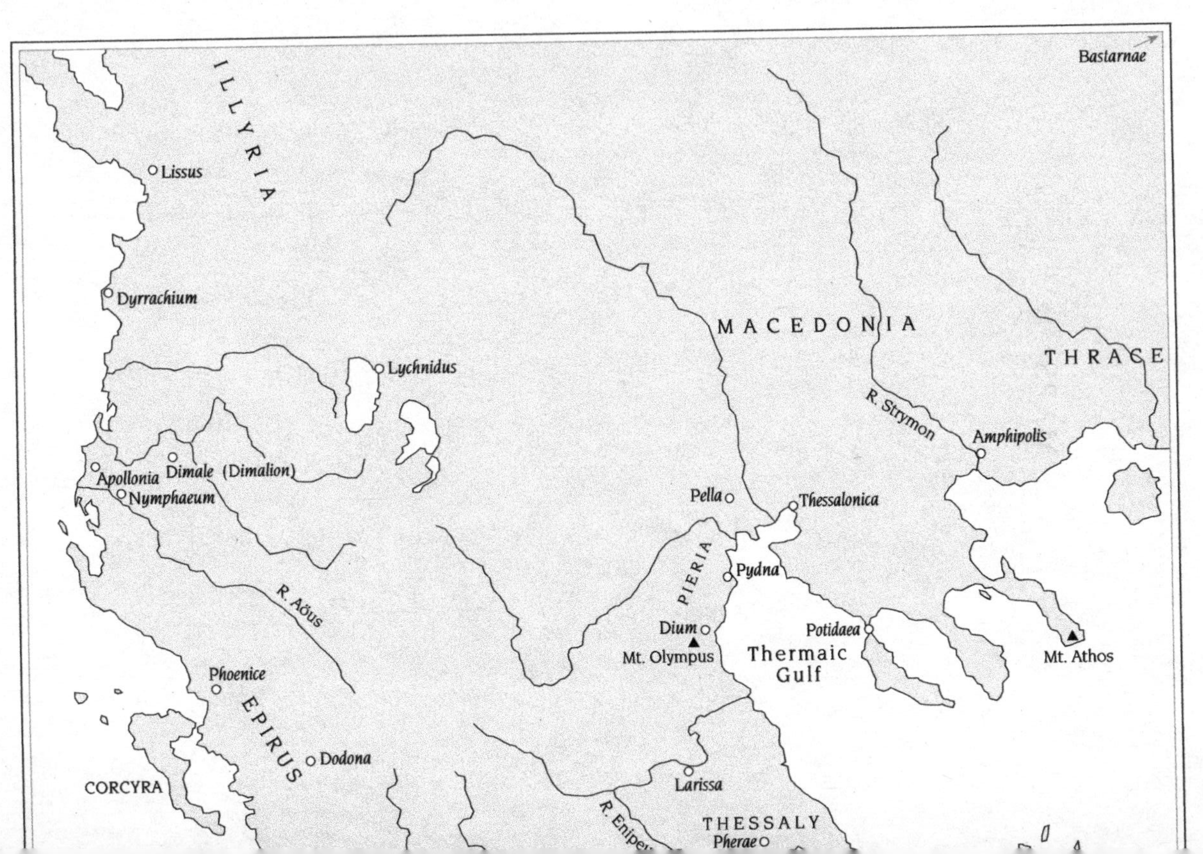

Bastarnae
ILLYRIA
Lissus
Dyrrachium
MACEDONIA
THRACE
Lychnidus
R. Strymon
Amphipolis
Apollonia
Dimale (Dimalion)
Nymphaeum
Pella
Thessalonica
PIERIA
Pydna
R. Aõus
Dium
Mt. Olympus
Potidaea
Thermaic Gulf
Mt. Athos
Phoenice
EPIRUS
Dodona
CORCYRA
Larissa
THESSALY
Pherae

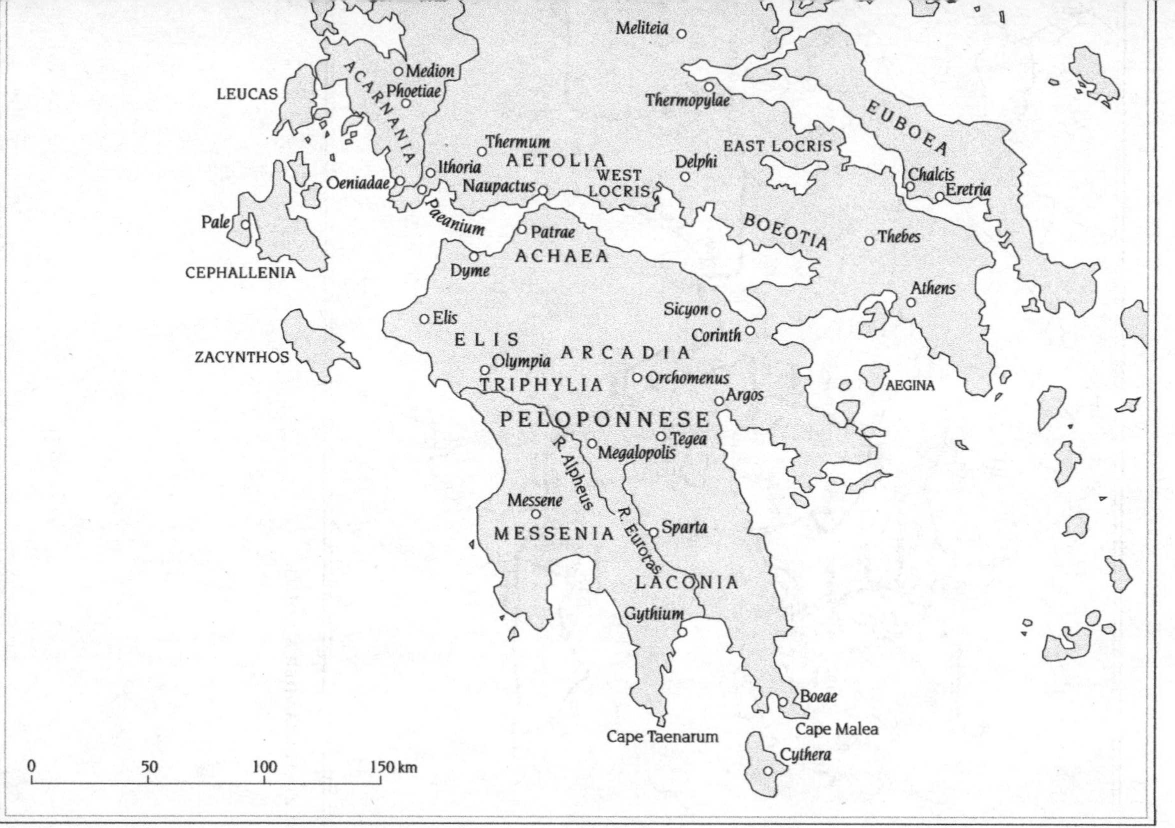

Meliteia
Medion
Phoetiae
ACARNANIA
LEUCAS
Thermopylae
EUBOEA
Thermum
AETOLIA
Ithoria
EAST LOCRIS
Delphi
WEST LOCRIS
Oeniadae
Naupactus
Chalcis
Eretria
Pale
Paeanium
Patrae
BOEOTIA
Thebes
ACHAEA
CEPHALLENIA
Dyme
Athens
Sicyon
Elis
Corinth
ELIS
ARCADIA
ZACYNTHOS
Olympia
Orchomenus
TRIPHYLIA
AEGINA
Argos
PELOPONNESE
Tegea
Megalopolis
R. Alpheus
Messene
R. Eurotas
Sparta
MESSENIA
LACONIA
Gythium
Boeae
Cape Taenarum
Cape Malea
Cythera
0
50
100
150 km

MAP I. GREECE

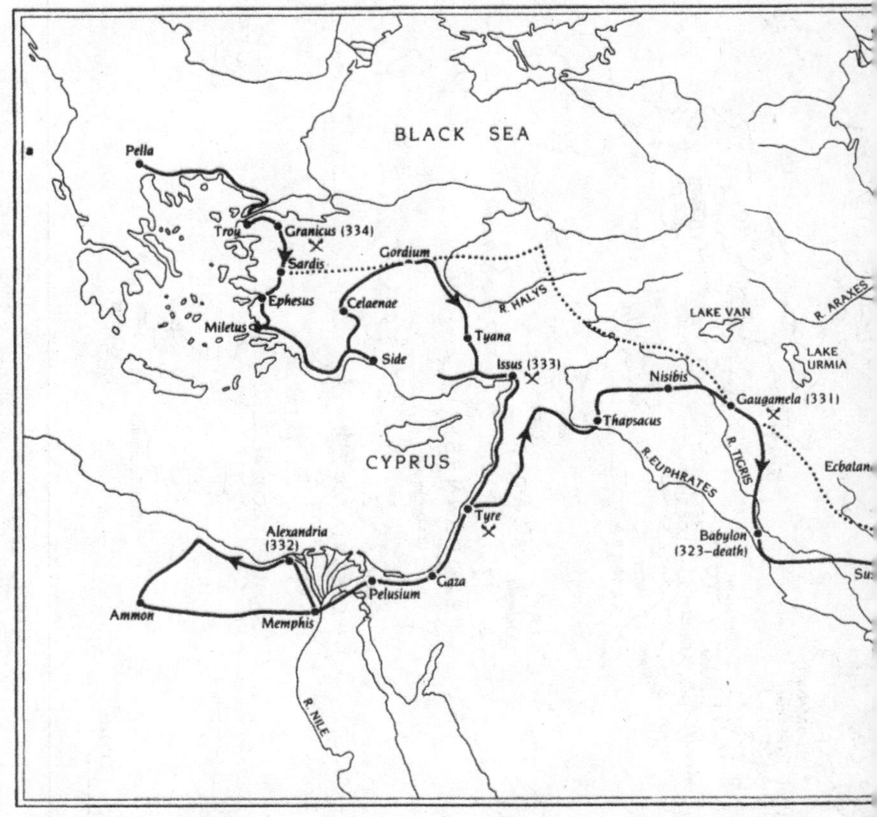

MAP 2. ALEXANDER'S ROUTE

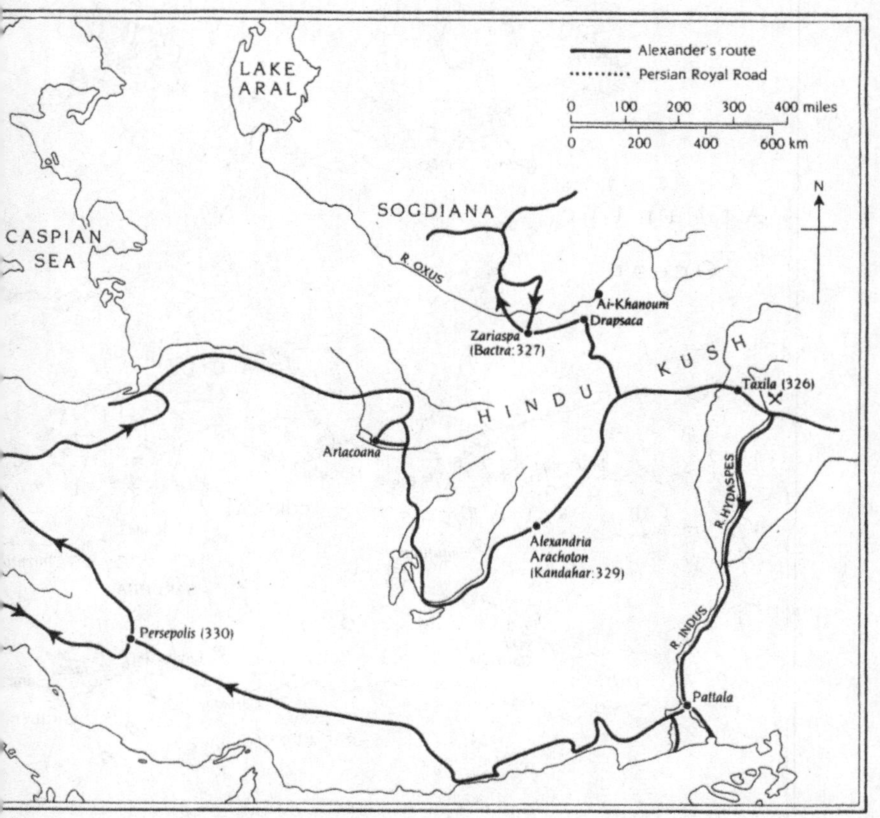

Alexander's route
Persian Royal Road
0 100 200 300 400 miles
0 200 400 600 km
N
LAKE ARAL
CASPIAN SEA
SOGDIANA
R. OXUS
Ai-Khanoum
Drapsaca
Zariaspa (Bactra: 327)
HINDU KUSH
Taxila (326)
Artacoana
R. HYDASPES
Alexandria Arachoton (Kandahar: 329)
R. INDUS
Persepolis (330)
Pattala

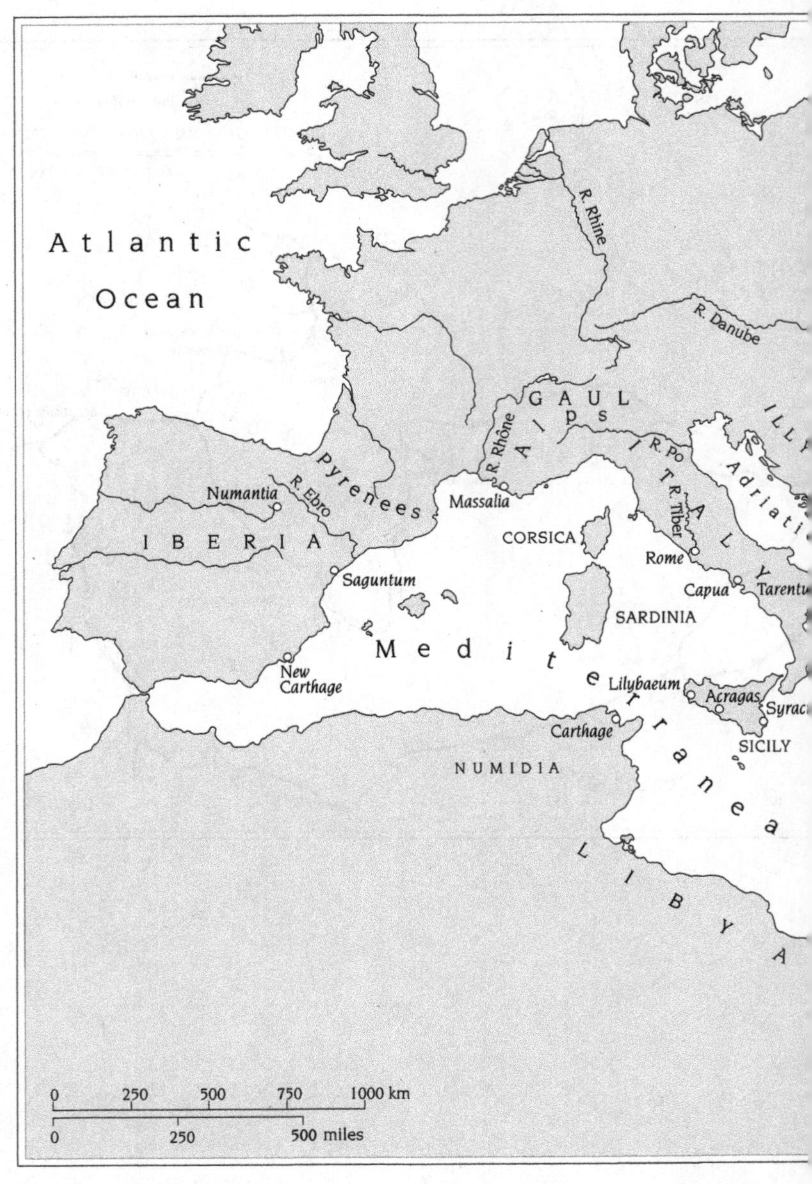

MAP 3. THE MEDITERRANEAN

R. Don
Caspian Sea
Lake Maeotis
Black Sea
R. Danube
Sinope
THRACE
Byzantium
Chalcedon
BITHYNIA
PONTUS
MACEDONIA
Propontis
Hellespont
EPIRUS
Aegean Sea
Pergamum
ASIA MINOR
CAPPADOCIA
Taurus Mts
R. Tigris
MESOPOTAMIA
R. Euphrates
GREECE
Ephesus
CARIA
PAMPHYLIA
Athens
Megalopolis
Antioch
RHODES
SYRIA
Babylon
CRETE
CYPRUS
Berytus
Sidon
Tyre
COELE SYRIA
Sea
Jerusalem
Gaza
Alexandria
Raphia
Pelusium
EGYPT
R. Nile

HELLENISTIC LIVES

ALEXANDER

INTRODUCTION

Alexander the Great (356–323 BCE) was one of the most successful and ruthless military leaders in antiquity. His overthrow of the Persian empire made possible the Greco-Macedonian domination of the East that has come to be known as the Hellenistic period. He came to the Macedonian throne after the assassination of his father in 336 and quickly established his authority, eliminating rivals, securing the frontiers, and destroying the rebellious city of Thebes. Within two years of his accession he had led his army into Asia Minor, leaving a senior general, Antipater, in charge of Macedon and Greece. In a series of three major battles he defeated the forces of the Persian empire, first at the Granicus river (334) in northern Asia Minor, then at Issus (333) in the south, and finally, after a detour to Egypt, at Gaugamela (331) near the heart of the empire. With the death of the fleeing Persian king Darius III at the hands of his own entourage, Alexander became ruler of this vast empire. It was not, however, undisputed. There was resistance further east, especially in Bactria and Sogdiana (roughly Tajikistan, Afghanistan, and Uzbekistan), which was brutally suppressed over the course of several years. Alexander inspired intense loyalty among his Macedonian soldiers but, faced with Alexander's determination to move further into India amid the blast of the monsoon rain, they finally refused to follow. In 325, abandoning any idea of further campaigning in the East, he led his army down the Indus river to the sea and then westwards through the inhospitable Gedrosian desert. By 323 he was back in Babylon where, at the age of only 33, he died. Reportedly he had many plans for what he would do next but few for how the empire might continue without him.

The *Alexander* is one of the longest of the *Lives*. Plutarch opens it with a prologue that emphasizes that he is writing biography, not history, conscious perhaps that Alexander is so dominant in the historical narrative that it might not be easy to make a clear distinction between biography and history in this case. But where history is about deeds and events, biography is about character. A joke or casual action, suggests Plutarch, might tell the reader more about the character of the subject than a major victory would. Alexander's great victory at Issus, for example, is covered in little more than a sentence, but his capture of Darius' mother, wife, and daughters as a result of the battle gives Plutarch the opportunity to devote several chapters to anecdotes that demonstrate Alexander's impressive self-control.

In practice, Plutarch offers a fairly full narrative in the first half of the Life, interspersed with anecdotes that illuminate the king's character. Once Alexander's victory at Gaugamela is reached, however, the narrative becomes less important, at least until he arrives in India and his soldiers impose a limit on his ambition. The several years that Alexander spent fighting in Bactria and Sogdiana, for instance, are given very cursory treatment. Instead Plutarch focuses on episodes that allow the reader to think about how Alexander handled the pressures of absolute monarchy. The first half emphasized Alexander's self-control and his receptiveness to reason, but at the same time it signalled the aspects of his character that, if not kept under control, could prove destructive, his impulsiveness and his fondness for drinking, both of which are related to the heat, even fieriness, of his body (4). Gaugamela is represented as a conclusion: the Persian empire is at an end, Alexander is now king of Asia and revenge has been taken for the Persian invasions of Greece (35). The text marks this with a literal line of fire as the people of Babylon sprinkle inflammable naphtha in a path leading to Alexander's quarters, then light it to create a swift wall of light burning up the street. This becomes part of an extended digression on naphtha and its qualities. It is not hard to see this as a metaphor for the fiery Alexander himself, impetuous, compelling, destructive, blazing a trail through the Persian empire, and suddenly extinguished.

The following chapters (36–56) focus more on Alexander as king of Asia than as conqueror. There is the negative: his drunken burning of Persepolis and killing of Cleitus, who had earlier saved his life; the conflict with the Macedonian nobles over the adoption of Persian customs at court; and his suppression of conspiracies against him. He looks an increasingly lonely figure, who has alienated his friends and supporters. At the same time, however, Plutarch does not ignore the positive: he emphasizes Alexander's generosity to those of all ranks. Nor is it as simple as Alexander alienating those around him. He remains as relentlessly active and hardy as ever, determined to pursue his ambitions of conquest, but it is those around him who start to prefer luxury and lack the resolve to persist. As he puts it at one point (40): 'Don't you realize that there's no point in our winning unless we avoid imitating the losers?' The final part of the Life *is* replete with intimations of death (61–77). His beloved horse Bucephalas dies; Alexander himself is almost killed in battle; the tomb of Cyrus, the founder of the Persian empire, is robbed; the Indian philosopher Calanus incinerates himself on a funeral pyre; the death of Alexander's close friend Hephaestion is marked by an elaborate funeral; and there are omens of all sorts as Alexander approaches Babylon.

The Life of Alexander is paired with that of Julius Caesar. This comparison did not begin with Plutarch. It is there already in the early first century CE, when Velleius Paterculus (2.41) wrote that in the greatness of his thinking, the speed of his warfare, and the endurance of dangers Caesar was very like Alexander (but an Alexander who was sober and not angry). In Caesar's lifetime, however, it was Pompey the Great who was most readily compared to Alexander, due to his early success and his victories in the East, but the longer he lived the less appropriate the comparison became (*Pompey* 46). Nonetheless Plutarch presents Caesar as measuring himself against Alexander; thus he tells how Caesar wept when he thought how little he had achieved in comparison with Alexander at the same age (*Caesar* 11). Alexander and Caesar may not have had age in common but they were both great conquerors, one in the West, the other in the East, they were both fiercely ambitious, and in both cases their tremendous success led former comrades to conspire against them. Their careers also gave an opportunity to examine not only the nature of monarchic power but also the elevation of men to the level of the divine. Nor was the comparison without contemporary resonance. Caesar was the forerunner of the emperors, and the emperor at the time was Trajan, a man who was himself compared to Alexander.

One of the problems with the study of Alexander is that, although his extraordinary achievements generated an immediate outpouring of historical writing, frustratingly, none of this survives. Thus modern historians are left with an Alexander whose mythology has been refined over several centuries. The earliest surviving account is contained in book 17 of Diodorus' world history, written in the first century BCE, some 250 years after Alexander's death. The most reliable history of Alexander, although not without error, is considered to be that of Arrian, written some years after Plutarch around the mid-second century CE and known by the title *Anabasis*. In addition to these two Greek histories there are two Latin works: a highly rhetorical history of Alexander by Quintus Curtius Rufus from the first century CE, and Justin's epitome of Pompeius Trogus' world history, the original written at the time of Augustus, the abridgement made anywhere between the second and fourth century CE.

In gathering together material for the Life Plutarch read widely, but there is no indication whether he relied more on one historian than another, for instance to provide the narrative framework for his account. He does, however, refer to numerous authorities, generally in support of a particular point or story. Many of these citations come from those early, lost writers. He cites more often those who had accompanied the expedition: the ill-fated Callisthenes of Olynthus, a pupil of Aristotle who wrote an adulatory and unrestrained account of the campaign until his death in 327; the Cynic Onesicritus of Astypalaea, chief helmsman of Alexander's fleet, who may have had a special interest in Alexander's philosophical background; Aristobulus of Cassandreia, a junior officer whose account was probably written in his old age; and Chares of Mytilene, the court chamberlain, with a predilection for court gossip. A list of fourteen writers is given in chapter 46, where Plutarch divides them into those who believed that Alexander met the Amazon queen and those who did not (the majority). These include his only mentions of Cleitarchus of Alexandria, whose popular and rather dramatic history was very influential, and of the memoir of Ptolemy I of Egypt, which would later provide the basis for Arrian's history. Listing these writers does not mean that Plutarch had read them all; he may have learnt the names of some from those he had read. Plutarch also makes extensive use of a set of letters said to have been written by Alexander himself, among which there are letters to his teacher Aristotle, his mother Olympias, and the governor of Macedon, Antipater. There are, however, serious doubts about the authenticity of most of these letters, although Alexander was known to keep copies of his correspondence (*Eumenes* 2).

Plutarch's Life offers a distinctive and highly readable treatment of Alexander. In contrast to the surviving histories, the narrative is but a structure for exploring broader questions about Alexander's life and character. It is rich in anecdotes, and although many may be apocryphal, their cumulative force is revealing about later interpretations of Alexander, as each age reimagined Alexander to suit its needs.

Beneker, J., 'Drunken Violence and the Transition of Power in Plutarch's *Alexander*', in J. Ribeiro Ferreira *et al.* (eds.), *Symposion and Philanthropia in Plutarch* (Coimbra, 2009), 193–200.

Bowden, H., *Alexander the Great: A Very Short Introduction* (Oxford, 2014).

Bosworth, A. B., *Conquest and Empire: The Reign of Alexander the Great* (Cambridge, 1988).

Carney, E., and Ogden, D. (eds.), *Philip II and Alexander the Great: Father and Son, Lives and Afterlives* (Oxford, 2010).

Cartledge, P., *Alexander the Great: The Hunt for a New Past* (London, 2004).

Cook, B. L., 'Plutarch's Use of "Legetai": Narrative Design and Source in *Alexander*', *Greek, Roman, and Byzantine Studies*, 42 (2001), 329–60.

Hamilton, J. R., *Plutarch, Alexander: A Commentary* (Oxford, 1969).

Hammond, N. G. L., *Sources for Alexander the Great: An Analysis of Plutarch's Life and Arrian's Anabasis Alexandrou* (Cambridge, 1993).

Heckel, W., *Who's Who in the Age of Alexander: Prosopography of Alexander's Empire* (Oxford, 2006).

—— and Yardley, J. C., *Alexander the Great: Historical Sources in Translation* (Oxford, 2004).

Holt, F., *Into the Land of Bones: Alexander the Great in Afghanistan* (2nd edn., Berkeley, 2012).

Lane Fox, R., *Alexander the Great* (London, 1973).

—— 'Tragedy and Epic in Plutarch's *Alexander*', *Journal of Hellenic Studies*, 108 (1988), 83–93 (reprinted in B. Scardigli (ed.), *Essays on Plutarch's Lives* (Oxford, 1995), 209–28).

Mossman, J. M., 'Plutarch, Pyrrhus, and Alexander', in P. Stadter (ed.), *Plutarch and the Historical Tradition* (London, 1992), 90–108.

Pearson, L., *The Lost Histories of Alexander the Great* (New York, 1960).

Pelling, C., *Plutarch: Caesar* (Oxford, 2011), 1–35.

Roisman, J. (ed.), *Brill's Companion to Alexander the Great* (Leiden, 2002).

Sansone, D., 'Plutarch, Alexander, and the Discovery of Naphtha', *Greek, Roman, and Byzantine Studies*, 21 (1980), 63–74.

Stewart, A., *Faces of Power: Alexander's Image and Hellenistic Politics* (Berkeley, 1993).

Wardman, A. E., 'Plutarch and Alexander', *Classical Quarterly*, 5 (1955), 96–107.

Worthington, I. (ed.), *Alexander the Great: A Reader* (2nd edn., London, 2012).

Worthington, I., *By the Spear: Philip II, Alexander the Great, and the Rise and Fall of the Macedonian Empire* (Oxford, 2014).

Zambrini, A., 'The Historians of Alexander the Great', in J. Marincola (ed.), *A Companion to Greek and Roman Historiography* (Oxford, 2007), 210–20.

ALEXANDER

[1] In this book I will write the biographies of King Alexander and of Caesar—the Caesar who overthrew Pompey.* Now, given the number of their exploits available to me, the only preamble I shall make is to beg the reader not to complain if I fail to relate all of them or to deal exhaustively with a particular famous one, but keep my account brief. I am not writing history but biography, and the most outstanding exploits do not always have the property of revealing the goodness or badness of the agent; often, in fact, a casual action, the odd phrase, or a jest reveals character better than battles involving the loss of thousands upon thousands of lives, huge troop movements, and whole cities besieged. And so, just as a painter reproduces his subject's likeness by concentrating on the face and the expression of the eyes, by means of which character is revealed, and pays hardly any attention to the rest of the body, I must be allowed to devote more time to those aspects which indicate a person's mind and to use these to portray the life of each of my subjects, while leaving their major exploits and battles to others.

[2] As regards Alexander's lineage, it has been reliably established that on his father's side he was descended from Heracles via Caranus and on his mother's side from Aeacus via Neoptolemus.* We also hear that after Philip had been initiated on Samothrace* along with Olympias, he fell passionately in love with her, and although he was only a young adult and she was an orphan, he went right ahead and betrothed himself to her, once he had gained the consent of her brother Arybbas.* On the night before they were to be locked into the bridal chamber together, the bride had a dream in which, following a clap of thunder, her womb was struck by a thunderbolt; this started a vigorous fire which then burst into flames and spread all over the place before dying down. And later, after they were married, Philip dreamt that he was pressing a seal on his wife's womb, and that the emblem on the seal was the figure of a lion. Although all his other diviners viewed the dream with suspicion and interpreted it as meaning that Philip needed to protect his marriage more securely, Aristander of Telmessus* said that the woman was pregnant, since no one puts a seal on anything empty, and that the child she

was carrying was impatient and lion-like. Moreover, a snake was once seen stretched out alongside Olympias' body while she was asleep, and they say that it was this incident more than anything that cooled Philip's passion and affection until he even stopped coming to her bed very often. This was perhaps because he was afraid that she would cast spells over him and drug him, or perhaps he refused to have sex with her on religious grounds, because she was the partner of a higher being. However, there is another version of this story, as follows. It is a long-standing tradition in this part of the world for all the women to be involved in the Orphic and Dionysian rites. The female practitioners are called Clodones and Mimallones, and there is a great deal of similarity between what they do and the practices of the Edonian and Thracian women on Mount Haemus (from whom, apparently, the word *thrēskeuein** came to be applied to extravagant and over-elaborate ceremonies). Olympias, it is said, outdid the other women in her efforts to achieve possession by the god and used to exhibit her inspiration in a wilder fashion: she would introduce great snakes into the meetings, tame ones, but they used to terrify the men by crawling out of the ivy and the ritual baskets and coiling themselves around the women's wands and garlands.*

[3] Be that as it may, the story goes that after the portent Philip sent Chaeron of Megalopolis to Delphi and he returned with an oracle from the god, instructing Philip to offer more sacrifices and honour to Ammon than to any other god, and adding that he was to lose whichever of his eyes he had applied to the chink in the door to glimpse the god in the guise of a snake sleeping with his wife.* Also, according to Eratosthenes,* when Alexander was setting out on his eastern campaign, Olympias accompanied him during the procession, told him in private the secret of his birth, and urged him to entertain ambitions worthy of his parentage. Others, however, maintain that she repudiated the idea on religious grounds and said, 'I wish Alexander would stop getting me into trouble with Hera.'*

Anyway, Alexander was born during the first quarter of the month Hecatombaeon (or Löos, to give it its Macedonian name), on the sixth, which was the day when the temple of Artemis at Ephesus was destroyed by fire.* It was in reference to this that Hegesias of Magnesia made a statement of sufficient frigidity to have extinguished that great conflagration: it is not surprising, he said, that the temple was burnt down, since Artemis was busy delivering Alexander.*

However, there happened to be a number of Magi resident in Ephesus at the time, and they all interpreted what had happened to the temple as an omen of further disaster; they ran to and fro, pummelling their faces and crying that Asia's ruin and perdition had been born that day.*

Philip had just succeeded in capturing Potidaea and three messages reached him more or less simultaneously. The first reported the defeat of the Illyrians by Parmenio in a great battle, the second brought news of his victory at the Olympic Games in the horse race, and the third told him of Alexander's birth. He was already delighted with all this, of course, but his diviners raised his spirits even higher by declaring that since the boy's birth coincided with three victories he would be invincible.

[4] His physical features can be seen particularly clearly in the statues of Lysippus, who was, in fact, the only sculptor Alexander regarded as good enough to portray him. Lysippus has perfectly captured what many of Alexander's Successors and Friends* tried to imitate, the way he held his neck cocked with a slight inclination to the left, and his melting gaze.* Apelles' famous picture, *The Wielder of the Thunderbolt*,† has not accurately reproduced his complexion, but makes him too dark and swarthy.* He had a pale complexion, they say, and his skin used to take on a ruddy tinge especially around the chest and face. Moreover, his skin used to emit a delightful odour and, as I have read in Aristoxenus' *Memoirs*, his mouth and whole body used to be bathed in a fragrance which filled his clothes. This was perhaps due to the unusually hot and fiery blend of the humours in his body; at any rate, according to Theophrastus, fragrance is a result of the coction of liquids by heat.* That is why most spices, and certainly those with the nicest scents, grow in the dry and fiery places of the world: the sun draws off the moisture, which lies like a source of corruption on the surface of the bodies of the plants. It was the heat of Alexander's body, presumably, which gave him his fondness for drink, and also made him impatient.

Even as a child, however, his self-discipline was apparent in his stubborn disregard for physical pleasures and the composure with which he approached them, which contrasted with his intensity and impetuosity in other respects; moreover, his ambitious desire for recognition gave his mind a certain dignity and detachment beyond his years. For he did not feel attracted towards recognition *tout court*, whatever its source, as Philip did, with his tendency to preen himself on his rhetorical skill like a sophist and to engrave his successes at Olympia in the chariot-race on his coins. On the contrary, when people in Alexander's retinue asked him whether he might like to compete in the foot-race at the Olympic Games, since he was a fast runner, he said, 'Yes, if I could have kings to compete against.' By and large, he seems to have been opposed to athletics; at any rate, although he instituted a great many tragic and musical competitions (for both the pipes and the lyre), and also rhapsodic contests, games involving all kinds of hunting, and quarterstaff matches, he showed no interest in offering prizes for boxing or pankration.*

[5] Once, when Philip was out of the country, Alexander received the members of a delegation from the Persian king and came to be on very good terms with them. He won them over with his friendliness, and because rather than asking any childish or trivial questions he tried to find out how long the roads were and the nature of the route into the interior, whether or not the king was inclined to go to war, and what martial ability and military resources the Persians had. They were so impressed that they regarded Philip's well-known ingenuity as nothing compared to his son's eagerness for high endeavour.

Anyway, Alexander never used to greet the news that Philip had captured an important city or won a famous victory with particular delight; instead he used to say to his friends, 'Lads, my father's going to pre-empt me in everything. By the time he's finished, there'll be nothing important left for me to present to the world, no splendid victories to be won with your help.' Since he had set his sights on excellence and fame, rather than pleasure and wealth, he thought that the more he received from his father, the less he would accomplish by himself. And so, since the strengthening of Macedonia's position meant, to his mind, that more and more achievements were being squandered on his father, he did not want him to bequeath an empire which would afford him wealth, luxury, and enjoyment, but one which would provide him with conflicts, wars, and opportunities for distinction.

We hear, of course, of a great many people who were concerned with his welfare, as instructors, tutors, and teachers, but chief among them was Leonidas, a man of stern temperament and a relative of Olympias. Although he himself did not mind the title of tutor,* since he thought that the job involved noble and admirable work, other people called him Alexander's instructor and mentor because of his moral gravity and his kinship to the boy. However, the person who assumed both the mannerisms and the title of tutor was Lysimachus, an Acarnanian by birth. He was basically a man of no culture, but he won favour by his habit of referring to himself as Phoenix, Alexander as Achilles, and Philip as Peleus,* and became second in importance to Leonidas.

[6] When Philonicus of Thessaly brought Bucephalas* to Philip with an asking price of thirteen talents, they went down to the plain to assess the horse and found him to be intractable and quite unmanageable. He refused to accept anybody on his back or to submit to the commands of any of Philip's companions, but just kept resisting them all. Philip was starting to get annoyed and to tell Philonicus to take the horse away, on the grounds that he was wild and uncontrollable, but Alexander, who was there, said, 'What a horse they are losing! And all because they're too inexperienced and feeble to manage him!'

At first Philip made no reply, but then, when Alexander kept on interrupting him and showing how deeply upset he was, he said, 'Who are you to criticize your elders? Do you think you know more than them or can manage horses better?'

'Yes,' Alexander replied, 'I do think I could manage *this* horse better than others have done.'

'If you don't succeed in doing so, what penalty are you prepared to pay for your cheek?'

'I guarantee to pay the price of the horse,' he said.

There was laughter at this, but as soon as the two of them had settled the terms of the wager Alexander ran over to the horse, took hold of the reins, and turned him to face the sun—apparently because he had noticed that the horse was made jittery by the sight of his shadow stretching out and jerking about in front of him. He ran alongside the horse for a short while, caressing him, until he saw that he was bursting with energy and that his spirit was up, at which point he unhurriedly shrugged off his cloak, jumped up, and sat safely astride him. Then he pulled a little on the bit with the reins and kept him in check without hitting him or tearing his mouth. When he saw that the horse was no longer a threat and was eager for a gallop, he gave him his head, urging him on more stridently now, and kicking with his heels. At first Philip and his companions were in an agony of silent suspense, but when Alexander made a perfect turn and started back jubilant and triumphant, everyone else cried out loud, but his father—so we are told—actually shed tears of joy, and when Alexander had dismounted he kissed him on the head and said, 'Son, you had better try to find a kingdom you fit: Macedon is too small for you.'

[7] Now, Philip could see that although Alexander was stubborn when it came to resisting coercion, he was easily led by reasoned argument to the proper course of action, so he not only tried for his own part to use persuasion rather than order him about, but also, because he did not entirely trust the teachers of cultural studies and the usual curriculum to take care of him and educate† him well (since education was, in his opinion, a matter of considerable importance and, as Sophocles puts it, 'a job for bridles a-plenty and rudders too'),* he sent for the most famous and learned of the philosophers, Aristotle. The fee he paid him was noble and appropriate: Aristotle's home town, Stagira, had been depopulated by Philip, and its inhabitants had scattered far and wide or been sold into slavery, but he now brought them back and resettled the town.*

Philip gave Aristotle and Alexander, as a place of resort where they could go and study, the sanctuary of the Nymphs at Mieza, where even now people point out the stone seats and shady walks Aristotle used to frequent.* It looks as though Alexander not only received from Aristotle his ethical and political doctrines, but also took in his more profound, secret teachings, which Aristotle's successors used to call the 'oral' and 'esoteric' teachings and did not offer to the public. For later, during his campaign over in Asia, he heard that some aspects of this secret teaching had been published by Aristotle in books, and he wrote him a candid letter in defence of philosophy, the text of which is as follows: 'Greetings from Alexander to Aristotle. It is wrong of you to have published your oral doctrines. How am I to stand out from everyone else if the ideas which constituted my education become common property? I would rather be distinguished by my knowledge of these excellent teachings than by my power. Farewell.' In his response, Aristotle encouraged this ambition of Alexander's and tried to justify what he had done with these teachings by saying that they both were and were not public knowledge. And it is in fact true that his treatise on metaphysics† is useless for either teaching or learning, but was originally written as an *aide-mémoire* for those already trained in the subject.

[8] I imagine that Aristotle was chiefly responsible for giving Alexander his interest in medicine as well, which extended beyond mere fascination with the theory, because he helped his friends when they were ill: as we can tell from his letters, he prescribed certain treatments and regimens for them. He was also interested in literature, studious, and fond of reading. He regarded and referred to the *Iliad* as a handbook on warfare, and carried about with him Aristotle's recension of the text, which he called 'the *Iliad* of the casket' and always kept under his pillow along with his dagger, according to Onesicritus.* When he was deep in Asia and had no access to any other books, he told Harpalus* to send him some, and Harpalus sent him Philistus' works,* a lot of tragedies by Euripides, Sophocles, and Aeschylus, and the dithyrambic poetry of Telestes and Philoxenus.*

Although at first he admired Aristotle and felt just as much affection for him as for his father (as he himself used to say, on the grounds that while his father gave him life, Aristotle gave him the gift of putting that life to good use), he later came to view him with some suspicion. It never reached the point where he actually did him harm, but the fact that his acts of kindness towards Aristotle failed to exhibit their original intensity and warmth is sufficient proof of his estrangement from him. But the passionate attraction towards philosophy which he had all his life, both as an innate gift and as a product of his education, never left him, as we can tell from his respect for Anaxarchus, the fifty talents he sent Xenocrates, and his great interest in Dandamis and Calanus.*

[9] While Philip was away on a campaign against Byzantium, Alexander was appointed regent of Macedonia in his absence, despite being only sixteen years old, and given responsibility for the royal seal. During his period of office, some of the Maedians* rose up in rebellion against Macedonia; Alexander defeated them, captured their main settlement, expelled all the natives from it, brought in a mixed population of soldiers and civilians, and renamed the place Alexandropolis. He also went and took part in the battle of Chaeronea against the Greeks, and is said to have led the charge against the Theban Sacred Band. Even today one is shown an ancient oak growing next to the Cephisus which is called 'Alexander's Oak' because he pitched his tent against it; it is quite close to the communal grave of the Macedonian dead.*

These exploits of his made Philip extremely proud of his son, of course; in fact, he did not even mind it when the Macedonians described Alexander as their king and Philip as their general. But troubles at home, when as a result of Philip's marriages and love-affairs a kind of infection spread from the women's quarters to the whole kingdom, caused a great many recriminations and fierce quarrels between father and son, which Olympias, who was a jealous and vituperative woman, spitefully exacerbated by egging Alexander on. The most open quarrel was provoked by Attalus on the occasion of Philip's wedding to Cleopatra, a young woman whom Philip, despite being past the age for such things, had married after falling in love with her when she was still a girl. Attalus was Cleopatra's uncle, and he drunkenly called on the Macedonians to pray to the gods for a legitimate heir to the throne to be born to Philip and Cleopatra.* This irritated Alexander, who said, 'So, you swine, you consider me a bastard, do you?', and threw a cup at him. Philip got up to attack Alexander and drew his sword, but luckily for both of them his anger and the wine he had drunk made him stumble and fall. Alexander taunted him and said, 'Gentlemen, there lies the man who was getting ready to cross over from Europe to Asia,* but who trips up on his way over to one couch from another!' After this drunken brawl Alexander took Olympias and set her up in Epirus, while he stayed among the Illyrians.

While he was there, Demaratus of Corinth,* who was a guest-friend of the household and a man who was used to speaking his mind, came to visit Philip. Once the preliminary greetings and expressions of affection were over, Philip asked about the state of inter-Greek *entente cordiale*. 'It is really very good of you, Philip,' said Demaratus, 'to express concern for Greece when your own household is overrun, thanks to you, with so much conflict and trouble.' This brought Philip to his senses; he sent messengers to Alexander and with Demaratus' help persuaded him to return home.

[10] As an incentive for Philip to enter into an alliance with him, Pixodarus, the satrap of Caria,* wanted to marry his eldest daughter to Philip's son Arrhidaeus,* and he sent Aristocritus to Macedonia to see to the matter. Once again stories and lies began to reach Alexander's ears from his friends and his mother, to the effect that Philip was planning to use an illustrious marriage and important state affairs to promote Arrhidaeus and settle the kingdom on him.

Disturbed by the stories, Alexander sent the tragic actor, Thessalus, to Caria, to talk to Pixodarus and convince him that he ought to ignore the illegitimate son, who was also weak in the head, and think instead about contracting a marriage alliance with Alexander. This idea was far more attractive to Pixodarus than his earlier scheme, but when Philip realized what was going on, he entered† Alexander's room (taking with him one of Alexander's close friends, Philotas,* the son of Parmenio), berated his son with harsh words, and accused him of betraying his high birth and his felicitous position by finding attractive the prospect of becoming the son-in-law of someone who was not only a mere Carian, but was a slave to a foreign king. Philip dealt with Thessalus by writing to the Corinthians and demanding that they return him to Macedonia in chains, and he banished several of Alexander's Companions from Macedonia—Harpalus and Nearchus, and also Erigyius and Ptolemy—though they were later recalled by Alexander and held in the highest honour by him.*

When Pausanias, who had been assaulted at the instigation of Attalus and Cleopatra, murdered Philip for failing to recompense him, most of the blame attached itself to Olympias, on the grounds that she had encouraged the young man in his anger and incited him to do the deed, but Alexander did not come out of the affair spotless either.* It is said that once, after the assault, Pausanias happened to meet Alexander; when he started complaining, Alexander quoted the line from the *Medea*, 'The giver of the bride, the groom and the bride too'.* However, he did in fact hunt down Pausanias' accomplices and punish them, and he was furious with Olympias for the brutal way* she dealt with Cleopatra while he was out of the country.

[11] The kingdom that Alexander inherited at the age of twenty was surrounded on all sides by bitter resentment, deep hatred, and danger. Not only were the native tribes on his borders chafing at their lack of freedom and missing their traditional monarchies, but also, although Philip had gained control of Greece by force of arms, he had not had the time to tame the people and accustom them, so to speak, to the Macedonian yoke; all he had done was introduce changes and shake things up, and then he had left them, due to his inexperience, in a state of considerable commotion and instability. The Macedonians were concerned about the critical situation and thought that Alexander should ignore Greece altogether, without using any force there, while attempting to win back the revolting

native tribes by conciliatory moves and to appease their rebellious feelings before they really got started. Alexander, however, adopted the opposite approach and resolved to win safety and security for Macedonia by bold and confident gestures, in the belief that if he were seen to relax his proud stance at all, he would be set upon by all his enemies.

So he took an army and swiftly overran the country up to the Danube, which put an end to any rebellious stirrings among the native tribes and brought the wars there to an end, and he defeated King Syrmus of the Triballians in a major engagement.* Then, as soon as he heard that the Thebans had risen up against him and that the Athenians had joined them, he led his army through the pass of Thermopylae, asserting that he wanted Demosthenes, who had dismissively called him a child when he was in Illyrian and Triballian territory, and a youth when he had reached Thessaly, to see before the walls of Athens that he was a man.* He drew close to Thebes, but wanted to give them a chance even then to repent of what they had done, so he demanded the surrender of Phoenix and Prothytes, and proclaimed a pardon for anyone who came over to his side. But the Thebans responded by demanding, in their turn, that Alexander should surrender Philotas and Antipater,* and they proclaimed that anyone who wanted to help them liberate Greece should join their ranks; and so Alexander committed his troops to war.

The Thebans fought with courage and determination, and excelled themselves against an enemy who vastly outnumbered them, but when the Macedonian garrison also came down from the Cadmeia* and attacked them in the rear, they were surrounded. Most of the Theban soldiers fell in the actual battle, and the city was captured, plundered, and razed to the ground. Alexander did this mainly because he expected the Greeks to be terrified at the enormity of the disaster and to cower in fear, but also as a specious way of gratifying his allies' grievances, since the Phocians and Plataeans had complained to him about the Thebans. He separated out priests, all those who were guest-friends of Macedonians, Pindar's descendants, and everyone who had voted against insurrection, and sold the rest into slavery.* About 30,000 were sold into slavery, while over 6,000 had died in the battle.

[12] Here is one out of many examples of the kind of savagery that afflicted the city at this time. Some Thracians broke into a house

belonging to Timocleia, a well-respected and virtuous woman, and while his men were looting the building, the leader raped her and defiled her, and then demanded to know if she had gold or silver hidden anywhere. She said that she had, took him out alone into the garden, and pointed to the well, where, she said, she had thrown her most valuable possessions when the city's fall was imminent. As the Thracian leant over and peered down the well, she came up behind him and pushed him in, and then hurled a great many stones down on top of him until he was dead. When she was brought before Alexander in chains by the Thracians, he could tell straight away from her demeanour and the way she walked that she was a woman of dignity and pride, because she showed no fear or concern as her captors led her in. When Alexander asked her who she was, she replied that she was the sister of Theagenes, the Theban general who had deployed his men against Philip in defence of the liberty of Greece and had fallen at Chaeronea. Alexander was impressed with the way she replied, as well as with what she had done, and told her that both she and her children could have their freedom and leave.*

[13] He also came to terms with the Athenians, despite the fact that they were deeply troubled by the catastrophe that had befallen Thebes. In fact, although the celebration of the Mysteries was under way, they were so upset that they abandoned it; they also showed nothing but kindness to any Theban refugees who sought safety in Athens.* Nevertheless, perhaps because, like a lion, his anger was sated, or perhaps because he wanted to offset an act of terrible and grim ferocity with one of clemency, he not only dropped all the charges against them, but even told the Athenians to keep well abreast of events, because, if anything should happen to him, they would be the rulers of Greece.* However, on more than one occasion later the Theban disaster is said to have caused him remorse and to have made him treat quite a few people with greater leniency. At any rate, he used to say that both the business with Cleitus, which happened when he was drunk, and the cowardice of the Macedonians when they were up against the Indians, which robbed his expedition and his glory of their crowning achievement, were due to the vengeful anger of Dionysus;* and later, whenever any of the Theban survivors came to him with a petition, he granted it. Anyway, that is what happened to Thebes.

[14] Following a conference held by the Greeks at the Isthmus, at which they decided to join Alexander's expedition against Persia, he was formally put in charge.* A great many people—not only politicians, but philosophers too—gained audiences with him to tender their congratulations, and he hoped that Diogenes of Sinope, who was living in Corinth at the time, would follow their example. Diogenes, however, continued to live an untroubled life in Craneium, without paying the slightest attention to Alexander, so Alexander paid him a visit and found him relaxing in the sun. Diogenes raised himself up a bit when the huge crowd of people appeared and looked at Alexander, who greeted him and asked him if there was anything he wanted. 'Yes,' replied Diogenes, 'move aside a little, out of my sunlight.' The story goes that Alexander was so struck at being held in such contempt, and so impressed with the man's haughty detachment, that while the members of his retinue were ridiculing and mocking Diogenes as they left, he said, 'But as for me, if I were not Alexander, I would be Diogenes.'*

He went to Delphi, because he wanted to hear what the god had to say about his proposed expedition to the East, but his visit happened to coincide with a run of inauspicious days, when the delivery of oracles is traditionally forbidden. At first he merely sent for the prophetess, but when she refused to officiate and cited tradition by way of explanation, he went up to her residence himself and started to drag her against her will towards the temple, whereupon, apparently overcome by his forcefulness, she said, 'You are invincible, my son.' On hearing this, Alexander declared that this was the only prophecy he needed—that she had given him the response he wanted.

A number of supernatural portents marked the start of his eastern expedition. For instance, at about that time, the wooden statue of Orpheus at Leibethra* (it was made out of cypress wood, in fact) sweated profusely. Everyone was frightened at this omen, but Aristander told Alexander not to worry, because his achievements would form the theme of songs and tales, and it would cost poets and musicians a great deal of sweat and toil to celebrate them in verse.

[15] The most conservative estimates of the size of his army make it consist of 30,000 foot and 4,000 horse; the most generous give it 43,000 foot and 5,000 horse.* To provide this army with supplies he had, according to Aristobulus, no more than seventy talents; Duris claims that he had enough food for only thirty days, and Onesicritus

adds that he was 200 talents in debt as well.* But although he set out with such meagre and restricted resources, he did not board his ship until he had discovered how things stood with his Companions,* and had given one of them a farm, another a village, and another the income from some hamlet or harbour. After he had used up and distributed almost all the royal properties, Perdiccas* asked, 'But what are you leaving for yourself, my lord?' 'My hopes,' he replied. 'All right,' said Perdiccas, 'then that's what *we*'ll have too; after all, we're joining you on this expedition.' Then he refused to accept the property that had been assigned him, and some others of Alexander's Friends followed his example. But Alexander was happy to gratify anyone who accepted his offer and who wanted what he was giving, and in this way he distributed and gave away most of his Macedonian properties. This goes to show how determined he was, and how he prepared himself mentally for his expedition.

And so he crossed the Hellespont.* At Troy, he offered up a sacrifice to Athena and poured libations to the heroes. At Achilles' tombstone,† he anointed himself with plenty of oil, ran a foot-race, naked as custom demands, with his Friends, and crowned the tombstone with a garland, pronouncing Achilles fortunate for the true friend he found during his lifetime and the great herald he found after his death.* While he was walking about and seeing the sights of the city, someone asked him if he would like to see Alexander's lyre;* he replied that he had not the slightest interest in that lyre, but was looking for the one Achilles had used to sing of the glorious achievements of brave men.

[16] Meanwhile, since Darius' generals had gathered together a considerable army and deployed it at the crossing of the river Granicus, it was presumably going to be necessary to fight at the gateway to Asia, so to speak, for the right to enter the Persian empire.† However, most of the Macedonians were concerned about the depth of the river and the unevenness and ruggedness of the further bank which they would have to make their way up in the thick of battle, and some were also of the opinion that they should not break with the tradition that in the month of Daisios Macedonian kings generally do not go out to war. However, he sorted out the latter objection by telling them to treat the month as a second Artemisios,* and when Parmenio tried to stop him fighting a decisive battle, on the grounds that it was too late in the day, he said that the Hellespont

would be embarrassed to see him afraid of the Granicus after having succeeded in crossing *it*, and he plunged into the river with thirteen cavalry squadrons.*

Since he was riding towards an enemy armed with missiles and was making for precipitous terrain which was defended by both armed men and cavalry, and since the current was strong enough to sweep men away and overwhelm them, this seemed to be an insane tactic, reckless and ill-advised. Nevertheless, he persevered with the crossing and, albeit with a great deal of difficulty, gained the opposite bank, which was wet and treacherously muddy—whereupon he was immediately forced to fight in disarray and to take on wave after wave of assailants, before he could get the men who were crossing the river into some kind of order. The enemy yelled as they charged into the attack, matching horse against horse, wielding their spears and then their swords when their spears were broken. Alexander himself was a particular target, for he was easily recognizable by his shield and by the amazingly tall white plumes which flanked the crest of his helmet. At one point he was hit by a javelin, which pierced the joint of his breastplate, but he came to no harm. Then Rhoesaces and Spithridates,* two high-ranking officers, bore down on him simultaneously. He evaded Spithridates and got in the first blow against Rhoesaces, but his spear snapped on his breastplate, so without further ado he turned to his sword. While Alexander was engaged with Rhoesaces, Spithridates rode up on his blind side, reared up straight away on his horse, and brought a Persian sword down on his head. He sheared off the crest and one of the plumes, and the helmet only just managed to withstand the blow—in fact, the flat of the sword touched the ends of the hairs on Alexander's head. Spithridates was raising himself up again for another blow,† but before he could strike, Cleitus the Black* ran him through with his spear. At the same moment Rhoesaces fell too, cut down by Alexander's sword.

While the cavalry engagement was hanging precariously in the balance like this, the Macedonian phalanx was crossing the river, and the foot-soldiers from both sides joined battle. The Persians, however, did not put up a very spirited resistance and before long all of them had turned and fled, with the exception of the Greek mercenaries, who grouped together at a certain hill and begged Alexander for mercy. In response, guided by anger rather than reason, he led a charge against them. Alexander lost his horse to the thrust of a sword through the ribs (but he was on a different horse, not Bucephalas), and it was in this fight that the Macedonians ran the greatest risk and sustained their heaviest losses in terms of numbers of men killed or wounded, because they were up against desperate men who were skilled fighters.

It is said that the losses on the Persian side were 20,000 foot and 2,500 horse, while, according to Aristobulus, Alexander lost thirty-four dead, of whom nine were foot-soldiers. Alexander commissioned bronze statues of the dead, which Lysippus sculpted.* He wanted the Greeks to feel involved in the victory, so, apart from sending the Athenians in particular 300 of the shields he had captured, he also had the rest of the spoils inscribed for general appreciation with a highly ambitious legend: 'Alexander the son of Philip and all the Greeks except the Spartans dedicate this booty won from the barbarians who live in Asia.'* But he sent almost all the items such as cups and purple-dyed garments that he took from the Persians to his mother.

[17] This battle immediately brought about substantial changes in Alexander's affairs: even Sardis, the bulwark of Persian mastery of the sea, surrendered to him, and he annexed various other places as well. The only cities that offered any resistance were Halicarnassus and Miletus, but he captured them by force of arms and subdued all the territory around them.* But then he was undecided about what to do next. He was often attracted to the idea of meeting Darius in battle and gambling everything on the outcome of the encounter, but he also often thought he should undergo a training programme first, so to speak, and build up his strength on the resources and wealth of the coast, before heading inland to face Darius.

Near the city of Xanthus in Lycia there is a spring which is said to have overflowed its banks and changed course at this time, apparently without anything causing it to do so, and in the process to have brought up from its depths a bronze tablet with ancient writing on it, which made it clear that the Persian empire would be overthrown and brought to an end by Greeks. This gave Alexander fresh heart, and he hurriedly set about clearing up the coastal region as far as Phoenicia and Cilicia. His rapid progress through Pamphylia has turned out to provide a number of historians with material for vivid and high-flown language; they claim that the sea providentially made way for Alexander, although it generally surged in from the open sea and hardly ever revealed the faint and exposed paths that run under the cliffs and gullies of the mountainside.† In fact, Menander makes a joke about this miracle in one of his comedies:

> What an Alexandrine situation this is! Anyone I look for
> Will appear as if by magic, and of course if I have to pass
> Through the sea at any point, it'll open up for me.*

However, in his letters Alexander himself makes no mention of anything supernatural like this, but just says that he set out from Phaselis and made his way through the country along the Ladder, as the road is called. This also explains why he spent several days in Phaselis. During his stay there he noticed that a statue of Theodectes, who was a citizen of Phaselis, had been set up in the main square after his death, and one day, drunk after his evening meal, he led a band of revellers there and they tossed quite a few of their garlands on to the statue's head—a nice, if flippant, way of thanking the man for the time they had spent together after he had been introduced to him by Aristotle and philosophy.*

[18] Next he put down a rebellion among the Pisidians and conquered Phrygia.* When the city of Gordium capitulated to him (this is the city which is said to have been the capital of Midas' kingdom in the olden days), he saw the famous cart with its lashing made out of the bark of a cornel tree, and heard the story which the natives there believe, that whoever undid the knot was destined to become the ruler of the whole world. Most writers say that since the ends of the knot were hidden, and since the strands were twisted and turned over and under one another time and time again, Alexander could not find a way to undo it, and so he cut through the knot with his sword until a number of ends were exposed. However, Aristobulus says that he undid it very easily, by removing from the pole the dowel, as it is called, which joined the lashing to the cart, and then pulling the yoke away from under the cart.

He went on to annex Paphlagonia and Cappadocia. When he heard of the death of Memnon,* who of all Darius' generals on the coast was the one who had been likely to make a great deal of trouble for him and cause him countless setbacks and delays, he felt even more positive about his prospects for marching towards the interior. In any case, Darius was already on his way down from Susa, with his confidence boosted not just by the size of his army (he had 600,000 men under him),* but also by a dream which the Magi had interpreted in a manner designed to please him rather than to accord with probability. In the dream he saw the Macedonian infantry consumed by a raging fire and himself being waited on by Alexander, who was dressed in the clothing he, Darius, had been accustomed to wear in days gone by, when he was the king's courier; then Alexander seemed to pass into the precinct of Bel and disappear. All this was, it seems, the god's way of suggesting that Macedonian affairs were destined to become brilliant and glorious, and that Alexander would gain control of Asia (just as Darius had when he stopped being the royal courier and became king), but before long would die at the height of his fame.

[19] Darius was even more encouraged by the length of Alexander's stay in Cilicia, which he took to be a sign of cowardice. In fact, however, it was the result of an illness, which some writers attribute to exhaustion, others to his having bathed in the river Cydnus and caught a chill. Most of his doctors lacked the confidence to treat him; they thought that the risks of the treatment outweighed any help it could provide, and they were afraid of the criticism failure would earn them from the Macedonians. However, Philip of Acarnania* saw that Alexander was in a bad way, and trusted in his friendship; he could not bear the idea of not making absolutely every effort to help him, even if the cost proved to be his life, and did not see why he should stay out of danger when Alexander was in danger, so he prepared a medicine and persuaded him to drink it, however unpleasant he might find it, since he was so eager to regain his strength for the war.

Meanwhile Parmenio sent Alexander a letter from the camp in which he advised him to be on his guard against Philip, who had been suborned, he said, by an offer from Darius of vast sums of money, and even marriage to his daughter, to murder Alexander. Alexander read the letter and then put it under his pillow, without having shown it to any of his Friends. When the time for Philip's appointment with Alexander arrived, and he came in with his associates, carrying the medicine in a cup, Alexander handed the letter over to him while happily accepting the potion without the slightest hesitation. The ensuing wonderful scene could have come from the theatre: one of them was reading the letter and the other drinking the potion, and then they both looked at each other, but not with the same significance, since Alexander was displaying his goodwill and trust in Philip with his cheerful and open countenance, while Philip was distraught at the accusation, and alternated between calling on the gods with his hands raised to heaven and throwing himself down by Alexander's couch with words of encouragement and the advice to listen to his instructions. For at first the drug proved too powerful for Alexander's body and, so to speak, expelled and submerged his energy, with the result that he lost the power of speech and grew very faint, with a near total loss of use of his senses.* Philip soon brought him back around, however, and once he had recovered he showed himself to the Macedonians, who could not regain their morale until they had actually seen Alexander.

[20] In Darius' army there was a Macedonian exile called Amyntas* who knew Alexander quite well. When he saw that Darius was intending to march to meet Alexander within the confines of the mountains, he begged him to stay where he was and fight on the broad, open plains, since his army vastly outnumbered Alexander's. When Darius replied that he was worried about the enemy running away before he had made contact with them, and that he did not want Alexander to escape, Amyntas said, 'Well, you can put your mind at rest on this score, at any rate, my lord. He will come against you; in fact, he's probably on his way already.'

However, Darius was not convinced that Amyntas was right, so he mobilized his troops and made his way into Cilicia. Meanwhile, Alexander was marching into Syria to meet him. But they missed each other in the night, so they turned their armies around again—a piece of good fortune that delighted Alexander, and he hurried on to meet Darius in the mountains, while Darius was just as eager to extract his forces from the mountain passes and get back to the place he had used earlier for an encampment. For by now he realized that he had done himself a disservice by advancing into country which was unsuitable for cavalry manoeuvres because of the sea and the mountains and the river—the Pinarus—running through the middle of it, and which was so frequently broken up that it favoured the small numbers of the enemy force.

So Fortune provided Alexander with the battle site, but his tactics made a more important contribution towards victory than her provisions. Given the fact that he was so greatly outnumbered by the barbarians, he did not give them a chance to surround his army, but he outflanked their left wing with his right wing, which was under his personal command, got on their flank, and routed the Persians ranged against him. He was so prominent in the fighting that he was wounded in the thigh by a sword. Chares* says that it was Darius who wounded him—that the two of them met in hand-to-hand combat—but in his letter to Antipater about the battle Alexander does not say who wounded him, only that he had been wounded in the thigh by a dagger, and that no serious harm came to him as a result of the wound.

Although he won an outstanding victory* and killed over 110,000 enemy troops, he failed to capture Darius, who fled with a head-start of four or five stades, but he did capture his chariot and his bow before turning back from the pursuit. He found his Macedonian troops plundering the Persian camp of its riches, which were extraordinarily plentiful, despite the fact that the enemy had come to the battle lightly equipped and had left most of their baggage in Damascus. They had kept Darius' tent for him, which was filled with magnificent slaves and furniture, and a great deal of money. He lost no time in stripping off his armour and heading for the bath, saying, 'Let's go and wash the sweat of battle off in Darius' bath.' But one of his Companions said, 'No, in *Alexander's* bath. The losers' possessions must pass to the victor, and that should be acknowledged in the way we speak.' When Alexander saw the bowls, pitchers, wash-basins, and perfume-jars, all of gold and elaborately wrought,† when he smelt how marvellously the forechamber was scented with aromatic herbs and spices, and when he passed from there into a pavilion which was quite remarkable for its height and size, and for its gorgeous couch and tables, not to mention the actual food served up on them, he looked at his Companions and said, 'This, I suppose, is what it was to be a king.'

[21] As he was settling down to eat his evening meal, someone told him that among the prisoners were Darius' mother, his wife, and two of his unmarried daughters, and that at the sight of Darius' chariot and bow and arrows they had struck their breasts and burst out into tears of grief, because they assumed that Darius had been killed. After a long pause, feeling more strongly about their misfortune than he did about his own good fortune, Alexander sent Leonnatus* with instructions to tell them not only that Darius was still alive, but that there was no reason for them to be frightened of him; it was true, he said, that he was fighting Darius for supremacy in Asia, but they would have everything that they had come to expect during Darius' rule.

The women appreciated how merciful and compassionate these words were, but his actions proved even more kind. He gave them permission to bury any Persians they wanted, and to use clothing and jewellery from the spoils for this purpose; he let them keep all the attendants and tokens of prestige they had formerly possessed, and they even enjoyed a larger allowance than they had previously been given. But the noblest and most kingly favour these high-born and virtuous women received from him while they were his prisoners was that he protected them from hearing even the slightest hint or implication of anything that would cause them shame; they lived such a secluded and isolated life that it was as though they were being looked after in the hallowed women's quarters of some temple rather than in an enemy camp. And yet it is said that there was no queen on earth who could approach Darius' wife in beauty—that she was a match, then, for Darius himself, who was more handsome and tall than any other man alive—and that the daughters took after their parents. Alexander, however, considered the ability to conquer his enemies less important for a king than the ability to control himself, so he did not lay a finger on them. In fact, before his marriage the only woman he was intimate with was Barsine,* who was the widow of Memnon and was captured at Damascus. Since Barsine had been brought up in the Greek fashion, was a good woman—and was, besides, the granddaughter, via her father Artabazus, of a king's daughter—Alexander decided (at Parmenio's instigation, according to Aristobulus) to take her as his mistress, seeing that she was beautiful and had nobility to match her beauty.† But faced with the exceptional beauty and stature of these other captive women, Alexander merely used to remark, as a joke, that Persian women are a torment to the eyes.* But he used to match their physical beauty with a beautiful demonstration of self-control and restraint, and pass them by as though they were no more than lifeless statues.

[22] Also, when Philoxenus, the military governor on the coast, wrote to ask whether he wanted to buy two extraordinarily good-looking boys who were being offered for sale by a man called Theodorus of Tarentum, who was staying with him, Alexander was furious. In a raised voice he asked his Friends over and over again what baseness Philoxenus could possibly have observed in him that he should spend his time procuring such shameful creatures for him, and he wrote a long, rude letter back to Philoxenus in which he told

him to send Theodorus and his wares to perdition. He also once rebuked Hagnon* in no uncertain terms for having written offering to buy and bring him Crobylus, a young man who was highly thought of in Corinth.

When he heard that two Macedonians called Damon and Timotheus, who were serving under Parmenio, had seduced the wives of some mercenaries, he wrote to Parmenio with orders that, if they were found guilty, their punishment should be death, because they were no better than wild beasts whose sole purpose in life is the ruination of human beings. In this letter he also wrote about himself, and I quote: 'In my own case, no one could accuse me of even listening to talk of the beauty of Darius' wife, let alone seeing her or wanting to see her.' And he used to say that there was nothing better than sleep and sex for reminding him that he was not a god, presumably on the assumption that both tiredness and pleasure arise from the same flaw in our nature.

He was also very self-controlled about food. One out of many examples of this is his remark to Ada, whom he referred to as 'mother' and made queen of Caria.* She used to express her fondness for him by sending him lots of savouries and pastries every day, and eventually sent him the best chefs and pastry-cooks she knew. But he told her he had no need of any of them, because he already had better cooks, given him by his tutor Leonidas—a night's marching to get him ready for the morning meal, and short rations to prepare him for the evening meal. 'And Leonidas also used to come and open the chests where I kept my bedding and clothing,' he said, 'to make sure my mother hadn't put some delicacy or extravagance in there.'

[23] He also had less of a penchant for wine than was generally thought. He gained this reputation because he drew out the time he took over each cup, but it was time spent talking rather than drinking, since he was constantly presiding over some lengthy conversation or other, at any rate when he had plenty of time.* When action was called for, unlike other generals he was not detained by wine, sleep, some trivial pursuit or other, marriage, or a show—as is proved by his life, which for all its brevity he packed with exploit after major exploit. When he had time on his hands, however, he would get up and sacrifice to the gods, and then immediately sit down to eat his morning meal. Then he would go on to spend the day hunting or arranging his affairs or teaching some aspect of warfare or reading. If

he was on a leisurely journey he would try to improve his archery during it, or practise mounting and dismounting from a moving chariot; as we can learn from the Royal Diary,* he also often used to hunt foxes and birds for fun. Once he had found quarters for the night, he would ask his bakers and cooks, while he was busy with bathing or washing, whether they had everything they needed for his evening meal. He used to take to his couch and eat his evening meal late, after dark, and take an astonishing amount of care and consideration at the table to make sure that everyone got equal—and equally generous—portions.

As I have already said, he would prolong the after-dinner drinking with conversation. Although he was basically better company than any other monarch, and had all the social graces, during these conversations he tended to flaunt his achievements in a disagreeable manner and become too boastful. And not only did he indulge in self-glorification, but he also allowed himself to be ridden by flatterers, who made things difficult for any particularly refined people present, because they had no desire to try to beat the flatterers at their own game and yet did not want to lag behind in praising Alexander; they found the first option degrading, but the second was risky. After he had finished drinking, he would wash, and then go to sleep, often until midday, but occasionally for the whole of the next day.

He was also self-controlled where savouries were concerned. In fact, when especially rare fruits and fish were brought to him from the coast he used to have them sent to each of his Companions, often until he was the only one left with nothing. But his evening meals were magnificent affairs, and the cost of them increased along with his successes, until in the end it reached 10,000 drachmas. It stopped there, however, and this was the stipulated maximum amount which those who entertained Alexander were to spend.

[24] After the battle of Issus he sent men to Damascus and seized the Persians' money, baggage, children, and wives.* The Thessalian cavalry did particularly well from the booty: they had displayed exceptional bravery in the battle and Alexander sent them on this mission on purpose, because he wanted them to do well from it. But there was more than enough to go around everyone else in the army as well, and after this first taste of gold and silver and women and an eastern way of life, the Macedonians raced like hounds which have found the scent to pursue and track down Persian wealth.

However, Alexander decided that he should first gain control of the coast. As soon as he arrived there, the various kings of Cyprus came and surrendered to him, and all of Phoenicia did the same, except Tyre.* During the seven-month siege of Tyre, in which he used earthworks and siege-engines by land and a fleet of 200 triremes on the seaward side, he had a dream in which Heracles, standing on the city wall, reached out his right hand to him in greeting and spoke his name.* Meanwhile a number of Tyrians dreamt that Apollo told them that he was leaving them and going to join Alexander, since he did not like what was happening in the city. The people of Tyre treated the god as if he were a common mortal caught in the act of deserting to the enemy: they tied ropes around his cult statue and nailed it down to its base, calling him a collaborator with Alexander. Alexander had another dream in which a satyr seemed to tease him from a distance and then eluded him when he tried to catch him, but eventually surrendered after Alexander had run around after him, pleading with him over and over again to give up. His diviners split the word *satyros* in two and told him, not implausibly, '*Tyre* will be *yours*.'* One is shown a spring there and told that it is near where Alexander dreamt of the satyr.

While the siege was in progress, Alexander led a campaign against the Arabians who live around the Anti-Lebanon range. During this campaign he exposed himself to considerable danger, thanks to his tutor Lysimachus, who insisted on accompanying him, saying that he was no less brave nor any older than Phoenix.* When the expeditionary force got near the mountains they abandoned their horses and continued on foot, and while the others went on a good way ahead, Alexander refused to leave Lysimachus, who was too tired to keep up. Even though night was drawing in and the enemy were close by, he stayed behind to encourage and support him. Before he knew it, he had become separated from the main body of the army and was left with only a few men. It was dark and bitterly cold, and the terrain where they bivouacked was harsh. Then he saw, not far away, a number of enemy campfires dotted about. Since he had no doubts about his fitness, and was used to constantly encouraging the Macedonians when they got into difficulties by exerting himself, he ran over to the nearest fire, stabbed two of the Arabians who were grouped around it with his dagger, stole a brand, and brought it back to his men. They lit a good-sized fire, scared some of the enemy into immediate flight, and later routed others who attacked them. After that they spent the rest of the night in their camp without further danger. The source for these events is Chares.

[25] Here is how the siege came to an end. There came a period when the bulk of the army was resting, on Alexander's orders, after all the fighting they had been doing, and he used to lead just a few men in attacks on the city walls to keep the enemy on their toes. Then Aristander the diviner made a sacrifice and when he saw the omens he declared with some confidence to those who were present that the city would certainly fall that month. This provoked sceptical laughter, since it was already the last day of the month, but Alexander did not like to see Aristander in a predicament and always shared his commitment to his predictions. He therefore gave instructions that the day was no longer to be counted as the thirtieth of the month, but the twenty-eighth instead, and then he got the trumpeters to sound the attack and made an assault on the walls in greater strength than he had originally intended. A spectacular fight developed, and not even the troops who had remained behind in the camp could resist joining in, but ran over to help their comrades. At that point the Tyrians gave up, and so Alexander did take the city on that day.

Later, while he was laying siege to Gaza,* the largest city in Syria, a lump of earth, which had been dropped from a bird flying in the sky, fell on to his shoulder. The bird then landed on one of the siege-engines and accidentally got caught in the skein of sinews they were using to tighten and twist the ropes. This omen too turned out just as Aristander predicted: Alexander was wounded in the shoulder, but took the city. He sent a great deal of the booty to Olympias, Cleopatra,* and his friends, but he also had 500 talents of frankincense and 100 of myrrh transported back for his tutor, Leonidas, remembering an aspiration he had conceived as a child. Apparently, during a sacrificial ritual, Alexander had scooped up incense with both hands and burnt it as an offering on the fire, and Leonidas had said to him, 'Alexander, when you've conquered the land which produces incense, you'll be able to burn it this extravagantly, but for the time being go easy with what you've got.' So now Alexander wrote to Leonidas: 'I have sent you frankincense and myrrh in abundance, so that you don't have to stint the gods any more.'

[26] When he was brought a casket which was, in the estimation of those who had appropriated Darius' property and baggage, the most valuable item there, he asked his Friends what they thought was

important enough to be kept in it. Various suggestions were made, but he himself said that he would put the *Iliad* there for safe keeping.* This story is vouched for by quite a few reliable sources. And if there is truth in what the people of Alexandria say, on the authority of Heraclides, Homer was no sleeping partner on his campaign, but made a positive contribution. For they say that after Alexander had conquered Egypt, he wanted to found, as a memorial, a major, populous Greek city, named after himself, and on the advice of his chief engineers he already had a site more or less measured out and enclosed, but then one night while asleep he had an amazing dream in which a distinguished-looking man with a good head of grey hair came up to him and quoted the following lines:

> There is a certain island in the restless, churning sea
> Lying before Egypt: Pharos is the name men give it.*

So he got up straight away and went to Pharos, which in those days was still an island a little north of the Canobic mouth of the Nile, although now it has been connected to the mainland by a causeway.† When he saw the place—a spit of land like a moderately wide isthmus between a large lake and the sea, which ends in a large natural harbour—he appreciated its exceptionally favourable situation and declared that Homer had turned out to be as clever an engineer as he was remarkable in other fields; and he commanded his designers to draw up the plans for the city, making it conform to the topography of the place. There was no chalk to hand, so they took some barley and on a level patch of dark soil they marked out a circle whose lower arc was drawn up from its skirt, so to speak, until, by uniformly contracting the area, it formed the shape of a military cloak. Their royal master was delighted with the design, but suddenly a vast number of birds from the river and the lake, of all kinds and sizes—so many that it was as if a cloud passed across the sky—swooped down on to the place and devoured every last grain of barley. Even Alexander found this omen disturbing, but the diviners told him that there was no cause for alarm, because the city founded here by him would be self-sufficient to a very high degree and would supply the needs of all kinds of men, so he told his overseers to get on with the work.

Meanwhile, he himself set out on the long, tough, and arduous journey to the shrine of Ammon.* There are two reasons why the journey is dangerous: the first is the unavailability of water, which means that the route actually passes through desert for quite a few days, and the second is the possibility of a fierce south wind descending on travellers as they are passing over an immense area of deep sand. This, of course, is the wind which, in the famous story from long ago about Cambyses' army, whipped up a huge heap of sand until the plain was a surging sea, buried 50,000 men, and killed them.* Almost everyone else used to take all this into consideration, but it was never easy to get Alexander to change his mind once he had decided on a course of action. By yielding to his assaults, Fortune had strengthened his determination, and his passionate nature boosted his ambition until he became invincible against things,† and not only his enemies, but even places and opportunities succumbed to his will.

[27] At any rate, the help he luckily received from the god during this journey when the going was difficult has met with more credence than the oracles the god subsequently delivered—or rather, in a sense the oracles have gained credibility because of these lucky events. In the first place, heavy rain and persistent showers from Zeus not only relieved them of the fear of thirst, but also smothered the dryness of the sand until it became moist and compact, and so cleared the air and made it easy to breathe. Again, when the markers which the guides were following were obliterated, and the travellers were wandering aimlessly around and getting separated from one another in their ignorance of which way to go, some crows appeared and took on the role of expedition leaders: they would fly swiftly on ahead as long as the party stayed with them, and would wait for them if the others fell behind and slowed down. But the most astonishing thing, as reported by Callisthenes, is that the birds used their cries to recall any members of the party who went astray during the night, and cawed until they had got them back on to the tracks left by the rest of the party in its journey.*

Once he had passed through the desert and reached his destination, the prophet of Ammon gave him the god's greetings in terms implying that the god was his father.* When Alexander asked whether any of his father's assassins had escaped him, the spokesman told him not to speak such sacrilegious words, because he had no mortal father, so Alexander changed the question and asked whether he had punished all of *Philip's* assassins. Then he turned to his empire and asked whether it was the god's will that he should rule over the whole world. The god replied that such was his will, and that Philip had been paid the full quota of justice, and Alexander presented the god with magnificent offerings and the men with money.

This is the account most writers give of the god's prophecies, but Alexander himself in a letter to his mother says that he received some secret oracles which he would tell her and her alone when he returned. Some writers say that the prophet wanted, out of politeness, to address Alexander in Greek with the words '*O paidion*', 'My son', but, not being a Greek-speaker, he made a mistake with a sigma at the ending and said '*O paidios*' instead, substituting a *sigma* for the *nu*. Alexander, they say, was delighted with this slip in pronunciation, and word got out that the god had addressed him as the son of Zeus, *O pai Dios*.

It is also said that while he was in Egypt he attended a lecture by the philosopher Psammon,* and was particularly ready to accept his argument that, since the ruling and dominant part of anyone is divine, it follows that all men are ruled by the god. However, the story goes on, he himself had an even better and more philosophical idea on this matter, when he said that while the god is the common father of all men, he regards men of exceptional virtue as peculiarly his own.

[28] He generally behaved haughtily towards barbarians and made it seem as though he were fully convinced of his divine birth and parentage, but kept his assumption of divinity within reasonable bounds and did not overdo it when he was dealing with Greeks. All the same, in a letter to the Athenians about Samos he said, '*I* would not have given you that free and illustrious city; you received it from the person who was then your master and who was called my father'—that is, Philip. But on a later occasion, when he had been wounded by an arrow and was in great pain, he said, 'What you see flowing here, my friends, is blood and not "ichor, which flows in the veins of the blessed gods".'*

Once there was a huge clap of thunder which terrified everyone. Anaxarchus the sophist was there and he asked Alexander, 'Could you, as the son of Zeus, do that?' Alexander laughed and said, 'No, I don't want to frighten my friends, which is what you would have me do, when you cast aspersions on my banquets because you see the table laden with fish rather than satraps' heads.' For we hear that once, when Alexander sent some little fish to Hephaestion,* Anaxarchus really did say this, as if he were disparaging and mocking those who wear themselves out and risk their lives in the pursuit of fame and fortune when they have little or no advantage over others in terms of pleasure or satisfaction.* Anyway, it is clear from what I have said that Alexander had not actually become affected or puffed up, but used belief in his divinity to dominate others.

[29] After returning to Phoenicia from Egypt,* he discharged his duties to the gods with sacrificial rituals, processions, and competitions for both dithyrambic and tragic choruses which were spectacular not only for their trappings, but also for the degree of rivalry between the competing companies. For the producers were the kings of Cyprus, performing exactly the same function as is performed at Athens by those who are chosen by lot from the tribes, and they proved remarkably competitive and eager to outdo one another. The contest between Nicocreon of Salamis and Pasicrates of Soli was especially fierce. Both of them were assigned for their productions the most famous actors—Athenodorus for Pasicrates, and for Nicocreon Thessalus, one of whose greatest fans was Alexander himself. However, Alexander did not reveal his interest in Thessalus until the votes had been counted and Athenodorus had been declared the winner. But then, apparently, as he was on his way out of the theatre, he remarked that although he approved of the judges' decision, he would happily have given up a part of his kingdom in order not to have seen Thessalus beaten. Nevertheless, when Athenodorus, who had been sentenced by the Athenians to pay a fine for failing to appear at the Dionysia, asked Alexander to write a letter to them about his case, although he refused to do so, he did send them the fine at his own expense. Also, when Lycon of Scarphe was having a good day at the theatre and inserted into the comedy in which he was acting a line containing a request for ten talents, Alexander laughed and gave him the money.

Darius wrote Alexander a letter, and sent a delegation of his friends as well, to ask him to accept 10,000 talents as a ransom for the prisoners, to keep all the land west of the Euphrates, to marry one of his daughters, and to enter into a treaty of friendship and alliance with him.* Alexander told his Companions about the offer, and Parmenio said, 'If I were Alexander, I'd accept it.' 'So would I, by Zeus,' replied Alexander, 'if I were Parmenio.' And in his letter back to Darius he said that if Darius came to him, he would be treated with every courtesy, but that otherwise he, Alexander, would presently be marching against him.*

[30] Before long, however, he had cause for regret, when Darius' wife died in childbirth. It was easy to see that he was upset at having lost such an excellent opportunity to display his kindness, and he spared no expense in her funeral rites. Now, the eunuchs of her bedchamber had been taken prisoner along with the women, and one of them escaped from the encampment and made his way on horseback to Darius. When the eunuch, whose name was Tireos, told Darius the news about his wife's death, Darius struck his head in grief and cried out, 'Alas for the god of the Persians, if it is fated that the king's sister-wife should be taken prisoner, and as if that were not enough that she should also have died without gaining a royal funeral!'

But the eunuch replied, 'My lord, as far as her funeral is concerned, and the question whether she received all the honour that was her due, you have no cause to find fault with the wretched god of the Persians. My mistress Stateira, while she was alive, and your mother and children, did not lack any of the blessings and advantages they had enjoyed before, except the opportunity to see the light of your countenance, whose splendour I pray the Lord Oromazes* may cause to shine once more. Moreover, in death, she not only received the full array of funeral ornaments, but was even honoured with the tears of your enemies. For Alexander is as kind in victory as he is terrible in battle.'

In his grief and distress, these words filled Darius with absurdly misguided suspicions. He drew the eunuch deeper into the tent and said, 'If you have not followed the Fortune of the Persians in siding with the Macedonians—if I, Darius, am still your master—tell me, as you revere the great light of Mithras and the right hand of your king, was the evil that befell Stateira for which I am now shedding tears not the least of it? Did I suffer more pitiful wrongs while she was still alive? Would my misfortune not have been more compatible with my honour if I had met with a savage, grim enemy? For what proper relationship between a young man and the wife of his enemy could lead him to pay her so much honour?'

Even while he was still speaking, Tireos had thrown himself down at his feet and begged him not to say such terrible things, which wronged Alexander, demeaned his dead sister-wife, and robbed himself of the greatest consolation for his misfortunes—the idea that he was being beaten by a man who could rise above human nature; he said that Darius should even admire Alexander for a display of restraint in dealing with the Persians' womenfolk that surpassed the courage he had displayed in dealing with the Persians themselves. Leaving the eunuch still swearing awesome oaths to the truth of what he had been saying, and giving further examples of Alexander's restraint and noble principles, Darius went out to his companions and, with his hands raised to heaven, spoke the following prayer: 'Gods of my race and my kingdom, I pray above all that, by your leave, I may recover the Persian empire and see it once more established in as good and sound a state as when I received it, so that, once I have defeated Alexander, I may repay him for the kindness he has shown me, in the hour of my misfortune, concerning those whom I hold dearest. But if in fact the moment of destiny has come—the moment owed to the equilibration and mutability of things—and it is time for Persian dominance to cease, I pray that no man may sit on the throne of Cyrus* unless it be Alexander.' The majority of my sources record these events and words as I have written them down.

[31] Alexander gained control over all the territory west of the Euphrates and then marched to meet Darius, who was coming down against him with an army of a million men.* During this march one of Alexander's Companions, thinking it a laughing matter, told him that for fun the camp-followers had divided themselves into two groups, and appointed a person to command and lead each of the groups, one of whom they called Alexander, the other Darius. They had started by throwing lumps of soil at one another, then moved on to using their fists, and by the time the fight had been broken up, which had not been easy since a lot of people had become involved, in the heat of their desire for victory they had gone as far as wielding sticks and stones. When Alexander heard this he ordered the leaders themselves to fight each other in single combat. He himself gave arms and armour to the one called 'Alexander', while Philotas did the same for 'Darius'. The army watched the duel, and everyone regarded the result as an omen for the future. The two fought fiercely, but 'Alexander' won, and received as a reward twelve villages and the right to wear Persian clothing.* This story has been recorded for us by Eratosthenes.

The great battle against Darius did not in fact take place at Arbela, as most writers say, but at Gaugamela. The word apparently means 'home of the camel', and gained its name when an ancient king escaped from his enemies on the back of a dromedary, and then settled the animal there, gave the job of looking after it to some villages, and set aside some of his revenues for its upkeep.* Be that as it may, there was an eclipse of the moon in the month Boedromion at around the time of the beginning of the celebration of the Mysteries at Athens, and on the eleventh night after the eclipse,* with the two armies visible to each other, Darius had his army take up battle-stations and held a review of his troops by torchlight. Alexander, however, let his Macedonians rest, while he himself was busy performing certain secret rituals and sacrificing to the god Fear in front of his tent, along with his diviner, Aristander.

When the older men among his Companions, particularly Parmenio, saw the whole plain between the Niphates range and the Gordyaean mountains lit up by the Persians' fires, and heard the confused hubbub of voices and the noises echoing from the enemy camp as if from some vast sea, they were astounded at the huge numbers facing them and, after talking things over among themselves, came to the conclusion that it would be extremely difficult for them to engage and repel an enemy force of this size in broad daylight. So they approached the king, once he had finished with his sacrifices, and tried to persuade him to attack the enemy during the night and so to conceal the most fearful aspect of the coming battle under a blanket of darkness. Alexander gave a celebrated reply to this advice—'I am not a thief, to steal my victory,' he said—but it struck some people as a childish and foolish response, and they thought he was being flippant in the face of terrible danger. His reply seemed to others, however, to indicate that he was not dismayed by the situation and had correctly judged the future, in the sense that he would not give Darius a pretext for summoning up the courage for another attempt if he lost this time, by blaming his defeat on the night and the darkness, as he had blamed Alexander's previous victory over him on the mountains, the narrowness of the passes, and the sea. After all, they reasoned, as long as Darius could draw on the enormous resources of the vast territory at his disposal, he would never stop fighting because he had run out of weapons or men; no, he would do so only when he had lost his pride and confidence, and this would happen only when the point had been brought forcibly home to him by a crushing defeat in broad daylight.

[32] Alexander lay down in his tent, once the men had left, and is said to have spent the rest of the night so much more soundly asleep

than usual that in the morning, when his officers came to his tent,† they were surprised to find him still asleep, and they issued orders on their own initiative that the men were to take their morning meal before doing anything else. Then, given the urgency of the occasion, Parmenio entered the tent, stood by Alexander's couch, and spoke his name two or three times. When he had woken him up like this, he asked him how he could possibly sleep as if he had already won, instead of being on the point of fighting the most important battle of his life. Alexander smiled and said, 'What do you mean? Don't you think victory is already ours, now that we no longer have to wander around in a huge, desolate land in pursuit of Darius, while he refuses to give battle?'

Nor was it only before the battle that he demonstrated his calibre and showed how serenely confident he was in his assessment of the situation: he did the same during the actual fighting too. On the left wing, where Parmenio was in command, the battle turned and surged against them when the Bactrian cavalry burst violently into the Macedonian ranks with a terrific roar and Mazaeus sent horsemen around the outside of the Macedonian infantry to attack the men posted to defend the baggage. These two manoeuvres panicked Parmenio into sending messengers to Alexander to tell him that camp and baggage were lost unless he moved a strong body of men immediately from the front to help those in the rear. Now, this happened to be exactly the moment when Alexander was signalling the men around him to attack. After listening to the message delivered by Parmenio's men, he described Parmenio's behaviour as over-hasty and irrational, and said that in his panic he had forgotten that in any battle the winners are going to gain their enemies' possessions as well, while the losers had to forget about their valuables and their slaves, and make sure only that they died fighting with honour and glory.

After sending this message back to Parmenio, he proceeded to put his helmet on, but he had been wearing the rest of his armour ever since leaving his tent. He wore a belted Sicilian undergarment and on top of this a breastplate consisting of two layers of linen, which he had found among the booty captured at the battle of Issus. His helmet, the work of Theophilus, was made out of iron, but it gleamed as though it were pure silver; attached to it there was a neckpiece, also of iron, and set with precious stones. He had a marvellously well-tempered sword, of incredible lightness, which was a gift from the king of

Citium, and he was such a highly trained swordsman that a sword was invariably the weapon he chose to use during battles. He was wearing a cloak which did not quite go with the rest of his gear, since it was of a more elaborate design. It was the work of Helicon, a weaver from former times, and had been presented to Alexander by the city of Rhodes as a mark of respect. It was another item he always used to wear into battle.* As long as he was merely riding past his men, and perhaps slightly rearranging the infantry lines, or offering some encouragement or advice, or conducting a review, he would use a different horse, and spare Bucephalas, who was now past his prime; but whenever he was going into action Bucephalas would be brought up, and as soon as Alexander had swapped horses he would begin the attack.

[33] On this occasion he addressed the Thessalians and other Greeks at length, until they reassured him by shouting for him to lead them against the Persians. Then he shifted his spear into his left hand, leaving his right hand free to invoke the gods. According to Callisthenes, he called on the gods to defend and support his Greek troops, seeing that he really was the son of Zeus. Meanwhile, Aristander the diviner, wearing a white robe and crowned with a golden garland, rode in front of the lines, pointing out to them an eagle which hovered high in the sky over Alexander's head and directed its flight straight at the enemy. This sight boosted the troops' morale a great deal, and then, after speaking words of encouragement and assurance to one another, the infantry phalanx rolled on like a flood after the cavalry, which was charging at full speed against the enemy.

The Persians gave way before the front lines had clashed, and a fierce pursuit began, with Alexander herding the defeated enemy into the centre where Darius was.* For he had caught sight of Darius in the distance—just a glimpse deep into the centre of the ranks of the Royal Cavalry assigned to protect him—a tall, fine figure of a man, standing on a high chariot, and protected by many magnificent horsemen who were drawn up in a very tight defensive formation around his chariot. But the awful sight of Alexander near at hand, driving the retreating troops into the ranks of those who had maintained their positions, terrified most of the royal guards, and they scattered. The bravest of them, however, the crack troops, were cut down in front of the king and fell on top of one another until they formed a barrier against the Macedonians' charge, entwining themselves in their death-throes about men and horses.

With all these horrors before his eyes, and with the troops deployed to protect him being pushed back against him, Darius tried to turn his chariot around and drive away. This was not easy, however, since the wheels locked as they became entangled with the massed corpses, and the horses, terrified† at the number of the dead, refused to go on, and began to rear and plunge so much that the charioteer was beginning to lose control. So Darius abandoned his chariot and his armour, and fled, we are told, on the back of a horse which had recently given birth.* But it is generally held that he would not have escaped if further horsemen had not come from Parmenio and called Alexander away, because a considerable body of enemy troops still held together there and were continuing to resist.

Parmenio is commonly criticized as having been sluggish and ineffective in this battle, perhaps because he was by then too old and tired for acts of daring, or perhaps, as Callisthenes says, because he resented and found oppressive the unbridled arrogance of Alexander's power. At any rate, at the time in question Alexander was so irritated by his summons that he did not tell his men the truth. Instead he made out that he was glutted with the slaughter and, using the bad light as an excuse as well, had the trumpeters sound the recall. And as he was riding up to the danger area, he was informed that the enemy had been utterly defeated and put to flight.

[34] Given its outcome, this battle was generally believed to mark the complete overthrow of the Persian empire, and Alexander was proclaimed king of Asia. He made magnificent sacrifices to the gods and rewarded his Friends with fortunes, estates, and military commands. Because he was anxious to win the favour of the Greeks, he wrote an open letter pointing out that all tyrants had been deposed and that they now enjoyed political freedom. He also wrote to the Plataeans in particular, promising to rebuild their city because their forefathers had allowed the Greeks to locate their fight for freedom on Plataean territory.* And he sent a portion of the spoils to the people of Croton in Italy, as a mark of respect for the determination and bravery of the athlete Phayllus. For during the Persian Wars, when everyone else in Italy rejected the Greeks' requests for help, he fitted out a ship at his own expense and sailed to Salamis to play his part in the battle.*† These acts of Alexander's show how he favoured all forms of bravery, and how he felt protective and supportive of noble deeds.

[35] Next he attacked Babylonia, and soon subdued the whole country. What he found most astonishing there was the chasm of fire in Adiabene,*† where flames constantly shoot up into the air like a fiery fountain, and the stream of naphtha, which is so extensive that it forms a lake quite close to the chasm. Naphtha is basically similar to asphalt, except that it is so sensitive to fire that it is ignited, even before a flame has touched it, just by the radiance around the flame, and often sets fire to the intervening air as well. In order to demonstrate its qualities and power, the Babylonians lightly sprinkled the street leading up to Alexander's quarters with the substance, and then stood at one end of the street and applied their torches—for night was drawing in—to the moistened spots. The first spots caught fire straight away, and the fire spread too quickly for the eye to follow; as quick as thought, it shot down to the other end until there was an unbroken wall of fire all the way down the street.

There was a man called Athenophanes, who came from Athens, and was one of those whose job it was to tend to the king's body while he was being oiled and bathed, and to divert his mind with suitable relaxing pleasantries. At the time in question a young boy called Stephanus, who was particularly, even ridiculously, ugly, but had a beautiful singing voice, was also in attendance on Alexander in the bathroom, and Athenophanes said, 'Shall we take some of that substance, my lord, and conduct an experiment with it on Stephanus? If it sets fire to him without being extinguished, I would have to say that there is nothing that can withstand it and that its power is truly formidable.' For some reason the boy also enthusiastically offered himself for the experiment, and as soon as he had smeared the substance on himself and handled it, flames burst out all over his body, and he was so completely covered with fire that Alexander became completely panic-stricken with fear. Luckily there were lots of people there with bowls of water in their hands for his bath, otherwise the boy would have been beyond help and the flames would have spread. Even as things were his body was so completely on fire that they only just managed to extinguish the flames, and afterwards he was in a terrible state.

It is quite plausible, then, for some people, in trying to salvage the veracity of the myth, to say that this is the substance Medea smeared on the crown and the cloak, as portrayed in the tragedy.* They argue that it was not the crown and the cloak that started the fire, and that it did not start spontaneously either, but that a flame was brought near them and then a rapid attraction and connection, imperceptible to the senses, took place. The rays and emanations which proceed from a flame that is some distance away usually do no more than impart light and heat to things, but in the case of objects which have an airy dryness or a sufficiently oily moisture they gather, combust, and rapidly transform the material.

There has been considerable discussion about the origin of <naphtha . . . >,† or whether, on the contrary, the liquid which acts as a fuel for the flame flows out of the ground, which has an oily and combustible nature. For Babylonia is so very fiery that grains of barley often jump out of the ground and are hurled up into the air, as if the places where this happens throbbed with inflammation; and during the hot season the people there sleep on skins filled with water. When Harpalus was left in charge of the country, he was keen to embellish the palace gardens and walks with Greek plants, and whereas he managed to get other plants to take, ivy was the only one the soil always rejected and killed: ivy thrives in cool soil, and therefore could not survive in soil with a fiery composition. But perhaps impatient readers will complain less at digressions like this if they do not go on for too long.

[36] When Alexander took control of Susa,* he found 40,000 talents of coined money in the palace, as well as countless furnishings and valuables, including, according to my sources, 5,000 talents of purple cloth from Hermione,* which still had a fresh, bright colour, despite having lain in storage for 190 years. The reason for this, they say, is that honey was used when dyeing the purple cloths, and white olive-oil on the white cloths, since honey and white olive-oil retain their brilliance and gleaming appearance after that many years. Moreover, according to Dinon,* the Persian kings used to have water fetched from the Nile and the Danube and stored up along with everything else in their treasury, or *gaza*, as a way of confirming the extent of their empire and their mastery over the whole world.

[37] Persis is a difficult country to get into, owing to its ruggedness, and it was guarded by crack Persian troops, since Darius had taken refuge there.* So Alexander found a guide who showed him a roundabout way in, which involved only a slight detour. The guide was bilingual, since his father was Lycian and his mother Persian, and it was this, they say, that the Pythia had predicted in a prophecy

she gave when Alexander was still a child, to the effect that a Lycian would be Alexander's guide on his march against the Persians.

. . . † A terrible massacre of prisoners took place there. Alexander himself writes in a letter that, since he thought it would be to his advantage, he gave the command for the people to be slaughtered. He found as much coined money there as at Susa, and they say that it took 10,000 pairs of mules and 5,000 camels to transport all the rest of the furnishings and valuables out of the city. When Alexander saw a colossal statue of Xerxes, which had been rudely knocked over by the press of the huge numbers of people forcing their way into the palace,* he stood by it and said, as if he were talking to a living person: 'Shall I leave you lying there, to pay for your expedition against Greece, or shall I wake you up because of your noble self-assurance and excellence in other respects?' Eventually, after pondering the matter in silence for quite a while, he left the statue lying there and walked on. He wanted to give his troops a break—and it was wintertime, anyway—so he spent four months there. It is said that the first time he sat on the royal throne under the golden canopy, Demaratus of Corinth, a loyal old family friend of his, burst into tears, as old men will, and declared that the Greeks who had died before they could see Alexander seated on Darius' throne had missed a rare treat.

[38] Later, just when he was about to set out against Darius, he happened to get involved in a heavy drinking-party with his Companions, at which even women were present, who had come to join their lovers for a revel. The most famous of these women was Thais, a courtesan who originally came from Attica, and was there with Ptolemy, who later became king.* As the drinking went on, partly as a graceful way of complimenting Alexander and partly to amuse him, she was induced to deliver a speech which was in keeping with the customs of her native country, but was too high-flown for her. She said that although the high life they were enjoying that day in the extraordinary palace of the Persian kings made her exhausting travels through Asia seem worthwhile, she would still prefer, during the revel, to burn down Xerxes' residence, since he had destroyed Athens by fire;* and she said that she wanted to start the fire herself, with Alexander merely looking on, so that word might get around that the women in Alexander's entourage had avenged Greece more thoroughly than all his fine generals with their battles on sea and land.

Her words were greeted with tumultuous applause, and Alexander, won over by the enthusiastic prompting of his Companions, leapt to his feet and led the way, with a garland on his head and a torch in his hand. The others followed him with cries of revelry and surrounded the palace, and they were joined by some other Macedonians who had heard what was going on and ran up with torches. Their mood was good, because they hoped that burning the palace to the ground was the act of someone who was thinking of home and was not intending to live in foreign lands. But although some accounts claim that this is how it happened, others say it was a premeditated act.* In any case, everyone agrees that Alexander soon changed his mind and ordered the fire extinguished.*

[39] Alexander was born very generous,* and became even more so as his affairs prospered. He was also blessed with kindness, without which no gift is really welcome. I will mention a few instances. Once when Ariston, the commander of the Paeonians, had killed one of the enemy, he brought the man's head to Alexander to show it off to him,* and he said, 'It is a Paeonian custom, my lord, for this gift to be rewarded with a golden cup.' Alexander laughed and said, 'Yes, an empty cup, but I'll give you one full of wine.'

On another occasion one of the Macedonian rank and file was driving a mule which was carrying some of the king's gold, and when the beast became too tired to continue, the man hoisted the load on to his shoulders and proceeded to carry it himself. Alexander happened to see the man struggling along and had the situation explained to him, and so, when the man was about to put the load down, he said, 'Don't give up. Just keep on going to your tent, and take the gold there for yourself.'

He was usually more annoyed by people refusing gifts than by people asking him for something. In a letter to Phocion he said that in the future he would not treat him as a friend if he rejected his gifts.* Serapion, one of the young lads Alexander used to play ball with, never got any presents because he never asked him for any, and he in his turn, when he joined in their games, never threw the ball to Alexander. Eventually Alexander said, 'Why don't you give me the ball?' 'Because you don't ask for it,' Serapion replied. Alexander laughed at this and gave him a lot of presents.

There was a fairly cultured crowd of people with whom Alexander used to drink and tell jokes, and one of them, Proteas,* once seemed to have incurred his anger. Proteas' friends apologized for him, and Proteas himself pleaded with him with tears in his eyes, until Alexander said he forgave him—at which point Proteas said, 'In that case, my lord, first give me something to prove it.' And Alexander arranged for him to be given five talents.

That his Friends and Bodyguards* used to give themselves considerable airs over the valuable presents he gave them is proved by a letter from Olympias to Alexander in which she says, 'You should find some other way to do your friends good and show them how highly you think of them,† because at the moment you're making them all your kingly equals, and while you're guaranteeing them plenty of friends, you're leaving yourself none.' Olympias often wrote to him like this, and he used to keep her letters secret, except that once, when Hephaestion also read, as he usually did, a letter that had been left open, Alexander did not stop him, but slipped off his ring and applied the seal to his lips. And he once offered one of the sons of Mazaeus* (who had been the most influential person in Darius' court) an additional, larger province to govern, even though he already had one; Mazaeus' son refused, however, and said, 'My lord, previously there used to be only one Darius, but now you have made many Alexanders.' He gave Parmenio Bagoas' residence,* in which, it is said, there was found clothing worth more than 1,000 talents, and he wrote to Antipater warning him of plots against his life, and recommending that he keep bodyguards by him. He sent his mother a great many presents, but he refused to let her meddle in his affairs or interfere with his strategies; when she scolded him for this, he remained unruffled by her anger. Once, however, when Antipater* wrote him a long letter complaining about her, he remarked, after reading it, that Antipater was unaware that a single tear shed by a mother erases 10,000 letters.

[40] When Alexander noticed that his courtiers had become spoiled by luxurious living and were vulgarly flaunting the extravagance of their lifestyles—for instance, Hagnon of Teos used to wear silver nails in his boots, Leonnatus had the dust he used for his exercising transported by camel train from Egypt, Philotas owned hunting-nets 100 stades long, they infinitely preferred myrrh to oil as an unguent before going to be scraped clean, and they surrounded themselves with masseurs and chamberlains—he criticized them gently and reasonably.* He found it astonishing, he said, that people who had fought so many major battles could forget that working for others

makes for a better night's rest than being worked for by others, and could fail to appreciate, from a comparison between their own lives and those of the Persians, that, on a scale from slavery to kingship, wallowing in luxury was way down at the bottom and hard work was way up at the top. 'And yet,' he went on, 'how can anyone look after a horse on his own, or work on a spear or a helmet, if he has grown unaccustomed to using his hands on his very own body? Don't you realize', he added, 'that there's no point in our winning unless we avoid imitating the losers?'

And so he pushed himself to work even harder. He exposed himself to hardship and danger at war and out hunting—so much so that a Spartan ambassador who had watched him kill a huge lion said, 'Well fought, Alexander! You gambled with the lion for your kingdom!' This is the hunt depicted by the group of statues dedicated by Craterus at Delphi; he commissioned Lysippus and Leochares between them to make bronze figures of the lion and the hounds, of the king engaged with the lion, and of himself coming to help.*

[41] Although Alexander continued to risk his life in the pursuit of excellence for himself and in trying to motivate the rest of his men to seek it too, their wealth and their pretensions had by now made his Friends want only a life of luxurious ease, and they resented Alexander's detours and expeditions so much that it gradually got to the point where they would curse him and malign him. At first he remained perfectly calm about this, saying that a king was bound to have people wish him harm when he was trying to do them good, and even the slightest favours he did his close friends showed how much he continued to like and value them. Here are a few examples, to prove the point.

In a letter to Peucestas* he told him off for having written to tell everyone else apart from him that he had been bitten by a bear, and said, 'But write to me now, and tell me how you are and whether any of the people you'd gone hunting with left you in the lurch—in which case I'll punish them.' Once when Hephaestion was away on some business Alexander wrote and told him how Craterus had been accidentally wounded in the thigh by Perdiccas' light spear when they were hunting mongooses for fun. After Peucestas recovered from an illness, Alexander wrote to Alexippus the doctor to thank him. When Craterus was ill, Alexander not only personally performed certain sacrifices for him, as a result of a dream he had, but told him to follow his example as well; he also wrote to the doctor, Pausanias, who wanted to use hellebore* on Craterus, partly to express his anxiety and partly to advise him how to use the drug. He imprisoned the first people to bring him news of Harpalus' flight and desertion, who were called Ephialtes and Cissus, because he assumed that they were lying to get Harpalus into trouble.*

Once, when Alexander was having the invalids and veterans sent back home, Eurylochus of Aegae got himself included on the sick-list even though there was nothing wrong with him, and when he was caught he confessed that he was in love with Telesippa and was trying to follow her to the coast, since she was leaving. Alexander asked about her family, and when he heard that she was a free-born courtesan, he said, 'Well, Eurylochus, I'll help you pursue Telesippa, but we must be sure to win her round by arguments or presents since she is from a free-born family.'*

[42] For his friends he also wrote the kind of letter one can scarcely believe he would have had time for. When a slave belonging to Seleucus* ran away to Cilicia, for instance, he wrote giving orders for him to be hunted down; in another letter he praised Peucestas for apprehending Nicon, a slave belonging to Craterus, and in another to Megabyzus he talked about how to deal with a house-slave of his who had taken refuge in the sanctuary,* telling him to entice the slave outside the sanctuary, if possible, and then apprehend him, but not to touch him inside the sanctuary.

It is said that when he first began judging capital cases he used to listen to the prosecutor's speech with a hand placed over one of his ears, so that it might be kept unsullied and unbiased for the defendant. Later, however, all the accusations he had heard began to make him less tolerant, since there were enough true ones to have paved the way for the false ones and given them credibility. Above all, abuse would drive him mad and make him harsh and implacable, because he loved his reputation more than his life and his kingdom.

At the time in question,* then, he marched out against Darius, with the intention of engaging him in yet another battle, but when he heard that the king had been arrested by Bessus, he dismissed his Thessalian troops and sent them home, after distributing among them a bonus of 2,000 talents on top of their pay. His pursuit of Darius proved so long and arduous—they rode 3,300 stades in eleven days—that most of his men fell by the wayside, thanks particularly to the shortage of water.*† This was the point at which he came across some Macedonians carrying skins of water from the river on their mules; it was midday, and as soon as they noticed that he was desperately thirsty, they filled a helmet with water and brought it to him. He asked them who the water they were carrying was for. 'For our sons,' they said. 'But as long as you are alive we can always have other sons, even if we lose the ones we've got at the moment.' This made him accept the helmet, but then he looked around and saw that all the horsemen in the vicinity were craning their necks and staring at him expectantly, so he gave the helmet back without drinking from it. He thanked the men for their kindness, and said, 'If I'm the only one to get a drink, it will have a bad effect on the morale of my men.' At this display of his self-control and noble principles, the horsemen shouted out for him to lead the way, and whipped their horses into action. As long as they had such a king, they said, he could trust them not to feel tired or thirsty or even to consider themselves mortal at all.

[43] The same commitment to the task infused the whole army, but it is said that Alexander was accompanied by only sixty men when he burst into the enemy camp. They rode over piles of discarded silver and gold, past carts laden with women and children which had been abandoned by their drivers and left to wander aimlessly, and concentrated on chasing the men who had got away first, because they supposed that Darius would be among them. Eventually he was found lying in a wagon, his body riddled with javelin wounds, close to death. Nevertheless, he asked for something to drink and took a drink of cold water. Then he said to Polystratus, who had given him the water, 'My misfortunes can get no worse than this, that I cannot return this favour you have done me. But Alexander will repay you for your good turn, and the gods will repay Alexander for his kindness towards my mother, wife, and children. Here, take my hand: I offer it to him through you.' With these words he grasped Polystratus' hand and died.

When Alexander arrived and saw what had happened, he took off his own cloak and used it to cover and wrap the body, without attempting to disguise his grief. And later, once he had tracked Bessus down, he scattered his body, like slingshot, in various directions. Two upright trees were bent down until they met, and a part of Bessus' body was tied on to each of the trees, which were then released, so that as each tree sprang back up it took with it the part of Bessus' body that was attached to it.* At the time in question, however, he sent Darius' mother her son's corpse, adorned with a king's regalia, and let his brother Exathres* join the ranks of his Companions.

[44] Meanwhile he took the pick of his fighting force and went down into Hyrcania, where he saw a gulf of the open sea which looked as though it was at least as big as the Black Sea, but was less salty than the rest of the sea. His enquiries brought him no clear information about it, and his best guess was that it was an overflow from Lake Maeotis. Long before Alexander's expedition, however, natural scientists were aware of the truth and as a result of their researches reported that this is the most northerly of the four gulfs which run in from the outer sea, and is known as both the Hyrcanian Sea and the Caspian Sea.*

While he was in this part of the world some native tribesmen ambushed the attendants of Alexander's horse Bucephalas and captured it. Alexander's fury knew no bounds, and he sent a messenger threatening to kill them all, including their children and womenfolk, unless they sent the horse back to him. But when they did come, and not only brought the horse with them, but surrendered their towns to him as well, he treated all of them with kindness and gave those who had captured Bucephalas ransom-money.

[45] Next he marched into Parthian territory, and it was here, during a lull in the fighting, that he first wore non-Greek clothing, perhaps because he wanted to associate himself with local customs, on the grounds that the sight of what is familiar and congenial goes a long way towards winning people over, or perhaps this was a sly attempt to get the Macedonians to adopt the practice of doing obeisance before him,* by gradually getting them used to putting up with changes in his way of life. However, he did not approve of the famous Median style of clothing, which is so thoroughly alien to Greek tastes, and he did not take to trousers or *kandys* or *tiara*, but adopted a kind of balanced blend of Persian and Median clothing, which was more simple than the latter and more stately than the former.* At first he used to wear these clothes only when meeting non-Greeks and when he was with his Companions at home, but then he began to be seen by ordinary people in these clothes when out riding and when holding audiences.

His fellow Macedonians did not like to see him dressed like this, but they were so impressed with his outstanding qualities in other respects that they thought they should let him get away with some things which pleased him or increased his prestige. For despite the fact that, in addition to all the other wounds he had received, he had recently been hit in the shin by an arrow which splintered and dislocated the shin-bone, and on another occasion had been hit on the neck by a stone, which had caused his sight to become clouded and to remain so for quite some time, he did not stop taking serious risks with his life, and in fact he crossed the river Orexartes (mistaking it for the Tanaïs), routed an army of Scythians, and pursued them for 100 stades—all while suffering from dysentery.

[46] It was after he had crossed the Orexartes that the queen of the Amazons* paid him a visit—a visit that is recorded in most writers, such as Cleitarchus, Polycleitus, Onesicritus, Antigenes, and Ister. But Aristobulus and Chares the Chamberlain are joined by Hecataeus of Eretria, Ptolemy, Anticleides, Philon of Thebes, Philip of Theangela, Philip of Chalcis, and Duris of Samos in claiming that this visit is a fiction. And it looks as though Alexander supports them, because he wrote a very precise and detailed letter to Antipater in which he says that the Scythian king offered him his daughter in marriage, but he does not mention any Amazon. And there is a story that many years later Onesicritus was reading the fourth book of his history to Lysimachus,* who had become king by then, and when he came to the bit about the Amazon, which is contained in this book, Lysimachus smiled gently and said, 'And where was I at the time?' Anyway, our admiration for Alexander will not be decreased if we disbelieve the story of the Amazon or increased if we believe it.

[47] Alexander was worried about the Macedonians refusing to continue with the campaign, so he left the remainder of the army where it was, but he had the best of his troops with him in Hyrcania*—20,000 foot and 3,000 horse—and he won them over† by telling them that at the moment the barbarians could see them face to face,† but that if all they did was cause havoc in Asia and then leave, the enemy would regard them as no better than women and not hesitate to attack them. Nevertheless, he left it up to them to leave if they wanted to, and asked that if they did so they should testify that in his attempt to make the whole world subject to the Macedonians, he had been left behind with his friends and those who were prepared to continue with the campaign.† This is almost a verbatim quote from a letter of his to

Antipater, and he goes on to say that after he had finished speaking they all shouted out loud, calling on him to take them wherever he wanted in the world. Once these elite troops had met this test of their loyalty, it proved easy to win over the main body of the army, which readily followed his lead.

After this, then, he began to assimilate his way of life even more closely with that of the easterners, and also tried to get them to adopt Macedonian customs. He was of the opinion that while he was far away political stability would follow from fusion and cooperation, achieved through goodwill, rather than from the use of force. This is also why he issued instructions that 30,000 selected children were to learn Greek and to be trained in the use of Macedonian weaponry, and appointed a large number of people to oversee this project.* Moreover, although in Rhoxane's case he fell in love with her beauty and grace when he saw her dancing at a banquet, the marriage was also held to fit in quite well with the policy he was pursuing.* For the barbarians were reassured by the bond the marriage formed, and they particularly appreciated the self-restraint he demonstrated in refusing to lay a finger even on the only woman he ever fell for until it had been sanctioned by law.

Moreover, when he saw that among his closest friends Hephaestion approved of what he was doing and joined him in modifying his habits, whereas Craterus stuck to the traditional ways, he used Hephaestion for conducting business with foreigners, and Craterus for Greeks and Macedonians. And, to put it succinctly, he loved Hephaestion best, but respected Craterus most; he was constantly saying that, in his opinion, while Hephaestion was loyal to Alexander, Craterus was loyal to the king. This helps to explain why there was bad feeling festering between Hephaestion and Craterus, so that they often clashed. Once, in fact, while they were in India, they even got into a fight, with drawn swords, and their friends were taking sides and coming up to help, when Alexander rode up and told Hephaestion off in front of everyone, calling him a reckless, crazy fool for failing to understand that without Alexander he was nothing. After also giving Craterus a severe dressing-down in private, he brought the two of them together and had them make friends again, and he called on Ammon and all the other gods to witness that although these were the two men he loved most in the world, if he found them quarrelling again he would kill them both, or at least the one who started the quarrel. After this, we are told, neither of them said or did anything to offend the other, even as a joke.

[48] Philotas the son of Parmenio was one of the most highly respected Macedonians, with a reputation for bravery and endurance, and for being second only to Alexander himself in his generosity and loyalty towards his companions.* At any rate, there is a story that on being asked for some money by one of his close friends, he ordered it to be given to him, but the steward told him that he had none to give. 'What?' said Philotas. 'Not even a cup or a cloak?' However, his haughty pride, opulence, concern for bodily comfort, and lifestyle were offensive in a private citizen, and also his affectation of lofty aloofness was awkward in its clumsy vulgarity and speciousness. All this only made him an object of suspicion and envy; and even Parmenio felt compelled to say to him once, 'Please don't make so much of yourself, my son.'

Now, Alexander had in fact been hearing bad things about Philotas for very many years. For after Darius' defeat in Cilicia and the seizure of the property in Damascus, there was found among the prisoners of war, who were brought into the Macedonian camp, an attractive woman called Antigone, who came originally from Pydna. She became the property of Philotas. Now, he used to speak freely to her, as young men will to a lover when they are under the influence of wine, in a self-important and boastful fashion, and in telling her the great importance of his own and his father's achievements, he used to say that it was thanks to them that Alexander, whom he described as a callow youth, was enjoying the title of ruler. Antigone told this to one of her close friends, and he of course told somebody else, until eventually the tale reached Craterus, who fetched the woman and secretly took her to see Alexander. When he heard what she had to say, he told her to carry on meeting Philotas and to come and tell him everything she learnt from him.

[49] Philotas had no idea that this trap was being set for him, and during his times together with Antigone he would often, in his anger and pride, criticize the king and express disapproval of him. In spite of the incontestable evidence that had come his way against Philotas, Alexander restrained himself and put up with it without saying or doing anything, perhaps because he felt he could confidently rely on Parmenio's loyalty, or perhaps because he was afraid of Philotas' and Parmenio's reputation and power.

Now, at this point in time, a Macedonian from Chalaestra called Dimnus† was plotting against Alexander's life, and he invited a young man called Nicomachus, with whom he was in love, to join the conspiracy. Nicomachus refused, and told his brother Cebalinus about the enterprise, whereupon Cebalinus went to Philotas and asked him to get them an audience with Alexander, because they had urgent and important news to communicate to him. Philotas, however, for reasons that are obscure, did not take them to see Alexander, saying that the king was busy with other, more important matters. In fact, he turned them down twice. They now became suspicious of Philotas and approached someone else instead, who got them in to see Alexander. They started by denouncing Dimnus, and then they gradually revealed that Philotas had twice done nothing when they were trying to obtain an audience with him.

This made Alexander furious, and when Dimnus resisted arrest and was killed by the man Alexander had sent to take him into custody, the thought that proof of the intrigue had been lost worried him even more. In his bitter rage against Philotas he attracted to himself those who had long hated Philotas, who now spoke their minds and said that it was careless of the king to imagine that Dimnus, a man from Chalaestra, would undertake such a bold enterprise all by himself; they said that he was no more than a hired hand, or rather a tool set to work by a greater agency, and that the source of the plot should be sought among those who had the most to gain from its concealment.

Once the king had opened his ears to this kind of argument and insinuation, Philotas' enemies began to denounce him in countless ways, and the outcome was that he was arrested and questioned, with the Companions standing by during the torture, while Alexander listened from behind a curtain which had been hung up as a divider. And they say that when Philotas pitifully and miserably begged Hephaestion for mercy, Alexander said, 'How could anyone as feeble and cowardly as you, Philotas, have taken on such a formidable task?' No sooner was Philotas dead than Alexander sent men to Media and had Parmenio killed too—Parmenio, who had been Philip's colleague in many great victories, who had been almost the only one of Alexander's older Friends to have encouraged him to invade Asia, who had given the lives of two of the three sons of his who were on active service, and who was now murdered along with the third of these sons.* These measures of Alexander's made a number of his

Friends afraid of him, especially Antipater, who entered into secret negotiations with the Aetolians and exchanged pledges with them. Aetolian fear of Alexander stemmed from the time they had destroyed Oeniadae and he had said, on hearing about it, that the Aetolians would not be punished by the sons of Oeniadae, but by him.

[50] Soon after this there occurred the business with Cleitus too,* and although at first sight it might seem more savage than what happened to Philotas, if we consider both the cause and the circumstances we find that the act was not premeditated, but that, unluckily for the king, Cleitus' drunkenness and anger furnished his spirit* with an excuse. Here is what happened. Some fruit from Greece was brought up from the coast to Alexander, and he was most impressed with how fresh and attractive it was, so he called Cleitus because he wanted to show him the fruit and give him some. Cleitus happened to be in the middle of performing a sacrifice at the time, but he left it and came over—with three of the consecrated sheep following him. When Alexander heard about this, he consulted his diviners, Aristander and Cleomenes of Laconia, who said that it was a bad omen, and so he ordered sacrifices to be carried out without delay to avert any danger from Cleitus. For in fact, two nights earlier, he had had a strange dream, in which Cleitus and Parmenio's sons were seated together all dressed in black, and all dead. However, the sacrifices for Cleitus had not yet been performed when he hurried to come and have dinner with Alexander, who had sacrificed to the Dioscuri.*

A vigorous drinking-session was initiated, and songs by a certain Pranichus (or Pierion, on some accounts) were sung, which had been composed to embarrass and mock the Macedonian generals who had recently been defeated by an eastern army. The older men protested and rebuked both the poet and the singer, but Alexander and his companions were enjoying the song and told the man to continue. Cleitus, who was drunk by then and was in any case bad-tempered and insubordinate, was particularly angry. He said that in front of barbarians and enemies* it was wrong to abuse Macedonians, who were far better men than those who were mocking them, just because they had met with a piece of bad luck. Alexander retorted that for Cleitus to make cowardice out to be a piece of bad luck was no more than special pleading. Cleitus stood up and said, 'Well, this "cowardice" kept you safe once, for all your divine parentage, when you left your back exposed to Spithridates' sword, and it was Macedonian blood and these wounds of mine that made you grand enough to disown Philip and call yourself a son of Ammon!'

[51] Alexander was furious. 'Damn you!' he hissed. 'Do you think you're going to get away with it every time you talk like that about me and set the Macedonians at one another's throats?'

'I'm not getting away with it even now, Alexander,' Cleitus replied. 'Look at how I'm rewarded for all my troubles. The lucky ones are those who have already died, to my mind, because they didn't live to see us Macedonians flogged with Median rods and having to beg Persians for an audience with our king.'

At these candid words of Cleitus', Alexander's Friends got to their feet too and hurled abuse at him, while the older men present tried to calm things down. But Alexander turned to Xenodochus of Cardia and Artemius of Colophon* and said, 'Don't you get the impression that the Greeks strut around among the Macedonians like demigods among animals?'

Cleitus refused to back down, and he told Alexander to say what he wanted to say for all to hear,† or alternatively not to invite to dinner men who were free and spoke their mind, but to surround himself with barbarians and slaves, who would do obeisance before his Persian belt and pure white tunic. At this Alexander could no longer contain his anger. He picked up one of the apples that was lying on the table, threw it at Cleitus, and hit him with it. Then he began to cast about for his sword, but one of his Bodyguards, a man called Aristonous,*† quickly removed it before he could lay his hands on it. Everyone else stood around him and begged him to calm down, but he leapt to his feet and called out in Macedonian* for the Hypaspists, which was a prearranged signal indicating serious trouble; then he ordered the trumpeter to sound the alarm and punched him when he hesitated and refused to do so. Afterwards, then, this trumpeter was congratulated for the crucial part he played in preventing panic in the camp.

Cleitus was still seething, but his friends just managed to push him out of the dining-room. He started to come in by another door, insolently and brashly quoting the following lines from Euripides' *Andromache*: 'Alas! What evil customs rule in Greece . . .'*† This was when Alexander grabbed a spear from one of the guards, and as Cleitus stepped towards him while drawing aside the curtain which covered the door he ran him through. As soon as Cleitus fell to the ground with a gasp and a bellow of pain, Alexander's anger vanished.

When he came to himself and saw his Friends standing speechless, he pulled the spear from Cleitus' body before anyone could stop him and made as if to stab himself in the throat—but was stopped by his Bodyguards, who pinioned his hands and carried him struggling into his bedroom.

[52] A night of bitter tears followed, and the next day, worn out by his cries of grief, he lay without saying a thing, sighing deeply. His Friends were worried by his silence and insisted on coming in to see him. He ignored what they all said, but when Aristander the diviner reminded him of the dream he had had about Cleitus and of the portent, as if to suggest that it had all been fated for a long time, he seemed to relax, so they brought in the philosopher Callisthenes, a relative of Aristotle's, and Anaxarchus of Abdera. While Callisthenes tried to deal with his suffering by tactful and gentle means, using euphemisms and circumlocutions to avoid giving pain, Anaxarchus, who had always had an idiosyncratic way of going about philosophy, and had acquired a reputation for despising and belittling convention, shouted out, as soon as he was in the room: 'Look at Alexander, the idol of all the world! Here he lies prostrate with grief, as afraid of people's rules and criticism as a slave, when people should really regard him as their rule and standard of right and wrong, since by his victories he has gained the right of rulership and authority, and need never be enslaved and cowed by superficial opinion. Don't you realize', he concluded, 'why Zeus has Justice and Right seated beside him? It is to ensure that every action performed by anyone in a position of authority is right and just.'

Anaxarchus may have alleviated the king's pain with this kind of argument, but he also considerably increased his conceit and his inclination to disregard rules. Moreover, he succeeded in making himself incredibly popular, while putting Alexander off Callisthenes, whose company was in any case too exacting to be pleasant. There is a story that once at dinner there was a discussion about the climate and the weather, and when Anaxarchus started to raise objections and argue against Callisthenes, who was siding with the view that it was more cold and stormy there than in Greece, Callisthenes said, 'But you have to admit that it's colder here than there. After all, you used to go through winter there wearing only a thin cloak, but here you lie down for your meals with three blankets on top of you.'* This, of course, only added to Anaxarchus' irritation with Callisthenes.

[53] Callisthenes used to annoy all the other sophists and flatterers as well, who did not like to see that the young men found his discourses interesting, and that the older men found the way he lived just as attractive. In fact, his life was so orderly, dignified, and self-sufficient that it tended to confirm the reason given for his trip abroad—that he had travelled up country to Alexander because he desired the honour of bringing his fellow citizens back home and repopulating the country of his birth.* Not only did the way others admired him make him an object of resentment, but he himself also sometimes supplied his detractors with ammunition to use against him, in that he would usually refuse invitations to dinner, and when he was in company his serious and silent manner made it seem as though he disapproved and disliked what was going on. Once, in fact, Alexander said about him, 'I can't stand a clever man who doesn't apply his intelligence to himself.'*

We are told that once at one of Alexander's dinners, to which he had invited a great many guests, Callisthenes was ordered, during the drinking-session, to give a speech eulogizing the Macedonians, and he spoke so eloquently on the topic that everyone gave him a standing ovation and threw their garlands at him. So Alexander quoted Euripides, 'Speaking well is no great problem, given good material for one's speech,'* and went on to say: 'Why don't you prove your eloquence by giving a speech criticizing the Macedonians, to teach them their faults so that they can improve?' And so the man set about his palinode and turned to outspoken and detailed criticism of the Macedonians. After showing that Greek feuding was the cause of Philip's rise to power, he said: 'But in times of civil strife even criminals become respectable.'* This made the Macedonians hate him, with a deep and bitter hatred, and Alexander said that Callisthenes had not proved his ingenuity so much as his ill-will towards the Macedonians.

[54] We have this story on the authority of Hermippus, who says that Stroebus, Callisthenes' reader, told it to Aristotle. And, Hermippus adds, when Callisthenes realized that the king was angry with him, as he was leaving he muttered two or three times under his breath the line 'Patroclus too is dead, who was a far braver man than you.'* So Aristotle seems to have hit the mark in saying that Callisthenes was a capable and powerful speaker, but lacked common sense.

Nevertheless, by his vehement objection on philosophical grounds to the act of obeisance*—he was the only one openly to discuss the issues which were secretly alarming all the best and oldest Macedonians—he averted the practice and so saved the Greeks from serious humiliation, and Alexander from even worse dishonour. This cost him his life, however, since he was generally thought to have used force rather than persuasion on the king. Chares of Mytilene says that once during a symposium, after drinking from a bowl, Alexander handed it to one of his Friends, who stood up to face the hearth, drank from the bowl, did obeisance before Alexander, and then kissed him, before resuming his place on his couch. Everyone else did the same, one after another, and then the bowl reached Callisthenes. Alexander was not watching what he was doing, but was talking to Hephaestion. After drinking, Callisthenes went over to kiss him—but Demetrius, whose surname was Pheidon, said, 'My lord, don't kiss him: he's the only one who hasn't done obeisance before you.' When Alexander refused to kiss him, Callisthenes said in a loud voice: 'All right, then, I'll go away, the poorer by a kiss.'

[55] The first consequence of the tension developing between Alexander and Callisthenes was that Hephaestion was believed when he said that Callisthenes had promised him he would do obeisance before Alexander, and had then gone back on his word. Secondly, people like Lysimachus and Hagnon stuck close to Alexander and claimed that the haughty way the sophist went around smacked of the intention to overthrow the monarchy, and that young men flocked to him and followed him around as though he were the only free man to be found among all those countless thousands of people.

In this context, when the conspiracy of Hermolaus* and his associates came to light, the accusations Callisthenes' enemies made against him seemed plausible. They said that when Hermolaus had asked him how he could become the most famous person in the world, Callisthenes had replied, 'By killing the most famous person in the world.' They also said that he had encouraged Hermolaus in his attempt by telling him not to be put off by the golden couch, but to remember that he was approaching a man, who was capable of falling ill and being wounded. And yet even when pressed to the limit, not one of Hermolaus' accomplices denounced Callisthenes. In fact, when he wrote immediately after the event to Craterus, Attalus, and Alcetas,* Alexander himself says that under torture the youths confessed that they had made this attempt by themselves and that no one else had been in on the plot. In a later letter to Antipater, however, he accuses Callisthenes of complicity and says, 'The youths were stoned to death by the Macedonians, but I shall punish the sophist myself, along with those who sent him and those who harbour in their cities men who intrigue against me.' These words are an unequivocal expression of his feelings about Aristotle, since Callisthenes, as a relative (his mother Hera was Aristotle's cousin), had been brought up in Aristotle's home.

As for Callisthenes' death, some say that he was hanged by Alexander, and others that he was imprisoned and died of disease, but Chares says that after his arrest he was kept in prison for seven months so that he could be tried before the congress* with Aristotle present, but that around the time when Alexander was wounded in India, Callisthenes died a vastly overweight, louse-ridden man.

[56] But this happened later. Meanwhile, Demaratus of Corinth, who was by now getting on in age, conceived the ambition to travel up country to see Alexander, and having done so declared that the Greeks who had died before they could see Alexander seated on Darius' throne had missed a rare treat.* However, he did not get to enjoy the king's goodwill towards him for long, because he died after a debilitating illness. He received a magnificent funeral, and the army raised as a memorial of his death a mound eighty cubits high and with an enormous base. His remains were taken down to the coast on a spectacularly decorated four-horse chariot.

[57] Alexander was poised to set out across the mountains into India,* but he could see that his army was by now bogged down by the weight of all the booty they had taken. At dawn one day, therefore, after the baggage had been packed on to the carts, he began by burning his own and his Companions' booty, and then gave orders to set fire to the Macedonians' takings as well. In the end, the deed proved to be considerably less difficult and formidable in the execution than it was in the planning. For only a few men found it unwelcome, while the majority set to with a will. Shouting and cheering, they shared essentials with those who needed them, and burnt and destroyed with their own hands anything that was superfluous. Their enthusiasm filled Alexander with energy and resolution, and in any case by this stage of his career his men had come to fear him, as an implacable punisher of wrongdoing. There was, for instance,

the occasion when one of his Companions, a man called Menander to whom Alexander had given command of a military outpost, refused to stay* where he had been posted, and Alexander killed him; then there was Orsodates, a Persian who rose up in revolt against him, whom Alexander personally shot with his bow.

When a sheep gave birth to a lamb with a mark on its head which in both shape and colouring was like a tiara with testicles on either side of it, Alexander found the portent disgusting and had himself purified by the Babylonians whom he invariably kept around for this kind of purpose. He told his Friends that he was not worried for his own sake, but for theirs, in case after his death the gods might confer power on an ignoble and impotent man.* However, a more promising portent occurred, and Alexander's spirits lifted. Proxenus, the Macedonian whose job it was to supervise those who took care of the king's furnishings, was excavating a site for Alexander's tent beside the river Oxus when he uncovered a spring of oily and fatty liquid. When they skimmed the surface off, it immediately bubbled up pure and translucent, seemingly identical to olive-oil in smell and taste, and completely indistinguishable as far as its brightness and oily texture were concerned. And yet this was a country where there were no olive-trees growing. The water of the Oxus itself is also said to be very soft, and consequently to make one's skin sleek if one bathes in it. In any case, a letter of Alexander's to Antipater shows how incredibly pleased he was at the portent: he counted it one of the most important omens the god had ever given him. His diviners, however, interpreted the portent as signifying a campaign in which glory would be won by a great deal of effort and hard work, since oil is a gift from the god to men 'for the relief of their weariness'.*

[58] And so Alexander was often in dangerous situations during battles, and sustained serious wounds, but it was the shortage of essential supplies and the severity of the weather that took the greatest toll of the army. But Alexander was determined that fortune would fall to daring, strength to courage: he was convinced that there was no position so impregnable that it could keep brave men out, and none so secure that it could keep cowards safe. It is said that during the siege of Sisimithres' stronghold, which was built on such a sheer and inaccessible rock that his men despaired of taking it, Alexander asked Oxyartes what kind of man Sisimithres was. When Oxyartes replied that he was a terrible coward, Alexander said, 'So you for one

are saying that we can take this rock, since it is insecure at the top.'* And in fact the rock did fall to him as a result of Sisimithres' fear. During his assault on another rock, just as precipitous, with a detachment of younger Macedonians, he said to one of them, whose name was Alexander,* 'Well, we expect to see *you* fight bravely because of your name.' And when the young man died fighting brilliantly, Alexander's grief knew no bounds.

When the Macedonians were reluctant to advance on the city of Nysa,* because there was a deep river by it, Alexander stood on the riverbank and said, 'What an utter fool I am! Why did I never learn to swim?' And he was ready to try to cross even though he was carrying his shield.† After he had called a halt to the fighting, a delegation came from the besieged stronghold to ask for terms; first of all, they were astonished to find him unkempt and still wearing his armour, and then, when a pillow was brought for him, he told the oldest member of the delegation, a man called Acouphis, to take it for his seat. Acouphis, impressed by his self-possession and kindness, asked him what it would take for them to be on good terms with him. 'I'd like to see them make you their ruler,' Alexander replied, 'and send me their 100 best men.' Acouphis laughed and said, 'But I'll be doing a better job as ruler, my lord, if I send you my worst men, not my best.'

[59] Taxiles' kingdom in India* is said to have been as large as Egypt and to have contained excellent land, both for livestock and arable farming. He is also supposed to have been a man of considerable intelligence. When he met Alexander, after they had exchanged greetings he said, 'Why do we have to fight and make war on each other, Alexander? It's not as if you have come to steal our water or essential foods, which are the only things men with any sense should feel compelled to fight for. As for other forms of wealth and what men call possessions, if I'm better off than you in these things, I'll happily do you a good turn, and if I'm worse off, I have no objection to being in a position to thank you for any good turn you do me.'

Alexander liked the man a great deal. He took him by the hand and said, 'Do you really think these welcoming words of yours can avert a battle arising from our meeting? No, I won't let you prevail. I shall fight to the bitter end, pitching my generosity against yours, to make sure that you don't get the better of me in kindness.' Eventually, after he had received a great many gifts and had given even more, Alexander presented Taxiles with 1,000 talents of coined money—which really upset his Friends, but went a long way towards disarming the hostility of many of the natives.

The best fighters among the Indians were mercenaries whose strenuous defence of various cities which called them in did Alexander a great deal of harm. Once, after he had entered into a truce with them at one of these cities, he ambushed them on the road as they were leaving and annihilated them all.* This act of his is like a stain on his military achievements, since he generally fought in accordance with the rules of war and behaved as a king should. Moreover, the philosophers irritated him just as much as these mercenaries, by vilifying any kings who joined him and inciting the populations of autonomous cities to rebel against him. So he hanged a great many of them too.*

[60] He himself has described the course of his battle against Porus* in his letters. He says that the Hydaspes flowed between the two armies and that Porus kept his elephants constantly stationed on the opposite bank† to guard the crossing. Under these circumstances, then, he had his men make a great deal of random noise every day as they went about their business in the camp, so that the enemy would get used to it and not view it as a reason for alarm. Then on a stormy, moonless night he took an infantry detachment and the pick of his cavalry quite a way from the enemy, and crossed over to a small island in the river. While he was there the rain started pelting down, and his troops were struck by frequent thunderbolts and buffeted by high winds. Although he could see that some of his men were being burnt to death by the thunderbolts, he set out from the island and began to make his way over to the opposite bank. But the Hydaspes had been whipped up and swollen by the storm and, as it rushed down, it gouged a deep channel and quite a bit of its water began to flow down this new channel. His men could find no sure footing on the ground between the two currents, since it was slippery and broken up. It was at this point, we hear, that he said, 'Men of Athens, you'll probably find incredible the terrible dangers I face in order to win your good opinion.'

But that is from Onesicritus. Alexander himself says that they abandoned their rafts and crossed the channel in their armour, wading through chest-high water. After they had crossed he rode with the cavalry twenty stades ahead of the infantry, his idea being that if the enemy attacked with their cavalry he would easily overcome them, and if they moved up their infantry his own infantry would still have time to reach him. And in fact one of these two possibilities did happen: he was attacked by a force consisting of 1,000 horsemen and sixty chariots, and he routed them, capturing all the chariots and killing 400 of the horsemen.

Porus now realized that Alexander himself had crossed the river, and he advanced towards him with his whole army, except for a small force he left behind to stop any Macedonians who tried to ford the crossing. Alexander's chief worries were the elephants and the sheer size of the enemy army, so while he charged one of the wings, he ordered Coenus to lead the Macedonian right wing into the attack. The enemy was routed, and on both sides the troops who were pushed back retreated towards the elephants and became crowded together at the centre. From then on, for seven hours or more until the enemy finally gave up, the battle was fought at close quarters.

This is the account of the battle given by its prime mover in his letters. Most writers agree that Porus was four-and-a-half cubits tall, and that because of his height and massive body he fitted his elephant just as well as a horseman does his horse—and this despite the fact that his was the largest elephant in the army. This elephant also showed astonishing intelligence and concern for its royal master: while he was still safe and sound, the creature bravely warded off and beat back attackers, but once it sensed that he was failing because of the number of times he had been struck by missiles and wounded, it became afraid that he might slip off. It calmly lowered itself down on to its knees, and then gently took hold of each of the spears with its trunk and pulled them out of his body.

Porus was taken prisoner, and when Alexander asked him how he should treat him, he replied, 'As a king should.' Alexander went on to ask him if he had anything else to add, but he said, ' "As a king should" covers everything.' So Alexander not only let him rule over his former kingdom with the title of satrap, but also gave him extra territory, once he had subdued its autonomous inhabitants,† which is said to have included fifteen peoples, 5,000 notable towns, and countless villages. He also made one of his Companions, Philip, the satrap of another territory three times the size of this satrapy of Porus'.

[61] Another thing that happened after the battle against Porus was that Bucephalas died—not immediately afterwards, but some time later. He died, according to most writers, from wounds for which he was undergoing treatment, but Onesicritus says that he

died of old age, a broken-down old horse, aged thirty at the time of his death. Alexander took his death very hard, since he felt exactly as though he had lost a close and loyal friend, and he founded in his memory a city on the banks of the Hydaspes, which he called Bucephalia. There is also a story that when Alexander lost a dog he loved called Peritas, which he personally had brought up, he founded a city named after it. Sotion says he heard this from Potamon of Lesbos.*

[62] Now, the battle against Porus took the edge off the Macedonians' appetite for war and checked their advance further into India. It had not been easy for them to repel Porus, who had taken to the field with 20,000 foot and 2,000 horse, and so they strongly resisted the pressure coming from Alexander to cross the Ganges as well*—a river, they discovered, which was thirty-two stades wide and 100 fathoms deep, and whose further shores were covered with huge numbers of armed men, horses, and elephants. For they were hearing reports that the kings of the Gandaritae and the Praesians were waiting for them with 80,000 horse, 200,000 foot, 8,000 chariots, and 6,000 war elephants. Nor do these reports seem to have been exaggerated, because Sandrocottus,*† who reigned there not long after this, gave Seleucus 500 elephants, and overran and conquered the whole of India with an army of 600,000 men.

At first, then, Alexander shut himself up in his tent and lay there in sullen anger, refusing to feel any gratitude for what he had already achieved unless he could cross the Ganges as well; in fact, to his way of thinking, withdrawal was the same as an admission of defeat. But his Friends gave him plausible reasons for not feeling so bad, men from his army stood by the entrance to his tent with tears and protestations, and between them they implored him to change his mind. Eventually he relented and began to break camp, and while doing so came up with a number of tricks and subterfuges designed to influence the Indians' impressions of him. For instance, he had an unusually large suit of armour made, and oversized horses' mangers and particularly heavy bits, all of which he left behind, scattered here and there as if casually cast aside. He also set up altars to the gods,* which are still used for sacred purposes by the kings of the Praesians when they cross the river: they perform sacrifices in the Greek manner at them. Sandrocottus, who was then just a young man, actually saw Alexander, and he often used to say in later years that Alexander came very close to gaining control of the land, since the king at the time was hated and despised for his iniquity and low birth.*

[63] Next Alexander had large numbers of rafts and oared ferry-boats built and began to make his way at a leisurely pace down the rivers, because he wanted to see the outer sea.* Not that the voyage was entirely idle or unwarlike, however: he used to land and attack the settlements he came across. All of them, without exception, fell to him, but when he took on the people known as the Malli, who have the reputation of being the best fighters in India, he came very close to being cut down. After sweeping the defenders off the walls with a hail of missiles, a ladder was placed against the wall and he was the first up it, but then the ladder was broken and he found himself exposed to the missiles of the Indians who lined the bottom of the wall below him. Despite being almost alone he crouched down and leapt into the middle of the enemy, and luckily landed on his feet. As he brandished his weapons, the Indians saw a flash of flame* and an apparition moving in front of his body, and so at first they fled and scattered. But when they saw that he was supported by only two Hypaspists, they rushed up, and while he defended himself against those who fought him at close range, trying to pierce his armour and wound him with their swords and spears, one of them stood back a little and fired an arrow from his bow with such energy and force that it penetrated his breastplate and lodged in his ribcage. The force of the blow pushed Alexander back and he sank to his knees, while his assailant charged up with his Indian dagger drawn, and Peucestas and Limnaeus defended their king. Both of them sustained wounds, which proved fatal for Limnaeus, but Peucestas held out, and Alexander killed the Indian. However, he had received a number of wounds, and finally a blow on the neck from a club forced him to rest his back against the wall, with his eyes still fixed on his enemies. Meanwhile his Macedonian troops had formed a solid mass around him and, now unconscious of his surroundings, he was snatched away and taken to his tent. In no time at all a rumour had arisen in the camp that Alexander had been killed, but, although it was a difficult and time-consuming task, they sawed off the wooden shaft of the arrow, so that they could then ease off the breastplate and get down to cutting out the head of the arrow, which was embedded in one of his ribs, and is said to have been three fingers wide and four long. During its removal, therefore, Alexander passed out and came

very close to death, but he pulled through.* Even after he was out of danger, he remained weak for a long time and had to keep to a regimen and a course of treatment; but one day he heard outside his tent the Macedonians clamouring in their desire to catch sight of him, so he got a cloak and went out to them. Then, after sacrificing to the gods, he boarded his ship again and continued on his way down river, conquering plenty of territory and major cities on his way.

[64] He captured the ten gymnosophists* who had been the ringleaders behind Sabbas' rebellion* and had therefore done the Macedonians a very great deal of harm. They were reputed to have the ability to answer questions cleverly and pithily, so Alexander put difficult questions to them, with the warning that he would kill the first one to give an incorrect answer, and then the rest, one after another, on the same principle. He started with the oldest one, and asked him whether, in his opinion, the living or the dead were more numerous: 'The living,' he said, 'because the dead no longer exist.' The second was asked whether the earth or the sea produced larger creatures: 'The earth,' he said, 'since the sea is part of the earth.' The third was asked which animal was the greatest nuisance: 'An animal as yet undiscovered by man,' he replied. The fourth was asked why he had persuaded Sabbas to revolt, and he replied: 'Because I wanted him either to live an honourable life or to die an honourable death.' The fifth was asked which came first, in his opinion, day or night: 'Day,' he said, 'by a day.' And when the king looked puzzled, he added that hard questions are bound to have hard answers. So Alexander moved on to the sixth gymnosophist and asked him how a man could best win popularity: 'By being extremely powerful,' he said, 'without being an object of fear.'

That left three gymnosophists. One was asked how a man might become a god: 'By doing something', he answered, 'that a man cannot do.' The next one was asked which was stronger, life or death: 'Life,' he said, 'because it carries so much suffering.' And the last one was asked how long a man should live: 'Until he has stopped considering death preferable to life,' he replied. So then Alexander turned to the judge and told him to deliver his verdict. He said that they had each given a worse answer than the one before. 'In that case,' Alexander said, 'you will be the first to die for giving this verdict.' But he said, 'No, my lord, unless you were lying when you said that the first to die would be the one who gave the worst answer.'

[65] He gave these gymnosophists gifts and let them go, but there were others who were particularly highly regarded and lived in peace and isolation. He sent Onesicritus, a philosopher who was a follower of Diogenes the Cynic, to ask them to pay him a visit. Onesicritus tells us that Calanus dealt with him brusquely and rudely, ordering him to strip naked before listening to what he had to say, and telling him that otherwise he would not talk to him even if he had been sent from Zeus. Dandamis, however, was more even-tempered: he listened while Onesicritus spoke about Socrates, Pythagoras, and Diogenes, and then remarked that for all their obvious natural talents, they had lived in too much awe of convention.* Other writers claim, however, that Dandamis said absolutely nothing except: 'Why did Alexander bother to come all the way here?'

However, Taxiles did manage to persuade Calanus to pay Alexander a visit. Calanus' real name was Sphines, but since he greeted people he met in the Indian language and said '*Kale*' instead of 'Hello', he came to be called Calanus by the Greeks. This is the man who is also said to have given Alexander a famous illustration of government. He threw a dry and shrivelled hide on to the ground and stepped on the edge of it, which pressed it down there, but made it rise up everywhere else; then he went all the way around the edge, pressing down on each bit in turn and showing what happened. Finally, he stood in the middle of the hide, and that checked it and kept the whole hide still. This was meant to be a vivid demonstration of how important it was for Alexander to put pressure on the middle of his empire and not travel far away from it.

[66] His voyage down the rivers to the sea took seven months.* After emerging into the Ocean with his fleet, he sailed back to an island which he called Scilloustis (although others knew it as Psiltoucis), where he landed and sacrificed to the gods. He carried out a survey of the open sea and of as much of the shoreline as was accessible, and then, after praying that no one might ever beat his record and go further than he had gone in this expedition, he turned back. He ordered the fleet to sail along the coast, keeping India on their right, and he put Nearchus* in overall command, with Onesicritus as chief helmsman. Meanwhile, he himself made his way by land through the territory of the Oreitae, where things could not have gone worse for him.* He lost so many men that by the time he left India his fighting force had been reduced by more than three-quarters—and this was an army which

had once consisted of 120,000 foot and about 15,000 horse. But serious illnesses, inadequate food, scorching heat, and above all starvation carried them off, since they were crossing an uncultivated land, inhabited by people who eked out a miserable existence with the few wretched sheep they owned—sheep they usually fed on sea-fish, and which therefore had offensive, foul-smelling flesh. At last, after sixty days, they made their way across this region and reached Gedrosia, where they immediately had more than enough of everything, supplied by the nearest satraps and kings.

[67] After recruiting fresh troops from Gedrosia, then, he set out on a riotous seven-day journey through Carmania. He himself was pulled along at an easy pace by eight horses, on a dais fixed on a tall, conspicuous, oblong scaffold, feasting continuously with his Companions, day and night. He was followed by an enormous train of wagons, each with some means of protecting its passengers from the sun—either purple-dyed or embroidered canopies, or boughs which were kept constantly green and fresh. These carts carried the rest of his Friends and the officers of his army, all of whom wore garlands and were drinking. There was not a shield or helmet or pike to be seen, but all the way along the road there were soldiers ladling wine out of huge jars and vats with bowls, cups, and beakers, and drinking to one another's health, some doing so even while they marched along, others lying by the side of the road. The whole place resounded with the frequent strains of wind-pipes and reed-pipes, of song and lyre, and with the shrieks of Bacchic women. They accompanied their disorderly and meandering progress with games of Bacchic licence, as if the god himself were present and were taking part in the revel.*

And when Alexander reached the palace of Gedrosia,* he again gave his army a break while he celebrated a festival with a public procession. There is a story that he was watching a choral competition, rather the worse for drink, and his boyfriend Bagoas, after winning the dancing contest, made his way through the audience, still in his costume, and sat down beside him. At this sight the Macedonians applauded and called out for Alexander to kiss him, until he put his arms around him and gave him a loving kiss.

[68] While he was there Nearchus came up to see him. Alexander listened with delight to his account of his voyage, and became enthusiastic about the prospect of himself taking a large fleet and sailing down the Euphrates, around the coasts of Arabia and Libya, and

through the Pillars of Heracles into the inner sea. He got to the stage of having all kinds of ships under construction at Thapsacus,* with sailors and helmsmen pouring in from all over the place, but the difficulty of his return journey so far, the wound he had received fighting the Malli, and rumours of the heavy losses his army had sustained, raised doubts about whether he would survive the planned expedition. These doubts encouraged rebellion among the subject peoples, and caused his military governors and satraps to act with gross injustice, greed, and brutality, until the whole of the empire was riddled with turmoil and instability. Olympias and Cleopatra had even fallen out with Antipater and divided his principality between them, with Olympias taking Epirus and Cleopatra Macedonia. When Alexander heard about this he remarked that Olympias had made the wiser choice, because the Macedonians would not put up with being ruled by a woman.*

So Alexander ordered Nearchus to put to sea again, since he had made up his mind to fill the whole coastline with settlements,† while he himself went down and set about punishing those of his military governors who had abused their powers. He personally killed Oxyartes, one of the sons of Aboulites, by running him through with a pike, and when Aboulites failed to furnish him with provisions, but brought him 3,000 talents of coined money instead, he gave orders that the money was to be offered to the horses. When they refused to touch it, he said, 'What use are these provisions of yours to us?', and threw Aboulites into prison.

[69] The first thing he did in Persis was pay the womenfolk their money, in accordance with the custom by which whenever Persian kings arrive in the country they give some gold to every woman there. This explains why some of them, we hear, did not go there very often, and Ochus* not even once: he was so mean that he preferred voluntary self-exile from the country of his birth.

Secondly, when he discovered that the tomb of Cyrus had been broken into, he had the person who had committed the crime put to death, even though the culprit was an eminent Macedonian from Pella called Poulomachus.* After reading the inscription on the tomb, he had a Greek version transcribed underneath the original. This is how the Greek version reads: 'Sir, whoever you may be and wherever you may be from, know that I am Cyrus, who gained the Persians their empire. Therefore do not begrudge me this earth which covers my body: it is not so very much.' This reminder of the uncertainty and instability of things profoundly moved Alexander.

It was here that Calanus, who had been suffering for a short while from an intestinal disorder, asked for his funeral pyre to be built. After riding to the pyre on horseback, he offered up a prayer, purified himself with a sprinkling of water, and consecrated some of his hair, before climbing up on to the pyre. He greeted the Macedonians who were present, urged them to make that day one of pleasure and of drinking with the king—and told them that he would soon be seeing the king in Babylon.* Then he lay down and covered his head. The approach of the flames did not make him move; he stayed exactly as he was when he lay down, and made an acceptable sacrifice of himself in accordance with the traditional practice of the sophists of his country. Many years later in Athens another Indian, when meeting with Caesar, did the same as Calanus, and even today people point out his tomb, which is called 'The Tomb of the Indian'.*

[70] After leaving the funeral pyre, Alexander called a lot of his Friends and officers from the army together for a banquet, and proposed that they should hold a contest in drinking undiluted wine, with a garland for the winner. Promachus managed to down four choes, which was the largest quantity, so he received the prize of a garland, which was a talent in weight, but he lasted only another three days before dying.* In fact, according to Chares, forty-one of the company died from the after-effects of the drink as well, when severe cold followed upon their drinking.

At Susa he arranged a mass marriage of his Companions.* He himself took Stateira, Darius' daughter, for his wife, and in assigning his men their brides he tried to match excellence with excellence. Then he held a wedding-feast not only for them, but also for any Macedonians who had got married earlier. According to my sources, there were 9,000 guests at the feast, and not only was every single one given a gold drinking-bowl for the libations, but everything else was on just as spectacular and astonishing a scale. And, if any of them were in debt, Alexander paid off their creditors, which cost him in all 9,870 talents. When Antigenes the One-Eyed got himself falsely listed as a debtor and produced someone who claimed that he had lent him money against his bank, Alexander paid the man back the money, but then, when the deception was found out, he was so angry that he banished Antigenes from his court and stripped him of his command. However, Antigenes was a brilliant soldier, and while still a young man, during Philip's siege of Perinthus,* despite having been wounded in the eye by a bolt from a catapult, he refused to let the bolt be removed or to rest until he had pushed the enemy back and pinned them inside the walls. On the occasion in question, then, his shame at being disgraced knew no bounds, and it was clear that his grief and depression were going to make him do away with himself. Alexander did not want to see that happen, however, so he forgave him and told him to keep the money.

[71] The 30,000 boys he had left to be trained and educated* had developed manly physiques and handsome features, and displayed remarkable skill and agility in their exercises. Alexander himself was delighted with their progress, but the Macedonians were saddened and frightened by the thought that the king would pay them less attention. So when he sent the sick and disabled back down to the coast, they called it a foul insult for him first to make the fullest possible use of people, and then to discard them in disgrace and toss them back to their homelands and parents, just because they were no longer the men he had recruited. They asked him why he did not send them all away and regard all Macedonians as useless now that he had these young blades to help him sweep across the world and bring it all under his control.

This made Alexander furious. In his rage he cursed them thoroughly, dismissed his guards, and brought in Persians to do the job instead, using them to make up his units of bodyguards and attendants. When the Macedonians saw him being escorted by Persians, while they were excluded and reviled, they were humbled, and after talking the matter over came to the conclusion that they had been driven almost out of their minds by jealous rage. In the end they came to their senses and, without carrying arms or wearing armour over their tunics, went to Alexander's tent. With cries and tears of grief, they put themselves in his hands and asked him to deal with them as their iniquity and ingratitude deserved, but he refused to accept their petition, although in fact his attitude had already begun to soften. They would not go away, however: they stayed just as they were by his tent for two days and nights, without lessening their lamentations or their appeals to their lord and master. On the third day he emerged from his tent and when he saw their pitiful and wretched state he wept for a long time before gently telling them off and speaking kindly to them.* Then he dismissed those who were *hors de combat*, after giving them magnificent gifts, and told Antipater in a letter that they should have the right to wear garlands and have the front seats whenever any public games were being held or there was a production at a theatre. He also made the sons of those who had died stipendiary orphans.

[72] At Ecbatana in Media,* as soon as he had dealt with matters that needed his urgent attention, he became involved once again with theatrical productions and public festivals, since 3,000 performers had arrived from Greece. Sometime around then Hephaestion contracted a fever, but with a young man's impatience he refused to submit to a strict regime. As soon as the doctor, Glaucus, had left, he went to the theatre and ate a morning meal of boiled chicken, accompanied by a large cooler of wine, whereupon he was taken ill, and died a short while later.

Alexander went out of his mind with grief at his death.* He immediately gave orders that all horses and mules were to be shorn as a sign of mourning, and that the fortifications of the cities thereabouts were to be dismantled; he had the wretched doctor impaled on a stake, and banned playing the pipes and all music in the camp for a considerable period of time, until he received an oracle from Ammon, telling him to worship Hephaestion as a hero and to institute sacrificial rituals in his honour.* He used warfare as a means of consolation, and went out after men as if he were going out hunting. So he not only conquered the Cossaeans,* but slaughtered all the adult male inhabitants, and described this massacre as an offering to Hephaestion. He planned to spend thousands upon thousands of talents on his tomb and on an elaborate funeral, and since he wanted to get more than his money's worth in terms of craftsmanship and originality of design, he was desperate to get as the architect Stasicrates,* who was breaking new ground with structures displaying splendour, boldness, and ostentation. For instance, at a previous meeting between the two men Stasicrates had said that there was no mountain better suited than Athos in Thrace for being given the form and shape of a man, and so, if Alexander gave him the go-ahead, he would turn Athos into an effigy of him that would surpass all others in terms of endurance and prominence, holding in its left hand a city of 10,000 inhabitants, and dispensing with its right hand a mighty river whose waters would flow into the sea. Alexander had turned down this offer, but now he was busy working with his architects to develop and devise far more extraordinary and expensive projects.

[73] Alexander next set out for Babylon.* *En route* there he was rejoined by Nearchus, who had completed his voyage into the Euphrates from the great sea, and Nearchus told him of the advice some Chaldaeans he had met had given him, to the effect that Alexander should keep away from Babylon. Alexander ignored this advice, however, and continued on his way—and then, just as he reached the city walls, he saw a large number of crows wheeling about in the air and striking at one another, and some of the crows fell dead at his feet. Next, on receiving a report that Apollodorus, the military governor of Babylon, had commissioned a sacrifice to try to see what the future held for Alexander, he summoned the diviner, Pythagoras, who made no attempt to deny that he had performed the rite. When Alexander asked him what the entrails had been like and received the reply that the liver had had no lobe, he exclaimed, 'Ah! What a powerful omen!' He did not punish Pythagoras, however, and he regretted having ignored Nearchus' advice. In fact, he spent most of the time camped outside Babylon or cruising up and down the Euphrates.

There were also a number of other omens that worried him. For instance, the largest and most handsome lion in his menagerie was set upon and kicked to death by a tame donkey. And once he had stripped to oil himself for a ball-game, and when the time came for him to get his clothes again, the young men he had been playing with saw a man sitting in silence on Alexander's throne, wearing the royal diadem and robes. When he was asked who he was, there was a long pause before he pulled himself together at last and said that his name was Dionysius and that he came from Messene. He went on to tell them that he had been brought there from the coast, because he had been accused of some crime or other, and had been in prison for a long time; then a short while ago, he said, Sarapis had come and released him from his chains and brought him there, with instructions to take the robes and the diadem and sit down without saying a word.*

[74] After hearing the man's story, Alexander did away with him, as the diviners recommended, but he remained depressed—no longer confident of the favour of the gods and suspicious of his friends. He was especially afraid of Antipater and his sons.* One of these sons, Iolas, was his chief cup-bearer, but the other, Cassander, had only

recently joined him, and when he saw some easterners doing obeisance before Alexander, he could not stop himself laughing, because he had been brought up in the Greek manner and had never seen anything like that before. Alexander lost his temper, grabbed hold of Cassander's hair violently with both hands, and pounded his head against the wall. On another occasion, when Cassander wanted to respond to some men who were lodging complaints against Antipater, Alexander interrupted him and said, 'What do you mean? Do you think people would make such a long journey if they had no genuine grievances and just wanted to lie?' Cassander said that the very fact that they had travelled so far from the evidence proved that they were lying, but Alexander laughed at him and said, 'This is just another one of those sophisms you followers of Aristotle have devised for arguing either side of a case, but you'll suffer for it if I find that you've done these men the slightest wrong.'

In short, it is said that fear of Alexander took hold of Cassander's mind with such terrible force and became so deeply embedded there that many years later, when he was king of Macedon and master of Greece, he was walking around Delphi looking at the statues, when he suddenly glimpsed a statue of Alexander and became so terrified that his body shuddered and trembled, he nearly fainted at the sight, and it took a long time for him to recover.*

[75] Anyway, now that Alexander had abandoned himself to superstition, there was no unusual or odd event, however insignificant, that did not appear to his troubled and terrified mind to be an ominous portent. All over the palace people could be found performing sacrifices, ritual purifications, and divinations—and filling Alexander with inane fear. This shows that while contemptuous doubt of the supernatural is an awful thing, superstition is terrible as well: like water, it always finds its way down to the lowest level and <. . .>†

Nevertheless, when he received the oracles from the god about Hephaestion, he set aside his grief and turned once more to sacrificial feasts and drinking. Once he gave a spectacular banquet in honour of Nearchus, and then, although he had taken his customary bath before going to bed, when Medeius asked him to a drunken party, he accepted the invitation. After spending the whole night and the next day there drinking, he began to feel feverish. The fever was not brought on by his having drained Heracles' goblet, nor did it follow a sudden pain in the back as if he had been stabbed by a spear, even though both these stories can be found in authors who felt obliged to write as if they were creating the tragic and emotive finale of a great drama.* Aristobulus, however, says that he had a severe fever, and that as a result of his raging thirst he drank some wine, after which delirium set in, and he died on the thirtieth of Daisios.*

[76] But here is the account of his illness recorded in the Royal Diary.* On the eighteenth of Daisios he slept in the bathroom because of his fever. The next day, after bathing, he went back to his bedroom and spent the day playing dice with Medeius. In the evening he took his bath, performed the sacrificial rites to the gods, ate a light meal, and had a fever throughout the night. On the twentieth he had another bath, made a sacrifice as usual to the gods, and passed the time on a couch in the bathroom, listening to Nearchus' tales of his voyage and the great sea. On the twenty-first he did the same again, but was running a worse fever; he passed an uncomfortable night and was extremely feverish the next day. He had his bed moved to beside the large swimming-pool, where he lay and had a discussion with his generals about the lack of officers in some regiments, and how they should go about assessing men to fill the vacancies. On the twenty-fourth he was extremely feverish and had to be carried outside to perform his sacrifices, and he told his senior officers to wait in the palace courtyard, while the regimental commanders and the commanders of the units of 500 were to spend the night outside the palace. On the twenty-fifth he was carried to the palace on the other side of the river, where he got a little sleep, but the fever did not abate. When his officers came in to see him, they found him incapable of talking, and the same thing happened again on the twenty-sixth. Under these circumstances the Macedonians believed that he had died, and they came crying and shouting to his door; they threatened the Companions until they had no choice but to open the doors for them, and then one by one, dressed only in their tunics, they all filed passed his couch. It was also on this day that Peithon* and Seleucus were sent to the sanctuary of Sarapis* to ask if they should bring Alexander there, but the god told them to leave him where he was. And then he died late in the afternoon of the twenty-eighth.

[77] This is an almost verbatim transcript of the account in the Royal Diary. No one had any suspicion at the time that Alexander had been poisoned, but five years later, we hear, on the strength of information she had been given, Olympias had a large number of men put

to death, and scattered the remains of Iolas' body, on the grounds that it was he who had administered the poison.*

There are some writers who claim that Aristotle put Antipater up to the deed, and that the collection of the poison was entirely Aristotle's doing. They say that they have this on the authority of a certain Hagnothemis, who in his turn heard it from King Antigonus. The alleged poison was freezing-cold water from a certain cliff in Nonacris which† people gather in the same way one collects delicate dew, and store in a donkey's hoof, which is the only container that can keep it in, since it is so cold and acidic that it eats its way through everything else.* However, most writers take the story about the poisoning to be nothing but a fabrication, and it is strong support for their case that throughout the period when Alexander's officers were quarrelling among themselves,* which lasted quite a few days, his body lay untended in various warm, unventilated spots, but stayed fresh and unblemished, without showing any signs of decay.*

Now, Rhoxane happened to be pregnant, which made the Macedonians especially proud of her, but she was jealous of Stateira. She used a forged letter to trick her into coming, and once she had got her there she killed her and her sister, threw the bodies into a well, and filled it in. Perdiccas was in on the plot and helped her carry it out, because immediately following Alexander's death he was the one who gained the most power, by attracting the support of Arrhidaeus, who was, so to speak, a cipher of kingship, since his mother was an undistinguished commoner called Philinna, and an illness had made him weak in the head. This was neither an accident nor congenital: as a boy, they say, his cleverness and natural gifts were plain to see, but then his mind became ruined when he was poisoned by Olympias.*

DEMOSTHENES

INTRODUCTION

The Athenian Demosthenes (*c.*384–322 BCE) was a passionate anti-Macedonian politician, who has long been regarded as one of the greatest exponents of Greek oratory. His career as a public speaker began early, when he successfully prosecuted his guardians for mismanaging the estate that had been bequeathed to him by his late father. He spent some time as a speech-writer for hire before gradually becoming more involved in politics. He did not immediately appreciate the danger posed by Philip II of Macedon, who in less than a decade had transformed a minor kingdom into a major force. But from the late 350s, with Philip now master of Thessaly, Demosthenes spoke out increasingly against Macedon. In 349 he delivered his three *Olynthiacs*, urging the defence of Olynthus in the Chalcidic peninsula, but they failed to prevent the capture and destruction of the city the following year. In 346 both Demosthenes and his fellow orator Aeschines were involved in negotiating a peace with Philip known as the Peace of Philocrates. This highly contentious agreement was rapidly denounced by Demosthenes, and led to years of hostility between the two men that found bitter expression in the law-courts, beginning with Demosthenes' unsuccessful prosecution of Aeschines in 343 and concluding with the latter's exile in 330 after his own failed prosecution of Ctesiphon for proposing that Demosthenes be honoured with a crown. Unusually the speeches of both Demosthenes and Aeschines survive in each case (Demosthenes, *On the False Embassy* and *On the Crown*; Aeschines, *On the False Embassy* and *Against Ctesiphon*).

In the years after the peace, Demosthenes became more and more influential in the Athenian Assembly. It was then that the majority of his powerful anti-Macedonian speeches, the *Philippics*, were delivered. When Philip advanced into central Greece in 338, it was Demosthenes who negotiated the alliance with Thebes that led the two cities to make their ill-fated stand against Macedon at the battle of Chaeronea. This failure did little to dent Demosthenes' popularity in the short term; the same year he was invited to give the oration over the war dead and not long afterwards he was presented with the crown. But his influence appears to have declined during the years of Macedonian rule, so much so that in early 323 he went into exile after being found guilty of accepting a substantial bribe from the renegade Macedonian Harpalus, who had taken temporary refuge in Athens. On the death of Alexander later that year he was back in Athens supporting the Greek rebellion against Macedon, a conflict that has come to be known as the Lamian War. With the defeat of the Greek forces at Crannon in 322 he fled to the island of Calauria, where he chose to commit suicide rather than hand himself over to the Macedonians.

Demosthenes may have advocated resistance to Macedon, but he was not a military figure. This makes him unusual among the subjects of the *Lives*, who for the most part had significant military careers. Plutarch paired Demosthenes with the Roman orator and politician Cicero, a man with similarly limited military experience. In both cases their fame and political success rested on their skill in oratory. The comparison between the two men did not originate with Plutarch. The speeches that Cicero delivered against Antony had long been known as the *Philippics*, a name originally given to them in jest by Cicero himself (*Letters to Brutus* 2.3.4). Plutarch, however, appears to have taken the comparison much further than anyone else had done previously. It was, he suggested, as if Nature and Fortune were each struggling to make the men as similar as possible. Not only were they alike in character, both being eager for honour, champions of freedom, and prone to cowardice, but they also faced the same challenges, namely an obscure family background, conflict with kings and despots, loss of a daughter, exile and honourable recall, and a death that coincided with the end of freedom (3). Plutarch may shape his narrative to highlight these similarities, but they also give him an opportunity to explore the different ways people react to the same event. For example, when Demosthenes lost his daughter, he put aside his grief to celebrate the news of Philip II's death. Although Plutarch was critical of the Athenians celebrating the death of a man they had earlier honoured, he approved of the way Demosthenes put the affairs of state before his own personal grief. Dwelling on it should be left to women. Plutarch here allows himself an extended discussion of how grief should best be handled, a discussion that looks forward to Cicero's excessive grief at the loss of his own daughter in childbirth (*Demosthenes* 22, *Cicero* 41).

The Life of Demosthenes assumes that the reader will have a good knowledge of the broader historical context and even of Demosthenes' own career. Even so, it is quite patchy, perhaps because as a politician rather than a military man he does not lend himself to an easy narrative, perhaps also because that narrative anyway is one of failure. After a brief review of his early life (4–5) Plutarch devotes several chapters to his development and standing as an orator (6–11). Next comes his opposition to Philip, but there is no mention of his speeches in defence of the Olynthians and little of the controversial Peace of Philocrates; instead Plutarch emphasizes Demosthenes' consistency and powers of persuasion as the narrative builds towards the battle of Chaeronea (12–22). The reign of Alexander begins positively with Demosthenes challenging Macedon, but ends with him despondent and in exile for taking bribes (23–6). In the final section of the Life Plutarch treats Demosthenes' heroic suicide at length, his final act of resistance to Macedon. There were, he says, many different versions of Demosthenes' death. Significantly, he prefers the story that Demosthenes died after chewing on a pen loaded with poison, a story which reminds the reader right at the end that Demosthenes' power lay in words, just as Cicero's Life would end with his murderers cutting off the hands that wrote the *Philippics*.

Plutarch cites an impressive array of sources in this Life. On the death of Demosthenes alone he names four different writers, the philosopher Ariston of Chios, the biographer Hermippus of Smyrna (who had learnt the story from an otherwise unknown Pappus), the Alexandrian scientist Eratosthenes, and Demosthenes' nephew Demochares. He was familiar with the historians of period, such as Theopompus of Chios, who appears seven times, and Duris of Samos, who is cited twice, and philosophers, such as Theophrastus and Panaetius. Especially important are contemporary speeches, both those of Demosthenes himself and those of his rival Aeschines, although clearly they will have offered very different perspectives. In these cases, however, we know that Plutarch has drawn his information from them because the originals survive, but he does not always explicitly acknowledge them as authorities. In particular Plutarch makes considerable use of *On the Crown*, in which Demosthenes set out a defence of his whole career and which helped establish the enduring image of him as the defender of Greek freedom against Macedonian aggression.

Cooper, C., 'The Moral Interplay between Plutarch's *Political Precepts* and *Life of Demosthenes*', in A. G. Nikolaidis (ed.), *The Unity of Plutarch's Work: 'Moralia' Themes in the 'Lives', Features of the 'Lives' in the 'Moralia'* (Berlin, 2008), 67–83.

Habicht, C., *Athens from Alexander to Antony*, trans. D. L. Schneider (Cambridge, Mass., 1997).

Harris, E., *Aeschines and Athenian Politics* (Oxford, 1995).

Lintott, A., *Plutarch: Demosthenes and Cicero* (Oxford, 2013).

MacDowell, D. M., *Demosthenes the Orator* (Oxford, 2009).

Mossman, J. M., 'Is the Pen Mightier Than the Sword? The Failure of Rhetoric in Plutarch's *Demosthenes*', *Histos* 3 (1999), 77–101.

Roisman, J., Worthington, I. (eds.), and Waterfield, R. (trans.), *Lives of the Attic Orators: Texts from Pseudo-Plutarch, Photius, and the* Suda (Oxford, 2015).

Sealey, R., *Demosthenes and His Time: A Study in Defeat* (Oxford, 1993).

Worthington, I. (ed.), *Demosthenes, Statesman and Orator* (Oxford, 2000).

Worthington, I., *Demosthenes of Athens and the Fall of Classical Greece* (Oxford, 2013).

Zadorojnyi, A., 'King of his Castle: Plutarch, *Demosthenes* 1–2', *Cambridge Classical Journal* (*Proceedings of the Cambridge Philological Society*), 52 (2006), 102–27.

DEMOSTHENES

[1] According to the author of the encomium of Alcibiades, written for his victory in the chariot-race at Olympia—whether it was Euripides, as the prevalent tradition maintains, or someone else—the first prerequisite for human happiness, Sosius Senecio,* is citizenship of 'a far-famed city'. But true happiness seems to me to depend almost entirely on a man's character and disposition, and so I think that it is as little affected by being born in an obscure and humble city as it is by being borne by a mother who is ugly and small. After all, it would be ridiculous to suppose that Ioulis (which occupies only a fraction of the already small island of Ceos), or Aegina (which someone from Athens once suggested should be removed, as an eyesore afflicting Piraeus),* both places which bear good actors and poets, could never produce a man of justice, self-reliance, intelligence, and high principle. For even if skills are likely to wither in obscure and humble cities, since the reasons for their development are generally profit and fame, there is nowhere that excellence cannot take root, like a tough and hardy plant, as long as it meets with a noble nature and an unflagging spirit. And from this it follows that the same applies to me too, and it would be right for me to attribute any defects in my thinking or habits not to the insignificance of the land of my birth, but to myself.

[2] However, when one has undertaken to compose a historical treatise out of material that is not readily available or locally published, but which is mostly to be found scattered here and there in books that are unavailable at home, his primary and foremost need truly is to live in 'a far-famed city', one that is cultured and populous. Not only does he have access there to an abundance of books of every description, but he can also bring up in conversation and ask about all those points that have eluded writers, but have been preserved with a high degree of conspicuous reliability in people's memories. And then he can come up with a work that lacks no essential piece of information.

Now, the city where I live is small,* and I refuse to desert it in case it becomes any smaller; but while I was in Rome and travelling in Italy I was too busy with public business and lecturing on philosophy to become proficient in Latin. So it was late in the day and

I was getting on in years when I began to read Latin literature—and a strange thing happened to me, strange but true. It was not so much that, by learning the language, I came to understand and recognize the events that were being described, as that, thanks to my prior knowledge, however acquired, of the events, I found I could follow the gist of the words also. I have no doubt that gaining an appreciation of the beauty and concision of the Latin language, its figures of speech, its rhythmicity, and all its other graceful features, is a fine and delightful accomplishment, but the study and practice involved are arduous, and are suitable only for those who have more free time than I did, and whose age still permits the fulfilment of such aspirations.

[3] In this fifth book of parallel Lives,* then, as I write about Demosthenes and Cicero, I shall use their achievements and their political careers to consider what they were like and assess their characters relative to each other, but I shall not make any attempt to compare their speeches or decide which of them was the more pleasing or brilliant orator. After all, as Ion says,* 'A dolphin's strength is useless on dry land'—a saying which† the ever-excessive Caecilius* ignored when he rashly published his comparison of Demosthenes' and Cicero's use of language. But then, I suppose, the injunction 'Know thyself'* would not be held to be divine in origin if self-knowledge were within everyone's reach.

My approach is justified by the fact that the deity who formed Cicero seems to have made him fundamentally identical to Demosthenes. It is not just that he imbued his nature with many of the same characteristics—desire for distinction, for example, and commitment to political freedom, and lack of courage in the face of war or physical danger—but he even included in his life many of the same contingencies. For I doubt that another two orators could be found both of whom rose to power and prominence from obscure and insignificant origins, came into conflict with kings and despots, lost daughters, suffered banishment from their homelands, returned with honour, fled again, were captured by their enemies, and died at the precise moment that their fellow citizens lost their freedom. In fact, supposing that Nature and Fortune were to engage in a trial of skill, as sculptors do, it would be hard to decide which of them had made the two men more perfectly alike—Nature in respect of their characters or Fortune in respect of their circumstances. But I shall write first about the one who came first in time.

[4] Demosthenes senior, the father of Demosthenes, came from a good family, according to Theopompus,* but was called 'the Cutler' because he owned a large workshop and skilled slaves who were employed in this business. As for what the orator Aeschines says about Demosthenes' mother—that her father, Gylon, had been banished from the city for treason, and that her mother was not Greek—I am not in a position to confirm it, or deny it as a slur.*

At the age of seven Demosthenes was left by his father in affluent circumstances, with an estate the total value of which came to just under fifteen talents. But he was ill used by his guardians,* who appropriated some of the estate for themselves and neglected the rest, until in the end even Demosthenes' teachers could not be paid. That was one reason, then, why he seems not to have received the kind of education that would have suited and been expected of a free-born boy, and another was his physical weakness and delicacy. His mother refused to let him exert himself, and his personal attendants did not force him to either, because he was always a skinny and sickly child.

That is also apparently how he came by the insulting nickname 'Batalus':* it was given him by other children to tease him for his physique. There are two accounts of who Batalus was: some say he was a camp pipe-player, the subject of a playlet by Antiphanes* satirizing his effeminacy, others that he was a composer of immoral verses and drinking-songs. Apparently, also, the word *batalos* was used in those days in Athens for a part of the body that one does not mention in polite company. As for 'Argas', which we are told was another of Demosthenes' nicknames, this was given to him either because of his characteristic fierceness and mordancy (*argas* being a poetic word for 'snake'), or because of his manner of speaking, which grated on his audiences (Argas being the name of a composer of vulgar and irritating songs).

[5] His attraction towards oratory is said to have come about as follows. The orator Callistratus was going to court for the case about Oropus,* and the trial was eagerly anticipated, not only because of Callistratus' powers as a speaker—at the time his reputation had never been higher—but also because of the notoriety of the case. So when Demosthenes heard his teachers and the personal attendants arranging among themselves to attend the trial, he begged and implored his own attendant to take him to the hearing, until he had got his way.* Thanks to his acquaintance with the public slaves

who opened the courts, this attendant of his secured the boy a place where he could sit and listen to the speakers without drawing attention to himself.

Callistratus' victory won him an extraordinary degree of adulation, and at the sight of the large following that surrounded the man and showered him with congratulations, Demosthenes wanted his glory for himself. But what impressed him and struck him even more was the power of Callistratus' speech, its ability to overcome and quell all opposition. And so he abandoned all his other studies and childish pursuits, and devoted himself to the study and practice of declamation, with the intention of one day joining the ranks of the public speakers himself. He took Isaeus as his rhetoric teacher,* even though Isocrates* was teaching at the time, either because (as some say) as an orphan he could not afford the ten mnas Isocrates asked for his course, or because for practical purposes he preferred the vigour and subtlety of Isaeus' style. But Hermippus* claims to have read in an anonymous treatise that Demosthenes had studied with Plato and that his speeches were very heavily indebted to the philosopher. He also quotes Ctesibius as saying that Callias of Syracuse and some other people surreptitiously supplied Demosthenes with the handbooks written by Isocrates and Alcidamas* for him to study.

[6] Be that as it may, when Demosthenes came of age he instituted proceedings against his guardians, and the first speeches he wrote were to prosecute them.* They kept finding loopholes and filing counter-suits, but thanks to the fact that, to borrow an idea from Thucydides, he assiduously honed his technique in a situation where failure would bring real danger,* Demosthenes eventually won. Even though he was unable to recover a single penny of his patrimony, he gained confidence and a good deal of practice at public speaking; and now that he had glimpsed the distinction and power that the law-courts could bring, he ventured to enter public life and engage in politics. They say that Laomedon of Orchomenus took up long-distance running at the advice of his doctors, to combat a disorder of the spleen, and then, after he had made himself fit in this way, he set his sights on the crown games and became a champion *dolikhos*-runner.* Likewise, Demosthenes first stripped off and turned to public speaking to recover his property, but once this had enabled him to become a clever and powerful speaker, he found himself, as soon as he entered the realm of politics (the equivalent of the crown

games), taking first place over those of his fellow citizens whose arena was the speaker's platform.

In actual fact, though, when he first addressed the Athenian people he was heckled and mocked for his inexperience. The length of his clauses was felt to detract from their clarity and his arguments seemed forced, so that his speech came across as harsh and excessive. Moreover, by all accounts his voice was weak, his articulation unclear, and his delivery impaired by shortness of breath, which broke up his clauses and made his meaning hard to grasp. Eventually he abandoned the Assembly, but Eunomus of Thria, a very old man at the time, caught sight of him slouching gloomily around Piraeus and told him off. 'Listening to you speak,' he said, 'one could almost be hearing Pericles himself, and yet you're throwing your talent away. What a feeble and pathetic thing to do! You don't have the guts to stand up to the masses, and in your idleness you're letting your body get out of condition, when you should be preparing it for the struggles ahead.'*

[7] On another occasion, so the story goes, when he had met with a hostile reception in the Assembly and was walking home disturbed and upset, his friend Satyrus the actor* accompanied him and followed him into his house. Demosthenes began to complain to Satyrus that, although there was no more conscientious public speaker in Athens and he had worked himself almost to the bone on his speeches, he had not found favour with the people—that drink-besotted, ignorant sailors were listened to and made the speaker's platform theirs, while he was ignored. 'You're right, Demosthenes,' said Satyrus, 'but I'll soon have the problem fixed. All you have to do is recite for me from memory a passage of Euripides or Sophocles.' Demosthenes did so—but then Satyrus repeated the passage after him, and by speaking it in character and with the appropriate delivery he transformed it so thoroughly that its immediate impact on Demosthenes was that of a completely different passage.

Now that he realized the considerable contribution delivery makes to the elegance and charm of speech, he came to consider practice more or less a complete waste of time unless attention were also paid to how the words should be expressed and spoken. As a result, he built an underground study (which still exists today), where he would go every day without fail to work on his delivery and train his voice.* In fact, he often used to stay there for two or three months on end, with one side of his head shaved so that he would be too embarrassed to step outside, however much he wanted to.

[8] Furthermore, when he met people on the outside, spoke with them, and did business with them, he would make that too the basis and starting-point for study. As soon as the meeting was over, he would go down into his study and review the whole transaction from beginning to end and the arguments used at each stage. Then again, if he had heard any formal speeches being delivered, he would go back over them in his mind, and analyse them into their basic propositions and sentiments; and he used to come up with all sorts of corrections and alternative ways to put things that he had said to someone or someone had said to him.

The upshot of all this was that he came to be regarded as someone who lacked natural talent. It was said that his rhetorical skills and power were the products of hard work, and the idea seemed to be confirmed by the fact that one rarely heard Demosthenes speaking off the cuff. In fact, although the Athenian people often called on him by name if he was sitting in the Assembly, he only ever stepped up to speak if he had given the matter some prior thought and preparation. He came in for a lot of teasing from the other politicians for this, and especially from Pytheas,* who once said that Demosthenes' arguments smelled of wicks. To this Demosthenes replied acerbically: 'Yes, Pytheas, my lamp and yours are indeed privy to different secrets.' Generally, however, he did not quite deny the allegation, but used to admit that his speeches were neither fully written out nor completely spontaneous. In fact, he maintained that practised speeches were the mark of a true democrat: preparation is a kind of deference to the people, whereas being unconcerned about how the masses will feel about what one says is the mark of an oligarch, one who prefers force to persuasion. And, as further evidence of his reluctance to speak off the cuff, people point out that whereas Demades* often used to stand up and speak spontaneously in defence of Demosthenes when he had been shouted down, Demosthenes never returned the favour.

[9] But why, then, did Aeschines disparage him as 'remarkably bold when it's a matter of making speeches'?* Why was Demosthenes the only one to get to his feet and respond to Python of Byzantium's torrent of anti-Athenian invective?* At Olympia, when Lamachus of Smyrna* was reading out the eulogy he had written of the kings, Alexander and Philip, with its frequent slurs against the Thebans

and Olynthians, why was it Demosthenes who stepped up? He gave a detailed account, supported by examples, of all the good the people of Thebes and Chalcidice had done Greece, and all the trouble for which the Greek flatterers of Macedon had been responsible, and won the audience over to his point of view so completely that the sophist slunk away from the festival out of fear at the outcry.

It would be reasonable to conclude that, while Demosthenes basically found little of relevance to himself in Pericles, he emulated and imitated the style and tone of his delivery, and his refusal to rush into speaking or to extemporize on any and every issue, presumably because he took these to be the sources of Pericles' greatness. But he had no interest in momentary glory and, if he could help it, he rarely left his talent at the mercy of Fortune. Nevertheless, the speeches that he delivered in person display more boldness and courage than those he wrote for others, if we are to trust Eratosthenes,* Demetrius of Phalerum,* and the comic poets. Eratosthenes, for example, reports that Demosthenes often worked himself up into a frenzy while speaking, and Demetrius informs us that when Demosthenes swore his famous metrical oath to the Athenian people—'By Earth I swear, by springs, by rivers, and by streams'—it was as though he were possessed by a god.

As for the comic poets, one sneers at him as 'Mr Much-ado-about-nothing', and another mocks his use of contrast in the following lines:

A. He takes and he takes back: it's all the same.
B. Now, there's a phrase Demosthenes would've liked to take over.*

Unless, by Zeus, this was another of Antiphanes' jokes about Demosthenes' speech on Halonnesos,* in which he advised the Athenians not to *take* the island from Philip, but to *retake* it, differing from them over the number of syllables the word should contain.

[10] Nevertheless, it was Demades who was universally acknowledged to be unbeatable when he relied on his natural talent; an impromptu speech from him was held to be better than all Demosthenes' studied preparations. But then there is also Theophrastus' assessment of the two speakers, as recorded by Ariston of Chios.* When he was asked for his opinion of Demosthenes as a speaker, he replied: 'Just right for Athens.' And Demades? 'Too much for Athens.'

Ariston also records the claim of Polyeuctus of Sphettus,* one of the Athenian politicians of the time, that Demosthenes may have been the greatest speaker, but Phocion was the most effective, since he expressed more meaning in fewer words than anyone else. And there is a story that, whenever Phocion mounted the platform to respond to something Demosthenes had said, Demosthenes himself used to tell his friends: 'There stands the knife that prunes my speeches.' But this is ambiguous. Was Demosthenes affected by Phocion's style of speaking or by his lifestyle and reputation, in the belief that a single word and a nod from a man of honour is more potent than many a fine phrase?*

[11] The exercises he adopted for his physical defects (according to Demetrius of Phalerum, who names his source as Demosthenes himself when he was an old man) were as follows. In order to get rid of his mumbling and a tendency to stammer—in other words, in order to articulate clearly—he used to recite passages while holding pebbles in his mouth, and to train his voice he used to talk while running or climbing slopes, and recite a few sentences or verses at a single breath. He also had a large mirror at home and he would declaim while standing in front of it.

Once, we hear, a man came to ask for his support in court and described how he had been beaten up by someone. 'But *you* weren't the victim,' said Demosthenes. 'None of this happened to *you*.' The man raised his voice and shouted: 'What, Demosthenes? I wasn't beaten up?' 'By Zeus,' Demosthenes said, '*now* I hear the voice of a victim, a man who has been wronged.' This shows how important he thought a speaker's tone of voice and delivery were for making him believable.

Although the masses found his delivery wonderfully pleasing, men of culture, such as Demetrius of Phalerum, thought the artificiality of his style demeaning, vulgar, and feeble. But Hermippus tells us that when Aesion* was asked to compare the orators of old with those of his own day, he said that it would be impossible not to find the old orators impressive to listen to live, with their orderly and stately manner of speaking, but that Demosthenes' speeches made for much better reading, being far superior in their arrangement and power.

Now, it goes without saying that in his written speeches severity and acerbity predominate, but he had a sense of humour as well, as is shown by his spur-of-the-moment responses. For instance, Demades once said: 'Demosthenes teach *me*? That would really be the sow teaching Athena!'* And Demosthenes retorted: 'The Athena he's talking about is the one who was caught whoring recently in Collytus.' Or again, when the thief known as 'Brazen' was teasing him for the sleepless nights he spent writing, Demosthenes said: 'Yes, I'm sure *you* find it annoying if I light my lamp.' And then he went on: 'Athenians, you shouldn't be surprised if burglaries take place, when our thieves are made of brass and our walls of mud.' I could mention further witticisms, but I shall say no more on this: we should turn to his achievements and political career, and use them to shed light on all the other facets of his personality and character.

[12] He embarked on a public career after the outbreak of the Phocian War, as he himself tells us, and as can be gathered from his *Philippics*, some of which fall after the conclusion of the war, while the earliest of them touch on the latest events of the war.* We also know that he was thirty-two years old when the speech he wrote for the prosecution of Meidias* was ready for delivery, but still had no power or standing in the political world—a fact which worried him enough, I think, to have been the main reason why he settled out of court. 'For no sweet-tempered man was he, nor kind of heart;'* on the contrary, he was ruthless and unrelenting in redressing wrongs against himself. But he could see what a difficult task he had set himself, and he felt that it would be beyond his powers to bring down a man like Meidias, who was well protected by money, eloquence, and friends, and so he gave in to those who were interceding on his behalf. But I feel sure that the 3,000 drachmas in itself would not have been enough to blunt Demosthenes' rancour if he had expected to win and had been capable of it.

The defence of Greece against Philip furnished him with a noble basis for his public career, and it did not take long for his admirable efforts in that cause to attract attention. He became famous for his eloquence and his bluntness, until he was not only admired in Greece, but was treated with respect by the king of Persia and was more on Philip's mind than any other politician in Athens. Even his enemies admitted that they had taken on a distinguished opponent. At any rate, both Aeschines and Hypereides describe him as such, even while denouncing him.

[13] I am at a loss, therefore, to understand what Theopompus was thinking of when he said that Demosthenes was temperamentally

unstable and incapable of staying true to the same activity or people for long. After all, it seems clear that he stuck with the faction and position he took up at the start of his political career right to the end, and that not only did he not change during his lifetime, but he even sacrificed his life in order not to change. He was no Demades, who defended the inconstancy of his policies by arguing that while he may often have belied his own earlier views, he had always remained true to the interests of the city. He was no Melanopus* who, despite being a political opponent of Callistratus, was often paid by him to change his position, and used to tell the Athenian people: 'It's true that the man is my enemy, but the good of the city comes first.' He was no Nicodemus of Messene* who, after first attaching himself to Cassander, and then supporting Demetrius instead, denied that he had changed—his position being that it was best to obey whoever was in power.

No, we cannot describe Demosthenes as a trimmer and a turncoat, for what he said or what he did. He stuck with just one register, so to speak, and always sang in the same key throughout his career. The philosopher Panaetius* said that the assumption underlying the majority of Demosthenes' speeches was that the only true goal in life was honour. He referred specifically to *On the Crown*, *Against Aristocrates*, *On the Exemptions*,* and the *Philippics*, and it is true that Demosthenes never, in any of these speeches, recommends the most pleasant or easy or profitable measures to his fellow citizens, but frequently expresses the view that safety and security should take second place to the honourable and proper course of action. In fact, if he had complemented the loftiness of his principles and the nobility of his sentiments with courage in war and incorruptibility in all his dealings, he would deserve to be ranked as an orator not with Moerocles, Polyeuctus, and Hypereides,* but alongside Cimon, Thucydides, and Pericles* of old.

[14] At any rate, among Demosthenes' contemporaries, Phocion was held to be in no way inferior to Ephialtes, Aristeides, and Cimon,* despite the fact that he was the spokesman for an unpopular policy and was thought to favour Macedon. Demosthenes, however, could not be relied on under arms, as Demetrius tells us, and was not absolutely impregnable by bribery. Even though he stood firm against offers from Philip and Macedon, he was vulnerable to Asian gold from Susa and Ecbatana,* and his resistance was swept away by

it. There may have been no one better at praising the past glories of Athens, but he was not so good at imitating them.

All the same, leaving aside Phocion, he surpassed all the other politicians of his day even in his conduct. He certainly left all his contemporaries behind when it came to speaking bluntly to the people, opposing the desires of the masses, and seizing on their faults, as we can tell from his speeches. Then there is also the story recorded by Theopompus.† The Athenians were pushing Demosthenes to prosecute a certain case and created an uproar when he refused. He stood up and said: 'Athenians, you'll get advice from me whether or not you want it, but you'll never get me to accuse a man falsely, however much you want it.'

Then again, his position in the Antiphon affair* was highly anti-democratic. Even though Antiphon had been acquitted by the Assembly, Demosthenes arrested him and brought him before the Areopagus Council, taking no thought for the offence this would cause the people. He proved him guilty of having undertaken to set fire to the dockyards for Philip, and the man was handed over to the authorities by the Council and put to death. Moreover, when he took the priestess Theoris* to court for inculcating dishonesty in Athenian slaves, among many other crimes, he asked the court for the death penalty and had her killed.

[15] It is said that Apollodorus' speech *Against Timotheus*, which enabled him to secure the general's conviction as a debtor, was written for him by Demosthenes; certainly, the speeches Apollodorus* delivered in response to Phormio and Stephanus were—which did Demosthenes' reputation no good, because Phormio also went to court with his response to Apollodorus written by Demosthenes, for all the world as though he were selling the rival litigants the daggers to use against each other from one and the same cutlery shop.*

Among his public speeches, *Against Androtion*, *Against Timocrates*, and *Against Aristocrates* were written for others, before Demosthenes had embarked on a public career; he seems to have been only twenty-seven or twenty-eight years old* when these speeches were delivered. But the two speeches *Against Aristogeiton* were delivered by Demosthenes in person, as was *On the Exemptions*.* This latter speech was written, according to Demosthenes' own account, to help Ctesippus, the son of Chabrias, and some say that he was motivated by the fact that he was courting the young man's mother.

But it was not she who became his wife, but a woman from Samos, as Demetrius of Magnesia* reports in his *People with the Same Name*. We do not know whether the speech *On the False Embassy* was actually delivered, despite the fact that Idomeneus* assures us that Aeschines was acquitted by only thirty votes. This seems unlikely to be true, if we are to trust the evidence of both of their respective speeches *On the Crown*, neither of which contains a clear or unequivocal statement to the effect that the earlier case came to trial.* But I had better leave this question for others to decide.

[16] Even in peacetime, Demosthenes made no secret of his position. Nothing the Macedonian king did passed without invective from him, and he never missed an opportunity to whet and kindle the Athenians' anger against him. That is why Philip took more note of him than of anyone else in Athens, and when Demosthenes went to Macedon as one of a ten-man ambassadorial commission,* although Philip listened to them all, he took particular care to respond to any point he raised. But otherwise he showed him no respect or courtesy, and tried instead to win Aeschines and Philocrates* over to his cause. Hence, when Demosthenes found these men praising as unrivalled Philip's abilities as a speaker, his good looks, and even, by Zeus, his capacity for wine, Demosthenes could not refrain from responding, with bitter sarcasm, that the first was a quality to be praised in a sophist, the second in a woman, and the third in a sponge, but none of them was praiseworthy in a king.

[17] But before long, with Philip incapable of keeping the peace and the Athenians constantly being stirred to action by Demosthenes, the scales tipped towards war. Demosthenes first urged the Athenians to do something about Euboea, which had been enslaved for Philip by his tyrants, and, acting on a proposal drafted by him, they invaded the island and drove out the Macedonians.* His second step was to help the people of Byzantium and Perinthus,* when Philip was making war on them. He persuaded the Athenians to forgive the two cities, to forget any grievances they might retain against them from the Social War, and to send an army there to keep them safe, which it did.

He next toured the Greek states on behalf of Athens, and as a result of the discussions he held and his rousing words, he got almost all of them to unite against Philip. In the end they raised a force of 15,000 foot and 2,000 horse, not counting the citizen levies, and willingly contributed money and pay for the mercenaries.

This was the occasion, according to Theophrastus, when the allies demanded that their contributions be capped, and the demagogue Crobylus* quipped: 'War does not feed on fixed rations.'

With all Greece on tenterhooks, people by people and city by city the Athenians began gaining as allies the Euboeans, Achaeans, Corinthians, Megarians, Leucadians, and Corcyraeans. But the greatest challenge still awaited Demosthenes. It was imperative for him to bring the Thebans into the alliance, because their land bordered that of Athens, they had a battle-ready army, and at the time there was no one in Greece with a more formidable reputation in the field. But the fact that Philip had recently courted the Thebans' favour with benefactions during the Phocian War* made it unlikely that they would change their minds, and the worst problem was that the squabbles that broke out between the two cities as a result of their proximity meant that the enmity between them, with its potential for warfare, was constantly erupting afresh.

[18] Meanwhile, however, Philip's morale was riding high as a result of his success at Amphissa, and he launched a surprise attack on Elatea and took possession of Phocis.* Panic seized the Athenians, and no one dared to ascend the speaker's platform; no one had any idea what to say, and helpless silence gripped the Assembly. The only one to come forward was Demosthenes. He advised the people not to give up on the Thebans and, having restored their spirits and given them, as usual, some hope for the future, he was sent to Thebes as one of a team of ambassadors. Philip too sent his own representatives to respond to the Athenians—the Macedonians Amyntas, Cleander, and Cassander, as Marsyas informs us,* and the Thessalians Daochus and Thrasydaeus.

The Thebans had to decide what it was best for them to do, but every single one of them could vividly imagine the horrors of war, since their wounds from the recent Phocian conflict were still raw. Nevertheless, as Theopompus tells us, Demosthenes' powers of persuasion fanned the embers of their courage and fired their determination. He convinced them that all other considerations were irrelevant, and in the end they rejected fear, calculation of expediency, and indebtedness as motives, and were inspired by his words to choose the honourable course of action.*

There was no mistaking the importance and brilliance of this coup by Demosthenes, in that Philip immediately sent an embassy to sue for peace,* the Greeks faced the future with hope and high spirits, and it was not just the Athenian generals who served Demosthenes by carrying out his orders, but the Boeotarchs as well. In effect, Demosthenes directed all the assemblies that took place at the time, in Thebes just as much as in Athens. Nor was his popularity and power in the two places unconstitutional or undeserved, as Theopompus asserts; it was exactly what the situation demanded.

[19] It seems, however, that, in its determination to bring Greek freedom to an end at that moment in time, some agency beyond human control—Fortune, or a cycle in the affairs of man—opposed Demosthenes' plans. Many predictions came to light about the future, including dire omens uttered by the Pythia* and an ancient oracle in verse from the *Sibylline Books*,* that went as follows:

> May I be aloof from the Thermodon conflict,
> Looking down as an eagle from the clouds and the sky.
> The victim weeps and the victor is brought low.

Now, this 'Thermodon' is supposed to be a little river here in Chaeronea, a tributary of the Cephisus, but, as far as I know, there is no stream with that name today. My best guess is that the stream now called the Haemon was called the Thermodon in those days: this is the river that flows past the sanctuary of Heracles where the Greeks made their camp, and I conjecture that after the battle it was filled with blood and corpses and gained its new name as a result.* But, according to Duris,* Thermodon is not a river. He claims that while some soldiers were digging a trench around a tent they were erecting, they unearthed a statuette in stone, which was identified by an inscription as 'Thermodon carrying a wounded Amazon in his arms'. And in this context† he refers to another verse oracle:

> What a prospect awaits you, dark-hued bird,
> At the Thermodon conflict: human flesh aplenty!

[20] Anyway, this issue is too complex to resolve now, but Demosthenes is said to have had complete confidence in the Greek forces. Inspired by the might and determination of so many men challenging the enemy, he ordered them to pay no attention to oracles or listen to prophecies, and even suggested that the Pythia was biased in favour of Philip. He reminded the Thebans about Epaminondas and the Athenians about Pericles, arguing that these men had regarded

omens and so on as excuses for cowardice and had made reason their touchstone.* Up until this point, then, no one could fault him; but in the battle, so far from covering himself in glory or doing anything congruent with his fine words, he completely disgraced himself by breaking rank, discarding his arms and armour, and taking to his heels. As Pytheas used to say, he felt no shame even before the motto on his shield, which was inscribed in letters of gold with the words 'With Fortune's Blessing'.

In the first flush of victory, Philip paid a drunken visit to the battlefield to crow over the corpses, and chanted the opening of the decree drawn up by Demosthenes, giving the words metrical values and rhythm: 'Proposed by Demosthenes, son of Demosthenes, of Paeania.' But when he sobered up and realized the magnitude of the struggle in which he was involved, he shuddered at the skill and power of the orator, who had forced him to risk his empire and his life on the outcome of a few brief hours. Demosthenes' reputation even reached the king of Persia, and he wrote to his satraps on the coast. He sent them money for Demosthenes, and ordered them to make a particular point of cultivating him among the Greek politicians, since he had the power to distract the Macedonian king and keep him busy with turmoil in Greece. It was Alexander who brought this business to light, when he subsequently found in Sardis some letters written by Demosthenes, and the files of the king's generals, which showed how much money he had received.*

[21] At the time in question, however, in the aftermath of the Greek defeat, Demosthenes' political rivals went after him. They arranged for him to be audited and brought indictments against him, but the Athenian people not only pronounced him innocent on all counts, but continued to honour him. So far from treating him as one who wished them harm, they urged him to resume his political career, even to the extent of giving him the job of delivering the eulogy in honour of the fallen troops, whose bones had been collected from Chaeronea and brought home for burial. So far from being crushed into ignobility by the defeat, as Theopompus writes in his hifalutin way, they proved that they did not regret his advice by showing him particular honour and respect.

So Demosthenes delivered the eulogy, but he still refused to introduce political proposals under his own name. Instead, to exorcise the spirit of misfortune that was haunting him, he used to inscribe the name of each of his friends in turn, and continued to do so until Philip's death alleviated his gloom. Philip did not long survive his victory at Chaeronea, and this is presumably what the last words of the oracle were foretelling: 'The victim weeps and the victor is brought low.'

[22] Demosthenes had secret intelligence of Philip's death and, anticipating the boost the news would give to Athenian morale, he came forward with joy on his face to address the Council. He told them he had had a dream which had led him to expect great good fortune for Athens, and before long the messengers arrived with news of Philip's death. The Athenians immediately performed a thanksgiving sacrifice and decreed a crown for Pausanias,* and Demosthenes came forward to speak, wearing a brilliant-white robe and with a garland on his head, even though his daughter had died six days earlier. Aeschines, our source for this episode, criticizes Demosthenes for it and charges him with hating his own child.* But it was petty and spiteful of Aeschines to hold that a gentle and affectionate disposition is indicated only by grief and mourning, and to rule out the possibility of enduring misfortune calmly and serenely.

Speaking for myself, I have to say that I think the Athenians were wrong to wear garlands and sacrifice to mark the death of a king who, at the height of his success, had treated them so moderately and kindly after their defeat. It was unforgivable, as well as petty, for them to honour the man during his lifetime and award him Athenian citizenship, but then to express immoderate delight when he was struck down by someone else—to dance a jig on the corpse and sing victory songs, as though they had performed a deed of valour themselves. But I approve of what Demosthenes did: he left his domestic misfortunes, the weeping and wailing, to his womenfolk, and occupied himself with what he thought was in the city's best interests. I believe that there is something statesmanlike and virile about focusing always on the common good and finding relief from domestic business and events in politics, just as I believe that it is far more regal† to maintain one's dignity than it is to behave like actors playing the part of kings or tyrants, whom we see on stage weeping and laughing, not because they actually want to, but because the plot demands it.

Besides, we feel obliged not to leave someone who has met with misfortune prostrated by what has happened, without comfort; we feel moved to speak words of consolation to him and to turn his mind towards more pleasant matters, just as we might tell people with eye disease to avert their gaze from bright and glaring colours towards pale, soft shades instead. But, surely, there could be no better way to relieve a person's distress than by making it possible for him to blend his private affairs with the public affairs of a prosperous country, until the better overwhelms the worse and all trace of it is lost. Anyway, I was moved to say all this by seeing that Aeschines' words stir pity and other womanly feelings in a lot of people.

[23] With Demosthenes again fanning the flames, the Greek cities united. The Thebans, armed in part by Demosthenes, set upon their garrison and killed a number of men, and preparations were under way in Athens to join them for war. Demosthenes ruled the Assembly, and he wrote letters to the king's generals in Asia,* trying to arrange an attack from there on Alexander, whom he described as a mere boy and a Margites.* But once he had settled affairs in Macedon, Alexander personally led an army of invasion into Boeotia. Athenian courage evaporated, Demosthenes' ardour was quenched, and the Thebans, betrayed by the Athenians, fought on alone and lost their city.*

There was pandemonium in Athens. Envoys were sent to Alexander, with Demosthenes among them, but he abandoned the mission at Cithaeron and turned back, out of fear of the king's anger. Alexander immediately sent the Athenians a demand for the surrender of a number of democratic politicians—ten, according to Idomeneus and Duris, but the most trustworthy writers, and the majority, name eight: Demosthenes, Polyeuctus, Ephialtes, Lycurgus, Moerocles, Demon, Callisthenes, and Charidemus.*

This was when Demosthenes told the fable about the flock of sheep who surrendered their dogs to the wolves, comparing himself and his political allies to dogs defending democracy and calling Alexander 'the lone wolf of Macedon'. And he added: 'You know how traders carry around a sample of their wares in a bowl, and use just these few grains of wheat to sell the rest? Well, the same goes in our case too:† you're failing to appreciate that you're surrendering yourselves, the entire city, not just the few of us.' We have this story on the authority of Aristobulus of Cassandreia.*

The Athenians' deliberations had reached an impasse when Demades, who had been given five talents by the men, declared his willingness to go on an embassy to the king and petition him on their behalf. Presumably, he was relying on his friendship with Alexander—or perhaps he expected to find him glutted like a lion, sated with gore. Be that as it may, it was Phocion* who persuaded the king to be lenient and restored normal relations between him and Athens.

[24] Alexander returned north, leaving the pro-Macedonians in power in Athens and Demosthenes diminished. When Agis of Sparta rebelled, Demosthenes made a half-hearted attempt to support him, but the Athenians refused to join the uprising and he cowered back down. Agis fell in battle and the Spartans were crushed.*

Just then, the indictment of Ctesiphon in the matter of the crown came to trial.* The suit had been drawn up in the archonship of Chaerondas, a short while before the battle of Chaeronea, but it came to court in the archonship of Aristophon, ten years later. The case attracted more attention than any other public trial, partly because of the fame of the speakers, but also because of the principled behaviour of the jurors. The fact that Demosthenes' persecutors were then at the height of their power and had the backing of Macedon did not influence them to vote against him, and they acquitted him decisively; in fact, Aeschines failed to gain twenty per cent of the votes,* and he left Athens immediately and spent the rest of his life as a teacher in Rhodes and Ionia.

[25] Not long afterwards, Harpalus* reached Athens in his flight from Asia. He had run from Alexander partly because he was troubled in his mind about the bad things his extravagant lifestyle had led him to do, and partly because he was afraid of the king, who had by now turned against his Friends. He proposed to entrust himself, along with his money and ships, to the Athenian people. As soon as he sought refuge there, all the other politicians, eyeing up his wealth, offered to support his petition and set about persuading the Athenians to take him in and keep him safe. But Demosthenes' position—at first, anyway—was that they should throw Harpalus out, or run the risk of plunging the city into war for no compelling or justifiable reason. A few days later, however, while an inventory was being taken of his treasure, Harpalus noticed that a Persian cup had taken Demosthenes' fancy. Demosthenes was closely examining its chasing and design, and Harpalus told him to heft the cup in his hand and feel the weight of the gold. Demosthenes was amazed at how heavy it was and asked how much it would fetch, and Harpalus said with a smile:

'For you it will fetch twenty talents.' And as soon as night had fallen, he sent Demosthenes the cup along with twenty talents.

Harpalus, it seems, was good at telling a man who was drawn to gold by the melting look on his face and the gleam in his eyes. Demosthenes could not resist the bribe. He let down his defences, and by admitting this garrison, so to speak, he committed himself to Harpalus' cause. The next day, he went to the Assembly with his neck well and thoroughly wrapped in woollen scarves and bandages, and when he was asked to get up and speak, he shook his head as though he had lost his voice. But the wags there jeered and suggested that the previous night the orator had caught not tonsilitis but moneyitis. Later, the whole Assembly became aware that he had been bribed, and when he asked for a chance to defend himself and try to change their minds, they angrily refused and shouted him down. And someone got to his feet and said sarcastically: 'But, Athenians, you *must* listen to the man with the cup!'*

Under the circumstances, then, they banished Harpalus from the city and instigated a vigorous search for the money and valuables which the politicians had grabbed, in case they ever had to account for it. In the course of the investigation, they even entered people's houses, omitting only the house of Callicles,* the son of Arrhenides. They would not let this house be searched, Theopompus reports,† because Callicles had just got married and his new bride was inside.

[26] Putting a bold face on the matter, Demosthenes introduced a proposal that the Areopagus Council should conduct the investigation into the affair and that those whom they found guilty should then be punished. He was one of the first people condemned by the council, however, and when he came to court he was fined fifty talents and imprisoned. But out of shame at the accusation, he says,* and because he was physically too weak to endure confinement, he escaped, partly by stealth, partly by connivance.

Anyway, he had not fled far from the city, it is said, when he heard some of his fellow citizens behind him, enemies of his. He wanted to hide, but they called out his name and drew near. They said they had brought money for his travel expenses, and begged him to take it. That was why they were following him, they said, and they also tried to cheer him up and told him not to be too upset by what had happened. At this, Demosthenes burst into a greater flood of tears and said: 'How can I not be upset, when I'm leaving a city where my enemies are the kind of people rarely found as friends elsewhere?'

He did not suffer exile bravely. He spent most of the time on Aegina or in Troezen, sitting and gazing towards Attica with tears in his eyes. There are extant, then, some resentful sayings of his that do not sit well with his spirited efforts as a statesman. We hear, for instance, that, as he was leaving the city, he stretched out his hands towards the Acropolis and said: 'Lady Athena, guardian of the city, how is it that you like the three most savage creatures in the world—the owl, the snake,* and the Athenian people?' Then again, he would try to dissuade the young men who came and visited him from entering politics. He used to tell them that if he had originally been faced with a choice between two roads, one leading to a career as a public speaker in the Assembly, and the other heading straight for destruction, and if he had known in advance all the evils that accompany a political career—the fear, envy, lies, and lawsuits—he would have taken the road that led straight to death.

[27] Now, Demosthenes was still in exile when Alexander died.* The Greek states united once again, and Leosthenes showed his mettle by pinning Antipater* in Lamia and starting to circumvallate the town. Pytheas and Callimedon 'the Crab',* who were in exile from Athens, put themselves at Antipater's service and travelled around Greece with his Friends and envoys, trying to dissuade the Greeks from listening to the Athenians and rising in rebellion. But Demosthenes joined the Athenian ambassadors to support their efforts, and worked with them to try to get the cities to make a concerted attack on the Macedonians and throw them out of Greece.*

In Arcadia, according to Phylarchus,* Pytheas and Demosthenes even bandied insults in the assembly in the course of their speeches, the one pro-Macedonian and the other pro-Athenian. This is the occasion when Pytheas is supposed to have said that, just as bringing ass's milk into a house is a sure sign of trouble, so a city must be sick to accept an Athenian embassy. But Demosthenes turned the image against him and retorted that, just as ass's milk restores health, so an Athenian embassy delivers a city from its troubles.

The Athenian people were pleased with Demosthenes for his help and rescinded his exile. The proposal was introduced by Demon of Paeania,* a cousin of Demosthenes, and a trireme was sent to Aegina to fetch him. His escort on the way up from Piraeus to the city included every archon and priest without exception, and in fact almost all the rest of his fellow citizens also met him and gave him an enthusiastic reception. According to Demetrius of Magnesia, Demosthenes even raised his hands and thanked the gods for having blessed him on that day with a more honourable return from exile than Alcibiades, because he had persuaded rather than forced his fellow citizens to take him back.*

His fine was still outstanding, however, because it was not legally possible simply to remit a sentence, but they found a cunning way around the law. During the festival of Zeus the Saviour, it was usual for people to be paid for preparing and decorating the altar. So on this occasion they gave the job to Demosthenes and paid him fifty talents, the amount of the fine, for performing this service.

[28] But he did not get to enjoy the country of his birth after his return for long, because the Greeks were soon crushed. In Metageitnion the battle of Crannon took place, in Boedromion the garrison entered Munychia, and in Pyanepsion* Demosthenes died. Here is how it happened.

When news arrived that Antipater and Craterus were marching on Athens, Demosthenes and his associates quickly slipped out of the city, and the people sentenced them to death, on the proposal of Demades. They scattered here and there, but Antipater sent men to find them wherever they were and arrest them. He gave command of this task force to Archias 'the exile-hunter', who came originally from Thurii and, we hear, had formerly been a tragic actor; in fact, Polus of Aegina, the unrivalled master of tragic acting, is said to have been his student. Hermippus reports that Archias was a pupil of the rhetorician Lacritus,* while Demetrius says that he attended Anaximenes' lectures.*

Anyway, Archias found the orator Hypereides, Aristonicus of Marathon, and Himeraeus, the brother of Demetrius of Phalerum, on Aegina, where they had taken refuge in the sanctuary of Aeacus. He forcibly removed them from the sanctuary and sent them to Antipater at Cleonae, where they were put to death. Hypereides' tongue, it is said, was cut out while he was still alive.*

[29] When Archias found out that Demosthenes was seated as a suppliant at the altar of the temple of Poseidon on Calauria,* he sailed over to the island in dispatch boats with some Thracian spearmen. On landing, he tried to persuade Demosthenes, with

a guarantee of fair treatment, to leave the temple and go with him to Antipater. But it so happened that, the night before, Demosthenes had had a strange dream, in which he was contending with Archias for first prize as a tragic actor and was beaten, despite an excellent performance and a transfixed audience, thanks to his lack of resources and financial backing. Hence, however benignly Archias spoke to him, in the end Demosthenes just sat there, looked up at him, and said: 'Archias, I never found you convincing as an actor, and you're not going to persuade me now with your promises either.'

At this, Archias lost his temper and began to threaten him, and Demosthenes said: 'Now I hear the true voice of Macedon; you were playing a part before. Well, give me a little time, please, so that I can write to my family.' With these words, he withdrew inside the temple. He took a roll of papyrus and, as though he were about to start writing, he raised his pen to his mouth and chewed on it, which was a habit of his when he was thinking and writing. He kept the pen there for some time, and then covered his head and began to shake it. The spearmen standing at the entrance laughed at what they took to be a sign of his cowardice and taunted him for his womanly weakness, but Archias came up to him and asked him to get up, repeating the same promises of reconciliation with Antipater. By now Demosthenes could feel that the poison had taken hold and was going about its deadly business, so he uncovered his head, looked at Archias, and said: 'Not long to wait now. Soon you can play the part of Creon in *Antigone* and throw this body of mine out unburied.* Beloved Poseidon, I shall leave your sanctuary before I die. If it were up to Antipater and the Macedonians not even your temple would have been left undefiled.' He then asked for support, since he was already shaking and unsteady, and left the temple, but got no further than the altar before he fell, and breathed out his soul with a sigh.

[30] Ariston says that Demosthenes got the poison from the pen, and this is the version I have followed above, but someone called Pappus, who was Hermippus' source for the story, has a different version. According to him, after Demosthenes had fallen by the altar, the papyrus was found to have the beginning of a letter written on it—'Demosthenes to Antipater'—but no more, and the puzzling swiftness of his death was explained by what the Thracians guarding the entrance said: that they had seen Demosthenes taking the poison into his hand from a strip of cloth, putting it to his mouth, and

swallowing it, though at the time, they claimed, they had supposed that it was money that was being swallowed. And, when questioned by Archias, the girl who had been attending Demosthenes said that he had worn that strip for a long time as an amulet. Eratosthenes too says, on his own authority, that Demosthenes kept the poison in a hollow band, and that this band was worn by Demosthenes as a bracelet.

A great many people have written about Demosthenes' death, and I do not feel obliged to go through all the differences between them. I shall mention only the view of Demochares,* who was a relative of Demosthenes, that he was killed not by poison, but by the gods, who showed how much they honoured and cared for him by snatching him out of the Macedonians' cruel hands with a swift and painless death. He died on 16 Pyanepsion, the grimmest day of the Thesmophoria,* when the women celebrants fast in the temple of the goddess.

This was the man who, before long, was properly honoured by the Athenian people with the erection of a bronze statue and a decree awarding the senior member of his family maintenance at public expense in the Prytaneum.* The famous inscription on the base of his statue ran as follows:

> If your strength had matched your intelligence, Demosthenes,
> Never would Greece be ruled by a Macedonian warlord.

The suggestion that Demosthenes himself composed these lines on Calauria, as he was about to take the poison, is of course sheer nonsense.

[31] Shortly before my stay in Athens, the following incident is supposed to have occurred. A soldier who had been summoned to a tribunal by his commanding officer placed a few gold coins, all he had, in the hands of Demosthenes' statue, which had interlaced fingers. The money could not be seen, because a lot of leaves from a small plane tree that grew near by lay in a heap over it—perhaps a breeze had accidentally deposited them there, or perhaps the man himself who put the money there covered it up in this way—and remained unseen for quite a long while. When the man returned and found his money still there, word got out about what had happened, and a competition arose among the wags of the city to compose epigrams on the theme of Demosthenes' incorruptibility.

Demades did not enjoy his hateful fame for long before the justice due to Demosthenes brought him back to Macedon, to perish as he deserved at the hands of those he had so demeaningly flattered. This was not the first time he had given offence to the Macedonians, but now there was no escaping the charges brought against him, because a letter of his emerged in which he urged Perdiccas* to attack Macedon and save the Greeks, who were attached to Macedon, he said, only by 'an old and rotten thread'—in other words, Antipater. When Deinarchus of Corinth* denounced Demades for this, in a fury Cassander slaughtered his son at his side, and then gave orders for Demades to be killed as well. It took the worst of misfortunes for him to learn the truth of what Demosthenes had often told him, but he had never believed: that traitors sell themselves first.

So, Sosius Senecio, there is your Life of Demosthenes, drawn from both written and oral sources.

PHOCION

INTRODUCTION

Phocion (402–318 BCE) was an Athenian politician and general, who until the last years of his life had a successful but largely unremarkable career. He had a reputation for integrity and at some point acquired the name Phocion the Good. He was said to have held the generalship an unprecedented forty-five times, an extraordinary number and perhaps an exaggeration. Nonetheless our knowledge of his military career is sketchy at best. He commanded part of the fleet at the battle of Naxos in the 370s and may have played a decisive role in that victory. In the 340s his campaigns on behalf of Athens took him to Euboea, Megara, and Byzantium, but nothing is known of any military activity in the intervening two decades. In contrast to Demosthenes, who was aligned with the supporters of democracy and opponents of Macedon, Phocion's sympathies were oligarchic and he became friends with various prominent Macedonians. Had he died a few years earlier than he did, he would probably now be treated as a minor figure in the history of fourth-century Athens. But the Athenian failure in the Lamian War (323–322) that followed Alexander's death changed all that. Despite being around eighty years old, Phocion played a leading part in the peace negotiations with Antipater, the governor of Macedon. The price of peace was a Macedonian garrison and a new constitution which restricted political participation to those who met a property qualification. This Macedonian-backed regime did not last much beyond the death of Antipater in 319. A power-struggle ensued between Antipater's son Cassander and Polyperchon, the man designated as his successor. Caught between these two rivals, Phocion and his regime were overthrown and he himself was executed by the Athenian people in 318. His body and those of his associates were then unceremoniously expelled from Attica and dumped across the border.

In many ways Phocion seems an odd choice for a Life. He did little that would make an impact on the historical tradition until he was in his eighties. Cornelius Nepos, a Roman writer of the first century BCE, included him among his short biographies of distinguished commanders, but began by saying that Phocion was better known for his virtues than for his military achievements. In practice Nepos had little to say about anything that Phocion did until he reached the controversial arrangement with Antipater at the very end of his life. It is the same with Diodorus, whose focus is on Phocion's trial and execution. Even Plutarch devotes almost half the Life

(22–38) to the period after the death of Alexander, and what precedes is often more anecdote then narrative. The apparent absence of earlier achievement is indirectly addressed by Plutarch when one of the leading advocates of resistance to Macedon challenges Phocion, asking what good he had done the city in all his generalships, to which Phocion replies, 'Quite a lot, actually. My fellow citizens are buried in their own private tombs' (23).

The early chapters of the Life (4–11) cover his philosophical education (under no less a teacher than Plutarch's own philosophical guide, Plato), his military service with Chabrias, his rather bad-tempered relationship with the Athenian people, and his popularity with the allies. Then follows a short section on his military campaigns of the 340s (13–15), before moving on to Chaeronea and its aftermath, in particular Phocion's relationship with the Macedonians, in which it is made clear that despite being offered huge amounts of money he always turned it down (16–22). Phocion comes across as a man who was stubborn, honest, frugal, and always had Athens' best interests in mind, although a reading of Diodorus (18.64–7) shows that a less sympathetic interpretation was possible.

Phocion is paired with Cato the Younger, a Roman senator whose suicide in 46 BCE marked the end of the Roman Republic in the eyes of many. The Life of Phocion is one of a cluster of roughly contemporary Greek Lives, each of which is coupled with a Roman from the end of the Republic. In addition to Phocion's pairing with Cato, there are Alexander with Caesar, Demosthenes with Cicero, and Demetrius Poliorcetes with Antony. Together they suggest that the late fourth century was the end of an era and that one can read the fall of the Republic back on to Greece. Plutarch sees both Phocion and Cato as good men who were not prepared to deviate from their principles and beliefs to win the favour of the people. Indeed, Phocion's exasperation with and lack of sympathy for democracy are the subject of a whole series of anecdotes in the Life (8–10). But there is also a second parallel at work in this pair of Lives. It is with the philosopher Socrates, another man with conservative political views who was executed at the command of the Athenian people. The comparison is implicit for much of the Life of Phocion, only becoming explicit at the very end: 'But what happened to Phocion reminded the Greeks of Socrates, and they felt that on both occasions the city had been equally at fault and equally visited by misfortune.' Cato too recalls Socrates in his Life, particularly in the manner of his death, which follows a careful reading of Plato's *Phaedo*, the dialogue that treats the death of Socrates; but where Cato offers deliberate imitation, Phocion manages to be like Socrates without even trying, even in death. Plutarch was a Platonist, so the representation of Phocion as another Socrates suggests that in this case he sympathized more strongly than usual with his subject.

In striking contrast to the Life of Demosthenes, Plutarch here makes very few references to any sources he might have used. There are two citations of Duris of Samos, one on Phocion's character and appearance (4) and the other on how Alexander the Great addressed him in letters, a point for which Alexander's chamberlain Chares of Mytilene is also cited (17). In addition to these, the often slanderous Idomeneus of Lampsacus is cited for a questionable story about Phocion's father (4). But all these references are on fairly minor and incidental points. Plutarch gives no indication of what other sources he may have used, although a strong case has been made for Demetrius of Phalerum, whose work Plutarch used in the Life of Demosthenes. This man was an ally of Phocion who was condemned to death *in absentia* and subsequently returned to lead a pro-Macedonian, oligarchic government from 317 to 307. It would have been under his auspices that Phocion was honoured with a statue and his bones finally given a proper burial.

Bayliss, A. J., *After Demosthenes: The Politics of Early Hellenistic Athens* (London, 2011), 129–51.

Bearzot, C., *Focione tra storia e trasfigurazione ideale* (Milan, 1985).

Do Céu Fialho, M., 'The Interplay of Textual References in Plutarch's *Life of Phocion*', in F. Frazier and D. F. Leão (eds.), *Tyché et Pronoia: la marche du monde selon Plutarque* (Coimbra, 2010), 195–206.

Duff, T. E., *Plutarch's Lives: Exploring Virtue and Vice* (Oxford, 1999), ch. 5.

Gehrke, H.-J., *Phokion. Studien zur Erfassung seiner historischen Gestalt* (Munich, 1976).

Lamberton, R., *Plutarch* (New Haven, 2001), 117–25.

—— 'Plutarch's Phocion: Melodrama of Mob and Elite in Occupied Athens', in O. Palagia and S. V. Tracy (eds.), *The Macedonians in Athens 322–229 BC* (Oxford, 2003), 8–13.

Palagia, O., and Tracey, S. V. (eds.), *The Macedonians in Athens 322–229 BC* (Oxford, 2003).

Trapp, M., 'Socrates, the *Phaedo*, and the Lives of Phocion and Cato the Younger', in Pérez Jiménez *et al.* (eds.), *Plutarco, Platón y Aristóteles* (Madrid, 1999), 487–99.

Tritle, L., *Phocion the Good* (London, 1987).

—— 'Plutarch's "Life of Phocion": Analysis and Critical Report', *Aufstieg und Niedergang der römischen Welt*, II.33.6 (1992), 4258–97.

PHOCION

[1] The orator Demades, who owed his influence in Athens to the fact that his policies were pro-Macedonian and pleasing to Antipater, used to say that he should be forgiven for all the measures he proposed and speeches he delivered that contravened the city's dignity and traditions—that he had no choice, because he was at the helm of a shipwrecked city. This statement—perhaps rather an exaggeration coming from Demades—would seem to be true, instead, of Phocion's political career. For Demades was himself a piece of flotsam from the wreckage of Athens, and his life and political career were so amoral that Antipater said of him in his old age that he resembled a sacrificial victim after the sacrifice was over: nothing left but tongue and belly.* But the good Phocion found himself pitted against a heavyweight opponent, so to speak: all the misfortunes of Greece in those violent times overshadowed his goodness and made his reputation less brilliant than he deserved. Even though we do not have to agree with Sophocles' assertion of the weakness of goodness, when he says

> True, my lord: no trace of good sense remains
> When things go wrong. It takes its leave,*

we should still allow Fortune this much power in her struggle against good men: sometimes, when she makes them the recipients of unjustified accusations and slanderous lies instead of the honour and gratitude they deserve, she weakens confidence in their goodness.

[2] Now, it is widely believed that the ordinary citizens of a community are more likely to abuse its good men when things are going well for them, because they get carried away by their importance and strength. In fact, the opposite is the case: it is disaster that turns men sour. Disaster makes them irascible and short-tempered, and then it is hard for them to listen to advice without taking offence, since they find every reasonable and forceful assertion annoying. Anyone who tells them off for a mistake is taken to be casting their misfortune in their teeth, and speaking one's mind is considered a sign of disdain.* Just as honey hurts a part of the body that has been wounded or injured,* so truth and good sense often sting and irritate men when things are going badly, unless the advice is given in a kind and

easygoing manner. (That, by the way, is why Homer describes pleasant things as 'heart-easing',* because they put up no opposition or resistance to the part of the soul that feels pleasure, but make things easy for it.) An inflamed eye likes to linger on dull colours, lacking in brilliance, and avoids those that are bright and glaring, and the same goes for a community too: the weakness induced by unwelcome and unfortunate circumstances makes it too timid and sensitive to put up with plain speaking just when it needs it most—when events cannot be blamed for its errors. And that is why it is hazardous to be a politician in such a community: anyone who says what the people want to hear will perish along with them, while anyone who refuses to indulge them will perish before them.

Learned men tell us that the sun's motion is neither the same as that of the vault of heaven, nor absolutely opposed and contrary to it; they say that it takes an oblique and slanting course, so that it describes a smooth, curving, coiling† spiral, thanks to which everything is kept safe and attains the best possible blending. The same goes for the administration of a community as well: an overly straight approach, one which resists the popular will in everything, is as rough and hard as the alternative—being carried along by and favouring the general populace's errors—is risky and hazardous. But the kind of administration and governance of men that makes concessions and yields to their desires if they are obedient, but then demands in return what is in their best interests—and men do often meekly give valuable service, as long as they are not tyrannized and oppressed—that is what keeps a community safe. It takes effort and hard work, however, and involves the kind of aloofness that is rarely found in combination with a sense of fairness. But if the combination is achieved, no rhythm or attunement is more harmonious and melodious than this blending, which is said also to give God the means to govern the universe without compulsion, using persuasion and reason to direct material necessity.*

[3] The combination was found in Cato the Younger* as well. The masses never found his ways winning either, and he never endeared himself to them. If he shone in public life, it was not by seeking popularity. In fact, Cicero says that the reason he was turned down for the consulship was because in his political career he behaved as though he were living in Plato's ideal state rather than among the dregs of Romulus.* His experience strikes me as identical to what happens

to fruit that appears out of season: people enjoy the sight of it and admire it, but they make no use of it. Likewise, when Cato's old-fashioned values appeared, after an absence of many years, in a corrupt society with debased ways, they earned him plenty of fame and glory, but they were irrelevant to people's needs, because his goodness was unsuited to the times—too weighty, too substantial. Although his country had not already been laid low, as Phocion's had, and was only beset by storm and surge, and although he was denied the rudder and the helm, and was responsible only for sails and ropes in support of those with greater power, he still gave Fortune a hard fight. For even though Fortune did succeed in destroying and overthrowing the Republic, using others as her instruments, Cato and his goodness made things difficult for her and slowed her down, so that she had to fight every inch of the way for many years before winning.

The comparison I am making between Cato's goodness and Phocion's does not depend on general similarities, such as their both being good men and good statesmen. It is true that virtue is not homogeneous: Alcibiades and Epaminondas were both brave, but in different ways; Themistocles' intelligence differed from that of Aristeides; and what justice meant to Numa was different from what it meant to Agesilaus. But with Cato and Phocion, search as one might for the most minute differences, their virtues are indistinguishable, down to the last detail, in character and form, and in overall moral colouring. It is as though in both of them kindness was mixed with severity in the same proportions, courage with circumspection—as though they bore a similar blend of concern for others with disregard for their own safety, and of careful avoidance of wrongdoing with vigorous pursuit of justice. This means that the discernment and discovery of the differences between them call for the precision instrument, so to speak, of very fine reasoning.

[4] The brilliance of Cato's lineage, as I shall show later, is generally accepted; but Phocion's background was perfectly respectable and elevated, in my view. After all, if Idomeneus* had been right to say that his father was a pestle-maker, then Glaucippus,* the son of Hypereides, would certainly have included his lowly birth among the countless other slurs he collected and retailed in his speech. Nor, if Idomeneus were right, would Phocion have enjoyed such a liberal and sound education: he studied in the Academy with Plato while he was still in his teens, and then later with Xenocrates,* and devoted

himself from an early age to the noblest pursuits. For no one in Athens found Phocion easily moved to laughter or tears, nor (this is all from Duris) did they ever see him washing in a public bath-house or with his hand outside of his cloak.* That is, if he happened to be wearing a cloak* in the first place: when he was out of town and on campaign, he never wore shoes or warm clothing unless the cold was so extreme as to be unbearable. In fact, there was a joke among the men who served alongside him: How can you tell if it's a bad winter? Phocion's wearing a cloak.

[5] Despite the fact that he was the kindest and most considerate of men, his features made him seem grim and forbidding, so that anyone outside his immediate circle found it difficult to be alone with him. That is why, when the Athenian people were laughing at some remark of Chares' about Phocion's frown, he said: 'This frown of mine has never hurt you, but the laughter of Chares* and his kind has often reduced the city to tears.' The same goes for his manner of speaking as well: with its wholesome sentiments and ideas, there was nothing malign about it, but it had a somewhat imperious, harsh, and unpleasing brevity.

Zeno* used to say that a philosopher had to dip his words in sense before speaking them out loud, and Phocion used to pack the most sense into the fewest words. This is probably what Polyeuctus of Sphettus was thinking of when he said that Demosthenes was the best public speaker, but Phocion the cleverest. For just as a coin contains the maximum spending-power in the smallest bulk, so skilful speech seems to communicate a great deal with few words. In fact, Phocion himself, we hear, was once walking about behind the stage while the theatre was filling up, deep in thought, when one of his friends said to him: 'You seem to have something on your mind, Phocion.' 'Indeed I have,' he replied. 'I'm wondering whether I can shorten the speech I'm about to give to the Athenian people.' And Demosthenes, who was otherwise highly contemptuous of his fellow orators, used to say calmly to his friends when Phocion got up to speak: 'Here's the knife that prunes my speeches.' But perhaps Demosthenes was thinking of Phocion's character. After all, a mere word or nod from a good man inspires as much confidence as any number of elaborate arguments and phrases.*

[6] As a young man, Phocion attached himself to the retinue of the general Chabrias.* This not only gained him valuable military

experience, but he also occasionally corrected the general's behaviour. Although Chabrias was basically lethargic and slow to take action, in battle his spirit rose and caught fire, and he used to hurl himself into the fray along with the boldest of his men, with too little thought for his own safety. And this, of course, is how he did eventually get himself killed on Chios, trying to be the first to drive his trireme ashore and force a landing. Phocion, then, who was becoming known for combining caution and effectiveness, used to put fire into Chabrias when he was holding back and restrain him when he was getting too carried away.

Chabrias, who was a good-natured and decent man, began to appreciate Phocion's qualities and to give him responsibilities and commands; and the critical importance of the missions with which he was being entrusted brought him to the attention of the Greeks. And then, at the battle of Naxos,* Chabrias secured Phocion's reputation and assured him no small measure of glory by putting him in charge of the left wing, where the fighting turned out to be fiercest and the battle was swiftly brought to an issue. Seeing that this was the first sea-battle the Athenians had fought on their own against the Greeks since the fall of the city, and that it was a success, they thought the world of Chabrias and began to take note of Phocion as a capable commander. The victory coincided with the Great Mysteries,* and from then on, every year on 16 Boedromion, Chabrias used to put on a Festival of Wine in Athens.

[7] Some time later, we hear, when Phocion was setting out, on Chabrias' orders, to collect the islanders' contributions,* Chabrias offered him twenty ships. But Phocion replied that, if his mission was to fight, this was too small a force, and that if he was going as a friend to friends, a single ship was enough. He set off in his own trireme, talked things over with the cities, held fair and frank meetings with their leaders, and then returned with a flotilla of ships sent by the allies, bringing the Athenians their money.

Phocion not only displayed constant devotion and respect for Chabrias while he was alive, but took good care of his family after his death, which included trying to make something worthwhile of his son, Ctesippus.* Even when he found the young man to be wayward and unmanageable, he did not stop reprimanding him and covering up his disgraces. On one occasion, however, the story goes, the young man was with him on campaign, and was making a thorough nuisance of himself, plaguing Phocion with irrelevant questions and advice, as though he were sharing the command and had a right to criticize him. And Phocion said: 'Chabrias, Chabrias, what a high price I'm paying for your friendship, in putting up with your son!'

He could not help noticing that Athenian politicians of the time had split the War Department off from the speaker's platform, as though they were separate provinces. Some of them, such as Eubulus, Aristophon, Demosthenes, Lycurgus, and Hypereides,* only addressed the Assembly and introduced measures, while others, such as Diopeithes, Menestheus, Leosthenes, and Chares,* advanced their careers by military commands and warfare. He wanted to revive and restore the kind of rounded public service, so to speak, that had been provided by Pericles, Aristeides, and Solon,* which covered both spheres at once. For each of these men had proved himself, in the words of Archilochus:

> Both at once—companion in arms of the Lord Enyalius
> And expert in the gift of the lovely Muses.*

And each of them was aware that the city's patron deity was a goddess of war and of civic life at the same time, and was addressed as such.*

[8] Phocion organized his life on the same principle, and so combined proposing measures that were designed to bring about peace and quiet with serving as general not only more often than any of his contemporaries, but more often than anyone ever had. He did not seek the position or canvass for it, but neither did he avoid it or turn it down when the city called upon him. It is widely agreed that he held the generalship forty-five times, even though he did not attend the election meeting even once, but always had to be summoned from elsewhere for the vote.

Unintelligent commentators have expressed surprise at this, seeing that Phocion very often opposed the Athenian people and never said or did anything to win their favour. But in fact the Athenian people behaved no differently from kings, who are said to enjoy the presence of their flatterers at mealtimes. That is, they treated their more clever and amusing politicians as entertainment, but when they wanted a leader they were never anything but sober and serious, and they would call on the most severe and sensible of their fellow citizens, even though he was the sole or chief opponent of their whims and wishes. Once, in fact, when an oracle from Delphi was read out in the Assembly, to the effect that while all other Athenians were of one mind, there was one man who dissented from the city, Phocion stepped up and told them not to worry—that he was the one they were looking for, because he was the only one who disapproved of everything they did.* Once a proposal he was making to the assembled people went down well, and faced with the unanimous acceptance of what he had said, he turned to his friends and asked: 'I haven't just said something wrong, have I? I didn't mean to.'

[9] Once the Athenian people were soliciting contributions for a public sacrifice. Everyone else gave something, except Phocion. After being asked a number of times, he replied: 'Ask these rich people. I'd be ashamed to give you money when I'm still in debt to him'—and he pointed to Callicles,* the banker.

Once, when they would not stop bawling and shouting at him, he told them the following story: 'A cowardly man was setting out for war when he heard some crows cawing, so he put down his weapons and stayed where he was. After a while, he picked them up again and set off, but the crows cawed again and he stopped. Eventually, he said: "Croak as you may, you won't get a taste of me!" '*

Then there was a time when the Athenians wanted him to launch an expedition against the enemy, and he would have nothing to do with it. When they started decrying him as a weakling and a coward, he said: 'You can make me brave as little as I can make you cowardly. But each of us knows what the other is like.'

Once, at a time of danger, the people were furious with him, and demanded that he submit to an audit of his conduct as general: 'See to your safety first, my friends,' he said.

Then there was a time when a war frightened them into humility, but as soon as it was over they began to assert themselves and to denounce Phocion for denying them victory. 'Lucky you!' he said. 'If you didn't have a general who knows what you're like, you'd have been ruined long ago.'

Once, when the Athenians were refusing to let a territorial dispute with the Boeotians* go to arbitration, and wanted to make war on them instead, he advised them to play to their strength rather than their weakness, and fight with words rather than weapons.

One day, when he was trying to make a speech, and the people would not let him and refused to listen to his advice, he said: 'You can force me to do something I don't want to do, but you will never get me to speak against my better judgement.'

When Demosthenes, one of his political opponents, warned him that one day, in a fit of madness, the Athenians would put him to death, he replied: 'And they'll kill you in a fit of sanity.'

On a hot day once, after listening to Polyeuctus of Sphettus advising the Athenians to go to war against Philip, he saw that the man, who was overweight, was panting and sweating furiously. 'What a good idea', he said, 'for you to be persuaded by this man to vote for war! Why, he's in danger of suffocating just from telling you his thoughts! What do you think he'll do in his breastplate and shield with the enemy near by?'

On another occasion, Lycurgus was going on and on, in the course of a speech in the Assembly, about what an appalling person Phocion was, above all because, when Alexander had demanded the surrender of ten Athenian citizens,* Phocion had advised the Athenians to obey. And Phocion said: 'But I've often given them sound and expedient advice. It doesn't mean they listen to me.'

[10] There was a man called Archibiades, who was nicknamed Laconistes* because he let his beard grow to an extraordinary length, only ever wore a light cloak, and went around with a scowl on his face. One day, during a noisy session of the Council, Phocion called on him for support, to testify to the truth of what he was saying. But when Archibiades got to his feet, the advice he gave was what the Athenians wanted to hear. So Phocion took him by the beard and said: 'Why didn't you cut this short, then, Archibiades?'

At meetings of the Assembly, the sycophant Aristogeiton* was always calling for war and trying to rouse the people to action. One day, during the registration of troops, he walked up leaning on a stick and with both legs bandaged. Phocion, who was standing on the speaker's platform, spotted him when he was still some way off and called out: 'Here's another one. Register Aristogeiton too as lame and unfit for service.'

One might wonder, then, how and why such a rude and grumpy man came to be called 'the Good'. But I think that a human being, like a wine, may be simultaneously sweet and dry—an unusual, but not impossible combination—just as there are also wines (and people) that appear sweet, but on further acquaintance turn out to be extremely unpleasant and harmful. And yet we are told that Hypereides once said in the Assembly: 'The question you should be asking, Athenians, is not only whether I'm hateful, but whether I've been bribed to be hateful'—as though it were only those who made themselves hated and disliked for greed whom the Athenians feared and censured, and not, rather, those who used their power to gratify malicious arrogance, or anger, or some rivalry.

Anyway, Phocion was never moved by personal hostility to harm any of his fellow citizens—in fact, he did not even regard any of them as an enemy—and, if he was brusque, intractable, and stubborn, he took it only as far as was necessary to resist those who opposed the measures he was taking for his country. In all other walks of life he was unfailingly courteous, polite, and kind. In fact, he even helped his adversaries when they were in trouble and stuck by them when they were in danger. When his friends told him off for appearing in court on behalf of some worthless individual, he replied that good men did not need help. And when the sycophant Aristogeiton, after he had been found guilty, wrote and asked him to come and see him, he agreed and set out for the prison; and when his friends tried to stop him, he said: 'No, let me go. Where better to see Aristogeiton?'

[11] At any rate, it is certainly true that the allies and islanders treated as enemies Athenian emissaries who were under the escort of any other general. They strengthened their walls, blocked harbour entrances, and brought livestock, slaves, and families in from the countryside. It was only if Phocion was in command that, wreathed in garlands and smiles, they would venture far out in their own ships to meet the emissaries, and would take them into their own homes.

[12] When, in the process of gradually taking over Euboea, Philip began bringing forces over from Macedon and installing tyrants in the cities to make them his own, Plutarch of Eretria contacted the Athenians and asked them to prevent the island from falling into Macedonian hands.* Phocion was sent out as general with only a small force, since he expected the Euboeans to rally enthusiastically to his side. But instead he found the island filled with traitors, beset by civil strife, and riddled with corruption, all of which made his situation extremely dangerous. He therefore occupied a hill, which was separated by a deep ravine from the plains around Tamynae, and there he gathered and concentrated the best of his troops. He ordered his officers to ignore the exodus from the camp

and departure for Athens of the undisciplined, the whingers, and the unfit. If they stayed, he said, their lack of discipline would cause trouble and impair the effectiveness of his men, while back in Athens their awareness of what they had done would make them less likely to denounce him and would deter them from bringing false accusations against him.

[13] When the enemy advanced against him, he ordered his men to remain quietly under arms until he had finished sacrificing, and then he waited quite a while, either because the omens were unfavourable or because he wanted to draw the enemy closer. So it was Plutarch, thinking that Phocion was holding back because he had no stomach for a fight, who initiated the action by charging forward with his mercenaries. When they saw this, the cavalry could hold back no longer, and rode straight for the enemy, racing out of the camp in a disorderly fashion and attacking in small groups.

This first wave was defeated and thoroughly scattered, and Plutarch fled the field. At this, some of the enemy, no longer expecting the slightest resistance, came up to the camp and began to hack away at the palisade, trying to breach it. But just then the sacrifices finished, and the Athenians immediately poured out of the camp, routed their assailants, and cut most of them down as they fled among the entrenchments. Then Phocion halted his phalanx, to allow those who had been scattered in the earlier rout to rally and rejoin them, while he fell on the enemy with the elite troops.* A fierce battle took place, and although everyone fought with verve and with little regard for personal safety, honours went to Thallus, the son of Cineas, and Glaucus, the son of Polymedes, who had been assigned positions right by Phocion. But Cleophanes also made a crucial contribution to the battle: by calling the cavalry back from their flight and shouting at them to go and support the general, he got them to return and confirm the infantry victory.

Afterwards, Phocion threw Plutarch out of Eretria and captured Zaretra, a critically placed fortress on the narrowest stretch of the island, where the sea pinches it on both sides. Then he released any prisoners he had taken who were Greek, since he was afraid that the Athenian people might in their anger feel compelled, thanks to the orators, to mistreat them. [14] After these successes, Phocion sailed back to Athens. Before long, the allies came to miss his honesty and integrity, and the Athenians were made aware of his experience and grit. For Molossus, his successor, handled the war so incompetently that he even got himself taken alive by the enemy.*

But now Philip embarked on a highly ambitious project, and invaded the Hellespont at full strength, intending to annex the Chersonese, Perinthus, and Byzantium at one go. The Athenians urgently wanted to send help and, thanks to vigorous efforts by the public speakers, it was Chares who got the job. He duly set sail, but his achievements fell far short of the army's potential. The cities would not even let his ships into their harbours, and he roamed from place to place, mistrusted by everyone, soliciting money from the allies and being treated with contempt by the enemy. Eventually the Athenian people, stirred into action by the public speakers, became angry with Chares and regretted their decision to help Byzantium.* But then Phocion got to his feet and said that they should not be angry with their allies for their lack of trust, but with their generals for their lack of trustworthiness. 'Thanks to them,' he said, 'you are becoming feared even by those who rest all their hopes of salvation in you.'

His words took effect, and the people changed their minds again. They instructed Phocion to raise a fresh army and go to help their allies on the Hellespont himself. This proved to be the decisive factor in the preservation of Byzantium. Phocion's standing was already high there, but when Leon, the best of the Byzantines and an old friend of Phocion's from the Academy, personally guaranteed his good conduct, the Byzantine people refused to let him make camp outside the town, as he had intended; they opened their gates, made him welcome, and brought the Athenians in to live with them. As a result of being trusted like this, the Athenian soldiers behaved with irreproachable restraint and fought with the utmost determination. So Philip was driven from the Hellespont for a while, and whereas previously he had been thought invincible and irresistible, his reputation plummeted. Phocion even managed to capture some of his ships, recover towns that Philip had garrisoned, and land troops to plunder and raid at a number of places in Philip's territory. Eventually, however, he was wounded on one of these raids by some of the defenders and sailed back to Athens.

[15] When the Megarians made a secret appeal to Athens for help, Phocion was afraid that the Boeotians might get to hear about it and send a force first.* He therefore convened an Assembly early in the morning and told the Athenian people the news from Megara;

and, once his proposal had been officially approved, he had the trumpeter give the signal and led the Athenians, once they had collected their weapons, straight from the Assembly. The Megarians were delighted that he had come. He fortified Nisaea and built two 'legs' from the town all the way down to it.* With the city connected to the sea, the Megarians had little need to worry about a land-based attack, and at the same time were brought into dependency on Athens.

[16] The time came when the Athenians were fully committed to hostility with Philip. In Phocion's absence, others were put in charge of the war, but when he returned from the islands, he made it his first priority to try to persuade the Assembly to accept the peace terms Philip was offering,* arguing that the Macedonian king was not being belligerent and was terrified at the prospect of war. One of the sycophants who used to hang out by the People's Court interrupted him. 'Phocion,' he said, 'the Athenians are already up in arms. Do you dare to divert them from their purpose?' 'Yes,' he replied, 'even though I'm aware that in wartime I command you, but in peacetime you will command me.'

This attempt of his to persuade the Assembly was unsuccessful; Demosthenes got his way instead, with his recommendation that the Athenians should fight as far from Attica as possible. 'Sir,' said Phocion to Demosthenes, 'the question is not where we should fight, but how we might win. As long as we're winning, the war will be distant, but when people are losing every terror is close at hand.' After the defeat,* when the troublemakers who wanted change in Athens dragged Charidemus* to the speaker's platform and insisted on his being made general, the best men of the city became frightened. They brought the members of the Areopagus Council into the Assembly, and begged the people with tears in their eyes to entrust the city to Phocion, and eventually they prevailed.

Although Phocion's position was basically that Philip was being generous, and that they should accept his measures, he argued against Demades' proposal that the city should join the rest of the Greeks in subscribing to the common peace and attending the conference,* saying that they first needed to find out what demands Philip would make of the Greeks. Thanks to the crisis, Phocion's advice was rejected, but as soon as he saw that the Athenians were beginning to regret their decision, because they had to supply Philip with triremes and cavalrymen, he said: 'That's what I was afraid of; that's why I objected to Demades' proposal. But you committed yourselves to the agreement, so you mustn't complain. Cheer up! Remember that our ancestors too were sometimes rulers and sometimes subjects, and that, by acting honourably in both circumstances, they kept Athens safe and all Greece too.' When Philip died, Phocion tried to block a proposal in the Assembly for a thanksgiving sacrifice, pointing out that an expression of joy would be despicable—and also that the army they had faced at Chaeronea was smaller by only one man.*

[17] When Demosthenes was busy pouring scorn on Alexander even as he was advancing on Thebes, Phocion said to him: '"You fool, why purposely provoke a savage man",* who's driven by vaunting ambition? With the world ablaze on our doorstep, why are you fanning the city into flame? This is exactly why I take on the burden of generalship, to make sure that, willy-nilly, these people survive.'

After the destruction of Thebes,* with Alexander demanding the surrender of Demosthenes, Lycurgus, Hypereides, and Charidemus, and the Athenian people pinning their hopes on Phocion, they clamoured to hear what he had to say, and eventually he got to his feet. He had one of his friends stand by his side, the man whose company he enjoyed most, his dearest and most trusted friend. 'The men in question', he said, 'have reduced the city to such a state that even if it was the surrender of Nicocles* here that was being demanded, I would recommend you to obey. I mean, if my death would save all of you I would count myself lucky to be able to make the sacrifice. Athenians,' he continued, 'I feel sorry for the Theban refugees who have come here, but there's no point in giving the Greeks more to weep about than Thebes. Rather than fight the victors, then, it is better for both them and us to negotiate and try to obtain concessions.'

And so, we hear, when Alexander was handed a copy of the first Athenian decree, he hurled it to the ground, spun on his heels, and left the envoys; but he accepted the second one, because it was brought by Phocion, and Alexander had heard from his older advisers that even Philip had expressed admiration for the man. Not only did Alexander grant Phocion an audience, then, and hear his petition, but he even listened to his advice—that if peace was what he wanted, he should end the war, but if he wanted glory, he should leave the Greeks alone and make war on the Persians instead. Much of what he said was shrewdly designed to appeal to Alexander's nature and wishes, and in this way he managed to bring about a change of heart. In fact, he calmed his anger so successfully that Alexander told him that the Athenians should keep well abreast of events, because, if something happened to him, it was they who should properly become the rulers of Greece.

At a personal level, Alexander honoured Phocion with friendship and guest-friendship, and treated him with greater respect than he treated almost all those who had known him all his life. At any rate, Duris says that when Alexander had become 'the Great' by defeating Darius, he stopped using the expression 'Greetings' in his letters, except when he was writing to Phocion; Phocion was the only one, along with Antipater, to whom he used this form of address. Chares of Mytilene* reports this as well.

[18] As for the business with the money, it is generally accepted that Alexander sent Phocion 100 talents* as a personal gift. When the money arrived in Athens, Phocion asked the men who had brought it why Alexander had picked him out of the entire Athenian population for such generosity. They replied: 'Because, in his opinion, you are the only one with moral integrity.' 'In that case,' said Phocion, 'he should let me earn this opinion by actually *being* moral.'

When they accompanied him home and saw how frugally he lived—his wife was kneading dough, and Phocion drew his own well water to wash his feet—they pressed the money on him even more urgently, and indignantly said that it was shocking for a friend of the king to be living in such wretched conditions. Phocion happened to spot an old working-class man walking by in filthy clothes, and he asked the men whom they considered worse off, him or this poor old man. 'How can you even ask?' they exclaimed, and he said: 'Yet he lives off less than me and does all right. But the basic point is this: if I don't make use of it, it will do me no good to have all that money, and if I do make use of it I'll be blackening both the king's and my reputation in Athens.' And so the money returned home from Athens, but it had proved to all Greece that the one who had no need of it was richer than the one who was offering it.*

Alexander was annoyed, and wrote again to Phocion, saying that he did not consider anyone who needed nothing from him to be a friend, but even then Phocion refused to accept the money. He did, however, ask for the release of the sophist Echecratidas, Athenodorus 'the Imbrian', and two Rhodians, Demaratus and Sparton;* they had been arrested on various charges and were being held in prison in Sardis.

Alexander released them straight away, but later, when he was sending Craterus back to Macedon, he told him to give Phocion one of four cities in Asia,* whichever one he chose out of Cius, Gergithus, Mylasa, and Elaea, and he made it even more plain that he would not take it well if the gift were refused. But Phocion turned it down, and not long afterwards Alexander died. Even today one can see Phocion's house in Melite,* decorated with bronze plates, but otherwise plain and unpretentious.

[19] As for his marriages, no information has come down to us about his first wife, except that she was the sister of Cephisodotus the sculptor.* But the second had as great a reputation in Athens for modesty and simplicity as Phocion did for goodness. Once, some newly written tragedies were being shown in Athens, and the actor who was to play the part of the queen asked the producer for plenty of richly arrayed handmaidens. When the producer said no, the disgruntled actor kept the audience waiting by refusing to make his entrance. Eventually the producer, Melanthius, pushed him out into the open, saying in a loud voice: 'Look at Phocion's wife! Don't you know that she only ever walks out with a single servant? Yet here you are giving yourself airs and ruining our womenfolk!' His voice was audible and the audience greeted his words with loud applause and catcalls. And another story about this wife: once, when an Ionian visitor showed off her golden jewellery, her hair-bands and necklaces studded with precious stones, Phocion's wife said: 'My husband, now in his twentieth year as general of the Athenians, is all the embellishment I need.'

[20] When his son Phocus wanted to compete in the Panathenaic Games, Phocion let him take part in the Dismount,* not for the sake of victory, but for the good that the physical training and exercise would do him, given that the boy was otherwise fond of partying and led an irregular life. After Phocus won, invitations to victory dinners poured in, almost all of which Phocion declined, granting this distinction to one man only. When he turned up for the banquet and saw the magnificence of the preparations, including bowls of spiced wine that were brought to the guests as they entered, for them to wash their feet, he called his son over and said: 'Phocus, stop your friend spoiling your victory!'

Later, wanting to get this kind of lifestyle completely out of his son's system, he took him to Sparta and had him join the young men who were being trained according to the famous 'regime'.* The Athenians took offence at this, as though Phocion were scorning and disdaining their own way of doing things. And Demades said to him: 'Phocion, why don't we try to persuade the Athenians to adopt the Spartan constitution? Just say the word, and I'm ready to draw up the proposal and introduce it.' But Phocion replied: 'Yes, with the scent of perfume strong on you and such a fine cloak on your shoulders, you're obviously the right man to commend Lycurgus to the Athenians and advise them on messing together.'*

[21] When Alexander wrote asking the Athenians to send him triremes,* the public speakers balked, but the Council asked to hear what Phocion had to say. 'Well,' he said, 'my advice is that you should either have military superiority or else be on good terms with those that do.' Pytheas was just then beginning his public career in Athens, but he already had a glib tongue and a bold attitude. 'Simmer down!' Phocion said to him. 'You're just a slave,* newly acquired by the people.'

When Harpalus* fled from Asia to escape Alexander and arrived in Attica with a huge amount of money, those who were in the habit of using their position as politicians to enrich themselves raced to see him and vied with one another to see who could be bribed first. He scattered and tossed in their direction some trifling sums from his deep coffers to keep them sweet, but he wrote to Phocion with an offer of 700 talents, and the suggestion that all the rest of the money, and himself along with it, should be committed to Phocion's exclusive care. Phocion's reply was blunt, however—that Harpalus would regret it if he did not stop trying to corrupt Athens—and for a while Harpalus was put in his place and stopped making a nuisance of himself. Before long, however, when the Athenians were debating what to do about him, Harpalus noticed that those who had taken money from him had changed their tune and were now denouncing him, to cover up their guilt, while Phocion, who had taken nothing, was considering how to keep him safe without jeopardizing the common good. Encouraged by this, he renewed his attempt to win Phocion's favour, but, search as he might for a chink in his defences, he found him to be a fortress, completely impregnable by money.

Harpalus did, however, form a close friendship with Charicles, Phocion's son-in-law, and ruined his reputation by making him his right-hand man and agent for everything. [22] For instance, when the courtesan Pythonice died, who had been loved by Harpalus and had borne him a daughter, he wanted to build a costly monument to her memory,* and he made Charicles responsible for it. This was rather demeaning work, and the completed tomb only compounded the disgrace. The tomb is still there in Hermeion, on the Athens–Eleusis road, and there is nothing about it that justifies the thirty talents which Charicles is said to have charged Harpalus for the job. Now, it is true that, after Harpalus' death, responsibility for his child was taken over by Charicles and Phocion and they gave her upbringing their best attention; but when Charicles was prosecuted over the Harpalus affair, and asked Phocion to help him and put in an appearance alongside him in court, Phocion refused. 'I took you as my son-in-law, Charicles,' he said, 'on the understanding that you would never be anything but honest.'

When Asclepiades, the son of Hipparchus, broke the news of Alexander's death to the Athenian people, Demades told them not to believe it, on the grounds that if it were true the whole world would already smell of his magnificent corpse. Seeing that the Athenian people were bent on rebellion, Phocion tried to dissuade them and check their impulsiveness, but speaker after speaker leapt up to the podium and cried out that the news Asclepiades had brought was true, and Alexander really was dead.* 'Well,' said Phocion, 'if he's dead today, he'll still be dead tomorrow and the day after. So we can take time over our deliberations, or rather we can deliberate in safety.'

[23] But Leosthenes soon plunged Athens into the War for Greece.* Seeing that Phocion disapproved of this, Leosthenes asked him with a sarcastic laugh what good he had done the city in all his generalships. 'Quite a lot, actually,' replied Phocion. 'My fellow citizens are buried in their own private tombs.' And once, when Leosthenes was making overconfident and extravagant claims in the Assembly, Phocion said: 'Young man, your words are like cypress trees: they reach impressively high, but they bear no fruit.' At this, Hypereides got to his feet* and asked: 'So, Phocion, *when* will you advise the Athenians to go to war?' And Phocion replied: 'When I see the young men ready to stand firm in battle, the rich ready to pay the war levy, and the politicians ready to keep their thieving hands off public money.'

The army put together by Leosthenes* was an object of general admiration, and Phocion was frequently asked his opinion of Athens' preparations. 'Good for a sprint,' he said, 'but it's the long-haul aspect of the war that I'm worried about, since the city has now run out of money, ships, and men.' And events proved him right. Leosthenes' early successes—defeating the Boeotians in battle and pinning Antipater in Lamia—were undeniably brilliant. At this point, with the city entertaining high hopes, holding one thanksgiving festival after another, and offering constant sacrifices to the gods, some people are said to have asked Phocion, in an attempt to prove that he had made a mistake: 'But you'd be happy to have Leosthenes' achievements to your credit, wouldn't you?' 'Of course,' he said. 'But I'm also happy with the advice I gave.' Again, when good news was daily pouring in by letter and messenger from the army, he asked: 'But when will all these victories of ours come to an end?'

[24] After Leosthenes' death, there were those in Athens who were afraid that Phocion would be put in command and would negotiate an end to the war. They therefore primed someone, a relative nobody, to get up in the Assembly, claiming to be a friend and former fellow student of Phocion, argue that he was irreplaceable, and advise the Athenian people to keep him safely out of harm's way, and give Antiphilus* command of the army. The Athenians agreed, and Phocion stepped up and said that the man had never been a friend of his, close or otherwise, and that they had certainly not been students together. 'But from today onwards,' he told him, 'I shall count you my friend, because of the good your advice here has done me.'

When the Athenians were determined to attack the Boeotians, Phocion at first spoke out against the idea, and some of his friends told him that he would be put to death if he kept opposing the Athenian people. 'That wouldn't be right if I'm doing them good,' he said, 'only if I'm out of line.' Later, however, seeing that they kept up their clamouring and would not let the matter drop, he told the town crier to announce that every adult Athenian male under sixty years of age was to find five days' worth of provisions and set out with him straight after the Assembly. This provoked uproar, with the older men jumping up and shouting out their objections. 'I don't see why you're making such a fuss,' he said. 'I'll be going with you as your general, and I'm eighty years old.' For a while, then, he quietened them down and got them to change their minds.

[25] However, when the coast came under attack by Micion, who landed at Rhamnous with a large force of Macedonians and

mercenaries and set about ravaging the countryside,* Phocion led the Athenians out against him. While they were on the march, men approached Phocion from all sides with tactical advice, some suggesting that he should seize a particular hill, others with ideas about where he should send the cavalry or where to make camp. 'Good Heracles!' he said. 'What a lot of generals I have, and how few soldiers!' After he had drawn up his heavy infantry for battle, one of the men advanced quite a way ahead of the rest, but then, when challenged by an enemy soldier, he retreated in fear back to the line. 'Shame on you, young man!' Phocion said to him. 'You've deserted your post twice—once the post assigned by your general, and then the one you chose yourself.' Then he attacked the enemy lines, and drove them into flight, with considerable loss of life, including that of Micion himself. Meanwhile, in Thessaly, Leonnatus and the Macedonians he had brought from Asia had joined Antipater, but even so the Greek forces carried the day, and Leonnatus fell.* In this battle, Antiphilus commanded the heavy infantry, and Menon of Thessaly* the cavalry.

[26] Not long after this, Craterus crossed over from Asia with a large army, and another pitched battle was fought, at Crannon.* Although the Greeks lost, it was not a major defeat in terms of loss of life. The problem was that the senior officers on the Greek side were too young and too fair to command obedience—and at the same time Antipater was testing the resolution of the Greek cities, and to their great shame they withdrew their forces and threw away their freedom. Antipater immediately advanced on Athens, and Demosthenes and Hypereides fled.* Although Demades was finding it impossible to pay off even the smallest portion of what he owed the state by way of fines for court cases he had lost—he had been convicted seven times for introducing unconstitutional measures and the consequent loss of his rights as a citizen debarred him from public speaking—he was given permission under the circumstances to address the Assembly and he proposed that ambassadors should be sent to Antipater with full powers to negotiate peace terms.

In their fear, the Athenian people approached Phocion, telling him that he was the only one they could trust. 'Had you trusted me enough to take my advice in the first place,' he said, 'we wouldn't now be wondering how to cope with this crisis.' Anyway, once Demades' proposal had been passed into law, Phocion was sent to Antipater, who had made camp on the Cadmeia while preparing to invade Attica.* Phocion's first request was that Antipater should stay where he was for the peace negotiations. Craterus said that it was unfair of Phocion to ask them to inflict themselves on land belonging to their friends and allies, when they could be despoiling enemy territory, but Antipater took him by the hand and said: 'No, we should do Phocion this favour.' But otherwise he gave the Athenians the same rejoinder that Leosthenes had given him at Lamia—that they should leave it to the victors to dictate the terms.

[27] Phocion returned to Athens, and once the Athenians decided to proceed on that basis, seeing that they had no choice, he went back to Thebes, accompanied this time by the rest of the ambassadors chosen by the Athenians. One of them was the philosopher Xenocrates,* whose goodness was universally acknowledged and recognized, and it was therefore expected that, however abusive or cruel or hostile a man may be, the mere sight of Xenocrates would engender in him a degree of deference and respect. But Antipater was a hard-hearted and perverse man, so that was not how things worked out at all. First, he refused to greet Xenocrates, though he offered all the other ambassadors his hand. Xenocrates is supposed to have responded to this by saying that this was just Antipater's way of expressing shame to him for his ruthless plans for Athens, and he was right to do so. But then Antipater interrupted Xenocrates whenever he tried to speak, and his hostile antagonism reduced him to silence.

After listening to what Phocion had to say, however, Antipater stated his conditions for a treaty of friendship and alliance with the Athenians: they were to surrender Demosthenes and Hypereides, restore their property-based ancestral constitution,* accept a garrison on Munychia,* and also pay the costs of the war and an additional indemnity. All the other ambassadors regarded these terms as generous and were happy to accept them, except for Xenocrates, who said that the settlement was fair if Antipater regarded them as slaves, but harsh for free men. Phocion pleaded with Antipater and tried to convince him that there was no need for a garrison, and Antipater is said to have replied: 'Phocion, I'd gladly grant you any concession you like—but not if it would encompass our ruin, yours and mine.' But there is an alternative version of the story, according to which Antipater asked Phocion whether, if he let the Athenians off the garrison, Phocion would guarantee that Athens would keep the peace and not make a nuisance of itself. Phocion did not immediately reply, and Callimedon, nicknamed 'the Crab',* an aggressive man and no friend of democracy, leapt to his feet and said: 'Antipater, are you going to trust this man and his empty words? Aren't you going to carry out your plans?'

[28] So the garrison was installed under the command of Menyllus,* a decent man and a friend of Phocion. But, as it turned out, the order was merely a way of asserting authority, and the occupation of Munychia was more a display of arrogant power than a measure that served any practical purpose. The timing of the occupation also greatly increased the Athenians' distress. For the garrison was installed on 20 Boedromion, during the Mysteries, on the day when the Athenians process with Iacchus from the city to Eleusis, and the disruption of the ceremony led very many people to compare the gods' earlier behaviour with the present. In the past, they said, the mystic sights and sounds had coincided with the city's greatest successes and had been accompanied by consternation and dismay on the part of their enemies.* But now the gods were looking down impassively as Greece suffered in ways that were bound to cause serious disruption to these same rites; now the most sacred festival of the calendar, the one that pleased the gods more than any other, was being besmirched by its association with their worst misfortunes.

Not only had the priestesses of Dodona, a few years earlier, published an oracle that the city was to 'guard the heights of Artemis'* against occupation by outsiders, but now, during the days of the festival, the straps which are wound around the mystic chests turned a sallow, necrotic colour when dyed, instead of the normal crimson, and, even more ominously, all the objects unrelated to the festival that were being dyed in the same bath took on the right colouring. Moreover, when one of the initiates was washing his piglet* in the Cantharus harbour, a monstrous shark seized him and devoured the entire lower half of his body up to his belly—a clear warning from heaven that they would lose the lower, coastal district, but retain the upper city.

Anyway, thanks to Menyllus, it was not the garrison that upset people, but more than 12,000 men were now deemed too poor for citizenship.* Of these, some stayed in Athens, where they presumably suffered all the indignities of non-citizens, while those who abandoned the city in order to avoid this fate and moved to Thrace, where

Antipater gave them land and a city, were like refugees from a city that had capitulated.

[29] I have written elsewhere about the deaths of Demosthenes and Hypereides,* respectively on Calauria and at Cleonae. It is hardly an exaggeration to say that these deaths inspired the Athenians with a passionate longing for Alexander and Philip. There is a story from later that, after Antigonus Monophthalmus had been killed and those responsible for his death had initiated an oppressive and harsh regime, a peasant in Phrygia who was digging on his land was asked what he was doing, and he said with a sigh, 'I'm looking for Antigonus.'* Many people were moved now to say much the same kind of thing† when they remembered how the magnanimity and generosity of those two kings had made it easy for their anger to be pacified. This was not the case with Antipater, however; although he disguised his power by making himself look like an ordinary man, with mean clothing and a simple way of life, he was in fact a more oppressive and tyrannical master for his wretched subjects than Philip and Alexander.

Despite this, Phocion did often successfully petition Antipater to remit sentences of exile, and he arranged for those who were in exile (such as Hagnonides* the sycophant) to live in the Peloponnese, rather than being driven out of Greece 'beyond the Ceraunian mountains and Cape Taenarum', like everyone else who was banished.* His administration of Athens was moderate and lawful,* and he managed to keep men of education and culture continually in office, while teaching the troublemakers and agitators, who were fading into insignificance just by being denied positions of power and opportunities for disturbance, to be content with tilling the soil. When he saw that Xenocrates was paying the resident alien's tax, he offered to have him registered as a citizen, but Xenocrates refused, saying that he had served as ambassador to try to abort this version of Athens, and so he could not very well be a member of it.

[30] Menyllus too† offered Phocion 100 talents as a personal gift, but Phocion replied that Menyllus was a lesser man than Alexander and, having refused such a gift before, he had no more reason to accept it now. And when Menyllus asked him to take it for his son Phocus, if not for himself, Phocion replied: 'If Phocus changes his ways and sobers up, his inheritance will be enough, but as things are now nothing is enough.'

Antipater once wanted him to do something improper, and

Phocion replied rather brusquely: 'Antipater cannot have me as a friend and a flatterer at the same time.'* And Antipater himself is supposed to have said that he had two friends in Athens, Phocion and Demades, one of whom never accepted his gifts, while the other never had enough of them. And indeed, while Phocion made no secret of the poverty in which he had grown old, even though he had served the Athenians so often as general and counted kings as friends, Demades used to flaunt his wealth even if it involved breaking the law. For instance, there was a law in Athens at the time that no non-Athenian was to take part in a choral festival, or the producer would be liable to a fine of 1,000 drachmas; but Demades laid on a chorus of a hundred dancers, none of whom was an Athenian—and brought with him to the theatre the fine of 1,000 drachmas for each of the hundred dancers! And at his son Demeas' marriage ceremony he said: 'When I married your mother, my boy, no one noticed, not even the neighbours. But the costs of your wedding are being met in part by kings and dynasts.'

The Athenians used to pester Phocion to get Antipater to remove the garrison. He always refused the mission, however—though he did persuade Antipater not to demand prompt and immediate payment of the money—perhaps because he did not expect to win the argument, or perhaps because he saw that the people behaved with more restraint when they were afraid, and became easier to manage politically. So the Athenians called on Demades instead, and he had no hesitation about taking on the mission. Off he went to Macedon with his son, but some deity seems to have been at work, and he arrived at a time when Antipater was seriously ill and Cassander had assumed control.* But Cassander had found a letter that Demades had written to Antigonus Monophthalmus* in Asia, in which he asked Antigonus to come and take charge of affairs in Greece and Macedon, which were hanging 'by an old and rotten thread'—Demades' scornful description of Antipater. As soon as Cassander heard that he had arrived, then, he had him arrested. First, he had Demeas slaughtered in his father's presence, so close that the blood pooled in the folds of Demades' clothing and he was spattered with gore; and then, after rebuking him savagely and at length for his ingratitude and treachery, he put him to death.

[31] After Antipater's death, Cassander revealed his true intentions and seized control, even though Antipater had given the Generalship

to Polyperchon and made Cassander his second-in-command.* Cassander quickly sent Nicanor* to replace Menyllus as garrison commander, and ordered him to seize Munychia before Antipater's death became public knowledge. Everything went according to plan. A few days later, when the Athenians heard the news of Antipater's death, they railed at Phocion, alleging that he had been privy to the information and had kept quiet for Nicanor's sake. Phocion ignored them, but he held meetings and discussions with Nicanor, and made sure that he was gentle and generous in his dealings with the Athenians. Above all, he persuaded him to become Master of Games, and in that capacity to arrange some of the events and meet some of the costs.

[32] Meanwhile Polyperchon, who had the king in his care* and was determined to outmanoeuvre Cassander, wrote a letter to Athens in the name of the king, proclaiming the restoration of the democracy and saying that all Athenian citizens were to participate in the political process, in accordance with their ancestral constitution.* The letter was cunningly designed to undermine Phocion, because Polyperchon's intention, as his actions a short while later showed, was to gain control of Athens. He did not think he would succeed, however, unless Phocion were banished, and he thought that the best way to ensure his banishment was if the disfranchised citizens regained their political dominance, and demagogues and sycophants once again occupied the speaker's platform.

The letter stirred some unrest, and Nicanor, wanting to address the Athenians, attended a meeting of the Council in Piraeus, under a guarantee of safe conduct from Phocion. Dercyllus, the general responsible for the Athenian countryside, tried to arrest him, but Nicanor got wind of the attempt and evaded the trap. It looked as though he was going to take immediate reprisals against the city, but Phocion, who was criticized for having let the man go without detaining him, said that he trusted Nicanor and did not expect him to act vengefully. In any case, he said, he would rather be known as a victim of crime than as a criminal.

Now, such a sentiment might certainly seem high-minded and noble coming from a man who was speaking only for himself, but someone who gambles with his country, and does so when he is general and head of state, is running the risk, I think, of transgressing a higher and more important obligation, to do right by his fellow citizens. Phocion could not claim that it was fear of plunging the city into war that had made him let Nicanor go; he excused his behaviour on other grounds, citing the obligations of honour and justice, in the hope that Nicanor would respect his reasons and do nothing, or nothing that injured Athens. No, the fact of the matter is, apparently, that Phocion absolutely trusted Nicanor. In fact, when he was forewarned about Nicanor's hostile intentions towards Piraeus, and heard from many sources that he was transporting mercenaries to Salamis and corrupting some of the residents of Piraeus, he dismissed the warnings as untrue and unreliable.* Even when Philomelus of Lamptrae proposed that the entire citizen levy should stand armed and ready, awaiting orders from Phocion, their general, he still did nothing, right up until the time when Nicanor brought his troops down from Munychia and dug defensive trenches around Piraeus.

[33] Under these circumstances, Phocion was at last willing to lead the Athenians into battle, which provoked cries of outrage and contempt, but just then Polyperchon's son Alexander arrived with an army.* In theory, he was there to help the people of Athens against Nicanor, but in fact he wanted to gain control of the city if he could, seeing that it had turned against itself. The Athenian exiles who had joined his army of invasion quickly entered the city, and when the foreign residents and disfranchised citizens flocked to them, a motley and disorderly Assembly was held, at which Phocion was removed from office and a fresh board of generals was appointed. If Alexander had not been spotted having a private conference with Nicanor by the city wall, and if the number of occasions on which they met had not made the Athenians suspicious, Athens would not have escaped the danger it was in.

The orator Hagnonides lost no time in attacking Phocion and denouncing him as a traitor. At this, Callimedon and Charicles fled the city in terror,* and Phocion, along with those of his friends who remained by him, set out for Polyperchon's camp. They were accompanied by Solon of Plataea and Deinarchus of Corinth,* who owed Phocion a favour and were said to be close to Polyperchon. But Deinarchus fell ill and they were held up for a long time in Elatea, while in Athens the people adopted a proposal brought forward by Archestratus and championed by Hagnonides, and sent a delegation to denounce Phocion.

Both groups found Polyperchon at the same time. He was

marching south with the king, and had reached a village in Phocis called Pharygae, which lies at the foot of Mount Acrurium (Mount Galata, nowadays). There Polyperchon set up the golden canopy and seated the king and his Friends beneath it.* He had his men snatch Deinarchus right out of the queue approaching the king and take him away for torture and death, and then he let the Athenians speak—but they reduced the meeting to chaos by screaming accusations and counter-accusations at one another. Eventually, Hagnonides stepped up and said: 'You should cage us all up together and send us back to explain our conduct to the Athenians.'

This made the king laugh, but the Macedonian and foreign bystanders wanted to hear what the Athenians had to say, since they had nothing better to do with their time, and they signalled the envoys to go ahead with their denunciation of Phocion. But the whole thing was very unfair, in that Polyperchon hardly ever let Phocion finish a sentence, and eventually Phocion thumped his stick down on the ground and stepped back in silence. Then, when Hegemon* said that his loyalty towards the Athenian people could be confirmed by Polyperchon, Polyperchon angrily shouted back: 'How dare you lie about me in front of the king!' At this, the king leapt to his feet and lunged at Hegemon with a spear,* but Polyperchon quickly threw his arms around him. At that point the meeting broke up.

[34] Guards surrounded Phocion and his companions and, seeing this, those of his friends who were luckily standing some way off covered their faces and fled to safety. Phocion and the rest were taken to Athens by Cleitus,* ostensibly to stand trial, but in reality they had already been condemned to death. The manner of their conveyance made it even worse: they were carried on carts through the Cerameicus* to the theatre, and when Cleitus had brought them there he kept them under guard until the archons had gathered enough people for an Assembly. No one was excluded; even slaves, foreigners, and the disfranchised were allowed in, and the speaker's platform and the theatre were made freely available to every man and woman.*

The king's letter to the Athenian people was read out, the gist of which was that he had no doubt of the men's treachery, but he left it up to them, as free and autonomous agents, to reach a verdict. Then Cleitus introduced the prisoners. At the sight of Phocion, the best of the Athenians covered their faces, bowed their heads, and wept. One of them, however, had the courage to get to his feet and say that, since the king had entrusted such an important trial to the Athenian people, slaves and foreigners had no place in this Assembly and should leave. But the suggestion did not go down well with most of the people there, and they cried out: 'Stone them! Stone the oligarchs, the opponents of democracy!'

No one undertook to speak for Phocion, and it was only with considerable difficulty that he was able to make himself heard. 'Do you want to kill us fairly or unfairly?' he asked. 'Fairly,' came the reply from some quarters. 'And how will you know the rights and wrongs of the case,' he asked, 'if you refuse to listen?' This argument fell on deaf ears, however, so he drew closer and said: 'I am guilty. I admit it, and the penalty I propose for my crimes against the state is death.* But why kill these men here with me, Athenians? They've done nothing wrong at all.' Many voices called back: 'Because they're friends of yours.' At this, Phocion gave up and spoke no more. But Hagnonides read out a proposal he had prepared and brought with him, to the effect that the Athenian people were to vote on the guilt of the accused by a show of hands, and that in the event of a guilty verdict the penalty was death.

[35] After the proposal had been read out, some people wanted to add that Phocion was to be tortured to death, and they called for the wheel be fetched and the executioners summoned. But Hagnonides could see that Cleitus disapproved, and he too thought it would be a savage and disgusting thing to do, so he said: 'We'll torture that crook Callimedon, Athenians, when we catch him. But in Phocion's case—no, that's not part of my proposal.' At this, an honest Athenian called out: 'Quite right too. For if we torture Phocion, what shall we do when it's your turn?'

So the wording of the proposal was ratified as it stood. When it came to the show of hands, no one remained seated; all rose to their feet—a great many of them had put on celebratory garlands too—and they condemned the men to death. With Phocion at the time were Nicocles, Thoudippus, Hegemon, and Pythocles; Demetrius of Phalerum,* Callimedon, Charicles, and a few others were condemned to death *in absentia*.

[36] After the Assembly had broken up, the men were taken off to prison. All the rest of them wept and groaned as they walked along, with friends and relatives clinging to them; but Phocion had the same look on his face that he used to have when he was being escorted

from the Assembly as general, and people were amazed by this composure and detachment. But his enemies ran alongside him sneering, and one of them even came up and spat in his face. At this, it is said, Phocion looked towards the archons and said: 'Will someone please stop this indecency?'

When Thoudippus reached the prison and saw the hemlock being crushed, he protested and bewailed his fate, saying he did not deserve to die with Phocion. And Phocion said: 'So Phocion isn't good enough company for you to die with?' When one of his friends asked if he had any message for his son Phocus, he said: 'Yes, I do. Tell him not to hold a grudge against the Athenians.' And when Nicocles, his most faithful friend, asked his permission to drink the poison before him, Phocion said: 'That's a hard and upsetting thing to ask of me, Nicocles, but I've never refused you anything in my entire life, and I'm not going to start now.' But the hemlock ran out when Phocion was the only one who had not yet drunk it, and the gaoler refused to crush more unless he was given twelve drachmas, the cost of the dose.* After some delay, Phocion called in one of his friends and asked him to give the man the money, saying: 'It seems that in Athens one can't even die for free!'

[37] The date was 19 Munychion,* and as the Athenian cavalry passed the prison in the course of their parade in honour of Zeus, some of them removed their garlands, while others looked towards the prison doorway with tears in their eyes. Everyone—everyone whose mind had not been warped into cruelty by anger and malevolence—thought it had been the height of impiety not to wait for that day to pass, to keep the city pure of public bloodshed during a festival.*

His enemies, however, seem to have felt that their victory was incomplete, and they decreed that Phocion's body was to be taken beyond the borders, and that no Athenian citizen was even to attend the burial and light the pyre. This deterred his friends from doing anything with the body, but a man called Conopion, who used to hire himself out to perform this service, transported it over the border at Eleusis, found fire there in Megaris, and burnt it. But Phocion's wife, who had gone there with her maidservants, heaped up some earth as a cenotaph and poured libations over it. Then she returned home under cover of darkness, with the bones hidden inside her clothes, and buried them next to the hearth. 'Hearth of our home,' she said, 'to you I consign these remains, all that is left of a good man. I pray that you will return them to his ancestral tomb once the Athenians have come to their senses.'

[38] And so it turned out. Before much time had passed, events taught the Athenian people how great a champion of justice and guardian of moderation they had lost. They erected a statue of him in bronze, and gave his bones a state funeral.* As for his accusers, Hagnonides was condemned and put to death by the Athenians themselves, while Epicurus and Demophilus fled the city, but were tracked down and punished by Phocion's son.

It is clear from the stories about him that Phocus did not turn out well at all.* Once, for example, he was in love with a girl who was being brought up in a brothel, and he happened to hear Theodorus the atheist conversing dialectically in the Lyceum. The gist of his argument was: 'If it is no disgrace to ransom a man one loves, the same goes for a woman one loves too. By the same token, if it is no disgrace to ransom a male friend, the same goes for a girlfriend.' Convinced by his desire of the soundness of the argument, Phocus bought his girlfriend's freedom.

But what happened to Phocion reminded the Greeks of Socrates,* and they felt that on both occasions the city had been equally at fault and equally visited by misfortune.

EUMENES

INTRODUCTION

Eumenes (*c*.362–316 BCE) came from Cardia in the Thracian Chersonese, better known today as the Gallipoli peninsula. Despite being Greek rather than Macedonian, he became a significant figure in the wars of the Successors that followed Alexander's death. His earlier career, however, is poorly known. He was from a leading family in Cardia and moved to the court of Philip II in the late 340s at the age of nineteen. Serving as the king's secretary, he continued to hold that position under Alexander and went on to accompany him on the Persian expedition. At some point, however, he took on a more military role, eventually in 324 replacing Perdiccas as Cavalry Commander. In the developing conflict after Alexander's death Eumenes was aligned with Perdiccas, the regent for the king's heirs, and proved an adept military commander, defeating Craterus, one of the senior Macedonian generals, just after the latter had crossed into Asia Minor. But when Perdiccas was killed attacking Ptolemy in Egypt, Eumenes was without his most important ally. Shortly afterwards, at Triparadeisus, the new regent Antipater established a fresh settlement for the Macedonian empire, one which had no place for Eumenes or any other adherents of Perdiccas. Antigonus Monophthalmus was given the Generalship of Asia and the task of dealing with Eumenes. The death of Antipater in 319 brought Eumenes a temporary reprieve, when his successor Polyperchon sought to restrain Antigonus by giving Eumenes the command of Asia. This allowed Eumenes official access to the royal resources of the empire, and so he headed eastwards to take advantage of the wealth of Iran. Here two major battles were fought; the first, at Paraetacene, was indecisive; the second, at Gabene, was ultimately disastrous for Eumenes, because Antigonus succeeded in capturing Eumenes' baggage camp and with it the soldiers' families. Disgruntled and determined to get back what they had lost, the soldiers handed Eumenes over to Antigonus and 'the pest from the Chersonese' was soon executed.

This brief narrative of Eumenes' career, however, omits one distinctive feature of the wars of the Successors. These were wars fought between men who knew one another well, and this is something that Plutarch brings out very effectively. The potential for conflict is evident right at the beginning of the Life, when Eumenes gets into several disputes with Hephaestion. But after Alexander's death any conflict is on quite a different scale. The two most significant opponents of Eumenes in the Life are Craterus and Antigonus. In both cases Plutarch chooses to emphasize the friendship between Eumenes and his enemy. He draws a moving picture of Eumenes holding the hand of the dying Craterus as tears pour down his face, a marked contrast to Diodorus' account of the same battle, in which the two men never meet. Antigonus' task is to hunt Eumenes down, but when the siege of Nora is interrupted for negotiations between the two, they 'embraced and greeted each other with warmth and affection, since they were old friends and had been close to each other' (10). At the end of the Life, when Eumenes is captured, Antigonus has to decide whether or not to kill his friend. The corpse is then cremated and the ashes returned to Eumenes' family in a silver urn, just as the ashes of Antigonus' own son Demetrius would later be returned to his family by Seleucus (*Demetrius* 53).

The *Eumenes* is the shortest of the *Parallel Lives*. Eumenes' early life and career under Alexander are covered rather sketchily, but even so a series of anecdotes in the second chapter paints a surprisingly negative picture of Eumenes as self-interested and given to petty quarrels. The focus of the Life is very much on the period after Alexander's death, which has already been reached by chapter 3. This suggests that Plutarch's material was primarily taken from narrative histories of the wars of Successors, but unfortunately in this Life he makes almost no reference to the sources he has used. In his opening sentence he cites the roughly contemporary historian Duris of Samos on the lowly background of Eumenes' father, but straight away rejects it for an alternative account, for which he gives no authority. Hieronymus of Cardia is usually identified as a major source for the Life, due to similarities with histories that are believed to have drawn heavily on his work, notably book 18 of Diodorus' Universal History. Hieronymus' history covered the period from the death of Alexander at least as far as the death of Pyrrhus in 272. As a historian of Eumenes, especially of the wars he fought with Antigonus, his position was complex. On the one hand, he was closely associated with Eumenes; he was a compatriot, he had served under him and may even have been his nephew. On the other hand, he transferred his allegiance to the victorious Antigonus after Eumenes' death and remained in the service of the Antigonids for the rest of his long life.

In the *Parallel Lives* Eumenes was paired with the maverick Roman commander Quintus Sertorius, who established himself in Spain as the alternative to the Sullan government in Rome. Plutarch draws out many similarities between the two men, both in their character and in the course of their lives, but Sertorius' patriotism means that he elicits more sympathy from the reader than the self-serving Eumenes. Unusually, in this case the Roman life precedes the Greek and so

Plutarch's introductory thoughts on the key points of comparison between the two men appear there:

> Both were talented commanders adept at using cunning in warfare; both were driven from their homeland; both were leaders of foreign soldiers; in death both experienced a violent and unjust fortune; for they were both plotted against and done away with by the very men with whom they were defeating their enemies.

The themes of leadership and cunning appear throughout the Life of Eumenes, often together as he finds ways to ensure the loyalty of his men, both the officers and the troops, something that was all the more difficult as a Greek among Macedonians. He borrows from those who dislike him the most so that they have a vested interest in keeping him alive. Fearing that the capture of the enemy baggage train would slow his army down, he warns the man in charge of it to increase security, an approach which he justifies on the grounds of friendship. When he is faced with Craterus, he ensures that as few as possible know that the opposing army is being led by the celebrated Macedonian general, as he fears soldiers might desert to his opponent. But Eumenes' reputation for cunning did not begin with Plutarch. Not only is it found in earlier writers, such as Cornelius Nepos in his Life of Eumenes, but there are also further stratagems that do not even appear in Plutarch, such as the forged letter designed to undermine the popularity of his ally and rival Peucestas (Diodorus 19.23). But the stratagems that Plutarch reports tend to be to Eumenes' credit, whereas the story of the letter suggests that he was no better than those around him, plotting against them as much as they were plotting against him. In the end, however, all his leadership skills and guile were not enough in a world where distinguishing enemy from friend was no easy matter and loyalty was secondary to self-interest.

Anson, E., *Eumenes of Cardia: A Greek among Macedonians* (Leiden, 2004).

Bosworth, A. B., 'History and Artifice in Plutarch's *Eumenes*', in P. Stadter (ed.), *Plutarch and the Historical Tradition* (London, 1992), 56–89.

—— *The Legacy of Alexander: Politics, Warfare, and Propaganda under the Successors* (Oxford, 2002).

Geiger, J., 'Plutarch on Hellenistic Politics: The Case of Eumenes of Cardia', in I. Gallo and B. Scardigli (eds.), *Teoria e prassi politica nelle opere di Plutarco, Atti del V Convegno plutarcheo* (Naples, 1995), 173–85.

Hadley, R. A., 'A Possible Lost Source for the Career of Eumenes of Kardia', *Historia*, 50 (2001), 3–33.

Roisman, J., *Alexander's Veterans and the Early Wars of the Successors* (Austin, Tex., 2012).

Schäfer, C., *Eumenes von Kardia und der Kampf um die Macht im Alexanderreich* (Frankfurt a.M., 2002).

Waterfield, R., *Dividing the Spoils: The War for Alexander the Great's Empire* (Oxford, 2011).

EUMENES

[1] According to Duris,* the father of Eumenes of Cardia was driven by poverty to work as a carter, and yet the boy received the kind of education at school and in the gymnasium that one would expect of a free-born child. While he was still young Philip came to town and passed some time watching the boys and young men of Cardia compete at pankration* and wrestling. Eumenes performed well, attracted Philip with his obvious intelligence and courage, and was taken into his entourage. The alternative account seems more plausible, however: that Eumenes was advanced by Philip* because of the king's guest-friendship with and affection for his father.

After Philip's death, he was found to be no less intelligent or loyal than any of the men close to Alexander, and he was held in as much respect as any of Alexander's friends and familiars, even though his title was just Chief Secretary. During the Indian campaign, in fact, he was entrusted with a mission for which he was given command of a force on his own,* and after Hephaestion's death, when Perdiccas was promoted to the vacant position, he replaced Perdiccas as Cavalry Commander.* That is why the Macedonian troops laughed at Neoptolemus,* the commander of the Hypaspists, for saying—this was after Alexander had died—that while *he* had taken up shield and spear to follow Alexander, Eumenes had taken stylus and writing-tablet. They knew that Alexander had recognized Eumenes' worth and had honoured him in a number of ways, including a close marriage alliance. For at the mass wedding* of Persian women to his Companions, he gave Apama and Artonis,* the sisters of Barsine, respectively to Ptolemy and Eumenes, and Barsine, the daughter of Artabazus, was the first woman Alexander had known in Asia and the mother of his son Heracles.*

[2] Eumenes often incurred Alexander's displeasure, however, and, thanks to Hephaestion, even found himself in some danger. The first occasion was when Hephaestion assigned Euius the pipe-player a house which Eumenes' slaves had already claimed as their master's quarters. Taking Mentor with him, Eumenes stormed off to Alexander in a rage, complaining that he might as well throw away his weapons and take up the pipes or acting.* At first Alexander sympathized with

him and told Hephaestion off in no uncertain terms, but before long he changed his mind and was angry with Eumenes, more for having hectored him than for speaking bluntly to Hephaestion.

The next occasion was when Alexander was sending Nearchus with a fleet to the outer sea,* and he asked his Friends for money, because the treasury was out of funds. Eumenes' contribution was supposed to be 300 talents, but he gave only 100, and claimed that it had taken time and effort for his stewards to collect even this much for him. Alexander uttered not a word of reproach, but he did not believe him in the slightest. He told his slaves to set fire secretly to Eumenes' pavilion, his intention being to catch Eumenes in a lie as his valuables were being carried out of harm's way. But before that could happen the pavilion burnt to the ground, and Alexander's correspondence was destroyed, to his regret. The gold and silver melted by the fire was found to weigh more than 1,000 talents, but Alexander did not take any of it. He did, however, write around to all his satraps and generals, asking them to send copies of the lost correspondence, all of which he turned over to Eumenes.

Then there was another time when Eumenes fell out with Hephaestion, this time over a gift, and insults flew thick and fast between them. At the time this made no difference to Eumenes' status, but Hephaestion died a short while later, and in his excessive grief Alexander dealt harshly and heavy-handedly with everyone he suspected of having envied Hephaestion while he was alive and of being glad he was dead. His suspicions fell above all on Eumenes, and he repeatedly brought up the way the two of them had quarrelled and traded insults. But Eumenes was cunning and plausible, and found a way to turn potential ruin into salvation. What he did was seek safety in Alexander's desire to honour Hephaestion and gratitude for favours received. He suggested honours that would particularly grace the dead man, and made a generous and unsolicited contribution towards the cost of building his tomb.*

[3] After Alexander's death, the infantry and the Companions formed opposing camps, and although Eumenes' sympathies lay with the Companions, he played the part of neutral mediator between the two sides, making out that, as a foreigner,* it was no business of his to meddle in Macedonian squabbles. He stayed in Babylon even after all his fellow Companions had left, and he succeeded in calming most of the infantry down and reconciling them to the idea of compromise.*

Once they had recovered from the initial chaos, the generals met and distributed satrapies and generalships. Eumenes received Cappadocia, Paphlagonia, and the southern coastline of the Black Sea up to Trapezus. All this territory still lay outside Macedonian control, under the rulership of Ariarathes,* but Leonnatus and Antigonus* were supposed to escort Eumenes to his province with a large army and install him as satrap. Antigonus ignored Perdiccas' dispatches, since he was already getting above himself and thinking himself superior to everyone else, but Leonnatus marched from the interior to Phrygia to take the satrapy for Eumenes. But then Hecataeus, the tyrant of Cardia, came to see him, and asked him instead to relieve Antipater and the Macedonians who were under siege in Lamia.*

Leonnatus decided to go over to Greece, and he invited Eumenes to join him and tried to make peace between him and Hecataeus. There was a hereditary feud between them, based on political differences, and Eumenes had often openly denounced Hecataeus' tyranny and asked Alexander to restore freedom to Cardia. At the time in question, then, Eumenes refused to play a part in the campaign against the Greeks, giving as his reason his fear that Antipater, who had long hated him, would do away with him as a favour to Hecataeus.

Leonnatus took him into his confidence and laid bare all his plans. He only claimed to be helping Antipater. That was just a pretext and, as soon as he reached Europe, he intended to lay claim to Macedon. He showed Eumenes some letters from Cleopatra, in which she invited him to come to Pella and marry her.* But Eumenes broke camp and left under cover of darkness, taking his baggage with him. It is not clear whether he did this out of fear of Antipater, or because he had given up on Leonnatus, seeing him as unstable and prone to sudden, erratic impulses.

Eumenes had 300 horsemen, 200 armed slaves, and gold worth 5,000 talents of silver. That is what he took with him when he fled to Perdiccas and revealed Leonnatus' plans. He immediately became a man of importance in Perdiccas' court and one of his chief advisers, and before long he was installed in Cappadocia with the help of an army that was commanded by Perdiccas in person. Ariarathes was taken prisoner,* the territory subdued, and Eumenes proclaimed satrap. He put his friends in charge of the cities, appointed garrison commanders, and arranged both the judiciary and the administration as he saw fit, without the slightest interference from Perdiccas. Then, when Perdiccas left, he went too, not just because he was his courtier, but also because he wanted to stay close to the kings.*

[4] Perdiccas, however, was confident that he could subdue the lands against which he was proceeding on his own, and at the same time he felt that the places they were leaving behind needed a firm and reliable hand at the helm, so he sent Eumenes back from Cilicia. On the face of it, he was being sent to his own satrapy, but in fact his task was to restore order in neighbouring Armenia, which had been thrown into chaos by Neoptolemus. And warped though Neoptolemus was by vain pride and pretensions, Eumenes still tried to restrain him by talking to him as a friend.

Faced with the insolence and presumptuousness of his Macedonian troops, Eumenes set about raising a cavalry unit as a counter-force. He recruited local men who had the resources to serve on horseback by offering them immunity from taxation, and he equipped those of his own men whose loyalty was beyond question with horses that he bought for them. He stimulated their pride with decorations and rewards, exercised and drilled them to develop their physical skills, and when they saw the ease with which Eumenes had gathered about him a cavalry unit of at least 6,300 men, the unruly Macedonians were intimidated and the rest were given fresh heart.

[5] Once they had defeated the Greeks, Craterus* and Antipater invaded Asia, with the intention of deposing Perdiccas. The rumour was that they were planning to attack Cappadocia, so Perdiccas, who was himself campaigning against Ptolemy,* made Eumenes commander-in-chief of the forces in Armenia and Cappadocia. He also put his instructions in this regard down in writing, with letters to Alcetas* and Neoptolemus telling them to take their orders from Eumenes, and one to Eumenes telling him that the conduct of the war was entirely at his discretion.

Alcetas, however, flatly refused to take part in the campaign, on the grounds that the Macedonians in his army were too much in awe of Antipater to fight him, and were so loyal to Craterus that they were ready to receive him with open arms, and Neoptolemus turned traitor. When his intrigues were discovered, he ignored a summons to explain himself and instead drew up his forces for battle. This was the first occasion when Eumenes reaped the benefits of his foresight and planning. For even as his infantry were being defeated, his cavalry first routed Neoptolemus' cavalry and captured the baggage train, and then they made a massed charge against Neoptolemus' infantry, who had lost formation while pursuing Eumenes' men, and forced them to surrender. And after an exchange of pledges, Eumenes incorporated Neoptolemus' men into his own army.

Neoptolemus gathered a few of the stragglers and fled to Craterus and Antipater. They had already contacted Eumenes with an invitation to change sides. He would continue to enjoy the satrapies he currently held, they said, and would also receive further troops and territory from them provided he healed the rift between himself and Antipater, and did not open one up between himself and Craterus. After hearing their offer, Eumenes replied that his enmity with Antipater was of such long standing that friendly relations were impossible between them, since Antipater persisted in treating Eumenes' friends as enemies; but he was ready, he said, to effect a reconciliation between Craterus and Perdiccas, and to bring them together on fair and equitable terms, such that if either of them was wronged by another's aggression, the other would help as long as he had breath, and would lose his life rather than go back on his word.†

[6] After receiving this response from Eumenes, Antipater and his officers were weighing up the entire situation at their leisure when Neoptolemus reached their camp in flight from the battlefield. He told them about the engagement and asked for help—help from both of them, preferably, but at any rate from Craterus, because the Macedonians had an extraordinary longing for him. They had only to see his cap and hear his voice, Neoptolemus said, and they would rush to his side, armed and ready.

What Neoptolemus was saying about Craterus' standing was true. After Alexander's death, he was the one most people longed for. They remembered how he had even deliberately incurred Alexander's wrath by repeatedly resisting the king's inclination to play the Persian, and by sticking with traditional Macedonian ways even as they were being undermined by luxury and affectation. At the time in question,* then, Craterus sent Antipater to Cilicia, while he and Neoptolemus advanced towards Eumenes with a sizeable portion of the army. Craterus expected to take Eumenes by surprise, with his men relaxed and celebrating their recent victory.

Now, that Eumenes had advance warning of Craterus' approach

and took precautionary measures might be seen as a sign of sound leadership, but it hardly represents the apex of brilliance. However, not only did he prevent the enemy gaining any knowledge of his weaknesses, but he even concealed the identity of the opposing general from his own troops, and launched them against Craterus before they knew whom they were up against—and I know of no other general with this achievement to his credit. The rumour he spread was that Neoptolemus and Pigres* were returning to the fray with a force of Cappadocian and Paphlagonian cavalry.

Eumenes was intending to break camp and leave under cover of darkness, but then he fell asleep and had an odd dream, in which two Alexanders were getting ready to fight one another, each with a single phalanx at his command, but then Athena arrived to help one of them and Demeter the other. After a fierce struggle, the Alexander who was supported by Athena was beaten, and Demeter wove for the victor a garland out of ears of grain she harvested herself. A favourable interpretation of the dream occurred to Eumenes straight away, seeing that he was fighting for control of extremely fertile land, which at the time in question had an abundance of fine cereals standing in the ear. In fact, the whole land was under cultivation and the fields, thick with waving grain, were a picture of peace. And his interpretation was further confirmed when he discovered that the enemy's watchword was 'Athena and Alexander'.*

He too then issued his own watchword, 'Demeter and Alexander', and ordered all his men to pick ears of grain with which to entwine their weapons and make garlands for themselves. He was often tempted to speak up and tell his officers and generals whom they would be meeting in the coming battle, because he did not like being the only one in possession of such a critical secret and concealing it from others. But he stuck by his decision and entrusted the battle to his original plan.

[7] The force he deployed to do battle with Craterus consisted of two mercenary cavalry units, but no Macedonians, since he thought there was a very good chance that, if the Macedonian troops recognized Craterus, they would go over to him. The commanders of the cavalry units were Pharnabazus, the son of Artabazus,* and Phoenix of Tenedos, and Eumenes ordered them to charge at full gallop as soon as the enemy were within sight, without giving them time to manoeuvre or raise a battle-cry, and without receiving

any herald they might want to send. He himself, with his personal guard of the 300 best horsemen, rode over to the right wing to engage Neoptolemus.

Craterus was taken aback to see Eumenes' cavalry, once they had crossed the intervening hill and come into view, making a determined and vigorous charge. He bitterly reproached Neoptolemus for having misled him into thinking that the Macedonians would desert, and then, urging his officers to show their mettle, he launched his own counter-attack. The initial clash was violent, spears were quickly shattered, and the battle became a sword-fight. Craterus' courage would not have disgraced Alexander, and many of his opponents fell or fled before him, but eventually he was wounded by a Thracian, who rode at him from the side, and he fell from his horse. No one riding past him realized who it was lying there on the ground, except for Gorgias, one of Eumenes' generals. He dismounted and stood guard over the man, who was now in the final throes of a painful death.

Meanwhile, Neoptolemus had encountered Eumenes. Despite the ferocity of their mutual hostility and loathing, they failed to spot each other during the first two charges, but as soon as they recognized each other in the course of the third manoeuvre, they galloped with drawn swords, whooping, straight for each other. Their horses slammed together with the force of warships and, letting go of the reins, they grabbed hold of one another, each trying to tear off the other's helmet and rip the breastplate from his shoulders.

In the course of these struggles their horses ran out from under them, and they tumbled to the ground, where they continued to grapple and wrestle. Then, as Neoptolemus was trying to stand up, Eumenes struck him a crippling blow with his sword in the back of the thigh, and it was he who got to his feet instead. Neoptolemus supported himself on one knee, with the other leg incapacitated, and fought back valiantly from below, but he was incapable of inflicting life-threatening wounds, and a slashing blow to the neck laid him low. In a rage, spurred on by his long loathing for the man, Eumenes began to strip his armour from him, cursing him all the while, but Neoptolemus still had his sword in his hand, and he surprised Eumenes with a blow under the breastplate, where it reaches and skirts the groin. But Eumenes was more shocked than hurt, since Neoptolemus was too weak to deliver an effective blow.

After stripping the corpse of its armour, Eumenes remounted his horse and galloped over to the other wing, ignoring the pain from the open wounds on his thighs and arms. He expected to find the enemy still in formation, but learnt instead that Craterus had died. He rode up and dismounted, finding him still alive and conscious. With tears pouring down his face, he grasped his enemy's hand. He gave free rein to his loathing for Neoptolemus, and free expression to his sorrow, not just for Craterus' fate, but also for his own sense of duty, which had compelled him to fight a dear friend, and either kill or be killed.*

[8] This was Eumenes' second victory within about ten days, and although the combination of skill and courage that had won him it attracted people's admiration, he also earned a great deal of envy and hatred from allies and enemies alike, as an upstart foreigner who had used Macedonian weaponry and manpower to kill the greatest and most distinguished Macedonian of them all. Ironically, if Perdiccas had known of Craterus' death in time, *he* would have become the greatest Macedonian. But Perdiccas was killed in a mutiny in Egypt* two days before news of the battle reached his camp, and in their anger the Macedonian troops immediately condemned Eumenes to death. With Antipater's backing, Antigonus was given command of the war against Eumenes.*

When Eumenes came to Mount Ida and found the royal herds that were pastured there, he took all the horses he needed, but sent a list to the managers.* At this, we hear, Antipater said with a laugh: 'I'm impressed by Eumenes' foresight. He clearly expects to account to us for royal possessions, rather than us to him.'

Since he had cavalry superiority, Eumenes wanted to give battle in Lydia, on the plains near Sardis, and at the same time he was anxious to put on a show of strength for Cleopatra.* But at her request—she wanted to avoid giving Antipater any cause for complaint—he marched off to inner Phrygia and took up winter quarters in Celaenae. Here he was faced with challenges by Alcetas, Polemon, and Docimus for supreme command of the army (to which he responded by saying: 'It's just as the proverb says: of pestilence there is no end'), and in order to fulfil his promise to give the soldiers their pay within three days, he sold them the villas and castles that lay round about, which were bursting with slaves and livestock. The brigade commander or mercenary captain who made the purchase then put the place under siege with engines and artillery provided by Eumenes, and the soldiers divided all the booty among themselves and put it towards what they were owed.

The upshot was that Eumenes' popularity rose again, and when leaflets appeared at one point in the camp, circulated by the enemy officers, offering a reward of 100 talents and further honours to anyone who killed Eumenes, the Macedonian troops were furious. They decreed that Eumenes should be surrounded at all times by a bodyguard of 1,000 leading soldiers, who would take turns to protect him and spend the nights close by his quarters. The decree was put into effect, and the chosen men were delighted with the way he honoured them with gifts of the kind normally given by kings to their Friends. For Eumenes was able to distribute purple-dyed caps and military cloaks, and to a Macedonian there is no gift that is more particularly the prerogative of the king.*

[9] Now, even people of no real worth get puffed up with pride when they meet with good fortune, and gain a certain aura of grandeur and dignity as they gaze from the height of their success, but true greatness and strength of will are revealed more by a man's conduct during setbacks and failures.* Eumenes is a case in point. First, after treachery had led to defeat by Antigonus at Orcynia* in Cappadocia, even with the enemy in pursuit he did not let the traitor slip away during the flight and make his way to the enemy, but arrested him and hanged him. Then he doubled back in the direction from which the pursuit was coming, bypassed the enemy without being seen, and arrived back at the place where the battle had been fought. He made camp there, collected his dead, and burnt the bodies on pyres—one for officers and one for other ranks—made of planking torn from the surrounding villages. Then he buried the bones under a common mound and left. Even Antigonus, when he reached the spot later, expressed admiration for his courage and steadfastness.

Second, when he happened upon Antigonus' baggage train, he could easily have taken many prisoners and gained a great deal of booty in the form of slaves and riches garnered from so many wars and raids. But he was worried that the burden of all that plunder might slow his men down in their flight and undermine their ability to endure life on the move, especially for the length of time he felt he needed if he was to deter Antigonus and stand any chance in the war. But since it was virtually impossible to stop the Macedonian troops taking anything valuable they found lying within their reach, he told them to get some rest and feed their horses, in preparation for meeting the enemy, but then secretly sent a message to Menander, the man responsible for the enemy's baggage. Claiming to be concerned for him as a friend, Eumenes advised Menander to take precautions. As soon as possible, he should leave his present position in level, low-lying land and withdraw to the nearby foothills, which were inaccessible to cavalry and impossible to encircle.

Menander was not slow in recognizing the danger. He left, and Eumenes sent out scouts, making no secret of this mission, and told his troops to arm themselves and tack up their horses, as though he were going to lead them against the enemy. But, of course, the scouts reported that there was no way they could get at Menander, given the ruggedness of the terrain where he had taken refuge, and Eumenes led his army away with a show of annoyance. When Menander told Antigonus what had happened, the Macedonians were grateful for what Eumenes had done and began to feel less hostile towards him. He could have enslaved their children and disgraced their wives, but he had spared them and let them go. But Antigonus is supposed to have said: 'No, my friends, he didn't let them go for your sake, but because he saw them as so many shackles impeding his flight.'

[10] After this, with nowhere for him to settle and the enemy hot on his heels, Eumenes persuaded most of his men to leave, perhaps out of concern for their safety, or perhaps because he wanted to shed the burden of an army that was too small to give battle, but too large to hide.* He took refuge in Nora, a fortress on the border between Lycaonia and Cappadocia, with 500 horse and 200 heavy infantry, and there again, if any of his friends asked permission to leave, because they could not stand the harsh conditions and cramped way of life in the fortress, he sent them on their way with thanks and no hard feelings.

When Antigonus came to Nora and suggested that they meet before the siege began, Eumenes' response was that, while Antigonus had many friends and officers to take his place, he himself now had no successor among the men under his command, and so Antigonus should send him hostages if he wanted to treat with him. And when Antigonus asked to be addressed as a superior, Eumenes replied: 'I call no man my superior as long as I am master of my sword.'

But once Antigonus had complied with Eumenes' demand and sent his nephew, Ptolemy, into the fortress, Eumenes emerged, and they embraced and greeted each other with warmth and affection, since they were old friends and had been close to each other.

The conference went on for a long time. So far from confining himself to the issues of safety and an end to the war, Eumenes even demanded that he be confirmed in his satrapies and that all his privileges should be restored. Everyone at the conference was astonished at this, and impressed by his bold self-assurance. At the same time, the Macedonians began to crowd around, eager to see who Eumenes was, because since Craterus' death he was the most talked-about man in the army, and Antigonus became frightened in case Eumenes came to any harm. At first he roared at the men to stay away and hurled stones at them as they pressed in, but in the end he wrapped his arms around Eumenes and barely managed to take him off to a place of safety, ordering his guards to hold back the crowd.

[11] Antigonus next built a wall around Nora and decamped, leaving behind a small force to watch Eumenes, who was now under close siege. Now, the fortress had plenty of grain, and more than enough water and salt, but nothing else edible, not even savouries to go with their bread. Nevertheless, Eumenes made use of what there was to contrive a convivial way of life for his companions, by inviting them all in turn to join him at his table, and by sweetening their shared meals with graceful conversation and good cheer. Besides, he had a pleasing appearance. He did not look at all like a veteran, worn down by warfare; his features were refined and youthful, and his whole body was as well muscled as a perfect example of the sculptor's art, with limbs that were remarkably well proportioned. And although he was not a brilliant speaker, there was a subtlety and plausibility about his use of language, as we can tell from his letters.

The most detrimental factor of the siege on his companions was the restricted space. Their quarters were small, and they were living in a place with a total circumference of two stades, which meant that neither men nor horses were getting exercise before eating or being fed. Eumenes did not just want to alleviate the energy-sapping boredom of inactivity, but he also needed to find a way to keep them fit in case an opportunity for flight should present itself. So he allocated the men the largest building in the fortress, fourteen cubits long, as a place to walk, and ordered them gradually to increase their pace;

and he had every horse first supported by great straps that were fastened to the roof and wrapped under its chest, and then raised up into the air by pulleys until its hind legs were resting on the ground, but the tips of its front hoofs barely grazed it. With the horses suspended like this, the grooms would stand next to them and work them up into a frenzy of rage and fury by screaming at them and whipping them, until they reared and pranced on their hind legs, while striving to stamp the ones that were up in the air down on to the ground. In this way they stretched every muscle in their bodies, with sweat pouring from their limbs and foam from their mouths, and were thoroughly exercised for both speed and strength. They were also fed pre-pounded barley, so that they could process it more quickly and digest it better.

[12] The siege had been going on for some time when Antigonus learnt that Antipater had died in Macedon and that the dispute between Cassander and Polyperchon had thrown the country into chaos.* Antigonus' ambitions now broke their bounds and he saw himself taking over the entire empire, but he wanted to be on good terms with Eumenes and to gain his help towards achieving his goals. So he sent Hieronymus* to Eumenes to arrange a truce, and proposed a form of words for the oath, but Eumenes altered the wording and left it up to the Macedonians who were besieging him to decide which version was more fair. As a formality, Antigonus had mentioned the kings in the preamble to the document, but had otherwise made himself the recipient of the oath of loyalty. What Eumenes did was add Olympias and the kings to the oaths, so that Antigonus was not the sole recipient of his oath of loyalty and he was promising to have the same friends and enemies not just as him, but as Olympias and the kings as well. The Macedonians felt Eumenes' version to be more fair, and once he had taken the oath they put an end to the siege and wrote to Antigonus, for him to swear fidelity to Eumenes as well.

Meanwhile, however, Eumenes ransomed all the Cappadocian hostages he had been holding in Nora in exchange for horses, mules, and tents, which were brought by the men who came for the hostages. Then he collected those of his troops who were still at large in the countryside, where they had scattered after his flight, until he had a force of almost a thousand horsemen, and with these he rode off and made his escape. He was afraid of Antigonus, and rightly so, because

Antigonus had not only ordered the wall to be rebuilt and the siege resumed, but had written angrily back to the Macedonians for having accepted Eumenes' alterations to the oath.

[13] While Eumenes was in flight, letters reached him from those in Macedon who were alarmed at the rise of Antigonus. Olympias* invited him to come and take over the upbringing of Alexander's young son, whose life she felt to be in danger, and Polyperchon and King Philip ordered him to take command of the army in Cappadocia and make war on Antigonus. They even gave him permission to take 500 talents from the treasury at Cyinda* to improve his own personal position, and to draw on the treasury for as much as he needed to prosecute the war.

Polyperchon and Philip had also written in this regard to Antigenes and Teutamus, the commanders of the Silver Shields.* On receipt of the letter, they tried to make it seem as though they welcomed Eumenes as their general, but it was not hard to see that they were filled with envy and longed to dispute his leadership, since they considered it beneath their dignity to occupy a lower rung on the ladder than him. Eumenes therefore mollified their envy by not taking the money, making out that he had no need of it. But their jealous coveting of his command—the jealousy of men who were neither capable of leading nor willing to be led—he treated with a dose of superstition.

He claimed that Alexander had appeared to him in a dream,* and had gestured to a pavilion that was equipped for a king and had a throne in it. He had then told him that, if they met there as a council, to deliberate and do business, he himself would be present and would put his hand to every plan and enterprise that they began in his name. It was not difficult for Eumenes to persuade Antigenes and Teutamus of the truth of this vision, since they refused to go to his pavilion and he too had no desire to be seen at others' doorways. So they erected a royal pavilion and a throne dedicated to Alexander's use, and that was where they held their most important meetings.

As they marched inland, they were met by Peucestas, who was a friend, along with the other eastern satraps, and they joined forces.* Although the Macedonian troops were greatly encouraged by the number of the reinforcements, and by the quality of their equipment, the satraps themselves had become so used to wielding power since Alexander's death that they had become wilful, and enervated by soft living. This meant that there was a clash of minds that were used to the exercise of sole power and had been enfeebled by barbarian trumpery, and they quarrelled among themselves and found it difficult to get along. At the same time, however, they went overboard in courting the favour of the Macedonian troops, and spent extravagantly on banquets and sacrifices, until before long they had turned the camp into a tavern for festive debauchery, and the army into a mob who appointed generals at the prompting of persuasive speakers, as in democracies.

Eumenes realized that, while they found one another merely contemptible, they found him threatening, and were looking for an opportunity to do away with him. So he pretended that he needed money and borrowed heavily from those who disliked him most, thinking that uncertainty about their loans would cement their loyalty and make them refrain from killing him. The upshot was that the wealth of others was his shield, and whereas men generally *give* money to ensure their safety, he managed the unique feat of gaining security by taking it.

[14] As long as they were in no danger, the Macedonian troops allowed themselves to be corrupted by those who were prepared to bribe them, these would-be generals with their bodyguards, and hung around their patrons' doorways. But when Antigonus encamped close by with a large army and the situation all but cried out for a true general, it was not just the ordinary soldiers who looked to Eumenes: every single one of those who were great in times of peace and easy living caved in and held the post assigned to him without a word of complaint. But it so happened that, when Antigonus tried to cross the river Pasitigris,* none of the others were even aware of his movements, although they were on the lookout, and only Eumenes confronted him. In the ensuing battle he inflicted heavy casualties on the enemy, choked the river with corpses, and took 4,000 prisoners.

It became particularly clear when Eumenes fell ill that the Macedonian troops may have considered the others good for entertaining them with splendid feasts and festivals, but Eumenes was the only one they thought of as a competent leader and general. Peucestas, for example, expected to be treated as the most important man in the army because he had put on a splendid banquet* for them in Persis and had given every man in the army a victim for sacrifice.

But only a few days later the men found themselves marching against the enemy, while Eumenes, critically ill, was being carried on a litter away from the column, where it was quiet and his sleep would not be disturbed.

Before they had gone far, the enemy suddenly appeared, cresting a range of hills and descending on to the plain. At the sight of Antigonus' personal guard marching with perfect discipline, their golden armour reflecting the sunlight and glinting down from the ridge, and of the castles on the backs of the elephants and the purple robes with which the beasts were arrayed when going into battle, the vanguard halted and began to call out at the tops of their voices that they wanted Eumenes. They would go no further, they said, unless he was their general. They grounded their weapons, gave the order to halt, and told their officers to do nothing—to avoid battle and not to take any risks in relation to the enemy without Eumenes. When all this reached Eumenes' ears, he had his bearers speed up and take him to his men at the double. He opened the curtains on either side of the litter and joyfully offered the men his right hand. Without further delay, after hailing him in Macedonian,* they picked up their weapons. They clattered their pikes against their shields and raised their battle-cry, hurling defiance at the enemy now that their leader was with them.

[15] Hearing from prisoners that Eumenes was ill and, in fact, in a bad enough way to be confined to a litter, Antigonus thought it would be relatively easy to crush the others while he was indisposed, and he lost no time in bringing his army up for battle. But while the enemy was deploying, he rode past their lines—and halted for quite some time in amazement at the sight of the efficient and orderly way in which they were going about it. But then the litter was seen being carried across from one wing to the other, and Antigonus said to his Friends, with his usual guffaw: 'Ah, that's what we're contending against!' And he immediately pulled his forces back and made camp.*

But this brief respite only turned Eumenes' men once more into a mob. They mocked their officers and spread themselves for the winter over almost all Gabene, with a gap of about a thousand stades between the rearguard's quarters and the van. When Antigonus discovered this, he launched a surprise attack. He took a route that was difficult and waterless, but direct and short, because he hoped to fall on them while they were dispersed in their winter quarters, which would make it hard for most of them to link up with their commanding officers. But then he came to a stretch of uninhabited desert, where savage winds and severe frosts began to play havoc with the march. All his men could do to alleviate the difficulties in which they found themselves was light a lot of fires. And that is how the enemy came to know he was there: some of the natives who lived on the hills overlooking the desert were astonished at the sight of so many fires and sent messengers to Peucestas on dromedaries.

Terrified completely out of his wits by the news, and seeing that the others were in the same state, Peucestas was ready to flee, and raise troops above all from those they would come across on the way. But Eumenes tried to calm them down and quell their fears by promising to slow the enemy down and delay the expected time of their arrival by three days. They agreed to let him try, and he sent out messengers ordering his forces and everyone else to leave their winter quarters and assemble as quickly as possible, while he and the other officers rode out of camp on a separate mission. He occupied a spot that was visible from afar to anyone travelling across the desert, measured it off, and ordered a large number of fires to be lit at regular intervals, as in an encampment.

When the fires were lit on the mountainside, they were plainly visible to Antigonus' men. Antigonus was dismayed and disheartened by the thought that the enemy had known about his approach all along and were coming to meet him. He had to make sure that he was not forced to pit his men, while they were worn out and exhausted from the march, against troops who were fresh and had spent an easy winter, so he abandoned the short-cut and took his men through villages and towns at an easy pace, in order to refresh them. But no attempt was made to check his progress, as one would have expected from an enemy who was encamped near by, and when the local inhabitants told him that they had seen no army, but that the place was covered with burnt-out fires, Antigonus realized that he had been out-generalled by Eumenes. Angrily, he brought his army up to decide the conflict in pitched battle.

[16] Meanwhile, most of Eumenes' forces had assembled and, impressed by his intelligence, were demanding that he and he alone should command them. This was not to the liking of the commanders of the Silver Shields, Antigenes and Teutamus, who took it as an affront and began to intrigue against him. They convened a meeting of

most of the satraps and generals, and the unanimous conclusion of their discussion about when and how to kill Eumenes was that they should make use of him for the coming battle, and then do away with him as soon as the battle was over. But Eudamus, the commander of the elephant unit, and Phaedimus secretly brought news of the decision to Eumenes, not so much out of loyalty or a sense of duty as because they wanted to make sure they did not lose the money they had lent him.

Eumenes thanked them and retired to his pavilion, where he remarked to his friends that he was living in a menagerie of wild beasts. He then drew up his will, and shredded and destroyed his papers, since he did not want any secrets to get out after his death and lead to his correspondents being prosecuted and persecuted. Having settled his affairs, he convened his council to try to decide whether to cede victory to his enemies, or whether to escape via Media and Armenia and attack Cappadocia. He came to no decision while his friends were there, but after turning things over in his mind, schooled to versatility by his changing fortunes, he set in motion the process of drawing up his forces for battle.*

He spoke words of encouragement to the Greek and barbarian contingents, but was himself urged to be sanguine by the Macedonian phalanx and the Silver Shields, who were sure that their opponents would not stand their ground against them. For they were the oldest of those who had campaigned under Philip and Alexander; they were athletes of war, so to speak, who up until then had never lost a battle or suffered defeat, and many of them were seventy years old, while none of them was under sixty. And so, as they bore down on Antigonus' forces they shouted: 'You miserable curs! You're sinning against your fathers!' They fell in a rage on Antigonus' phalanx and completely overwhelmed it. Not a single man stood his ground against them, and most of them died in hand-to-hand combat.

Even though Antigonus was being decisively defeated in this part of the field, the cavalry engagement went his way, thanks to Peucestas' thoroughly careless and cowardly performance, and he seized Eumenes' entire baggage train. He owed this success not only to his ability to keep a cool head in the face of danger, but also to the help offered by the terrain. For the battle was fought on an immense plain, the surface of which was only lightly covered with loose soil consisting of a gritty, dry salt, and when, during the course of the battle, the rapid movements of all those horses and men disturbed the surface, a fine, chalky dust arose, which whitened the air and darkened the sight. This made it easier for Antigonus to gain possession of the enemy's baggage without being noticed.

[17] As soon as the battle was over, Teutamus sent a delegation to negotiate for the baggage,* and Antigonus promised to return it to the Silver Shields, and to treat them generously in other respects as well, once Eumenes was in his hands. And so the Silver Shields came to an appalling decision, to hand the man over alive to his enemies. They first approached him and kept a close eye on him without arousing his suspicions, by pretending to be complaining to him about the loss of their baggage, or urging him not to be disheartened since he had won the battle, or denouncing the other senior officers. Then they leapt on him, snatched his sword from his grasp, and tied his hands tightly with his belt.

As he was being led through the midst of the Macedonians by Nicanor, the man sent by Antigonus to fetch him, he asked permission to address them, not because he wanted to appeal to them or try to get them to change their minds, but to explain to them where their best interests lay. Silence fell, and standing on a rise he stretched out his bound hands and said: 'You Macedonian cowards! Do you imagine there is any victory over you that Antigonus would have preferred to the one you've awarded him by handing your general over in bonds? I can hardly believe that you would acknowledge yourselves defeated, despite your victory, because of your baggage! It's as though you think that victory depends on possessions, not on prowess. And then you ransom your baggage by surrendering your general! Well, I may be in custody, but I am undefeated, since I beat my enemies. My downfall is due to my friends. As for you, I urge you, in the name of Zeus, the lord of hosts, and of the gods who protect oaths, to kill me yourselves, right here and now—not that it makes any difference if I meet death there in his camp, for it will still be your doing. Antigonus won't tell you off for killing me: he *wants* Eumenes dead, not alive. If you don't want to sully your hands, one of mine will be enough to do the deed, if you untie me. But if you don't trust me with a sword, throw me, bound as I am, to be trampled by the elephants. If you do that, I absolve you of all guilt in my case, and declare that there have never been soldiers who have treated their general with greater propriety and justice.'

[18] Eumenes' speech moved most of the crowd to bitter remorse, but the Silver Shields called out for him to be taken away and told the others not to listen to his blethering. It was hardly the end of the world, they argued, if a pest from the Chersonese was done away with, who had worn out the Macedonians with war after war. But it was unthinkable for the soldiers who had best served Alexander and Philip to be deprived in their old age, after all their efforts, of the prizes they had earned, and to beg their bread from others; and it was horrendous that their womenfolk had spent the past two nights in the beds of their enemies. And with these words they hurried him off.

The size of the mob frightened Antigonus—Eumenes' camp had completely emptied—and he sent out his ten most formidable elephants and a large body of Median and Parthian spearmen to disperse them. But he could not stand the sight of Eumenes, because it reminded him of their long friendship, so when the men who had fetched him asked how they should guard him, he said: 'As you would an elephant or a lion.' A little later, however, in a compassionate mood, he ordered Eumenes' heavy fetters removed and allowed one of his personal slaves in to clean him. He also gave permission for his friends to spend the daylight hours with him, if they wanted, and to bring him whatever he needed. Then he spent quite a few days wondering what to do with his prisoner. He was open to ideas and offers, with his son Demetrius and Nearchus of Crete doing their best to keep Eumenes alive, and almost everyone else resisting them and arguing for his death.*

It is said that Eumenes asked Onomarchus, his gaoler, why Antigonus, with his deadly enemy in his power, was neither speedily putting him to death nor magnanimously letting him go. Onomarchus' insolent reply was that it was too late now for Eumenes to show courage in the face of death: he should have done so in battle. 'But, as Zeus is my witness,' Eumenes said, 'I did show courage in battle. Ask those who came up against me. In fact, I'm not aware of ever having met anyone better than me.' And Onomarchus said: 'Well, now that you have, why don't you just wait on his pleasure?'

[19] Once Antigonus had decided to kill Eumenes, he stopped his food, and after two or three days of deprivation Eumenes was at death's door. But then they unexpectedly broke camp, and a man was sent to do away with him. Antigonus gave the corpse to his friends,

and let them burn it and collect his remains in a silver urn for delivery to his wife and children.*

So Eumenes died. But, ironically, the gods reserved the punishment of the officers and men who had betrayed him for Antigonus himself. Giving as his reason their impiety and savagery, he sent the Silver Shields on to Siburtius, the governor of Arachosia,* telling him to do all he could to wipe them off the face of the earth and ensure that none of them ever returned to Macedon or set eyes upon the Greek Sea.

DEMETRIUS

INTRODUCTION

Demetrius Poliorcetes (*c*.336–*c*.283 BCE) was the son of one of the most formidable of the Successors, Antigonus Monophthalmus. Born in Macedon, he was brought up in Antigonus' satrapy of Phrygia, and by his late teens was commanding the cavalry during the final stages of his father's campaign against Eumenes. Antigonus went on to build up a substantial Asian empire that caused serious concern among his rivals, who responded by forming a coalition against him. Entrusted by his father with the defence of Syria, the young Demetrius suffered a heavy defeat against the experienced Ptolemy at the battle of Gaza in 312. Despite a peace agreement the next year, it was not long before Demetrius was taking the war to mainland Greece, where in 307 he 'liberated' Athens by expelling the pro-Cassander government of Demetrius of Phalerum. Any ambitions in this direction, however, had to be temporarily put aside to fight Ptolemy, who was defeated by Demetrius in a tremendous sea-battle off Cyprus in 306. The result was that Ptolemy lost the island and with it naval dominance in the eastern Mediterranean. Victory also gave both Antigonus and Demetrius the opportunity to claim the title 'king' for themselves, a move that was soon to be imitated by their rivals. Antigonid aggression continued with Demetrius leading an assault on Rhodes, where he conducted his famous and ultimately unsuccessful siege, earning himself the sobriquet Poliorcetes, the Besieger. He then returned to the mainland, where he did much to undermine Cassander's and also Ptolemy's influence in Greece, invading the Peloponnese and setting up a new Hellenic League modelled on Philip's League of Corinth. But before he could take this any further he was recalled to Asia to assist his father against a renewed coalition. At the great battle of Ipsus in 301, Antigonus was killed and Demetrius fled, leaving their Asian territories to be divided up among the victors.

Demetrius, nonetheless, recovered from this disaster, and by 294 had managed to take advantage of divisions within the family of the deceased Cassander to install himself as king of Macedon. Not content with Macedon and mainland Greece, he looked to expand into Asia Minor, no doubt with a view to reclaiming territory lost at Ipsus. Not for the first time, a coalition was formed against him, but this time there was no major battle. As Macedon came under increasing external pressure, Demetrius found himself the victim of a military coup. After six or seven years in power he was forced out. Now he made a final attempt to re-establish himself in Asia Minor, leaving his son Antigonus Gonatas in charge of what was left of his mainland garrisons. The attempt was a failure and he was forced to surrender to Seleucus, who kept the demoralized king under house arrest for several years until the latter's death in 283 (or perhaps 282). But Demetrius' death did not mean the end of Antigonid power. Antigonus Gonatas went on to claim the Macedonian throne in 277, and held it for almost forty years.

Not surprisingly, perhaps, the reversal of fortune is a pervasive theme in the Life. The point is made explicitly in chapter 35: 'But no other king had to suffer such sudden and major shifts of Fortune; no other king was affected so often by Fortune's ebb and flow, so that he was raised high and then brought low again, only to recover his strength once more' (cf. chapters 1, 5, 28, 30, 31, 45, 49–50). Demetrius himself is presented as being very conscious of the role fortune plays. His response to his first major setback, his defeat at Gaza at the hands of Ptolemy, displays the maturity of a seasoned commander accustomed to changes of fortune (5). Finally, when cornered by Seleucus, he realizes that 'there will be no more changes of fortune' (49). Yet, at the same time this emphasis on fortune seems to deny him credit for his successes. Indeed, Seleucus is in fear not of Demetrius' military ability but his 'reckless determination and his luck, which always converted certain disaster into stunning success' (48).

The Life of Demetrius enables Plutarch to explore a key moment in the early Hellenistic period, the transition of the Successors from satraps and warlords to kings. This, he believes, was not simply the addition of a title. It transformed the way the various Successors thought about themselves, how they behaved, and how they treated others. No longer was there a need to conceal their power. Plutarch makes an interesting analogy, which resonates through the rest of the Life: 'As soon as an actor puts on a costume, he also changes the way he walks, the sound of his voice, his posture at table, and the way he addresses others, and the same went for these men too' (18). Plutarch's Demetrius is an untiring actor, for whom kingship is a performance, a flamboyant figure swaggering around Macedon in his purple and gold clothes. In Athens he instructs the Athenians to hold their assembly in the theatre and enters by a passage used by actors (34). Whereas Pyrrhus captured something of the courage of Alexander, Demetrius, in common with so many of the other kings, was more like an actor impersonating Alexander (41). When he is toppled as king of Macedon, he exchanges his ostentatious clothing for something less conspicuous so as to slip away unnoticed, the behaviour of an actor whose role is defined by his costume rather than that of a true king (44). If kings are performers, then this is made possible by an audience that collaborates in the charade, a circumstance most vividly depicted in the extended discussion of flattery and the excesses of ruler cult in Athens (10–13). Theatre permeates the Life of Demetrius, the comic giving way to the tragic as it progresses (28), until finally Plutarch brings his 'Macedonian drama' to a close (53). The theme reappears in the *Aratus*, but there, interestingly, it is voiced not directly by Plutarch but by Demetrius' son Antigonus Gonatas, who in a speech at a banquet suggests that the Achaean politician Aratus, after his visit to Alexandria, now realizes that at the Ptolemaic court 'everything is just play-acting and trumpery' (*Aratus* 15). Yet Antigonus' highly manipulative speech before an audience of assembled diners is itself an example of just this sort of play-acting as he seeks to win Aratus over.

Particularly prominent in the Life of Demetrius is the city of Athens, which repeatedly shares centre-stage with Demetrius. The attitude of the Athenians to him mirrors the rise and fall of his fortunes. They make him the object of cult after the liberation of 307, ban him from the city after Ipsus, hesitantly accept him as he re-established himself in the 290s, and rebel against him after he loses the throne of Macedon. Athenian flattery of Demetrius is all the more striking when set alongside the stubborn resistance of the Rhodians, who not long afterwards withstood a siege by Demetrius for a whole year.

Demetrius' Roman counterpart is Mark Antony, ally of Caesar, the lover of Cleopatra, and losing party in the civil war with the future emperor Augustus. These two men are included in the *Parallel Lives* as examples of how not to live one's life: both were 'men who lived recklessly and . . . became infamous for their iniquity'. Not only did they have similar characters (prone to love-affairs and drinking, soldierly, generous, extravagant, and overbearing), they also met with similar fortunes (1). But whereas Demetrius kept the pleasure and work sides of his life separate, a point made explicitly by Plutarch (2, 19), Antony's defeat in the civil war and resulting death were due to his inability to achieve this separation. The one occasion when Demetrius comes close to this, his narrow escape from his enemies during a rendezvous with the famous beauty Cratesipolis, can be seen as a comic prelude to Antony's destructive relationship with Cleopatra. Although Plutarch professes not to be including these biographies for their entertainment value, they are among the most readable of the Lives and it is hard to imagine that Plutarch was unaware of this, especially given the influence of the theatre on the way he presents them.

In this Life Plutarch cites and quotes from many writers, especially poets, as a way of reflecting on what he is relating, but in spite of this he gives little away about his sources for Demetrius' career. It is most likely that he drew much of his narrative from the historian Hieronymus of Cardia, whose work is believed to lie behind Diodorus, books 18–20. Hieronymus knew the events well due to his longstanding presence in the Antigonid court, during which time he served Antigonus Monophthalmus, Demetrius, and Antigonus Gonatas (see further the introduction to *Eumenes*). But there is much scope for speculation and some supplementary material would probably have come from writers such as the near-contemporary Duris of Samos and the Athenian politician Demochares, the nephew of Demosthenes. Diodorus provides a useful check on Plutarch, but the surviving books end just short of the battle of Ipsus, leaving Plutarch's Lives of Demetrius and Pyrrhus as crucial sources for the early history of the third century BCE.

Beneker, J., *The Passionate Statesman: Erōs and Politics in Plutarch's Lives* (Oxford, 2012), ch. 4.

Billows, R., *Antigonos the One-Eyed and the Creation of the Hellenistic State* (Berkeley, 1990).

Chaniotis, A., 'Theatricality beyond the Theater: Staging Public life in the Hellenistic World', in B. Le Guen (ed.), *De la scène aux gradins: théâtre et représentations dramatiques après Alexandre le Grand dans les cités hellénistiques* (Toulouse, 1997), 219–59.

Duff, T. E., 'Plato, Tragedy, the Ideal Reader and Plutarch's *Demetrios and Antony*', *Hermes*, 132 (2004), 271–91.

Habicht, C., *Athens from Alexander to Antony*, trans. D. L. Schneider (Cambridge, Mass., 1997), 67–97.

Holton, J. R., 'Demetrios Poliorketes, Son of Poseidon and Aphrodite: Cosmic and Memorial Significance in the Athenian Ithyphallic Hymn', *Mnemosyne*, 67 (2014), 370–90.

Martin, T. R., 'Demetrius "the Besieger" and Hellenistic Warfare', in J. B. Campbell and L. Tritle (eds.), *The Oxford Handbook of Warfare in the Classical World* (Oxford, 2013), 671–87.

Mikalson, J. D., *Religion in Hellenistic Athens* (Berkeley, 1998), 75–104.

Monaco, M., 'Folly and Dark Humor in the *Life of Demetrius*', *Ploutarchos*, 9 (2011/12), 51–61.

Pelling, C., *Plutarch: Life of Antony* (Cambridge, 1988), esp. 18–26.

Sweet, W. E., 'Sources of Plutarch's *Demetrius*', *Classical Weekly*, 44 (1951), 177–81.

Thonemann, P., 'The Tragic King: Demetrios Poliorketes and the City of Athens', in O. Hekster and R. Fowler (eds.), *Imaginary Kings: Royal Images in the Ancient Near East, Greece and Rome* (Munich, 2005), 63–86.

Waterfield, R., *Dividing the Spoils: The War for Alexander the Great's Empire* (Oxford, 2011).

Wehrli, C., *Antigone et Démétrios* (Geneva, 1968).
Wheatley, P. V., 'The Young Demetrius Poliorcetes', *Ancient History Bulletin* 13 (1999) 1–13.
—— 'Lamia and the Besieger: An Athenian Hetaera and a Macedonian King', in O. Palagia and S. V. Tracy (eds.), *The Macedonians in Athens 322–229 BC* (Oxford, 2003), 30–6.

DEMETRIUS

[1] It seems to me that the idea that the arts resemble the senses first occurred to people principally because they noticed the equivalence of their discriminatory powers, that enable us to grasp the opposites as they occur in the one domain or the other. For this power is common to both the arts and the senses, although they differ in what they do with the opposites they distinguish. Our senses are designed equally for the discernment of white *and* black, sweet *and* sour, soft (or yielding) *and* hard (or resistant). Their job is to be moved by every single thing they encounter and, as they are moved, to refer the experience to the mind. But since the arts, in conjunction with reason, deliberately choose and adopt what is appropriate to them, and avoid and reject what is alien, they are in themselves chiefly concerned with the one set of qualities, and take only an incidental interest in the others, just so as to be able to protect themselves against them.

The art of medicine, for instance, is concerned with the nature of disease, and music-making is concerned with the nature of dissonance, only in order to produce their opposites. And since the most perfect of all the arts—moderation, justice, and practical wisdom—base their decisions on what is harmful, disgraceful, and wrong just as much as on what is good, right, and useful, they hold no brief for the kind of guilelessness that is the result of inexperience of the negative side of things, but regard it as foolish ignorance of matters which someone who intends to improve his life absolutely must know. That is why in the old days, during their festivals, the Spartans used to force their helots to drink a lot of neat wine and would then introduce them into their symposia, as a way of showing the younger generation what drunkenness was like.

Now, although, in my opinion, the method of improving some by degrading others is quite inhumane and uncivilized, I may still be forgiven if I include in my exemplary Lives one or two pairs of men who lived recklessly and, finding themselves in positions of power at critical periods of history, became infamous for their iniquity. My reason for doing so is certainly not to entertain or divert my readers by introducing variety into my work. But just as Ismenias of Thebes* would get his students to listen to both good and bad pipe-playing, and used to say, '*That's* how to play' and '*That's* how not to play', and just as Antigeneidas* was convinced that young people would get more pleasure from listening to pipes well played if they also had experience of the opposite, so I think we shall be more ready to observe and imitate the lives of better men if we have before us accounts of the lives of men of reprehensible wickedness.

This book will therefore consist of the Lives of Demetrius Poliorcetes and of the Roman general Antony, men who confirmed the truth of Plato's view that the vices of great men are as great as their virtues.* Both men shared similar qualities—they were given to love-affairs and drinking, soldierly, generous, extravagant, and overbearing—and their fortunes were consequently similar as well. Over the course of their lives they experienced great successes and great setbacks, made huge gains and suffered huge losses, and met with unexpected disasters and equally surprising recoveries. Moreover, at the times of their deaths one was a captive of his enemies and the other was right on the brink of this calamity.

[2] So, then, Antigonus Monophthalmus* had two sons by Stratonice, the daughter of Corrhagus, one of whom he called Demetrius after his brother, and the other Philip after his father. That is what the majority of the sources say, but some claim that Demetrius was not Antigonus' son, but his nephew—that his father died when he was still a baby, and then his mother immediately married Antigonus, so that he was thought to be Antigonus' son. Be that as it may, Philip, who was a few years younger than Demetrius, died early.

Demetrius was tall (though shorter than his father), and was so incredibly attractive and exceptionally handsome that no sculptor or painter ever managed to catch his likeness. For his features possessed at one and the same time both grace and dignity, grimness and beauty, and his youthful vigour was blended with an aura of heroism and regal majesty, which was very hard to capture. In much the same way, his character too naturally tended to overawe and charm people at one and the same time. For although he was very good company, and although there was no king to rival him for refinement when he was relaxing over drinks and delicacies and food, none could match him either when it came to the energy and determination he brought to seeing an enterprise through to its completion. Hence the god he modelled himself on more than any other was Dionysus,* for his combination of terrible fearsomeness in war with his ability to turn to relaxation and pleasure when war is over.

[3] He was exceptionally close to his father, and his devotion to his mother proved that he honoured his father too out of genuine loyalty, not to appease his power. Once Demetrius returned from hunting to find Antigonus busy with some embassy or other, and he came up to his father and kissed him, and then sat down next to him just as he was, javelins in hand. When the ambassadors were leaving with their answers, Antigonus called out after them in a loud voice: 'Gentlemen, when you deliver your report about us, please include what you have seen about our feelings for each other'—the implication being that his good relations with and trust in his son were a source of strength for the royal house and a proof of its power. Empire is such a thoroughly divisive thing, it seems, and so riddled with distrust and disloyalty, that the greatest and most senior of Alexander's Successors boasted of not being afraid of his son, and of allowing him near his person, spear in hand. But in fact the Antigonid house was more or less the only one not to be disfigured by such troubles for a great many generations—or rather, Philip V was the only one of Antigonus' descendants to have killed a son.* But in almost all the other dynasties sons were frequently put to death, and so were mothers and wives, while the assassination of brothers was like a geometrical axiom for them, regarded as a common postulate and a way for kings to secure their rule.

[4] In his early years, Demetrius had a kind and friendly nature, as the following anecdote shows. Mithradates,* the son of Ariobarzanes, was a friend of his and a classmate from the same age-group. He was a courtier of Antigonus, and although his loyalty was and was known to be solid, Antigonus became suspicious of him as a result of a dream. In this dream, Antigonus saw himself advancing across a large and beautiful plain, sowing gold-dust as he went; at first a crop of gold sprang up from the dust, but a little later, when he returned,† he found nothing but stubble. In his annoyance and fury, he heard some people saying that it was Mithradates who had harvested the golden grain and that he had then gone off to the Black Sea coast.

Antigonus was very disturbed by the dream, and after getting his son to promise not to say anything, he described it to him and said that he was fully resolved to get rid of Mithradates and put him to death. Demetrius was extremely upset about this, and when the young man joined him, as usual, to pass time with him, Demetrius, constrained by his promise, did not dare to say anything or utter a word of warning out loud. But he gradually drew him aside from their friends, and when they were alone he wrote with the butt-spike of his spear in the ground, with Mithradates looking on: 'Fly, Mithradates!' Mithradates understood and fled at night to Cappadocia, and before long Antigonus' dream became reality. For Mithradates gained control of large tracts of good land and founded the line of Pontic kings, which was brought to an end by the Romans in its eighth generation.* Anyway, this anecdote goes to show that Demetrius was temperamentally inclined towards decency and justice.

[5] But just as the effect of Strife on Empedocles' elements is to produce conflict and warfare among them, and especially on those that touch or come into contact with one another,* so the continuous warfare waged by all Alexander's Successors against one another flared and blazed up all the more readily when interests and territories were contiguous. The fighting that broke out at the time between Antigonus and Ptolemy* was a case in point. Antigonus was busy in Phrygia, but when he heard that Ptolemy had sailed over from Cyprus and was raiding Syria, ravaging the land and carrying the cities by force, he sent his son to deal with the threat. Demetrius was twenty-two years old,* and this was the first time he had been given full responsibility for a critical campaign.

As one might have expected, however, given that an untried youngster was up against a man who had graduated from Alexander's wrestling-school and had honed his skills in many great conflicts of his own, Demetrius was defeated in a battle fought near the city of Gaza, with 8,000 of his men captured and 5,000 dead.* He also lost his pavilion, his war chest, and all his personal effects, but Ptolemy returned them to him, along with his Friends, and added† a generous and courteous message to the effect that they should fight only for glory and empire, not for everything indiscriminately. On getting his things back, Demetrius prayed that he would not long be in debt to Ptolemy, but would soon be in a position to repay him in kind, and his attitude towards defeat was not that of a stripling who had suffered a setback at the start of a career, but that of a sober general who was accustomed to changes of fortune. So he busied himself with levying men and manufacturing arms and armour, kept the cities in hand, and drilled his new recruits.

[6] When Antigonus heard about the battle, he said that it was one thing for Ptolemy to have defeated beardless youths, but now he would be fighting men. Nevertheless, not wanting to extinguish or curb his son's pride, he did not refuse him when he again asked to be allowed to fight on his own, but gave his permission. Not long afterwards, Ptolemy's general Cilles arrived with a formidable army, intending to drive Demetrius out of Syria altogether. He was not anticipating any difficulty, given Demetrius' earlier defeat. But Demetrius caught Cilles unawares with a surprise attack, routed his men, and captured the camp, general and all.

Despite the fact that he took 7,000 prisoners and hugely enriched himself, what pleased him about the victory was not what he would gain by it, but what he could give away; more than the wealth or the glory of the victory, he enjoyed his ability to discharge the debt he had incurred as a result of Ptolemy's kindness. He did not go ahead with this of his own accord, however, but wrote to his father. When Antigonus said yes, giving him *carte blanche* to deal with everything as he saw fit, he loaded Cilles and the king's Friends with gifts and sent them back to Ptolemy. This defeat drove Ptolemy out of Syria, and brought Antigonus down to the coast from Celaenae, delighted at the victory and eager to see his son.*

[7] Demetrius' next mission was to subdue the Nabataean Arabs.* He rose confidently to the challenge posed by encountering waterless tracts of desert, struck terror into the barbarians, and returned home laden with booty he had seized from them, including 700 camels. Then, when Seleucus, the ruler of Babylonia (who had lost his empire to Antigonus some years earlier, but had subsequently recovered it* by his own efforts), marched east with his forces, intending to add the peoples bordering on India and the regions around the Caucasian mountains to his empire, Demetrius hoped to find Mesopotamia undefended. He made a sudden crossing of the Euphrates and entered Babylon before anyone could stop him. He swept Seleucus' garrison from one of the citadels (Babylon has two), made it his, and installed 7,000 of his own men. But after telling his men to take everything they could carry away as plunder from the land, he returned to the coast, leaving Seleucus more securely established in his dominions than before, because, by ravaging the land and treating it as though it no longer belonged to him and his father, he was felt to have renounced their claim to it.

When Ptolemy put Halicarnassus under siege, however, Demetrius lost no time in bringing up armed support and snatched the city from his grasp [8] and, on the strength of the glory they gained as a result of this achievement, Antigonus and Demetrius hatched an astonishing plan: to free Greece, all of which had been enslaved by Cassander and Ptolemy.* None of the kings ever fought a more noble or just war, in the sense that the resources Antigonus and Demetrius had amassed by humbling the barbarians were now expended on the Greeks, in an honourable and glorious cause.

Antigonus decided to make Athens his prime target. When one of his Friends suggested to him that, if the city fell to them, they should occupy it with their own garrison, seeing that it was a gangplank into Greece, Antigonus rejected his advice. He said that the goodwill of the Athenians was a better gangplank, one that could not be troubled by any swell, and that, thanks to its fame, Athens would soon blazon what they had done to all men, as though the city were a beacon visible by the whole world.

With a war chest of 5,000 talents and a fleet of 250 ships, Demetrius sailed against Athens, where the city itself was being administered for Cassander by Demetrius of Phalerum* and there was a garrison in Munychia.* By a combination of good luck and good planning, he appeared off Piraeus—it was 26 Thargelion*—before anyone realized what was happening. In fact, when his fleet first hove into sight, everyone started to get ready to welcome them, thinking they were Ptolemy's ships.* Eventually, when the Athenian generals realized what was going on, they sent help, and confusion ensued, of the kind one might expect when men are having to resist a surprise landing by enemy forces. For Demetrius was already inside: finding the mouths of the harbours unbarred, he had swept past them. But once he could be seen by everyone, he hoisted a signal on his ship, calling for an end to the fighting and for silence. In the hush that followed, he had a herald stand by his side and announce that his father had sent him to free the Athenians with the help of Good Fortune, expel the garrison, and restore their laws and their ancestral constitution.*

[9] At this proclamation, most of his opponents immediately laid their shields on the ground at their feet and applauded. They called out to Demetrius, inviting him to land, and hailing him as their benefactor and saviour. Moreover, Demetrius of Phalerum decided to accept

the conqueror on any terms, even if he had no intention of keeping any of his promises, and he sent a delegation to ask for a meeting. After a friendly meeting with these men, Demetrius sent them back to the Phalerean with one of his father's Friends, Aristodemus of Miletus.* The proposed constitutional changes meant that the Phalerean became more afraid of his fellow citizens than he was of the enemy, but Demetrius took care of him. Out of respect for the man's standing and integrity, he arranged for him to be safely escorted at his own request to Thebes, while he himself insisted that, for all his desire to see Athens, he would not do so until he had completely freed it by getting rid of the garrison. He surrounded Munychia with a palisade and a trench, and meanwhile sailed against Megara, which had been garrisoned by Cassander.

But when he found out that Cratesipolis,* the wife of Polyperchon's son Alexander and a famous beauty, was in Pagae† and would not be displeased to see him, he left his army at Megara and made his way there with an escort of just a few light-armed men. Then he told them to make themselves scarce and pitched his tent apart, so that the woman could join him discreetly. But some of his enemies found out and charged down at him. Terrified, he grabbed a cheap cloak and ran away, narrowly avoiding falling ignominiously into hostile hands thanks to his lack of self-control. But his enemies got away with his tent and valuables.

When Megara fell, his soldiers turned to looting, but the Athenians put in a strong plea that the citizens be spared, and Demetrius expelled the garrison and freed the city. In the midst of all this activity, he remembered the philosopher Stilpo,* a man who was famous for having chosen a life of perfect retirement.† He sent for him and asked him whether anyone had taken anything from him. 'No,' Stilpo replied, 'I haven't seen anyone stealing knowledge.' But almost all the household slaves in the city had been stolen, and at the end of a subsequent conversation Demetrius had with the philosopher, he said, as he was departing, 'Well, Stilpo, I'm leaving your city free.' 'True,' said Stilpo. 'You've left us none of our slaves.'

[10] Demetrius returned to Munychia and made camp there. At last, once he had driven out the garrison and demolished the fortress, he went up to Athens itself, at the Athenians' insistent invitation, and called a general assembly of the people. He restored their ancestral constitution, and also assured them that 150,000 *medimni* of grain

and enough ship-quality timber for 100 triremes would be coming from his father. It was fourteen years since the Athenians had lost their democracy. In the years after the Lamian War and the battle of Crannon, the constitution had been nominally an oligarchy, although the power of the Phalerean was such that it was actually a monarchy.*

Demetrius had demonstrated magnificence and greatness in his benefactions, but now the extravagance of the honours the Athenians decreed for him turned him offensive and oppressive. The Athenians were the first to call Demetrius and Antigonus kings—a title the two of them had so far conscientiously avoided—even though this was the only kingly attribute remaining to those who followed Philip and Alexander which it had been assumed would remain special and distinctive of them alone; and the Athenians were also the only ones to have them registered as saviour gods. In fact, they abolished the traditional office of eponymous archon, and instead inscribed the name of the annually elected Priest of the Saviours at the head of their decrees and contracts.* They also decreed that the figures of Antigonus and Demetrius were to be embroidered into the robe of Athena* alongside the gods, and they declared the spot where Demetrius had first descended from his chariot sacred and established an altar there to Demetrius Descendent. They also added two new tribes, Demetrias and Antigonis, and increased the membership of the Council from 500 to 600, since each tribe supplies fifty members.

[11] The inventor of these ingenious and extravagant acts of obsequiousness was Stratocles,* and the most outrageous idea of all also came from him. He proposed that, whenever an official delegation was sent, in accordance with a decision of the Assembly, to Antigonus or Demetrius, the members of the commission should not be called 'ambassadors', but 'witnesses', just like those who go to Delphi and Olympia and conduct the traditional sacrifices for their cities at the time of the Greek festivals.

This was not the only manifestation of Stratocles' brazen shamelessness. He lived a scandalous life, and it was said that his grandstanding and coarseness were attempts to imitate the unprincipled familiarity with the Athenian people that had once been the hallmark of Cleon.* His mistress was called Phylacion, and one day she bought brains and neck at the market for his dinner. 'Oh, no!' he said. 'You've bought the kinds of things we politicians kick around for sport!' At the time of the battle of Amorgos,* which was a defeat for the Athenians, Stratocles rode through the Cerameicus, before word of the battle had arrived, with a celebratory garland on his head. He told the assembled people that it had been an Athenian victory, proposed a thanksgiving sacrifice, and arranged for meat to be distributed tribe by tribe. When the wrecks were brought home from the battle a short while later, the people were furious and called on him to explain himself. He boldly faced the uproar and said: 'What harm have I done you? For two days, you've been happy.' This is a good example of Stratocles' audacity.

[12] But, as Aristophanes puts it, some things are hotter even than fire.* And so someone else brought forward a proposal that outdid Stratocles in servility: that, whenever Demetrius came to Athens, he should be received with the honours paid to Demeter and Dionysus, and that whoever laid on the most splendid and costly reception should be given a sum of money from the public treasury for a dedication. And in the end they renamed one of the months (Munychion became 'Demetrion'), one of the days (the old and new became 'Demetrias'),* and one of the festivals (the Dionysia became the 'Demetria').*

The gods very often showed their displeasure, however. For instance, the robe on which the Athenians had decreed that the figures of Demetrius and Antigonus were to be embroidered alongside Zeus and Athena† was torn in two when a storm broke out as it was being escorted through the Cerameicus. Or again, all around their altars the earth was thick with hemlock, a plant which generally did not grow at all elsewhere in Attica. And the day of the Dionysia was so unseasonably cold that the parade was cancelled, and the subsequent settled frost was so heavy that not only were all the vines and fig trees scorched by the cold, but also most of the cereal crops were ruined in the blade.

This is the context of the following attack on Stratocles by Philippides, who was no friend of his, in one of his comedies:*

> Thanks to him, frost scorched the vines;
> Thanks to his sacrilege, the robe was torn in two,
> Because he gave divine honours to men.
> These are the things that undermine the democracy.
> Don't blame comedy!

Philippides was one of Lysimachus' Friends and was often responsible for the king's benefactions to Athens.* Lysimachus even thought that it was a good omen for him to bump into Philippides and catch sight of him when he was embarking on an enterprise or setting out on an expedition. It was Philippides' character that made the king like him, since he never made a nuisance of himself and was not constantly meddling, as courtiers tend to. Once, in the course of a conversation with him, Lysimachus said: 'Philippides, is there anything of mine you'd like me to give you?' And Philippides replied: 'Anything except a state secret, my lord!' I have deliberately mentioned Philippides alongside Stratocles for the sake of the contrast between the playwright and the politician.

[13] But the most extraordinary and bizarre honour Demetrius received was proposed by Dromocleides of Sphettus, to the effect that they should get an oracle from him on the matter of the dedication of the shields at Delphi.* I shall transcribe the exact words of the decree: 'For good fortune, it has been resolved by the people that the people are to choose one man from the citizen body to go to the Saviour and, having obtained a favourable sacrifice, enquire of the Saviour how the restoration of the dedications might be effected in the most pious, honourable, and efficient manner. The people are to act on whatever response the Saviour gives.' This kind of mockery of the man by the Athenians was the ruin of Demetrius, who was mentally unstable anyway.

[14] During his sojourn in Athens at this time Demetrius married Eurydice, a widow. She was descended from Miltiades of old, and had been married to Ophellas, the governor of Cyrene, until his death, when she had returned to Athens.* The Athenians were inclined to regard this marriage as his way of thanking and honouring the city, but Demetrius was rather cavalier when it came to marriage, and had a number of wives at the same time. The most famous and respected of them was Phila, because she was the daughter of Antipater and had previously been married to Craterus, who was remembered by the Macedonians with more affection than any of Alexander's Successors.*

It seems that Antigonus persuaded Demetrius to marry Phila when he was still very young, even though she was not the same age as him, but older.* And the story goes that Antigonus dealt with his son's reluctance by whispering the following Euripidean line into his ear: 'You'll never get anywhere unless you marry, however much it may go against the grain'—substituting off the top of his head 'unless you marry' for Euripides' similarly formed 'unless you're servile'.* But Demetrius respected Phila and his other wives so little that he consorted freely and frequently with both courtesans and free women, and none of the kings of the time had a worse reputation for this kind of self-indulgence.

[15] When his father summoned him to fight Ptolemy for possession of Cyprus, he had to obey, but he did not like abandoning the war for Greece, which was the nobler and more glorious enterprise. He therefore wrote to Cleonides,* Ptolemy's commander of the garrisons at Sicyon and Corinth, offering him money to set the cities free. Cleonides turned him down, however, and Demetrius wasted no further time. He put to sea and, once he had supplemented his forces, sailed against Cyprus, where he joined battle with Menelaus, the brother of Ptolemy, and promptly defeated him. But then Ptolemy himself appeared with a huge land army and navy combined. Threatening and taunting messages passed between them, with Ptolemy suggesting that Demetrius should sail away to avoid being crushed by his army when it was fully assembled, and Demetrius offering to let him go if he agreed to withdraw his garrisons from Sicyon and Corinth. The battle was nervously anticipated not just by the two protagonists, but all the other dynasts as well anxiously awaited the outcome, which hung in the balance and left the future uncertain. For they felt that the victor would gain not just Cyprus or Syria, but would immediately be propelled to a position of overall supremacy.*

[16] Ptolemy deployed with 150 ships under his own command, while Menelaus was to wait until battle was fully joined and then launch an attack from Salamis with sixty ships, take Demetrius' fleet in the rear, and destroy his formation. But Demetrius ranged only ten ships against Menelaus' sixty; that was all it took to block the narrow harbour-mouth. He brought up his land army and occupied any headlands that projected into the sea, and then put to sea himself with 180 ships. He engaged the enemy with such overwhelming force that Ptolemy was utterly routed. After the defeat, Ptolemy himself raced away with just eight ships (which were the only survivors: seventy were captured along with their crews and the rest were destroyed in the battle), but all his attendants, Friends, and womenfolk, who had been huddled in transport vessels lying at anchor near

by, and all his weaponry, money, and artillery as well—absolutely everything fell into Demetrius' hands and was taken back to his camp.

Among the prisoners was the celebrated Lamia,* who had originally come to people's attention as an artiste—she had no little skill with the pipes, apparently—but became famous later for her sexual expertise. Anyway, at the time in question, even though her beauty was fading and Demetrius was much younger than her, she charmed him into submission and conquered him so thoroughly that she was the only one of the women he wanted, even though he was wanted by all the rest of them.

After the battle, Menelaus gave up as well and surrendered Salamis to Demetrius, along with his fleet and a land army of 1,200 horse and 12,000 hoplites. [17] Demetrius further embellished this already brilliant victory by his tact and humanity: he buried the enemy dead in magnificent style, released the prisoners, and gave the Athenians 1,200 sets of armour from the spoils.

The messenger he sent to deliver a first-hand report of the victory to his father was Aristodemus of Miletus, who was the leading yes-man in his court and had, it seems, seized this opportunity to concoct the last word in flattery as a way of crowning Demetrius' achievement. After sailing over from Cyprus, he would not let the ship come to land, but ordered the crew to drop anchor and stay quietly on board, while he left on his own in the tender and made his way inland to Antigonus, who was waiting anxiously for news of the battle and was as keyed up as men tend to be when so much is at stake. At the time in question, then, he became even more agitated when he heard that Aristodemus had arrived. He could scarcely keep himself from rushing out to meet him, and he sent his servants and Friends, one after another, to get the news. Aristodemus said nothing to any of them, however, but gradually drew near, stony-faced and in complete silence.

Antigonus, utterly distraught, could restrain himself no longer. He went to the doorway to meet Aristodemus, who was now being escorted by a large number of people, all hurrying to the palace. When he came up to Antigonus, he stretched out his hand and cried out in a loud voice: 'Greetings, King Antigonus! We met Ptolemy* at sea and defeated him. Cyprus is ours, along with 16,800 prisoners.' 'Greetings to you too, by Zeus!' replied Antigonus. 'But you'll pay for tormenting us like this: the reward due to you as bringer of good news will be slow in coming!'

[18] This was the cue for the general populace to hail Antigonus and Demetrius for the first time as kings. Antigonus' Friends immediately bound his head with a diadem,* and Antigonus sent Demetrius a diadem along with a letter addressing him as king. When the Egyptians heard about this, they proclaimed Ptolemy king as well, in case anyone got the impression that the defeat had dented his self-assurance. And then the practice spread, by a process of emulation, to the rest of the Successors. Lysimachus also began to wear a diadem, as did Seleucus in his meetings with Greeks; he had already been styling himself king in his dealings with the barbarians in his realm for a while. As for Cassander, even though the rest of them addressed him as king when they wrote to him or of him, he himself made no changes to the way he styled himself in his letters.*

There was more involved in this than the mere addition of a title and change of style. As soon as an actor puts on a costume, he also changes the way he walks, the sound of his voice, his posture at table, and the way he addresses others, and the same went for these men too. Calling themselves kings stirred their pride, fuelled their ambitions, and imbued their lives and interactions with others with authority and dignity. Another consequence was that they began to pass down harsher judgements, since they no longer had any need to conceal their power, which is what had previously made them, on the whole, quite diplomatic and lenient with their subjects. All it took was just one word from a flatterer, and the new dispensation spread throughout the whole world.

[19] Fired up by what Demetrius had achieved on Cyprus, Antigonus immediately launched an expedition against Ptolemy in Egypt, with him leading the army by land and Demetrius shadowing him along the coast with a huge fleet. But the outcome of the attempt was revealed to Medeius,† one of Antigonus' Friends, in a dream.* He dreamed that Antigonus himself, with his whole army, was taking part in a two-stade race. He made a fast, strong start, but then his strength began gradually to fail, and in the end, after he had made the turn, he was so weak, and his breathing was so ragged, that he could hardly stay on his feet. And so, after encountering many difficulties on land himself, and after Demetrius had almost been driven by a ferocious storm and heavy seas on to a bleak, harbourless stretch of

coastline, and had lost many ships, Antigonus returned from Egypt without having achieved anything.

By then Antigonus was almost eighty years old and was reluctant to get involved in campaigns, more because of his bulk and weight than because of his advanced age. He began to rely on his son instead. Demetrius was now making a good job of handling matters of the greatest importance, thanks to his luck and experience, and Antigonus had no problem with his son's luxurious and expensive lifestyle, or with his drinking. It was true that, in times of peace, Demetrius gave himself over to these vices, and indulged freely and excessively in his pleasures when he was not otherwise occupied, but in wartime he was as sober as a natural teetotaller.

There is a story dating from the time when Lamia's power over Demetrius was common knowledge, that once, when he returned from abroad, he greeted his father with a kiss, and Antigonus said with a laugh: 'You seem to think you're kissing Lamia, boy!' And on another occasion, when Demetrius had been drinking for several days and excused himself by saying that he had been troubled by a flux, Antigonus said: 'So I heard. But was it Thasian or Chian "flux"?'* On yet another occasion, when Antigonus found out that Demetrius was ill, he went to visit him and met a member of the fair sex at the entrance. He went in, sat down by the bed, and held his son's hand, and Demetrius said that the fever had left him now. 'I don't doubt it, my boy,' Antigonus said. 'It met me at the doorway just now on its way out!'

Antigonus tolerated Demetrius' excesses in this way because he found him otherwise competent. When Scythians drink and get intoxicated, they lightly pluck the strings of their bows to summon back their courage from the relaxed state induced by indulgence. But Demetrius was as single-minded about serious business as he was about enjoying himself, and he kept these two activities separate, so that his readiness for war was never impaired.

[20] As a general, however, he seems to have been better at getting an army ready for war than at putting it to work. He wanted to have a surplus of everything for every eventuality, and he was insatiable when it came to the construction of ships and machinery on a large scale, and to the designing of them, which afforded him particular pleasure. For he was intelligent and inventive, and employed his ingenuity not on trivia or useless diversions, as other kings did,

who played the pipes, or painted, or chased metal. Aeropus of Macedon,* for instance, in his spare time would make little tables and lamps. Attalus Philometor* used to grow medicinal plants—not just henbane and hellebore, but also hemlock, aconite, and datura; he would sow and plant them himself in his palace gardens, and made it his business to know the properties of their juices and berries, and the right time to gather them. And the Parthian kings prided themselves on their ability to sharpen and hone the points of their weapons by themselves.

In Demetrius' case, however, even his manual work was on a regal scale, and his researches had a grandeur about them, while his products displayed, along with their ingenious originality, a certain loftiness of intention and purpose, so that they seemed to deserve a king's labour, not just his favour and funding. The scale of his inventions intimidated even his friends, and their beauty delighted even his enemies. This is not just a neatly phrased sentiment, but the literal truth. His enemies would stand and gaze in astonishment at his 'sixteens' and 'fifteens'* as they sailed by their shores, and his city-takers* amazed the people whose cities they were trying to take. The facts bear this out. After all, none of the kings was a more bitter enemy of Demetrius than Lysimachus; but when Demetrius had Soli in Cilicia under siege and Lysimachus brought up his forces against him, Lysimachus wrote and asked for a demonstration of his siege-engines in operation and ships under sail, and after the demonstration he removed his forces, much impressed. And although the Rhodians suffered a long siege at his hands, when the war was over they asked to be given some of his engines, to remind them not just of his power but of their own bravery.

[21] Demetrius' war with the Rhodians,* who were allies of Ptolemy, saw the largest of his city-takers deployed against their walls. It had a square base, with each side of the frame at the bottom measuring 48 cubits, and it rose to a height of 66 cubits, converging towards the top, with its sides narrower high up than at the base.* The space inside was divided into storeys, with many rooms, and the side which faced the enemy was riddled with windows on every floor, through which poured a variety of missiles, since the whole thing was filled with men armed with every kind of weapon imaginable. The fact that it did not totter or lean as it moved, but stayed upright and stable on its base, well balanced and advancing forward with much loud screeching and

straining, simultaneously terrified the mind and pleased the eyes of anyone watching.

Two iron breastplates also arrived from Cyprus for his use in this war, each of which weighed only forty mnas.* To demonstrate their durability and strength, Zoïlus, the designer, suggested that Demetrius fire a catapult bolt at one of them from a distance of twenty paces. The iron remained intact where the bolt struck, showing no more than a faint scratch such as might have been made by a stylus. Demetrius wore this one himself, and the other was worn by Alcimus of Epirus, the best fighter and the strongest man in the army—the only one whose panoply weighed two talents, while everyone else's weighed just one.* He fell in battle at Rhodes near the theatre.

[22] But the Rhodians put up a spirited defence, and although Demetrius was unable to accomplish anything worthy of note, he struggled on, incensed by the fact that the Rhodians had captured a ship which was bringing him letters, blankets, and clothing from his wife Phila, and had sent it, just as it was, to Ptolemy. Rhodian behaviour in this instance did not match the politeness of the Athenians. During the war with Philip they captured some of his couriers, and although they read all the rest of the letters, they left the one from Olympias unopened and returned it to him intact, with her seal unbroken.*

Nevertheless, although Demetrius was extremely irritated by this, he refused to retaliate when an opportunity presented itself immediately afterwards. It so happened that Protogenes of Caunus was still working on his portrait of Ialysus when Demetrius found it, almost finished, in one of the suburbs of the city, and took possession of it. When the Rhodians sent a herald, begging him to spare the picture and leave it unharmed, Demetrius replied that he would sooner burn a portrait of his father than destroy the product of so much artistic labour—for the painting apparently took Protogenes seven years to complete. And Apelles says that he was so astounded by the painting when he saw it that words failed him, and it was only later that he was able to say: 'What painstaking work! An astonishing painting!'* He added, however, that it lacked the graceful touches that raised his own work to the heavens. Be that as it may, this painting was one of the many crammed together in the same place in Rome that were consumed in the fire.*

The Rhodians continued their resistance until an Athenian delegation arrived and got Demetrius to make peace with them—he had only been looking for an excuse—on the condition that they would be allies of Antigonus and Demetrius except in a war against Ptolemy.

[23] But now the Athenians were asking Demetrius for help, since Cassander had the city under siege.* He sailed there with a fleet of 330 ships and a large number of hoplites, and not only drove Cassander out of Attica, but stayed close on his heels and kept him on the run all the way to Thermopylae,* where he gained Heraclea, which voluntarily surrendered to him, and 6,000 Macedonian troops came over to his side. On his return, he freed all the Greeks south of Thermopylae, entered into an alliance with the Boeotians, and took Cenchreae. He also reduced Phyle and Panactum, fortresses in Attica which were garrisoned by Cassander, and gave them back to the Athenians.

Although the Athenians had already effusively exhausted every honour that could be awarded him, they still found ways to give their flatteries at this time too an air of freshness and originality, by assigning him the rear chamber of the Parthenon as his quarters, for instance. While he was living there it was said that Athena made him welcome and looked after him as his hostess, even though he was not a very well-behaved guest and was scarcely as unassuming as one should be when lodging with a virgin. And yet once, when Antigonus found out that Demetrius' brother Philip had been billeted on a household that included three young women, even though he said nothing directly to him, he sent for the quartermaster and said to him, in Philip's presence, 'Now, sir! Could you please release my son from these confined quarters?'

[24] Demetrius should have restrained himself in the presence of Athena, at the very least because she was his elder sister, or so he liked to claim; but instead he polluted the Acropolis so much by his disgusting behaviour with free-born boys and citizen women that the place seemed to be at its most pure when he limited his debauchery to the company of the famous prostitutes Chrysis, Lamia, Demo, and Anticyra. For the sake of Athens, I should refrain from revealing all the details, but the virtue and modesty of the young teenager Democles should not go without a mention. He first came to Demetrius' attention because of his nickname, which betrayed his beauty: he was

called Democles the Fair. Many admirers had tried to seduce him with gifts or bully him into submission, but he refused all of them, and ended up by avoiding the wrestling schools and gymnasium, and going to bathe at a private bath-house. One day Demetrius, who had been watching for his opportunity, entered the bath-house after him and found him alone. When the boy saw that there was no help and no escape, he took the lid off the cauldron and killed himself by leaping into the boiling water.

Democles did not deserve this fate, but at least his attitude was worthy of his country and commensurate with his beauty. The same cannot be said of Cleaenetus, the son of Cleomedon, who obtained from Demetrius letters ordering the remission of a fine of fifty talents that his father had incurred and presented these letters to the Assembly. He not only disgraced himself, but also made trouble for the city as a whole, because, after letting Cleomedon off his fine, they passed a decree forbidding the introduction by an Athenian citizen of letters from Demetrius into the Assembly. When Demetrius heard about this decree, he was furious, and the terrified Athenians not only rescinded the decree, but also put to death or sent into exile those who had proposed the bill and spoken in its favour.

They also passed a further decree: 'Resolved by the people: whatever King Demetrius should ordain is righteous in the eyes of the gods and just in the eyes of men.' When one of the better sort said that Stratocles was mad to propose such a thing, Demochares of Leuconoe* replied: 'He would indeed be mad not to be mad.' For Stratocles had done very well for himself by his flattery. Demochares, however, was attacked for what he had said and sent into exile. That is how things stood in Athens, where they thought they had obtained their freedom when they got rid of their garrison.

[25] Demetrius next campaigned in the Peloponnese.* None of his enemies there put up any resistance, but chose flight and abandoned their cities instead. He gained the region known as the Headland and all Arcadia except Mantinea, and he purchased the freedom of Argos, Sicyon, and Corinth with a 100-talent bribe to their garrisons.

At Argos it was time for the festival of Hera, and Demetrius acted as Master of Games, joined the Greeks in their celebrations, and married Deidameia, the daughter of King Aeacides of Molossis and sister of Pyrrhus.* At Sicyon he told the inhabitants that their city was in the wrong place and persuaded them to move it to its current site; and at the same time as changing its location, he also changed its name from Sicyon to Demetrias. And at the Isthmus there was a general assembly, well attended by delegates from all over Greece, and he was proclaimed Commander of Greece, the position occupied earlier by Philip and Alexander.*

In actual fact, though, elated by his current run of luck and the strength of his position, he felt himself to be far superior to Philip and Alexander. At any rate, Alexander never denied any of the other kings their title, did not declare himself King of Kings, and frequently gave his permission for men to be called and to be kings. But Demetrius used to jeer and scoff if the title 'king' was applied to anyone other than himself and his father. The series of toasts he liked to hear over drinks hailed him as king, Seleucus as master of elephants, Ptolemy as admiral, Lysimachus as treasurer, and Agathocles of Sicily as island governor.* When the other kings heard about this, they all found it amusing except for Lysimachus, who was furious that Demetrius would consider him less than a man, seeing that it was usually eunuchs who were employed as treasurers. In any case, none of the kings loathed Demetrius as much as Lysimachus did. As a way of sneering at him for his affair with Lamia, he used to say that this was the first time he had ever seen a whore playing a tragic role; but Demetrius claimed that his whore was more chaste than Lysimachus' Penelope.*

[26] Anyway, to resume, when Demetrius was getting ready to leave the Peloponnese and return to Athens, he wrote to the Athenians that he wanted to be initiated into the Mysteries as soon as he got back, and to receive the full course of initiations, from the Lesser Mysteries up to the final revelation.* But this was unprecedented and unlawful, since the Lesser Mysteries are celebrated in the month of Anthesterion, the Great Mysteries in Boedromion, and at least a year has to elapse between the Great Mysteries and the revelation. Nevertheless, when the letter was read out, the only person to protest was the Torch-bearer, Pythodorus,* and he got nowhere. Instead, on Stratocles' proposal, they voted to change the name of the current month and treat it as Anthesterion instead of Munychion,* and they initiated Demetrius in the Lesser Mysteries at Agra. Then they changed Munychion again, this time to Boedromion, and Demetrius received the remaining initiation and the revelation at

the same time. That is why Philippides' attack on Stratocles included the line:

> He compressed a year into a single month.

And, with reference to the Parthenon being used as Demetrius' lodgings:

> He took the Acropolis for a vulgar inn
> And introduced courtesans to the virgin goddess.

[27] Much that went on in the city in those days infringed both good taste and the law, but the following is the incident that is said to have annoyed the Athenians most. They were ordered to come up with 250 talents in short order and give it to him, and they instituted a rigorous compulsory levy, but when he saw that they had collected the money he told them to give it to Lamia and her fellow courtesans to buy soap. It was the shame more than the financial loss that upset people, the idea of it rather than the doing of it. But there is an alternative version according to which it was the Thessalians whom he treated like this, not the Athenians.

Then there was a separate occasion when Lamia demanded money of her own accord from a number of people for a dinner she was preparing for the king. The meal was so expensive that it became famous enough for Lynceus of Samos* to write a version of it. This is also the context of the rather nice description of Lamia by a comic poet as 'a true city-taker'. And Demochares of Soli used to call him Demetrius 'the Myth', because he too had his Lamia.*

Lamia's success and the affection Demetrius felt for her aroused the jealousy and envy not only of Demetrius' wives, but also of his Friends. At any rate, once some of his Friends arrived at Lysimachus' court on a diplomatic mission from Demetrius, and in a moment of spare time Lysimachus showed them deep scars on his thighs and arms, which had been caused by a lion's claws, and told them the story of how he had fought the beast when he had been shut up with it on the orders of Alexander, his king.* They laughed and said that their king too bore bite wounds on his neck from a fearsome beast—Lamia!

People found it odd that he complained at first about the disparity between his age and Phila's, but fell for Lamia and loved her for so many years, even when she was past her prime. At any rate, once, when Lamia was playing the pipes at dinner, Demetrius asked Demo, also known as Mania, 'How does she strike you?' 'As an old woman, my lord,' she replied. And on another occasion, when some sweets had been served, Demetrius said to Demo, 'Look at all the things Lamia sends me!' 'That's nothing to what you'll get from *my* mother,' Demo replied, 'if you sleep with her too.'

Another anecdote about Lamia that has come down to us concerns her refutation of the famous judgement of Bocchoris.* Once, in Egypt, someone was in love with the courtesan Thonis, but she was asking for a great deal of money. But one night he dreamt that he slept with her, and afterwards his desire for her vanished. Thonis took him to court to try to get her money, and after listening to her argument, Bocchoris ordered the man to count out the full amount of the money she was demanding and to wave it to and fro in its sack; and he told Thonis to take for herself the shadow it cast, since what is seen in a dream is a shadow of reality. But Lamia queried the fairness of this judgement, on the grounds that, while the dream may have quenched the young man's ardour, the shadow did not put an end to the courtesan's desire for the money. Anyway, so much for stories about Lamia.

[28] But the changing fortunes and activities of the subject of this Life draw my account from the comic back to the tragic stage. For all the other kings formed a coalition and combined their forces against Antigonus, so Demetrius left Greece and joined his father. Belying his age, Antigonus was eagerly looking forward to the war, and this made Demetrius all the more optimistic. Now, it is arguable that if Antigonus had made a few slight concessions and had relaxed his excessive desire for dominion, he would have retained his position of supremacy to the last and bequeathed it to Demetrius. But he was an overbearing and scornful man, with a way of talking to others that was as disagreeable as the way he behaved towards them, and many young and powerful men had been antagonized and angered by him. But he used to say that he would scatter the coalition and alliance that they formed at that time with a single stone and a yell, as if they were a flock of birds after seeds in a field.

The army under Antigonus' command consisted of more than 70,000 foot, 10,000 horse, and 75 elephants, while the other side had 64,000 foot, 500 more horse than him, 400 elephants, and 120 chariots. But when he was near them, something shifted in his mind—not his resolve so much as his expectations. He usually approached battles with arrogance and disdain, speaking loudly and confidently, and he often even cracked a joke or made some humorous remark when the enemy was close at hand to show how calm he was and how little he thought of them. But now he was noticeably pensive and reticent, and he presented his son to the troops and recommended him as his successor. But what everyone found most odd were the one-to-one meetings with Demetrius in his tent, whereas usually he kept his plans to himself and did not reveal them even to his son. Typically, he would form his plans on his own, and only then give his orders openly and put into effect the course of action he had decided on by himself. At any rate, there is a story that when Demetrius was still quite young he asked his father when they were going to break camp, and Antigonus replied angrily: 'Are you worried that you'll be the only person not to hear the trumpet?'

[29] But, to resume the narrative, their resolve was also crushed by bad omens. Demetrius dreamt that Alexander, dressed in gleaming armour, asked him what watchword they were going to issue for the battle. 'Zeus and Victory,' he replied. 'I'm off to the other side, then,' said Alexander, 'where I'm welcome.'* And with the phalanx already forming up for battle, Antigonus tripped as he was setting out, fell flat on his face, and hurt himself badly; but he pulled himself to his feet, raised his hands to heaven, and asked the gods for victory—or a painless death before defeat.

When the two sides engaged,* Demetrius, who had the best and largest force of cavalry on the field, clashed with Antiochus, the son of Seleucus.* Up to the point at which the enemy turned and fled, Demetrius fought a brilliant battle; but he ruined his chances of victory by pursuing them with excessive zeal and determination, so that the elephants could block his return and prevent him from linking up with the infantry. Seleucus, noticing that the enemy phalanx was unprotected by cavalry, had his horsemen wheel all around it, keeping the soldiers in constant fear of attack, but without actually attacking, so as to give them the opportunity to change sides. And that is what happened: a large body of men which had become separated from the rest chose to change sides, and then the rest turned to flight. Many of the enemy were heading for Antigonus' position, and someone in his entourage said: 'It's you they're after, my lord.' 'Of course,' Antigonus replied. 'Who else could be their target? But Demetrius will come and help us.' Right up until the end, this was what he expected, and he kept looking out for his son, but a volley of javelins laid him low. All the rest of his adjutants and Friends abandoned him, and only one man remained by his body, Thorax of Larisa.

[30] So the battle was decided. The victorious kings then proceeded to slice up the whole of Antigonus' and Demetrius' domain like an enormous carcass, each taking his portion, and they also redistributed among themselves the provinces they had possessed before. Demetrius escaped with 5,000 foot and 4,000 horse, and rode furiously for Ephesus. He was so short of money that everyone thought he would plunder the sanctuary,* but in fact he was afraid of his troops doing just that, so he did not stay long in Ephesus, but sailed for Greece. He was pinning almost all his remaining hopes on Athens, where he had left ships, money, and his wife Deidameia, and where, he believed, the loyalty of the Athenians would secure him a safer haven than he would find anywhere else. Hence, when he reached the Cyclades and was met by Athenian envoys who told him he had better stay away from Athens, since the people had decreed that no king was welcome in the city—they had already sent Deidameia to Megara with a fitting escort and the honour due to her rank—he was beside himself with rage, even though he had otherwise taken his misfortune in his stride, without cringing or cowering at the radical change in his circumstances. But the unexpected dashing of his illusions about the Athenians, the fact that their apparent loyalty had proved, when tested by circumstances, to be an empty pretence, was hard for him to bear.

It rather looks as though the excessive awarding of honours by the masses is no true measure of their loyalty towards kings and dynasts. Such honours are good only if they are freely given, but fear—for honours may be awarded out of fear just as much as affection—robs them of their value. Hence sensible men consider what they have actually achieved and accomplished rather than the statues and portraits and deifications they have been awarded, and only then either trust them as genuine honours or mistrust them as having been conferred by people who felt compelled to do so. After all, it is not uncommon for the people of a city, even while they are conferring honours, to hate the recipients for accepting them immodestly and arrogantly even from people who do not really want to confer them.

[31] Be that as it may, at the time in question Demetrius felt himself to have been very badly treated, but there was nothing

he could do to retaliate, so he wrote a letter of mild rebuke to the Athenians and asked to have his ships returned to him, one of which was a 'thirteen'. After collecting them, he sailed to the Isthmus, but things were not going well for him. His garrisons were everywhere being thrown out and everyone was deserting him for the enemy. So he left Greece in Pyrrhus' hands* and sailed for the Chersonese, where he accomplished two things: he weakened Lysimachus, and he enriched his men and prevented the break-up of his army, which was beginning to recover and once again be a force to be reckoned with. The other kings did nothing to help Lysimachus, whom they considered as obnoxious as Demetrius and more of a danger, because of his greater strength.

Not long afterwards, Seleucus sent and asked for the hand of Stratonice, Demetrius' daughter by Phila. He already had a son, Antiochus, by his Persian wife Apama,* but his empire was large enough for more than one successor, in his opinion; and he needed the connection with Demetrius, since Lysimachus had taken one of Ptolemy's daughters for himself and another for his son Agathocles.* For Demetrius to gain Seleucus as a relative was an unexpected piece of good fortune, and he took Stratonice to Syria with his entire fleet as her escort. On the way he made land as necessary, but he also raided Cilicia, which had been given by the kings after the battle with Antigonus to Pleistarchus, Cassander's brother, as his share of the spoils. Pleistarchus regarded Demetrius' landings as an infringement of his territory, and he wanted to remonstrate with Seleucus for having become reconciled with the common enemy independently of the other kings, so he went to pay him a visit.

[32] When Demetrius heard about this, he set out from the Cilician coast to Cyinda. Finding that the treasury still held 1,200 talents of valuables, he packed it all up and had it stowed on his ships before anyone could react, and then quickly sailed away. Once Phila had joined him, Seleucus met him at Rhosus, and from the outset their meetings were unmarred by deceit or dishonesty, and conducted in a regal fashion. First Seleucus entertained Demetrius under canvas in his camp, and then Demetrius held a reception for Seleucus on board his 'thirteen'. There were also occasions for relaxation and casual conversation, and they spent whole days together without guards or weaponry, until Seleucus returned to Antioch in splendid style with Stratonice.

Demetrius next occupied Cilicia, and sent his wife Phila to her brother Cassander to refute Pleistarchus' charges. Meanwhile, Deidameia sailed from Greece to join him, but she fell ill and died soon after her arrival. Then Seleucus brokered a reconciliation between Demetrius and Ptolemy, and Demetrius became betrothed to Ptolemy's daughter Ptolemais.

So far, Seleucus had been all tact, but now he asked Demetrius to sell him Cilicia, and when Demetrius refused he became angry and demanded that he give him Sidon and Tyre.* But people thought Seleucus was wrong to bully Demetrius like this. He was lord of all Asia from India to the Syrian coast, and yet he still felt so badly off and impoverished that, for the sake of two cities, he was harassing a man whose daughter he had married and who had suffered a severe setback. Nothing could more clearly demonstrate how right Plato was to suggest that anyone who wants to be truly well off should not increase his possessions, but decrease his dissatisfaction, because a man who never curbs his love of money is never free of poverty or want.*

[33] Demetrius was not intimidated, however, and said that even after ten thousand defeats like Ipsus he would still refuse to pay to have Seleucus as his son-in-law. He strengthened the cities with garrisons, but the news that Lachares* had exploited political divisions to impose himself as tyrant on the Athenians made him hope that all he had to do was appear and the city would immediately fall to him. He brought an immense fleet safely over the open sea, but as he was sailing up the Attic coast he was caught by a storm and lost most of his ships, along with a not inconsiderable number of men.

Demetrius was unharmed, however, and he began a desultory war against Athens, but that was getting him nowhere, so he sent agents to gather another fleet, while he invaded the Peloponnese and put Messene under siege. During an assault on the city walls, he came close to losing his life when a bolt from a catapult struck him in the face, piercing his jaw and entering his mouth. Once he had recovered, he regained some rebel cities and then invaded Attica again. He gained Eleusis and Rhamnous, ravaged the land—and hanged the trader and the captain of a grain ship that was bound for Athens. Others were therefore frightened into steering clear of Athens, and the city was soon in the grip of a terrible famine. It was not just the shortage of grain, but there was a dearth of other commodities as well. At any rate, a *medimnus* of salt cost 40 drachmas, and wheat was selling for 300 drachmas a *medimnus*.

The Athenians gained a brief respite when 150 ships appeared off Aegina, sent by Ptolemy to help them, but then Demetrius was joined by fleets from both the Peloponnese and Cyprus, until altogether he had 300 ships. At this, Ptolemy's ships weighed anchor and fled, and the tyrant Lachares abandoned the city and took to his heels.

[34] Although the Athenians had decreed that any mention of peace and reconciliation with Demetrius was punishable by death, they immediately opened the gates nearest to his camp and sent a delegation to him. It was not that they expected mercy from him, but starvation left them no choice. Here is one typically grim story from the many that date from the famine: a mouse corpse fell from the rafters of a room where a father and son were sitting in utter despair, and they leapt up and fought each other for it. In another story from the same time, the philosopher Epicurus* kept his companions alive by rationing the number of beans to be distributed among them.

These stories illustrate the desperate plight of the city when Demetrius entered it. He ordered a general assembly in the theatre and, with the stage building bristling with weaponry and the stage itself ringed by bodyguards, he made his entrance by one of the upper passages used by the actors. All this only added to the terror of the assembled Athenians, but his first words put an end to their fears: without raising his voice or uttering a bitter word, he gently told them off, as a friend would, and said he had no further quarrel with them. He went on to say that he was making them a gift of 100,000 *medimni* of grain, and he restored the offices that were most agreeable to the people.*

When the orator Dromocleides saw that the people could hardly find words to express their joy and were reaching for even more extravagant ways to express their gratitude than those usually proposed from the speaker's platform by demagogues, he brought in a proposal 'that Piraeus and Munychia should be surrendered to King Demetrius'.* This decree was passed, and Demetrius took it upon himself to install a garrison on the Museum Hill as well, to make sure that the people of Athens would not become restive again and interrupt his other enterprises.

[35] With Athens secured, Sparta immediately became his next target. King Archidamus* came out to meet him at Mantinea, but

Demetrius defeated him and routed his army, and then invaded Laconia. In a second battle right by Sparta itself he took 500 prisoners and killed 200, and seemed poised to take the city, which had never fallen in its history. But no other king had to suffer such sudden and major shifts of Fortune; no other king was affected so often by Fortune's ebb and flow, so that he was raised high and then brought low again, only to recover his strength once more. And so, in the midst of his worst setbacks, we hear, he used to cry out to Fortune Aeschylus' line: 'It's you who fan me into flame, you who reduce me at will to ashes.'*

So now, just when his rise towards imperial power seemed unstoppable, the news arrived that Lysimachus had first taken from him his cities in Asia Minor, and that Ptolemy had then taken all Cyprus, with the exception only of Salamis, where Demetrius' children and mother were bottled up and under siege. But, like the woman in Archilochus who 'treacherously bore water in one hand and fire in the other',* after drawing him from Sparta with this grim and terrifying news, Fortune immediately gave him fresh hope of major success. This is what happened.

[36] After Cassander's death, the eldest of his sons, Philip, ruled Macedon for only a short while before dying.* Cassander's other two sons were at daggers drawn, and when one of them, Antipater, murdered his mother Thessalonice, the other, Alexander, summoned Pyrrhus' help from Epirus and Demetrius' from the Peloponnese.* Pyrrhus got there first and took over a large slice of Macedon as the price of his assistance, and from then on loomed menacingly on Alexander's borders.* But the young man was far more worried by the fact that his letter had drawn north a man as formidable and famous as Demetrius at the head of an army, and he went to meet him at Dium. He greeted him warmly as a friend, but told him that the situation no longer required his presence. The upshot was an atmosphere of mutual distrust, and once, when Demetrius was walking over to dinner at the young man's invitation, someone informed him of a plot to kill him that very evening, while they were drinking after the meal.

Demetrius remained unruffled. He slowed his pace down a little, ordered his officers to hold their troops armed and ready, and told his attendants and slaves—he had a far larger entourage than Alexander—to join him in the dining-room and to stay close until he got up from the table. These arrangements deterred any attempt by Alexander, and before long Demetrius left the dinner, alleging that his health did not allow him to take wine. The next day he set about breaking camp, telling Alexander that something had come up that required his attention. He apologized for leaving sooner than expected, and told Alexander that they would get together on another occasion, when he had the time.

Delighted that Demetrius was leaving the country of his own free will, not as an enemy, Alexander escorted him as far as Thessaly. But when they reached Larisa, they renewed their mutual invitations to dinner and their plots against each other's lives. It was this above all that delivered Alexander into Demetrius' hands. Alexander was reluctant to take any precautions, because he did not want to prompt Demetrius to take counter-measures against him, and so he held back in order to ensnare him more completely and ended up suffering the fate he had been devising for his enemy.† For he accepted a dinner invitation from Demetrius at his lodgings, and when Demetrius got up from the table before the meal was finished, Alexander was so frightened that he got up as well and followed close behind Demetrius as he walked to the door. When Demetrius reached the entrance, where his own bodyguards were posted, he spoke just these few words: 'Kill the man behind me.' Then he stepped outside, and Alexander was cut down by the soldiers. The same thing happened to Alexander's Friends when they came to help, and one of them is supposed to have said, as he was being butchered, that Demetrius had been just one day ahead of them.

[37] Naturally enough, the Macedonian camp seethed with anxiety all night. Dawn found them still troubled, but despite their fear of Demetrius' army there was no immediate threat. In fact, Demetrius sent a messenger to ask them for a meeting and an opportunity to explain his actions, and they decided to keep their hopes alive and grant him an audience. When he came, he found that long speeches were unnecessary. The Macedonians hated Antipater for murdering his mother and there was no better man available, so they proclaimed Demetrius king of Macedon* and then returned straight home with him. The change of ruler was not unwelcome to the Macedonians there either, who had never forgotten or forgiven Cassander for his crimes against Alexander the Great after his death.* And in so far as the memory of the elder Antipater's moderation still lingered,

Demetrius reaped the benefit of this too, because he was married to Phila and his son by her, who was by then a young man and was serving under his father, was his heir.*

[38] In the midst of this brilliant success, Demetrius received news that Ptolemy had released his children and mother,* and had sent them on their way laden with gifts and honours. He also heard that the daughter of his who had been married to Seleucus was now the wife of Antiochus, Seleucus' son, and was styled queen of the barbarian eastern satrapies.* What happened, apparently, was that Antiochus fell in love with Stratonice, who was still a young woman, even though she had borne Seleucus a baby. Antiochus was in a terrible state, and tried long and hard to resist his feelings, but eventually, filled with self-loathing for his scandalous lust and incurable sickness, and for succumbing to irrational impulses, he sought a way to die, and to this end he denied himself food and generally disregarded his bodily needs.

As he gradually became weaker and weaker, he pretended that he was suffering from some ailment or other. But it was a simple matter for Erasistratus,* his doctor, to see that he was in love, even if it was less easy for him to guess who he was in love with. In order to find out, he spent all his time in Antiochus' chambers, and whenever a beautiful boy or woman came in, he carefully examined Antiochus' face and watched for changes in those parts of the body that are particularly responsive to the tendencies of the soul. When anyone else came in, Antiochus remained unchanged; but whenever Stratonice paid him a visit, as she often did, either on her own or in Seleucus' company, he suffered from the full range of symptoms described by Sappho:* he became tongue-tied, his vision blurred, he broke out into sudden sweats, he suffered from irregular palpitations of the heart, and finally, to mark the total collapse of mental resistance, he became bewildered and dazed, and his face lost all colour. In addition to these symptoms, Erasistratus also took into consideration the fact that, in all probability, if the king's son were in love with anyone else, he would not insist on keeping it secret and taking the secret to his grave.

Erasistratus was under no illusions about the difficulty of the report he had to deliver, but he took the risk one day, trusting in the affection Seleucus felt for his son, and told him that the young man was sick with a love that could never be consummated or satisfied. Seleucus asked in surprise what he meant by saying that it could never be satisfied. 'By Zeus!' exclaimed Erasistratus. 'Because it's my wife he's in love with!'

'Well, Erasistratus,' said Seleucus, 'can't you give my son your wife? You're my friend, and you can see that in times of trouble he's my only support.'

'No,' said Erasistratus, 'and you wouldn't have done that either, even though you're his father, if it were Stratonice Antiochus wanted.'

'My friend,' replied Seleucus, 'I wish that somehow, by divine or human agency, his feelings could be realigned and pointed in that direction instead. You should know that I would happily sacrifice even my kingdom to keep Antiochus safe.'

Seleucus was in a highly emotional state and wept freely as he spoke; and Erasistratus took him by the hand and said: 'You have no need of me. You're not just the best father, husband, and king. You're also the best doctor your household could hope for.'

So Seleucus summoned a general assembly of the Macedonians and said that it was his will and his decision to make Antiochus king of all his eastern territories, with Stratonice as his queen, and that they would live together as man and wife. He added that he did not expect any opposition to the marriage from his son, who was accustomed to obey him in everything and carry out all his commands, but that if the woman objected to the unusual arrangement, his Friends should explain matters to her—that is, they should persuade her to consider a king's every decision not just fair and right, but for the best too. Anyway, that was the reason, we hear, for the marriage of Antiochus and Stratonice.*

[39] After Macedon, Demetrius had next gained Thessaly as well. Since he already had most of the Peloponnese and, outside the Peloponnese, Megara and Athens were his, he next marched against the Boeotians. At first they made reasonable attempts to arrange a pact of friendship with him, but then Cleonymus the Spartan* arrived in Thebes with an army. The Boeotians' confidence rose, and when Peisis of Thespiae, the most important and powerful man in the league at the time, added his encouragement to that of Cleonymus, they came out in rebellion.

But when Demetrius brought up his engines and put Thebes under siege, Cleonymus took fright and stole away, and the terrified Boeotians surrendered. Demetrius installed garrisons in their cities, fined them heavily, and left the historian Hieronymus* as their governor and commander. This settlement, and especially his treatment of Peisis, earned him a reputation for leniency. After Peisis fell into his hands, so far from doing him harm, he treated him with civility and kindness, and made him the polemarch of Thespiae.

Before much time had passed, however, Lysimachus was captured by Dromichaetes,* and Demetrius' response was to hurry off to Thrace, hoping to find it undefended. But the Boeotians revolted again, and at the same time news arrived that Lysimachus had been released. Demetrius furiously retraced his steps with all speed, but he found that the Boeotians had already been defeated in battle by his son Antigonus, and he put Thebes under siege once more.

[40] Meanwhile, however, Pyrrhus had invaded Thessaly and had been seen as far south as Thermopylae, so Demetrius left the siege in Antigonus' hands and marched against him. Pyrrhus beat a hasty retreat. After stationing a force of 10,000 hoplites and 1,000 horse in Thessaly, Demetrius renewed the pressure on Thebes. He brought up his city-taker, but the effort required to heave the monster slowly along was so great that in two months it had hardly advanced two stades. The Boeotians put up a determined defence, and Demetrius often forced his men to fight and risk their lives out of combativeness, rather than because there was any real need. Antigonus became very upset at the not inconsiderable loss of life and asked: 'Why are we letting these men's lives be thrown away unnecessarily, father?' The question annoyed Demetrius and he replied sharply: 'Why should that upset *you*? Do you owe the dead wages?'

But he did not want his men thinking that he was merely wasteful of others' lives; he wanted them to see that he exposed himself to danger as well—and he was wounded in the neck by a bolt from a catapult. Despite the severity of the wound, he did not slacken his efforts, and Thebes fell to him once again. The Thebans were in an agony of terror at his entry into the city. They expected the worst, but after having thirteen men executed and a few more sent into exile, he pardoned everyone else. And so it turned out that Thebes was captured twice in the ten years or so since it had been repopulated.*

At the time of the Pythia, Demetrius undertook an extremely unusual project. Since the Aetolians occupied the passes around Delphi, he held the games and the festival in Athens, claiming that it was peculiarly appropriate for the god to be honoured there, since he was their ancestral deity and was said to be the founder of their line.*

[41] From Athens, Demetrius returned to Macedon, and then marched against the Aetolians. It was not just that he was constitutionally incapable of inactivity, but he also found that his men's loyalty increased when they were out on campaign, while they tended to be restless and troublesome at home. After ravaging the Aetolians' farmland, he left Pantauchus there with one division of the army, while he marched against Pyrrhus, who was also advancing to meet him. But they missed each other, and while Demetrius laid waste to Epirus, Pyrrhus swooped down on Pantauchus. In the ensuing battle, the two generals exchanged blows and wounded each other,* but Pyrrhus routed Pantauchus' forces, taking 5,000 prisoners and killing a substantial proportion of the rest.

This defeat was particularly damaging to Demetrius' cause, in the sense that any hatred Pyrrhus might have incurred for his success was outweighed by the admiration he received for having in large part been personally responsible for the victory. In fact, this battle was the foundation of his great and glorious reputation in Macedon, and many Macedonians were moved to say that he was the only one of the kings in whom a trace of Alexander's courage could be detected.* The rest of the kings, they felt, and especially Demetrius, merely made a show of the great man's weight and substance, as if they were actors on a stage.

And there was indeed a strong streak of theatricality about Demetrius. It was not just the extravagance of his clothing and headgear—his cap with its double headband, his purple-dyed cloaks bordered with gold—but he even had gold-dyed slippers made for his feet out of layers of felt dyed with pure purple. He also had a riding-cloak that took ages to make, an extraordinary piece of work, depicting the world and the heavenly bodies. It was left half-finished at the time of his downfall, and no one dared to wear it, even though quite a few of his successors on the throne of Macedon were flamboyant characters.

[42] People had never seen anything like it before, but this ostentation of his was not the only thing that annoyed them; they also found his self-indulgent way of life offensive, and especially the difficulty of getting an audience or a meeting with him. He tended either not to make time for meetings, or to be brusque and harsh with those who did get to see him. For instance, even though he took the Athenians more seriously than he did any other Greeks, he still kept one of

their embassies waiting for two years, and once, when just a single ambassador arrived from Sparta, he was annoyed at what he took to be a slight. 'What's the meaning of this?' he asked. 'The Spartans have sent just one man for the meeting?' The ambassador's reply was neat and typically laconic: 'Yes, my lord. He's meeting only one man.'

One day, when he was out riding, he seemed to be in a more receptive mood than usual and to be not unhappy at the prospect of meeting his subjects; and when people crowded around and handed the drafts of their petitions up to him, he accepted them all and tucked them away in his cloak, to the delight of the petitioners, who were carefully watching what he did. But when he came to the Axius bridge,* he shook out his cloak and pitched all the petitions into the river. This was deeply resented by the Macedonians, who felt that Demetrius' conduct was more arrogant than regal, and they recalled, or listened to those who recalled, how fair and impartial Philip had been in such matters. On another occasion, an elderly woman accosted him in the street and insistently asked for an audience; and when Demetrius said that he had no time, she hurled back at him: 'Then don't be king!' Stung to the quick, Demetrius returned home deep in thought and for many days afterwards he postponed all other business and made time for people who wanted an audience, starting with the old woman.

There is, after all, no aspect of a king's work that is more important than the administration of justice. Timotheus* may be right to call Ares a tyrant, but, in Pindar's words, 'Law is king of all.'* Then again, according to Homer, kings receive from Zeus, to 'uphold' and preserve, not city-takers and bronze-beaked ships, but 'his divine ordinances', and it is not the king who is best at war, or most aggressive, or most bloodthirsty, whom Homer describes as an 'intimate' or disciple of Zeus, but the one who is best at dispensing justice.* But Demetrius relished the surname he was given, even though it ran counter to the king of the gods: where Zeus is called 'Protector of Cities' or 'Guardian of Cities', Demetrius was known as Poliorcetes, 'Besieger of Cities'. In other words, he replaced something honourable with something dishonourable, the product of mindless force, and allowed his name to be linked with injustice.

[43] Anyway, Demetrius next came very close to losing Macedon, when Pyrrhus stormed in and advanced as far as Edessa while he lay critically ill in Pella. But as soon as he was on the road to recovery, he drove Pyrrhus out with considerable ease, and then entered into

a pact of sorts with him, because he did not want to be constantly clashing and jockeying for position with him, to the detriment of his main project. And this project was nothing less than the recovery of all the territory that had formed his father's empire.

The scale of his preparations was commensurate with the magnitude of his hopes and the ambitiousness of this project. He had already put together a land army of 98,000 men, with a cavalry contingent of 12,000 besides. At the same time, he was laying down keels for a fleet of 500 ships, divided among his bases at Piraeus, Corinth, Chalcis, and Pella, and he paid personal visits to each of these places, explaining what had to be done and helping with the designs of the ships.

It was not just the number of ships that were being built, but their size* that aroused universal astonishment. This was, after all, the first appearance in history of a 'fifteen' or a 'sixteen'. In later years, Ptolemy IV Philopator actually built a 'forty', which was 280 cubits long and 48 cubits high from ground to sternpost; it had a crew of 400 non-oarsmen and 4,000 oarsmen, and it also had room for almost 300 hoplites on the gangways and deck. But it was only for show, and since it hardly differed from a stationary structure on land, there was considerable danger and difficulty involved when it was in motion, and it was brought out only for display, not for use. But the beauty of Demetrius' ships did not make them less serviceable in war, and so far from being hampered by their excessive bulk, their speed and effectiveness were even more remarkable than their size.

[44] While this enormous force, larger than any since Alexander's time, was getting ready to sail for Asia, the three kings—Seleucus, Ptolemy, and Lysimachus—united against Demetrius.* Their next move was to send a joint embassy to Pyrrhus, asking him to strike at Macedon and to disregard a truce which had gained Demetrius the right to initiate war against anyone at whim, but had given Pyrrhus no guarantee that he would not come under attack. Pyrrhus was receptive to the idea, and Demetrius quickly became embroiled in major warfare. Ptolemy arrived in Greece with a sizeable fleet and tried to get the cities to rise up in rebellion against him, and at the same time Lysimachus and Pyrrhus invaded Macedon from Thrace and neighbouring Epirus respectively, and set about plundering the land.

Demetrius left Greece to his son and undertook the defence of Macedon himself. He made Lysimachus his first target, but then news arrived that Pyrrhus had taken Beroea. It did not take long for this information to reach the Macedonian troops, and it triggered a breakdown of discipline in Demetrius' camp. The only sounds to be heard were weeping and wailing, and angry curses aimed in his direction; and the men, unwilling to stay put, began to drift away—to their homes, in theory, but in reality to Lysimachus.

Demetrius therefore decided to put as much distance as possible between his men and Lysimachus, and to turn against Pyrrhus. His thinking was that Lysimachus was a Macedonian like his men, and was popular with them because of Alexander, while Pyrrhus was a foreign interloper and would not be chosen by the Macedonians over himself. But he was completely mistaken in this. The Macedonians had always admired Pyrrhus' military genius, and from time immemorial they had regarded the best soldier as the best king; moreover, at the time in question they also heard how leniently he had been treating his prisoners, and they wanted to be rid of Demetrius anyway, whether that meant going to Pyrrhus or elsewhere. So when Demetrius approached Pyrrhus' position and made camp near by, they continued to desert, at first in secret and in small numbers, but later the entire camp was openly in motion and there was complete chaos.

Eventually, some of his men found the courage to come up to Demetrius and suggest that he should leave and save himself. They told him that the Macedonians were no longer prepared to fight to support his self-indulgent lifestyle. Demetrius found what they were saying very reasonable, compared with the abuse he was receiving from every other quarter. He went into his pavilion and, as though he were an actor rather than a true king, he changed his famously flamboyant cloak for a drab one, and stole away unnoticed. Most of his men immediately fell to looting his pavilion, tearing it apart and fighting among themselves over the plunder, but then Pyrrhus appeared and took control of the camp. In fact, he occupied it without meeting any resistance. And so all Macedon was divided between him and Lysimachus, after Demetrius had held the throne securely for seven years.*

[45] So Demetrius was driven from his kingdom and found refuge in Cassandreia.* But it tormented his wife Phila to see him once again out of power and in exile; there was no king more ill-starred, she felt, and she gave up all hope. Cursing her husband's Fortune for

being constant only in times of trouble rather than when things were going well, she drank poison and died. But Demetrius made up his mind to cling to the wreckage, and he went to Greece and began to gather around himself the generals and friends he had there.

The image applied by Sophocles' Menelaus to his own misfortunes is relevant here:

> E'er whirls my fate on Fortune's wheel,
> And e'er it changes, just as the moon
> Has no power to remain the same to our sight
> For two successive nights. First she emerges
> New born out of darkness, her face
> Growing more fair as she expands.
> But just as she attains the peak of her splendour
> She begins once more to waste away to nothing.*

This image could be applied even more aptly to Demetrius' fortunes as they waxed and waned, expanded and collapsed. Just at the moment when he seemed to have been completely eclipsed and extinguished, his power shone forth again, and expanding resources restored his hopes once more.

This was also the first time he had visited the cities of Greece as an ordinary citizen, stripped of all the trappings of royalty, and someone who saw him like this in Thebes rather neatly referred the following lines of Euripides to him:

> Having exchanged his divine form for that of a mortal,
> He is here, by Dirce's waters and Ismenus' streams.*

[46] As soon as he had embarked upon the royal road of hope and had once again gathered together the materials and paraphernalia of royalty, he gave the Thebans back the right of self-government. The Athenians revolted, however. They erased the name of Diphilus from the list of those who give their name to the year, where it had been inscribed as the Priest of the Saviours, and voted to return to the traditional practice of choosing archons.* And when they realized that Demetrius was stronger than they had expected, they asked Pyrrhus to send help from Macedon.

Demetrius attacked them in a rage and put the city under a close siege, but the Athenians sent the philosopher Crates, a well-known intellectual, to negotiate with him.* Partly thanks to Crates' persuasiveness in presenting the Athenians' pleas, and partly because of thoughts triggered by Crates' clarification of where his best interests lay, Demetrius raised the siege, gathered all the ships he had, put on board a force of 11,000 foot and his cavalry, and sailed for Asia, where he intended to get Caria and Lydia to secede from Lysimachus. At Miletus he was welcomed by Phila's sister Eurydice, who was accompanied by Ptolemais, one of her daughters by Ptolemy, whose betrothal to Demetrius had earlier been arranged by Seleucus. Demetrius now married her, with Eurydice giving her away.*

Straight after the wedding Demetrius turned his attention to the Greek cities. Many of them attached themselves voluntarily to his cause, but many others were forced into submission. He also took Sardis, and a few of Lysimachus' generals deserted over to his side, bringing money and men with them. But when Lysimachus' son Agathocles advanced against him with an army, Demetrius marched up from the coast to Phrygia. His plan was to seize Armenia, if he could, and then stir up rebellion in Media and gain control of the eastern provinces, where a displaced king could find plenty of places to hole up and hide out.

Agathocles followed him, however, and although Demetrius had the advantage in their engagements, he found himself in difficulties because his supply lines had been cut and his soldiers were prevented from foraging. His men also suspected that he was taking them off to Armenia and Media. Then, at one and the same time, the food shortage got worse, and during a botched crossing of the Lycus river a large number of soldiers were whisked away by the current and lost their lives. But the men retained their sense of humour, and one wag posted in front of Demetrius' pavilion the first words of *Oedipus at Colonus*, slightly altered:

> O child of aged, blind Antigonus, what lands are these
> To which we've come?*

[47] In the end, however, hunger was compounded by disease, as is inevitable when men are on emergency rations, and, after losing 8,000 men in all, Demetrius began to retrace his steps with the remainder. When he reached Tarsus, he wanted to leave the farmland there unscathed, because it formed part of Seleucus' realm at the time and he had no desire to antagonize him. But this proved

impossible, because his men were by then completely desperate, and Agathocles had fortified the passes of the Taurus mountains against his return. So Demetrius wrote to Seleucus, pouring out a torrent of bitter complaints about his bad luck, and begging and imploring him at length to have pity on a man who was a relative, and whose suffering deserved sympathy even from his enemies.

For some reason Seleucus was moved by the letter, and he wrote to his regional generals there, ordering them to maintain Demetrius himself in a manner befitting a king, and to supply his troops with ample provisions. But then Seleucus was approached by Patrocles,* a trusted Friend with a reputation for shrewdness, who said that although the expense of maintaining Demetrius' army was not very great, he should still not allow him to linger there. Time and again, he argued, Demetrius had proved himself to be the most aggressive and daring of the kings, and his circumstances at that moment in time were of the kind that might induce even less violent men to throw caution to the winds and go on the rampage.

Patrocles' advice roused Seleucus to action, and he set out for Cilicia at the head of a large army. Demetrius, dismayed and frightened by Seleucus' sudden change of heart, pulled back to a part of the Taurus range that was particularly easy to defend. He then contacted Seleucus, asking for permission to carve out for himself a kingdom among the unconquered barbarians, where he could end his unsettled, refugee existence and live out the rest of his life. If Seleucus could not do that for him, he asked him at least to continue to maintain his troops where they were for the winter, and not to drive him out, destitute and naked, into the hands of his enemies.

[48] Seleucus found the whole thing highly suspect, but told him that he could, if he liked, winter for two months in Cataonia, provided that he handed over his foremost Friends as hostages. At the same time, he began to fortify the passes into Syria against him. Demetrius was now surrounded on all sides, cornered like a wild beast, and felt he had no choice but to fight back. He raided the countryside, and every time Seleucus attacked him, Demetrius came off best in the engagement. On one occasion Seleucus launched his scythed chariots against him, but Demetrius stood his ground, routed Seleucus' troops, and then drove away the men who were fortifying the passes into Syria and took them over himself.

Demetrius was now in a state of feverish excitement and, seeing that his men's morale was once again riding high, he began to prepare for the final contest with Seleucus. The Syrian king found himself in a bind: he had refused an offer of help from Lysimachus, whom he mistrusted and feared, but he was reluctant to engage Demetrius on his own, since he was worried about the man's reckless determination and his luck, which always converted certain disaster into stunning success. But meanwhile Demetrius had been stricken by a serious illness, which was not only physically debilitating but also brought about his final downfall, as some of his men deserted to the enemy and others drifted away. It took forty days, and even then he had scarcely recovered, but he set out with his remaining soldiers for Cilicia, as far as his opponents could tell or guess. But then, in the middle of the night, without any signal being given, he set out in the opposite direction, crossed the Amanus mountains, and plundered the plain all the way up to Cyrrhestica.*

[49] Seleucus arrived and took up quarters near by, but one night Demetrius aroused his men and marched against him. Seleucus was asleep and remained in ignorance for a long time, until some deserters came and warned him of the danger. He leapt in terror from his bed and ordered the alarm to be sounded, while simultaneously pulling on his boots and calling out to his Companions that they had locked horns with a ferocious beast.

The hubbub in the enemy camp alerted Demetrius to the fact that he had lost the element of surprise, and he beat a hasty retreat. Seleucus counter-attacked at dawn. Demetrius entrusted the left wing to one of his Friends and routed the enemy troops facing him, but then Seleucus dismounted, removed his helmet, and advanced towards Demetrius' mercenaries, armed only with a light shield. As he walked forward, he showed them who he was and urged them to change sides. They had been aware for a while, he said, that his constant aim for all these months had been to spare them, not Demetrius. At this, they hailed and acclaimed him king, and deserted *en masse* over to his side.

Demetrius, realizing that he would now meet with no more changes of fortune, disengaged and fled towards the Amanus pass, where he plunged into a dense wood with some of his Friends and attendants, not many in all, and waited for nightfall. His plan was to see if he could take the Caunus road and break through to the coast there,* where he expected to find his fleet at anchor. But then it was brought to his attention that they did not have enough provisions even for that day, and he began to ponder alternatives. At this juncture, however, one of his companions, Sosigenes, turned up with 400 gold pieces in his belt and, hoping that this would help them reach the coast, they set out under cover of darkness towards the pass. But the sight of enemy campfires there forced them to give up on that route, and they pulled back to where they had been before. It was a diminished band, however, since some had run away, and those who remained were less resolute than before. One of them summoned up his courage and suggested that Demetrius should surrender himself to Seleucus. At this, Demetrius drew his sword and threatened to kill himself, but his Friends gathered round, calmed him down, and persuaded him to do as the man had suggested. So Demetrius sent a messenger to Seleucus, telling him that he was putting himself in his hands.

[50] On receiving Demetrius' message, Seleucus remarked that Demetrius owed his life not to his own Fortune, but to *his* Fortune, which had already blessed him in so many ways and was now presenting him with the opportunity for a display of mercy and decency. He summoned his quartermasters and told them to put up a pavilion fit for a king, and to do all they could to prepare a grand reception for Demetrius and to take care of his needs on a munificent scale. There was a man called Apollonides in Seleucus' camp who had been close to Demetrius, and Seleucus immediately sent him off to put Demetrius at his ease and reassure him that in him he would be meeting a man who was a friend and a relative. Once Seleucus' attitude was common knowledge, his Friends—a few at first, but then most of them—sped off to Demetrius, vying with one another to get there first, in the belief that Demetrius would very soon occupy a very prominent position in Seleucus' court.

This not only soured Seleucus' pity, however, but it also gave malign and malevolent individuals the opportunity to deflect and destroy his kindness. What they did was convince him that there was a real danger that, as soon as the man appeared, serious mutinies would break out in the camp. So, not long after Apollonides had reached Demetrius, beaming his pleasure, and while the rest of the visitors were arriving with amazing tales of Seleucus' intentions, and when Demetrius had at last changed his mind, following his terrible misfortune and defeat, and no longer saw surrender as shameful, as he had before, because of his new optimism and confidence for the future—just then Pausanias turned up with a mixed force of 1,000 infantry and cavalry. Without warning, he had his men surround Demetrius and isolate him from everyone else, and then, without giving him even a glimpse of Seleucus, he took him off to the Syrian Chersonese.*

From then on he had a strong guard set over him there, but Seleucus kept him supplied with enough creature comforts and money, flawless food was prepared for him every day, and the royal rides, walks, and parks stocked with game were placed at his disposal. Moreover, any of his friends who had joined him in exile was allowed to spend time with him, and despite his situation a few people used to come for a visit from Seleucus' court, conveying the king's best wishes and encouraging him to look forward confidently to his release the moment Antiochus arrived with Stratonice.*

[51] Under these circumstances, Demetrius wrote to his son, and to his officers and friends in Athens and Corinth, telling them not to trust any letters or documents bearing his seal, and entrusting his affairs in general and the cities to Antigonus' care. When Antigonus heard of his father's capture, he was very upset and dressed as though he were mourning his death. He wrote letters to all the other kings, and to Seleucus himself, begging for mercy and offering to surrender all that was left of his and his father's possessions. Above all, he offered himself as a hostage for his father. Many cities and dynasts supported his petition, but not Lysimachus, who even promised Seleucus a large amount of money if he killed Demetrius.* But Seleucus was wary of Lysimachus anyway, so this just made him even more inclined to regard him as a savage barbarian, and he kept Demetrius in custody, awaiting the pleasure of his son Antiochus and Stratonice.

[52] At first Demetrius endured his lot and acquired habits that made his situation more bearable. Early on in his captivity he found ways to exercise, by taking advantage of what possibilities there were for hunting or riding, but later he gradually developed a distaste for these activities and lost all interest in them. He devoted himself instead to drink and dice, and that was how he spent most of his time. Perhaps he was trying to escape the reflections that occurred about his situation when he was sober, drowning thought in drunkenness; or perhaps he had come to realize that this was the life he had

always basically wanted and sought, and that he had been led astray by folly and vainglory, and had made a great deal of trouble for both himself and others by trying to find in weaponry, fleets, and armies the good which he had now unexpectedly found in idleness, leisure, and relaxation. After all, what other goal do bad kings have in mind when they undertake wars and run risks? They are so corrupt and stupid that they not only make self-indulgent pleasure their object instead of virtue and goodness, but do not even know what really gives them pleasure or how to indulge themselves.

After three years in custody in the Chersonese, Demetrius succumbed to sickness (brought on by inactivity, overeating, and wine) and died. He was fifty-four years old. Seleucus came in for some criticism, and he bitterly regretted having been so suspicious of Demetrius at the time. He wished that instead he had behaved like Dromichaetes, a barbarian from Thrace who had treated Lysimachus with regal generosity after his capture.*

[53] Even Demetrius' burial had a dramatic and theatrical aspect. When Antigonus heard that his father's remains were on their way home, he put to sea with his entire fleet and sailed for the islands to meet them. The jar, which was of beaten gold, was handed over, and he placed it in his largest flagship. On his way back, wherever he made land, the cities wreathed the jar with garlands and sent men, dressed for mourning, to represent them at the funeral and to escort the ashes home. As the fleet sailed into Corinth, the urn, decorated with royal purple cloth and a diadem, was clearly visible in a prominent position on the prow, with an honour guard of young men standing by it. Moreover, the most famous pipe-player of the day, Xenophantus,* sat near by playing the most solemn of tunes; and as the rowers took their timing from him, the plashing of the oars corresponded with the phrasing of the music.

But it was Antigonus himself who stirred the most pity and sorrow in the spectators crowding the shoreline, when they saw how he grieved and wept. After the urn had been draped with ribbons and wreaths at Corinth, Antigonus took the remains to Demetrias* for burial—to the city named after his father and formed by the synoecism of small villages in the region of Iolcus.

The family Demetrius left behind were: two children by Phila, Antigonus and Stratonice; two sons called Demetrius—one of them, Demetrius the Thin, by an Illyrian woman and the other, who came to rule Cyrene, by Ptolemais; and Alexander, who lived all his life in Egypt, by Deidameia. He is also said to have had a son called Corrhagus by Eurydice. His descendants ruled Macedon by continuous succession until the line ended with Perseus, during whose reign the Romans conquered Macedon.*

But now that the Macedonian drama is over, it is time to bring on its Roman counterpart.*

PYRRHUS

INTRODUCTION

Pyrrhus (319–272 BCE) was king of the Molossians, the most powerful of the tribes of Epirus, a region in north-western Greece bordering on Macedon. He is best known as the first Hellenistic monarch to confront the Romans in battle, but his reputation in antiquity went well beyond this. Hannibal, in conversation with Scipio Africanus, was said to have named Pyrrhus among the greatest generals of all time, usually as second to Alexander, although in this Life he holds first place. During the fourth century Epirote affairs, and the monarchy in particular, had repeatedly been subject to Macedonian intervention. It was for this reason that Pyrrhus was brought up in exile after the overthrow of his father Aeacides when he was little more than a baby. He occupied the throne briefly between the ages of twelve and seventeen, at which point he was expelled. Joining his brother-in-law Demetrius Poliorcetes, he fought at the battle of Ipsus in 301 and then spent several years as a hostage at the court of Ptolemy I in Egypt. Here he so impressed the king and his wife that he not only acquired a royal bride, he also obtained support for a successful attempt to reclaim his throne. Back in power, he did much to strengthen Epirus and expand its territories, even for a while taking possession of part of Macedon.

In 281, however, he accepted the invitation of Tarentum, a Greek city in southern Italy, to help them against the growing power of Rome, an invitation that led to some six years campaigning in the West. He twice defeated the Romans in battle, at Heraclea in 280 and at Asculum the following year, but his losses were heavy and he was faced with an enemy that appeared to have no difficulty calling up fresh troops from its allies. He was reputed to have said, 'One more victory like that over the Romans and we shall be completely undone' (21), hence the phrase 'a Pyrrhic victory'. Shortly after Asculum he crossed the straits to Sicily to assist the Syracusans in their campaign to drive the Carthaginians from the island. After initial successes, he fell out with his allies and abandoned Sicily for southern Italy, where in 275 he was defeated by the Romans at Malventum (later given the more auspicious name Beneventum). In the end his western campaigns achieved little. Returning to Greece, he won and lost the Macedonian throne in a matter of months before turning south and campaigning in the Peloponnese, where he was killed in a misjudged attempt to seize Argos.

Although Pyrrhus is often considered together with the other early Hellenistic kings, he differed from them in important ways. They or their fathers were Macedonians who had campaigned with Alexander, and only took the title of king for themselves later while laying claim to part of his territory. Pyrrhus, on the other hand, was born after Alexander's death and was a member of the Epirote royal family. As a result, his approach to international relations differs from those who were fighting among themselves for a share of Alexander's empire. Instead, he views the world from a more traditional Epirote perspective: holding back Macedon and keeping an eye on events in the West. Crossing to Italy would have been a radical step for other kings of the period, constrained as they were by what Alexander had done, but for Pyrrhus it was almost what was expected of him. His great-uncle Alexander the Molossian had himself gone west to help the Tarentines in 334 (on that occasion against Lucanians). Nonetheless, Pyrrhus was at the same time very much part of the complex network that tied together the emerging Hellenistic dynasties: his great aunt was Olympias, mother of Alexander; his sister Deidameia married Demetrius Poliorcetes; and he himself, during his time at the Ptolemaic court, married Ptolemy I's stepdaughter Antigone (see the family tree).

Plutarch's Pyrrhus is a man who is restless, easily bored, and ever ready to take on new projects, the more grandiose the better. There are echoes of his ancestor Achilles and of Alexander in his depiction, but despite being an immensely talented military commander, he never lives up to his potential. His Life, far from offering a series of great achievements, is a succession of abandoned ventures and wasted campaigns, whether in Macedon, Italy, or Sicily. Pyrrhus made no attempt to consolidate what he had gained; instead, greed, the desire for more, drove him on to seek further conquests regardless of the damage he caused to others (see especially chapters 26 and 30). This is expanded on in a dialogue between Pyrrhus and his adviser Cineas, presented in the manner of the familiar model of a wise man talking to a ruler. Here Pyrrhus' obsession with constant warfare and conquest is challenged. Cineas asks him what he will do after his next conquest, and the answer is always to pursue yet another conquest, first Italy, then Sicily, then North Africa. But what, says Cineas, would they do when it was all over? When Pyrrhus replies that they could then spend their time drinking and conversing, Cineas points out to him they could do that now if they chose to (14).

Plutarch sees this greed and the incessant warfare that resulted as a key feature of Hellenistic monarchy (7, 9, and 12), just as in the Life of Demetrius he sees theatricality as another important feature. Thus, even though these two men may not have been the two most significant kings of the period, he is able to use their Lives to explore the character of Hellenistic kingship more broadly. That Plutarch was pondering similar problems in the two Lives is evident in the way they overlap, most obviously in chapter 12, which contains almost the same words as *Demetrius* 41, albeit with the order reversed and applied to Pyrrhus rather than Demetrius: 'He had found that the Macedonians were better behaved out on campaign than when they had time on their hands, and, in any case, he was constitutionally incapable of inactivity.' Furthermore, both Lives draw attention to the role of Alexander as a model for his Successors, but, in contrast to the other kings who merely put on a show of being like Alexander, Pyrrhus recaptured the spirit of the great Macedonian (*Pyrrhus* 8, *Demetrius* 41). In both Lives, too, Plutarch reflects on the purpose of war and questions the motives of the perpetrators; Cineas' challenge to Pyrrhus can be taken together with Plutarch's own strongly worded criticism of Demetrius at the conclusion of the latter's Life (*Demetrius* 52).

The fragmented nature of Pyrrhus' career would suggest that Plutarch made use of several sources to build up his account. He cites a number of writers during the course of the Life, usually on specific points where two authorities disagree. Thus he reports the contrasting casualty figures for the battle of Heraclea given by the contemporary historian Hieronymus of Cardia and the Augustan Dionysius of Halicarnassus (17), and the disagreement between Hieronymus and Phylarchus on the size of a trench dug to protect Sparta (27; for Phylarchus, see the introduction to *Agis and Cleomenes*). At other times he reveals that his sources disagree, but he does not tell the reader who they were (3 and 4). Hieronymus is likely to have been an important source, just as he surely was in the Lives of Eumenes and Demetrius (see further the introduction to *Eumenes*). There may, however, have been others who were used by Plutarch but not cited, such as the third-century historian Timaeus of Tauromenium, who is known to have written on Pyrrhus' activities in the West. Plutarch also mentions Pyrrhus' own military treatises, but it is not clear whether he had read them (8).

Pyrrhus' counterpart in the *Parallel Lives* is the Roman general Gaius Marius, but, unusually, there is no prologue or concluding comparison to guide the reader. Marius was one of the most successful of Rome's military commanders, victorious over Jugurtha in North Africa and the invading Cimbri and Teutones in Northern Italy in the closing years of the second century BCE. He shared with Pyrrhus a passion for warfare and conquest, but what especially united the two men in Plutarch's mind was their desire to pursue this even at the expense of their own happiness. After the conversation with Cineas, Pyrrhus 'could see the great happiness he was leaving behind, but he could not give up his dreams for the future' (14). Marius is rather less self-aware. In spite of living for seventy years, holding an unprecedented seven consulships, and being enormously wealthy, he 'still lamented his fate and felt that he was dying without having attained and achieved all that he desired' (*Marius* 45). Cineas' arguments were as relevant to Marius as they were to Pyrrhus.

Pyrrhus is paralleled with a Roman in a quite different way from most of the other Greeks who appear in the Lives. With Pyrrhus, the parallel lives converge as the king becomes the first of Plutarch's subjects to meet a Roman. His first impressions are, therefore, very important. Watching the Roman camp from a distance, he is struck by its orderliness, and he says to one of his associates, 'Megacles, there's nothing barbarian about these barbarians' discipline' (16). This observation is reinforced by the chapters that follow (17–21), which are as much about the nature and character of the Romans as they are about Pyrrhus. Appius Claudius and Fabricius, in particular, stand out as virtuous, honourable men, defying Pyrrhus' attempts to win them over, in marked contrast to the later Romans of the Life of Marius. Plutarch may call the barbarianness of the Romans into question, but he also queries the Greekness of the Molossians. It is surely no coincidence that the opening chapter of the Life draws attention to the barbarian background of the Molossian kings themselves before they adopted Greek customs and language.

Buszard, B., 'The Decline of Roman Statesmanship in Plutarch's *Pyrrhus-Marius*', *Classical Quarterly*, 55 (2005), 481–97.

—— 'Caesar's Ambition: A Combined Reading of Plutarch's *Alexander-Caesar* and *Pyrrhus-Marius*', *Transactions of the American Philological Association*, 138 (2008), 185–215.

Davies, J. K., 'A Wholly Non-Aristotelian Universe: The Molossians as Ethnos, State and Monarchy', in R. Brock and S. Hodkinson (eds.), *Alternatives to Athens: Varieties of Political Organization and Community in Ancient Greece* (Oxford, 2000), 234–58.

Duff, T. E., *Plutarch's Lives: Exploring Virtue and Vice* (Oxford, 1999), ch. 4.

Edwards, J., 'Plutarch and the Death of Pyrrhus: Disambiguating the Conflicting Accounts', *Scholia*, 20 (2011), 112–31.

Franke, P. R., 'Pyrrhus', in F. W. Walbank *et al.* (eds.), *The Cambridge Ancient History*, 7.2: *The Rise of Rome to 220 BC* (2nd edn., Cambridge, 1989), 456–85.

Garouphalias, P., *Pyrrhus: King of Epirus* (London, 1979).

Hackens, T., *et al.* (eds.), *The Age of Pyrrhus: Papers Delivered at the International Conference: Brown University, 8–10 April 1988* (Louvain-la-Neuve, 1992).

Hammond, N. G. L., *Epirus: The Geography, the Ancient Remains, the History and Topography of Epirus and Adjacent Areas* (Oxford, 1967).

Lévêque, P., *Pyrrhos* (Paris, 1957).

Mossman, J. M., 'Plutarch, Pyrrhus, and Alexander', in P. Stadter (ed.), *Plutarch and the Historical Tradition* (London, 1992), 90–108.

—— '*Taxis ou Barbaros*: Greek and Roman in Plutarch's *Pyrrhus*', *Classical Quarterly*, 55 (2005), 498–517.

Schepens, G., 'Plutarch's View of Ancient Rome: Some Remarks on the Life of Pyrrhus', in L. Mooren (ed.), *Politics, Administration and Society in the Hellenistic and Roman World* (Leuven, 2000), 349–64.

—— 'Rhetoric in Plutarch's *Life of Pyrrhus*', in L. Van der Stockt (ed.), *Rhetorical Theory and Praxis in Plutarch* (Leuven, 2000), 413–41.

Zambon, E., *Tradition and Innovation: Sicily between Hellenism and Rome* (Stuttgart, 2008).

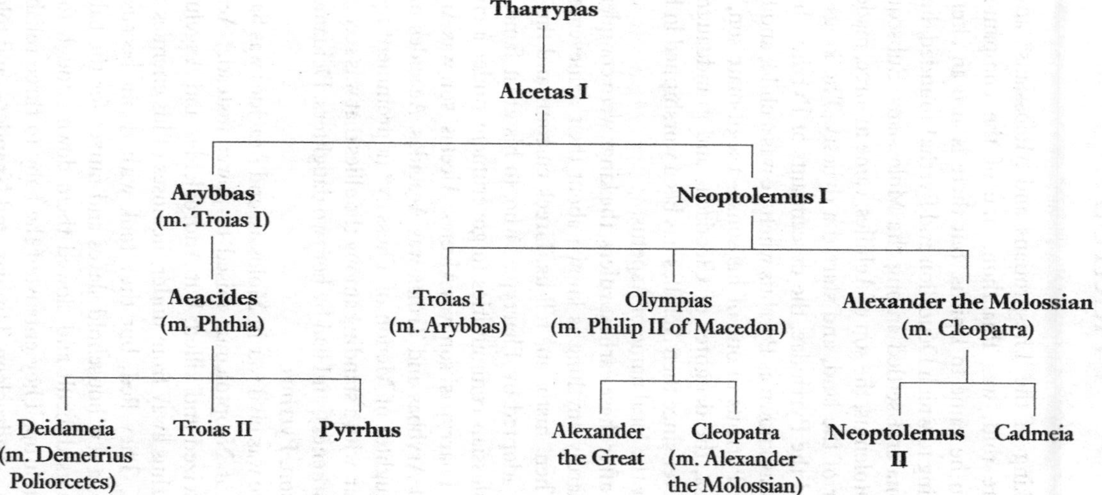

PYRRHUS AND THE AEACID FAMILY TREE

PYRRHUS

[1] The first king of the Thesprotians and Molossians* after the Deluge, we are told, was Phaethon, one of the companions of Pelasgus* when he came to Epirus, but there is also an alternative version according to which Deucalion and Pyrrha* founded the sanctuary at Dodona and settled among the Molossians. Subsequently, however, Neoptolemus, the son of Achilles, came in force, made himself the master of the land, and started a dynasty. The kings of his line were called the Pyrrhidae, the descendants of Pyrrhus, because Neoptolemus was known as Pyrrhus when he was a child, and he also gave the name Pyrrhus to one of his sons—a legitimate son, borne him by Lanassa, the daughter of Cleodaeus and granddaughter of Hyllus.* And ever since then Achilles has been worshipped in Epirus as a god, under the local name of Aspetus.

For a while, after these earliest rulers, the kings were complete barbarians, and hardly anything is known about their achievements or their reigns. Then, historians tell us, Greek customs and the Greek language were adopted by Tharrypas, who, to his great fame, introduced the Molossian communities to government under a civilized code of laws.* Tharrypas' son was Alcetas; Alcetas' son was Arybbas; and the son of Arybbas and Troias was Aeacides. Aeacides married Phthia, the daughter of Menon of Thessaly* (a prominent figure in the Lamian War, with a standing among the allies that was second only to that of Leosthenes), and had by her two daughters, Deidameia and Troias, and a son, Pyrrhus.

[2] But there was civil war in Molossis, and Aeacides was banished and the sons of Neoptolemus raised to power instead.* Aeacides' friends were seized and killed, but Androcleides and Angelus stole the infant Pyrrhus away from under the noses of his enemies as they came for him. They fled, but they took with them, because they had no choice, a few household slaves and nurses for the baby, and this made things difficult and slowed them down enough for their enemies to catch up. They entrusted the baby to three reliable and fit young men—Androcleon, Hippias, and Neander—and told them to fly at full speed and make for the village of Megara in Macedon. Meanwhile they held up their pursuers, first by pleading with them

and then by fighting them off, until late in the afternoon. Then, having finally beaten them off, they raced after the men who had Pyrrhus.

The sun had already set and they were nearing their destination when they suddenly found themselves thwarted. The river that flows by the town, when they came up to it, had a wild and savage appearance, and proved to be completely uncrossable. It was in spate, its waters swollen by rainfall, and the gloom made everything more hazardous. They realized that there was no way they could cross it on their own, burdened as they were with the baby and the women who were looking after him. But then they spotted some of the local inhabitants standing on the far bank of the river, and decided to ask for their help in making the crossing. They held up Pyrrhus for them to see, and shouted out pleas for help, but the rumbling and roaring of the river drowned them out.

There was a pause, with one lot shouting and the others failing to understand, but then someone had a good idea. He tore a strip of bark from an oak tree and scratched a message with a brooch explaining what they wanted and the child's situation. Then he wrapped the bark around a stone, to weight it for its flight, and threw it across—though some say that he fixed the bark around a javelin and hurled it across. When the people on the other side read the message and realized how critical things were, they cut logs, lashed them together, and set out across the river. And, as chance would have it, the first of them to make land and take Pyrrhus in his arms was called Achilles. The rest of the Molossians were helped across by various of the others.

[3] So they outstripped their pursuers and reached safety. From Megara they made their way to Illyris, to the court of King Glaucias,* and, finding him at home with his wife, they put the baby down on the floor between them. This gave Glaucias food for thought, since he was afraid of Cassander, who was an enemy of Aeacides. He sat in silence for a while, trying to decide what to do, and while he was doing so Pyrrhus crawled over, without any prompting, and pulled himself upright at his knees by grasping his robe. The king laughed at first, but then felt sorry for the boy, who seemed to be clinging to him† and weeping, for all the world as though he were a suppliant. But some historians do not have Pyrrhus supplicating Glaucias; they say it was an altar the baby grabbed hold of, and that Glaucias took it to be a sign from heaven that the child stood hugging the altar. He immediately handed Pyrrhus over to his wife, telling her to bring the

boy up as one of their own children, and then, a little later, refused to give the child up to his enemies when they demanded his return, even when Cassander offered him 200 talents. And when the boy was twelve years old, Glaucias used his army to restore him to Epirus and set him on the throne.*

Pyrrhus' features were more stern than majestic. He was short of teeth, in the sense that his upper jaw was one continuous bone, with faint creases marking where the gaps should have been. He was supposed to be able to help people with enlarged spleens. He would sacrifice a white cock, and then, with the patient lying flat on his back, press steadily down on the internal organs with his right foot. He refused no one this treatment, however poor or humble, and the gift of the cock he had sacrificed pleased him more than any other token of gratitude. It is said that the divine power of his right big toe* was proved after his death: the rest of his body was burnt up by the flames of the pyre, but the toe was found in pristine condition, untouched. But I have got ahead of myself.

[4] When he was about seventeen years old,* and seemed to be securely established on the throne, he happened to make a journey abroad for the wedding of one of Glaucias' sons—one of his foster-brothers. But the Molossians conspired against him, banished his friends, stole his property, and put themselves in Neoptolemus' hands.* With his throne lost, and nothing in the world to call his own, Pyrrhus attached himself to Demetrius, the son of Antigonus, who was married to his sister Deidameia. She had been promised, while still young, to Rhoxane's son Alexander, but that was not destined to happen, and when she reached a marriageable age Demetrius took her as his wife.*

Despite his youth, Pyrrhus took part, on Demetrius' side, in the great battle fought by all the kings at Ipsus,* where he routed his opponents and fought with distinction. Even after Demetrius' defeat, he did not abandon him: he looked after the cities in Greece which had been left in his care,* and after Demetrius came to terms with Ptolemy, Pyrrhus went to Egypt as a hostage.* When he was out hunting or in the gymnasium, he made sure Ptolemy noticed how valiant and brave he was, and, since Berenice* was clearly the most influential of Ptolemy's wives, as well as being the most honest and intelligent of them, he did his best to win her favour. He was very good at charming his superiors and profiting from it, and so it was he who was chosen, out of many eminent young suitors, to marry Antigone, a daughter of Berenice's by Philip, who was her husband before her marriage to Ptolemy.

[5] With his standing even higher as a result of this marriage, and since Antigone was a good wife to him, he arranged to be given money and an army, and to be sent to Epirus to recover the throne.* Most of the Epirotes welcomed him back, since they loathed Neoptolemus for the oppressive brutality of his regime, but Pyrrhus did not want to drive Neoptolemus into the arms of one of the other kings, so he made peace with him and settled their differences, on the understanding that they would share power. As time went on, however, people subtly set them against each other and sowed the seeds of mutual suspicion. But the affair that stirred Pyrrhus to decisive action is said to have gone like this.

Passaron, a Molossian town, is the location for a ritual in which the kings sacrifice to Zeus Areius and then exchange oaths with their people; the kings swear to uphold the laws as rulers, and the people swear to uphold the laws as defenders of the kingdom. So both kings were present for this procedure. They and their respective Friends spent time with one another, and plenty of gifts were given and received. In the course of the gift-giving, Gelon, a member of Neoptolemus' inner circle, took Pyrrhus warmly by the right hand and made him a present of two teams of plough oxen. Pyrrhus' cup-bearer, a man called Myrtilus, asked for the oxen, but Pyrrhus said no and gave them to someone else. Gelon noticed Myrtilus' disgruntlement and invited the cup-bearer to dinner—where, according to some writers, he drunkenly had his way with the beautiful boy. Then he tried to persuade him to throw in his lot with Neoptolemus and poison Pyrrhus. Myrtilus listened to his arguments, and pretended to approve and find them persuasive, but he went and informed Pyrrhus. On Pyrrhus' orders, Myrtilus also arranged a meeting between Gelon and Pyrrhus' senior cup-bearer, Alexicrates, to get him involved as well, because Pyrrhus wanted more than one witness to vouch for the crime.

Gelon had no inkling of the trap, and neither did Neoptolemus. In fact, thinking that the plot was well under way, Neoptolemus was unable to keep it to himself, but used to talk openly and gleefully about it to his Friends. Once, having drunk deep at his sister Cadmeia's house, he let his tongue run away with him. He thought that he could not be overheard, because there was no one near except for Phaenarete, the wife of Samon, the manager of Neoptolemus' flocks and herds, and she was lying on a couch with her face turned to the wall, apparently asleep. But, unknown to him, she heard everything and the next day she went to Antigone, Pyrrhus' wife, and recounted everything she had heard Neoptolemus telling his sister.

Pyrrhus did nothing there and then in response to this information, but he picked a day of sacrifice, invited Neoptolemus over, and killed him at dinner. He knew that the leading men of Epirus were on his side and had been encouraging him to get rid of Neoptolemus. They did not want him to be content with just a small portion of the kingdom, but to follow his natural bent and take on larger projects. At the same time, he also suspected that he was doing away with Neoptolemus before Neoptolemus could do away with him.

[6] To commemorate Berenice and Ptolemy, when Antigone gave birth to a baby boy he named him Ptolemy, and Berenicis was the name he gave a city he founded on the Epirote Chersonese. After this, although he had plenty of grandiose projects in mind, he pinned his hopes first and foremost on matters near at hand, and found an excuse to get involved in Macedonian affairs. This is what happened.

When Cassander's eldest son Antipater killed his mother Thessalonice and banished his brother Alexander, Alexander asked for help from Demetrius, but also invited Pyrrhus to come.* Demetrius was too busy to appear straight away, and when Pyrrhus came he demanded, as the price of his aid, that he be given both Stymphaea and Parauaea from Macedon, and from more recently acquired territories Ambracia, Acarnania, and Amphilochia.* The young man acceded to these demands. Pyrrhus took possession of these places, secured them with garrisons, and then set about plundering Antipater as a way of gaining the rest of Macedon for Alexander.

King Lysimachus* was otherwise engaged, but anxious to help Antipater. Knowing that the last thing Pyrrhus wanted to do was displease Ptolemy or deny him anything, he sent Pyrrhus a forged letter, purporting to be from Ptolemy and ordering him to accept an offer of 300 talents from Antipater and bring his campaign to an end. As soon as Pyrrhus opened the letter, however, he realized that this was a trick by Lysimachus, because instead of Ptolemy's usual way of addressing him—'From father to son, greetings'—the letter read: 'From King Ptolemy to King Pyrrhus, greetings'. Pyrrhus railed at Lysimachus, but went ahead with making peace, and they met to swear their oaths over sacrificial victims. A bull, a boar, and a ram were brought up to the altar, but the ram dropped down dead of its own accord. Everyone else found this merely amusing, but the seer Theodotus told Pyrrhus not to swear the oath, since the gods, he claimed, were indicating that one of the three kings would die. So Pyrrhus withdrew from the peace treaty.

[7] Alexander's problems had already been resolved, but it was too late to stop Demetrius. As soon as he arrived, however, he realized that Alexander no longer needed him and was frightened of him, and after only a few days together their mutual distrust led them to plot against each other's lives. It was Demetrius who seized his chance and struck first; he killed the boy and was proclaimed king of Macedon.*

On top of the facts that Demetrius already held a grudge against Pyrrhus and that Pyrrhus had been conducting raids in Thessaly, greed, the innate disease of dynasties, combined with the fact that they were neighbours, made for a potentially explosive situation, and the tension got even worse after Deidameia's death.* Now that both of them occupied Macedonia, they were thrown together and there were more frequent pretexts for hostility. So Demetrius first attacked the Aetolians, and after defeating them in battle, he left Pantauchus there with a good-sized army and marched against Pyrrhus. As soon as Pyrrhus found out, he set out to confront Demetrius as well, but they mistook their routes and bypassed each other. Demetrius went on to invade and plunder Epirus, but Pyrrhus came up against Pantauchus and brought him to battle.* The two sides engaged and the fighting was fierce, especially in the part of the field where the generals were.

Pantauchus was acknowledged to be the best of Demetrius' generals—the bravest, the most competent, and physically the fittest—and, bold and self-assured, he challenged Pyrrhus to single combat; and Pyrrhus, the most daring and valiant of the kings, in his determination to show the world that the glorious name of Achilles* belonged to him for his prowess, not just by heredity, advanced through the front ranks to confront him. After the initial hurling of spears, they drew their swords and fought at close quarters with skill and aggression. Pyrrhus, wounded once himself, wounded his opponent twice—on the thigh and the neck—and Pantauchus turned and ran. Pyrrhus brought him down, but Pantauchus was snatched away by his friends before Pyrrhus could finish him off. Fired up by their king's victory and filled with admiration for his courage, the Epirotes overwhelmed the Macedonian phalanx and cut it to pieces. Many Macedonians were killed by their pursuers as they fled, and 5,000 were taken alive.

[8] So far from filling the Macedonians with anger or hostility towards Pyrrhus for their defeat, this battle made those who had fought against him and witnessed what he had done think all the more highly of him. They admired his prowess, and his reputation grew. In fact, they used to compare his looks, his briskness, and his gestures to those of Alexander the Great, and they imagined that in him they could see the contours, so to speak, and traces of Alexander's fervour and forcefulness in battle. The other kings, they felt, reflected Alexander with their purple robes and honour-guards, and in the way they inclined their heads* and spoke in a lofty tone of voice, but the only one who displayed anything of his genius with weaponry and troops was Pyrrhus.

One can find evidence of Pyrrhus' tactical and strategic expertise in the military treatises he wrote.* It is also said that when Antigonus was asked who was the best general, he replied: 'Pyrrhus, if he makes old age.' Antigonus was commenting only on his contemporaries, but Hannibal (as mentioned in my Life of Scipio)* thought that Pyrrhus' experience and skill made him the best general ever, with Scipio second and himself third. In short, Pyrrhus seems to have been a lifelong student and scholar of military science, on the grounds that there is no subject more worthy of a king's attention. Everything else he seems to have counted as irrelevant, no more than garnishing. We hear, for instance, that once at a party he was asked whether he thought Python or Caphisias better on the pipes, and he replied that Polyperchon* was a good general, as though warfare were the only thing a king should look into or know anything about.

He treated his friends fairly and equably, but he was very dogged and determined when it came to repaying favours. At any rate, when Aeropus died, he took it badly. 'Death was inevitable for Aeropus as it is for all of us,' he said, 'but it was wrong of me to have failed to demonstrate how grateful I was to him. I deeply regret my constant postponements and delays.' The point is that, while a financial debt can be repaid to one's creditor's heirs, when it is a matter of returning a favour, it upsets a good and honest man if his creditor is unaware of it.

In Ambracia there was a man who was always criticizing and cursing Pyrrhus, and people thought he should send him away. 'No,' he said, 'let him stay here. I'd rather have him revile me where only a few people can hear him. I don't want him to go around abusing me to all mankind!' And once he was interrogating some young men who had spoken disparagingly of him when they were drunk, and he asked them whether the report he had received about what they had said was true. 'Yes, my lord,' replied one of the young men. 'And we'd have said even more if the wine hadn't run out.' Pyrrhus laughed and let them go.*

[9] After Antigone's death he took several more wives, always to increase his position and power. He married the daughter of King Autoleon of Paeonia; Bircenna, the daughter of Bardyllis of Illyris; and Lanassa, the daughter of Agathocles of Syracuse,* who presented him with the city of Corcyra,* which had been captured by Agathocles, as her dowry. His sons, in order of age, were Ptolemy (by Antigone), Alexander (by Lanassa), and Helenus (by Bircenna). He brought them all up to be good and fiery fighters, making this the focus of their education right from the hour of their birth. For instance, there is a story that one of them, while he was still a boy, asked him which of them would inherit the kingdom. 'The one with the sharpest dagger,' Pyrrhus replied. But this is no different from the famous curse from the play, that the brothers should 'divide their house with sharpened steel'.* This just goes to show the savagery and brutality of any enterprise that is driven by greed.

[10] After this battle* Pyrrhus returned home a happy man, covered in glory, with his fame and his pride riding high. The people of Epirus began to call him 'the Eagle', and he said: 'It is thanks to you that I am an eagle. How could I not be, with your weapons the wing-feathers that allow me to soar?' A little later, when he was informed that Demetrius was critically ill, he made a sudden incursion into Macedon. This was only meant to be a plundering raid, but he came very close to taking over the entire country and making himself king without a fight, since he advanced as far as Edessa without meeting any opposition. In fact, large numbers of men came over to his side and joined his ranks. But the emergency forced Demetrius from his sick-bed, despite his weakness, and before long his Friends and commanders had assembled a good-sized force. They advanced resolutely and determinedly to meet Pyrrhus, who offered no resistance, since

the primary purpose of his expedition was plunder, but retreated, losing a portion of his army on the way to Macedonian attacks.

Even though it had not proved difficult or time-consuming to drive Pyrrhus out of the country, he remained on Demetrius' mind. Demetrius had big plans—nothing less than the recovery of his father's kingdom with an army of 100,000 men and a navy of 500 ships—and he did not want trouble with Pyrrhus, nor did he want to leave the Macedonians with an awkward and hostile neighbour. So, since he did not have time to fight him, he settled his differences with him and made peace, leaving himself free to concentrate on the other kings.

After they had come to this agreement, however, Demetrius' plans were betrayed by the scale of his preparations, and the other kings became afraid.* They sent messengers and letters to Pyrrhus, expressing their surprise that he should have passed up what had been a perfect opportunity for him and was waiting to fight on Demetrius' terms. They also found it surprising, they said, that even though he could drive Demetrius out of Macedon—for Demetrius had thrown the country into considerable turmoil and was in disarray himself—he was waiting to fight the decisive battle for the sanctuaries and tombs of the Molossians at Demetrius' convenience, which would be when he had grown great. And this was especially strange, they said, given that Pyrrhus had just lost both Corcyra and his wife to the man. For Lanassa had withdrawn to Corcyra, complaining that Pyrrhus paid more attention to his barbarian wives than to her, and since she wanted to be a queen she had invited Demetrius to be her husband, knowing that there was no king who was more ready to wed than him. And Demetrius had indeed sailed there, married her,* and installed a garrison in the city.

[11] At the same time as writing to Pyrrhus along these lines, the kings also moved quickly against Demetrius, before his preparations were complete. Ptolemy arrived in Greece with a sizeable fleet and tried to get the cities to rise up in rebellion against him, and Lysimachus invaded upper Macedon from Thrace and proceeded to plunder it. Pyrrhus timed his excursion to coincide with theirs and marched on Beroea, rightly expecting Demetrius to go and confront Lysimachus and leave lower Macedon undefended.

That night Pyrrhus dreamt that he was summoned to an audience with Alexander the Great, and that when he went he found him lying ill in bed. Despite his indisposition, Alexander spoke to him in a kind and friendly fashion, and promised to do all he could to help. 'My lord,' Pyrrhus ventured to ask, 'how will you be able to help me if you're ill?' 'By the power of my name,' said Alexander, and led the way astride a Nesaean stallion.*

Fired up by this dream, Pyrrhus marched swiftly across the intervening territory and took Beroea. He stationed most of his men there and gave his generals the job of winning over the rest of the country. When Demetrius heard about the loss of Beroea and realized that there were mutinous rumblings from the Macedonians in his camp, he was afraid to advance any further towards Lysimachus. He was worried that if his men came close to a king who was a Macedonian of high renown, they would go over to his side. So he turned around and led his men against Pyrrhus instead, thinking that his men would detest him as a non-Macedonian. But when Demetrius made camp close to Pyrrhus' position, people began to come there from Beroea, and a lot of them sang Pyrrhus' praises, saying that he was invincible in battle and a military genius, and reported how leniently and humanely he was treating his prisoners. Some of these visitors were Pyrrhus' agents, pretending to be Macedonians, who suggested that now was the time to get rid of Demetrius and his oppressive regime, and to go over to Pyrrhus instead, a man who was considerate of ordinary people and treated his troops well.

The upshot was that most of the army was in a state of high excitement, and they went in search of Pyrrhus. They looked all over the place, because, as it happened, he was not wearing his helmet, but then, when he realized what was going on, he put it on, and they could tell by its prominent crest and goat's horns who he was. Then the Macedonians ran up to him and asked for the password to his camp, while others crowned themselves with garlands of oak because they could see that the members of his entourage were wearing them. Eventually some of Demetrius' men found the courage to come up to him and suggest that it was probably a good idea for him to give up and slip away. Demetrius realized that the disturbance in the camp was, in effect, the same sort of advice, and he sneaked away in fear for his life, wearing a cap and a plain cloak. So Pyrrhus came and took the camp without a fight, and was proclaimed king of Macedon.

[12] Then Lysimachus arrived, claiming that Demetrius' downfall had been his doing as much as Pyrrhus', and demanding

a share of the kingdom. Pyrrhus did not know how far he could trust the Macedonians, and this uncertainty made him agree to Lysimachus' proposal. So they divided the cities and the land between them.* This kept them happy and stopped them fighting each other for a while, but not much time had passed before they realized that, so far from ending their enmity, the division of Macedon was a cause of recrimination and friction. After all, when men whose greed recognizes no limits set by sea or mountain or desert, and whose desires overleap even the boundaries that define Europe and Asia—when such men are neighbours, with adjacent territories, it would be foolish to think that they could remain content with what they have, without doing each other wrong. No, war between them is constant, because intrigue and envy are second nature to them, and they treat the two words, 'war' and 'peace', as though they were coins, making use of whichever one gives them an advantage, without taking right and wrong into consideration. In fact, they are better men when they make open war than when they employ terms such as 'justice' and 'friendship' to describe the intervals, the breaks they take from injustice. Pyrrhus is a good example of this. It was because he wanted to check the resurgence of Demetrius—to stop his power recovering from what one might describe as a critical illness—that he offered to help the Greeks and went to Athens.*

While in Athens, he walked up to the Acropolis and sacrificed to the goddess, and when he came down, later that same day, he said that while he appreciated the loyalty and faithfulness of the Athenian people towards him, it would be sensible of them never to admit any king into the city again, but to bar their gates against them all. He next made peace with Demetrius, but then, a short while later, after Demetrius had set sail for Asia, at Lysimachus' instigation he tried to stir up rebellion in Thessaly, and also attacked Demetrius' garrisons in the Greek cities. He had found that the Macedonians were better behaved out on campaign than when they had time on their hands, and, in any case, he was constitutionally incapable of inactivity.

Demetrius' final defeat in Syria* removed Lysimachus' greatest fear, and as soon as he had time he set out against Pyrrhus. He found him encamped near Edessa, and the first thing he did was attack and take his supply convoys, until provisions were scarce in Pyrrhus' camp. Next, he wrote to and met with the leading Macedonians, in an attempt to seduce them away from Pyrrhus. He said it was wrong of them to choose as their master a man who was not a Macedonian and whose forebears had always been subject to the Macedonian people, while spurning men who had been Alexander's friends and familiars. So many of them were won over by him that Pyrrhus became afraid and left, taking his Epirote and allied troops with him, and so lost Macedon in the same way that he had gained it. And it follows that kings are in no position to criticize the ordinary people of their kingdoms for changing position to suit their selfish interests, because they are only imitating their rulers, who are models of faithlessness and treachery, and believe that the less a man observes justice the better it is for him.

[13] Now that he had been driven back to Epirus* and had given up on Macedon, Pyrrhus had the chance quietly to enjoy what he had and to live in peace, ruling his own people. But for him the inability to disrupt others' lives and his own along with them was as boring as being becalmed at sea and, like Achilles, he hated having nothing to do, 'but wasted his heart away in idleness, yearning for battle-cry and war'.*

To satisfy his need, Pyrrhus found an opportunity for new adventures in the war being fought between Rome and Tarentum.* The Tarentines lacked the resources to prosecute the war, and at the same time the defiance of their popular leaders, who were unsavoury characters, blocked any possibility of a negotiated settlement. So they decided to appoint Pyrrhus their commander-in-chief and invite him to take charge of the war, because he was more likely than any of the other kings to be available, and because none of the others could rival his skill as a general. Some of the older and wiser Tarentines objected strenuously to the decision, but they were booed and forced out of the assembly by the hawks, and in view of this the rest stayed away.

However, there was one good man, Meton by name, and when the day arrived for the decision to be ratified by the assembly, he reeled into the meeting, where the people were already in session, wearing a garland from the night before and carrying a torch, as drunken revellers do, with a pipe-girl leading the way. Now, in a democracy crowds tend to be unruly, and his appearance was greeted with both applause and laughter, but no one did anything stop him. On the contrary, they called for a tune from the pipe-player and a song from Meton, and he stepped forward into the open, making it look as though he was about to do as they suggested. But when silence fell, he said: 'People of Tarentum, you're quite right to indulge those who want to have fun and party while they can. In fact, if you're sensible, *all* of you will enjoy your freedom now, because things are going to be very different when Pyrrhus reaches the city. Our lives and lifestyles are going to be turned upside down.' Most of the Tarentines agreed with him, and a murmur of approval ran through the assembly, but there were men there who were afraid of being surrendered to the Romans if peace were made, and they told the people off for tolerating such a disgusting display of drunkenness. And the Tarentines, with one accord, threw Meton out of the meeting.

So the decree was passed and a delegation consisting of representatives from the confederation of Italian Greek cities, not just the Tarentines, was despatched to Epirus. They bore gifts for Pyrrhus, and told him that they needed a man of intelligence and high rank to take command of the war, and that he would find waiting for him there substantial armies provided by the Lucanians, Messapians, Samnites,* and Tarentines, amounting to 20,000 horse and a total of 350,000 foot. Pyrrhus' interest was aroused, and the ambassadors' message convinced the Epirotes too. They committed themselves enthusiastically to the expedition.

[14] Now, there was a man called Cineas,* a Thessalian, who was well known for his intelligence; he had studied under the orator Demosthenes, and was held to be the only speaker of the time, or almost the only one, who reminded his audiences of Demosthenes' skill and seemed to evoke his brilliance. He was attached to Pyrrhus' court, and represented him on missions to the cities of Greece, in which capacity he confirmed Euripides' view that 'every achievement of hostile weaponry can also be won by speech'.* At any rate, Pyrrhus used to say that Cineas' words had won him more cities than his own weapons, and he always held him in high regard and treated him as one of his most valued friends.

At the time in question, then, when Cineas saw that Pyrrhus had committed himself to Italy, he drew him into the following conversation, one day when he found him with some spare time. 'People say, Pyrrhus,' he began, 'that the Romans are good fighters and have many warlike peoples at their command. If, by the grace of the gods, we defeat them, what shall we do after the victory?'

'The answer's obvious, Cineas,' Pyrrhus replied. 'Once the Romans have been conquered, there will be no city there, Greek or barbarian, to challenge us, and all Italy will fall to us. And you should know better than anyone how large and fertile and rich in resources Italy is.'

After a short pause, Cineas went on: 'And after we've taken Italy, my lord, what then?'

Pyrrhus still could not see where he was going with this. 'Neighbouring Sicily beckons to us,' he said, 'a prosperous and populous island, and easy to capture. Ever since Agathocles passed on, you see, Cineas, there's been nothing but infighting there. The cities have descended into anarchy, and only the shrill tones of demagogues can be heard.'

'That may well be true,' Cineas said, 'but will that mark the end of the campaign, the capture of Sicily?'

'If the gods grant us victory and success,' Pyrrhus said, 'these conquests will be merely the prelude to true greatness. For who could keep his hands off Libya and Carthage, once they come within striking distance? Agathocles came very close to taking Carthage just by slipping quietly out of Syracuse and sailing there with a few ships. And it goes without saying that, once we've taken Carthage, none of our enemies, who now treat us with scorn, will offer any further resistance.'

'You're right,' said Cineas, 'because with a power-base as great as that we will obviously be able to recover Macedon and put our leadership of Greece on a firm foundation. But what shall we do next, when we rule it all?'

Pyrrhus laughed and said: 'We'll have plenty of time on our hands, my friend. We'll meet every day for drinks and conversation, and have a fine old time together.'

Now that he had brought Pyrrhus to the heart of the matter, Cineas said: 'But what's to stop us meeting for drinks now, if we want to, and spending time together? We can do that already—so, without lifting a finger, we already have exactly the privileges we're planning to gain, with severe disruption not just of others' lives but of our own as well, through bloodshed and massive effort and all the dangers of warfare.'

Pyrrhus was troubled by what Cineas had said, but not enough to change his mind. He could see the great happiness he was leaving behind, but he could not give up his dreams for the future.* [15] So first he sent Cineas to Tarentum with a force of 3,000 soldiers, and then, once a large number of ships had been sent over from Tarentum—transport vessels for cavalry, decked warships, and any kind of ship that could serve to convey troops—he embarked 20 elephants, 3,000 horse, 20,000 heavy infantry, 2,000 bowmen, and 500 slingers.

Finally everything was ready and he set sail, but when he was halfway across the Ionian Sea an unseasonably strong wind from the north suddenly arose and swept the convoy off course. Pyrrhus himself managed, at the cost of a great deal of effort and danger, to weather the violence of the storm and make land, thanks to the courage and determination of his crew. The remainder of the fleet, however, was thrown into chaos and scattered. Some of the ships missed Italy altogether and were driven off into the Libyan and Sicilian Seas. The rest failed to round Cape Iapygia before nightfall, when rough and heavy seas dashed them against a harbourless stretch of shoreline that was choked with rocks. All except the royal flagship were wrecked.

As long as the swell was from the direction of the open sea, the great ship held her own, with her size and strength keeping her safe against the pounding of the waves. But then the wind veered and came at her from the land, and since the ship was standing prow on to the powerful surge, she was in danger of being broken up. But the risk of harm where they were seemed less than leaving the ship once again at the mercy of a raging sea and furiously gusting winds, and so Pyrrhus jumped up and leapt into the water. His Friends and bodyguards all immediately hastened and strove to help him, but they were badly hampered by the darkness, the crashing of the breakers, and the fierce undertow. It was only after daybreak, when the wind was beginning to die down, that he at last made it ashore, completely exhausted physically and sustained in the face of disaster only by sheer grit and strength of will. But then the Messapians—it was their shore he had been cast up on—ran up eagerly to help with whatever they had to hand, and at the same time some of the ships that had survived came up. They held hardly any cavalrymen, fewer than 2,000 infantrymen, and two elephants.

[16] Pyrrhus took these men and set out for Tarentum, and Cineas advanced to join up with him, when he heard of his approach. In Tarentum, Pyrrhus at first did not coerce the Tarentines in any way or force through any measures. But then those of his ships that had survived the storm sailed in and most of his army was reassembled—and at that point Pyrrhus began to realize that the majority of the

Tarentines were incapable of saving either themselves or others unless forced to it. So, since they let him do the fighting for them, while they stayed indoors and occupied themselves with bathing and social activities, he closed the gymnasia and the walkways, where on their state's behalf, as they took their ease, they outgeneralled the Romans in theoretical battles. He also banned drinking-parties, revels, and merry-making in general as inappropriate under the circumstances, instituted a call-up, and tolerated no excuses or evasions from those who were listed as due to serve. The upshot was that a number of people left the city, denouncing as 'slavery' their inability to live as they wanted, because they were unaccustomed to authority.

At the time when Pyrrhus learnt that the Roman consul Laevinus* was marching against him with a sizeable army, plundering Lucania as he came, he had not yet been joined by his allies. Nevertheless, the idea of delaying and doing nothing as the enemy approached was anathema to him, and he took to the field with his forces. He sent a herald on ahead to the Romans, however, to ask whether they might like to receive compensation from the Italian Greeks, as a way of avoiding war, with himself as adjudicator and arbitrator. But Laevinus replied that the Romans did not want Pyrrhus as an arbitrator and were not afraid of him as an enemy either, so Pyrrhus marched on and made camp on the plain between Pandosia and Heraclea.

When he found out that the Romans were making camp near by, on the far side of the Siris, he rode over to the river to watch. He was impressed by what he saw of their discipline, their pickets, and the orderly layout of their camp, and he said to one of his Friends, who happened to be nearest to him: 'Megacles, there's nothing barbarian about these barbarians' discipline,* but we'll soon find out what they're capable of.' Since he was no longer sure of the outcome, he decided to wait for his allies, and he posted a guard on the bank to deter any Roman attempt to cross the river before he was ready. But the Romans were anxious to forestall the arrival of Pyrrhus' reinforcements, and they attempted the passage. While their infantry set out across the river by means of a ford, the cavalry rode across at many points, threatening to encircle the Greeks on the other bank, who therefore retreated. Pyrrhus was rattled when he heard this, but he got word to the officers in command of the infantry to draw their men up immediately for battle and to wait under arms, while he rode out ahead with the cavalry, who were 3,000 strong, hoping to catch the Romans out of formation while they were still crossing the river and spread out. Instead, however, he was greeted by massed shields on the riverbank and the cavalry advancing on him in good order.*

Pyrrhus had his men close up and rode into the attack at their head. All eyes were immediately drawn to him, thanks to the beauty and splendour of his extravagantly chased armour, and he proved by his deeds that he was as great a warrior as men said.† Above all, while playing a full and active role in the actual fighting, defending himself vigorously against everyone who took him on, he remained rational and clear-headed, and steered the course of the battle as though he were surveying it from a distance, galloping in a hundred different directions and ordering up reinforcements for those who seemed hard pressed.

At one point, a Macedonian called Leonnatus noticed that an Italian was waiting for an opportunity to attack Pyrrhus: he was keeping his horse on a parallel course and mirroring every change of position or direction that Pyrrhus made. 'My lord,' he said, 'do you see that barbarian there, mounted on the black horse with white feet? He has some great and fearful deed in mind, if I read him aright. He has steeled his nerves and summoned up his spirit, and it's you he's watching, you he's intent on. He doesn't care about anyone else. Please be on your guard against the man.' And Pyrrhus replied: 'Leonnatus, no man can escape his destiny, but he or any other Italian who engages me at close quarters will regret it.'

Even while they were talking, the Italian took a firm grip of his spear, turned his horse, and charged at Pyrrhus. And then, at one and the same time, the Italian wounded the king's horse with his spear and Leonnatus rode up and did the same to the Italian's horse. Both horses fell, but Pyrrhus' Friends gathered around and snatched him out of danger, while the Italian—a Frentanian called Oplacus, the captain of a cavalry troop—fought on and died.

[17] This episode taught Pyrrhus to be more cautious, and so, when he saw that his cavalry were starting to give way, he called up his heavy infantry and deployed them for battle, but before advancing on the Romans he gave one of his Friends, Megacles, his cloak and armour, and disguised himself more or less as him. The Romans withstood his advance and battle was joined. For a long time the outcome hung in the balance; the battle swayed back and forth seven

times, it is said, as the pursuers became the pursued and then the pursuers again. In fact, although the king's exchange of armour with Megacles was opportune, in the sense that it saved his life, it came close to losing him the battle and turning victory into defeat.

This is what happened. Many of the enemy made Megacles their target, and the one who struck him first and laid him low, a man called Dexius, tore the helmet and cloak from the body and rode over to Laevinus, displaying them and calling out that he had killed Pyrrhus. When the spoils were carried past the phalanxes and held up for all to see, the Romans whooped with joy, but morale in the Greek ranks plummeted and they lost their stomach for the fight. But then Pyrrhus found out what was happening and rode past with his face uncovered, stretching out his right hand to his men and letting them recognize him by his voice.

The worst problems for the Romans were caused by Pyrrhus' elephants*—their horses became terrified even before they got close to the creatures and bolted with their riders—and in the end Pyrrhus led his Thessalian cavalry against them while they were in disarray and swept them off the field. The slaughter was terrible. Dionysius* reports Roman losses as not far short of 15,000 (though Hieronymus* says 7,000) and places Pyrrhus' losses at 13,000 (fewer than 4,000, according to Hieronymus). But these were the best of Pyrrhus' troops, and the Friends and generals that he lost were those he tended to rely on and trust the most. But still, he captured the Roman camp after they had abandoned it, won over to his side some of Rome's allied cities, plundered a great deal of farmland, and advanced to within 300 stades of Rome. After the battle, Lucanians and Samnites turned up in large numbers, and although Pyrrhus told them off for being late, it was easy to see that he was pleased and proud that he had defeated a large Roman army with just the men he had with him and the Tarentines.

[18] The Romans retained Laevinus as general, despite what we are told Gaius Fabricius* said—that it was not a matter of the Epirotes having defeated the Romans, but of Pyrrhus having defeated Laevinus—in other words, it was not the army that had lost them the battle, but Laevinus' generalship. But the Romans resolutely brought their legions back up to strength and raised fresh levies, and their war rhetoric was so confident and uncompromising that Pyrrhus became worried and decided to make contact with them first, to see if

they were disposed to come to terms. His thinking was that it would be extremely difficult for him to capture Rome and win outright victory—he thought it was beyond his present capabilities, in fact—whereas a pact of friendship with them after having defeated them in battle would greatly enhance his international standing.

Cineas, his chosen representative, therefore met with the authorities in Rome, but all the gifts he sent their wives and children from the king were refused, with the Romans and their wives unanimously replying that they would wait until peace had been officially sanctioned, and then they too would find ways to express their goodwill and gratitude to the king. Moreover, none of the tempting and generous offers Cineas made in the Senate was welcomed or leapt at, even though Pyrrhus was not only prepared to release the prisoners of war without ransom, but was also promising to help the Romans complete their subjugation of Italy; and in return for these favours he was asking only that he should become a friend of Rome and that the Tarentines should be left alone, and nothing else at all.

Now, it was widely known that most members of the Senate were inclining towards peace. Not only had they lost a major battle, but they expected another one, with an even larger army ranged against them, now that the Italian Greeks had joined Pyrrhus. At this point Appius Claudius* intervened. He was a distinguished Roman, who had been forced out of public life and into retirement by a combination of old age and failing eyesight, but when news of the king's offers began to circulate and the rumour took hold that the Senate was going to vote for peace, he could not restrain himself. He ordered his attendants to pick him up, and had himself carried on a litter through the Forum and into the Senate house. When he reached the entrance, his sons and sons-in-law took over, gathered around him, and escorted him into the Senate, where out of respect and regard for the man the senators fell silent.

[19] Claudius got straight to his feet. 'Romans,' he said, 'in the past it's been the loss of my eyesight that I've found hard to bear, but what's upsetting me now is that I'm not deaf as well as blind—that I can hear the disgraceful decisions and resolutions you're making, to the detriment of the great name of Rome. What has become of the assertion the whole world heard so often on your lips, that if the famous Alexander the Great had come to Italy and had engaged us in battle when we were young and our fathers in their primes, songs

would not now be celebrating his invincibility, but instead he would have fled or possibly fallen, and either way would have added to Rome's glory? You're showing now that this was no more than idle bragging. How? By being afraid of Chaonians and Molossians, whom the Macedonians never regarded as anything but war booty, and by trembling before Pyrrhus, whose entire life has been spent in the retinue and court of one or another of Alexander's Bodyguards,* and who now wanders here and there in Italy—not so much out of any desire to help the Greeks here as to escape his enemies back home—promising to establish our leadership with the help of an army that failed to enable him to hang on to just a small part of Macedon. What you need to realize is that, if you make him your friend, you will not so much be getting rid of him as inviting the Italian Greeks to sneer at you as people anyone can get the better of. That's what will happen if you allow Pyrrhus to leave without paying for his insolence—to leave, in fact, with the extra reward of having made Rome a place that Tarentines and Samnites laugh at.'

This speech by Claudius revived the Senate's commitment to the war, and they sent Cineas back with their response: that only once Pyrrhus had left Italy would they discuss friendship and alliance, if he still felt the need, but that as long as he was in Italy and under arms the Romans would prosecute the war with all their might, even if he should overwhelm ten thousand Laevinuses in battle.

Cineas is said to have combined this business of his in Rome with making a determined effort to observe how the Romans lived and understand what made their political system so good, and to meet and talk with the best men. And it is said that one of the items in his report to Pyrrhus was a statement to the effect that the Senate had seemed to him to be a council made up of many kings.* As for the general population, he told Pyrrhus that he was afraid they might turn out to be fighting a Lernaean Hydra of some kind,* seeing that the consul had already gathered twice as many men as they had faced in the earlier battle, and that there were still many times this number of Romans who were capable of bearing arms.

[20] After this, Gaius Fabricius arrived at the head of a delegation to negotiate for the prisoners of war. As Cineas had reported, there was no one in Rome whom the Romans held in greater esteem than Fabricius, as a good man and a good soldier, but he was extremely poor. Pyrrhus met with him privately and tried to persuade him

to accept money from him, not to try to corrupt him—perish the thought!—but as a token of friendship, he said. Fabricius refused the offer, and Pyrrhus left it at that for the time being. The next day, however, he wanted to give Fabricius, who had never seen an elephant, a shock, and he told his men to station the largest of them behind a curtain to the rear of them as they talked. This was done, and at Pyrrhus' signal the curtain was drawn aside and the elephant suddenly raised its trunk, held it over Fabricius' head, and emitted a terrifying, strident blast. But Fabricius calmly turned to Pyrrhus and said with a smile: 'I am as little disturbed by your elephant today as I was by your money yesterday.'

Over dinner the conversation ranged far and wide, but the most common topic was Greece and its philosophers. At one point, Cineas mentioned Epicurus* and summarized Epicurean ideas about the gods, politics, and the purpose of life. They held that pleasure was the highest good, he explained; they shunned political life on the grounds that it damaged and played havoc with happiness; and they resettled the gods far from gratitude and anger, or any concern with us human beings, in a life free from care and filled with pleasure. And even before he had finished speaking, Fabricius cried out in prayer: 'Heracles, please may Pyrrhus and the Samnites follow these teachings for the duration of the war with us!'

Pyrrhus was impressed by the self-assurance and strength of character the man displayed, and this increased his desire for friendship with Rome, rather than war. He even privately invited Fabricius to join his court after the peace, and live with him as the foremost of all his companions and generals. But Fabricius, we hear, said quietly to him: 'No, that wouldn't do you any good, my lord. You see, if the men who now honour and admire you get to know me, they'll want me as their king rather than you.'

That was typical of Fabricius, but Pyrrhus listened without taking offence or losing his temper, and described him to his Friends as a man of principle. He made him solely responsible for the prisoners of war, on the understanding that, if the Senate rejected peace, they were to be returned to him, once they had greeted their relatives and celebrated the Saturnalia.* And they were indeed returned to him after the festival, with the Senate decreeing the death penalty for any of them who stayed behind.

[21] Some time later, during Fabricius' consulship,* a man entered

his camp and came to see him, bringing a letter from Pyrrhus' doctor. In this letter, the doctor undertook to kill Pyrrhus with poison, provided that the Romans promised to be properly grateful to him for having brought the war to an end without their having to fight any more battles. But Fabricius found the man's treachery distasteful and, as soon as he had gained his colleague's agreement, he wrote to Pyrrhus, warning him of the plot. Here is the text of the letter:

Gaius Fabricius and Quintus Aemilius, consuls of Rome, to King Pyrrhus, greetings. It looks as though you are as poor a judge of friends as you are of enemies. You will see, once you've read this letter, that the men you're fighting are decent and honest, while you have surrounded yourself with treacherous villains. And you should know that we are not telling you this out of the kindness of our hearts, but to ensure that your downfall does not make people think badly of us and assume that we had to use treachery to win the war because we were unable to do so by our own prowess.

After reading the letter, Pyrrhus satisfied himself as to the existence of the plot and punished the doctor. He then offered Fabricius and the Romans the prisoners of war without ransom, and sent Cineas back to try once again to get him a peace treaty. But the Romans did not think it right that they should be given the men for free, even as an expression of gratitude from an enemy or as a reward for their honesty, and they released the same number of Tarentines and Samnites to him. But they refused to discuss friendship and peace until Pyrrhus had left the shores of Italy with his weaponry and his army, and sailed back to Epirus on the ships that had brought him.

The upshot of all this was that another battle was required of him, so he gathered his army and set out. He met the Romans near the town of Asculum,* but his forces were restricted to terrain that was unsuitable for cavalry, with a tree-fringed river† and broken ground, and gave his elephants no opportunity to charge and engage the enemy phalanx. Many of his men were wounded or killed, but he fought on until nightfall before disengaging. The next day, by strategic manoeuvring, he ensured that the battle took place on level ground and that his elephants could engage with the enemy's ranks. He secured the broken ground early with a guard and interspersed large numbers of javelineers and archers among the elephants. Then he had the infantry close ranks and led them fast and furiously forward in battle array.

The Romans had no room, as on the previous day, to fall back or extend their line beyond Pyrrhus' flanks. They engaged the enemy head on, on level ground. Since they were anxious to repel the heavy infantry before the elephants came up, they wielded their swords with reckless ferocity among the enemy pikes, focused entirely on wounding and slaying, and unconcerned about what happened to them. It is said that their line began to crumble, eventually, at the exact spot where Pyrrhus himself was bearing down on his immediate opponents, but in fact he owed his victory largely to the overpowering strength of his elephants. The Romans' prowess was of no use to them; it was as though they were in the path of a tsunami or a ruinous earthquake, and their only thought was to get out of the way. They could see no point in standing their ground only to die in vain, or in taking terrible losses without gaining the slightest advantage, so they turned and fled to their camp, which was not far away.

According to Hieronymus, Roman casualties in the battle were 6,000, and Pyrrhus' losses, as recorded in the Royal Notebooks,* amounted to 3,505. According to Dionysius, however, Asculum was not the site of two battles, and the Romans were not unequivocally beaten either. All he mentions is a single battle, in which the two sides fought until sunset and then finally separated. He also says that Pyrrhus was wounded in the arm by a lance, that his baggage train was plundered by Daunians, and that between them Pyrrhus and the Romans lost over 15,000 men.

The two sides disengaged, and Pyrrhus is said to have remarked to someone who was congratulating him: 'One more victory like that over the Romans and we shall be completely undone.'* For by then he had lost a large part of the army he came with, and almost all his Friends and generals, who were irreplaceable. He could also see that, while the enthusiasm of his allies in Italy was waning, the Roman army was quickly and easily brought back up to strength—it was as though there were a spring that flowed straight from their home into their camp—and so far from being demoralized by their defeats, the resentment they felt towards the enemy gave them extra strength and determination.

[22] Even while he was pondering these difficulties, he was faced with prospects which gave him fresh grounds for optimism, but

placed him in a quandary. What happened was that a delegation from Sicily and messengers from Greece arrived at the same time. The Sicilians offered to give him charge of Acragas, Syracuse, and Leontini, and asked him to help them expel the Carthaginians and free the island from tyrants,* and the messengers from Greece brought news that Ptolemy Ceraunus had perished fighting the Celts, along with his army, and that now would be the perfect moment for him to appear in Macedon, which was crying out for a king.* Pyrrhus roundly cursed Fortune for bringing him two such glorious opportunities at one and the same moment, and for a long time he hesitated over his decision, because he could see that he would lose one or the other of the two possibilities that had come his way.

Eventually, the proximity of Sicily to Libya* led him to regard the Sicilian enterprise as the one with the greater potential. As soon as he turned his thoughts in that direction he despatched Cineas, as usual, for preliminary discussions with the cities. Meanwhile, he installed a garrison in Tarentum, against the protests of the Tarentines, who demanded that he either do what he came to do and help them in their war against the Romans, or withdraw his troops from their land altogether and leave their city as he found it. Pyrrhus gave them a high-handed response—that they should avoid battle and await his convenience—and set sail for Sicily.

As soon as he reached the island his hopes began to be realized, since the cities readily surrendered to him, and if he ever had to fight or use force his opponents never put up any kind of resistance. Attacking with an army of 30,000 foot and 2,500 horse, and a fleet of 200 ships, he set about driving the Carthaginians off the island and making their possessions his own. The strongest of their fortresses was Eryx,* and it was well stocked with defenders too, but he decided to try to take it by direct assault on its walls. When his army was ready and he had donned his armour, he stepped forward and prayed to Heracles, vowing an athletic festival and a sacrifice in recognition of the hero's valour, if he let the Sicilian Greeks see that he, Pyrrhus, was a worthy descendant of his warrior ancestors and deserved his present success.

Then he had the trumpet sound the start of battle. After raking the walls with missiles to scatter the barbarians, he brought up his ladders. He was the first to mount the wall, and fought off all the many men who challenged him, pushing some of them to their deaths off the wall to one side or the other, but slaying far more with his sword, until the bodies lay in heaps around him. He himself was completely unscathed, but his appearance struck terror into his opponents, proving that Homer was right, and was talking from experience, when he said that courage was the only one of the virtues that not uncommonly allows a man to be moved to ecstasy and acts of divinely inspired madness.* And after the city had fallen, he performed a magnificent sacrifice to the god and organized a variety of athletic contests for the entertainment of the public.

[23] The Mamertines, as the barbarians in Messsana were called, were causing the Greeks a great deal of trouble, and had even reduced some of them to tributary status. There were a lot of them and they were good fighters—hence their name, in fact, which means 'people of Ares' in Latin—but Pyrrhus arrested and executed their tribute-collectors, and then defeated them in battle and extirpated many of their garrisons.* Meanwhile, the Carthaginians were inclining towards a negotiated solution, and were promising him money and ships once there was friendship between them. But this was not enough to satisfy Pyrrhus' ambitions, and he told them that the only way there could be peace and friendship between them was if they completely evacuated Sicily and made the Libyan Sea the border between themselves and the Greeks.*

Flushed with the run of good fortune he was enjoying, and still pursuing the prize that had drawn him there in the first place, he decided to make an attempt on Libya first. A lot of his ships needed their crew numbers making up, and the way he dealt with the cities as he went about collecting oarsmen was high-handed and tactless; he bullied them in an oppressive and irascible manner, and penalized them for defaulting. He had not started out like this; in fact, at first he had made exceptional efforts to try to win the cities over by dealing graciously with them, never doubting them, and never antagonizing them. But now, instead of trying to make himself popular, he was fast becoming a tyrant, and in addition to the reputation he already had for severity, he gained a name for ingratitude and mistrust.

Nevertheless, the Sicilian Greeks could see the necessity of what he was doing and put up with it, despite their resentment. But then there was the business with Thoenon and Sosistratus. These men, eminent Syracusans, had been in the forefront of the attempt to persuade Pyrrhus to come to Sicily, had entrusted Syracuse to him as soon as he arrived, and had provided invaluable support for his Sicilian conquests. But Pyrrhus began to doubt them, and while he did not want to take them with him to Libya, he did not want to leave them behind either. Sosistratus became afraid and made himself scarce, but Pyrrhus found Thoenon guilty of conspiring with Sosistratus and put him to death.

The change in Pyrrhus' circumstances was instantaneous and immediate: the cities conceived a violent hatred for him, and either went over to the Carthaginians or made overtures to the Mamertines. Everywhere he looked, he saw nothing but secession, rebellion, and a determination to unite against him. But then letters arrived from the Samnites and Tarentines, who were finding it difficult to hold out under war conditions on the resources of the cities alone—they had been completely cut off from their farmland—and begged for his help. This gave him a specious pretext for leaving the island without its seeming to be flight or failure, but in truth he scrambled back to Italy because gaining control of Sicily was beyond him and he was seeking a way off the island as one would off a ship that was in trouble. And we are told that he looked back at the island as he was leaving and said to his companions: 'What a wrestling-ground we're leaving for the Carthaginians and Romans!'—a guess that came true only a few years later.*

[24] But the barbarians joined forces against him as he was leaving. He lost many ships to the Carthaginians in a battle in the strait, and then, after escaping to Italy with the rest, he came up against the Mamertines, who had crossed over to Italy ahead of him with an army of at least 10,000 men. They were too frightened to face him in open battle and attacked him in the hills, throwing his entire army into confusion, causing the loss of two elephants, and inflicting heavy casualties on the rearguard. Pyrrhus rode back in person from the van to keep the enemy at bay, in a desperate attempt to fight off men who were expert soldiers and whose blood was up. And soon their morale was further boosted, when Pyrrhus took a blow on the head from a sword and temporarily withdrew from the fighting.

One of the Mamertines, a giant of a man dressed in gleaming armour, ran out far ahead of the rest and called on Pyrrhus in a defiant tone of voice to show himself, if he was alive. Pyrrhus turned back in a rage, in spite of the efforts of his guards. He pushed his way through them, his features darkened with anger, smeared with blood, and terrible to behold. He got the first strike, swinging his sword down on the barbarian's head—and so strong was his arm and so keen his tempered blade that he cleaved him all the way down, so that the two halves of his body fell apart simultaneously to either side. At this the barbarians checked their advance, dumbfounded by what Pyrrhus had done, which seemed to them to be the work of some superior being, and he completed the rest of his journey without further trouble. He reached Tarentum with 20,000 foot and 3,000 horse, supplemented this force with the pick of the Tarentines, and without further ado led them against the Romans, who were encamped in Samnium.

[25] But few of the Samnites joined him. Their power had been broken and their pride humbled by many defeats at Roman hands, and in addition they harboured quite a grudge against Pyrrhus for having sailed off to Sicily. Pyrrhus divided his forces into two. He sent one division to Lucania, to occupy one of the two consuls there and prevent him from reinforcing his colleague, and he led the other division against Manius Curius,* who was safely encamped near the city of Beneventum, awaiting aid from Lucania. Another reason for Curius' inactivity was that there were occasional omens and sacrifices that contraindicated action, according to his seers.

Pyrrhus was therefore in a hurry to attack Curius before the reinforcements arrived, and he set out by night to assault his camp with the pick of his men and the best of his elephants. But it took him so long to complete the roundabout and densely wooded route he had chosen that his men's torches began to fail and they found themselves uncertain of their whereabouts. The further delay this caused used up what darkness remained, and at daybreak he was clearly visible to the enemy as he advanced on them from the heights.

Pyrrhus' appearance threw the Roman camp into turbulent disarray, but the sacrifices were propitious and circumstances were leaving Curius no alternative but armed resistance. He led his men out of the camp, engaged the first of Pyrrhus' men to come up, and routed them. Their panic infected the rest of Pyrrhus' army, and they all turned to flight, during which considerable numbers died, and some of the elephants were left behind and fell into enemy hands. This victory brought Curius down on to level ground, fighting all the way, and he again routed the enemy, this time in open battle. At one point of the field, however, his men were overwhelmed by the elephants and driven back to their camp. Curius called up the many pickets he had standing guard over the camp, who were armed and still fresh. They emerged from their vantage-points and forced the elephants into retreat with their javelins. As the elephants fled through the friendly ranks behind them, they sowed chaos and panic, and this gave victory to the Romans—and not just victory, but also the upper hand in the struggle for dominion. For their brilliant performance in these battles gave them such confidence and strength, and such a reputation for invincibility, that Italy fell to them straight away and Sicily not long afterwards.*

[26] So Pyrrhus' ambitions for Italy and Sicily were wrecked, after six years of warfare there. His courage remained undaunted, however, even in defeat, and while he was acknowledged to be more than a match for any of the kings of his time in terms of military experience, skill, and daring, people also thought that what he gained by his exploits he lost by being overambitious. They said that he was too driven by desire for what he did not have to take the time that was needed to secure what he had. That is why Antigonus used to say he was like a gambler who makes plenty of good dice-rolls, but does not know what to do with them.

He returned to Epirus with 8,000 foot and 500 horse, and began to look around for a war that would give him the funds to maintain this force, since he had no money. Joined by some Celts, he invaded Macedon (where Antigonus, the son of Demetrius,* was on the throne), intent on no more than plunder and pillage. But after a number of cities had fallen to him and 2,000 soldiers had come over to him, he raised his sights and marched against Antigonus. They met at the Narrows, and the entire Macedonian army broke and ran at Pyrrhus' onslaught. But the large body of Celts who formed Antigonus' rearguard put up a stiff resistance, and this led to a ferocious battle, and ultimately to the slaughter of most of the Celts. Antigonus also lost all his elephants when the officers responsible for the unit surrendered after being trapped.

With these substantial additions to his forces, and guided by his run of luck rather than by clear thinking, Pyrrhus advanced on the Macedonian phalanx, which was already in terrified disarray as a result of its earlier defeat. They therefore made no attempt to engage Pyrrhus or fight him, and all he had to do to cause the defection of Antigonus' entire infantry corps, to a man, was raise his arm and call on the generals and senior officers by name. Antigonus fled, but still held some of the coastal cities.

Of all his victories, Pyrrhus thought that the one that most enhanced his reputation was his defeat of the Celts, and he dedicated the most beautiful and striking of the spoils from the battle in the sanctuary of Athena Itonis,* with the following elegiac inscription:

> The shields hanging here, taken from the insolent Celts,
> Pyrrhus of Molossis gave to Athena Itonis
> After annihilating the army of Antigonus. No cause for surprise:
> The Aeacidae have always been brave spearmen.*

As soon as the battle was over, Pyrrhus proceeded to recover the cities. When he gained control of Aegae, one of a number of harsh measures he imposed on the city was to leave it with a garrison of the Celts who were serving under him. But the lust of the Celtic race for money knows no bounds, and they set about digging up the tombs of the kings who had been laid to rest there, stealing anything valuable and insolently scattering the bones.* Pyrrhus made little of this incident and was widely held not to have taken it seriously enough. Perhaps he put off punishing the barbarians because of lack of time, or perhaps he let them off simply because he was afraid of them, but in any case the Macedonians thought the worse of him for it.

His situation in Macedon was still far from secure and stable when his thoughts veered once more towards fresh prospects. First, he poured scorn on Antigonus, saying that it was shameless of him to be still dressing in purple and not to have adopted the clothing of an ordinary man. Second, when the Spartiate Cleonymus came and invited him to attack Sparta, he leapt at the chance.*

Cleonymus was of royal lineage, but had failed to win the Spartans' affection or trust—they thought he had a tyrannical and autocratic temperament—and Areus was on the throne. The fact that he had been passed over for the throne was the fundamental, long-standing cause of the grudge he bore his fellow citizens, but there was also the matter of his marriage. In later life, Cleonymus had married a beautiful woman of royal lineage called Chilonis, the daughter of Leotychidas, but she was madly in love with Acrotatus, the son of Areus, a young man at the peak of his youthful beauty. So the marriage was a source of unhappiness for Cleonymus, since he loved his wife, and also brought him into disrepute, because everyone in

Sparta knew that his wife was making it a mockery. It was this combination of domestic friction and political grievance that induced Cleonymus, in his anger and resentment, to invite Pyrrhus to Sparta.

Pyrrhus answered the invitation with 25,000 foot, 2,000 horse, and 24 elephants, and the scale of his preparations immediately showed that he was not trying to gain Sparta for Cleonymus, but the Peloponnese for himself. He never admitted it out loud, of course, and denied it to the Spartans themselves, in the person of the ambassadors they sent to meet him at Megalopolis. What he told them was that he had come to free the cities from their subjection to Antigonus, and he called on Zeus to witness that he was planning to send his younger sons there for a Spartan education,* if nothing stopped him, in order to give them, in due course of time, this unique advantage over other kings. He used these lies to mislead every delegation that came to him while he was still on his way, but no sooner had he reached Laconia than he turned to pillage and plunder. When the Spartan ambassadors protested about his making war on them without prior declaration, he replied: 'But you Spartans don't warn others of your intentions either. We know that.' Whereupon one of the Spartans at the meeting, a man called Mandrocleidas, said (in his Spartan dialect): 'Well, if ye're a god, we shall suffer nae hairm, since we're doing ye nae wrong. But if ye're a man, there'll aye be someone more strang than ye.'

[27] After this, Pyrrhus continued marching down towards Sparta. Cleonymus was pushing for an immediate assault on the city, but Pyrrhus, it is said, was worried that his men might sack the city if they attacked it at night, so he waited, saying that whatever they would achieve by night, they would achieve by day as well. After all, the suddenness of the attack had caught what few troops there were in the city unprepared, and Areus was away in Crete helping the Gortynians in their war. In fact, this proved to be the main thing that saved the city, that its defencelessness and weakness made it seem less of a threat. For Pyrrhus bivouacked for the night, since he was expecting no resistance anyway, while Cleonymus' friends and helots smartened up his house and got it ready in anticipation of Pyrrhus' coming for dinner.

The first decision the Spartans took that night was to send their womenfolk off to Crete, but the women objected. Archidamia* even came before the Council of Elders with a sword in her hand and, speaking for all the women of Sparta, berated the men for expecting them to live on after the destruction of Sparta. The Spartans next decided to run a trench parallel to the enemy camp, and to place their carts at either end of the trench, packed in earth up to the middle of their wheels, so that they would be fixed firmly enough to serve as a solid barricade against the elephants. But as they were beginning to put this plan into effect, the women arrived, married and unmarried, some with their tunics tucked up under their cloaks, others wearing just their tunics, to help the men past military age in their work. They suggested that those who were due to fight should go and rest, and then they were assigned a stretch to work on and dug a third of the trench all by themselves. According to Phylarchus,* the trench was six cubits wide, four cubits deep, and eight plethra long, but Hieronymus makes it smaller.

At daybreak, with the enemy starting to stir, the women handed the men their weapons and committed the trench to their defence and protection, reminding them that while victory in battle before the eyes of their fellow citizens was sweet, it was glorious to lay down their lives like true Spartans and die in the arms of their mothers and wives. But Chilonis stayed by herself, away from the others, with a noose around her neck, because if the city fell she had no desire to fall into Cleonymus' hands.

[28] While Pyrrhus and his hoplites mounted a frontal attack on the many Spartan shields arrayed against them, and on a trench that was uncrossable and too crumbly to afford his men a secure footing, his son Ptolemy took 2,000 Celts and a company of picked Chaonians, followed the trench to its end, where the carts were, and tried to get through there. But the carts were positioned so close together, and sunk so deep in earth, that they made it difficult for Ptolemy and his men to mount an assault—though no more difficult than they made it for the Spartans to put up a defence. The Celts began to dig the wheels out from the earth and drag the carts down to the river, but young Acrotatus saw the danger. He ran with 300 men back through the city and got around behind Ptolemy, making use of dips in the ground to avoid being spotted. Then he attacked Ptolemy's men from behind and forced them to turn and fight him. Ptolemy's men were now crowding one another into the trench and tripping over the carts, and in the end they were bloodily repulsed.

The older Spartans and most of the women had watched Acrotatus' display of valour, and when he came back again through the city to resume his allotted post, covered with blood and glowing with pride at his victory, he struck the women as taller and more handsome than before, and they envied Chilonis her lover. But some of the older men followed him and called out: 'Acrotatus, hie thee and lie with Chilonis! Just be sure to make brave sons for Sparta!'

Meanwhile, Pyrrhus was involved in a fierce battle. Many Spartans fought with distinction there, but none more so than Phyllius, who stood his ground for longer than anyone and killed more of the attackers. And when he realized that his strength was failing as a result of all the wounds he had received, he made way for one of the men from the rank behind him, and collapsed among his comrades, to make sure that his body did not fall into enemy hands.

[29] The two sides disengaged when it grew dark, and while asleep that night Pyrrhus had a dream in which he saw Sparta being struck by thunderbolts hurled by an eagle,* until the whole city was in flames, and in his dream he was exultant.† Awakened by this rush of emotion, he ordered his officers to prepare the army for battle, and described the dream to his Friends as a sign that he was going to take the city by storm. His interpretation met with general and admiring assent, with the exception of Lysimachus, who did not like the sound of it and explained his concerns. Places struck by thunderbolts are forbidden to mortal men, he said, and so the gods might be warning Pyrrhus that the city was not to be entered by him. But Pyrrhus said that the idea that such places were sacrosanct was arrant nonsense, designed to fool the masses, while they, being armed and ready, should act on the assumption that 'one omen is best of all, to fight in defence of Pyrrhus'.* And then he got to his feet and at daybreak led his men against the city.

But the Spartans defended their city with extraordinary grit and courage. The women were there too, distributing missiles, bringing food and drink where they were needed, and recovering the wounded. The Macedonians set about filling the trench by gathering large amounts of rubble and throwing it on top of the weapons and the dead bodies that lay there, and the Spartans went to try to stop them, but just then Pyrrhus was seen galloping into the city beyond the carts and the end of the trench. The Spartans who had been assigned the defence of that point raised the alarm, and the women screamed and ran, but just as Pyrrhus was riding over to attack the men who faced him there, his horse took a wound in the belly from a Cretan javelin, reared up, and in its death-agony threw Pyrrhus onto a slippery and steeply sloping patch of ground. While his companions gathered around in consternation, the Spartans raced up and succeeded in driving them all off with their javelins.

After this Pyrrhus called a general halt to the fighting, since he expected the Spartans more or less to give up, seeing that almost all of them were either dead or wounded. But at this point the Good Fortune of the city came to its rescue. Perhaps she was testing the Spartans' virtue, or proving just how powerful she could be when all seemed lost, but now, when the Spartans' situation was desperate, she brought one of Antigonus' generals, Ameinias of Phocis, from Corinth* at the head of a mercenary force and sneaked him into the city past the enemy. And then, just after Ameinias' arrival, their king, Areus, arrived from Crete with 2,000 soldiers. The women immediately split up and returned to their homes, since they did not expect to be involved any more in the fighting, while the men dismissed those who were too old for military service, but who had been called up as an emergency measure, and then deployed for battle.

[30] These reinforcements inspired Pyrrhus with a kind of competitive† determination to gain control of the city. But he achieved nothing apart from losing more men, so he pulled away from the city and plundered Laconia, since he planned to winter there. But destiny is inescapable. There was civil war in Argos between Aristeas and Aristippus, and since Aristippus was believed to be on good terms with Antigonus, Aristeas leapt at the chance to invite Pyrrhus to Argos.

For Pyrrhus, one prospect always evolved out of another. Since he made every success the starting-point for another adventure, and compensated for every failure with further enterprises, then as far as he was concerned neither defeat nor victory brought an end to the disruption he caused to his own and others' lives. He therefore lost no time in breaking camp and heading for Argos. But Areus, with men posted at the most difficult stretches of Pyrrhus' route and ambushes laid at many points, kept whittling away at the Celts and Molossians in the rearguard.

Now, Pyrrhus had been warned by his seer, after sacrifices in which the victims' livers had no lobes,* that he would lose a member of his family, but in the muddle and confusion of the moment his mind went blank, and he ordered his son Ptolemy to take his Companion Cavalry and go and help the rearguard, while he sped up the extraction of his army from the defile and led them out of danger. Ptolemy found himself involved in a desperate struggle. And then, while the men assigned to defend him were engaged with an elite Spartan company under the command of Eualcus, a man called Oroesus, from Aptera in Crete—an aggressive man and a strong runner—dashed around the outside of them. He found Ptolemy already fighting furiously, and felled him with a thrust.

After Ptolemy's death his men turned and fled. The Spartans gave chase, sweeping all before them, and before they knew it they found themselves on level ground and cut off by Pyrrhus' heavy infantry. Pyrrhus, who was devastated by the news he had just received of his son's death, had his Molossian cavalry turn and attack them. He himself rode at their head and gorged himself on Spartan blood. He had always appeared unbeatable in battle and terrifying to his enemies, but for sheer aggression and violence none of his previous battles came close. When he spurred his horse at Eualcus, the Spartan stepped aside and only just missed taking off Pyrrhus' hand with his sword, the hand that was holding the reins, but he hit the rein instead and severed it. Since Pyrrhus was at the same time running Eualcus through with his lance, he fell off his horse. Now on foot, Pyrrhus and his men proceeded to slaughter the entire elite company over Eualcus' body. This terrible waste of Spartan lives, when the war was already over, was caused entirely by the desire of the respective leaders to cover themselves with glory.

[31] After this blood-sacrifice, so to speak, for his son, and these magnificent funeral games, with his grief largely sated by his burst of fury against his enemies, he carried on towards Argos. But he found Antigonus already encamped on the hills overlooking the plain, so he made camp at Nauplia, and the next day sent a herald to Antigonus, calling him the bane of his people and challenging him to come down to the plain and decide the Macedonian throne by battle. But Antigonus replied that what was important to him, as a general, was timing rather than force, and that if Pyrrhus was tired of life, there were plenty of other roads available to him that led to death.

But then envoys came from Argos to both Pyrrhus and Antigonus, asking them to leave and allow the city to be neutral and on good terms with them both. Antigonus assented and offered his son to the Argives as a hostage, but Pyrrhus, while agreeing to leave, failed to provide any token of good faith, and the Argives therefore remained uncertain of him. But Pyrrhus had been clearly shown what the future held, when the decapitated heads of some cattle he had sacrificed were observed sticking out their tongues and licking at their own puddled blood. And in Argos the priestess of Apollo Lyceius ran out of the sanctuary, crying: 'I see Argos filled with corpses and running with blood! I see the eagle coming to join the battle! But the eagle has vanished!'

[32] In the dead of night Pyrrhus came up to the city walls. Finding that the gate they call the Throughway had been opened for his men by Aristeas, he had the Celts who were serving under him steal into the city, and they managed to occupy the city square without the alarm being raised. But his elephants could not fit through the gate, and this meant that their castles had to be removed and then replaced, with all the noisy confusion of working in darkness. And so the Argives had time to realize what was happening. They ran up to the Shield and the other defensible points of the city, and called on Antigonus for help.

Antigonus halted his men not far from the city and, while he waited outside with the reserves, he sent a large force inside under the command of his generals and his son. Areus arrived as well, with 1,000 Cretans and a company of Spartan light infantry, and the combined attack of all these men played havoc with the Celts. Then Pyrrhus entered the city past the Cylarabis gymnasium, with his men whooping and shouting. But he could tell from the feeble and unconfident tone of his Celts' answering whoops that they were rattled and hard pressed, so he sped up, forcing on the horsemen in front of him, who were finding the going difficult and dangerous in the city's ubiquitous gutters.

This was a night battle, so there was considerable uncertainty about what was happening and what orders were being issued. Men became lost and separated from their units in the streets, and since they could not see in the darkness, nor make out their officers' shouted commands, nor manoeuvre in the narrow streets, generalship was pointless, and both sides spent time in futile activity while waiting for daybreak. But when it grew light, the sight of the Shield bristling with armed enemies shook Pyrrhus' confidence. Moreover, among the many votive offerings that had been set up in the city square he caught sight of a sculpture in bronze of a wolf and a bull poised for battle, and he remembered with a jolt of dread an oracle he had received long ago, that he was destined to die when he saw a wolf fighting a bull.

The Argives say that this sculpture commemorates an episode from their ancient history. When Danaus first landed there (at Pyramia in Thyreatis), he saw a wolf and a bull fighting while he was marching towards Argos. As he watched the fight, it occurred to him that the wolf stood for him, since like him it was an intruder attacking local residents, and after the wolf's victory he prayed to Apollo Lyceius* and assaulted the city. And he did indeed win, once Gelanor, who occupied the throne at the time, had been deposed by his political enemies. Anyway, that is the story of the sculpture.

[33] The sight of it unnerved Pyrrhus, and at the same time he was discouraged by his failure to attain any of his objectives. Retreat now began to seem the best option, but he was concerned about the narrowness of the city gates, so he sent a messenger to his son Helenus, who had been left outside with the bulk of the army, telling him to demolish a stretch of wall and shelter the men who came out through the breach if the enemy was making things difficult for them. But the man he sent was so rushed and flustered that he mangled his message, and as a result of his mistake the young prince took the remaining elephants and his best men, and marched in through the gates to reinforce his father.

Pyrrhus, however, was already in retreat. As long as he was in the city square, he and his men had room while they gave ground, and they could keep turning and fighting off their attackers. But once they had been forced out of the square and into the street that led to the gate, they began to encounter the relieving force coming at them from the opposite direction. Pyrrhus called on Helenus' men to fall back, but even those who heard the order—and that was only some of them—were prevented from carrying it out, however much they wanted to, by those who were piling in behind them from the direction of the gate.

The chaos was only compounded when the largest of the elephants was brought down right in the gateway, and lay there bellowing and blocking the way back, while at the same time one of the elephants already inside the city (its name was Nicon) was moving against the current of those who were trying to get out. Nicon was searching for its rider, who had fallen off wounded, and it was causing such a crush that friend and foe were intermingled and pressed up against one another. And when at last it found its rider, it lifted him up with its trunk and laid him to rest on its two tusks, and then began to retrace its steps, trampling everyone in its path to death, as though it were berserk.

Men were so tightly packed and crammed together that no one was able to act as an individual, but the crowd as a whole kept surging back and forth, or swaying from side to side, like a single body consisting of parts bolted together. Although a few fights did break out against enemy troops who were constantly being thrown their way or were pressing in behind them, they did more harm to themselves than to the enemy. For it was impossible for a man, once he had drawn his sword or couched his lance, to raise it or sheathe it again without its slicing into whomever happened to be there, and so they died just because they were in one another's way.

[34] Seeing the storm and surge raging around him, Pyrrhus took off the diadem which distinguished his helmet, handed it to one of his Companions, and then gave his horse its head and charged at his pursuers. As he engaged them, he took a spear in the chest. The wound was not fatal or even serious, though it pierced his breastplate, but Pyrrhus turned against the man who had struck him. Now, this man was an Argive of no social standing, the son of a poor old woman, who was watching the affray from the rooftops along with all the other women. When she saw that her son was fighting Pyrrhus, she was terrified for him, and she picked up a roof-tile with both hands and threw it at Pyrrhus. It struck him on the back of the head, just below the helmet, and crushed the vertebrae at the base of his neck. His vision blurred, his hands dropped the reins, and he slid from his horse and fell to the ground by the tomb of Licymnius.

Hardly anyone recognized him there, but a man called Zopyrus from Antigonus' army and two or three others ran over to where he lay. When they realized who it was, they dragged him into a doorway, just as he was beginning to recover consciousness. Zopyrus drew his Illyrian sword to cut off his head, but Pyrrhus fixed him with such a terrible glare that he lost his nerve. Even though his hands were trembling, Zopyrus still made the attempt, but he was so shaky and nervous that the blow did not fall true, but struck Pyrrhus across his mouth and chin, so that it took time and effort to cut right through and separate the head from the body.

Before long most people knew what had happened. Alcyoneus* ran up and asked for the head, to identify it, and then rode off with it to his father. Finding him sitting with his Friends, he tossed the head at him, but when Antigonus saw it and recognized who it was, he lashed out at his son with his staff and drove him away, calling him a godforsaken barbarian.* Then he covered his eyes with his cloak and wept at the memory of his grandfather and father, Antigonus Monophthalmus and Demetrius, both examples from his own family of the fickleness of Fortune.* And after seeing that Pyrrhus' head and body were properly attired for death, he burnt the corpse on a pyre.

Later, Alcyoneus came across Helenus wearing a plain cloak, trying to remain inconspicuous. He spoke kindly to him and took him to his father, and Antigonus said: 'This is better than before, my boy, but still not quite right. You shouldn't have left him wearing these shabby clothes, which shame us rather than him, since we're supposed to be the victors.' He treated Helenus with courtesy, saw that he was properly attired, and sent him back to Epirus. And he dealt gently with Pyrrhus' Friends, when he gained possession of his camp and took over his entire army.

ARATUS

INTRODUCTION

Aratus of Sicyon (271–213 BCE) was one of the most influential figures in the third-century Peloponnese. He transformed the Achaean League from a minor confederation of kindred cities into a significant political force whose membership extended well beyond the original Achaean core. Aratus spent his childhood in exile in Argos after his father was murdered by political opponents, but in 251, when he was aged about twenty, he and a group of exiles made a surprise attack on Sicyon, toppling the government of Nicocles, a man represented in our hostile sources as a tyrant. To give added security to his new government Aratus brought Sicyon into the Achaean League, even though the city was not ethnically Achaean. Only a few years later, in 245, he was elected to the Generalship, the chief magistracy of the league, an office he would hold almost every other year for the rest of his life (consecutive office-holding was not allowed). He thus had enormous control over the direction of the league. In particular he sought to undermine Macedonian power in the Peloponnese, first by his unexpected expulsion of the Macedonian garrison from the Acrocorinth, a key strategic point for the control of the region, then by making an anti-Macedonian alliance with the Aetolians, and finally by challenging the now vulnerable Macedonian-backed tyrannies in the Peloponnese. The tyrants of both Megalopolis and Argos responded by resigning their positions and bringing their cities into the league (in 235 and 229 respectively).

But expansion also brought the league into conflict with a revived Sparta under the energetic and innovative king Cleomenes III (see *Agis and Cleomenes*). Tension between the two was exacerbated by the anti-Spartan traditions of the league's new members, Megalopolis and Argos. Lacking the military strength to deal with Sparta, Aratus took a radical and controversial step. He sought help from his old adversary Macedon, whose king, Antigonus Doson, marched into the Peloponnese and defeated Cleomenes at Sellasia in 222. The price of this victory, however, was the Acrocorinth, which was to remain in Macedonian hands until the defeat of Philip V by the Romans in the Second Macedonian War (200–196). The arrangement not only brought Macedon back into the Peloponnese, but it also brought Aratus into the Macedonian court, where he was adviser to first Antigonus Doson and then Philip V, who succeeded to the throne in 221. This association with the Macedonian king thus gave Aratus great influence while at the same time restricting his freedom as Achaean leader. Nonetheless, he sought to use his new position to the advantage of the league, bringing Macedon in on Achaea's side against Aetolia in the Social War of 220–217. In the highly competitive world of the court, Aratus held his own, but his relationship with Philip deteriorated as the king became increasingly determined to strengthen Macedon's grip on the Peloponnese. So bad had their relationship become that, when Aratus died in 213, it was rumoured that Philip had had him poisoned.

The *Aratus* is different in character from the other Lives in this volume, because it was not written as part of the *Parallel Lives*. Instead it is a freestanding Life. It is not known when Plutarch wrote it, but most likely it is earlier than the *Parallel Lives*. It was dedicated to Polycrates of Sicyon, a man whose family claimed descent from Aratus. That alone would suggest that the reader should not expect anything unduly critical, but Plutarch also makes it clear that Aratus should be seen as a model for his descendants, in particular Polycrates' sons. Thus he is sending Polycrates the volume, 'so that, as they grow up, your sons Polycrates and Pythocles might be able to hear and read about the qualities they should imitate by having the example of a member of their own family before them' (1). The aim, therefore, is in part at least educational, highlighting Aratus' virtues and great achievements as an inspiration for the younger members of the family, and by extension younger readers more generally. Moreover, the Life differs in style from those of the *Parallel Lives*. Stories are narrated at much greater length and include dramatic set-pieces, such as Aratus' overthrow of Nicocles (4–9) or his seizure of the Acrocorinth (16–24), that would capture the imagination of the young. In contrast to this extended treatment of episodes early in his career, there is markedly less emphasis on his later years as an adherent of Macedon. The period from the aftermath of the victory over Cleomenes in 222 to Aratus' death in 213 is covered in a mere seven chapters (46–52).

Just before Plutarch begins his narrative of Aratus' career as an Achaean politician, he inserts a brief and important character study of his subject (10), which can usefully be compared with a similar passage in the second-century BCE Achaean historian Polybius (4.8). Aratus is a man for whom politics is everything. He puts public affairs ahead of his own personal interests, public interest before friendship. These are represented as positive attributes, but it would be easy to interpret them differently. In military matters he was a master of stratagem and undercover operations but a failure in open warfare, in which he was irresolute and lacking in confidence. But where Plutarch seems to see Aratus as being overly cautious on the battlefield, Polybius puts it down to cowardice and dismissively suggests that the Peloponnese was littered with memorials to his defeats. Plutarch later addresses the subject of Aratus' cowardice at greater length, suggesting that these were malicious stories put about by his enemies (29). In keeping with the educational aims of the *Aratus* and his own philosophical outlook, Plutarch sees Aratus' shortcomings as being due to the limitations of his education. He had already observed that, as a young man in Argos, Aratus had devoted himself to athletics rather than rhetoric (3). Plutarch's own criticism of Aratus largely stems from his decision to appeal to Macedon for help against Cleomenes (38, 44–5). That in turn led to the brutal treatment of the Argive Aristomachus and the massacre and enslavement of the Mantineans (both acts sufficiently controversial for Polybius to spend several chapters on them). But it is Aratus' renaming of Mantinea as Antigoneia, after the man who destroyed it and killed its citizens, that most galls Plutarch (45).

Fundamental to Plutarch's account of Aratus were the *Memoirs* written by Aratus himself. They covered his life down to 220, and may have been prompted by a need to justify the political about-turn that brought Macedon back into the Peloponnese. Plutarch cites them several times, and while he made considerable use of the content, was not impressed by Aratus' writing style: 'He was probably more eloquent than one might think from reading his published *Memoirs*, which he dashed off in a casual and offhand manner, using the first words that came to mind' (3). Plutarch did not, however, use them uncritically, and read them alongside the histories of Polybius and the pro-Spartan contemporary of Aratus, Phylarchus (38), two historians whose views of Aratus were diametrically opposed to each other. Polybius, who had himself read the *Memoirs*, wrote a generally favourable account of Aratus and his role in the growth of the Achaean League (see especially 2.38–70, 4.8, 4.82, and 7.11–12; see further introduction to the next set of Lives). Phylarchus, on the other hand, whose now-lost history spanned much of the third century, was very sympathetic to Cleomenes and was particularly strong in his condemnation of Aratus. Another source cited by Plutarch in the Life is Deinias (29), the author of a lost history of Argos and perhaps one of the assassins of the Sicyonian tyrant Abantidas (3).

Almagor, E., 'The *Aratus* and the *Artaxerxes*', in M. Beck (ed.), *A Companion to Plutarch* (Chichester, 2014), 278–91.

Beck, H., and Eckstein, A., 'Aratos of Sicyon', in I. Worthington (ed.), *Brill's New Jacoby* 231, <http://referenceworks.brillonline.com/entries/brills-new-jacoby/aratos-of-sicyon-231-a231> [on Aratus' *Memoirs*].

Golan, D., 'Aratus' Policy between Sicyon and Argos: An Attempt at Greek Unity', *Rivista storica dell'antichità*, 3 (1973), 59–70.

Gruen, E. S., 'Aratus and the Achaean Alliance with Macedon', *Historia*, 21 (1972), 609–25.

Haegemans, K., and Kosmetatou, E., 'Aratus and the Achaean Background of Polybius', in G. Schepens and J. Bollansée (eds.), *The Shadow of Polybius: Intertextuality as a Research Tool in Greek Historiography* (Leuven, 2005), 123–39.

Lolos, Y. A., *Land of Sikyon: Archaeology and History of a Greek City-state* (Princeton, 2011).

Mackil, E., *Creating a Common Polity: Religion, Economy, and Politics in the Making of the Greek Koinon* (Berkeley, 2013).

Marasco, G., 'The Hellenistic Age: Autobiography and Political Struggles', in G. Marasco (ed.), *Political Autobiographies and Memoirs in Antiquity: A Brill Companion* (Leiden, 2011), ch. 3.

Meadows, A., 'Polybius, Aratus, and the History of the 140th Olympiad', in B. Gibson and T. Harrison (eds.), *Polybius and his World: Essays in Memory of F. W. Walbank* (Cambridge, 2013), 91–118.

Pelling, C., 'Aspects of Plutarch's Characterisation', *Illinois Classical Studies*, 13 (1988), 257–74 (= C. Pelling, *Plutarch and History* (Swansea, 2002), ch. 13).

Porter, W. H., *Plutarch's Life of Aratus, with Introduction, Notes, and Appendix* (Cork, 1937).

Stadter, P., ' "The Love of Noble Deeds": Plutarch's Portrait of Aratus of Sicyon', in R. Ash, J. Mossman, and F. B. Titchener (eds.), *Fame and Infamy: Essays for Christopher Pelling on Characterization in Greek and Roman Biography and Historiography* (Oxford, 2015), chapter 11.

Walbank, F. W., *Aratos of Sicyon* (Cambridge, 1933).

ARATUS

[1] There is an ancient saying, Polycrates,* which the philosopher Chrysippus*—anxious, I suppose, to avoid saying anything negative—repeats in an altered or, as he would say, improved version: 'Who but a happy son will praise a father?' But Dionysodorus of Troezen* proves him wrong and quotes the correct version instead: 'Who but an *unhappy* son will praise a father?' And he says that the purpose of the saying is to silence the kind of man who has no good qualities of his own, but clothes himself in the virtues of an ancestor, and goes on and on about what a wonderful person he was. But men in whom, as Pindar puts it, 'of its own accord the noble temper of their bloodline shines forth'*—men like yourself, who seek the noblest example your family provides on which to model your life—would count themselves happy to keep the memory of the best of their forebears fresh in their minds, by listening to and telling stories about them whenever possible. For it is not that lack of their own good qualities forces them to praise others' virtues in order to gain a vicarious reputation for goodness themselves. No, it is rather that they see a connection between their own native qualities and those of their ancestors, whom they celebrate, therefore, as the founders not only of their families, but also of their lives.

That is why I have sent you this Life I have written of Aratus, your fellow countryman and forebear, whom you dishonour neither by your standing in society nor by your abilities. I have no doubt that you have taken care all your life to gain the most detailed and accurate knowledge of his achievements, but I have still sent it to you so that, as they grow up, your sons Polycrates and Pythocles might be able to hear and read about the qualities they should imitate by having the example of a member of their own family before them. For there is always someone better than oneself in every respect, and failure to recognize this is a sign of *amour propre*, not of culture.

[2] Immediately following the dissolution in Sicyon of what we may call the pure Dorian mode of aristocracy,* the city succumbed to factional feuding, with rival popular leaders vying for prominence. There was no end to its ailing and disordered condition, with one tyrant following another, until after the murder of Cleon they chose as

heads of state Timocleidas and Cleinias, men of the highest standing and greatest power in the city. But the political situation had only just achieved a measure of apparent stability when Timocleidas died, and Abantidas, the son of Paseas, made himself tyrant by killing Cleinias and banishing or murdering his friends and relatives. He also went to Cleinias' house with the intention of murdering his son Aratus, now a seven-year-old orphan, but in the turmoil the boy escaped among the other fleeing members of the household. Lost in the city, terrified and defenceless, he luckily slipped unnoticed into the house of a woman called Soso, who was the sister of Abantidas and the wife of Cleinias' brother Prophantus. She was a generous-hearted woman and, thinking that some god must have guided the boy to take refuge with her, she first hid him inside the house and then sent him secretly to Argos by night.*

[3] So Aratus was stolen out of the city and came to no harm—and an immediate effect of the episode was that the intense and burning hatred he held for tyranny began to take root and grow in him. He was brought up among his father's friends and guest-friends in Argos in the manner appropriate for a free-born boy, and when it became clear to him that he was going to develop into a tall, strong man he devoted himself to athletic training, and became good enough to compete as a pentathlete and win crowns.* His statues,* at any rate, certainly show him with a muscular body, and for all their intelligence and majesty his features still smack of the athlete's bulky diet and the mattock.* It may be that his devotion to athletics meant that he took less interest in rhetoric than a statesman should, but he was probably† more eloquent than one might think from reading his published *Memoirs*,* which he dashed off in a casual and offhand manner, using the first words that came to mind.

Some time later Abantidas was murdered by Deinias and Aristotle the logician.* The tyrant was in the habit of attending and playing an active part in all the philosophical discussions they held in the city square, and they encouraged him in this activity, laid their plans, and killed him. Abantidas' position was taken over by Paseas, his father, but Paseas was treacherously killed by Nicocles, who made himself tyrant instead. It is said that Nicocles bore a striking resemblance to Periander, the son of Cypselus—as close a resemblance as the Persian Orontes is said to have borne to Alcmaeon, the son of Amphiaraus, or as the young Spartan in Myrsilus' story did to Hector. According to Myrsilus, the young man was trampled to death by the mob of people who came to look at him when they became aware of the similarity.*

[4] Nicocles was tyrant of Sicyon for only four months, but he managed to do the city a great deal of harm in this time, and came close to losing it to an Aetolian plot.* By then Aratus was a young man, and was already held in exceptionally high regard for his noble birth and for a cast of mind which, as people were beginning to discover, was elevated and yet not impractical, since it had a down-to-earth quality and was tempered with more common sense than is usual in one so young. Hence the exiles looked to him above all for help, and his behaviour attracted the attention of Nicocles, who secretly kept him under observation and watched him to try to learn his future intentions. It never crossed his mind that Aratus might do anything as bold and risky as what he did, but he was concerned in case he was in communication with the kings, with whom he was on good terms, as they had been guest-friends of his father. Aratus had, in fact, tried to take that route, but Antigonus* had procrastinated and failed to keep his promises, and the prospect of help from Ptolemy* in Egypt seemed remote. So he decided to overthrow the tyrant on his own.

[5] The first people to whom he revealed his intentions were Aristomachus and Ecdelus,* the former one of the Sicyonian exiles, and the latter an Arcadian from Megalopolis, a philosopher and a man of action, who was a close associate of Arcesilaus,* the head of the Academy in Athens. On the strength of their enthusiastic response, he got in touch with the rest of the exiles,* but only a few of them joined the conspiracy, those who were ashamed to abandon hope, while the majority thought that Aratus' boldness was the product of naivety and even tried to argue him out of it.

Aratus had been planning to seize a stronghold in Sicyonia, as a base from which to make war on the tyrant, but then a Sicyonian who had broken out of prison there arrived in Argos. He was the brother of Xenocles, one of the exiles, and once he had been introduced to Aratus by Xenocles he told him that the stretch of wall that he had climbed over to safety was more or less level with the ground inside, since it had been built on a rocky hillside, while the external height of the wall was well within the reach of scaling-ladders. On receiving this information, Aratus sent two of his servants, Seuthas and Technon, to accompany Xenocles to Sicyon to reconnoitre the wall. He had decided to see if he could gamble everything on a single attempt, swiftly and covertly put into motion, rather than trying to match his private resources against a tyrant in a drawn-out war with overt fighting. So when Xenocles returned with the measurements of the wall and told him that, so far from being inaccessible, the place was not even hard to approach—though he added that it was hard to approach undetected, because of some little dogs belonging to a man who had a market garden there, which, for all their size, were extraordinarily fierce and uncontrollable—he immediately committed himself to the venture.

[6] Laying in a supply of arms raised no eyebrows, because it is hardly an exaggeration to say that in those days everyone robbed and raided everyone else, and the ladders were made openly by the engineer Euphranor, since his job screened him from the suspicion that would otherwise have fallen on him as one of the exiles. As for men, each of his friends in Argos provided him at short notice† with ten, while he himself armed thirty of his own slaves, and with the help of the robber chieftains Protus and Xenophilus he also hired a few soldiers, who were told that the purpose of the upcoming sortie to Sicyonia was to rustle the king's horses.*

Most of these men were sent ahead, a few at a time, to the fortified farmstead belonging to Polygnotus, with orders to wait there. Aratus also sent Caphisias ahead with four companions under his command, travelling light, with the job of reaching the gardener's place while it was still dark; that was the only way they could get in, so they were to pretend to be wayfarers, settle down for the night there, and lock up the gardener and his dogs. The ladders were broken down, packed in boxes for concealment, and sent ahead on wagons.

Meanwhile, some of Nicocles' spies had been spotted in Argos, and were said to be skulking around, keeping an eye on Aratus. The next morning, therefore, Aratus emerged from his house and showed himself openly in the city square, where he passed time with his friends. Then, after taking exercise in the gymnasium, he collected from the wrestling-ground some of the young men with whom he was accustomed to drink and relax, and went back home. And before long one of his slaves was seen carrying garlands through the city square, another buying lamps, and another talking to the women entertainers who regularly played the lyre and the pipes at symposia.

Seeing all this, the spies were completely taken in, and they said to one another with a laugh: 'It's true, then, that there's nothing more timid than a tyrant. Nicocles is the master of a powerful city and has a sizeable army at his command, yet he's afraid of a boy who wastes the meagre funds he has available in exile on the pleasures of daytime carousing!'

[7] The deception worked, then, and the spies left town. Straight after the midday meal Aratus rode out and joined the soldiers at Polygnotus' farmstead, before taking them on to Nemea, where he briefed them on the mission. This was the first most of them had heard about it, and he encouraged them with assurances of success. Then he told them the watchword, which was 'Apollo on high', and led them on towards the city. By adjusting his speed according to the movement of the moon, he had the advantage of its light while travelling, and reached the market garden, close to the city walls, just as it was setting.

Here he was met by Caphisias, and learnt that he had been unable to control the dogs, which had scampered away before he could catch them, and had managed only to lock up the gardener. The men's confidence evaporated at this, and the majority were in favour of aborting the mission, but they cheered up again when Aratus promised to take them back home if the dogs proved too troublesome. And with these words he sent forward the ladder-bearers, under the command of Ecdelus and Mnasitheus, while he slowly came up behind with his men.

Soon the dogs were running alongside Ecdelus' party, barking furiously, but they managed to reach the wall safely and prop their ladders up against it. Just as the first men were setting their feet on the ladders, however, the officer responsible for relieving the night watch started making the rounds with his bell, and the darkness and quiet were shattered by all the torches and commotion of the morning watch as they came up. But Ecdelus' men crouched down on the ladders and froze, and were never in any danger of being detected. But then another sentry detail approached that stretch of wall from the opposite direction, and this put them in terrible danger. But this second detail marched past along the wall without spotting them either, and as soon as they were out of sight Mnasitheus and Ecdelus climbed up. They secured the wall-walks in both directions, and then sent Technon to tell Aratus to make all speed.

[8] It was not far from the garden to the wall and the tower, which was guarded by a large hunting-dog. Perhaps the dog was a lazy one, or perhaps it had worn itself out the day before, but it did not react to Aratus' approach. But when the little dogs belonging to the gardener began yapping out a warning from the foot of the tower, it started to growl, faintly and indistinctly at first, but louder and louder as Aratus and his men passed by. Before long the whole place resounded with the baying of the hound, and the sentry who was posted across the way from the tower called out in a loud voice, asking the hunter who his hound was barking at so fiercely, and whether anything was amiss. 'There's nothing to worry about,' the hunter called back from the tower. 'It was just excited by the light of the sentries' torches and the ringing of the bell.'

Nothing could have encouraged Aratus' troops more; they now thought that the hunter was in on the plot and covering up for them, and that they would find plenty of other supporters in the city. But when they assaulted the wall they found that the danger was very far from over. The ladders wobbled violently unless only one man climbed up at a time and took it slowly, and time was pressing, because the cocks were already crowing and the farmers who regularly brought produce in to market from the countryside would start arriving at any minute. Aratus therefore quickly mounted the wall himself when only forty of his men had climbed up before him, and waited for only a few more from below before proceeding against† the tyrant's house and the praetorium, where the mercenaries were spending the night. His attack caught the mercenaries unprepared and he took them all prisoner, with no loss of life. As soon as he had secured the praetorium, he sent men around to his friends in the city, summoning each of them from their homes, and they flocked to him from all directions. Day was now breaking and the theatre was teeming with people, agitated by the vague rumours they had heard. In fact, they had no true idea of what was happening until the herald stepped forward and announced that Aratus, the son of Cleinias, was calling on his fellow citizens to seize their freedom.

[9] Then, convinced that the long-anticipated moment had arrived, they ran *en masse* to the tyrant's house to set it on fire. The towering flames that arose from the burning building were visible in Corinth,* to the astonishment of people there, who

came very close to setting out to see if help was needed. Nicocles escaped unnoticed through drains and fled the city, while Aratus' soldiers enlisted the help of the Sicyonians to extinguish the flames and then plundered the tyrant's mansion. Aratus did nothing to stop them, and he also donated the rest of the wealth accumulated by the tyrants to the public treasury. Not a single man from either the attackers or their enemies was killed or even scratched; Fortune kept the operation unsullied and free from the taint of kindred blood.

Aratus allowed back to Sicyon eighty exiles who had been banished by Nicocles and at least five hundred from the time of the previous tyrants, who had been uprooted for a long while—not far off fifty years, in fact. Most of these men came back impoverished and tried to reclaim their former possessions, but by going back to their farms and houses they made it very difficult for Aratus to know what to do. The city was threatened from outside, with Antigonus begrudging it its restored freedom, and now he could see that it was also tearing itself apart with internecine strife.*

Under the circumstances, then, he decided that the best course would be to incorporate the city into the Achaean League,* and that is what he did.* And despite being Dorians,* the Sicyonians had no objection to being called Achaeans and willingly accepted the Achaean political system, even though at the time the league was rather undistinguished and weak. Most of the member states were small, with farmland that was neither good nor extensive, and a coastline that lacked harbours and was washed by a sea that reached land for the most part in the form of breakers. Despite this, no one did more than the Achaeans to prove that the Greeks are invincible on those occasions when they organize themselves, work harmoniously together, and are guided by an intelligent leader. Although Greece's ancient heyday had more or less entirely passed them by, and although at the time in question the total resources available to all of the Achaean communities together did not amount to those of a single decent-sized city, nevertheless, thanks to their receptiveness to good advice and their capacity for cooperation, and thanks to their ability not to resent the appearance of a leader of unrivalled excellence, but to submit obediently to him, they not only managed to preserve their own freedom when they were surrounded by powerful cities, formidable armies, and aggressive tyrannies, but were also on very many occasions the liberators and saviours of fellow Greeks.

[10] Aratus was a principled politician, more attentive to public business than his own affairs, bitterly hostile towards tyranny, and always inclined to let the criterion of public expediency determine his friendships and enmities. The consequence of this seems to have been that, if he was never a true friend, in the strict sense of the word, he was at least a mild and moderate enemy, since his friendship or hostility towards others changed according to changing political circumstances. He was a passionate advocate of international concord, cooperation among states, and unanimity between council and popular assembly, which he saw as unconditional goods. And although he was undeniably irresolute and unconfident when it came to warfare and battle, he was brilliant at gaining the upper hand by deceit, and at ensnaring cities and tyrants by covert means. As a result, although he was often unexpectedly successful when he took a risk, he seems to have let just as many chances slip through cautious fingers.* For just as some animals have night vision, but are blind in the daytime (this is due to the fact that the fluid in their eyes is too thin and slight to be capable of merging with light), so there is apparently a certain kind of human skill or intelligence which is inherently liable to be confounded by formally declared warfare out in the field, but recovers its confidence for secret, covert operations. In naturally gifted people, this kind of inconsistency is the result of lack of education; like a crop that springs up spontaneously, without any husbandry, they have aptitude without knowledge. Anyway, the evidence will give us a chance to consider this question further.

[11] After committing himself and his city to the Achaeans, Aratus served in the league cavalry. His obedience to authority made him popular among his commanding officers, because despite all that he had done for the league in giving them the glory of his own name and the resources of the city of his birth, he served every incumbent Achaean General without expecting special treatment, whether he was from Dyme or Tritaea or somewhere even smaller. And when the king* sent him twenty-five talents as a personal gift, he accepted the money, but used it to create a charitable fund for the benefit of Sicyonian citizens, particularly those who lacked the means to ransom prisoners of war.

[12] The returning exiles refused to compromise, however, and

continued to make trouble for the people who now held their property, until Sicyon was close to self-destruction. Since, to his mind, only Ptolemy's generosity could save the city, Aratus decided to take ship and ask the king to fund his attempt to solve the problem. He put to sea from Mothone,† north of Cape Malea, in order to make use of the current through the strait. But there was a strong wind blowing and a heavy swell running from the open sea, and they were too much for the helmsman. They were swept off course and only just managed to make land on the island of Hydrea.†

But this was enemy territory, controlled and garrisoned by Antigonus. Aratus quickly disembarked before Antigonus' men could appear and, abandoning the ship, withdrew far inland. He was accompanied by one of his friends, a man called Timanthes,* and together they plunged into a thickly wooded part of the island, and passed a grim night. It was not long before the garrison commander arrived at the ship in search of Aratus, but Aratus' servants told him, as they had been instructed, that their master had fled the island immediately and sailed to Euboea. The officer believed this lie, but he declared the ship a prize of war, along with its cargo and Aratus' servants, and impounded it.

A few days later Aratus' situation was still desperate, but then, luckily for him, a Roman ship* anchored off the part of the island where he was dividing his time between climbing up to a lookout-point and keeping hidden. The ship was bound for Syria, but once he had been accepted on board Aratus persuaded the owner to take him as far as Caria. The voyage there was no less hazardous than what he had already been through, but he made it, and from there he crossed at last to Egypt. Ptolemy treated Aratus kindly, not just because of their family friendship, but also because he had been softened up by the paintings Aratus had sent him from Greece. Aratus had good taste in such matters, and whenever he came across a work of exceptional artistic quality, especially if it was by Pamphilus or Melanthus,* he would acquire it and send it to Ptolemy.

[13] At the time, Sicyon still had a flourishing reputation for the arts, and especially for fine painting, and it was held that only there had imperishable beauty found a home. In fact, even after he had begun to be admired, the great Apelles* went there and paid a talent to join the school of painters, not because he had anything to learn from them, but because he wanted the fame of having been associated

with them. So although one of the first things Aratus did after liberating the city was destroy the portraits of all the other tyrants, for a long time he hesitated over the portrait of Aristratus, who had been a contemporary of Philip of Macedon. For the picture, which showed Aristratus beside a chariot in which Victory was standing, had been painted by Melanthus with—we are informed by the geographer Polemon*—a contribution by Apelles.

It was a remarkable piece of work, and although its perfection tempted Aratus to be lenient, his hatred of tyranny finally prevailed and he ordered it removed and destroyed. At this, the painter Nealces, we are told, who was a friend of Aratus, begged him with tears in his eyes to spare it, and argued in the face of Aratus' intransigence that the tyrants were the enemy, not the tyrants' possessions. 'So let's leave the chariot and the Victory,' he said, 'and I'll make Aristratus himself disappear from the painting.' Aratus gave him the go-ahead, and Nealces erased† Aristratus and replaced him with just a palm-tree, not wanting to add anything more contentious. But apparently the feet of the otherwise erased Aristratus were overlooked under the chariot.

So Ptolemy, who was already inclined to like Aratus because of the paintings, took to him even more once he had got to know him, and gave him 150 talents for Sicyon, forty of which Aratus took with him straight away when he returned to the Peloponnese, and the rest Ptolemy sent to him later in separate tranches. [14] It was a major feat to procure such a large sum of money for his fellow citizens, when kings usually gave generals and politicians only a fraction of this amount, and that was to reward them for their crimes—for enslaving their countries and presenting them to the kings. But it was an even more significant accomplishment to use the money to reconcile rich and poor and establish concord between them, and to make the entire population safe and secure.*

Given how much power Aratus had, he displayed admirable restraint. He was appointed sole arbitrator of the exiles' claims and given complete control of their financial affairs, with absolute power, but he refused to work alone. He coopted fifteen other Sicyonians to join him. Even with their help, it was far from simple or straightforward, but eventually he managed to reconcile his fellow citizens with one another, settle their disputes, and restore harmony. For this, not only did the entire citizen body award him appropriate honours, but at their own expense the exiles erected a statue of him in bronze, with the following elegiac inscription:

It is true that word of this man's wisdom, and of what he has achieved
For Greece by his valour, has reached the Pillars† of Heracles.
But we have erected your statue to honour the goodness and justice
You displayed, Aratus, in arranging our restoration—a statue
Of our saviour, dedicated to the saviour gods, for the gift of equality†
And the sacred rule of law you gave the city of your birth.

[15] Aratus earned so much gratitude for his successful handling of this business that his position became unassailable by political rivalry. King Antigonus, however, was annoyed at the turn of events, and decided to try to win Aratus' friendship once and for all, or at least drive a wedge between him and Ptolemy. Among his friendly gestures, none of which was at all welcome to their recipient, he once sent Aratus in Sicyon portions of the victims from a sacrifice he was performing to the gods in Corinth. And at the well-attended banquet which followed the sacrifice, he made a speech for all his guests to hear. 'I used to think', he said, 'that this Sicyonian boy had no more going for him than a noble and patriotic spirit, but it looks as though he's also a competent judge of the lives and affairs of kings. After all, in the past he used to ignore us. He had his gaze fixed hopefully abroad, because all the talk he was hearing of elephants and fleets and palaces gave him a high regard for Egyptian wealth. But now that he has seen behind the scenes there and realizes that everything is just play-acting and trumpery,* he has come over entirely to our side. I myself welcome the young man. I have decided to involve him in all my affairs, and I require all of you to consider him a friend.' These words of his were a gift to the spiteful and malicious. They all tried to be the first to write to Ptolemy with a list of troubling charges against Aratus, and Ptolemy was moved to write an aggrieved letter to Aratus. But then, however highly prized friendship with kings and tyrants is, and however ardently men lust after it, it always brings envy and ill-will in its train.

[16] During Aratus' first Generalship of the Achaean League,* he conducted raids across the gulf on the Locrian and Calydonian coastlines, and took an army of 10,000 to help the Boeotians. But he arrived too late for the battle, which took place at Chaeronea. The Boeotians were defeated by the Aetolians with the loss of a thousand men, including the Boeotarch, Abaeocritus.†*

A year later, when he was General for the second time,* he set about putting into effect the seizure of the Acrocorinth.* This was not something he undertook merely for the sake of the Sicyonians or the Achaeans; the Macedonian garrison he was intending to drive from there was a tyranny that oppressed all Greece. Once, after defeating the Persian king's commanders, the Athenian general Chares described the victory in a letter to the Athenian people as 'sister to Marathon';* by the same token, this coup by Aratus might fairly be called the sister of the tyrant-slaying achievements of Pelopidas of Thebes and Thrasybulus of Athens, with the crucial difference that Aratus was acting not against fellow Greeks, but against foreign imperialists who had imposed their rule from outside.*

The point is that it is here that the Isthmus, acting as a barrier between the seas, joins and connects our mainland to the Peloponnese, so that, when garrisoned, the Acrocorinth, a tall mound rising from the heart of Greece, denies access to the entire Peloponnese by making communication and passage between the two halves of Greece difficult, and by impeding the execution of military manoeuvres by both land and sea. In other words, whoever holds the Acrocorinth with a garrison is thereby the sole lord and master of Greece, and Philip V was speaking no more than the earnest truth whenever he described the city of Corinth as the fetters of Greece.*

[17] That is why kings and dynasts were constantly fighting for control of the place, and why Antigonus' interest in it was indistinguishable from the most passionate variety of lust: he gave himself heart and soul to scheming how to gain it by stealth (an open attempt stood no chance) from whoever held it. So, after the death of Alexander,* in whose domain the citadel fell—he was allegedly poisoned by Antigonus—when his wife Nicaea took over the reins and became responsible for the security of the Acrocorinth, Antigonus immediately sent his son Demetrius* to her, flattering her with the prospect of a royal wedding and of marriage with a young man who would make a pleasant companion for an older woman. Although this use of his son as common bait netted him Nicaea, however, she would not give up the Acrocorinth, but kept it under a strong guard. But Antigonus continued to feign indifference: he celebrated their marriage in Corinth, and put on shows and arranged drinking-parties every day, for all the world as though he were so pleased and happy that he had nothing more on his mind than amusement and relaxation.

But then his moment came. Amoebeus* was giving a concert in the theatre, and Antigonus personally escorted Nicaea to the show in a litter decorated with royal trappings. Preening herself on this high honour, she had no idea what the future held. When they reached the point in the road where there was a turning up to the citadel, Antigonus gave orders that Nicaea was to be taken on to the theatre, but he turned his back on Amoebeus and the wedding celebrations, and raced up to the Acrocorinth with a speed that belied his years. Finding the gate locked, he knocked on it with his staff and ordered it to be opened, and the guards inside were so intimidated that they did so.

That is how he gained control of the place. He was beside himself with joy—so pleased that he used to drink and make merry in the streets, and carouse garlanded through the city square, attended by pipe-girls, greeting and addressing by name those he met. And he was an old man,* who should by then have become used to abrupt changes of fortune—which just goes to show that unexpected pleasure has more power than either grief or fear to drive a man out of his mind and disturb his composure. [18] Anyway, once Antigonus had taken possession of the Acrocorinth like this, he installed a garrison and made the philosopher Persaeus* and other men he especially trusted responsible for the city.

Now, Aratus had set things in motion even while Alexander was still alive, but then the Achaeans and Alexander had entered into an alliance, and he had cancelled the attempt. At the time in question, however, a fresh opportunity to act came his way. This is what happened.* There were four Syrian brothers living in Corinth, one of whom, Diocles, was a mercenary serving in the garrison. When the other three stole some of the king's coined gold, they brought it to a banker in Sicyon called Aegias, who was a business associate of Aratus. They disposed of some of the gold straight away, but the rest of it was being gradually exchanged for silver by one of the brothers, Erginus by name, in repeated visits to the banker.

As a result of the frequency of their meetings, Erginus and Aegias became friends, and on one occasion Erginus was drawn into a conversation with Aegias about the garrison. He told the banker that once, when he was going up to see his brother, as he was walking past the cliff-face he had noticed a sloping fissure leading† to a point where the citadel wall was at its lowest. Aegias said to him, as a joke: 'Why on earth, then, are you and your brothers breaking into the king's compound to get your hands on a few gold coins, when you could make yourselves hugely wealthy by selling just a little of your time? I mean, the penalty is death for burglars as well as traitors, if they're caught.' With a laugh, Erginus agreed to sound out Diocles—he did not trust the other two at all, he said—and a few days later, when he returned to Corinth, he undertook to show Aratus where the wall was no more than fifteen feet high, and guaranteed his and Diocles' help with everything else as well.

[19] Aratus promised them sixty talents if things went well, and in the event of failure, if he and they were still alive, a house and a talent each. Now, he was supposed to deposit the sixty talents for Erginus with Aegias, but he did not have that much money himself and he did not want to alert anyone else to the scheme by borrowing. What he did, then, was take most of his goblets and any pieces of golden jewellery his wife had, and leave them with Aegias as collateral. In other words, he was so excited by the prospect of satisfying his passionate desire to do good that he went one better even than Phocion and Epaminondas,* who, as he knew, were held to have been the best and most honest of the Greeks for having spurned huge bribes and preferred† the honourable course to the lucrative one. That is, he chose to commit his own money secretly and in advance to a project in which all the risks would be his and everyone else would remain in ignorance of what he was doing for them. Who could fail to find this admirable? Who could fail, even now, to feel an urge to support the man in his high-minded venture? He spent a fortune to place himself in great danger, and he pledged what are commonly held to be the most valuable possessions a man can have in order to infiltrate the enemy position by night and fight for his life, when all he had received by way of security from his fellow citizens were their hopes for a better future, and nothing else.

[20] The operation was risky enough in itself, but an unwitting mistake right at the beginning made it even more dangerous. Aratus' slave Technon was sent to meet up with Diocles and reconnoitre the wall. Even though he had never met Diocles face to face before, he thought he had a good enough sense of his general appearance from what Erginus had told him—that he had curly hair, a dark complexion, and no beard. So he went to the pre-arranged meeting-place—the

spot known as Bird Rock, outside the city—and waited for Erginus to arrive with Diocles.

But while he was waiting, by an unfortunate coincidence Dionysius, the eldest brother of Erginus and Diocles, turned up. Now, Dionysius was not one of the conspirators and knew nothing of the plot, but he looked like Diocles, and so Technon, prompted by the similarity to what he had been told to look for in Diocles, asked him whether he was related to Erginus. On hearing that he was his brother, Technon was absolutely convinced that he was talking to Diocles. Without asking his name or hesitating any further, he shook his hand, and began talking to him about his and Erginus' arrangements and asking how they were going.

Dionysius made no attempt to correct his mistake and, cunningly agreeing with everything Technon was saying, turned back towards the city, keeping the conversation going so as to draw Technon along with him without arousing his suspicions. But just as they were approaching the city and Dionysius was poised to arrest Technon, Fortune intervened again and Erginus met them. As soon as he saw that Technon had been tricked and they were in danger, he let him know, with a gesture of his head, that he should flee, and the two of them sped away to Aratus without further mishap. Aratus, however, was not inclined to despair. He immediately gave Erginus some money and told him to take it to Dionysius and ask him not to say anything. Erginus did as he was told, and even managed to bring Dionysius with him when he returned to Aratus' residence. Having got him there, they did not let him leave again, but tied him up, locked him in a storeroom, and put a guard on him. Then they began to prepare for action.

[21] When everything was ready, he ordered the bulk of his forces to stay under arms where they were for the night, while he took 400 picked men, only a few of whom knew what was at stake, and led them past the sanctuary of Hera towards the city gate there. It was the height of summer, there was a full moon, and the night was cloudless and clear enough to make them afraid that the guards might be alerted to their presence by the gleam of their weaponry in the moonlight. But by the time the first of them were approaching the wall, clouds had rolled in from the sea and cast the city and its surroundings into shadow.

At that point, while the rest of the men sat down and began to take off their boots (climbing ladders barefoot is quieter and less precarious), Erginus took seven young soldiers disguised as wayfarers, reached the gate without trouble, and killed the gatekeeper and the sentries posted with him. Meanwhile, the ladders were set up and Aratus had a hundred men scale the wall, telling the others to join up with him at the Acrocorinth as soon as possible. Then he pulled the ladders up after him and made his way through the city towards the citadel, elated by the fact that they had escaped detection and things were going well.

A little further on, they met four soldiers out on patrol with torches. The moon, which was still overclouded, stopped them being seen, but they could see the men approaching from straight ahead, so they withdrew into the shelter of some walls and buildings to ambush them. Three out of the four were killed in the attack, but, despite a head-wound from a sword, the fourth escaped, crying out that the enemy was within the walls. And before long trumpets were sounding the alarm, the city was stirring in response to the threat, the streets were filled with people running to and fro, many torches were starting to dispel the darkness both in the city below and up on the citadel, and indistinct shouting was breaking out from all quarters.

[22] Meanwhile, Aratus resolutely pressed on. He found the going past the cliff-face difficult, and his progress was pitifully slow and hesitant at first. In fact, he was in danger of straying from the path, which was completely overhung and overshadowed by the crags, and followed a tortuous and hazardous route up to the wall. But then, we are told, by some miracle the moon broke through the clouds and shone out, illuminating the most difficult stretch of the path, so that Aratus was able to reach the wall exactly where he was supposed to—and once he was there the clouds gathered again and everything was shrouded in darkness.

As for the 300 soldiers Aratus had left outside the walls at the gate near the sanctuary of Hera, they burst into the city to find it in turmoil and filled with torchlight. Unable to locate the path the others had taken or follow in their tracks, they huddled down all together under a rocky overhang and waited impatiently there. It was an anxious and stressful time for them, because when Aratus and his men came under fire from the citadel and the fighting began, the din of battle reached them from above. Cries rang out all around and echoed from the hills, jumbling all the sounds together so that it was impossible for them to tell where they were coming from and they had no idea what direction to take.

Just then, however, Archelaus, the commander of the king's forces, set out up the slope at the head of a large body of men, with shouts and trumpets blaring, to attack Aratus. But his route took him past the 300, and they rose up as if they had been lying in wait for him. They killed the leaders in their first charge, put the rest (including Archelaus) to panic flight, and pursued them until they were scattered about the city with no chance of reuniting. They had no time to rest on their laurels, however, because just then Erginus arrived from the force fighting up on the citadel, with news that the enemy Aratus had engaged were putting up a stiff resistance, so that there was a serious fight going on right at the wall and their help was urgently required. They told him to lead the way, and as they climbed up they called out to let their friends know that they were coming and inspire them with confidence.

The glint of their weaponry in the light of the full moon gave the enemy an exaggerated impression of their numbers, thanks to the length of time it took them to wind their way up, and at the same time the resonance typical of night-time made it seem as though their cries were issuing from many times the number of men. Eventually, with a concerted attack, they succeeded in driving the enemy troops out and gaining control of the Acrocorinth with its fortress. By now day was dawning and, as the first rays of the sun shone down upon their victory, the rest of Aratus' forces arrived from Sicyon. The Corinthians readily opened the city gates to welcome them, and helped them round up the king's men.

[23] When everything seemed safe, Aratus came down from the citadel to the theatre, which was filling up with an enormous crowd of people, all eager to see him and hear what his message to the Corinthians would be. With his Achaean troops posted at the entrances on either side of the theatre, he emerged from the stage building into view, still wearing his armour. He was so exhausted from his exertions and lack of sleep that he did not look his usual self, and his exultation and joy were overwhelmed† by physical weariness. But the assembled people greeted his appearance with effusive expressions of goodwill, so he grasped his spear in his right hand, and with his knee bent and body leaning a little at an angle he supported himself on it and stood there for a long time in silence, receiving their

congratulatory applause and acclamation for his valour and good fortune.

Once they had stopped and settled down, he pulled himself together and delivered a speech on behalf of the Achaeans that did justice to their achievement and persuaded the Corinthians to become Achaeans. He then gave them back the keys to the city gates, which had been denied them since the time of Philip II. As for Antigonus' generals, he let Archelaus go—he had been taken prisoner—but put Theophrastus to death, because he refused to leave of his own accord, while Persaeus had fled from the city as soon as the citadel fell and made his way to Cenchreae.* Later in life, we hear, when he had set himself up as a teacher, someone suggested that only a wise man could be a true general, and he replied: 'Well, I can assure you that I too used to be particularly attracted to this aspect of Zeno's teaching.* But I don't believe it any more. I was corrected by the youngster from Sicyon.' This story about Persaeus can be found in a number of writers.

[24] Within a few hours, Aratus had gained both the sanctuary of Hera* and Lechaeum.* He also took possession of twenty-five of the king's ships, and sold 500 horses and 400 Syrians. The Achaeans secured the Acrocorinth with a guard of 400 hoplites and fifty dogs, each with its own handler who lived in the fortress.

Now, the Romans used to express their admiration of Philopoemen by calling him 'the last of the Greeks',* in the sense that no great man was born in Greece after him. In my opinion, however, Aratus' capture of Corinth was the last significant Greek achievement, and it was on a par with the greatest of them not just in its boldness, but in the good fortune that attended it. This immediately became evident when the Megarians seceded from Antigonus and sided with Aratus, and Troezen and Epidaurus became members of the Achaean League. Moreover, in the very next expedition that he undertook, he invaded Attica and then sailed over to Salamis and plundered it.* It was as though the Achaean army had been released from confinement, and he could rely on them to do his bidding. Any Athenian citizens he captured he released without ransom, sowing the seeds there of rebellion against Macedon, and he entered into an alliance with Ptolemy,* granting him honorary leadership of the Achaean forces at war on land and at sea.

Aratus became so powerful within the league, in fact, that they elected him General every other year, and that was only because it was illegal to do so every year. In reality, however, and in terms of the policies they followed, he was the permanent head of state. For they could see that what mattered most to him was not wealth, or reputation, or the friendship of kings, or what was good for his native city, but purely and solely the growth of the Achaean League. It was his view that cities were vulnerable on their own and needed others to be safe—needed to bind themselves, so to speak, to the wider interests of a confederacy. Just as the parts of a body have life and the ability to cooperate because they are all interconnected, but wither and decay when the connection is broken and they become separate entities, in much the same way, he believed, cities are ruined by those who keep them apart, but are strengthened by mutual dependence, when as parts of a greater unity they gain access to wisdom of the whole.

[25] He hated to see the Argives enslaved, while the best of the league's neighbours were independent, and he put in motion a plot to kill their tyrant, Aristomachus. His intention was not only to bring the city into the league, but also to thank it for looking after him when he was a child, by giving it back its freedom. Men were found who would dare the deed, and Aeschylus and Charimenes the seer took charge of them, but they had no swords, because it was illegal to own one; the tyrant had stipulated severe penalties for anyone caught in possession of weaponry. Aratus therefore arranged for stilettos to be made in Corinth and sewn up inside saddle-cloths; these cloths were then draped over some mules, part of a train taking some odds and ends to Argos, and sent on their way. Charimenes, however, recruited a disreputable† character for the enterprise, to the annoyance of Aeschylus and the others, who gave up on the seer and proceeded to act on their own. When Charimenes found out, in the heat of the moment he informed against them just as they were walking up to stab the tyrant. Most of the conspirators, however, made their way swiftly out of the city square and escaped to Corinth.

But a short while later Aristomachus was killed by slaves, and Aristippus, an even more pernicious tyrant, took over from him before anything could be done.* Aratus therefore put together a force consisting of all those Achaeans he could find at short notice, and quickly set out to help, thinking that he would meet with an enthusiastic response from the Argives. But most of them were by now inured to slavery and accepted their lot, and when no one joined him he withdrew. All he had done was furnish grounds for the Achaeans to be charged with having gone to war at a time of peace. The case was heard before the Mantineans, and in Aratus' absence Aristippus, as plaintiff, won and the league was fined thirty mnas.* As for Aratus himself, Aristippus, moved by a combination of hatred and fear, now began to lay plans for his murder, with the help of King Antigonus. In almost every city they had agents looking for an opportunity to do the deed.

But for a head of state there is no safeguard to compare with true and stable loyalty. When both the common people and the power-possessors of a community are accustomed to be afraid *for* their leader, rather than *of* their leader, he sees with many eyes, hears with many ears, and has advance notice of events. And so I would like to interrupt my account at this point and explain how Aristippus lived—the kind of life that was his by virtue of his enviable tyranny and his absolute power, the glitter of which is so widely coveted and admired.

[26] Even though he had Antigonus as an ally, even though he kept a large number of troops to protect his person, and even though he had left none of his enemies alive in the city, he still used to have his bodyguards and sentries bivouac in the outer courtyard of his house. Immediately after dinner he would order all his household slaves to leave, and locked the door between the outer courtyard and the inner part of the house, before secreting himself and his mistress in a small upper chamber, which was accessed by a hatchway. Before lying down, he positioned his bed over this hatchway, and then his sleep was as troubled and fearful as you would expect from someone in his position. His mistress's mother used to remove the ladder and lock it up in another room, and then replace it at daybreak and call the grand tyrant down, and down he would creep like a reptile from its hole.

Aratus, however, used legal means, not weaponry, to secure unassailable power for himself, and it came to him by virtue of his excellence, not as a result of coercion. Dressed modestly in a cloak or simple cape, the declared enemy of all tyrants everywhere, his family to this very day is still one of the most distinguished in Greece. But few of the men who occupied citadels, kept bodyguards, and protected themselves, like timorous hares, with weaponry and locked doors and hatchways escaped violent death, and none of them has left a house or family or tomb to preserve his memory with honour.

[27] Anyway, none of Aratus' many attempts to take Argos and

topple Aristippus, by stealth or open warfare, was successful.* On one occasion, he actually managed to bring ladders to bear, scaled the wall at great risk with a few men, and killed any guards there who offered resistance. But then, at daybreak, the tyrant launched an all-out attack. While the Argives just sat and watched impassively and impartially, as though they were umpiring the Nemean Games rather than witnessing a battle in which their freedom was the prize,* Aratus fought back stubbornly and, despite taking a wound in the thigh from a spear-thrust, held his ground against his enemies' challenges until nightfall without giving way. Indeed, if he had been able to maintain the effort through the night, he would not have failed, since the tyrant was already contemplating flight and had sent many of his personal belongings on ahead to the coast. But unfortunately no one brought news of this to Aratus, and since he was also running low on water and disabled by his wound, he withdrew.

[28] After this, he abandoned the stealthy approach, and openly invaded the Argolid with his army and ravaged farmland. When a fierce battle with Aristippus took place at the river Chares, Aratus was accused of abandoning the battlefield and throwing victory away. Although the rest of his forces clearly had the upper hand—their pursuit of the enemy was already well advanced—he himself withdrew in disarray to his camp, not so much because he had been driven off the field by his opponents, as because he became unsure of victory and took fright.

When the rest of his men returned from their pursuit they were furious. Even though they had routed the enemy and the tally of the dead was well in their favour, they had allowed the losers to erect a trophy of victory over them. Out of shame, Aratus decided to risk a second pitched battle for the right to erect the trophy, and two days later he drew up his men again. But finding that the tyrant now had more men at his disposal and that they were resisting with greater determination, his courage failed and he went back home, after collecting the bodies of his dead under a truce.

His interpersonal and political skills, however, and his popularity were such that this lapse was not held against him, and he went on to gain Cleonae for the Achaeans and to hold the Nemean Games there, claiming that responsibility for the games belonged by right of tradition to the people of Cleonae. But the Argives also put on the games, and for the first time the inviolability and safety that were granted contestants counted for nothing, since everyone the Achaeans caught passing through their land who had taken part in the Argive games was treated as an enemy and sold into slavery. This just goes to show how fierce and implacable Aratus' hatred of tyrants was.

[29] A little later, it came to Aratus' notice that, although Aristippus had designs on Cleonae, he was too afraid to act while he, Aratus, was encamped at Corinth. He therefore issued a general call-up, ordered his men to bring enough food for several days, and marched down to Cenchreae, cunningly inviting Aristippus to attack Cleonae while he was supposedly out of the way. The plan worked, and Aristippus immediately advanced on Cleonae from Argos with his army. But as soon as night fell, Aratus turned back to Corinth from Cenchreae. After posting pickets on the roads, he led the Achaeans on towards Cleonae and they followed with such discipline, speed, and determination that they got there while it was still night, and not only had Aristippus no idea that they were on their way, but he was even unaware that they had arrived and were in a position to give battle.

At daybreak the gates were opened, the trumpet gave the signal, and Aratus led his men, screaming their war-cries, in a furious charge against the enemy. The Argive forces immediately turned to flight, and since the countryside was riddled with trails Aratus resolutely kept up the pursuit wherever he felt that Aristippus was most likely to be fleeing. The chase went on as far as Mycenae, in fact, and there the tyrant was overtaken and killed by a Cretan called Tragiscus, according to Deinias.* Apart from Aristippus himself, over 1,500 of his men also fell. But despite this brilliant success, achieved without any loss of life on his part, Aratus was denied the chance to capture Argos and give its citizens back their freedom, because Agias and the younger Aristomachus burst into the city with troops supplied by the Macedonian king and took control.*

Be that as it may, he had succeeded in largely depriving the tyrants' toadies of the right to tell their usual slanderous stories, designed to mock and ridicule him. These people curried favour with the tyrants by saying that the Achaean General used to get an upset stomach when battle was imminent; that he would feel faint and dizzy as soon as the trumpeter stood ready beside him; and that once he had drawn up his forces for battle and issued the watchword, he would ask his generals and captains if there was any reason for his presence, given that the die was already cast, and would then withdraw some distance away to await the outcome. These rumours were so prevalent that even in the philosophical schools, when the topic for investigation was whether heart palpitations, loss of colour, and loosening of the bowels at the appearance of danger indicated cowardice or an imbalance in the body's humours, a constitutional coldness, the name of Aratus inevitably came up, as an example of someone who was a good general but who always experienced these symptoms at a time of battle.

[30] The immediate next target of his scheming, now that he had done away with Aristippus, was Lydiadas of Megalopolis, who was ruling the city of his birth as tyrant.* Now, Lydiadas was at heart a noble and idealistic man, and unlike most autocrats he was not drawn towards this form of injustice as a way to indulge his immoderate desires and greed. But as a young man he had been fired by love of glory, and had foolishly allowed his pride to be fed by the lies and falsehoods that people tell about tyranny, to the effect that it is a blessed and wonderful state of affairs. Once he had made himself tyrant, however, he soon became wearied by the oppressiveness of a sole ruler's lot. Since he envied Aratus' success and at the same time feared his scheming, he decided to change direction and came up with a truly admirable plan, which would allow him not only to free himself from hatred and fear, and from the necessity of garrison and bodyguards, but also to be a benefactor of the land of his birth. He invited Aratus into Megalopolis, abdicated his rule, and brought his city into the Achaean League. And the Achaeans, full of praise for what he had done, elected him their General.*

Lydiadas at once conceived the desire to make a greater name for himself than Aratus, and in pursuit of this aim he did a lot of things which do not seem strictly necessary, including declaring war on Sparta. Aratus opposed this campaign, but was widely believed to have done so out of spite, and Lydiadas was elected General for the second time, at any rate, despite Aratus' express opposition and attempts to get the position awarded to someone else—not himself, because, as I have already said, he held the post every other year. So things continued to go well for Lydiadas up to his third Generalship,* and he was elected General every other year in alternation with Aratus. But then he began to make no secret of his hostility and repeatedly maligned Aratus before the Achaeans, and as a result he was cast aside and ignored, since this seemed to be a case of an assumed character trying to outdo genuine, unalloyed excellence. Just as in the fable of

Aesop the cuckoo asks the little birds why they avoid him, and they reply that one day he will turn into a hawk,* so Lydiadas could apparently never shake off the mistrust people felt because of his former tyranny, and this made it difficult for them to believe in the reality of his changed character.

[31] Aratus did his reputation no harm in the war against the Aetolians either.* At one point, when the Achaeans were eager to fight the Aetolians in front of Megara and the Spartan king Agis, who had arrived with his army, was also pushing for battle, Aratus opposed them, and despite all the insults he had to endure, and the scornful allegations of cowardice and timidity, he refused to be swayed by the appearance of disgrace into abandoning what he judged to be the expedient course of action, and he allowed the enemy to cross the Geraneia mountains and enter the Peloponnese unopposed. But then, when they unexpectedly took Pellene,* Aratus was a different man altogether. Without hesitation or delay, without waiting for his forces to muster and assemble from all quarters, he set out straight away against the enemy with just the troops he had readily available.*

Now, the Aetolians' strength had been thoroughly sapped in their hour of victory by indiscipline and unruliness. No sooner had they entered the city than the soldiers had spread out among the houses, brawling and fighting over the loot, while the officers had gone around seizing the Pelleneans' wives and daughters, with each man removing his helmet and putting it on a particular woman as a way of marking her as his property and stopping anyone else taking her. This is what was on their minds and occupying them when the news of Aratus' attack arrived like a bolt from the blue. Naturally, given their disarray, they became panic-stricken, and even before all of them knew of the danger the first of them had already lost a battle with the Achaeans at the city gates and in the suburbs, and had turned to flight. And as they were being driven back pell-mell, they made it impossible for those who were trying to rally and offer resistance to be effective.

[32] It so happened that, in the midst of all this chaos, one of the female captives, the daughter of a distinguished Pellenean called Epigethes and notable herself for her beauty and stature, was sitting in the sanctuary of Artemis,* where she had been left by the captain of the Aetolians' elite brigade, who had taken her as his prize and put his triple-crested helmet on her. All of a sudden she ran out to see what the commotion was about, and as she stood in the entrance of the

sanctuary and looked down on the fighting below with the helmet on her head, even her fellow citizens were struck by the superhuman majesty with which she seemed endowed, while the enemy took her to be the epiphany of a god and were so overcome by terror and dread that none of them made any attempt to defend himself.*

The Pelleneans themselves, however, tell a different story. They explain that the statue of the goddess generally remains untouched in the temple, and that on those rare occasions when it is moved by the priestess and taken out, no one looks directly at it, but everyone averts their gaze, because the sight of the goddess is too terrifying for people to endure. And it does not affect only human beings, but if it is carried through an orchard it even makes the trees unproductive, in the sense that they drop their fruit before their season. So the story they tell about the occasion in question is that the priestess carried this image out of the temple and turned it this way and that to face the Aetolians, so that they were driven out of their minds and robbed of their ability to think straight. Nothing like this appears in Aratus' *Memoirs*, however. According to him, after he had put the Aetolians to flight and had burst into the city in the course of pursuing them, he drove them out by main force and killed 700 of them. This action became particularly famous, and was brought vividly to life by the painter Timanthes in his depiction of the battle.*

[33] Nevertheless, when a formidable coalition of peoples and dynasts began to form against the Achaeans,* Aratus did not hesitate to approach the Aetolians with a view to friendship, and with the help of Pantaleon, the most powerful man in the Aetolian League, he not only brought the war to an end, but even arranged an alliance between the two leagues.* His desire to free the Athenians, however, earned him severe censure from the Achaeans, because despite the fact that they had a truce in place with the Macedonians and had called a halt to hostilities, he tried to capture Piraeus.

Now, in the *Memoirs* he published, he denies responsibility for this attempt on Piraeus, and blames it on Erginus, the man who had helped him with the Acrocorinth.* He says that Erginus attacked Piraeus of his own accord, and that while he was being pursued by the enemy after his ladder broke, he kept on calling out Aratus' name, as though he were there, and escaped from the enemy by means of this subterfuge. But this defence does not ring true. It is hardly likely that it would have occurred to Erginus, a Syrian holding no official position, to undertake such an important operation, unless he was acting on Aratus' orders, and his forces and the opportunity were provided by Aratus. In fact, Aratus himself confirms this, because he attacked Piraeus not two or three times, but over and over again,* like a desperate lover, and so far from being deterred by repeated failure, the extremely narrow margins by which his hopes were frustrated encouraged him to feel sure of eventual success. Once he even broke his leg while fleeing across the Thriasian plain.* It took a number of operations to make it better, and for a long time he had to be carried in a litter when out on campaign.

[34] After Antigonus' death and Demetrius II's accession to the throne,* Aratus redoubled his efforts against Athens, and had nothing but contempt for the Macedonians. Hence, when he was defeated in battle at Phylacia by Demetrius' general Bithys,* and it was widely rumoured that he was either a captive or a corpse, Diogenes, the commander of the Macedonian garrison at Piraeus, wrote to Corinth ordering the Achaeans to evacuate the city, now that Aratus was dead. But unfortunately for him, Aratus was in Corinth in person when the letter arrived, and so, highly entertained, everyone had a good laugh at the messengers' expense before dismissing them. And Demetrius himself sent a ship from Macedon to bring Aratus back to him in chains, while the Athenians took their inane flattery of Macedon to a new level by donning celebratory garlands as soon as they heard the report of his death. This made Aratus furious, and he immediately launched an expedition against them. He advanced as far as the Academy, but was then persuaded to leave them alone.

This made the Athenians appreciate the fundamental goodness of Aratus' character, and after Demetrius' death, when they committed themselves to recovering their freedom, it was him they turned to for help.* Despite the fact that he was not the Achaean head of state that year, and although he had long been bed-ridden by a protracted illness, he had himself taken in a litter to Athens in response to their plea for help, and he played a part in persuading Diogenes, the garrison commander, to return Piraeus, Munychia, Salamis, and Sunium to the Athenians for 150 talents, twenty of which Aratus contributed himself. An immediate result of this was that Aegina and Hermione joined the Achaeans, and the largest group of Arcadian communities became a tributary member of the league. So, with the Macedonians preoccupied by wars against their neighbours,* and with the Aetolians as their allies, the Achaeans were going from strength to strength.

[35] But Aratus had long-unfinished business to complete. He still found it intolerable that Argos, a neighbouring state, should be ruled by a tyrant, and he wrote to Aristomachus to try to persuade him to restore democracy to the city and bring it into the Achaean League. He argued that Aristomachus should imitate Lydiadas and become, with everyone's blessing and respect, the General of this great confederacy rather than being the threatened and hated tyrant of a single city. The argument worked, and Aristomachus asked Aratus to send him fifty talents, so that he could dismiss and pay off his troops.*

But Lydiadas, who was still General of the league and wanted to represent this project to the Achaeans as his own, wrote to Aristomachus even as the money was being raised, denouncing Aratus as an implacable enemy of tyranny, and convinced him to entrust the business to him instead. But when he brought the man before the Achaeans, the members of the Achaean council gave an unequivocal demonstration of their loyalty towards Aratus and their trust in him. For when Aratus angrily spoke out against the proposal, they drove Aristomachus out of the meeting, but later, when Aratus had been won over and came before them again to initiate discussion of the same matter,† they quickly and readily voted in favour of the proposal, and not only accepted Argos and Phlious* into the league, but a year later elected Aristomachus their General.*

Trading on his current popularity among the Achaeans, Aristomachus conceived the desire to invade Laconia, and summoned Aratus from Athens to help him. Aratus wrote back and tried to dissuade him from the campaign; he was reluctant to involve the Achaeans in a war with Cleomenes,* an aggressive man who was becoming dangerously strong. But when Aristomachus insisted, Aratus obediently returned and took to the field alongside him. This was the occasion when he prevented Aristomachus from joining battle when Cleomenes came upon them at Pallantium,* and was denounced by Lydiadas for having done so. But when Aratus and Lydiadas became rival candidates for the Generalship of the league, Aratus won the vote and was elected General for the twelfth time.*

[36] During this term of his as General he lost a battle against Cleomenes at Mount Lycaeum* and was forced to flee. But in the dark of night he became lost, and people assumed that he had been

killed. Once again this rumour gained wide currency in Greece, but he was rescued, rallied his scattered troops, and so far from being content just to have got away safely, he brilliantly turned the situation to his advantage by launching a surprise attack on the Mantineans, who were allies of Cleomenes—something no one had anticipated or foreseen as a possibility. The city fell to him, and he installed a garrison and enfranchised the resident aliens,* thereby at one stroke gaining for the Achaeans after they had been defeated in battle what they would have struggled to gain had they won.

Later that year the Spartans mounted an expedition against Megalopolis, and although Aratus came to the city's defence, he refused to take up Cleomenes' offer of battle, and resisted the Megalopolitans' demands that he should do so. It was not just that he simply lacked whatever it takes to be good at pitched battles, but also that, on this particular occasion, he was outnumbered by the enemy and was up against a man in the first flush of youthful boldness, when he himself had by now lost his edge and his desire for distinction had been reined in.* Besides, it seemed to him that the glory his opponent was trying to win for the very first time was already his, and that he should take care to conserve it.

[37] But at one point, during a sortie, his light-armed troops forced the Spartans back to their camp and got in among the tents. Even then, however, Aratus did not attack, but halted his heavy infantry at the lip of a ravine that was in their way and refused to let them cross. This made Lydiadas furious and, cursing Aratus, he ordered the cavalry up to his position and called on them to support the light-armed troops in their pursuit, to seize this chance of victory, and not to leave him to defend the city of his birth by himself.

Encouraged by the number and calibre of the men who fell in behind him, he attacked the enemy's right wing and put it to flight. During the pursuit, however, his ardour and love of glory got the better of him and he was drawn uncontrollably into awkward terrain, filled with cultivated trees and wide ditches. Here Cleomenes counter-attacked and Lydiadas fell, after giving his all in the noblest of causes, fighting at the gates of his native city. The survivors fled back to the phalanx, but their arrival there panicked the heavy infantry, and their defeat spread and infected the entire army. The debacle was largely blamed on Aratus, for his failure to support Lydiadas, and the Achaeans returned home with feelings running high and forced him to accompany them to Aegium.* They convened a general assembly there and voted to deny him money and to stop maintaining a mercenary contingent, so that if he ever wanted to go to war he would have to find the funds by himself.

[38] Aratus' first response to this humiliation was to consider giving up the seal of office and resigning his Generalship, but after thinking it over he stayed in place for the time being.* And in his capacity as General he led the Achaean forces to Orchomenus, where he fought and won a battle against Megistonous,* Cleomenes' stepfather, in which he killed 300 of the enemy and took Megistonous prisoner. But then, although he invariably served as General every other year, the next time it was his turn to stand, when his name was called he took an oath of exemption, and Timoxenus was elected General.*

Now, although the excuse he gave for his refusal was the rift between him and the Achaean people, this did not ring true, and the real reason was thought to be the situation the Achaeans found themselves in. The days when Cleomenes had been making only slow and steady progress were past, and he was no longer constrained by due political process. Once he had killed the ephors, redistributed the land, and added large numbers of *perioeci* to the citizen body he had absolute power,* and he immediately began to put pressure on the Achaeans and demand the leadership of the Peloponnese for himself.

As a result, people criticize Aratus for behaving like an irresponsible helmsman in giving up the tiller and handing it over to someone else when the Achaeans were beset by storm and surge. They maintain that the noble course would have been for him to remain at the helm, even if they did not want him there, and save the ship of state. Alternatively, if he thought that the situation was hopeless and the Achaeans too weak, it would have been better for him to have given in to Cleomenes' demands, rather than to have turned the Peloponnese once more into a barbarian stronghold* by bringing in Macedonian garrisons, or to have filled the Acrocorinth with Illyrian and Celtic weaponry, or to have made men whom he outclassed as both general and statesman, and at whom he constantly sneers in his *Memoirs*, the masters of the Peloponnesian cities, even under the euphemistic title of 'allies'. After all, even if Cleomenes was, as must be admitted, a lawless and tyrannical man, he was still a Heraclid* and a scion of Sparta, the least of whose citizens should have been more deserving of leadership than the most eminent Macedonian, to anyone who placed the slightest value on the nobility that Greek birth confers.

And the fact is† that when Cleomenes asked the Achaeans for supreme power he did so with the promise that he would repay them for the honour of that title by doing the cities a great deal of good, whereas when Antigonus* was proclaimed commander-in-chief, with unlimited powers on land and at sea, he refused to accept the position until the Achaeans had promised to pay him for his leadership with the Acrocorinth. Antigonus behaved, then, like Aesop's hunter:* he would not mount the Achaeans, even though they wanted him to and showed their submission to him in their diplomacy and their decrees, until they allowed him to bridle them with garrison and hostages.

It is true that Aratus finds every possible way to claim that the emergency left him no choice. But Polybius reports that, out of concern about Cleomenes' aggressiveness, Aratus had already been in secret communication with Antigonus for a while, well before the 'emergency', and had primed the Megalopolitans (who were suffering more than anyone from the war, with incessant plundering raids by Cleomenes) to ask the Achaeans to call in Antigonus.* And a similar account of this episode is given by Phylarchus too, although it would be wrong to trust him at all without Polybius to support him. For he is so prejudiced in favour of Cleomenes that his every mention of him is ecstatic, and he uses his history to denigrate one man and vindicate the other as though he were in a court of law.

[39] So the Achaeans lost Mantinea, which was retaken by Cleomenes, and they were also defeated in a major battle at the Hecatombaeum.* This defeat so demoralized them that they very soon wrote to invite Cleomenes to come to Argos with a view to assuming the leadership of the Peloponnese. But when Aratus learnt that he was on his way and had reached Lerna with his army, he became afraid, and sent envoys to ask him to bring only 300 men, seeing that he was coming to people who were his friends and allies, and to allay any suspicions Cleomenes might have he offered him hostages.* But Cleomenes upped sticks and left, declaring this demand to be nothing more than a way to humiliate and insult him, and wrote a letter to the Achaeans roundly rebuking and reviling Aratus. In return, Aratus too wrote a letter critical of Cleomenes, and their mutual recriminations and slurs escalated until they were pouring abuse on

each other's marriages and wives. And the upshot was that Cleomenes sent a herald to declare war on the Achaeans.

He came very close to seizing Sicyon with help from inside the city, but the attempt was thwarted and instead he attacked nearby Pellene, which he gained once the Achaean garrison commander had been expelled. Then, a little later, he also took Pheneus and Penteleium, at which point the Argives immediately came over to his side and the people of Phlious accepted his garrison. In short, the Achaeans could no longer count on any of their recent acquisitions, and Aratus was suddenly threatened by chaos, with the Peloponnese plainly unstable and rebellion being fomented everywhere by agitators in the cities.*

[40] The trouble was that no one† was satisfied or content with things as they stood. Many men, in fact, not only from Sicyon itself but also from Corinth, had been in open communication with Cleomenes, and had long been disloyal to the league out of desire for personal power. Aratus was given absolute authority* to deal with these men, and he put to death everyone in Sicyon who was found to have accepted bribes.

In Corinth, however, his attempt to discover who the offenders were and punish them aroused the anger of the ordinary people, who were already disaffected and unhappy with life under the Achaeans, and at a hastily convened assembly in the sanctuary of Apollo they decided to secede from the league, and to make their first step in that direction the killing or arrest of Aratus. They sent for him, and he came alone, leading his horse, as though he had no worries or suspicions.* At his arrival, many men leapt to their feet and began hurling abuse and accusations at him, but he kept his features and his speech calm and collected, and gently told them to sit down, pointing out that by standing and shouting in this disorderly manner they were making it impossible for those who were waiting by the entrance to come in.

As he was speaking, he gradually sidled away, as though he were going to hand his horse over to someone, and once he had slipped out of the precinct on this pretext he continued talking in an unflustered way to any Corinthians he met, telling them to make their way to the sanctuary, and before anyone suspected anything he was within reach of the Acrocorinth. Then he leapt on to his horse, sent word to Cleopater, the garrison commander, to stand firm and guard the Acrocorinth, and rode off to Sicyon. But he was accompanied by only thirty men; all the rest abandoned him and went their separate ways.

It did not take the Corinthians long to realize that he had fled, but the posse they sent after him failed to catch up with him. Then they called Cleomenes in and handed the city over to him, even though he felt that what they were giving him was no compensation for their mistake in letting Aratus get away. So once the inhabitants of the region known as the Headland had come over to his side and entrusted their towns to him,* he set about encircling the Acrocorinth with a wall and a palisade.

[41] Meanwhile, a few† Achaeans came and joined Aratus at Sicyon. They constituted an assembly, at which he was elected General with unrestricted powers, and he formed for his protection a bodyguard made up of his own fellow citizens. For thirty-three years* he had been the leading statesman in Achaea, and his power and glory had been unrivalled in Greece, but now he had no allies or resources, and was clinging to the wreckage of the league, so to speak, at the mercy of a storm-tossed sea and in constant danger. For the Aetolians turned down his request for aid, and even though the Athenians were ready to help, mindful of past kindnesses from Aratus, they were prevented from doing so by Eurycleides and Micion.*

Now, Aratus had property and a house in Corinth, but Cleomenes kept his hands off them, and preserved them from others' depredations as well. In fact, he arranged a meeting with Aratus' friends and managers, at which he told them to look after his property and to assume in all they did† that they would be submitting their accounts to Aratus. He also privately sent Tripylus to Aratus, and later his stepfather Megistonous,* promising him, among a number of other things, an annual allowance of twelve talents, double what he had been getting from Ptolemy, who had been sending Aratus six talents a year.* But at the same time he demanded that he should be proclaimed the leader of the Achaeans and that the Acrocorinth should be garrisoned by his Spartans as well as by the Achaeans.

Aratus replied that he was not in control of events, but the other way around,* and Cleomenes, thinking that he was being treated like a fool, immediately invaded Sicyonia. He plundered and devastated the land, and encamped before Sicyon itself for three months, while Aratus endured the siege and pondered whether to accept the condition on which Antigonus would agree to an alliance, which was that he should be given the Acrocorinth; without this, he was refusing to help.

[42] When the Achaeans met for their assembly at Aegium, therefore, they invited Aratus to attend, but with Cleomenes encamped by the city he was facing a dangerous journey. In fact, his fellow citizens tried to keep him in Sicyon. They pleaded with him and told him that they would not let him risk his life outside the city walls with the enemy near by, and before long he was surrounded by both women and children, who embraced him with tears in their eyes as though he were the common father and protector of them all. But he comforted them and allayed their fears, and, accompanied by ten friends and his son,* now a young man, he rode out to the coast, where there were ships lying at anchor. They went on board and were transported to Aegium to attend the assembly, at which the Achaeans voted to ask Antigonus for help and to give him the Acrocorinth. Aratus even sent his son to Antigonus as one of several hostages.* The Corinthians were furious at this betrayal, and they plundered Aratus' property and made a personal gift to Cleomenes of his house.

[43] As Antigonus marched south at the head of an army of 20,000 Macedonians and 1,300 horse, Aratus and the Ministers* eluded the enemy and travelled by sea to meet him at Pagae. Aratus was rather nervous about meeting Antigonus and wary of the Macedonians in general, seeing that he had made harming their interests the basis of his rise to power and that his political career had been essentially founded on his hostility towards the former Antigonus.* But men who seem to be rulers are really slaves to circumstance, and since in his opinion the situation left him absolutely no choice, he carried on despite his fears.

But when Antigonus was told of his arrival, although the way he greeted the rest of the party was nothing out of the ordinary, he received Aratus, even at this first meeting, with exceptional honour. And as he got to know him better and recognized his integrity and intelligence, he drew him into greater intimacy with himself. For Aratus proved not only to be of practical help in affairs of state, but also to be more pleasant company for the king in his leisure hours than anyone else. Hence, despite being young,* when Antigonus realized that a king could profit from friendship with such a man, he began to rely on him more, and more constantly, than he did even on any of the Macedonians in his court, let alone other Achaeans.

And so the portent displayed by the god on one of Aratus' sacrificial victims came true. Not long before this, when Aratus was sacrificing, a liver was found, we are told, that had two gall-bladders wrapped in a single piece of fat, and the seer told him to expect soon to become extremely close to what he loathed and hated most bitterly. At the time Aratus ignored the prophecy, since in any case he tended not to have much faith in sacrificial victims and seercraft, preferring to rely on reason. But later, when the war was going well, Antigonus laid on a banquet in Corinth and had Aratus, of all his many guests, recline next to him on his left. A short while later, he called for a blanket and asked whether Aratus was finding it cold as well. When Aratus admitted that he was indeed very cold, Antigonus told him to come closer, and when the blanket was brought the slaves covered both of them with it at once. Then Aratus remembered his sacrificial victim, burst into laughter, and told the king about the portent and the prophecy. But this incident took place later.

[44] At Pagae, as soon as Aratus and the king had exchanged oaths of friendship and alliance, they set out against the enemy, and some fighting took place near Corinth, where Cleomenes was well entrenched and the Corinthians put up stiff resistance.* But meanwhile an Argive friend of Aratus called Aristotle* wrote secretly to him, guaranteeing that he would get Argos to leave Cleomenes' alliance if Aratus brought him soldiers. After telling Antigonus, Aratus quickly set sail from the Isthmus to Epidaurus with a force of 1,500 men—but by then the Argives had already risen up in rebellion, attacked the troops Cleomenes had stationed there, and pinned them on the acropolis. When Cleomenes heard about this, he realized to his alarm that if the enemy occupied Argos there was no way he would be able to get safely back to Sparta, and so he left the Acrocorinth that same night and went to the defence of Argos.

He managed to reach Argos first, and inflicted a partial defeat on the rebels, but a little later Aratus arrived, and then Antigonus appeared with his army, and Cleomenes retreated to Mantinea.* After this, all the cities rejoined the Achaeans and the Acrocorinth was handed over to Antigonus. Aratus was elected General by the Argives and persuaded them to give Antigonus, as a personal gift, the property of the tyrants and the traitors. As for Aristomachus, he was tortured to death in Cenchreae and his body thrown to the fishes. Aratus came in for a great deal of criticism for this, on the grounds that, despite the fact that Aristomachus had not been a bad man, and had even cooperated with Aratus and agreed to abdicate his tyranny and bring the city in the Achaean League, he had allowed him to be killed without the due process of law.*

[45] Soon people began accusing him of everything else as well. They said, for example, that† the Achaeans had given Corinth to Antigonus as a personal gift as though it were just an ordinary village; that they had let him plunder Orchomenus and install a Macedonian garrison; and that they had made it illegal to contact any other king by letter or embassy without Antigonus' permission. They resented the fact that they were forced to maintain and pay the wages of the Macedonian troops, and put on sacrifices, parades, and athletic festivals in honour of Antigonus,* when it was the Sicyonians, Aratus' fellow citizens, who had taken the lead in this and had been the first to welcome Antigonus, when he came to their city as Aratus' guest.

In short, they laid everything at his door, not realizing that once he had handed over the reins to Antigonus, he was pulled along in the wake of the king's impetus, no longer the master of anything except his tongue, and even then it was dangerous for him to speak his mind. At any rate, it was perfectly plain that many of the king's actions annoyed Aratus—the business with the statues, for instance. In Argos, Antigonus put back up the statues of the tyrants that had been pulled down,* and pulled down the statues of the men involved in the capture of the Acrocorinth, with the sole exception of the one of Aratus. And however often Aratus begged him to reconsider, the king took not the slightest notice.

The Achaeans were also thought to have transgressed Greek conventions in their treatment of Mantinea. After gaining control of the city with Antigonus' help, they killed the most eminent and distinguished citizens, sold the rest of the men into slavery or sent them in fetters to Macedon, and enslaved the children and women, with one-third of the profits going to them and two-thirds to the Macedonians. Now, even if this fell under the law of reprisal*—for however appalling it is to treat men of the same race and blood like this out of anger, nevertheless, when the situation makes it necessary, 'even cruelty is sweet', as Simonides* says, thinking of the remedies and cures that are used for mental agony and torment—what Aratus went on to do to the city cannot be excused as either fair or necessary. After the city was given to the Achaeans by Antigonus, they decided to resettle it and Aratus was chosen to be the founder of the new settlement; and in his capacity as General of the league, he saw through a decree changing the name of the place from Mantinea to Antigoneia, which is the name it still bears today. And so the utter obliteration of 'lovely Mantinea'* seems to have been his doing, and the city continues to bear the name of the man who destroyed it and killed its citizens.

[46] Next, after Cleomenes lost the critical battle of Sellasia,* he abandoned Sparta and sailed away to Egypt, and Antigonus left for Macedon. Throughout, he had been nothing but honest and polite with Aratus, and when he got home, with his health already failing,* he sent Philip to the Peloponnese—his heir, who had barely reached young adulthood—with instructions to learn from Aratus especially, and with his help to get acquainted with the cities and become known to the Achaeans. And Aratus did indeed take the boy in hand, and returned him to Macedon full of affection for him personally, and with a keen interest in and commitment to the affairs of Greece.

[47] After Antigonus' death,* the Aetolians began to attack the Peloponnese. They had nothing but contempt for the apathy of the Achaeans, who had become used to relying for their safety on the protection of others, and as a result of sheltering behind Macedonian weaponry had sunk into a state of idleness and indiscipline. The primary purpose of the expedition the Aetolians mounted was to invade Messenia and ravage the land there, but on the way they also plundered Patrae and Dyme.

All this made Aratus furious, and he could see that Timoxenus, the Achaean General for that year, was reluctant to do anything, and kept putting things off because his term of office was almost over. But Aratus had already been chosen to succeed Timoxenus, so he anticipated the start of his year of office by five days so that he could go to the relief of the Messenians. But the Achaeans who made up his army were so physically unfit and mentally unprepared for war that he was defeated by the Aetolians at Caphyae.* Since he was thought to have gone about the campaign with rather too much ardour, his morale plummeted again. In fact, he lost interest and became discouraged to such an extent that he ignored all the many opportunities the Aetolians gave him and let them gad about, so to speak, in the Peloponnese and do pretty much whatever they wanted. And so the Achaeans once again reached out their hands to Macedon, and Philip was enticed down south to intervene in Greek affairs.* Bearing in mind especially his affection for Aratus, the Achaeans hoped to find him amenable to all their wishes and easy to manage.

[48] This was the first occasion when some members of the Macedonian court, chiefly Apelles and Megaleas,* tried to turn the king against Aratus. Philip believed their lies and gave his support in the elections to Aratus' opponents, favouring the appointment of Eperatus* as General of the league. But the Achaeans' utter contempt for Eperatus and Aratus' withdrawal meant that nothing went well, and Philip realized that he had been completely misled. So he transferred his favour exclusively back to Aratus, and as his situation improved, with an upturn in both his power and his popularity, he began to depend on Aratus and to see that he owed his good reputation and his growing strength to him.

It soon became clear to everyone that Aratus was just as good an instructor for a kingdom as he was for a democracy, when his principles and moral outlook began to, as it were, colour Philip's actions. So, for instance, the restraint with which the young king dealt with the Spartans when they transgressed, and the way in which his diplomacy in Crete brought the whole island over to his side in just a few days, and the astonishingly effective nature of the campaign he carried out against the Aetolians,* all enhanced Philip's reputation for following good advice and Aratus' for giving it. This gave Philip's courtiers all the more reason to dislike Aratus, and since slandering him to the king in private was getting them nowhere, they began to vilify him openly, and when they were in their cups they used to hurl outrageous abuse at him and make him the butt of crude jokes. Once they even chased him and pelted him with stones as he was returning to his tent after dinner. This made Philip furious, and he fined them twenty talents on the spot. Later, however, when he found them to be actively harming his interests and sowing discord, he had them executed.*

[49] But continuous success went to Philip's head and he let a number of strong desires grow within him. His innate badness began to force its way through and break up† the falsely assumed outer surface, gradually exposing and revealing his true nature.* First, he wronged the younger Aratus personally by carrying on an affair with his wife,* which he got away with for a while because he was lodging with the family as their guest. Second, he began to trample on the constitutional rights of the Greek cities, and it soon became clear that he was trying to shake himself free of Aratus' influence.

Suspicions were first aroused by his treatment of Messene.* The city had been torn apart by political feuding, and when Aratus' expedition was delayed, Philip got there a day before him, and immediately goaded the rival groups against each other. What he did was privately ask the Messenian generals if they did not have laws to restrain the masses, and also privately ask the democrats if they did not have hands to raise against those who ruled them like tyrants. As a result of this encouragement, the generals tried to arrest their democratic opponents, but the people rallied around their leaders and counter-attacked, killing the generals and almost 200 others.

[50] Not content with this horrific outcome, Philip was egging the Messenians on to commit even worse atrocities against one another when Aratus arrived. It was plain to see that he was angry himself with Philip, and when his son let loose a torrent of furious invective and abuse, Aratus did nothing to stop him. The young man seems to have been Philip's lover, and in the course of this tirade he told Philip that as far as he was concerned his charm had been erased for ever by what he had done, and that now there was no one on earth he found more repulsive. Philip made no response—surprisingly, since during the tirade he had more than once howled out in anger—but pretended that, as a moderate and diplomatic man, he had endured the tongue-lashing without getting upset. He merely gave his hand to the elder Aratus, raised him to his feet, and led him out of the theatre to Mount Ithome, where he wanted to offer a sacrifice to Zeus and look the place over. For Ithome is just as secure as the Acrocorinth, and with a garrison it becomes hard for neighbouring states to take and difficult to carry by force.

He made his way up to the sanctuary and sacrificed an ox, and when the seer brought him the entrails he took them in both hands and showed them to Aratus and Demetrius of Pharos,* leaning towards each of them in turn and asking them what they could see there, what message the victim bore for him: would he control the citadel or give it back to the Messenians? Demetrius replied with a laugh: 'If you think like a seer, you'll give the place up, but if you think like a king you'll grasp the ox by both its horns.' This was an oblique reference to the Peloponnese: Demetrius' meaning was that, if Philip gained Ithome in addition to the Acrocorinth, the entire Peloponnese would be his to rule and command.

Aratus, however, kept quiet for a while until, pressed by Philip for his opinion, he said: 'Philip, the Cretans have many lofty mountains. The Boeotians and Phocians have many citadels that tower over the earth. I imagine that the Acarnanians too have large numbers of wonderfully impregnable places, both inland and on the coast. You occupy none of these strong-points, yet all these peoples gladly do your bidding. Clinging to cliffs and crags is for brigands, but for a king there is no stronger or more secure defence than trust and gratitude. These are what open the sea route to Crete for you; these are the keys to the gates of the Peloponnese. And it is with their help that, young as you are, you are already the acknowledged leader there and master here.' He had not yet finished speaking when Philip passed the entrails back to the seer. Then he took hold of Aratus' hand, drew him closer, and said: 'Come with me. Let's walk together.' This was an acknowledgement that Aratus had forced him to change direction and he had accepted that Messene was not to be his.*

[51] Before long, however, Aratus began to withdraw from the court and gradually to extricate himself from his intimacy with the king. In fact, when Philip was planning to cross the mountains to Epirus and asked Aratus join the expedition, he refused and stayed at home, not wanting his reputation to suffer because of what Philip was doing. And the whole operation was a complete failure, with Philip losing his fleet to the Romans in the most ignominious manner possible.*

Afterwards, Philip returned to the Peloponnese. Once again, he tried to employ underhand tactics against the Messenians, but his schemes became known, and he turned instead to open aggression and plundered their farmland. Aratus now broke completely with Philip and would have nothing to do with him. By now he also knew of Philip's violation of the women's quarters of his household, a matter which upset him terribly, but which he kept hidden from his son. After all, even if his son knew of the insult, that was as far as it could go, since he would not be able to retaliate. For Philip does seem to have undergone a thorough and puzzling change, from mild-mannered king to pernicious tyrant, and from well-behaved youth to debauched adult. In reality, though, this was no change of character, but the manifestation at a time of security of corruption he had long been too afraid to reveal.

[52] For it finally became clear, from the way Philip dealt with Aratus, that his normal attitude towards him had always been a mixture of shame and fear. Although he wanted to see him dead and felt

that he could never be free, let alone a tyrant or a king, as long as he was alive, he made no attempt to employ violence against him. Instead, he ordered Taurion, a senior officer and one of his Friends, to find a stealthy way to get rid of him, preferably by poison, when Philip himself was not around. So Taurion got on good terms with Aratus and began to give him poison—not a powerful, fast-acting poison, but one of those that first produce gentle flushes of heat in the body and a dull cough, and only gradually induce death.† Aratus knew perfectly well what was going on, but since there was no point in challenging Taurion he endured his pain calmly and uncomplainingly, as though he were suffering from some ordinary and familiar ailment. But once, when one of his friends was in his room and exclaimed at the sight of him bringing up blood, Aratus said: 'This, Cephalon, is the cost of friendship with a king.'*

[53] That is how he met his death, in Aegium, in the year of his seventeenth Generalship.* The Achaeans wanted Aegium to be the site of his tomb and monuments commemorating his life as he deserved, but to the Sicyonians it was unthinkable for him to lie anywhere else but in Sicyon, and they persuaded the Achaeans to relinquish the body. But from time immemorial no burials had been allowed within the city walls, and this regulation was accompanied by strong feelings of superstition. So they sent envoys to Delphi to ask the Pythia about this ban, and she replied with the following oracle:

> Are you planning, Sicyon, a reward for your dead lord Aratus,
> Your saviour, in the form of ritual feasting for ever?
> Know, then, that what is a burden to this man and burdens you
> Is an impious affront to earth, sky, and sea.

When the envoys returned with this response, all Achaea rejoiced, and the Sicyonians put off mourning and turned to celebration. Garlanded and clothed in white, they lost no time in bringing the body home from Aegium and received it with paeans and choral dancing. They chose a conspicuous spot and buried him there as the Founder and Saviour of the City.* Even now, the place is called the Arateium, and they sacrifice to him there twice a year. The first sacrifice takes place on 5 Daisios (or 5 Anthesterion in the Athenian calendar), which is the anniversary of the day when he freed the city from tyranny, and so they call the festival the Soteria;* and the second on the day when, according to tradition, he was born.†

In the past, the first of these sacrifices used to be performed by the priest of Zeus the Saviour, and the second by the priest of Aratus, wearing a headband shot through with purple, rather than pure white. Songs were sung with a lyre accompaniment by members of the Guild of Dionysus,* and the gymnasiarch would lead the parade at the head of the boys and ephebes, who were then followed by the members of the Council, wearing garlands, and any other Sicyonian citizen who wanted to take part. Even nowadays the Sicyonians preserve slight traces of these practices in their devotions on these two days of the year, but most of the original forms of worship have lapsed, owing to the passage of time and the pressure of other business.

[54] Such, then, were the life and character of the elder Aratus, according to the information preserved in our sources. But Philip, true to the savagery of his abominable and tyrannical nature, drove the younger Aratus insane with drugs designed not to kill but to unbalance a man's mind. He became subject to weird and terrible urges, which caused him to behave oddly and drew him towards shameful and self-destructive experiences, so that although he died young, still in his prime, death came not as a disaster but as a relief and a release from suffering.*

Eventually, however, Philip paid the appropriate penalty to Zeus, the protector of hospitality and friendship, for this abhorrent crime. His defeat* by the Romans gave them the right to dictate the terms of his future existence. He was stripped of most of his empire, surrendered his entire fleet apart from five ships, undertook to pay an indemnity of 1,000 talents, and gave them his son as a hostage. It was only out of pity, in fact, that he was allowed to keep Macedon and its tributaries. But his habit of always killing the best of his subjects and his closest relatives made him an object of fear and hatred throughout the entire kingdom. The only good thing he had going for him in the midst of all this trouble was that he had an exceptional son*—but he killed him out of envy and jealousy of the honour paid to him by the Romans, and bequeathed his kingdom to his other son, Perseus, who, they say, was not legitimate, but suppositious, born of a certain Gnathaenion, a seamstress.* Perseus in his turn was paraded through the streets of Rome at Aemilius Paullus' triumph, and the succession of Antigonid kings ended with him.* But the descendants of Aratus were still living in Sicyon and Pellene in my day.

AGIS AND CLEOMENES

INTRODUCTION

Agis IV (died 241 BCE) and Cleomenes III (died 219 BCE) were kings of Sparta, who tried to revive Sparta by radical, revolutionary reforms. Sparta had long been in decline and was now far from being the powerful Greek state that had overcome Athens in the Peloponnesian War and dominated Greece in its aftermath. Defeat by the Thebans at Leuctra in 371 had been a turning-point in Spartan history, leading to the loss of Messenia and the foundation of the Arcadian city of Megalopolis on its borders. But Spartan decline was not only political. There was also a well-documented drop in the number of Spartan citizens, brought about, so Aristotle believed, by increasing inequality and the concentration of wealth in the hands of a few (*Politics* 2.1270a).

One of the distinctive and continuing features of the Spartan constitution was that it was overseen by two kings simultaneously, one a member of the Eurypontid family, the other of the Agiad family. By 244, when the youthful Agis IV succeeded to the Eurypontid throne, the decline in citizen numbers was such that there were said to be only 700 citizens remaining, of whom a hundred were very wealthy and the rest could barely retain their citizenship (*Agis* 5). It is unclear to what extent his short and turbulent reign sought to address this. He put into effect a cancellation of debts and was said to have proposed, but never carried out, a redistribution of land and extension of citizenship. Early in his reign he had his Agiad co-king Leonidas deposed and replaced with someone more amenable, but Leonidas later returned with the support of the wealthy and saw to the execution of Agis.

Leonidas continued as king until around 235, when his son Cleomenes, probably in his early twenties, succeeded him. In his early years Cleomenes seems to have established himself as king and achieved some military success against the Achaeans, but there was little to suggest that his reign would be anything out of the ordinary. Then, in 227, he pre-empted any opposition by staging a coup. Eighty citizens were sent into exile and fourteen were killed; the dead included four of the five ephors, the chief magistrates of Sparta. If these roughly matched the one hundred very wealthy citizens at the beginning of Agis' reign, then Cleomenes not only eliminated any opposition, he also acquired their extensive lands for redistribution. At this point he set about his reforms: cancellation of debts, redistribution of property, extension of citizenship, restoration of Sparta's traditional system of education, the *agōgē*, and the revival of the military messes, all of which was done in the name of the legendary Spartan lawgiver Lycurgus. The goal, therefore, was a return to Spartan greatness, and it went along with an increased emphasis on Spartan militarism. There are echoes here of Agis' failed programme of reform, and it was said that Cleomenes was influenced by his wife, who had previously been married to Agis.

Cleomenes' revolution not only increased Sparta's military strength, it also stirred up social unrest throughout the Peloponnese. Recognizing the changing balance of power in the region, Ptolemy III Euergetes switched his subsidy from the Achaean League to Cleomenes. All these factors would drive Aratus to take the controversial step of enlisting the help of the Macedonian king Antigonus Doson (see introduction to *Aratus*). But even a revitalized Sparta could not compete with the resources of Macedon, and Cleomenes was eventually defeated at Sellasia in 222. Afterwards he fled to Egypt to the court of Ptolemy Euergetes, where any hopes that he could make this a base from which to reclaim his throne were dashed when Euergetes died shortly afterwards. There, in 219, Cleomenes died leading a suicidal rising against Euergetes' unsympathetic successor, Ptolemy IV Philopator.

Cleomenes may have brought about a temporary resurgence in Spartan fortunes, but his failure also brought it to its lowest point: Sparta was occupied for the first time in its history and its dual monarchy was all but finished. The next decade or so left Sparta troubled and politically unstable, until the fifteen-year 'tyranny' of Nabis returned Sparta, temporarily at least, to the position of a major player in Peloponnesian politics. After Nabis' assassination in 193, however, Sparta would spend much of the century struggling to assert its independence from the Achaean League (see, for instance, *Philopoemen* 10, 12–16, Polybius 23.4, Livy 39.35–7).

This set of Lives is unique among the *Parallel Lives*, because the lives being paralleled are not those of two single individuals, one Greek and one Roman, but rather two pairs. Plutarch juxtaposes the two Spartan kings with two Roman brothers, Tiberius and Gaius Sempronius Gracchus, the tribunes of 133 and 123–122 respectively. Tiberius introduced an agrarian law, which distributed Roman public land in Italy to poor Roman citizens. A decade later Gaius initiated a much more ambitious and wide-ranging programme of reform. Both tribunes provoked vigorous opposition and both died violently. The comparison between the Roman tribunes and Spartan kings did not originate with Plutarch. It had already appeared in Cicero's *On Duties* (2.80), written in the mid-first century BCE, although there only Agis is mentioned by name. The key point of comparison for Cicero was their lack of respect for the rights of property. Plutarch had rather more sympathy for his subjects, and sees them as led astray by their desire for glory. By pursuing glory rather than virtue, they make themselves dependent on the opinion of others. For those 'whose sights are set on glory are the servants of the masses, and rulers in name alone' (1). The emphasis in his introduction is on the Gracchi, but these remarks apply equally to the Spartan kings, both of whom are said to have been eager for glory (7 and 44, where Cleomenes advocates always choosing 'the road that leads to glory rather than profit').

There has been considerable debate over the character, objectives, and general ethos of Cleomenes' reforms. On one level their purpose is clear enough: to make Sparta a more significant military power, by giving land to those without it and so increasing the citizen body. Significantly, the reforms did not take place on Cleomenes' accession in 235 but instead some years later, in 227, and the explanation for this time-lag may well be military. It is likely that they were introduced in response to an expansionary Achaean League, which would have appeared especially threatening after Megalopolis and Argos, both traditionally hostile to Sparta, had joined in 235 and 229 respectively (see *Aratus* 30 and 35). But Cleomenes' revolution was more complex than this. He was carrying out a wholesale revision of Spartan society, embracing its political structure (abolition of the ephorate and changing the role of the king), its system of landholding, and its citizenship. The cancellation of debts and the redistribution of land were important features of this programme, but they were also familiar slogans of contemporary Hellenistic revolution. As a result, the events in Sparta generated discontent among the lower classes of neighbouring states and anxiety among their elites (38). Aratus is reported as saying that the worst of Cleomenes' crimes were 'the abolition of wealth and alleviation of poverty' (37). Cleomenes' actions may have been very much of their time, but he justified this radical overhaul of the Spartan state by invoking Lycurgus, in the process rewriting the history of early Sparta. Instrumental in this reworking of the past was the Stoic philosopher Sphaerus, who was present in Sparta at the time and is credited by Plutarch with advising the king on the revival of some of the 'old' Spartan institutions (32). How much influence Stoic philosophy had on the revolution, or at least the packaging of it, is controversial.

While Cleomenes dominates his own Life, the naive and idealistic Agis is a more shadowy figure in his. Much of the action is in the hands of others, and it is only with his dramatic final days that he really comes to the fore. It is possible that his importance was inflated later, initially to provide a precedent for Cleomenes' actions, and then by Plutarch in order to have a figure that merited comparison to Tiberius. Certainly, the proposals that he planned but did not put into effect are suspiciously similar to those of Cleomenes (see notes to text).

Agis and Cleomenes offers an interesting companion piece to the *Aratus*, because the reign of Cleomenes is treated very differently. This variation in approach is partly a result of Plutarch's tendency to adopt the perspective of his subject, but also of his choice of sources for each Life. In the *Aratus* he made extensive use of Aratus' own *Memoirs*, whereas in *Agis and Cleomenes* his main source for the biographies of both kings was the contemporary historian Phylarchus, an admirer of Cleomenes and critic of Aratus (*Aratus* 38). Phylarchus' 28-book history spanned the years from Pyrrhus' invasion of the Peloponnese in the late 270s to the death of Cleomenes in Alexandria. His pro-Spartan, anti-Achaean stance did not endear him to the Achaean Polybius, whose scathing criticism has done much to tarnish Phylarchus' reputation, charging him with sensationalism and fabrication (Polybius 2.56–63). One feature of these Lives that is likely to derive from Phylarchus is the repeated emphasis on heroic Spartan women. This is most striking in the courage with which Agesistrata, the mother of Agis, faced her execution (20). Plutarch may have relied most on Phylarchus, especially for events within Sparta, but he was well aware that there were alternative views of the Spartan kings, and cites both Aratus and Polybius in this Life. No doubt other sources were used as well, but only the little-known Baton of Sinope is mentioned by name.

Africa, T. W., *Phylarchos and the Spartan Revolution* (Berkeley, 1961).

Cartledge, P., *Ancient Greek Political Thought in Practice* (Cambridge, 2009), ch. 9.

—— and Spawforth, A., *Hellenistic and Roman Sparta* (2nd edn., London, 2002), ch. 4.

Erskine, A., *The Hellenistic Stoa: Political Thought and Action* (London, 1990), ch. 6.

Hodkinson, S., *Property and Wealth in Classical Sparta* (London, 2000), esp. chs. 2 and 13.

Kennell, N. M., *The Gymnasium of Virtue: Education and Culture in Ancient Sparta* (Chapel Hill, NC, 1995).

Marasco, G., *Commento alle biografie plutarchee di Agide e di Cleomene* (Rome, 1981).

Pomeroy, S., *Spartan Women* (Oxford, 2002).

Powell, A., 'Spartan Women Assertive in Politics? Plutarch's Lives of Agis and Kleomenes', in A. Powell and S. Hodkinson (eds.), *Sparta: New Perspectives* (Swansea, 1999), 393–419.

Roskam, G., 'Plutarch's Life of Agis, or the Honourable Course of a Beginning Politician', in L. de Blois *et al.* (eds.), *The Statesman in Plutarch's Works*, vol. 2 (Leiden, 2005), 227–41.

—— 'Ambition and Love of Fame in Plutarch's Lives of Agis, Cleomenes, and the Gracchi', *Classical Philology*, 106 (2011), 208–25.

Shimron, B., *Late Sparta* (Buffalo, Col., 1972).

AGIS AND CLEOMENES

[1] There is nothing far-fetched or inherently unsound about the idea one occasionally hears that the Ixion myth* was made up with seekers of glory in mind—the story that he raped Nephele, the cloud, when he thought he had Hera, and that Centaurs were the outcome. For the glory that these people lust after is a phantom of true virtue, if I may put it that way, and their results, so far from being pure and unequivocal, are invariably a hybrid mixture of good and bad, since they veer this way and that in pursuit of their ambitions and in reaction to events. One is reminded of what Sophocles' shepherds say about their sheep:*

> Though their masters, we are in fact their slaves,
> Bound to obey them, though they say nothing.

This is a true analogy for the predicament of men in public life whose policies reflect the desires and whims of mobs: they make themselves slaves and followers in order to be known as leaders and rulers. Just as a lookout on a ship sees what lies ahead before the helmsman does, but still defers to him and obeys his orders, so men in public life whose sights are set on glory are the servants of the masses, and rulers in name alone.

[2] After all, a flawless man, a perfectly good man, would have no need of glory at all, except in so far as the trust of others opened up opportunities for him to act. Still, while a man is still young and idealistic, he should be permitted a degree of self-satisfied pride in glory gained from noble deeds because, as Theophrastus* says, the virtues that are budding and sprouting in people of that age are strengthened by praise when they get it right, and developed thereafter by pride. But excess, which is unsafe under any circumstances, is deadly in politics. If people gain access to great power when they do not see the good as a source of glory, but regard anything that brings them glory as good, they are driven completely and publicly out of their minds.

Antipater once asked Phocion to do something dishonourable, and Phocion said to him: 'You cannot have me as a friend and a flatterer at the same time.'* By the same token, the following message, or something like it, needs to be communicated to the masses: 'You cannot have a man as a leader and a follower at the same time.' Otherwise, the outcome is what happened to the snake in the fable, whose tail was fed up with always following its head.* The tail picked a quarrel with the head and demanded its turn as leader, but when it was given a go, it not only got itself into trouble by losing its way, but the head, compelled to follow the lead taken by a part of the snake that was blind and deaf, and so hardly suited for the job, was constantly being scraped along the ground. This is exactly what we invariably see happening to people whose sole concern as politicians is popularity. Once they have made themselves dependent on the fickle whims of mobs, they can never undo the damage or restore order.

I was moved to make these remarks about popular glory after noticing the powerful effect it had on the lives of Tiberius and Gaius Gracchus.* They were outstandingly gifted men, they received the best possible upbringing, and the political principles they espoused were of the noblest kind, but they were still ruined, and what brought them low was not so much a boundless desire for glory as fear of obscurity. Their motives were by no means discreditable: they had received in advance a great fund of goodwill from their fellow citizens, and they were ashamed to neglect what they saw as a debt. But they became engaged in a never-ending competitive spiral, whereby they strove to surpass the honours they were receiving with beneficial measures, and were honoured all the more thanks to the measures they were introducing out of gratitude. In this way, as a result of the equal devotion they had kindled in themselves for the people and in the people for themselves, they reached a point—the point at which what was not good became bad—where it was no longer possible for them to stop.

Anyway, you will make up your own mind about this after reading my account. For comparison with the Gracchi, let us have a pair of popular leaders from Sparta, the kings Agis IV and Cleomenes III. Like the Gracchi, they strengthened the political power wielded by the people, and revived a good, equitable constitution which had been waning for many years. Like the Gracchi, they were hated by the power-possessors of their time, who were reluctant to give up their usual greedy ways. The Spartan pair were not brothers, but their political measures were closely related and cut from the same cloth. Here is how it all began.

[3] When admiration for silver and gold first wormed its way into the city, things changed.* Avarice and stinginess arose as concomitants of the acquisition of wealth, and self-indulgence, hedonism, and extravagance characterized its possession and use. The upshot was that Sparta largely lost its nobility and its fortunes remained at a humiliatingly low ebb for many years, until the reign of Agis and Leonidas.

Agis was a Eurypontid,* the son of Eudamidas, and was the great-great-great grandson of Agesilaus, who invaded Asia and became the most powerful man in Greece.* Agesilaus' son was Archidamus III, who was killed by the Messapians at Manduria in Italy;* Archidamus' elder son was Agis III, and the younger one became Eudamidas I, who gained the throne after Agis had been killed at Megalopolis by Antipater, leaving no heir;* Eudamidas' son was Archidamus IV; he was succeeded by his son, Eudamidas II; and Eudamidas' son was Agis IV, the subject of this Life.

Leonidas, on the other hand, the son of Cleonymus, was an Agiad, from the other royal house, and was the great-great-great-great-great grandson of Pausanias, who defeated Mardonius at the battle of Plataea.* Pausanias' son was Pleistoanax, and Pleistoanax's son was the Pausanias who was banished from Sparta to Tegea.* He was replaced on the throne by his elder son Agesipolis, and when Agesipolis died childless, his younger brother Cleombrotus succeeded him;* Cleombrotus in his turn had two sons, Agesipolis II and Cleomenes, but Agesipolis died childless after only a few years on the throne, and his brother succeeded him. Cleomenes II was still alive when his elder son, Acrotatus, died, and his younger son, Cleonymus,* never became king either, even though he was living at the time of his father's death. Instead, Cleomenes' grandson Areus II did, the son of Acrotatus. When Areus died at Corinth, his son Acrotatus became king. He too died at Megalopolis, in the course of losing a battle to the tyrant Aristodemus, leaving his wife pregnant. When a baby boy was born, Leonidas, the son of Cleonymus, became his guardian, but the boy died before coming of age and so Leonidas became king.

Leonidas' subjects, however, did not find him a congenial ruler at all. The corruption of the citizenry had already brought about a general decline by then, but even so, Leonidas' rule was marked by a distinct departure from traditional ways. He had spent many years in satrapal courts and in the service of Seleucus,* and he transferred the pomp he found there into the Greek world of constitutional government, where it had no place.

[4] Agis, on the other hand, was a far more gifted and high-minded ruler than almost every Spartan king since the great Agesilaus, not just by contrast with Leonidas. Even though throughout his childhood he was surrounded by women, wealth, and luxury—for he was brought up by his mother Agesistrata and his grandmother Archidamia, who were the richest people in Sparta—before he was twenty years old he had set his face firmly and unequivocally against hedonism. He put aside the finery that was supposed to perfectly grace his elegant figure, and renounced and avoided all extravagance. Instead, he took pride in his thin cloak and made a point of adhering to traditional Spartan ways in his diet, bathing, and general way of life, and he used to say that there was no point in his being king unless he could use the position to restore their ancestral constitution and training regime.*

[5] Anyway, the decay and corruption of Spartan society set in almost immediately after they put an end to Athenian leadership of Greece and gorged themselves on gold and silver.* But they managed to keep the number of heritable households at the level stipulated by Lycurgus, with fathers passing their allotted farms on to their sons,* and somehow the continuing regularity and impartiality of this process saved them from other errors. But then a ruthless and cruel man called Epitadeus* gained power through his position as ephor, and because he had fallen out with his son, he proposed a measure making it permissible for a man to dispose of his household and farm to whomever he liked, either by gift during his lifetime or as a bequest.

Although he proposed the measure to satisfy a personal grudge of his own, his fellow Spartiates welcomed it and passed it into law out of greed—and destroyed what had been an excellent system. For now there was nothing to stop powerful people acquiring property by forcing the rightful owners from their inheritances, and before long wealth was concentrated in just a few hands.* The city as a whole became impoverished, and poverty not only left the dispossessed no freedom or time for noble pursuits, but made them envy and resent the rich. And so, of the fewer than 700 Spartiates who remained, only perhaps a hundred possessed land or even their allotted farm, while the general mass of Spartans sat idly in the city without resources or rights, defending themselves sluggishly and irresolutely against external threats, and constantly on the lookout for opportunities for revolutionary change.

[6] Under these circumstances, Agis rightly thought it would be a noble achievement if he could restore equality and replenish the number of Spartiates, and he began to sound people out. The younger Spartiates fell in with his plans more readily than he expected; like him, they stripped and dedicated themselves to the cause of justice, changing the way they lived in the name of freedom, as though they were changing their clothes. The older men, however, were mired in corruption, and most of them trembled with fear at the name of Lycurgus, as though they were slaves being returned to a master from whom they had run away. They told Agis he was wrong to find the present state of affairs unsatisfactory and to long to see Sparta's ancient dignity restored.

But Agis' initiative was welcomed, and his idealism encouraged, by Lysander, the son of Libys, Mandrocleidas, the son of Ecphanes, and Agesilaus. Lysander was the most distinguished man in Sparta, and Mandrocleidas had a cunning intelligence, seasoned with daring;* there was no one in Greece better at devising schemes. Agesilaus, however, who was Agis' uncle, despite being a powerful speaker, was basically a weak man, obsessed with money, and it was obvious that he was being pushed and spurred on by his son Hippomedon, who had earned a name for himself on many a battlefield and owed his considerable influence in the city to the affection of the younger generation. But the real reason why Agesilaus fell in with Agis' plans and played a part in the enterprise was the amount of money he owed, and his hope that by changing the constitution he would free himself of his debts.

As soon as Agis had gained Agesilaus' support, he tried with his help to win over his mother. She was Agesilaus' sister and, thanks to all the clients and friends she had, and the large number of people who owed her money, she had a great deal of influence in the city and often played an effective political role. [7] At first, however, she was aghast at what Agis was telling her, and tried to stop her son from proceeding with a scheme that seemed neither feasible nor worthwhile. But Agesilaus explained the benefits and advantages, and Agis himself begged his mother to support him financially in his bid for glory and renown. 'I can't match the other kings for wealth,' he said. 'The mere servants of satraps and slaves of Ptolemy's and

Seleucus' provincial governors have more money than all the kings of Sparta there have ever been. But if I, with my modest, simple, and honourable ways, can achieve something greater than satraps and kings with their self-indulgent ways—if I can share wealth equally among my subjects—I will gain the fame and honour that are due to a truly great king.'

These words of his completely changed Agesistrata's and Archidamia's minds. They were so excited by the young man's objectives, and so taken over by a kind of inspired enthusiasm for doing good, that they urged him to act, and to act quickly. Moreover, they sent for their male friends and appealed to them, and spoke to the other women, because they knew that Spartan men always obey their wives, and allow them to have a greater say in public affairs than they allow themselves in domestic affairs.

At that time, however, the women of Sparta controlled most of the wealth,* and it was this that made trouble for Agis and proved to be the chief obstacle to his enterprise. For the women were opposed to the project, not only because they would lose the luxuries which seemed to their vulgar taste to constitute happiness, but also because they realized that they would lose the respect and power they gained by being wealthy. So they approached Leonidas and asked him, as the older man, to take Agis in hand and call a halt to the business.

Now, Leonidas wanted to help the rich, but he was afraid of his subjects and their revolutionary fervour. He therefore did nothing overt to thwart Agis, but secretly tried to undermine and ruin the project by slandering him to the city's political leaders in his meetings with them. He used to say that Agis was gifting the property of the rich to the poor as a way to purchase tyranny, and by his land distributions and cancellation of debts was buying bodyguards for himself, not citizens for Sparta.*

[8] But Agis managed to get Lysander elected to the ephorate,* and lost no time in using him to introduce a proposal in the Council of Elders,* the main provisions of which were the cancellation of debts and a new division of the land, with the territory from the gorge at Pellana to Taygetus, Malea, and Sellasia making 4,500 lots, and the outer territory 15,000.* This outer territory was to be divided among those of the *perioeci* who were capable of bearing arms, while the inner territory was for the Spartiates themselves. Spartiate numbers were to be replenished from those *perioeci* and resident foreigners

who had been brought up as free men, and who were otherwise physically acceptable and in their primes. This body of Spartiates would then make up fifteen messes of 400 or 200 men,* and they would adopt the way of life that their ancestors had followed.

[9] This proposal met with no consensus among the Elders, however. Lysander next convened an assembly at which he talked over the issues with the citizens, and Mandrocleidas and Agesilaus asked them not to let the arrogance of a few men blind them to the debasement of Sparta. They should remember, they said, not only the earlier oracles that warned them of the lethal threat posed by love of money,* but also those they had recently received from Pasiphaë—from her sanctuary at Thalamae, that is, with its venerable oracle.*

Some say that Pasiphaë was one of the daughters of Atlas, and the mother by Zeus of Ammon, others that Thalamae was where Priam's daughter Cassandra died, and that it was because she revealed the truth to all that she came to be called Pasiphaë.* Phylarchus, however, says that she was a daughter of Amyclas called Daphne, and he tells the story of how she ran from Apollo's lust, was transformed into the plant that bears her name, and was honoured by the god with the gift of seercraft.*

According to Mandrocleidas and Agesilaus, then, the oracles from Pasiphaë agreed with them that all Spartiates should become equal in accordance with the terms of their original constitution as drawn up by Lycurgus. Finally, King Agis stepped forward and, after a brief exchange with the people, announced the very substantial contributions he was making to the constitution he was trying to establish. Most importantly, he was donating his own estate, which consisted not just of large tracts of both arable land and pasturage, but also of 600 talents of coined money apart from the land. And his mother and grandmother, and their friends and relatives—all the richest people in Sparta—were doing likewise.

[10] The people were astounded by the young king's magnanimity, and were delighted to find that after almost 300 years* a king had appeared of the calibre Sparta had been crying out for. But now Leonidas came out even more strongly in opposition. His thinking was that he would be forced to do the same as Agis and the others, but without reaping the same degree of gratitude for it from the Spartans; if *everyone* donated their property, only the person who did so first would receive credit for it. He therefore asked Agis if, in his opinion,

Lycurgus had been a fair and upright man. When Agis said yes, Leonidas went on: 'So can you tell me where Lycurgus made provision for either the cancellation of debts or the enfranchisement of foreigners? After all, he thought the state's health depended on the *expulsion* of foreigners.'

Agis replied that it came as no surprise to find Leonidas, who had been raised abroad and whose children were the offspring of his marriage to a satrap's daughter, unaware that Lycurgus had made lending and borrowing illegal, not just coined money, and had found the presence of foreigners in the country to be less of a problem than the presence of people whose principles and lifestyles were incompatible with Spartan ways. He conceded that Lycurgus had instituted the practice of expelling foreigners,* but argued that he did so not because he was hostile to them *per se*, but because he wanted to make sure that their lifestyles and habits did not infect his fellow citizens and make them see luxury, hedonism, and greed as desirable. After all, he pointed out, Terpander, Thaletas, and Pherecydes were foreigners, but because their songs and principles did not clash with Lycurgan institutions, they were held in exceptionally high honour in Sparta.*

'And what about you?' he said. 'You think the ephor Ecprepes was right to have taken an adze to Phrynis' lyre and cut off two of his nine strings, and you commend those who did the same thing again in Timotheus' case.* So why are you critical of my attempt to uproot luxury, extravagance, and pretentiousness from Sparta? Don't you realize that Ecprepes and the others were also trying to make sure that affectation and extravagance in the sphere of music did not advance to the point we've reached now in our lifestyles and habits, where intemperance and bad taste have made the city hideously out of tune with itself?'

[11] After this, while Agis became the champion of the people, the rich kept on begging Leonidas not to abandon them, and urgently lobbying the Elders, who had the power of deciding what measures to present to the people's assembly. They were successful, but only just: Agis' proposal was outvoted by one. But Lysander, who was still in office, decided to prosecute Leonidas under an ancient law that made it illegal for any Heraclid* to have children by a foreign woman and ordained death for anyone who left Sparta to live abroad. So after instructing others to talk up these charges against Leonidas, he and his fellow ephors began to watch for the sign.

What is this sign? Every nine years, the ephors pick a clear, moonless night and sit quietly, gazing up at the sky. If a star shoots across the sky from one particular zone to another, they conclude that the kings have offended the gods and they suspend their reign, until an oracle comes from Delphi or Olympia to exonerate them.* So this was the sign that Lysander now said he had been vouchsafed, and he proceeded against Leonidas, having found witnesses to testify that he had had two children by an Asian woman who had been given to him in marriage by one of Seleucus' officers, and that it was only because she found him hateful and abhorrent that he had reluctantly returned to Sparta, where he had become king in the absence of any other candidate.

While bringing this suit against Leonidas, Lysander also set about persuading Cleombrotus, who was Leonidas' son-in-law and of royal blood, to claim the throne for himself. Leonidas took fright and sought refuge as a suppliant at the altar of Athena of the Bronze House, and his daughter left Cleombrotus and joined him there.* And when he was summoned to attend his trial and stayed in the sanctuary, the court deposed him and made Cleombrotus king instead.

[12] At this juncture, Lysander's year of office came to an end. The newly appointed ephors raised Leonidas from his refuge, and arraigned Lysander and Mandrocleidas for the crime of supporting unconstitutional measures such as the cancellation of debts and reassignment of land. Faced with this threat, Lysander and Mandrocleidas tried to persuade the kings* to unite and disregard the ephors' resolutions. The ephorate, they argued, owed its power to dissension between the two kings, in the sense that the ephors used their vote to support whichever king spoke more effectively when the two of them disagreed about what was in the best interests of the state. When they were both in favour of the same policy, however, their power was unshakable and opposition to them would be illegal. It was the ephors' job, they said, to act as moderators and mediators when the kings were at odds, but when they saw eye to eye, the ephors should not intrude.*

The kings saw the force of the argument, and they and their friends descended on the city square, dissolved the board of ephors, and appointed others instead, one of whom was Agesilaus. They then formed a large number of the men of military age into an armed force and released those who had been thrown into prison—moves which terrified their opponents, who feared a massacre. But no blood was shed by the kings. In fact, when Agis found out that Agesilaus intended to kill Leonidas and had sent men to attack him on the road to Tegea, where he was retreating for safety, he despatched men he could trust to serve as an escort for Leonidas, and they brought him safely to Tegea.

[13] So the kings' project was going ahead smoothly and was making good progress, but just when it seemed that nothing could stop them, one man ruined and spoiled everything. It was Agesilaus. This was a most admirable project, worthy of Sparta at its best, and he destroyed it with the least admirable weakness a man can suffer from: avarice. He was one of the principal large-scale owners of good land, and he was also very heavily in debt. Since he could not pay off his debts and was unwilling to lose his land to his creditors, he persuaded Agis that it would cause too much social upheaval if both parts of the plan were realized at the same time, but that if the landowners were first conciliated by having their debts cancelled, they would later readily accept the redistribution of land without kicking up a fuss. This was Lysander's opinion as well, since Agesilaus was busy hoodwinking him too. So they collected all the mortgage deeds (or 'deeds of allotment', as the Spartans call them), brought them into the city square, and made a bonfire of them. As the flames rose, the rich and those who had held the mortgages left in great emotional turmoil, while Agesilaus crowed, as it were, that this was the brightest light and clearest blaze he had ever seen.

The people demanded that the redistribution of the land should also take place without delay, and the kings set it in motion, but Agesilaus kept obstructing it with other business of various kinds and finding pretexts for postponement. In fact, he managed to delay things until the whole business was overtaken by Agis' being required to take an army into the field, when the Achaeans, who had an alliance with the Spartans, called for their help. They were expecting an Aetolian invasion of the Peloponnese via Megara, and Aratus, the Achaean General, had written to the ephors in the course of putting together an army to see that this did not happen.*

[14] The ephors immediately sent Agis on his way, and he was filled with pride at the commitment and determination of the men under his command. Most of them were young and from poor families, and since they had been freed from the burden of their debts and hoped

to be assigned farms if they returned from the campaign, they wanted to impress Agis. The inhabitants of the cities they passed enjoyed the sight of them marching through the Peloponnese without damaging property, without drawing attention to themselves, and almost without making any noise, and all over Greece people were led to wonder in awe what kind of discipline a Spartan army must have had under the command of those famous leaders of old—Agesilaus, Lysander, and Leonidas I—seeing that all these soldiers displayed such respect and fear of a lad who was close to being the youngest man in the army. In fact, the young man was well worth seeing himself, since he clearly took pride in his ability to go without luxuries and endure hardship, and in wearing clothing and armour that were no more splendid than those worn by a person of no rank. But it was only the ordinary people of Greece who admired him, while the rich disapproved of his revolutionary ways and were frightened of the upheaval that would ensue if the common people elsewhere took his programme as their model.

[15] When Agis joined Aratus at Corinth, he found him still debating whether or not to fight and offer battle. Agis showed himself to be eager without being impetuous, and in favour of a course of action that was bold without being ill-advised. He said that, to his mind, they should fight—they should not abandon the gateway to the Peloponnese and let war inside—but that he would abide by whatever Aratus chose to do. Aratus was, after all, the older man and the Achaean General, while he had come to offer support and assistance, not to give orders and take command. Now, Baton of Sinope* claims that Agis refused a direct order from Aratus to fight, but that is because he has not read Aratus' account of this business. Aratus wrote,* in his defence, that since the farmers had already harvested almost all the crops, it seemed preferable to let the enemy in rather than risk everything in battle. So, having decided not to fight, he thanked the allies and dismissed them.

Agis returned home in high esteem, to find domestic affairs in Sparta in revolutionary turmoil. [16] For once Agesilaus had been freed of the debts that had restrained him before, he began to use his position as ephor to raise money by whatever illegal means it took. He even violated the traditional calendar and, though it was not the point of the cycle when the insertion of an intercalary month was required, added a thirteenth month to the tax year as a way of raising extra money. And then, out of fear of retaliation by the people he had wronged, and because he was universally hated, he began to maintain a company of swordsmen who used to act as his bodyguard as he walked from home to the ephors' chambers. As for the kings, he tried to convey the impression that, however contemptible he might find Cleombrotus, he had some respect for Agis, as a relative, at least, even if not as a king. He also let it be known that he would be serving a second term as ephor.*

Before long, then, Agesilaus' enemies decided to throw caution to the winds; they formed a caucus and openly brought Leonidas back from Tegea to resume his rule. This move also went down well with common people, who were furious at the deception that had been practised on them, given that no redistribution of the land had taken place. Agesilaus gained safe passage out of the city after an appeal to his fellow citizens by his son Hippomedon, who was trading on the universal popularity his courage had brought him. As for the kings, Agis took refuge in the sanctuary of Athena of the Bronze House, but Cleombrotus went as a suppliant to the sanctuary of Poseidon,* because he suspected that he would bear the brunt of Leonidas' anger. And indeed Leonidas did nothing about Agis, but took a company of soldiers to arrest Cleombrotus, and angrily accused him of plotting against him, usurping his throne, and helping to drive him into exile. He was particularly furious because Cleombrotus was his son-in-law.

[17] Cleombrotus had no response to make to these charges, and just sat there in helpless silence. Not so Chilonis, however, the daughter of Leonidas. Previously, out of sympathy for the wrongs being done to her father, she had left Cleombrotus, when he had usurped the throne, and had refused to abandon her father to his misfortune. She had joined him as a suppliant before his exile, and while he was in exile had never stopped grieving for his plight and cherishing her hatred of Cleombrotus. But at the time in question she had changed again, along with the changing circumstances, and could now be seen sitting beside her husband as a suppliant, with her arms around him and a child on either side of her. Everyone was moved to tears by her remarkable goodness and devotion.

Grasping her dishevelled clothes and unkempt hair, she said: 'Father, this wretched state you see me in is not due just to my feeling sorry for Cleombrotus. No, grief has remained my companion and consort ever since *your* downfall and exile. So, with you the victor and on the Spartan throne, should I live out my life in this misery? Or dress in royal splendour after seeing the husband of my youth murdered by you? If he cannot sway you with his pleas or move you to pity with the tears of his children and wife, his error of judgement will cost him more dearly than you want, since he will see me, the person he holds dearest in life, kill myself before I see him die. For why should I live, unable even to talk as an equal to other women, after failing to move either my husband or my father to pity by my pleas? No, as both wife and daughter, it has been my lot to share the misfortune and disgrace of the men in my life. My husband may have had some plausible reason for his actions, but it was nullified by me when I took your side and condemned what he had done. But now *you* are making his offence seem readily excusable, because you're making it plain by *your* actions that kingship is so important and so worth fighting for that it justifies murdering a son-in-law and disregarding a daughter's plea.'

[18] Following this impassioned appeal, Chilonis rested her chin on top of Cleombrotus' head and turned her eyes, blinded by tears of grief, on the people standing around. After conferring with his friends, Leonidas raised Cleombrotus from his refuge and sentenced him to exile, but he begged his daughter to stay. 'Don't leave me!' he said. 'I love you so, and I spared your husband's life as a gift to you.' But she was not moved. When her husband got up to leave, she gave him one of the children to carry, picked up the other one herself, did obeisance to the god's altar,† and left along with him. And if Cleombrotus' standards had not been warped by vainglory, he would have seen that, thanks to his wife, his exile was a greater blessing than his kingship.

With Cleombrotus out of the way, as soon as Leonidas had sacked the old ephors† and replaced them with others, he turned his attention to Agis. At first he tried to persuade him to leave the sanctuary and be joint king along with him. He told him that the Spartans had pardoned him, on the grounds that he had been duped by Agesilaus because he was young and idealistic. But Agis suspected a trap and stayed where he was, and Leonidas gave up trying to trick him with lies.

Amphares, Damochares, and Arcesilaus, however, were in the habit of visiting Agis in the sanctuary and talking with him there. Once, in fact, they even picked him up and took him to the bath-house, and then returned him to the sanctuary afterwards. They were all friends of his, but Amphares had recently borrowed some valuable clothing and goblets from Agesistrata,* and was actually intriguing against Agis and his womenfolk, so that he would not have to return these things. In fact, it is said that he became Leonidas' most loyal servant, and made sure that the ephors, of whom he was one, were hostile to Agis.

[19] Now, although Agis was basically living in the sanctuary, he used to visit the bath-house once in a while, so that was where they decided to arrest him, when he was outside the sanctuary. They waited until he was leaving the bath-house, and then they went up to him. After greeting him, they walked along with him, chatting light-heartedly as one would with a young friend. But at a certain point a side-street branched off the road in the direction of the prison, and when they reached this junction Amphares, by virtue of his office, grabbed hold of Agis and said: 'I am taking you to appear before the ephors, Agis, to give an account of the measures you have taken for the state.' Damochares, who was a tall, strong man, wrapped his cloak around Agis's neck and pulled him, while the others pushed him along from behind, all according to plan. No one came to his assistance, but the street emptied of people, and they threw him into prison.

Leonidas promptly appeared with a large company of mercenaries and surrounded the prison on the outside, while the ephors went inside to meet with Agis. They summoned to the building those members of the Council of Elders who shared their views, for all the world as though Agis were going to have a proper trial,* and asked him to explain his actions. The young man laughed at their hypocrisy, and Amphares called for him to suffer for his effrontery, but one of the other ephors, making out that he was offering Agis a concession and showing him a way of escaping the charges against him, asked if Lysander and Agesilaus had forced him to act as he did.

When Agis replied that he had not been forced to do anything by anyone, but that he had been drawn to the Lycurgan constitution just because he found it an admirable ideal, the man asked him a further question, whether he regretted what he had done. Agis replied that he could not regret such a noble project, even if he knew he would die for it. And so they condemned him to death, and ordered the executioners to take him to the Hold, which is what they call the chamber of the prison where convicted criminals are hanged. But the executioners could not bring themselves to lay hands on him, and the mercenaries who were standing by also turned away and refused the job, on the grounds that laying hands on the king's body was contrary to both law and custom. Damochares threatened them with punishment and cursed them, but in the end he dragged Agis off to the chamber himself.

Many people already knew about the arrest, and a noisy crowd had assembled at the entrance to the prison, carrying torches. Agis' mother and grandmother were there, crying out their demand that the Spartan king should be allowed a voice and a trial before his fellow citizens. But this only made the ephors press forward with the execution as quickly as possible, since they were afraid that more people would come in the night and break him out of prison.

[20] As Agis was on his way to be hanged, he saw that one of the executioners was sobbing uncontrollably. 'Shed no tears for me, my friend,' he said. 'Since I am innocent of any crimes that warrant death, I am a better person than my killers.' And with these words, he gave his neck without demur to the executioner's noose.

When Amphares appeared at the entrance, Agesistrata fell to her knees and begged him for mercy, in the name of their long intimacy and friendship. He raised her up, assuring her that Agis would not be hurt or killed, and gave her permission to go in and see her son if she wanted. She asked whether her mother could come in with her as well, and Amphares said that of course she could. He let both women inside and had the door locked again behind them.

Aged Archidamia, who throughout her long life had been the most highly regarded woman in Sparta, was the first of the two Amphares sent in to her death. Once she had been killed, he ordered Agesistrata inside, and she entered the chamber to find her son lying dead on the ground and her mother's corpse hanging with the rope around her neck. First, she helped the executioners lift her mother down. She laid her alongside Agis, tidied her up, and shrouded her body. Then she threw herself on her son's body, kissed his face, and said: 'Son, you were too cautious, too kind-hearted, and too considerate for your own good—or for ours either.' Amphares, who had been watching from the entrance and had heard what she said, stormed in and yelled at her. 'Since you shared your son's views,' he said, 'you can share his fate too.' And as Agesistrata got up and approached the noose she said: 'I pray only that this is for the good of Sparta.'

[21] When news of the tragedy reached the city and the three bodies were being brought out, the fear that gripped the people of Sparta was not so great that they hid their grief or their loathing of Leonidas and Amphares. Nothing as shocking or sacrilegious as this had ever happened in Sparta, they felt, since the Dorians first settled in the Peloponnese.* For apparently even enemy soldiers meeting a Spartan king in battle would hesitate before laying hands on him, and tended to turn aside out of fear and respect for his high status. Hence, in all the many battles the Spartans fought against other Greeks in the days before Philip of Macedon, only one king fell, and that was Cleombrotus I at Leuctra,* killed by a spear-thrust. The Messenians claim that Theopompus was another, slain by Aristomenes, but the Spartans say he was only wounded, not killed.*

Anyway, while there may be some dispute about that, Agis was certainly the first occupant of the Spartan throne to be put to death by ephors. His only crime was to have chosen to follow a noble and truly Spartan course of action, and he was of an age when men are generally pardoned for their mistakes. In fact, his friends had more reason to find fault with him than his enemies, seeing that he saved Leonidas' life* and trusted the rest of them, in his naive and kind-hearted fashion.

[22(1)] Directly after Agis' death, his brother Archidamus fled before Leonidas could arrest him, but his wife, who had a newborn baby,* was not so lucky. She was dragged from her house by Leonidas and forced to marry his son Cleomenes. Cleomenes was rather too young for marriage,* but Leonidas did not want Agiatis to be given to anyone else, since she had inherited a large estate from her father, Gylippus, not to mention the fact that she was by far the most beautiful and graceful woman in Greece.* She was also a good person, and so, although we hear that she begged passionately not to be forced into marriage, nevertheless, from the moment she started living with Cleomenes, she was a good and loving wife to the young man—though she never stopped hating Leonidas. Cleomenes, meanwhile, fell in love with her as soon as they were married, and even somewhat sympathized with his wife's devotion to Agis' memory. In fact, he often used to ask her about the past and he would listen carefully as she explained what Agis' intentions and policies had been.

Cleomenes was an idealistic and high-minded young man, and had no less innate strength of will than Agis when it came to resisting pleasures and luxuries, but there was no trace in him of Agis' over-cautious and unassertive temperament. In fact, his passionate nature served as a kind of goad, and he was irresistibly driven to do whatever noble deed presented itself at any given moment. The best thing of all, to his mind, was to have willing subjects, but he also thought it good to overcome those who were reluctant to obey him and force them to improve their lives.

[23(2)] He was appalled, therefore, at the state of affairs in Sparta under Leonidas. The citizens had been dulled by inactivity and pleasure, while the king took no interest in anything as long as he was left in peace to pursue a life of carefree luxury, surrounded by tokens of his abundant wealth. Public business was being neglected, because everyone was busy making sure of his own personal profit, and it was no longer safe even to mention 'training' or 'disciplining the younger generation' or 'endurance' or 'equality'. That was what had got Agis killed.

Cleomenes is also said to have dabbled in philosophy at an early age, when Sphaerus of Borysthenes* visited Sparta and taught a course designed specifically for ephebes and young men. Sphaerus had become one of the leading followers of Zeno of Citium, and it seems that he admired the manliness of Cleomenes' character and added fuel to the fire of his idealism. Once, we hear, Leonidas I was asked his opinion of Tyrtaeus as a poet and he replied: 'He's good for igniting youthful ardour.' (This is true: his poems used to inspire the young men of Sparta to give of themselves in battle and not to count the cost.)* But Stoicism is a dangerous and potentially harmful* doctrine for great-souled and impatient people; its beneficial potential is brought out best when it is diffused in the deep waters of a placid temperament.

[24(3)] When Cleomenes gained the throne on Leonidas' death,* he found that his subjects had by then become good for absolutely nothing at all. The rich ignored public business and were concerned only with personal pleasure and profit, and as a result of their wretched state at home the rest of his subjects had also lost their appetite for war and their commitment to the training regime.* Moreover, he found that he was king only in name, while it was the ephors who wielded real power. And so, before very long, he decided to shake things up and make some changes.

He was close to a man called Xenares, who had been his lover—or his 'inspirer', as the Spartans call it*—and he sounded him out with questions about Agis. What sort of king had he been? How had he come to embark on his course of reforms? Who had helped him? At first Xenares was happy to recall that time, and gave detailed accounts and descriptions of what had happened. But when he saw how emotionally involved Cleomenes was in the stories, and how extraordinarily excited he was by Agis' reforms, which he wanted to hear about over and over again, Xenares lost his temper and told him off for his unhealthy obsession, and finally called a halt to his visits and conversations with the young king. But he told no one the reason for their disagreement, saying only that the king knew why.

Xenares was going to be no help, then, and Cleomenes had no reason to believe that he would meet anything but the same disapproval from everyone else, so he began to lay his plans all by himself. Convinced that it would be better to introduce his reforms at a time of war rather than peace, he stirred up trouble between Sparta and the Achaeans. They had been giving him grounds for complaint anyway, because it had always been the intention of Aratus, the most influential man in the Achaean League, to make the Peloponnese a single political unit.* That had been his constant goal throughout all his many Generalships and his long political career, in the belief that there was no other way to make the Peloponnese unassailable by external enemies. Almost every Peloponnesian state had joined the league, with the only exceptions being Sparta, Elis, and those parts of Arcadia that were subject to Sparta, and so, immediately following Leonidas' death, Aratus had begun to provoke the Arcadians and to ravage their land, especially where it bordered Achaea, as a way of seeing what reaction he would get from the Spartans and Cleomenes, whom he dismissed as a callow youth.*

[25(4)] The ephors' initial response was to send Cleomenes to seize the Athenaeum in Belminatis, a point of entry into Laconia which was at that time the object of a legal dispute between the Spartans and the Megalopolitans.* When Cleomenes seized and fortified it, Aratus made no protest, but he set out one night for an attempt on Tegea and Orchomenus. Those who were supposed to betray these places to him backed out, however, and Aratus withdrew, hoping that his foray would draw no attention.

But Cleomenes wrote a sarcastic letter to him, in which he asked, as if it were just a friendly enquiry, what the purpose was of his nocturnal outing. Aratus wrote back that he had gone to stop Cleomenes building strongholds in Belminatis, having heard of his intention to do so, and Cleomenes sent him another letter, saying that he was sure Aratus was telling the truth, but 'What about all those torches and ladders? If it's not too much bother, do write and tell me why they joined your outing.' Aratus found Cleomenes' joke amusing, and asked what sort of person the youngster was. And Damocrates, a Spartan exile, replied: 'If you have any business with the Spartans, it would be a good idea to get a move on, before this cub grows claws.'

Cleomenes next took a few horsemen and 300 foot-soldiers and established a camp in Arcadia, but the ephors ordered him back, since they did not want to provoke war. But after he had pulled back, Aratus took Caphyae, and the ephors sent him out again. He seized Methydrium and laid waste to Argive territory, but then the Achaeans took to the field with an army of 20,000 foot and 1,000 horse, under the command of Aristomachus. Cleomenes met them at Pallantium and offered battle, but Aratus, cowed by Cleomenes' bravado, would not let Aristomachus run the risk and withdrew his forces.* His reward was abuse from the Achaeans and contemptuous derision from the Spartans, whose army was not even 5,000 strong. Flushed with pride, Cleomenes began to behave with more confidence towards his subjects, and he used to remind them of what an earlier Spartan king* had once said—that† when Spartans ask about an enemy, they do not ask how large their army is, but only where it is.

[26(5)] Cleomenes next went to help the Eleans, who had been attacked by the Achaeans. He fell upon the Achaeans near Mount Lycaeum as they were on their way home, and their entire army panicked and turned to flight. Achaean losses were heavy, and Cleomenes also took a great many prisoners; a rumour even spread through Greece that Aratus had been killed. But Aratus brilliantly turned the situation to his advantage: he marched straight from this defeat to Mantinea, took the city, and secured it with a garrison.* This was something that no one could have anticipated. Spartan morale plummeted and the ephors refused to send Cleomenes out on further expeditions.

Cleomenes therefore decided to write to Archidamus,* the brother of Agis, in Messene, and invite him to return. He was the rightful occupant of the Eurypontid throne alongside him, and

Cleomenes' thinking was that a whole and balanced kingship would blunt the ephors' power. But Agis' killers found out what he was up to and became frightened of being punished if Archidamus returned. So when Archidamus slipped secretly into the city, they welcomed him, helped to restore him to his throne—and then immediately killed him. Phylarchus says that this was done against Cleomenes' wishes, but it may be that he was prevailed upon by his friends and gave the man up to them. At any rate, most of the blame fell on them, since it was widely believed that they had put pressure on Cleomenes.*

[27(6)] Despite this setback, Cleomenes was still determined to stage his coup at the earliest possible opportunity, and he bribed the ephors to vote him a campaign. Many of the other Spartans were won over by his mother Cratesicleia, who shared his ideals and was helping him financially. It is even reported that it was for her son's sake that she took as a husband one of the most distinguished and powerful men in Sparta, even though she was not obliged to remarry.

So Cleomenes took to the field and seized the Megalopolitan fortress of Leuctra.* An Achaean force commanded by Aratus hastened to its relief, and Cleomenes deployed his men right under the walls of the town. In the battle, one division of his army was defeated, but Aratus called off the pursuit rather than let his men cross a deep ravine. This displeased Lydiadas of Megalopolis.* He forged ahead with his cavalry unit in pursuit of the fleeing enemy, and plunged into an area of vines and ditches and walls, where his men became separated and found themselves in difficulties. Seeing that they were vulnerable, Cleomenes unleashed his Tarentines and Cretans,* and although Lydiadas offered stiff resistance, he fell fighting.

Lydiadas' defeat gave fresh heart to the Spartans, and with a shout they fell on the Achaeans and put the entire army to flight, inflicting heavy losses. Under the post-battle truce, Cleomenes returned all the dead except for Lydiadas, whose body was brought on his orders to him. This was the man who had abdicated his tyranny, given his subjects back their freedom, and brought Megalopolis into the Achaean League, and Cleomenes sent his body to the gates of Megalopolis, magnificently arrayed in purple robes and a crown.*

[28(7)] Cleomenes was far more sure of himself after this victory, and he became convinced that it would not be difficult for him to seize power, if the plan he had for turning the war with the Achaeans to his advantage worked, so he set out to persuade Megistonous,* his mother's husband, of the necessity of getting rid of the ephors and sharing all property among the citizens of Sparta. With equality restored in Sparta, he said, they would rouse the city from its slumber and lead it towards dominion of Greece. Megistonous was won over, and brought in two or three of his friends as well.

By sheer coincidence, at much the same time one of the ephors had a remarkable dream while sleeping in the sanctuary of Pasiphaë.* He dreamt that four of the seats in the place where the ephors usually met and conducted their business had been removed, leaving only one, and that while he was puzzling over this a voice issued from the sanctuary, saying that it was in Sparta's best interests. When Cleomenes first heard about this dream from the ephor, he was troubled by the thought that the man had some inkling of what he was up to and was testing him, but he soon became convinced that the ephor's story was genuine, and his confidence returned.

He raised an army, making sure that it included all those Spartans who were most likely to be opposed to the coup, took Heraea and Asea, which were subject to the Achaeans, and brought a supply of grain for the people of Orchomenus. He then made camp close to Mantinea and completely wore out the Spartan contingents of his army with long treks up hill and down dale, until at their own request he left most of them in Arcadia, while he took the mercenaries and set off for Sparta. Along the way, marching slowly so as to catch the ephors at dinner, he confided his plans to those whose loyalty he had least reason to doubt.

[29(8)] When he was close to the city, Cleomenes sent Eurycleidas ahead to the ephors' mess. The cover was that Eurycleidas had come from the army with a message from Cleomenes for the ephors, but in fact Therycion and Phoebis, two of Cleomenes' foster-brothers (*mothakes*,* the Spartans call them), were following Eurycleidas with a small body of soldiers. Eurycleidas was in the middle of his address to the ephors when these men burst in with drawn swords and stabbed them.* The first one they struck was Agylaeus. He fell to the ground and seemed to be dead, but he slowly came to and dragged himself out of the room without being seen. He crawled into a small side-chamber, which housed a shrine of Fear. It was usually kept locked, but luckily for him it just happened to have been opened that day, and he was able to squeeze in and lock the door. But the other four ephors were killed, along with no more than ten others, who came to help. No one was killed unless he interfered, nor was anyone stopped from leaving the city, and even Agylaeus was spared when he emerged from the shrine the next morning.

[30(9)] The Spartans have shrines not just of Fear, but also of Death, and of emotions such as Laughter. They worship Fear not as a malignant deity to be warded off, but as the force on which the coherence of the state chiefly depends. This also explains why, as we learn from Aristotle, the ephors, on entering office, have a herald proclaim to their fellow citizens that they are to shave their upper lips and obey the laws, or risk the penalties for disobedience.* They specify the shaving of moustaches, I think, to get young men accustomed to obedience in even the most trivial matters. And it seems a reasonable hypothesis to me that in the old days Spartans used to think of courage not as fearlessness, but as fear of censure and terror of disgrace. For those who defy the law least defy their enemies most, and those whose major concern is to avoid shame are minimally worried about pain.

Whoever it was, then, who said that 'Fear and respect go hand in hand'* was absolutely right. So was Homer, with 'I feel respect for you, dear father of my wife, but also fear', and 'Silently, in fear of their leaders'.* After all, it is a common experience to feel the most respect for those one fears. And this also explains why the Spartans set up their shrine to Fear next to the ephors' mess, given that they invested the ephorate with almost absolute power.

[31(10)] Anyway, the next day Cleomenes posted a list of eighty citizens who were to leave town, and removed the ephors' seats, except one, which he intended for his use when he conducted official business. Then he called a general assembly and delivered a speech to justify his actions. Lycurgus, he said, had put Elders and kings in the harness together, and for many years they had formed the administration of the city, with no need of any other office. Later, however, the long war against the Messenians* had meant that the kings were too busy campaigning to administer justice themselves, and they had chosen some of their friends and left them behind in the city as their deputies. They called these people ephors, or 'overseers', and at first they only ever acted as the kings' assistants. But then they had gradually begun to arrogate more and more power to themselves, and in this way, before anyone realized it, they had created an office of their own.* He offered, as confirmation of his account, the survival to their own day of the ritual whereby, when the ephors summoned the king, he refused the first and the second summons, but got up and came to them at the third time of asking. And he claimed that Asteropus,* the man who had first given the office real sinew and strength, had not been ephor until many generations after the office had been created.

As long as the ephors kept within the bounds of moderation, he went on, it was better to put up with them. But when they usurped so much power that they subverted the traditional form of government by banishing kings or killing them without trial—when they threatened the lives of those who longed to see the revival in Sparta of the structure that had made it so perfect, a true heaven on earth—it was not to be tolerated. If he could have shed no blood while eradicating the imported influences that plagued Spartan society—luxury and extravagance, lending and borrowing—and the even older evils of poverty and wealth; if he could have been the doctor who cured his country painlessly, he would have considered himself the most fortunate king in history. But in fact, he said, he had Lycurgus' pardon for what he had been compelled to do, since Lycurgus had been neither king nor magistrate, but a private citizen, when with the intention of making himself king he had entered the city square with an armed retinue and forced the terrified king, Charillus, to seek refuge at an altar.*

It is true, Cleomenes said, that Charillus was a good man and a loyal patriot, and so had soon come to support what Lycurgus was doing and to accept his reforms, but Lycurgus' very actions proved how difficult it is to reform a political system without resorting to violence and terror. Cleomenes admitted that he had employed these tools, but only with the utmost restraint; he had done no more than remove those who were impeding Sparta's salvation. For everyone else, all land was to be public property and debts were cancelled. And an assessment and evaluation of foreign residents would take place, with the object of enrolling the best of them as Spartan citizens, so that they could be armed for the protection of the city. That, he said, would put an end to the sight they currently had to endure of their land being plundered by Aetolians and Illyrians just because there was no one to defend it.*

[32(11)] The next step Cleomenes took was to make his own property over to the state. He was followed by his stepfather Megistonous and all his other friends, who were followed in their turn by all the rest of the Spartiates as well, and then the land was reassigned. He even reserved an allotment for every man who had been exiled by him, and promised to let them come home when things had quietened down. Then he replenished the number of citizens with the most acceptable of the *perioeci*, and thus created a levy of 4,000 heavy infantry, whom he trained to use the two-handed pike rather than the spear, and to heft their shields by means of an arm-strap rather than a handle.*

After this, he turned to the training of the younger generation and the famous 'regime'.* Sphaerus was on hand to help him* with most of the reorganization, and before long they had made the appropriate adjustments to the structures of both the gymnasia and the messes. A few people had to be coerced into moderation, but most people willingly reduced the way they lived and adopted the old, frugal, Spartan regime. Nevertheless, he did not want to be thought of as an absolute ruler, and so he made his brother Eucleidas joint king along with him. This was the only time in Spartan history that both of their kings came from the same house.*

[33(12)] When Cleomenes found out that Aratus and the Achaeans believed that the revolution had made his position so precarious that he would not venture forth from Sparta or leave the city in the midst of such uncertainty and upheaval, it occurred to him that it would be both glorious and worthwhile for him to show the enemy just how ready his soldiers were. And so he invaded Megalopolitan territory, collected a great deal of booty, and caused widespread damage to the farmland.* The climax of the expedition, however, came after he had captured some members of the Guild of Dionysus* on the road from Messene. He had a theatre built, right there in enemy territory, put on a contest with forty mnas as the prize, and spent all of one day just sitting and watching. The point, of course, was not the show: it was a way of mocking his enemies and taunting them with a display designed to make it perfectly clear that he had power to spare. In fact, generally speaking, the Spartan was the only Greek or royal army that did *not* have in its train mimes, conjurers, and girls to dance or play the lyre, and was untainted by licentiousness, ribaldry, and merrymaking of any kind. The younger men spent most of their time training, the older men were invariably to be found instructing them, and to lighten their spare time they had their usual jokes, and their witty, laconic exchanges. I have written about the practical value of this kind of amusement in my Life of Lycurgus.*

[34(13)] Cleomenes himself was everyone's teacher in these respects. His life was simple and unpretentious, with nothing vulgar about it nor anything to distinguish him from ordinary people. It served as a kind of public model of self-discipline, and this created a bias in his favour when he was dealing with Greeks. For in their encounters with other kings, people were not so much overawed by their wealth and extravagance as disgusted by the arrogant self-importance that was manifest in the offensive and uncaring way they dealt with those to whom they granted an audience. But when they approached Cleomenes—a true king, not just a holder of the title—they were struck by the absence of purple-dyed robes or cloaks, or equipment such as sedan-chairs and litters. They found that doing business with him was not a frustrating and laborious experience, impeded by hordes of pages and doorkeepers or the intermediation of secretaries, but that he came to meet his visitors in person, dressed in ordinary clothes, and made time to talk graciously and kindly to his petitioners. And they were so charmed and captivated that they declared him to be the only true descendant of Heracles.*

His regular daily dinner was extremely meagre and Spartan, and eaten in a three-couch room, but if he was entertaining ambassadors or guest-friends, two further couches were added and his attendants made the table a bit more sumptuous, not with rich sauces and desserts, but in the sense that the servings were more generous and the wine more palatable. In fact, he criticized a friend of his when he heard that he had invited guest-friends for dinner and had served them black broth* and barley bread, the usual fare of the messes,* saying that there was no need to be too excessively Spartan on these occasions, with foreigners present.

Once the table had been removed, a bronze mixing-bowl filled with wine was brought in, along with a tripod to hold it, and two silver serving-jugs, each with a capacity of two *kotylae*.* No more than a few silver cups were provided, which were available for anyone's use, but no one had a cup pressed on him if he did not want it. No entertainment was laid on, but it was not missed, because Cleomenes' own conversation used to hold his guests' attention over the wine. Whether he was asking questions or explaining something, his tone was not disagreeably serious, but light, refined, and tasteful. For, in his opinion, the way the other kings went about snaring people, by tempting them and bribing them with money and gifts, was clumsy and dishonest. It seemed far better to him, and far more kingly, to attract people and win their affection with pleasing conversation and cogent argument, since the only difference between a hireling and a friend is that the one is captured by a man's money and the other by his character and conversation.*

[35(14)] First, then, the Mantineans invited him in. They surreptitiously admitted him into the city under cover of darkness, expelled the Achaean garrison with his help, and put themselves in his hands. He gave them permission to restore their traditional legal code and constitution, and then marched off to Tegea, all in a single day. Then, a little later, he took a circuitous route through Arcadia and descended on the Achaean town of Pharae, with the intention of either bringing the Achaeans to battle or discrediting Aratus if he turned tail and abandoned the region to him. I say 'Aratus' because, although Hyperbatas was the Achaean General that year,* Aratus had absolute power in the league.

The Achaeans took to the field with their entire levy and made camp by the Hecatombaeum at Dyme. When Cleomenes got there, he could see that it would be inadvisable to pitch camp, which would place him between Dyme, an enemy city, and the Achaean army, so he boldly offered the Achaeans battle and forced them to fight. He was overwhelmingly victorious. The Achaean phalanx broke and fled, with many of them losing their lives and many more falling alive into Cleomenes' hands. Then he marched on Langon, expelled the Achaean garrison, and returned the city to the Eleans.

[36(15)] Aratus usually became General every other year,* but now, with the Achaeans crushed, he refused to stand and turned a deaf ear to their appeals and pleas. But it was wrong of him to lay aside his power and hand the tiller over to someone else right in the middle of a major storm, as it were.* Cleomenes behaved better. Although the first demands he presented to the Achaean ambassadors struck them as outrageous, he told the second delegation they sent that all they had to do was surrender the leadership of the Peloponnese to him. That would heal the rift between them, and he would immediately return their prisoners and their fortresses.

The Achaeans were ready to accept peace on these terms and they invited Cleomenes to come to Lerna, where they would be holding their general assembly. Unluckily, however, as a result of drinking too much water after a strenuous day on the road, Cleomenes brought up a quantity of blood and lost his voice. He sent the most eminent prisoners back to the Achaeans, but postponed the conference and returned to Sparta.

[37(16)] And so Greece was ruined, when there had still been a faint chance that it could recover from its current plight and escape Macedonian overlordship and greed. But perhaps Aratus distrusted or feared Cleomenes, or perhaps he resented his sudden success and could not stand the thought that, after he had been at the helm for thirty-three years,* an upstart young man should at a stroke destroy both his glory and his power, and inherit dominion over a state that he had made great and had controlled for so long. Anyway, whatever his reasons, he first tried to coerce the Achaeans, but he found that they were too cowed by Cleomenes' bravado to pay any attention to him. In fact, they even thought that the Spartans' terms were fair, coming from people who were reviving the traditional form of organization of the Peloponnese. So Aratus then did something that would have been wrong for any Greek, but was especially disgraceful for him, and a betrayal of all that he had achieved and the policies he had followed: he invited Antigonus to Greece, and filled the Peloponnese with Macedonians, when as a young man it had been he who had earned the distrust and hostility of all the kings by driving the Macedonians from the Peloponnese with his liberation of the Acrocorinth,* and when this was the same Antigonus that he had used the publication of his *Memoirs** to vilify in every imaginable fashion.

Even though he boasts of all the difficulties and dangers he had to overcome in seeing that the Macedonians and their garrison were removed from Athens,* he still brought these same Macedonians armed into his own country, his own home, and even the women's quarters of his home.* In his opinion, a man who could trace his bloodline back to Heracles and was a king of Sparta—a man who had found that the strings, so to speak, of the ancestral constitution had lost their tension and was trying to retune it once again to the austere, Dorian mode of Lycurgan practices and habits—was not fit to become the titular head of Sicyon and Tritaea. Instead, to avoid eating barley bread and wearing a thin cloak, and to avoid what he denounced as the most heinous of Cleomenes' crimes, the abolition of wealth and alleviation of poverty, he prostrated himself and Achaea before a diadem and a purple robe, and subjected the Peloponnese to the edicts of Macedonians and satraps. And to avoid seeming to be under Cleomenes' thumb, he honoured Antigonus with festivals at which, properly garlanded, he performed sacrifices and sang paeans to a mortal man who was wasting away from consumption.* But I write this not so much to condemn Aratus, who was in many respects a true Greek and a great man, as to acknowledge with sadness whatever flaw it is in human nature that makes it impossible even for people with a remarkable and exceptional aptitude for virtue to achieve anything noble that is not tainted by imperfection.*

[38(17)] When the Achaeans returned to Argos for the rescheduled conference, and Cleomenes had arrived from Tegea, most people expected an end to the war. But Aratus had the security of knowing that the most important aspects of his agreement with Antigonus were already in place, and he was also afraid that Cleomenes might attain all his objectives by threatening the assembled Achaeans with force, if he could not win them over peacefully. So he demanded that Cleomenes should either accept 300 hostages and then present himself before them unaccompanied, or should bring his army up to the Cylarabis gymnasium* outside the city for the conference.

Cleomenes protested that this was not right. He should have been informed of these conditions straight away at the time, he said, not now; it was wrong to doubt him and drive him away when he already had one foot in their doorway. He addressed the issue in a letter to the Achaeans, but most of it was taken up with condemnation of Aratus, and once Aratus had returned the favour by publicly vilifying him,* Cleomenes wasted no more time. He returned home and sent a herald to the Achaeans to declare war—sending him, however, as Aratus reports, to Aegium* rather than Argos, so that he could get started on his preparations before they did.

There was turmoil in the Achaean League, and the member cities were inclining strongly towards secession. The common people hoped for a redistribution of the land and a remission of debts, while the leading citizens of many of the cities were unhappy with Aratus, and some of them were even openly angry with him for bringing the Macedonians to the Peloponnese. Cleomenes was encouraged by all this to invade Achaea, where he first took Pellene by surprise and expelled the Achaean garrison, and then gained Pheneus and Penteleium.

The Achaeans became afraid that there was treachery afoot in Corinth and Sicyon, and sent their cavalry and their mercenary contingents there from Argos to keep an eye on things, while the rest of them returned to Argos for the Nemean festival.* Cleomenes rightly thought that if he launched a surprise attack on the city when it was packed with festival-goers and spectators, they would panic. He led his army up to the walls under cover of darkness and succeeded in securing the rugged and defensible area near the Shield,* overlooking the theatre. The people were so terrified at this that not only did they offer no resistance, but they even accepted a garrison, handed over twenty of their fellow citizens as hostages, and entered into an alliance with the Spartans, under the overall leadership of Cleomenes.

[39(18)] The fall of Argos added greatly to Cleomenes' fame and power, since despite all their efforts past kings of Sparta had never succeeded in securing the city's allegiance. Even Pyrrhus, a military genius, failed to hold it: he managed to force his way inside, but then he lost his life there, along with many of his men.* So Cleomenes earned respect for his decisiveness and intelligence, and at the same time anyone who had laughed at him before for copying Solon* and Lycurgus with his cancellation of debts and equalization of property-holding now became absolutely convinced that he was responsible for the change in the Spartiates. Earlier their fortunes had been at such a low ebb and they were so incapable of helping themselves that the Aetolians had invaded Laconia and left with 50,000 slaves—allegedly prompting an elderly Spartan to say that the enemy had done the city a favour by lightening its load.* But now, only a short while later, when they had barely re-established contact with their ancestral customs and picked up the traces of their famous training regime, they put on a great display of courage and discipline for Lycurgus—it was as though he were there in the city alongside them—in the course of regaining the Peloponnese for Sparta and making it the leading state in Greece.

[40(19)] Immediately following the fall of Argos, Cleonae and Phlious came down on Cleomenes' side. Aratus happened to be in Corinth at the time, investigating alleged Spartan sympathizers, and the arrival of this news came as a big shock. Since he could see that the Corinthians too were inclining towards Cleomenes and wanted the Achaeans out, he summoned the citizens of Corinth to the council house and slipped away unnoticed to the city gates, where he mounted the horse he had waiting and fled to Sicyon.

Aratus informs us that everyone in Corinth was in such a hurry to reach Cleomenes at Argos that they wore out their horses, and that Cleomenes told them off for having let him slip through their fingers and escape. Nevertheless, Cleomenes sent Megistonous to him, to ask for the surrender of the Acrocorinth (which was garrisoned by Achaean soldiers) and offer a substantial financial inducement. Aratus replied, however, that he was not in control of events, but the other way around. This is the account Aratus has left us.

But Cleomenes marched from Argos to Corinth, receiving the surrender of Troezen, Epidaurus, and Hermione on the way. When he got there, he put the Acrocorinth under siege, since the Achaeans would not leave of their own accord, and arranged a meeting with Aratus' friends and stewards, at which he ordered them to take charge of Aratus' household and property, and keep it all safe and sound. Then he sent a second agent to Aratus, Tritymallus of Messene,* asking whether the Acrocorinth might not be garrisoned by a joint force of Achaeans and Spartans, and adding a personal promise that he would double whatever allowance Aratus had been receiving from King Ptolemy.* Aratus turned him down, however, and instead sent hostages to Antigonus, including his son, and persuaded the Achaeans to vote for giving the Acrocorinth to Antigonus. Cleomenes therefore overran and devastated some of Sicyon's farmland,* and when the Corinthians voted to make a personal gift to him of Aratus' property, he accepted it.

[41(20)] By the time Antigonus and his formidable army were crossing the Geraneia mountains,* Cleomenes had decided that it would be better not to fortify and guard the Isthmus, but the Oneia mountains*—in other words, that he should fight a war of attrition against the Macedonians by occupying strong-points rather than engage their experienced phalanx in pitched battle. This strategy did indeed make things difficult for Antigonus, since his grain stores were inadequate and, with Cleomenes dug in, entrance to the Peloponnese was hard.

After Antigonus had failed to slip past the enemy in the night by way of Lechaeum, and had lost some men in the attempt, Cleomenes' confidence could not have been higher, and his men attended to their evening meal elated by their victory. Antigonus' spirits were low, however, since he was being forced into a position where he had few options and none of them was plain sailing. He was planning to decamp to the Heraeum headland, and to ferry his army across from there by boat, but that would take a long time and an extraordinary amount of organization.

But in the late afternoon some men arrived by sea from Argos, friends of Aratus, inviting him to come, on the understanding that the Argives were ready to secede from Cleomenes. The prime mover of the insurrection was Aristotle,* but it had not been hard for him to win over the general populace, who were angry with Cleomenes for having failed to cancel debts as they had expected. So Aratus took 1,500 of Antigonus' men and sailed over to Epidaurus, but before he arrived Aristotle had already gathered his fellow citizens and attacked the garrison on the acropolis. Timoxenus was there as well to support him, with the Achaean garrison from Sicyon.

[42(21)] It was the second watch of the night when the news was brought to Cleomenes. He summoned Megistonous and angrily ordered him to march at once to the relief of Argos. He was angry with him because it had been Megistonous more than anyone who had quelled his doubts about the Argives and stopped him throwing those he suspected out of the city. So after sending Megistonous on his way with 2,000 soldiers, he kept a weather eye on Antigonus and tried to dispel the Corinthians' fears by telling them that nothing serious was happening at Argos, that it was just a minor disturbance involving a few people. But then Megistonous died fighting after gaining entrance to the city, and message after message began pouring in from the garrison, who were finding it difficult to hold out. Cleomenes became worried because, if the enemy gained control of Argos and closed the passes against his return, they could ravage Laconia without fear of retaliation and assault the walls of a defenceless Sparta. And so he led his army away from Corinth.*

Corinth was lost to him straight away, since Antigonus immediately entered the city and installed a garrison, but when Cleomenes reached Argos he committed himself to an assault on the walls and gathered his forces for the attempt as soon as they marched up. After securing the area of the vaults at the foot of the Shield,* he managed to climb the hill and join his men in the citadel, who were still holding out against the Achaeans. He also made some progress inside the city itself by having his Cretans* mount the walls and clear the streets of enemy troops with their arrows. But when he saw Antigonus leading his heavy infantry down from the hills to the plain, and the enemy cavalry already entering the city in droves, he realized that he was not going to win. He ordered all his men to gather at his point, brought them down safely, and led them away past the city wall.

It had taken Cleomenes very little time to make very great gains, and he came close to making the entire Peloponnese his with a single expedition, but it did not take him long to lose everything again. Some of the cities immediately withdrew from the alliance, and the rest soon surrendered to Antigonus.

[43(22)] So Cleomenes set out homeward from this catastrophic expedition with his army. By nightfall he had reached Tegea, where he was met by messengers from Sparta with news of an event that was just as calamitous to him as what he was already coping with: the death of his wife. Agiatis was the reason why he used to grow impatient out on campaign, even when things were going brilliantly, and would often return to Sparta; he loved her and thought the world of her. But even though he was stricken with grief, as any young man would be who had lost a particularly beautiful and virtuous woman, he did not let himself down or allow his dignity or principles to be swamped by anguish. He made sure that even his voice, demeanour, and appearance were no different from usual, and he continued to issue orders to his officers and take thought for the security of Tegea. At dawn the next day he started back to Sparta, and when he got there he assuaged his grief at home in the company of his mother and children, and then turned straight to thinking about affairs of state.

Ptolemy of Egypt was promising his support,* but wanted Cleomenes' children and mother as hostages, and for a long time Cleomenes was too embarrassed to tell his mother. He often entered her chambers and came right to the point of speaking, but said nothing, and she became suspicious and asked his friends if there was anything they knew of that he both wanted and did not want to tell her. But in the end Cleomenes screwed up his courage and spoke to her, and she laughed out loud and said: 'Is that what you couldn't bring yourself to tell me all those times when you meant to? Quick now, put me on board a ship and send me wherever you think this body of mine will serve Sparta best, before it dies of old age sitting uselessly here.'

When everything was ready, then, they travelled by land to Taenarum with an armed escort provided by his men. Just before boarding ship, Cratesicleia took Cleomenes into the temple of Poseidon. No one else was with them, and she held him and kissed him as he gave vent to his grief and distress. But then she said: 'Come, king of the Spartans. When we leave the temple, no one must see us weeping or letting Sparta down in any way. That much we can do; but our destinies are in the gift of the gods.'*

With these words, she composed her features, walked to the ship with her grandson, and told the captain to put to sea as soon as possible. When she got to Egypt, she found that Ptolemy was accepting proposals and embassies from Antigonus, and she heard that the Achaeans had invited Cleomenes to make peace, but that because of her he was afraid of ending the war without Ptolemy's permission. She therefore wrote and told him that he should do whatever was appropriate and good for Sparta, without living in constant fear of Ptolemy because of one old woman and a young child. This, then, is how Cratesicleia is said to have acquitted herself in her misfortunes.

[44(23)] After Antigonus had gained Tegea, and sacked Orchomenus and Mantinea, Cleomenes was reduced to Laconia itself.* He freed any helots who could put down five Attic mnas (thus raising a total of 500 talents),* armed 2,000 of them with Macedonian-style weaponry to counter Antigonus' White Shields,* and began to lay plans for a major undertaking, something that would take the whole world by surprise. Megalopolis was at this time no less important or powerful than Sparta, and it could call up help from the Achaeans and Antigonus, who was encamped on its flanks.* In fact, it was widely believed that Antigonus had been called in by the Achaeans largely at the Megalopolitans' insistence.* It was this city that Cleomenes planned to rip† from the Achaeans; no other word conveys the stunning speed of this famous achievement of his.

He ordered his men to bring five days' worth of rations and led them out of the city in the direction of Sellasia, as though he were going to ravage Argive territory, but then made for Megalopolis instead. After halting for a meal at Rhoeteium, he marched directly towards the city via Helissous. When he was quite close, he sent two brigades of Spartans on ahead, under the command of Panteus, with the task of seizing a certain section of wall between two towers, which Cleomenes had learnt was relatively free of Megalopolitan soldiers, compared with the rest of the fortifications. Meanwhile, he came on behind with the bulk of the army at a leisurely pace. Panteus in fact found much of the wall undefended, not only that particular stretch, and he immediately set about demolishing it here and undermining it there, killing any sentries he encountered. Cleomenes very soon joined him, and before the Megalopolitans knew what was going on he was inside the city with his army.

[45(24)] When at last the inhabitants realized to their horror what had happened, some of them immediately fled the city with whatever property came to hand, while others armed themselves and banded together to resist and attack the enemy. They could not muster enough strength to drive them out of the city, but they did at least make it possible for those of their fellow citizens who were fleeing to do so safely, and in the end no more than a thousand people were caught inside. All the rest managed to escape to Messene with their wives and children.

Most of those who fought in defence of the city survived as well, but a few were taken prisoner, not many altogether, but they included Lysandridas and Thearidas, men of great standing and influence in Megalopolis. The soldiers who captured them therefore took them straight to Cleomenes. Lysandridas saw Cleomenes when he was still some way off and called out: 'You have an opportunity here, king of the Spartans, for an achievement that will far outshine in kingly magnificence anything you've done before, and bring you undying fame.'

But Cleomenes guessed what he was going to ask and said: 'What do you mean, Lysandridas? Surely you're not going to suggest that I return the city to you, are you?'

'Yes, that's exactly what I mean,' Lysandridas replied. 'I don't think you should destroy such an important city, but fill it with friends and allies, men you can trust and rely on. And you can do that by returning Megalopolis to its citizens and making yourself the saviour of all those people.'

After a short pause, Cleomenes said: 'It's not easy to trust what you say, but I hope that I will always choose the road that leads to glory rather than profit.' And with these words, he sent Lysandridas and Thearidas to Messene along with a herald to proclaim his offer: that he would return Megalopolis to its citizens provided that they abandoned the Achaeans and joined him instead. Despite this diplomatic and generous offer from Cleomenes, Philopoemen would not allow the Megalopolitans to break their pledge to the Achaeans. In fact, he accused Cleomenes of intending not so much to return the city as to gain the citizens as well as the city, and threw Lysandridas and Thearidas out of Messene. This is the Philopoemen who later became the leader of the Achaeans and won an unrivalled reputation in Greece, as I have described in his Life.*

[46(25)] When news of the Megalopolitans' decision reached Cleomenes he was absolutely livid with rage. Although he had so far kept a close guard over the city, to keep it unharmed and inviolate, and no one had got away with stealing even the slightest of things, he now plundered it of its valuables, sent statues and paintings off to Sparta, and razed most of the city to the ground, including all the most important districts. Then he returned home, since he was worried about how Antigonus and the Achaeans would react.

But in fact they did nothing, because they were busy with a council meeting at Aegium. When Aratus mounted the speaker's platform he wept for a long time, shielding his face with his cloak. The Achaeans asked him in surprise to say what was troubling him, and he told them of the destruction of Megalopolis by Cleomenes. They were so dismayed by the speed and the extent of the catastrophe that the meeting broke up. Antigonus wanted to fight for the city, but his men were slow in emerging from their winter quarters, so he told them to stay where they were, while he went to Argos with just a small force.

It should be clear, then, that Cleomenes' second attempt on Argos was not a feat of reckless insanity, as was widely believed, but a carefully planned action, as Polybius says.* He knew that the Macedonians were dispersed in various cities for the winter, and he knew that Antigonus and his Friends were passing the winter in Argos with just a few mercenaries. So when he invaded Argive territory, his thinking was that Antigonus would either be shamed into fighting a battle that he would lose, or would turn the Argives against him by not daring to fight. And he was right. The sight of Cleomenes devastating farmland and making off with all their property was more than the Argives could bear, and they crowded around the doorway of the king's quarters, angrily demanding that he should either fight or pass his command on to better men. But Antigonus, as a wise general should, felt that it was taking unreasonable risks and throwing caution to the winds that was the shameful course of action, not offending the mob outside. He refused to make a sortie or allow his mind to be changed. Cleomenes brought his men right up to the city walls, taunting them and causing further damage, and then withdrew unmolested.

[47(26)] A short while later, however, when he heard that Antigonus was once again heading for Tegea, with the intention of invading Laconia from there, he quickly gathered his troops. Taking routes that would ensure no contact with Antigonus, he appeared at daybreak just outside Argos. He laid waste to the plain, not using scythes and swords to cut the grain, as everyone else did, but beating it down with large pieces of wood curved like a Thracian sword, which his men wielded almost playfully as they marched along, effortlessly flattening and destroying all the standing crops. But when they reached the Cylarabis* and were about to set fire to the gymnasium, Cleomenes stopped them, feeling that at Megalopolis he had acted angrily rather than honourably.

Antigonus' first response was to fall back immediately on Argos, and then he secured the heights and all the passes with pickets. In a show of nonchalance and disdain, Cleomenes sent heralds to Antigonus, asking for the keys to the Heraeum,* so that he could sacrifice to the goddess before leaving. After amusing himself with this mockery, he carried out the sacrifice in the lee of the locked sanctuary, and led his army away to Phlious. Then he drove the pickets off Mount Olygyrtus and returned home via Orchomenus.

This expedition by Cleomenes restored his subjects' pride and morale, and at the same time it also made his enemies think of him as a true leader, one who deserved his high status. After all, with the resources of just a single city he had taken on the Macedonian army, the entire Peloponnese, and the wealth of a king, and not only had he kept Laconia from harm, but he had done significant damage to enemy territory and had captured great cities. All this seemed to mark him as a man of extraordinary ability and great ambition.

[48(27)] But it seems likely to me that whoever first called money the sinews of every endeavour had military endeavours chiefly in mind. Similarly, Demades* was once being ordered by the Athenians to launch and man the war fleet when there was no money in the treasury, and he said: 'First you knead, *then* you make bread.'† And when Sparta's allies, with the Peloponnesian War looming, were calling on Archidamus* to fix their contributions, he is supposed to have said that war does not feed on fixed rations.

Athletes who have built up their bodies eventually outweigh

and outmatch those who are well proportioned and technically proficient, and in the same way Antigonus, who had plenty of resources to expend on the war, exhausted and outmatched Cleomenes, who had hardly enough to pay his mercenaries and feed his Spartan troops. In other respects, however, time was on Cleomenes' side, because events at home demanded Antigonus' attention. During his absence barbarians had overrun and devastated Macedonia, and at the time in question a large Illyrian army had invaded from the interior. It was their plundering that prompted the Macedonians to ask Antigonus to come home.

It was only by chance that this message did not reach him before the battle; if it had, he would have left straight away and that would have been the last the Achaeans saw of him for a long while. But Fortune likes to decide the greatest of events by a narrow margin, and she just barely tipped the scales of opportunity and means so that it was immediately after the battle of Sellasia, when Cleomenes had lost his army and his city, that the messengers arrived to call Antigonus home. This, more than anything else, is what made Cleomenes' downfall so tragic. If he had held out and continued refusing battle for just two more days, he would not have had to fight, and after the Macedonians had left he could have made peace with the Achaeans on terms of his choosing. But in fact the financial difficulties* of his that I have already mentioned forced him to stake everything on battle, and to pit his 20,000 men against 30,000. The numbers are from Polybius.*

[49(28)] Although his generalship in the battle was superb, and although his Spartans gave of their best and even his mercenaries acquitted themselves irreproachably, he was overcome by superior enemy weaponry and by the weight of their heavy infantry phalanx. Phylarchus, however, says that there was also treachery involved, and that this was the chief factor in Cleomenes' defeat.*

What happened was that, before deploying the rest of his forces for battle, Antigonus ordered his Illyrians and Acarnanians to make a wide circuit and without being seen to get behind the enemy's left wing, which was commanded by Eucleidas, Cleomenes' brother. But when Cleomenes could see no sign of Illyrian or Acarnanian weaponry as he looked out from his vantage-point, he became worried that Antigonus was using them for some such manoeuvre. He called for Damoteles, the officer in command of the *krypteia*,* and told him to find out by observation and enquiry how things stood in the rear and on either side of his battle-line. But Damoteles, who, we are informed, had already been bribed by Antigonus, told him that everything was fine there, and that he should not worry about them, but focus on fighting off the enemy soldiers who were engaging him head on.

Cleomenes trusted Damoteles and advanced against Antigonus. The force of his Spartiates' forward motion pushed the Macedonian phalanx back about five stades,* and Cleomenes followed, pressing them hard and keeping them on the defensive. But then on the other wing Eucleidas was outflanked, and when Cleomenes saw the danger he stopped and said: 'Dearest brother of mine, you are lost, lost! So noble you were! How the Spartiate boys looked up to you, and what songs the women sung about you!'

With Eucleidas and his men dead, the Illyrians and Acarnanians attacking from that direction and continuing to win, and his men losing formation and plainly too frightened to stand their ground, Cleomenes looked to his own safety. It is said that most of his mercenaries died, and all but 200 of the Spartans, who had numbered 6,000.

[50(29)] When he reached Sparta, the advice he offered those of his subjects who came out to meet him was that they should accept Antigonus. 'As for myself,' he said, 'I will continue to do what is best for Sparta, with my life or with my death.' Only when he saw that the women were running up to those who had fled with him, relieving them of their armour and offering them drinks, did he go home. But when the girl he had taken up with since his wife's death—a prostitute from Megalopolis, of free status—came up to him, as she did on his return from a campaign, to tend to his needs, he would not let himself take a drink, despite his great thirst, or sit down either, for all his exhaustion. Instead, just as he was, still in his armour, he placed his forearm against a pillar and leant his head on it, and after resting like this for no more than a few minutes, while running through all the possibilities in his mind, he set out with his friends for Gythium.* And there they boarded ships that had been kept ready against just this eventuality and put to sea.

[51(30)] Sparta surrendered to Antigonus the moment he arrived. He treated the people well, without disrespecting or insulting the dignity of the city, and even restored their former customs and constitution.* Then, after a public sacrifice to the gods, he withdrew, only two days after his arrival, when he received news of serious fighting in Macedon, with the farmland being plundered by the barbarians. Moreover, by now his consumption was at an advanced stage, with severe weight-loss and constant sputum. He did not take to his bed, however, but threw himself into the defence of his country and died a more glorious death than that, shortly after a decisive and massively bloody victory over the barbarians. In fact, it is reported by Phylarchus (as well as being plausible anyway) that his death was caused by internal bleeding brought on by the very shouting that he had to do in the course of the battle. In the schools* one used to hear it said that he gave a shout of joy after his victory—'O happy day!'—and then brought up a quantity of blood and died from a raging fever.

While all this was happening to Antigonus, [52(31)] Cleomenes sailed from Cythera and put in at another island, Aegila, before the final leg to Cyrene. But one of his friends, Therycion* by name—a man who sought the moral high ground in everything he did, and whose manner of speaking was therefore rather haughty and arrogant—spoke to him in private.

'My lord,' he said, 'we've passed up our chance of the noblest kind of death, death in battle, despite the fact that everyone heard us saying that Antigonus would never get the better of the king of Sparta without killing him. But we still have the possibility of choosing the second most glorious and noble form of death. What is the destination of this ill-advised voyage? A distant frying-pan rather than a close fire? I mean, if there's no disgrace in a descendant of Heracles being the slave of a descendant of Philip and Alexander, then we can save ourselves a long voyage by surrendering to Antigonus, who is likely to be a better man than Ptolemy, in so far as Macedonians are better than Egyptians. On the other hand, having refused to accept as our master the one who has defeated us in battle, why would we choose the one who has not? That will give people the impression that we think ourselves inferior to both kings, not just one of them—Antigonus because we're running from him, and Ptolemy because we're currying his favour.

'Or shall we say that we chose Egypt as our destination because of your mother? But when she shows you off to the women of Ptolemy's court, what a glorious sight you'll make—her son, a captive not a king, in exile! How everyone will envy her! No, as long as we are masters of our own swords and can gaze upon Laconia, let us put an end to our misfortunes here and now, and clear our names in the court of those who fell at Sellasia defending Sparta. Is that not better than sitting in Egypt and waiting for news of who Antigonus has made satrap of Sparta?'

When Therycion had finished, Cleomenes said: 'You poor fool, do you think your pursuit of death makes you brave?† There's nothing easier for men than dying; it is always an option for everyone. But you're choosing a more disgraceful form of escape than the one you chose a few days ago. Better men than us have surrendered to their enemies before now when Fortune let them down or they were overwhelmed by superior numbers, but anyone who gives up at the prospect of hardship and humiliation, or is cowed by the disapproval of others or by what men think of him, is the victim of his own weakness. A voluntary death should not be a way to avoid action, but an effective action in its own right; a selfish death is as shameful as a selfish life. But that is what your suggestion amounts to, in your haste to see the last of our current troubles, which is the only benefit or value the act would have. In my opinion, neither you nor I should abandon our hopes for our country. If they ever abandon us, there'll be nothing easier for us than dying, if we want to.'*

Therycion made no reply, but at the earliest possible opportunity he left Cleomenes, made his way to a remote stretch of beach, and killed himself.

[53(32)] But Cleomenes sailed from Aegila to Libya, and was then escorted through Ptolemy's kingdom to Alexandria. At first, when he and Ptolemy met, he found him no more than ordinarily kind to him, but that changed later. Once Ptolemy had some experience of Cleomenes' mind and had come to see how intelligent he was; once he began to appreciate the candour and charm contained within the typically Spartan artlessness of his daily interactions with people; and once he started to realize that, because Cleomenes would never disgrace his noble birth or bend his knee to Fortune, he was more trustworthy than the yes-men of the Egyptian court with their honeyed tongues, he came to hold him in great respect and to regret that he had neglected such a man and sacrificed him to Antigonus, with the consequent boost to Antigonus' reputation and power. So now he began to make amends with honours and gifts, and restored his spirits by promising to send him to Greece with ships and money, and restore him to his kingdom. He also gave him an annual allowance of twenty-four talents, some of which Cleomenes spent on looking after his own and his friends' needs in a simple and frugal fashion, while most of it went on charitable donations for Greek exiles living in Egypt.

[54(33)] But Ptolemy died before he could keep his promise to send Cleomenes home, and on his death the kingdom instantly became mired in debauchery and drunkenness, and the reins of power fell into the hands of women.* In the general climate of indolence, Cleomenes' interests were taken no further. The king's mind had been so thoroughly warped by women and wine that when he was at his most sober and serious he held religious rituals in the palace and used to process around the royal apartments, tambourine in hand, begging for the gods,* while critical matters of state were handled by his mistress Agathocleia and her mother Oenanthe, a former brothel-keeper.

Nevertheless, at first Cleomenes seemed to have a part to play. Ptolemy was afraid of the influence his brother Magas had over the soldiers thanks to the support of their mother,* and he enlisted Cleomenes' help and gave him a seat on a secret council as he deliberated whether or not to murder his brother. Everyone else advised Ptolemy to go ahead, with Cleomenes alone resisting the idea, saying that, on the contrary, in an ideal world Ptolemy would have *more* brothers, to help him secure and stabilize the state. When Sosibius, who had the king's ear more than any of his Friends, argued that Ptolemy would never be sure of the mercenaries as long as Magas was alive, Cleomenes replied that there was no need for worry on that score, because more than 3,000 of the mercenaries were from the Peloponnese; these men were loyal to him, and all he had to do was give them a nod and they would appear, armed and ready.*

At the time, this boast was one of the main things that reassured the king of his loyalty and made him appreciate his strength. Later, however, Ptolemy's weakness intensified his timidity, until he came to believe, as irrational people tend to, that the safest course was to fear and suspect everything and everyone, and then Cleomenes' boast began to make Ptolemy's courtiers worry about him and his influence over the mercenaries. It was common to hear him described as a lion among sheep, and in fact that is exactly the impression he must have given the king's men, with his fierce, intrepid eyes that took in all they saw.

[55(34)] Anyway, Cleomenes gave up asking for ships and men, but then he learnt that Antigonus had died* and that the Achaeans were embroiled in the Aetolian War;* with the Peloponnese in turmoil and falling apart, the very situation was positively imploring him to return. So he began to ask to be sent back alone, just himself and his friends, but his request fell on deaf ears. The king was too busy with women, Dionysian cults, and inebriated revelry to listen, and Sosibius, the head of state and the king's chief councillor, thought that although Cleomenes would be a formidable threat if he stayed in Egypt against his will, it would be even more dangerous to let him leave, given his adventurous and enterprising nature, and the fact that he had seen with his own eyes the rotten condition that Egypt was in.

But Cleomenes was not to be conciliated even by gifts. He was like the Apis bull,* which lacks for nothing and lives in apparent luxury, but in fact longs to live the life its nature fitted it for, with the freedom to run and prance, and is obviously miserable having its existence controlled by priests. Similarly, Cleomenes found no pleasure in his pampered life, but like Achilles 'wasted his heart away in idleness, yearning for battle-cry and war'.*

[56(35)] That was how things stood with Cleomenes when Nicagoras of Messene came to Alexandria, a man who concealed his hatred for Cleomenes under a veneer of affection. The reason for his hatred* was that he had once sold Cleomenes a fine estate, but had never been paid for it, presumably because† Cleomenes was strapped for cash, otherwise engaged, and preoccupied by warfare. So at the time in question, when Cleomenes, who happened to be walking along the quay, saw Nicagoras disembarking from his merchantman, he greeted him warmly, and asked what had brought him to Egypt. Nicagoras returned his greeting in a friendly fashion and explained that he was bringing the king some first-class warhorses, and Cleomenes laughed and said: 'You'd have done better to bring sambuca-girls* and degenerates. They're what the king likes to mount these days.'

At the time, Nicagoras smiled at the joke, but a few days later he reminded Cleomenes of the estate and asked if he might at last be paid for it, saying that he would not have bothered him about it if he had not lost a lot of money† disposing of his cargo. When Cleomenes explained that he was living on handouts* and had nothing left, Nicagoras stalked off and told Sosibius Cleomenes' joke. Sosibius was delighted to hear about it, but felt he needed a more serious charge to stir the king to action, and he persuaded Nicagoras to write a letter accusing Cleomenes of having planned to use any ships and troops he might get from Ptolemy to seize Cyrene, and to leave this letter with him. So Nicagoras wrote the letter and sailed away, and four days later Sosibius took the letter to Ptolemy as if he had just received it. This had the desired effect of enraging the young man, and they decided to set Cleomenes up in a large house, where he would be treated exactly as before—except that he would not be allowed out.

[57(36)] As if this were not distressing enough for Cleomenes, soon something else happened that made his prospects for the future look even more bleak. All the time he had been in Egypt, a friend of the king's called Ptolemy, the son of Chrysermus, had treated Cleomenes decently, and they had become close enough to enjoy free and frank conversation together. So when Cleomenes now asked Ptolemy to pay him a visit, Ptolemy came and spoke perfectly politely to him as he attempted to allay his suspicions and justify the king's treatment of him. But as he was leaving the house again, unaware that Cleomenes had followed him to the entrance, he lambasted the guards for the careless and casual watch they were keeping over such a ferocious creature, who was liable to break out at the slightest opportunity. Cleomenes overheard what he said and retreated before Ptolemy realized he was there.

As soon as he told his friends, they all saw the futility of the hopes that had sustained them until then, and made up their minds in the heat of the moment to pay the king back for his unfair and insulting treatment of them, and to die like true Spartans without waiting to be fattened up and slaughtered like sacrificial victims. It was outrageous, they said, for Cleomenes, who had refused to make peace with Antigonus, a man of war and energy, to sit waiting until this beggar-priest* of a king should make time to kill him, which he would do just as soon as he put down his tambourine and paused from drunken revelry.

[58(37)] Some time after they had come to this decision, it so happened that Ptolemy left town for Canopus.* Cleomenes and his friends first spread a rumour to the effect that the king had ordered their release, and then, acting on an Egyptian custom whereby the king sends food and presents to those who are about to be freed from confinement, his friends prepared plenty of food and so on for Cleomenes and had it delivered to the house. The guards, supposing that these things had come from King Ptolemy, were completely taken in, not least because Cleomenes went on to perform a thanksgiving sacrifice and to give a generous share of everything to them, while he and his friends reclined on couches with garlands on their heads and set about the feast.

It is said that Cleomenes moved the plan forward because he became afraid of a leak when he found out that one of his slaves, who was aware of the plot, had spent the night away from the house with his girlfriend. At midday, then, once he saw that the guards were in a drunken sleep, he put on his tunic with the stitching on the right shoulder unpicked, and charged out of the house, sword in hand, with his thirteen friends at his side, all with their tunics altered like his.

One of his friends, however, Hippitas, was lame, and although he resolutely joined them for the initial charge out of the house, he could see that he was slowing them down, and he told them to kill him, rather than ruin the venture by waiting for someone who was useless anyway. But they took a horse from an Alexandrian, who just happened to be leading it past their doorway, put Hippitas on its back, and raced through the streets, calling on the people to seize their freedom. Apparently, however, while the people of Alexandria had enough spirit to approve of Cleomenes' daring and admire it, not one of them had the courage to follow him and actively help him.

Be that as it may, three of Cleomenes' men caught Ptolemy, the son of Chrysermus, as he was leaving the palace, and killed him on the spot. And when they saw another Ptolemy, the man responsible for the security of the city, heading in their direction in his chariot, they charged straight at him, scattered his attendants and bodyguards, dragged him out of his chariot, and killed him. Next they made for the citadel, where they planned to break open the prison and make use of the large numbers of prisoners. But the guards quickly and effectively barricaded the prison, foiling this attempt by Cleomenes too, so that all he could do was roam aimlessly through the streets of the city. But no one joined him, and everyone ran from him in fear.

So Cleomenes called a halt and remarked to his friends: 'It's hardly surprising to find women in charge here, when people run from their freedom.' And he called on them all to meet death in a way that would dishonour neither him nor their past achievements. Hippitas was the first, struck down at his request by one of the younger men. After him, each of them calmly and unflinchingly stabbed himself, except for Panteus, the man responsible for the capture of Megalopolis.* As the most beautiful youth and the outstanding cadet of his generation, he had been the king's lover, and Cleomenes now ordered him to kill himself only when he knew that he and all the others were dead. In a short while, they were all lying on the ground, and Panteus walked over to each of them in turn and checked that they really were dead by jabbing them with his dagger. But when he pricked Cleomenes in the ankle, he saw him wince, so he kissed him and then sat down beside him. And once Cleomenes had breathed his last, he embraced him and stabbed himself to death over the corpse.

[59(38)] So died Cleomenes, the king of Sparta for sixteen years and a great man, as I have described.* News of what had happened spread throughout the entire city, and it proved too much for Cratesicleia to bear. Noble woman though she was, she broke down, threw her arms around Cleomenes' children, and gave voice to her grief. But suddenly the elder of the two children tore himself away and threw himself head-first from the roof. Though badly hurt, the suicide attempt was unsuccessful, and as he was picked up he complained loudly at not being allowed to die. But when Ptolemy heard what had happened, he had Cleomenes' body strung up in a leather sack and his children killed, along with his mother and her ladies-in-waiting.

One of these ladies-in-waiting was the wife of Panteus, a very beautiful and noble-looking woman. They had not long been married at the time of Cleomenes' defeat, and their love for each other could not have been stronger. Her parents had therefore locked her in her room to stop her sailing away with Panteus immediately, as she wanted. They kept a close eye on her, but before long she managed to get hold of a horse and a little money, and one night she made good her escape. She galloped to Taenarum, where she boarded an Egypt-bound ship that took her to her husband, and stayed by his side right to the end of their sojourn on foreign soil, without a word of protest or complaint.

It was she now who took Cratesicleia's hand as she was led away by the soldiers, supporting her robe and trying to keep her spirits up. In fact, Cratesicleia was not in the slightest frightened of death for herself, and the only favour she begged was that she should die before the children. But when they reached the place where the executioners usually did their work, they killed the children first, slaughtering them before Cratesicleia's eyes, and only then killed her. And all she said, in the extremity of her pain, was: 'Children, where have you gone?'

Panteus' wife, who was tall and strong, hitched up her robe, and quietly and calmly tended to each of the women as she was killed, and dressed them for burial as best she could. Finally, after all the others, she composed her own clothing and uncovered her head. She let no one come near or touch her except the man whose job it was to kill her, and met her end with exemplary courage, asking that no one should array her or cover her after her death. And so her modesty attended her death and preserved the guard she had placed on her body in life.

[60(39)] Sparta, then, laid on a dramatic competition, so to speak, in which there was nothing to tell between the women's tragedy and the men's, and proved under extreme conditions that virtue cannot be overwhelmed by Fortune. But a few days later, the guards posted to watch Cleomenes' body as it hung on a cross noticed that an enormous serpent had coiled itself around his head until his face was hidden and no carrion bird could alight there. Superstitious dread seized the king at this, and his fear prompted the women to perform further purificatory rituals, in view of the fact that it seemed as though he had killed a superior being, one who was high in the gods' favour. The Alexandrians even began visiting the place where Cleomenes hung to present their prayers and petitions, invoking him as a hero and a child of the gods, until the more sophisticated among them put an end to the practice. They explained that, just as rotting cows breed bees and horses wasps, and just as beetles are generated by decomposing donkeys, so human bodies produce snakes when the serum around the marrow pools and coagulates. It was observation of this phenomenon that led men in the old days to regard the snake above all other creatures as the familiar of heroes.*

PHILOPOEMEN and FLAMININUS

INTRODUCTION

The Lives of Philopoemen and Flamininus form the only case where Plutarch chose to pair a Greek and a Roman who were contemporaries. The two men even met each other, and they appear in each other's Lives. So although all the other Lives in this volume have been separated from their partners, in this instance we can print the full set, together with the concluding comparison. It is easy to forget that each Life was intended to be read as part of a larger whole. Here, however, it is possible to see the way in which Plutarch constructs the two Lives as a unity, exploring common themes and comparing and contrasting his subjects.

Philopoemen of Megalopolis (*c*.253–182 BCE) was a prominent Achaean politician and military leader, who held the Generalship of the Achaean League eight times in the late third and early second century. His career thus coincided with the establishment of Rome as a significant power in mainland Greece. He first distinguished himself in Achaea's war with the Spartan king Cleomenes in the 220s, after which he spent ten years as a mercenary commander in Crete. Returning in around 210, he was elected Cavalry Commander, the second-in-command of the league, and then General, and used his position to reform the Achaean army. After this, in keeping with Megalopolis' tradition of hostility to Sparta, he won a celebrated victory over the Spartan ruler Machanidas at Mantinea in 207, and a few years later was challenging his successor Nabis. Then, in 200, just as Rome and Macedon were embarking on the Second Macedonian War, he was off to Crete again, this time for six years. Yet, despite the considerable amount of time he spent on Crete, little is known about what he was doing there.

Much happened while he was away on his second Cretan expedition: first the Achaeans abandoned their alliance with Macedon and aligned themselves with Rome, then Philip V, the Macedonian king, was defeated by the Romans at Cynoscephalae, and finally the victorious Roman general Flamininus declared the freedom of the Greeks. Faced with this new situation, Philopoemen adopted a policy of friendship with Rome while at the same time promoting Achaean expansionism in the Peloponnese and asserting the league's independence. He continued fighting Nabis, and when the Spartan ruler was assassinated in 192 he forcibly incorporated Sparta into the Achaean League. By the time Messene and Elis were added a year later the league was effectively indistinguishable from the Peloponnese itself.

But Sparta and Messene were reluctant members. In 188 Philopoemen brutally suppressed opposition in Sparta, massacring a large number of leading Spartan citizens and making wholesale changes to the constitution. The troubled relationship between Achaea and Sparta would continue until Roman intervention in the 140s brought an end to the league itself. Philopoemen's attempt to suppress the Messenian secession of 182 fared less well. He was captured and died in a Messenian prison.

Titus Quinctius Flamininus (*c.*229–174 BCE) was a Roman politician and general, celebrated for his defeat of Philip V of Macedon. Plutarch refers to him throughout the Life as 'Titus', but for convenience and clarity this translation uses his cognomen 'Flamininus'. Flamininus achieved prominence very early in his career. After some successes in the Second Punic War he was elected to the consulship at an exceptionally young age, 'still under thirty years old' (*Flamininus* 2). He was then allocated the command in the war against Philip and quickly energized a hitherto rather sluggish campaign. He was able to exploit an early victory over Philip at the Aous gorge to win over some of Philip's allies, notably the Achaean League, which had supported Macedon since Aratus had called upon its assistance against Cleomenes in the 220s (see *Aratus* 38, 41–2). Then, in spring 197, he decisively defeated Philip at Cynoscephalae in Thessaly. In the post-war settlement Philip was forced to relinquish almost all possessions outside Macedon, but it was Flamininus' sensational announcement at the Isthmian Games of 196 that would resonate most deeply. The Greeks were to be free. Those places previously subject to Philip would be left free, without garrisons, subject to no tribute and governed by their ancestral laws. The Greek response was ecstatic, and Flamininus became the recipient of all sorts of honours, even divine ones. He remained in Greece until 194, overseeing its liberation and making war on his former ally, the Spartan ruler Nabis, who was reluctant to relinquish Argos. Two years later Flamininus returned to Greece to lead diplomatic efforts to keep as many Greek states as possible loyal to Rome in the face of Aetolian dissension and an imminent war with the Seleucid king Antiochus III. It is in these years in the late 190s that the lives of Flamininus and Philopoemen intersect. The relationship between the two men was fairly tense, with Flamininus wary of Achaean expansionism in the Peloponnese and Philopoemen determined not to do anything just because the Romans wanted him to.

Flamininus' career was in many ways a stellar one. He achieved the consulship by the time he was thirty and the censorship by the time he was forty, in both cases many years ahead of what would be expected of a Roman noble. His victory over Philip V brought him an unprecedented and lavish three-day triumph, and his celebrity helped ease his brother Lucius into the consulship of 192. But after the censorship in 189 Flamininus' career falters. His brother Lucius was expelled from the Senate by the censors of 184, his attempt to demand the extradition of Hannibal from the court of the Bithynian king Prusias resulted in the Carthaginian's suicide, and in 180 his intrigues to influence the Macedonian succession led to Philip executing Flamininus' preferred candidate. After that nothing is known of him until his death in 174.

This set of paired Lives allows the subject of the Greek encounter with Rome to be explored in depth from both sides, something that is also treated more briefly in *Pyrrhus*. It is likely, but not certain, that *Philopoemen* and *Flamininus* were written first. The narrative of Rome's rise to power, however, is of little interest to Plutarch. In the Life of Philopoemen the hero simply returns from Crete to a Greece in which Philip has been defeated. No explanation is given for the war or for Achaea's change of allegiance from Macedon to Rome during Philopoemen's absence. Inevitably the war itself does feature far more prominently in the Life of Flamininus, but even here it largely starts for the reader with the arrival of Flamininus in Greece. It is understanding Philopoemen and Flamininus that is important.

Nonetheless, Plutarch is concerned to place these men within a broader historical context and consider their implications for Greeks and Romans. From the opening chapter of *Philopoemen* there is a sense that this Life marks a conclusion and that Greek independence is coming to an end. Greece is in her old age and Philopoemen is the 'last of the Greeks', a remark all the more significant because it was said by a Roman. Philopoemen struggles to maintain Achaean independence, but ultimately he knows that fortune is against him (*Philopoemen* 17). But if Greeks now found themselves increasingly having to recognize Roman authority, what sort of people were the Romans? In the Lives of both Pyrrhus and Flamininus Plutarch raises and dismisses the suggestion that the Romans were in any real sense 'barbarians', a Greek term that not only distinguished Greeks from others, but also carried with it a strong sense of moral and cultural superiority. In both cases, meeting or seeing them was sufficient to render the idea nonsense (*Pyrrhus* 16, *Flamininus* 5). In fact, those who met him were delighted to find that Flamininus 'sounded and spoke like a Greek', and believed that 'they had found someone to champion their freedom'.

Freedom is a recurring and important theme in both Lives, and is one of the points on which the two men can be compared. Both are acclaimed as liberators in very similar settings. After Philopoemen had defeated and killed Machanidas, 'the tyrant of Sparta', he attended the festival at Nemea, entering the theatre with a troop of young soldiers just as a minstrel was reciting the opening lines of Timotheus' *Persians*: 'Glorious the great crown of freedom he is fashioning for Greece.' The crowd responded with a roar of approval for Philopoemen (*Philopoemen* 11). Later, in a carefully crafted performance, Flamininus would announce the freedom of the Greeks at the Isthmian festival. So loud was the cheering of the crowds that birds fell out of the sky (*Flamininus* 10).

Yet in neither case was freedom straightforward. Flamininus was offering freedom from Macedon, but turning to Rome came at a price: 'before long everything was subject to the Romans' (*Flamininus* 12). This was a conception of freedom that Philopoemen rejected, as he sought to maintain Achaea's independence in the face of encroaching Roman power. He would stand up to Rome in the interests of freedom as he had done in the past to Macedon; thus he makes a point of demonstrating that he can handle Sparta without Roman intervention. Despite Philopoemen's credentials as a liberator, he pursued a policy of Achaean expansionism and had no qualms about crushing Sparta and overthrowing its ancestral constitution, which was later put back in place by the Romans, an action that recalls their support of Greek freedom (*Philopoemen* 16–17). Philopoemen's pursuit of freedom had some sort of philosophical basis—that, at least, is the implication of his being taught by Ecdelus and Damophanes, two philosophers with a strong record of opposing tyranny (*Philopoemen* 1). But Flamininus, however Greek he may have seemed, had had no philosophical education, and his devotion to the freedom of Greece was driven instead by his ambition and his desire for glory (*Philopoemen* 15, *Flamininus* 1, 12).

Philopoemen comes across as a heroic figure, as befits the 'last of the Greeks', in a Life replete with echoes of the Homeric age. His childhood is compared to that of Achilles, he is an attentive reader of the more martial parts of the *Iliad*, the revived Achaean arms industry makes Plutarch think of the arming of Achilles, and the stoning of Messenian prisoners at his tomb brings to mind the killing of Trojan prisoners at the funeral pyre of Patroclus (*Philopoemen* 1, 4, 9, and 21). Philopoemen's way of reading the *Iliad* is but one symptom of his obsession with all things military (*Philopoemen* 3 and 4). For Flamininus, on the other hand, warfare was but a tool to achieve his ends; the Second Macedonian War was won as much by his diplomacy and charm as by his military tactics. Such people-skills, however, were a key area where Philopoemen fell short of his role model, the Theban general Epaminondas. Instead, he was contentious and prone to anger, characteristics that may have given him the necessary determination to uphold Achaean independence, but which could also work against him and, suggests Plutarch, his death may be one such example. Flamininus, on other hand, was intensely competitive, ever anxious that others would gain greater recognition than he did. His sense of rivalry comes out in both Lives, in his resentment of Philopoemen's popularity, his anxiety that the glory for winning the war would go to his successor, and his annoyance at the prominence given to the Aetolians in Alcaeus' poem (*Philopoemen* 15, *Flamininus* 7 and 9).

Plutarch's main source for both Lives was the historian Polybius, who was also a native of Megalopolis and whose family was so close to Philopoemen that he even carried the urn in his funeral procession. Polybius' *Histories* sought to explain Rome's rise to dominance in the Mediterranean in forty books, which covered the Carthaginian Wars and the wars fought in the Greek world. Much of the *Histories* is now lost, but enough survives to make comparisons with the text of Plutarch, enabling us to see how he has reworked his source material. For instance, in the prelude to Cynoscephalae, Plutarch has given both Flamininus and Philip speeches that do not appear in Polybius, each with an Alexander analogy (*Flamininus* 7, Polybius 18.22–4). In this fight for the future of Macedon and Greece Alexander thus becomes the measure of each.

Polybius also wrote a eulogistic life of Philopoemen, which no longer survives, but which was used by Plutarch for information on Philopoemen's childhood and early career. In contrast, Plutarch offers very little on the early life of Flamininus, presumably because he created the biography out of what could be found in narrative histories such as Polybius and Livy, where this type of material would not have been relevant. Livy's history of Rome was written in the late first century BCE, and its account of the events in the Greek East was largely drawn from Polybius, but Plutarch would have found much there on Roman politics and events in Rome itself. It is noticeable that he cites Livy for the scandal that finished the senatorial career of Flamininus' brother Lucius (*Flamininus* 18). Plutarch also names a number of other writers in support of various points of detail. Phylarchus (see introduction to *Agis and Cleomenes*) and Aristocrates of Sparta are cited in *Philopoemen*, while a number of Latin writers from the first century BCE are mentioned by name in *Flamininus*: Marcus Tullius Cicero, the rather more obscure Valerius Antias, and Gaius Sempronius Tuditanus (on all of whom see the notes).

Badian, E., *Titus Quinctius Flamininus: Philhellenism and Realpolitik* (Cincinnati, 1970), reprinted in C. Boulter *et al.* (eds.), *Lectures in Memory of Louise Taft Semple, Second Series, 1966–1970*. University of Cincinnati Classical Studies 2 (Norman, Okla., 1973), 271–327.

—— 'The Family and Early Career of T. Quinctius Flamininus', *Journal of Roman Studies*, 61 (1971), 102–11.

Baldson, J. P. V. D., 'T. Quinctius Flamininus', *Phoenix*, 21 (1967), 177–90.

Bremer, J., 'Plutarch and the "Liberation of Greece"', in L. De Blois *et al.* (eds.), *The Statesman in Plutarch's Works*, vol. 2: *The Statesman in Plutarch's Greek and Roman Lives* (Leiden, 2005), 257–67.

Derow, P., 'The Arrival of Rome: From the Illyrian Wars to the Fall of Macedon', in A. Erskine (ed.), *A Companion to the Hellenistic World* (Oxford, 2003), ch. 4; repr. in P. Derow, *Rome, Polybius, and the East* (Oxford, 2014), ch. 1.

Dmitriev, S., *The Greek Slogan of Freedom and Early Roman Politics in Greece* (Oxford, 2011).

Eckstein, A., *Rome Enters the Greek East: From Anarchy to Hierarchy in the Hellenistic Mediterranean, 230–170 BC* (Chichester, 2008).

Errington, R., *Philopoemen* (Oxford, 1969).

Gruen, E. S., *The Hellenistic World and the Coming of Rome* (Berkeley, 1984).

Pelling, C., 'The Moralism of Plutarch's *Lives*', in H. Hine, D. Innes, and C. Pelling (eds.), *Ethics and Rhetoric: Classical Essays for Donald Russell on his Seventy-fifth Birthday* (Oxford, 1995), ch. 15 (esp. section 3); repr. in C. Pelling, *Plutarch and History: Eighteen Studies* (London, 2002), ch. 10.

—— and Melandri, E., *Plutarco, Filopemene e Tito Flaminino: Introduzione e note* (Milan, 1997).

Pfeilschifter, R., *Titus Quinctius Flamininus. Untersuchungen zur römischen Griechenlandpolitik* (Göttingen, 2005).

Raeymaekers, J., 'The Origins of the Rivalry between Philopoemen and Flamininus', *Ancient Society*, 27 (1996), 259–76.

Swain, S., 'Plutarch's *Philopoemen* and *Flamininus*', *Illinois Classical Studies*, 13 (1988), 335–47.

Walsh, J. J., 'Syzygy, Theme and History: A Study in Plutarch's *Philopoemen* and *Flamininus*', *Philologus*, 136 (1992), 208–33.

—— 'Flamininus and the Propaganda of Liberation', *Historia*, 45 (1996), 344–63.

Waterfield, R., *Taken at the Flood: The Roman Conquest of Greece* (Oxford, 2014).

PHILOPOEMEN and FLAMININUS

PHILOPOEMEN

[1] Cleander of Mantinea* was second to none of his fellow citizens in birth and power, but he met with misfortune and was banished from his native city. He settled in Megalopolis, chiefly because of Craugis, the father of Philopoemen, who was a man of distinction in every field and a personal friend of his. While Craugis was alive, Cleander lacked for nothing, and after his death he repaid him for his hospitality by bringing up his orphaned son, as Achilles was brought up by Phoenix,* according to Homer, so that from his earliest years, as the boy's character developed, it gained a certain noble and kingly quality.

Once Philopoemen was out of childhood, however, Ecdelus and Demophanes of Megalopolis* became responsible for him instead. These men had become close to Arcesilaus* at the Academy, and were the chief advocates at that time of the political, practical application of philosophy. They even rid their homeland of tyranny by secretly arranging for Aristodemus to be assassinated; they helped Aratus expel Nicocles,* the tyrant of Sicyon; and, when the people of Cyrene turned to them at a time of political trouble and turmoil, they sailed there, restored order, and restructured the city along the best possible lines.* Nevertheless, they found time among their other achievements for bringing up Philopoemen, because they believed that with the help of philosophy they would make† this man a blessing for all Greece. For he was born late to Greece, so to speak, in her old age, the last in a line of great leaders, and so Greece absolutely doted on him and helped him grow in power and fame. And a Roman paid him the compliment of calling him the last of the Greeks,* in the sense that after him Greece bore no one great or worthy of her.

[2] Whatever some people think, he was not ugly, as we can tell from a statue of him that survives at Delphi.* Nevertheless, it was still possible for the Megarian hostess to make the mistake we hear about in the story, thanks to his nonchalance and lack of affectation. What happened was this. When she found out that the Achaean General was coming to their home, she set about preparing dinner in a tizzy, since

her husband happened to be away. Meanwhile, Philopoemen came into the house wearing a cheap cloak and, taking him to be a slave who had been sent on ahead, she ordered him to help with the chores. He immediately threw off his cloak and began to chop wood. When his host came in and saw him, he asked: 'What's going on, Philopoemen?' 'Oh,' Philopoemen replied in a Doric accent,* 'I'm just paying for mah poor appearance.' And Flamininus once made fun of his overall physique by remarking: 'Philopoemen, your arms and legs are lovely, but you have no belly!' He was in fact rather slender at the waist, but the joke was directed more at his resources, in the sense that although he had excellent hoplites and horsemen, he was often short of money. Anyway, these are the stories that are told about Philopoemen in the schools.*

[3] The ambitious side of his character, however, was not altogether untainted by the contentious desire to get the better of others, nor was it free from anger. He took Epaminondas* as his primary role model, but although he closely imitated his efficiency, intelligence, and indifference to money, Epaminondas' self-possession, gravity, and courtesy in dealing with political opponents were impossible for him to maintain, thanks to his quick temper and contentiousness. So Philopoemen gave the impression of being more suited for military than for political distinction. In fact, even as a child he was fond of military activities, and was an avid student of the subjects that bore on them, fighting in armour and riding.

He also seemed to have had a talent for wrestling, and when some of his friends and guardians suggested that he should take up athletics, he asked them whether it might have a negative effect on his military training. They told him the truth—that the physique and lifestyle required for athletics were completely incompatible with military life, especially in respect of the regimen and training involved. Athletes, they told him, both develop and maintain their condition by sleeping a great deal and regularly eating their fill, and by fixed periods of activity and inactivity; and so their condition is liable to be worsened by the slightest imbalance or departure from routine. A soldier, however, should be inured to every kind of inconstancy and irregularity, and above all should be able to cope easily with lack of food or sleep. This not only made Philopoemen shun and scorn athletics himself,* but in his later life he wielded punitive measures and expressions of contempt in a determined effort to banish athletics completely from the armies under his command, on the grounds that it took a perfectly serviceable body and made it useless and incapable of fighting when necessary.

[4] Once he had finished with schooling and education, he joined in the raids the Megalopolitans used to make on Laconia for plunder and booty, and made it his habit to be the first to go out and the last to return. In his spare time, he used to train his body and improve his agility and strength either by hunting or by working the land. He had a fine farm twenty stades from the city, where he used to go in the daytime after his morning or evening meal, and he would lay himself down on a rough bed of straw, just like any of his workers, to take his rest. In the morning he would get up and help his men with the vines or the cattle, and then return to the city and occupy himself with public business, along with his friends and the city officials. He spent his profits from military expeditions on horses, weaponry, and ransoming prisoners of war, and tried to increase his wealth by farming, which is the best line of business for a man of integrity. And he took it seriously, being convinced that the surest way for a man to keep his hands off others' property is for him to have property of his own.

He attended lectures and read books of philosophy, but not indiscriminately: he restricted himself to those he thought would help him attain distinction. Where the Homeric poems were concerned, he was interested only in those passages which, he felt, awoke and aroused images conducive to courage.* Otherwise, his favourite reading material was Evangelus' *Tactics*,* and he kept returning to the Alexander historians,* in the belief that words either end in action or they are no more than pointless chitchat, a way of passing an idle moment. He even used to ignore the diagrams as drawn in theoretical treatises on tactics, and would use actual physical locations to test ideas and make his studies. While out in the field, he would set his officers problems, and make his own investigations too into sloping terrain and broken ground, and into what happens to a phalanx in stream-beds or trenches or defiles—how its formation alters as it expands and then contracts again. Philopoemen seems, in fact, to have had an excessive enthusiasm for soldiering: he embraced warfare as affording the greatest variety of opportunities for excellence, and generally seems to have dismissed as useless men who had nothing to do with it.

[5] Philopoemen was thirty years old when King Cleomenes

of Sparta* launched a surprise night attack on Megalopolis, overwhelmed the guards, entered the city, and occupied the main square. Philopoemen led the resistance, but lacked the strength to drive the enemy out of the city, for all the determination and reckless fury with which he fought. But he did manage to sneak his fellow citizens out of the city, so to speak, by attacking those who were going after them and generally drawing Cleomenes in his direction. The upshot was that he only just managed to get away himself, the last to leave, unhorsed and wounded.

When Cleomenes wrote to the Megalopolitans at Messene, where they had gone, promising to return both city and land to them with their property intact, Philopoemen, seeing that his fellow citizens welcomed the offer and were eager to return, opposed them and argued them out of it. He explained that Cleomenes was not so much returning the city to them, as trying to gain its citizens as well, as a way of strengthening his hold on the city. He would prove incapable of staying and watching over empty houses and walls, he said: the dereliction would force him to leave. This argument changed the minds of his fellow citizens, but gave Cleomenes an excuse for damaging and razing most of the city before leaving, laden with booty.*

[6] Then King Antigonus came to help and marched with the Achaeans against Cleomenes.* Finding Cleomenes in possession of the heights and passes at Sellasia, Antigonus drew up his forces for battle near by; his plan was to attack and overrun the enemy positions. Philopoemen, with his Megalopolitan troop, was one of those assigned to the cavalry, and he had in support a good number of Illyrian infantry, who were stationed in the interstices of the line. Their orders were to wait and do nothing until on the other wing a red sheet was raised by the king on the end of a pike. But then the Illyrian officers led their men in an attempt to drive the Spartans off the field, while the Achaeans maintained discipline and kept themselves in reserve, as ordered. When Eucleidas, Cleomenes' brother,* realized that a gap had opened up in the enemy formation, he quickly ordered his most mobile troops to circle around, attack the Illyrians in the rear, detached as they were from the cavalry, and force them to turn.

But as the Spartan light-armed troops were harrying the Illyrians and throwing them into disarray, Philopoemen realized that it would be relatively easy to attack them and that the situation was crying out for it. He began by telling the king's officers, but they refused to listen; they thought he must be out of his mind, and looked down on him as one who had not yet earned the great reputation that might make him a plausible proponent of such an ambitious manoeuvre. He therefore gathered his fellow Megalopolitans and launched an attack of his own accord. The light-armed troops immediately panicked and turned to flight, with great loss of life.

Now Philopoemen was even more eager to urge the king's officers to action, and he was in a hurry to engage the enemy while they were scattered, so he abandoned his horse and set out on foot towards ground that was a jumble of stream-beds and gullies. As he struggled laboriously forward through the difficult terrain, laden down by his cavalry breastplate and other heavy equipment, both his thighs were pierced through by a single thonged javelin.* The wound was not life-threatening, but the force of the blow had driven the head of the javelin right through. At first, with the javelin restricting his movements like a shackle, he was completely immobilized; the javelin could not easily be pulled out through the wounds because of the thong, and his companions were reluctant to make the attempt. But the battle was at its most intense, and Philopoemen was impatient to join the fray, driven by his passion and desire for glory. By wiggling and moving his legs back and forth he broke the javelin in mid-shaft, and then he told his men to pull out each half separately.

Once he was free, he drew his sword and made his way through the front ranks to engage the enemy. This inspired his allies to emulate his bravery, and they fought with renewed determination. After the victory, then, when Antigonus was debriefing the Macedonians, he asked them why they had not waited for his command before bringing the cavalry on. In their defence, they said that they had not wanted to engage the enemy, but had been forced to do so by the premature attack launched by a youngster from Megalopolis.* At this Antigonus said with a laugh: 'Then that youngster has acted like a great commander.'

[7] The upshot was, of course, that Philopoemen became famous, and Antigonus, wanting to secure his military services, offered him a command and wealth. But Philopoemen turned down the offer, mainly because he knew himself well enough to realize that he found it irritating and unpleasant to be under someone else's command. He had no desire to be idle and do nothing, however, so he sailed to Crete to practise and study the art of war on service there.* In Crete he

trained for a long time with fighters who, in addition to being skilled in various kinds of warfare, were restrained and disciplined in their lives, and by the time he returned to the Achaeans he had gained such a name for himself that they immediately made him their Cavalry Commander.*

The cavalrymen he inherited, however, not only had inferior mounts—they used any old horses for each expedition as it came along—but they also usually avoided serving in person and sent others in their stead. The whole corps was appallingly inexperienced and, as a result, morale was low; and their commanders had persistently failed to address these problems because the cavalrymen were the most powerful group among the Achaeans and had a great deal of influence in the assignment of rewards and punishments.

Philopoemen, however, refused to kowtow to them or go easy on them. He even toured the cities of the league and played a part in stiffening the resolve of all the young men, one by one. He meted out punishment where necessary, had them drill and parade, and made them compete against one another in places where there would be plenty of spectators. As a result, before long he had made all of them incredibly fit and determined, and had got them to a state where both whole troops and individual horsemen could lightly and quickly wheel and turn, and there is no more important battlefield manoeuvre than this. He trained the whole unit to move with such ease that it resembled a single body moving by its own internal impulse.

At the battle of the Larissus river,* a closely fought action between the Achaeans and a joint army of Aetolians and Eleans, Damophantus, the Elean Cavalry Commander, rode out ahead of the rest of his men straight for Philopoemen. Philopoemen received his charge, got the first blow in with his spear, and laid Damophantus low. No sooner had he fallen than the enemy turned to flight, and Philopoemen gained a brilliant reputation as a man who could perform in battle as well as any of the younger men, and in counsel as well as any of the older men—as not just a highly competent soldier, but a superb general as well.

[8] The first to raise the Achaean League to a position of respect and power was Aratus; he found it in a wretched and fragmented state, united the sundered cities, and instituted a truly Greek and humane form of government.* What happened next was similar to what happens in running water in which a few small particles of

matter have begun to settle: as further particles are swept down, they encounter the first ones and are checked by them, and together form a strong bond and acquire solidity. In the same way, Greece at that time was drifting along city by city, in a weak and fragile state, but the Achaeans first formed themselves into a confederacy, and then they absorbed some of the surrounding cities by rescuing them and freeing them from their tyrants, and attracted others into the league by offering them political concord and granting them citizenship. Their intention was to form the Peloponnese into a single body, a single power.

While Aratus was alive, however, the Achaeans were usually dependent on Macedonian weaponry: they sought the friendship first of Ptolemy,* and then of Antigonus and Philip,* who were deeply involved in Greek affairs. But when Philopoemen became the leading man in the state,* the Achaeans were at last a match on their own for even their strongest opponents, and they stopped relying on foreign protection. For Aratus was thought to have a rather lackadaisical attitude towards battle, and (as I have said in his Life)* he owed most of his achievements to his sociability, his diplomacy, and his friendships with kings. Philopoemen, however, was a good soldier and not at all lackadaisical under arms, and he was also lucky and successful in his very first battles; and so thanks to him the Achaeans' pride increased along with their power, because under his command they became accustomed to winning most of their battles and carrying the day.

[9] Anyway, the first thing he did was change the Achaeans' inadequate battle formation and weaponry.* They had been using shields that were light and easy to carry, but were too narrow to protect a man's body, and their spears were much shorter than Macedonian pikes. This light equipment of theirs made them effective fighters at long range, but left them at a disadvantage when they directly engaged the enemy. They did not usually adopt any kind of battle formation or configuration that relied on small tactical units, and since the phalanx they employed lacked either a protective hedge of spears or close-order shields in the manner of the Macedonians they were easily pushed back and broken up.* Philopoemen explained all this to them and persuaded them to replace their light shields and spears with heavier shields and pikes; to wear protective helmets, breastplates, and greaves; and to practise a solid, stationary form of fighting, instead of fighting on the run with light weaponry.

Once he had persuaded the men of military age to adopt heavy arms and armour, he first raised their morale by convincing them of their invincibility, and then he changed their soft and extravagant habits for the better. They had been afflicted by vain and idle tastes too long for him to remove them completely: they loved expensive clothing, dyed their bed-sheets purple, and competed with one another over dinners and tableware.* But he began the process of diverting their fondness for self-adornment away from trivia and on to objects with some purpose and value, and before long he had persuaded and convinced them all to restrict the amount of money they spent on their daily bodily needs, and to be conspicuous for the splendour and ornateness of what they wore for soldiering and warfare.

So the sights of the city included piles of jars† and Thericlean vases* being cut up in the workshops; breastplates being gilded and shields and bridles silvered; heaps of decorated cavalry tunics and military cloaks.† The stadia were filled with colts being broken in and young men training in armour, and in the hands of the womenfolk helmets and plumes were being embellished with dyes. The mere sight of all this boosts morale and puts a man on his mettle, making him ready to take risks and face danger. Spending extravagantly on other forms of display weakens a man and makes him soft; it is a kind of titillation and stimulation of the senses that enfeebles the mind. But spending extravagantly on military equipment strengthens and enhances a man's spirit, and that is why Homer had Achilles exult in the sight of the new arms and armour laid out beside him, and burn to put them to use.*

Once Philopoemen had seen to their accoutrements in this way, he put the young men of military age through their paces and drilled them. The new tactics went down incredibly well with them, and they were enthusiastic and attentive students. The new formation seemed indestructible in its solidity, and the arms and armour were not only light and manageable, but so brilliant and beautiful that they took them up and wore them with pleasure. They were keen to try them out as soon as possible under battle conditions, to use them in a decisive victory over the enemy.

[10] There was a state of war at this time between the Achaeans and Machanidas, the tyrant of Sparta,* who was intending to use his considerable military might to take over the entire Peloponnese. So when news arrived that Machanidas had invaded Mantinea, Philopoemen

quickly led the army out to confront him. Both sides drew up their forces for battle near the city itself; both armies contained not only large numbers of mercenaries, but also almost their entire citizen levies. When battle was joined, Machanidas routed the javelineers and Tarentines* who had been posted out in front of the Achaean lines, but then, instead of immediately advancing against those who were still in the battle and scattering them, he set out after the fugitives, bypassing the Achaean phalanx, which had stayed in position.

Even though things had started so disastrously and the day seemed to be completely and utterly lost, Philopoemen put a brave face on it and made out that nothing terrible had happened. He could see what a great mistake the enemy were making—that in pursuing the fugitives they were separating from their phalanx and leaving empty space between them and it—so he did nothing to oppose them or check their pursuit, but let them pass by and open up a large gap. Then, as soon as he saw that the phalanx had been left exposed, he advanced on the Spartan hoplites, avoiding a frontal assault and attacking in flank. The Spartans were leaderless and had not been expecting to fight, because, with Machanidas off in pursuit, they had assumed they were winning and that victory was not in doubt.

Once Philopoemen had forced the Spartan hoplites back, with great loss of life (over 4,000 men are said to have been killed), he set out against Machanidas, who was returning with his mercenaries from the chase. But a wide and deep trench kept them apart, and the two commanders rode alongside it, parallel to each other on their respective banks, one wanting to cross the trench and escape, the other intending to stop him. It seemed to be not so much a fight between two generals as an encounter between a formidable hunter and a beast he had forced to turn at bay.

At this point, Machanidas' horse, a powerful, spirited creature, with both spurred flanks streaming blood, boldly attempted the crossing. With its chest up against the lip of the trench, it was struggling to gain a purchase on the other side with its forefeet. Then Simmias and Polyaenus, Philopoemen's constant companions in battle and his shield-fellows,* rode up together and cocked their spears at Machanidas. But Philopoemen got there first. Seeing that Machanidas' horse had its head raised in front of his enemy's body, he pulled his own horse a little aside. He held his spear firmly by the shaft, pushed it forward, and the strength of the thrust toppled the man from his horse. This is the stance of the bronze statue of Philopoemen that was erected in Delphi by the Achaeans, who were filled with admiration for his victory and his generalship that day.*

[11] There is a story about Philopoemen at the Nemean festival, in the year when he held the Generalship of the Achaean League for the second time;* this was shortly after his victory at Mantinea, when the festival gave him some time off. The story goes that after showing the assembled Greeks some of his phalangites in their decorated armour and having them go through their manoeuvres with their usual speed and verve, he later entered the theatre, during the lyric contest, with his men dressed in their military cloaks and purple-dyed tunics. All these young men were in peak physical condition and of much the same age, and their manner hinted not only at the great respect in which they held their commander, but also at the youthful pride they felt after the many noble contests they had come through. It so happened that, just after they had entered the theatre, the minstrel Pylades sang the opening of Timotheus' *Persians*:* 'Glorious the great crown of freedom he is fashioning for Greece.' The majesty of the poet's words were matched by the clarity of Pylades' voice, and all over the theatre people turned their gazes towards Philopoemen and joyful applause broke out. For the Greeks now expected to recover their long-lost status, and their confidence was almost as high as in the days of their pride.

[12] Just as colts grow attached to their usual riders, and are skittish and out of sorts if they have someone else on their backs, so, when it came to battle and facing dangers, the Achaean troops tended to lose heart and look around for Philopoemen if they had someone else in command. No sooner had they caught sight of him than their confidence grew, with a consequent upsurge in their vitality and energy. They could also tell from the behaviour of their enemies that he was the one general they were incapable of facing—that it took no more than his name and reputation to strike fear into them. King Philip of Macedon, for instance, was sure that the Achaeans would once again submit to him if Philopoemen were removed, and to this end he sent assassins to Argos;* but the plot was discovered, and Philip became an object of universal hatred and suspicion in the Greek cities.

The Boeotian siege of Megara is another example: the Boeotians expected the city to fall to them very shortly, but when they received news (false news, in fact) that Philopoemen was near by, on his way to help the Megarians, they immediately fled, leaving their scaling-ladders already up against the city walls.*

There was also the time when Nabis, the next tyrant of Sparta after Machanidas, suddenly seized Messene. It so happened that Philopoemen was out of office then, with no army under his command. He tried to persuade Lysippus, the incumbent Achaean General, to aid the Messenians, and when Lysippus refused (on the grounds that, with the enemy inside, the city's situation was hopeless), Philopoemen raised a force of his fellow Megalopolitans and went to help the Messenians of his own accord. The Megalopolitans did not wait for official permission or a vote, but followed the naturally better man as one who never needs the legitimacy of office. And even though Nabis had a strong position in the city, he put up no resistance. As soon as he heard of Philopoemen's approach, he slipped out through a back gate and left with his army, praying just to be able to escape, which he did. And so Messene regained its freedom.*

[13] Now, all this may have redounded to Philopoemen's credit, but his stay in Crete at the request of the Gortynians, who offered him command of their war, was held against him. People felt that his absence during the war the Achaeans fought against Nabis constituted desertion, or at least inappropriate expenditure of his energy on others. And yet the intensity of the war at that time was such that the Megalopolitans were living inside their city walls, and with their farmland devastated and the enemy encamped almost in the gateway of the city were using the side-streets to grow grain.

Philopoemen's fighting in Crete at this juncture and serving as a general abroad gave his enemies the opportunity to accuse him of deliberately shirking the war at home.* Others, however, felt that since the Achaeans had chosen other men as their heads of state and Philopoemen was out of office, his time was his own, and he had simply used it to meet the Gortynians' need for a commander. Inactivity was alien to him, and he wanted to exercise his skills as a general and a warrior—to keep them in constant use, just as he would any other possession. Further evidence for this comes from something he said once about King Ptolemy. Some people were singing Ptolemy's praises for drilling his troops on a daily basis and for setting himself a thorough and physically punishing schedule of training with weaponry, and Philopoemen remarked: 'But who can admire a king of his age who is constantly practising and never actually showing what he can do?'

Anyway, the Megalopolitans were displeased with him for his sojourn on Crete; they took it as treachery, and proceeded to sentence him to exile. But the Achaeans stopped them. They sent their General, Aristaenus,* to Megalopolis and, although he disagreed with Philopoemen over matters of policy, he vetoed the sentence. When Philopoemen subsequently found himself overlooked by his fellow citizens, he got many of the outlying villages to secede.* He taught them to claim that they had not been incorporated into the city and had never belonged to Megalopolis, and when they made use of this argument he came out in support of them, and was therefore instrumental in setting the Megalopolitans at one another's throats in the Achaeans' meetings.

But this happened later. In Crete the war in which he fought for the Gortynians was too devious and dirty for him to behave like a man of the Peloponnese and Arcadia. He adopted the Cretan style of warfare, and turned their cunning and crooked tactics,* their traps and ambushes, against them, making them look like mischievous children pitting foolish and pointless schemes against genuine experience.

[14] Philopoemen's stature grew as a result of these Cretan campaigns, and he returned to the Peloponnese covered in glory as a result of what he had achieved there. He learnt that Philip had been defeated by Flamininus,* and found the Achaeans and Romans at war with Nabis.* He was immediately elected head of state and decided to risk a sea-battle, in which he turned out to share Epaminondas' experience: that is, he found that his performance at sea fell far short of his ability and his reputation. In Epaminondas' case, some people claim that he deliberately returned from Asia and the Aegean islands without having achieved anything, because he was reluctant to give his fellow citizens a taste of the profits the sea could bring, in case they gradually and imperceptibly stopped being 'steady hoplites' (as Plato puts it), became sailors instead, and were corrupted.* But Philopoemen felt sure that his expertise with land forces would stand him in good stead fighting at sea as well—and so he came to recognize that success depends largely on rehearsal and that in every endeavour our abilities are greatly enhanced by practice. For not only did he come off worst in the sea-battle because of his inexperience, but he

even manned and launched an old but famous ship, unused for forty years, with a leaky hull that put the crew's lives in danger.*

The enemy now believed that he had altogether given up on the sea and was no threat in this regard, and continued their siege of Gythium* without taking any thought for him—so Philopoemen immediately launched an attack by sea and caught them unprepared, with their guard relaxed after their victory. After landing his men by night, he led them forward, and succeeded in setting fire to the enemy's tents, burning their camp to the ground, and inflicting serious casualties.

A few days later, as he was making his way across some rugged ground, Nabis suddenly appeared. The Achaeans were frightened: the difficulty of the terrain and the fact that it was already in enemy hands made it seem unlikely that they would escape with their lives. But Philopoemen paused, assessed the terrain, and demonstrated that there is nothing more important in warfare than tactical skill. He slightly altered the formation of his phalanx to adapt it to current conditions, and got them out of the impasse with no fuss or bother. Then he charged the enemy and put them to desperate flight. Noticing that the fugitives were not making for the city, but were scattering here and there over the countryside (which consisted of shrub-covered hills, with too many stream-beds and gullies to be suitable for cavalry), he checked the pursuit and encamped until daylight. At the same time, however, judging that the enemy soldiers would gradually make their way under cover of darkness towards the city in ones and twos, he placed a lot of men in ambush in the stream-beds and hills around the town, armed with daggers. A great many of Nabis' men lost their lives this way. They were not retreating en masse, but as individuals, seizing whatever chances of flight came their way, and so all around the city they swooped down like birds into their enemies' hands and were caught.

[15] This exploit made Philopoemen the darling of Greece, and he was conspicuously acclaimed by the Greeks in their theatres, to the secret chagrin of Flamininus, who was jealous of his own honour. As a Roman consul, he felt he deserved the Achaeans' admiration more than a man from Arcadia, and he thought that the good he had done Greece far outweighed what Philopoemen had done: after all, with a single proclamation he had freed all the Greeks who had been enslaved to Philip and the Macedonians.*

Next, Flamininus brought the war with Nabis to an end, but Nabis was assassinated by the Aetolians.* Philopoemen seized the opportunity presented by the chaos in Sparta and fell upon the city with an armed force. Although some of the Spartans dissented, he won the rest over, reorganized the city, and brought it into the league.* This made Philopoemen incredibly popular in Achaea: by acquiring such a great city, he had hugely increased the league's standing and strength. And it was indeed no small thing for Sparta to become part of Achaea. Moreover, he carried with him the best of the Spartans, who hoped to find in him someone to safeguard their freedoms, and therefore voted to give Philopoemen as a personal gift the 120 talents they raised by selling Nabis' house and property, after first sending an official delegation to announce their offer.

This gave Philopoemen the opportunity to make it perfectly plain that his reputation as a man of integrity was fully deserved. In the first place, no Spartan was prepared to go and offer a man like him a bribe; so great was their reluctance, in fact, that they used his guest-friend Timolaus* as their representative. Then, when Timolaus went to Megalopolis and stayed with Philopoemen, the dignified way he dealt with other people and the modesty of his way of life made it obvious that his character was quite impervious to the prospect of money. Timolaus therefore kept quiet about the bribe, and went back home after giving Philopoemen some other reason for his journey.

When Timolaus was sent back to Megalopolis a second time, the same thing happened, but then, on his third visit, when he met with Philopoemen he hesitantly explained what Sparta wanted to do for him. Philopoemen thanked him, and went in person to Sparta. He said that there was no point in trying to corrupt men of integrity who were already on their side and whose virtues were therefore available to them for free. He suggested that instead they should spend the money on bribing and buying off the troublemakers who were dividing the assembly; having accepted the money, they would have to keep quiet and make less of a nuisance of themselves. After all, he said, it was better to stop the mouths of one's enemies than one's friends. That is how exemplary his attitude was towards money.

[16] But when news arrived that the Spartans were again gripped by revolutionary fervour, Diophanes, the incumbent Achaean General, wanted to punish them. The Spartans committed themselves to war, and the entire Peloponnese was in turmoil. Philopoemen tried to calm

Diophanes down and cool his ardour by directing his attention to the broader situation: King Antiochus and the Romans were in Greece,* hovering over them with enormous armies, and that was something Diophanes, as head of state, should take into account in making his decisions. This was not the time, Philopoemen said, to be making trouble at home; to a certain extent, Diophanes should even overlook and ignore transgressions.

His advice fell on deaf ears, however. Diophanes joined forces with Flamininus for an invasion of Laconia, and they headed straight for Sparta itself. Incensed at this, Philopoemen boldly committed himself to an illegal course of action—impossible to justify, but a grand and majestic gesture. He slipped by them into Laconia and, even though he held no official position, he shut both the Achaean General and the Roman consul out of the city. He then restored calm in the city and brought the Spartans back into the league, as they had been before the troubles started.*

Later, however, when serving as league General, Philopoemen brought certain charges against the Spartans, which led to him restoring their exiles and putting eighty Spartiates to death (eighty according to Polybius, but Aristocrates says 350).* He also razed their defensive walls, and transferred a large chunk of their territory to the Megalopolitans. Moreover, he expelled all those who had been enfranchised by the tyrants and relocated them in Achaea—all except for 3,000, who disobeyed his order and refused to leave Sparta. These he sold into slavery and then, to add insult to injury, he used the money to build a stoa in Megalopolis.*

Gorging himself now on the Spartans, trampling on people who had already suffered more than they deserved, he treated their constitution with the most callous and criminal brutality. He abolished and did away with the regime instituted by Lycurgus, and forced Spartan boys and ephebes to adopt the Achaean form of training instead of their traditional one. His thinking was that their spirits would never be broken as long as they did things the Lycurgan way.* For a while, then, the Spartans were so crushed by calamity that they meekly and submissively let Philopoemen get away with hamstringing them, so to speak. Later, however, with the backing of the Romans, they shed the Achaean system of government and restored their ancestral constitution, in so far as that was possible after so much trouble and destruction.*

[17] Philopoemen was out of office in the year when war broke out in Greece between the Romans and Antiochus.* He could see that Antiochus was sitting in Chalcis,* doing nothing except lusting after young girls and marrying them, quite inappropriately for his age; he could also see that discipline had more or less completely broken down among Antiochus' Syrian troops and that they were ambling around the cities and living soft lives, with no sign of their officers;* and it irritated him that he was not the Achaean General at the time. In fact, he said that he begrudged the Romans their victory: 'If I'd been in command,' he remarked, 'I'd have cut them all down in their taverns.'

But after their defeat of Antiochus the Romans became more involved with Greek affairs, and they used their power to gain control of the Achaean League, thanks to the deference of the leading politicians. It was extraordinary how their strength grew in all respects, until the end which the wheel of Fortune was bound to reach was close at hand.* Under these circumstances Philopoemen, like a skilled helmsman struggling with rough seas, had no choice but to yield from time and time and give in to the prevailing situation. On most issues, however, he maintained his opposition, and kept trying to attract every powerful politician or man of action to the cause of freedom.

Aristaenus of Megalopolis was now the most influential man in the league, and he constantly courted the favour of the Romans. In his view, it would be a mistake for the Achaeans to oppose or displease them. It is said that once Philopoemen was listening to Aristaenus delivering a speech in the council. He was seething inside, but kept quiet—until in the end he could stand it no longer, and burst out furiously to Aristaenus: 'Why, man? Why are you in such a hurry to see the doom of Greece?'*

On another occasion, after his defeat of Antiochus,* the Roman consul Glabrio asked the Achaeans to allow the Spartan exiles to return home, and then Flamininus made the same request. Philopoemen, however, successfully blocked the move—not because he was hostile to the exiles, but because he wanted himself and the Achaeans to be responsible for their restoration; he did not want them to be in debt to Flamininus or Rome. And, in fact, when he was General the following year, he personally restored the exiles to Sparta. All this will give some idea of how, when faced with authority, his pride made him rather confrontational and contentious.

[18] At the age of seventy he became General of the Achaeans for the eighth time,* and could reasonably expect not just that his year of office would pass without warfare, but that events would allow him to live out the rest of his life in peace. For just as illnesses seem to abate the weaker one gets, so the Greek cities' rivalries faded as their power waned. But just when he was approaching life's finishing-post, running smoothly and well, some vengeful deity tripped him up.

This is what happened, according to my sources. First, at one of their meetings people were praising a man who had a reputation as a formidable general, and Philopoemen remarked: 'But why should we concern ourselves with a man who was taken alive by the enemy?'* Then, just a few days later, Deinocrates of Messene,* a man who had personally offended Philopoemen and was disliked by everyone else as well for his iniquity and immorality, got Messene to secede from the league. And then it became known that he was about to seize the village of Colonides. Philopoemen happened to be in Argos, sick with a fever, but when he heard the news he raced off to Megalopolis and reached it in a single day, a journey of over 140 stades. He raised a cavalry contingent from the highest strata of Megalopolitan society—it consisted, however, of very young men, who volunteered to serve under him because of the devotion and admiration they felt for him—and set out without further delay to save Colonides.*

They rode in the direction of Messene and encountered Deinocrates at Evander's Hill, where he was waiting for them. They succeeded in putting him to flight, but a troop of 500 horsemen, assigned to patrol the Messenian farmland, bore down on them, and when the others, those who had earlier been worsted, saw their friends harrying the Megalopolitans, they rallied and occupied the hills. Philopoemen was worried about being encircled, and did not want to put his men at risk, so he began to retreat over difficult ground. He brought up the rear himself, and made frequent sorties against the enemy, trying to make himself their target, but they did not dare to retaliate, and resorted to whooping and threatening his flanks from afar. The upshot was that, for the sake of his young troopers, he often had to be some distance away from them,† and, as he was escorting them like this one by one to safety, he suddenly found himself all alone and surrounded by considerable numbers of the enemy.

Still none of them dared to come to grips with him, but they hurled their javelins at him from some way off and forced him towards a rocky and precipitous stretch of ground, where he struggled to control his horse and kept spurring it on. Constant training had kept him fit, so his age was no problem and in no way impeded his escape, but the illness he was suffering from at the time had weakened him, and then the journey had exhausted him. He was heavy and stiff, then, and when his horse stumbled he was thrown to the ground. It was a bad fall: he banged his head, and lay unconscious there for a long while. His enemies even thought he was dead and started to roll him over and strip him of his armour. But then he raised his head and opened his eyes—and all of them piled into him at once. They pulled his hands behind his back, tied his wrists, and led him away, taunting and insulting a man who could not possibly have dreamt of this being done to him by Deinocrates.

[19] The inhabitants of Messene were beside themselves with joy at the news, and a crowd gathered at the city gates. But when they saw Philopoemen being ignominiously dragged along, for all his fame and past achievements and victories, most of them pitied him. They felt so sorry for him, in fact, that they shed tears and decried human ability as unreliable and meaningless. And so the generous thought crept up on the majority of the people there that they should remember the good he had done them in the past, and especially that he had restored their freedom by driving the tyrant Nabis from their city.* But there were a few who wanted to curry favour with Deinocrates, and called out for the man to be tortured and killed, as a troublesome and implacable enemy. Suppose he escaped, they said: Deinocrates should feel even more afraid of him now that he had taken him prisoner and humiliated him. But Philopoemen was taken to the 'Treasury', as it is called—an underground chamber into which no air penetrates or light from outside, and whose 'door' is an enormous boulder. They stowed him there, slammed the boulder into place, and posted an armed guard around the dungeon.*

Meanwhile, the Achaean cavalrymen had recovered from their flight. Since Philopoemen was nowhere to be seen, they took him to be dead, and for a long time they stayed where they were, crying out his name and telling one another that there was no honour in their safety, no way to justify it, since they had abandoned to the enemy the general who had risked his life to save them. Then they set off again together. They made enquiries, learnt of Philopoemen's capture, and informed the cities of the Achaean League. The Achaeans regarded his loss as a major catastrophe, so they not only decided to send envoys to ask the Messenians to return him, but they also prepared to go to war.

[20] But while the Achaeans were pursuing this course, Deinocrates was chiefly concerned to avoid any delay: that was the only thing that could save Philopoemen, he felt, and he wanted to forestall the Achaean initiative. So during the night, after almost all the Messenians had left, he opened the prison and sent in a public slave with poison and orders to give it to Philopoemen and to stand by him until he had drunk it. Philopoemen was lying down wrapped in his cloak, not asleep, but overcome by grief and troubled in his mind. When he saw a light, and then the man standing near him holding the cup of poison, he pulled himself together, weak as he was, and sat up. He took the cup and asked the man if he had heard anything about his cavalrymen, and especially Lycortas.* The man told him that most of them had got away, and Philopoemen nodded, looked at the man with perfect composure, and said: 'That's good, then. It didn't turn out all bad for us.' Without another word or sound he drained the cup and lay back down. He did not give the poison much work to do: he was so weak that his flame was soon extinguished.

[21] When news of his death reached the Achaean cities, the entire population was gripped by despair and grief. The council, however, had the men of military age assemble in Megalopolis, and the Achaeans proceeded straight to retaliation.* With Lycortas as their new General, they invaded Messenia and devastated the farmland until the Messenians agreed to open their gates to them. Deinocrates killed himself rather than face them. As for the rest, those who had called for Philopoemen's death were killed by the Messenians, while those who had also wanted him to be tortured were seized on Lycortas' orders, to be tortured to death themselves.

Once they had cremated Philopoemen's body and collected his ashes in an urn, they made their way home, not in a disorderly or haphazard fashion, but in a combined triumphal parade and funeral procession. For the very same men who had their heads crowned with wreaths could also be seen with tears in their eyes, and they brought their enemies with them in chains. The urn itself, borne by Polybius,* the son of the Achaean General, and escorted by the most eminent men of the league, was so covered with ribbons and wreaths that it was hardly visible. Then came the army, with the men in full armour and the horses richly caparisoned, the mood of the men poised between grief at their loss and joy at their victory. People emerged from the cities and villages on their route and came to meet the procession, as though they were welcoming Philopoemen back from a campaign, and they touched the urn and accompanied it into Megalopolis. There they were joined by the older men, the women, and the children, and now a cry of grief swept the entire army as they marched into the city,† which felt its loss keenly and painfully, and was sure that it had also lost its leading position in the league.

Philopoemen was buried, then, in the glorious fashion he deserved, and at his tomb the Messenian prisoners were stoned to death.* Many statues of him were erected and the cities officially and conspicuously honoured him in other ways as well.* Later, in the dark days of Greece following the destruction of Corinth,* a Roman tried to undo all of this by accusing Philopoemen, as though he were still alive, of being virulently hostile to Rome. A debate took place, at which Polybius responded to the man's misrepresentations, and neither Mummius nor the Roman legates could bring themselves to annul the honours awarded to such an illustrious man.* They were aware that he had not infrequently opposed the wishes of Flamininus and Glabrio, but they seem to have recognized the difference between what is good and what is necessary, between doing right and doing what is expedient, because they held, quite correctly and properly, that benefactors should always be rewarded and thanked by their beneficiaries, and that good men always deserve the recognition of other good men. Here ends the Life of Philopoemen.

TITUS QUINCTIUS FLAMININUS

[1] The man I am going to compare with him is Titus Quinctius Flamininus. The bronze statue of him in Rome readily lets us know what he looked like—the one that stands next to the great Apollo from Carthage, opposite the hippodrome, with a Greek inscription.* As for his character, he is said to have been prone to both anger and kindness, but not to the same degree, in the sense that, if he had to punish someone, he was lenient and soon forgot it, whereas he saw any act of kindness through to the end. He was as persistently loyal

to his beneficiaries as others are to their benefactors, and was always determined to look out for and look after those he had helped, as though they were his most prized possessions. He was, however, extremely ambitious for fame and glory, and this meant, first, that he was reluctant to let others share in his greatest and most significant achievements, and, second, that he preferred people who needed something from him to people who could do something for him. The former he regarded as the stuff of which virtue is made, and the latter as rivals in the quest for glory.

His upbringing was military: Rome was involved in those days in many great wars, and from their earliest years young Romans learnt on active service how to command. So Flamininus first saw action as a military tribune under the consul Marcellus in the Hannibalic War.* Marcellus was killed in an ambush, but Flamininus was appointed governor of the Tarentum region, and of Tarentum itself, which had just fallen to Rome for the second time.* He was thought to have handled the administrative aspects of the job just as well as he did the military side, and so, when colonists were sent out to two cities, Narnia and Cosa, he was chosen to lead them and found the colonies.*

[2] Largely as a result of all this success, he came to believe that he should bypass the intermediate offices that young men usually held—the tribunate of the people,* the praetorship, the aedileship—and go straight for the consulship. He returned to Rome with the wholehearted support of the colonists, but the tribunes Marcus Fulvius and Manius Curius opposed his candidacy, arguing that it would be a shocking breach of custom for a young man to force his way illegally* into the highest office while he was still uninitiated, so to speak, in the preliminary rites and mysteries of public life. But the Senate referred the decision to the people, and even though he was still under thirty years old they made him consul, with Sextus Aelius as his colleague.

When the lots were cast for provinces, Flamininus gained the war against Philip and the Macedonians.* It was a piece of luck for Rome that he gained a theatre where warfare and brute force were not the only tools a general needed, and the inhabitants were more likely to be won over by diplomacy and the personal touch. The kingdom of Macedon gave Philip a spearhead sufficient for battle, but in a drawn-out war his phalanx depended on the resources of Greece for its stamina, supplies, refuges, and its general effectiveness as a fighting machine. So unless a wedge were driven between Philip and the Greeks, it would take more than a single battle to decide the war. But the Greeks so far had had little to do with Rome;* in fact, this was the time when they were first really in contact, and so if the Roman general had not been a fair man who relied on words more than warfare—if he had not been persuasive when presenting a request and receptive to others' requests, and had not always been concerned above all to see justice done—the Greeks would not so readily have been content with foreign rule instead of what they had been used to. An account of his achievements will make this clear.

[3] Flamininus found that the generals who had held this command before him, Sulpicius Galba and Publius Villius,* had waited until late in the season to invade Macedon and had gone about the war sluggishly: they had wasted their time manoeuvring for position and sparring with Philip by sending out only skirmishers to secure roads and provisions. They had used up their year of office at home, enjoying their honours and busying themselves with politicking, and only then had they taken to the field. Flamininus had no intention of using this method of gaining an extra year's command, one as consul and one as proconsul. He was determined to make his year of office productive in the actual theatre of war, so he ignored all his honours and privileges, and asked the Senate only to let his brother Lucius join him as commander of the fleet.* Then he recruited, as the spearhead of his army, 3,000 veterans of Scipio's victories in Spain over Hasdrubal and in Libya over Hannibal,* selecting those who were still fit and determined, and sailed safely over to Epirus.

He found Villius and his army encamped close to Philip, who had for a long time been guarding the passes and narrows of the Apsus river.* But Villius had been stymied by the strength of Philip's positions, so after taking over his predecessor's troops Flamininus sent him home and began to consider the geography of the region. The terrain matches Tempe* for ruggedness, but lacks the beautiful trees and greenery, the clearings and sweet meadows that are found there. Massive, lofty mountains to left and right form a single ravine, deep and wide, through which the Apsus pours with the volume and speed of the Peneus. The river covers all the ground at the foot of the mountains, leaving a path only along a narrow and precipitous cutting by the side of the bed. It would under any circumstances be difficult for an army to make its way through the pass, and if it were guarded, it would be completely impossible.

[4] Some argued, therefore, that Flamininus should take the longer way round towards Lyncus via Dassaretis, where the going would be easy and the roads passable. But he was worried about advancing too far from the sea and finding himself in places where the soil was poor and hardly under cultivation: if Philip refused battle, shortage of provisions might force him to retreat back to the coast without having achieved anything, just like his predecessor. He decided, then, to attack in strength and try to force a passage through the heights.

With the mountains in the hands of Philip's phalangites, javelins and arrows rained down on the Romans' flanks from all directions. Men were beginning to be wounded, and then both sides were taking casualties as sharp encounters broke out between them, but the battle seemed to be deadlocked. Then some local shepherds came up to Flamininus and told him about a back route which the enemy had overlooked; they promised to show the way and have his men in position on the heights in three days at the outside. To confirm and corroborate their honesty they produced Charops, the son of Machatas, a leading man in Epirus who was well disposed towards the Romans and was secretly helping them out of fear of Philip.* Flamininus trusted Charops and despatched 4,000 foot and 300 horse under the command of a tribune, with the shepherds in bonds leading the way. They rested during the daytime, hiding in hollows and thickets, and travelled at night by the light of the full moon.

After sending this detachment on its way, Flamininus let his men rest for two days, except for the occasional skirmish to keep the enemy busy, and then at dawn on the day when those who had taken the back route were expected to show themselves on the heights he started out with all his men, both the heavy and the light contingents. He divided the army into three. He himself led his units in a column along the riverbed into the narrowest part of the ravine, pelted with Macedonian missiles and engaging at close quarters the enemy soldiers who challenged him wherever the going was difficult. Meanwhile, the other two divisions did their best to keep up with him, one on either side, clinging to the crags with a will.

The sun came up and a trickle of smoke, as faint and transparent as mountain mist, rose into the sky in the distance. The smoke came from the now-occupied heights behind the enemy, so they did not notice it. The Romans themselves were not sure what to make of it, but as they struggled painfully on they could only hope it was what they wanted to see. Then the smoke thickened and began to show black in the sky, and they could tell from the amount rising up that it was their friends' signal fire. With a whoop they drove forward determinedly. They pushed the enemy back on to particularly rough terrain, to the exultant cries of their friends in the enemy's rear, up on the heights.

[5] The entire enemy force turned immediately to headlong flight, but no more than 2,000 of them lost their lives, because the difficulty of the terrain made pursuit impossible. After plundering the Macedonian camp of its valuables, tents, and slaves, the Romans established their control of the narrows and set out through Epirus. They were far from the coastline and their supply ships, the monthly ration of grain had not been distributed, and there was little for sale; but, even so, the men retained their discipline and self-control, and spared the countryside, for all the abundant booty it offered. For Flamininus had found out that, as he passed or rather fled through Thessaly, Philip had uprooted the inhabitants from their cities and driven them into the mountains, put the cities to the torch, and allowed his men to steal everything of value that the inhabitants had left behind as too plentiful or too heavy to take with them. In effect, then, Philip had ceded the countryside to the Romans, and so Flamininus urged and ordered his troops to treat the land they marched through as though it had been given into their care and were their own.

And, indeed, their orderly behaviour immediately and perceptibly began to pay off. As soon as they set foot in Thessaly the cities came over to them, but that was not all: the Greeks south of Thermopylae could scarcely control their impatient longing to see Flamininus, and the Achaeans renounced their alliance with Philip and voted to side with the Romans against him.* And then, when the Aetolians (who were at this time especially staunch allies of the Romans)* demanded that the Opuntians allow them to take over their city and garrison it, the Opuntians resisted and turned to Flamininus. And when he came they put themselves in his hands and entrusted Opus to his protection.*

The story goes that the first time Pyrrhus looked down from a vantage-point and saw the Roman army drawn up for battle, he said that he saw nothing barbaric in this barbarian formation.* When people first met Flamininus they found themselves compelled to say much the same kind of thing. Macedonian propaganda had led them to expect a barbarian army under the command of a man who did nothing but subjugate and enslave by force of arms. But when they actually met him and found a nice-looking young man, who sounded and spoke like a Greek, and would never do anything dishonourable, they were incredibly charmed, and when they returned home they infected their cities with the warmth of their feelings for him, in the belief that they had found someone to champion their freedom.*

Philip seemed inclined to come to terms, and at their meeting* Flamininus offered him peace and the friendship of Rome, provided that he allowed the Greek cities their autonomy and withdrew his garrisons. Philip refused, and then at last even his partisans fully realized that, so far from coming to make war on the Greeks, the Romans had come to make war on the Macedonians for the sake of the Greeks.

[6] The process of gaining the support of the Greek states was, therefore, basically trouble-free. As he was peaceably passing through Boeotia, however, the leading men of Thebes came out to meet him. Brachyllas* had made sure that Theban sympathies lay with Macedon, but the Thebans greeted Flamininus respectfully, making out that they were on good terms with both sides. Flamininus received the deputation courteously, made them welcome, and continued quietly down the road, asking them for information on certain matters and explaining others, as a deliberate ploy to distract them until his troops had recovered from the march. Drawing the Theban delegates on like this, he entered the city along with them, which was not really what they wanted, but they were reluctant to try to stop him, seeing that he had a fair number of troops with him.

As if the city were not at his mercy, however, Flamininus appeared before the assembled Thebans and tried to persuade them to side with Rome. King Attalus backed him up and supported his appeal—but seems, in his eagerness to help, to have exerted himself beyond the capacity of his years. Right in the middle of his speech he suffered a fainting-fit or the onset of a flux, suddenly lost consciousness, and fell to the floor. Not much later, after he had taken his fleet back to Asia, he died.* But the Boeotians came over to the Roman side.

[7] When Philip sent envoys to Rome, Flamininus had his own representatives go there as well, to ensure that the Senate either voted to extend his command if the war continued, or, if there was to be peace, empowered him to negotiate the terms. He yearned so strongly for distinction that he was afraid of being robbed of his glory if another general was sent to take over the war. But his friends in Rome handled the matter for him so well that Philip failed to get what he wanted, and Flamininus retained command of the war as well. The news of the Senate's decision cheered him up immensely when it came, and he set straight out for Thessaly to confront Philip.* His army numbered over 26,000, including 6,000 foot and 400 horse provided by the Aetolians. Philip's army was much the same size.

The two forces advanced towards each other until they were near Scotoussa, where they were intending to fight the decisive battle. One might have expected that the troops on either side would have taken the other army's approach as a reason for fear, but that was not so. On the contrary, it increased their ardour and determination. The Romans were hoping to get the better of Macedonians who, thanks to Alexander, had the reputation in Rome of being as tough and effective as anyone; and the Macedonians, who considered the Romans better fighters than the Persians, were hoping, if they won, to prove Philip a greater general than Alexander. Flamininus therefore called on his men to be brave and resolute, seeing that they were going up against the best in the world and would be fighting in Greece, the fairest arena in the world. Philip, however, made a mistake. Either accidentally or because he was in too much of a hurry, he mounted the raised mound of a mass grave that happened to lie just outside his camp* and began to deliver a typically encouraging and inspiring pre-battle speech. But, disturbed by the fearful gloom with which his men greeted the omen, he refrained from battle that day.

[8] The following night was mild and wet, and just before dawn the clouds turned to mist. The entire plain was plunged into deep darkness, and a thick vapour rolled down from the hills into the space between the two armies, blanketing the region by the time the day was beginning to break. Both sides had sent men out to lay ambushes and reconnoitre, and these bands very quickly encountered one another. Fighting broke out at a place called Cynoscephalae, or

'Dog-heads', where the 'heads' are the small peaks of a dense range of hills, so called because that is what they look like. Inevitably, given the difficulty of the terrain, pursuit alternated with being pursued, and every time a body of men from either side withdrew in trouble they returned with reinforcements from their camp. Finally, when the air cleared and visibility was good, the full armies joined battle.

On the right wing, Philip had the better of it: he hurled his entire phalanx against the Romans from favourable ground, and not even the best of them could stand against the massed shields and wickedly projecting pikes. With his left wing turned and scattered over the hills, Flamininus gave it up as lost and quickly rode over to the other wing. He attacked the Macedonians where the rough and uneven ground had made it impossible for them to form a solid line or maintain any depth (which is critical for the strength of the Macedonian formation), and they were having to fight as individuals with heavy, unwieldy weaponry. For the Macedonian phalanx is like an invincible beast as long as it retains its solidity and the massed shields are locked together in a single formation; but once it has been broken up, each soldier loses even his individual effectiveness, partly because of the kind of weaponry he carries, and partly because his effectiveness is due not so much to himself as to his being part of a mutually supportive whole.*

So Philip's left wing was turned. Some of the Romans chased the fugitives, while others took those Macedonians who were still fighting in the flank and set about killing them. Before long even Philip's victorious right wing had to wheel about to face the new threat, and the soldiers began dropping their weapons and fleeing. At least 8,000 men lost their lives, and about 5,000 were taken prisoner.* Philip got safely away, however, and the Aetolians were blamed for this: they had turned to sacking and plundering the Macedonian camp while the Romans were still busy hunting down fugitives. In fact, they did such a thorough job that there was nothing left for the Romans when they returned.

[9] At first insults and angry words were exchanged, but later Flamininus grew more and more irritated by the Aetolians' constantly taking credit for the victory. The Aetolians made sure that their version was the first the Greeks heard and convinced them of it so successfully that they even gained pride of place in the inscriptions

and songs that poets and others composed in praise of the victory. The one that was most often on people's lips was this:

Unwept and unburied, traveller, on this Thessalian ridge
We lie, thirty thousand in number,
Brought low in war by the Aetolians, and by the Latins
Led by Titus from the plains of Italy
To bring great woe to Emathia. Philip's boldness has fled,
Passing quicker than a shy-footed deer.

This poem was written by Alcaeus to humiliate Philip, and he exaggerated the numbers of the dead, but it circulated so widely and was heard so often that it irritated Flamininus more than Philip.* Philip simply came up with an alternative and replied to Alcaeus with his own mocking couplet:

Unbarked and leafless, traveller, planted on this ridge
A cross of crucifixion looms, awaiting Alcaeus.

But Flamininus was hungry for the respect of the Greeks and he got excessively annoyed at this kind of thing. And so from then on he did what had to be done by himself, more or less ignoring the Aetolians. This did not go down well with them, and when Flamininus received a letter from Philip, and then an embassy, to discuss terms, they toured all Greece crying out that Philip was being sold peace, when war could be eradicated once and for all and the kingdom that had been the first to enslave* the Greek world could be destroyed. But while the Aetolians were bringing these charges and trying to stir the allies into discontent, Philip himself gave the lie to their suspicions when he came to the peace conference, by entrusting his affairs to the discretion of Flamininus and Rome.

The peace terms stipulated by Flamininus were as follows: he allowed Philip to retain his kingdom, but ordered him to stay away from Greece; he imposed an indemnity of 1,000 talents and removed his entire fleet, apart from ten ships;* and he took one of his sons, Demetrius, into custody and sent him to Rome as a hostage.* This was not just an excellent resolution of the current situation, but was also provident. For Hannibal of Carthage, the inveterate enemy of Rome, had been sent into exile and was already resident in Antiochus' court,* where he was encouraging the king to keep moving ahead while Fortune favoured him with following winds. Even without

Hannibal's encouragement, the scale of his achievements, which had earned him the title 'the Great', had already led Antiochus to contemplate the possibility of universal dominion, and it was above all the Romans against whom he was rousing himself to action. So if Flamininus had not seen this in the future and had not gone about the peace negotiations intelligently, the war with Antiochus would have found the war with Philip still in progress in Greece, and the two greatest and mightiest kings of the time would have united and made common cause against Rome, which would have been landed with fresh struggles and dangers no less formidable than those it had endured in the war against Hannibal. But by creating an interval of peace between the two wars, and by bringing the present war to an end before the impending one began, Flamininus denied Philip his last hope and Antiochus his first one.

[10] The ten commissioners sent to Flamininus by the Senate recommended that he should free the rest of the Greek cities, but keep his garrisons in Corinth, Chalcis, and Demetrias as insurance against Antiochus. But the enraged Aetolians raged at this, and stirred up the Greek cities by demanding that Flamininus free Greece from its 'fetters', which was Philip's usual way of describing these three places. They asked the Greeks whether they were happy to be wearing a collar that was more comfortable than the one they had had before, but no less burdensome—whether they were idolizing Flamininus as their benefactor when he had unshackled their feet, only to put a collar around their necks. Stung to anger by this, Flamininus kept petitioning the committee until at last he gained the legates' permission to remove the garrisons from the fetters as well, to complete the gift he was giving to Greece.*

At the Isthmian festival,* the stadium was packed with spectators watching the athletic competitions, for this was the first time for years that no war was being fought on Greek soil in the name of freedom and the festival was being celebrated at a time of certain peace. Then the trumpet sounded, the crowd fell completely silent, and a herald stepped forward into the open space and made the following announcement: 'The Roman Senate and Titus Quinctius Flamininus, proconsul, having defeated King Philip and the Macedonians, leave free, ungarrisoned, untaxed, and subject to their own ancestral laws the Corinthians, Phocians, Locrians, Euboeans, Phthiotic Achaeans, Magnesians, Thessalians, and Perrhaebians.'*

At first not everyone heard the announcement, or not well enough, and a confused buzz ran through the stadium, the noise of puzzled people asking one another for clarification and calling for the announcement to be repeated. But when silence fell again, the herald projected his voice more, to make sure he could be heard by everyone, and repeated the proclamation. A cry of joy arose, so unbelievably loud that it was heard on the coast. The spectators stood up; the athletes were forgotten; everyone leapt up eagerly to greet and salute the saviour and champion of Greece.

One often hears extravagant tales about the power of the human voice, but on this occasion their truth was verified by witnesses, when some crows that were flying overhead fell down into the stadium.* This is supposed to be caused by the splitting of the air: a sustained loud noise opens up a gap in the air so that it can no longer support flying creatures, but causes them to fall like people who step into a hole. But perhaps it might be more accurate to say that as the birds are flying past the sound acts like a blow from a weapon and they fall down dead. Alternatively, it is also possible that the air begins to circulate, and then, thanks to the size of the fluctuation, it forms itself, like a whirlpool at sea, into a downward-flowing spiral.

[11] Anyway, had Flamininus not noticed that, with the games abandoned, the crowd was racing towards him, and had he not speedily taken evasive action, it is doubtful whether he would have survived the crush of so many people pressing in around him from all directions at once. But by nightfall they had tired of cheering in the vicinity of his tent, and instead they greeted and embraced any friends and fellow citizens they met, and settled down to eat and drink with one another.

In the course of what was, naturally, an increasingly pleasant evening, people's minds and conversations turned to Greece. They spoke of the fact that, although the freedom of Greece had been the object of many wars, it had never been gained more securely or less painfully than now, when the cause had been championed by non-Greeks, and Greece itself had shed hardly a drop of blood or a tear of grief while winning the fairest and most precious prize of all. It was indeed true, they reflected, that however rare it was to find a man of courage or intelligence, there was no blessing rarer than a man of integrity. Commanders like Agesilaus, Lysander, Nicias, and Alcibiades* were brilliant at handling wars and winning battles on land and at sea, but they had no idea how to use their successes for generous and noble purposes. In fact, apart from the battles of Marathon, Salamis, Plataea, and Thermopylae, and Cimon's victories at the Eurymedon and on Cyprus,* every war Greece had fought had contributed to its own enslavement, and every trophy it had erected commemorated catastrophe and shame, since its ruination had invariably been caused by the destructive rivalry of its leaders. But now foreigners who were generally held to have no more than a faint spark of Greek ancestry and very little in common with them,* and who had therefore hardly been expected to form principles and policies in Greece's interest, had suffered and faced extreme danger in order to rid Greece of oppressive despots and tyrants, and make it free.

[12] These were the thoughts running through Greek minds, and events proved that the proclamation was not to be betrayed. Flamininus organized two expeditions simultaneously, sending Lentulus to Asia to free Bargylia and Stertinius to Thrace to rid the cities and islands there of Philip's garrisons;* meanwhile, Publius Villius sailed to Antioch to raise with Antiochus the issue of the freedom of the Greek cities within his empire.* Flamininus himself stopped at Chalcis and then went on to Magnesia, where he oversaw the departure of the garrisons and gave the cities back self-government.

He was appointed Master of Games for the Nemean festival at Argos,* and did an excellent job of directing it; he also used the occasion for a second public proclamation of freedom to the Greeks. Then he set out on a tour of the cities, where he established law and order, adjudicated a large number of disputes, reconciled the citizens with one another, and encouraged them to remain on good terms. He healed their political divisions and got them to take back their exiles, and prided himself just as much on persuading the Greeks to get on with one another as he did on his defeat of the Macedonians. And in the end the restoration of their freedom came to seem the least of his benefactions to them.

There is a story about the philosopher Xenocrates: he had been arrested by the tax-collectors and was being taken off to pay the resident-alien tax* when he was rescued by the politician Lycurgus, who also made sure that the men who were arresting him were punished for their insolence. Later, Xenocrates met Lycurgus' sons and said: 'Boys, I'm repaying your father very generously for his kindness: everyone thinks well of him for what he did!' Where Flamininus and the Romans were concerned, however, their benefactions to the Greeks not only made men think well of them, but quite rightly also made everyone trust them and submit to their authority. People did not just accept the officials who were sent to them, but actively asked for them, and entrusted themselves to them. Nor was it just regions and cities that did this, but kings too: when they found themselves wronged by other kings, they began to turn to Romans for help. And the upshot was that before long—and perhaps with divine assistance too—everything was subject to them.

Flamininus himself, however, regarded the freeing of Greece as his greatest accomplishment, and when he made a dedicatory offering at Delphi of some silver bucklers and his own shield, he had the following words inscribed:

> O sons of Zeus, who delight in feats of swift horsemanship,
> O Tyndaridae, noble princes of Sparta,
> Titus, born of Aeneas,* has given you the greatest of gifts:
> He has fashioned freedom for the sons of Greece.

He also dedicated a golden crown to Apollo, with the following inscription:

> It is only right,† son of Leto, for this gold-gleaming crown to rest
> On your ambrosial locks. It is the gift of the great man
> Who led the descendants of Aeneas to war. Apollo, near but far,
> Grant godlike Titus the glory he deserves for his prowess.

Corinth, then, has twice played the same role in Greek history. It was in Corinth that Flamininus gave the Greeks their freedom and autonomy on this occasion, and it was also in Corinth that Nero later, within my own lifetime, did very much the same. Both times, the proclamation was made during the Isthmian festival, but Flamininus used a herald, as I have said, whereas Nero delivered the speech in person from a platform in the main square, surrounded by the general populace.*

To resume, however. [13] Flamininus next went to war against Nabis,* the evil and lawless tyrant of Sparta. This was a perfectly honourable and justified war, but in the end he disappointed Greek hopes, in the sense that, although he could have removed Nabis, he chose instead to make peace with him and abandon Sparta to its undeserved slavery. Perhaps he was afraid that, if the war went on, another general would arrive from Rome and deny him the glory, or perhaps he was motivated by rivalry with Philopoemen and jealousy of all the honours he had been receiving. For Philopoemen was not just in general the outstanding Greek of his time, but had performed incredible deeds of outstanding daring in that particular war, and the Achaeans therefore honoured Philopoemen as much as they did Flamininus, and acclaimed him as loudly in their theatres. This annoyed Flamininus, who did not think an Arcadian, a general in minor border wars, deserved the Achaeans' admiration as much as a Roman consul who was championing the cause of Greece.* Still, Flamininus defended what he had done by arguing that he had brought the war to an end because, in his view, the death of the tyrant would have caused immense suffering for everyone else in Sparta.

The Achaeans voted Flamininus many honours, only one of which, I think, was commensurate with his benefactions, but he was as happy with this one as with all the rest put together. This is what it was. The Romans who had surrendered in the course of the Hannibalic War had been put up for sale all over the place and were working as slaves in various scattered locations. Twelve hundred of them were in Greece, in miserably reduced circumstances, and, as can be imagined, there were particularly heart-breaking incidents at the time in question, when an enslaved man encountered a free Roman who was his son or brother or friend. On the one side, men captured in war; on the other, men victorious in war.

For all the distress he felt at their predicament, Flamininus would not take these men back from their owners, but the Achaeans ransomed them at the rate of five mnas per man, gathered them all together, and handed them over to Flamininus just as he was about to set sail for Italy. He sailed home with a glad heart, then, feeling that he had been well paid for the good he had done, and had received the kind of recompense that a great man should, who loved his fellow citizens. This episode turned out to lend his triumph its most remarkable aspect. Following the custom of newly freed slaves, these men shaved their heads and wore felt caps, and paraded like that in Flamininus' triumphal retinue.

[14] The battlefield spoils displayed in the parade made a splendid sight—the Greek helmets and Macedonian shields and pikes—and there was also a great deal of money. Tuditanus† claims, in fact, that

3,713 pounds of gold bullion were carried in the triumph, and 14,514 gold 'Philips'.* In addition, there was Philip's indemnity of 1,000 talents—but the Romans were subsequently persuaded (largely by Flamininus) to let Philip off this, and at the same time they declared him an ally and released the son of his they had been holding hostage.*

[15] Then Antiochus invaded Greece* with a sizeable fleet and army, and began to foment rebellion and factional strife in the cities. The Aetolians, who had long since taken up a hostile and belligerent stance towards Rome,* were his allies in this venture, and suggested that the pretext he should give for the war was that he had come to free the Greeks. Being free already, the Greeks did not need to be freed, but, lacking a more plausible reason, the Aetolians explained to Antiochus that this was the best way to describe what he was doing. The Romans took the threat seriously, since Antiochus' military strength was well known, and despatched the consul Glabrio* to take command of the war. But for the sake of Greeks they also sent Flamininus as his legate.

The mere appearance of Flamininus in Greece strengthened the resolve of Rome's friends, and where he found cities on the verge of rebellion he administered the timely medicine of loyalty towards him, stopped them, and made sure that they did not stray. There were a few that got away from him, since they had already been thoroughly indoctrinated and bought by the Aetolians, but even though this made him furious, he still spared them after the battle—for Antiochus was defeated at Thermopylae* and fled straight back to Asia. But the consul, Glabrio, marched against the Aetolians and put some of their cities under siege, leaving it to King Philip to mop up the rest of the anti-Roman coalition.

With first the Dolopians and Magnesians and then the Athamanians and Aperantians being plundered by Philip, and with Glabrio himself first sacking Heraclea and then besieging Naupactus, which was in Aetolian hands, Flamininus felt sorry for the Greeks and sailed from the Peloponnese for a meeting with the consul. He began by remonstrating with Glabrio for letting Philip profit from a war that he, Glabrio, had won: there he was, wasting time over the siege of a single city to assuage his anger, while the Macedonians were gaining whole peoples and kingdoms in not inconsiderable numbers. Then, when some of the victims of the siege caught sight of him from the city wall, they called out his name and stretched out their arms towards him, begging for his help. At the time he said nothing, but just turned and left, with tears in his eyes; but later he talked to Glabrio, calmed him down, and arranged for the Aetolians to be granted a truce, to give them time to send an embassy to Rome to petition for favourable terms.*

[16] But the most serious and difficult fight he had with Glabrio was caused by his pleas on behalf of the Chalcidians, who had incurred the consul's wrath because of the marriage they had arranged for Antiochus, after the war had already started. It was a distasteful and inappropriate business, involving the lust of an elderly man for a young girl—the daughter of Cleoptolemus, apparently an exceptionally beautiful girl. Because of this marriage, the Chalcidians became very committed supporters of Antiochus and let him use their city as his headquarters for the war.* When Antiochus fled in haste from the battlefield, then, Chalcis was where he went. He picked up his young wife, his valuables, and his Friends, and sailed back to Asia, but Glabrio set out immediately for Chalcis in a rage. Flamininus went with him, trying to get him to relent and go easy on the Chalcidians, and in the end, by dint of appealing not just to him but to the authorities in Rome, he changed his mind and soothed his anger.

In gratitude for his protection, the Chalcidians dedicated to him the finest and most spectacular monuments they had. The inscriptions, of which the following are typical, can still be seen: 'By the will of the people, the gymnasium is dedicated to Titus and Heracles'; 'By the will of the people, the Delphinium is dedicated to Titus and Apollo.' Even today, they still elect a priest of Flamininus by a public show of hands, and after sacrificing to him and pouring a libation, they sing a special paean. It is too long to quote all of it, but here are its final words:

The Good Faith of Rome we revere
As our hearts' desire, and have sworn to cherish.
Sing, then, maidens,
Of great Zeus and Rome, of Titus and the Good Faith of Rome.
Ieie Paian!
O Titus, saviour!*

[17] Elsewhere in Greece the same thing happened: he received conspicuous honours and, thanks to his fundamental honesty, an incredible degree of loyalty, without which honours are empty.* It is

true that sometimes events or a point of honour caused him to fall out with people—Philopoemen, for instance, and then later the Achaean General Diophanes. But he did not bear a grudge, and he never let anger influence his behaviour; he went no further than expressing his point of view with as much candour as political debate allows. He was never vindictive (in fact, people often took him to be changeable and capricious), but was basically the best company in the world, and a charming but forceful speaker.

For instance, as a way of trying to dissuade the Achaeans from annexing the island of Zacynthos, he told them to beware of sticking their collective head, tortoise-like, too far out of the Peloponnese.* Then, the first time he met Philip to discuss the possibility of a truce and peace, when the king remarked on the fact that Flamininus had arrived with a large entourage while he had come alone, Flamininus replied: 'Yes, but that's your fault, for killing your friends and relatives.'* And once, in Rome, Deinocrates of Messene got drunk at a party and performed a dance wearing women's clothing. The next day, when he asked Flamininus to help him carry out his plan to get Messene to secede from the Achaean League, Flamininus told him he would think about it, but added that he was surprised that Deinocrates could dance and sing at a party when he had such an important enterprise under way.*

Then again, when Antiochus' envoys were detailing for the Achaeans the size of the king's army by running through a long list of regimental names, Flamininus told them how once, when dining with a friend, he had been taken aback by the number of meat dishes and wondered where his host had found such a variety for sale. His host replied that they were all pork dishes, which had just been differently prepared and flavoured. And Flamininus told the Achaeans: 'You shouldn't be surprised either, my friends, at this tale of Spear-bearers and Lance-bearers and Foot Companions: they're all just Syrians, differently armed.'

[18] After everything he had achieved in Greece and the war against Antiochus, Flamininus was appointed to the censorship. This is the most senior position in Rome and the crowning glory, so to speak, of a man's political career. His colleague was Marcellus, son of the five-times consul Marcellus.* They expelled from the Senate four men of no great distinction and, under coercion from the tribune Terentius Culleo, who persuaded the commons to carry the measure as a way of

spiting the nobles, they enrolled as citizens all who presented themselves as candidates, provided their parents had been free.*

Now, the two most distinguished and important men in Rome at the time, Scipio Africanus and Marcus Cato, were at odds with each other. Flamininus made Scipio Leader of the House,* on the grounds that he was the most honourable and eminent member of the Senate, but he fell out badly with the other, Marcus Cato.* This is how it came about. Flamininus had a brother, Lucius,* who was a completely different kind of person, above all because he was scandalously self-indulgent and cared nothing for decorum. Lucius had a young boyfriend whom he took everywhere and kept by his side even when he was in the field as a general or in a province as an administrator. Once, at a party, this boy told Lucius flirtatiously that it was a measure of his love for him that he had left a gladiatorial show to be with him, even though he had never in his life seen a man being killed. 'You see how I put your pleasure before mine,' he said. Lucius was charmed. 'No problem!' he replied. 'Your wish is my command!' He ordered a condemned prisoner to be fetched from the prison, summoned a subordinate, and ordered him to cut off the man's head in the middle of the symposium.

Valerius Antias* says that Lucius did this to gratify a girlfriend, not a boyfriend; and, according to Livy, Cato said in a speech that it was a Celtic deserter, not a prisoner. In Cato's version, the man turned up at the house with his family, and Lucius introduced him into the party and killed him with his own hand, to please his boyfriend. Cato probably put it this way to beef up his prosecution speech. That the man who was killed was a prisoner, not a deserter, and one who had already been condemned to death, is the version given by many others, including the orator Cicero, who in his *On Old Age* attributes the story to Cato himself.*

[19] So when Cato became censor* and purged the Senate, he expelled Lucius from it. Now, Lucius had consular rank, and the disgrace seemed to reflect badly on Titus too, so both brothers presented themselves humbly before the people, with tears in their eyes, and made what was supposed to be a reasonable request of their fellow citizens, that Cato should explain why and for what reasons he had brought such shame on a distinguished house. Cato promptly stepped up and, with his colleague standing beside him, asked Titus if he knew about the symposium. When Titus said no, Cato told him

the story, challenging Lucius to prove the falsity of anything he said. Lucius stayed silent, so that the people realized the justice of Cato's expulsion of Lucius and cheered him loudly off the platform.

Flamininus was very upset at what had happened to his brother. He allied himself with men who had long wanted to see Cato fall and he prevailed on the Senate to cancel and undo every public contract, lease, and tax-farming deal that Cato had arranged; he also had him brought up in court more than once on serious charges.* I would not like to say whether it was either morally right or politically expedient for him to take up a position of unremitting hostility towards a legally elected officer and an upstanding citizen of Rome, for the sake of a man who may have been a relative, but was a worthless individual, and whose punishment had been merited. But on a later occasion, when the theatre was packed with the ordinary people of Rome for a show and the senators, as usual, were seated in splendour up front, Lucius was spotted sitting somewhere at the very back, dishonoured and humiliated. People felt sorry for him and could not stand to see him like this. They kept on calling out to him and telling him to change places, until he did so; and his fellow ex-consuls let him sit with them.

[20] Now, the ambitious side of Flamininus' character met with approval as long as he was busy with the wars I have mentioned, which gave his desire for recognition enough material to work with. For instance, he became a military tribune for a second time, after holding the consulship, when there was no need for him to do so.* But once he was elderly and out of office, he increasingly came to be criticized for his inability to stop himself lusting after glory and behaving like a young man, despite the fact that he would not see action in the years that remained to him. His behaviour towards Hannibal, for instance, seems to have been motivated by some such impulse, and it turned most people in Rome against him.

After escaping into exile from Carthage, Hannibal spent some time with Antiochus, but after the battle in Phrygia* Antiochus was glad to make peace, and Hannibal fled again.* He wandered far and wide before finally settling in Bithynia under Prusias' protection. This was common knowledge in Rome, but Hannibal was too feeble and old for anyone to be concerned; it looked to them as though he had been cast aside by Fortune. But when Flamininus went to Prusias' court as an envoy from the Senate on some other business and actually saw Hannibal living there, it made him furious that he was alive. Prusias interceded on Hannibal's behalf time and again, imploring Flamininus to be merciful towards a man who was a suppliant in his court and a friend, but Flamininus was unmoved.*

There was an old oracle that appeared to refer to Hannibal's death, as follows: 'Hannibal's body in Libyssan soil shall lie.' Now, Hannibal assumed that this meant Libya and burial at Carthage, and saw himself ending his days there, but in Bithynia there is a sandy stretch of coastline with a small village on it, called Libyssa. Hannibal was living not far from this village, and since he never trusted Prusias, regarding him as weak, and feared the Romans, he had already riddled the house with seven subterranean escape-routes, leading from his own quarters. The tunnels ran in various directions, and all of them had concealed exits far from the house. So, at the time in question, when he heard of Flamininus' warrant, he planned to escape through the tunnels; but he found the king's guards waiting for him and decided to take his own life.

One account is that he wrapped a length of cloth around his neck, and told a slave to stand behind him, plant a knee in the small of his back, pull back sharply with all his might, and twist the cloth until he had choked him to death. Others say that he copied Themistocles and Midas and drank bull's blood. But Livy says that he had a potion prepared, and that as he took the cup he said: 'The Romans find it too long and tedious a process to wait for the death of their aged enemy, so let us put an end at last to their fear. But this is a shabby victory for Flamininus, and unworthy of his forebears, who wrote and informed Pyrrhus of the poisoning attempt* that was going to be made on his life, even though he was at war with them and had the upper hand.'

[21] These are the stories of Hannibal's death. When the news reached Rome, many senators were disgusted with Flamininus and found what he had done excessive and cruel; Hannibal had been like a bird, too old and tattered to fly, that had been allowed to live on as a pet, and Flamininus had killed him. And he had done it for no more pressing reason, they said, than personal glory: he wanted his name to be linked with the death. They compared the forbearance and magnanimity of Scipio Africanus, and admired him all the more. After defeating Hannibal in Libya, when he had never previously been beaten and remained a real threat, Scipio did not drive him into exile or demand his arrest by his fellow citizens; he treated him with

respect when they met before the battle, and afterwards, in settling the terms of the armistice, he did not crow and trample on the man in his misfortune.

There was apparently also a subsequent occasion when the two of them met in Ephesus. First, as they were walking around together, Hannibal took the more prestigious position, but Scipio did not let that bother him and walked on without making anything of it. And when their conversation came round to generals, and Hannibal asserted that Alexander had been the greatest general, followed by Pyrrhus and then himself, Africanus quietly said with a smile: 'What if I hadn't beaten you?' And Hannibal replied: 'Then I wouldn't have counted myself third, Scipio, but first.'*

Although people generally tended to admire Scipio and reviled Flamininus for claiming someone else's kill as his own, some thought he had been right. It was their view that as long as Hannibal was alive, he was a fire that just needed to be fanned into flame. They pointed out that what the Romans had found terrifying about Hannibal was not his physical strength or his sword arm, but his skill and experience, coming on top of his deep bitterness and hostility towards Rome. These things, they argued, do not decline in old age; a man's natural characteristics remain. But Fortune is changeable, and as it changes it tempts men whose hostility is forever fuelled by hatred with fresh hopes of success and calls them to new ventures. And in a sense, subsequent events came close to proving Flamininus right. First, Aristonicus,* a musician's son, used the name of Eumenes to stir all Asia into rebellion and warfare, and then Mithradates,* even after defeat by Sulla and Fimbria and the loss of so many men and generals, rose again in strength to fight Lucullus on both land and sea.

But Hannibal did not sink as low as Gaius Marius. Hannibal at least had the friendship of a king, and led his usual life, occupied with ships and cavalry and tending to troops. But the Romans mocked Marius in his misfortune, as he wandered in abject poverty in Libya—and then a short while later bowed down before him in Rome as they were being slaughtered and scourged.* When the future is taken into consideration, nothing in the present is either great or small; change ends only when existence ends. And so some writers say that Flamininus was not acting without authorization, but that the purpose of his and Lucius Scipio's mission was precisely to see to Hannibal's death.

My research has uncovered no further political or military activity by Flamininus after this. He did not die on the battlefield.* And now it is time to turn to the comparison.

PHILOPOEMEN and FLAMININUS COMPARED

[1] In terms of the amount of good they did the Greeks there is no point in comparing Philopoemen and Flamininus, and the same goes for a great many who were better men than Philopoemen. On the one hand we have wars fought by Greeks against Greeks, and on the other wars fought by a non-Greek to defend Greeks. And Philopoemen's departure for Crete when he was unable to protect his own fellow citizens from the attacks of their enemies coincided exactly with the time when Flamininus, having defeated Philip, was in the heart of Greece liberating people after people and city after city. Moreover, analysis of their battles shows that the number of Greeks killed by Philopoemen as General of the Achaean League was greater than the number of Macedonians killed by Flamininus in defence of Greece.

Their flaws stemmed in the one case from a desire for recognition, and in the other from a desire to get the better of people. The one was easily moved to anger and the other was hard to deflect from his course. For instance, Flamininus left even Philip the dignity of his kingship and treated the Aetolians tactfully, whereas out of anger Philopoemen denied his native city the contributions it received from its outlying dependencies. Then again, Flamininus was always a staunch friend to those he had benefited, but when he was angry Philopoemen was liable to undo the good he had done. For instance, although he had been a benefactor of Sparta, he later razed its walls and ravaged its farmland, and ended by changing and destroying its very constitution. He probably even threw away his life out of anger and the desire to get the better of a rival, since the attack he launched on Messene was untimely and over-hasty. Unlike Flamininus, as a general Philopoemen did not think everything through and try to avoid risks.

[2] Despite this, the number of Philopoemen's wars and victories certainly made him the more experienced general. Flamininus fought two battles to decide the war against Philip, whereas Philopoemen won countless battlefield victories, and left no one in any doubt

that they were due to skill rather than luck. Moreover, one of the two men became famous while drawing on the resources of Rome at the height of its power, while the other had only the resources of Greece when it was already in decline and past its peak, which meant that Philopoemen's success was his own work, whereas Flamininus' was a shared effort. And Flamininus had good soldiers in his command, while Philopoemen made his good when he took command. Then again, even though Philopoemen's battles were unfortunately all fought against Greeks, this very fact convincingly proves his proficiency. For where other things are equal, the more proficient man wins. And, in fact, although he fought the Cretans and the Spartans, both extremely warlike peoples, he proved himself craftier than the most cunning Cretans and bolder than the bravest Spartans. Furthermore, Flamininus had the materials of victory ready to hand, in the sense that he inherited the weaponry and formations he used, whereas Philopoemen himself reformed and changed the military system. In the one case, the critical factor in victory did not exist and was invented; in the other case it already existed in a serviceable form. On the battlefield, then, Philopoemen achieved a great deal that was important, while Flamininus did nothing. In fact, an Aetolian called Archedemus* used to tell a mocking story about Flamininus, about a time when he was charging the massed Macedonian troops at the double with a sword in his hand, and Flamininus was standing and praying with his hands stretched up to heaven.

[3] Moreover, everything worthwhile that Flamininus did was done when he was a general or an ambassador, whereas Philopoemen proved himself just as good and effective when he was out of office as when he was General of the Achaeans. It was while he was out of office that he drove Nabis out of Messene and gave the Messenians back their freedom, and it was while he was out of office that he shut the Achaean General Diophanes and Flamininus out of Sparta, thwarted their assault, and saved the Spartans. In other words, he was a natural leader who did not just operate within the guidelines of the law, but also knew how to override the law when the common good demanded it. He did not feel that the men he commanded had to have appointed him to command; he simply made use of them when a crisis arose, since as far as they were concerned the criterion for true generalship was seeing to their interests, not being appointed by them. So however great Flamininus' kind and equable treatment of the Greeks

was, Philopoemen's rough treatment of the Romans in the name of freedom was greater, because it is easier to be kind to people who need you than it is to antagonize people who are stronger than you.

If, after this study, it is still not easy to pinpoint the difference between the two men, ask yourself whether you will think I have done an adequate job as an umpire if I award the Greek the prize for military experience and generalship, and the Roman the prize for integrity and honesty.

EXPLANATORY NOTES

ALEXANDER

8 *overthrew Pompey*: Gaius Julius Caesar (100–44 BCE) defeated his former political ally Pompey at the battle of Pharsalus in August 48 BCE.

Heracles . . . Neoptolemus: this gives Alexander impressive heroic lineage on both sides of his family. On the Macedonian side the Argead dynasty's descent from Heracles through Argos was already known to Herodotus (8.137–8) in the 5th C. Caranus was reputed to be the mythical founder of the dynasty, although he may have been a relatively late addition to the family tree, given that he appears in neither Herodotus nor Thucydides. He was most likely added early in the 4th C. for reasons that are unclear, see W. Greenwalt, 'The Introduction of Caranus into the Argead King List', *Greek, Roman, and Byzantine Studies*, 26 (1985), 43–9. On the other side, the Molossian kings claimed descent from the Aeacus, the legendary king of Aegina, who was grandfather of Achilles and great-grandfather of Neoptolemus; see also *Pyrrhus* 1.

Samothrace: a small island in the north Aegean off the coast of Thrace; famous for its mystery cult of the Great Gods, it was under Macedonian control from the time of Philip II.

Arybbas: Olympias was of Molossian royalty; she was born *c.*373 and married Philip *c.*357. Arybbas was in fact Olympias' uncle rather than brother.

Aristander of Telmessus: a diviner and interpreter of dreams from Telmessus in Lycia, he would later accompany Alexander on his campaign: see chapters 14, 25, 31, 33, 50, and 52.

9 *thrēskeuein*: Plutarch deriving (rather questionably) this verb (meaning 'worship') from Thrēissai, meaning Thracian women.

wands and garlands: typical religious paraphernalia in the Dionysian mysteries that were heavily associated with women. Euripides vividly depicted scenes of Dionysiac abandon in his *Bacchae*, during which, for instance, snakes lick blood from the cheeks of ecstatic women (lines 767–8).

sleeping with his wife: Philip lost an eye during the siege of Methone in 354. The god Ammon was Zeus Ammon, who was importantly identified with the Egyptian Amun-Re, at whose sanctuary Alexander would later be addressed as son of the god: see chapters 26–7.

Eratosthenes: Eratosthenes of Cyrene, a 3rd-C. BCE scholar based in Alexandria.

Hera: wife of Zeus, who would not have been pleased to know that her husband had fathered a son by the Macedonian queen.

destroyed by fire: in July 356; such a synchronism was an omen therefore of the greatness of Alexander.

delivering Alexander: despite being a famously virginal goddess, Artemis was also a goddess of childbirth. Hegesias was a 3rd-C. rhetorician and historian, whose grandiloquent style was both famous and mocked; see, for example, Cicero's parody in *Letters to Atticus* 12.6. He wrote a history of Alexander.

10 *born that day*: the Magi, as Persian priests, here reflect a Persian perspective on what the birth of Alexander would mean for Asia and for the Persian empire in particular.

Friends: on these see note to p. 20.

melting gaze: the importance of looking like Alexander is fully discussed with excellent illustrations in A. Stewart, *Faces of Power: Alexander's Image and Hellenistic Politics* (Berkeley, 1993); see also *Pyrrhus* 8. Lysippus of Sicyon was responsible for a number of bronze sculptures of Alexander; see also chapters 16 and 40.

dark and swarthy: Apelles was a celebrated 4th-C. painter from Colophon, who made Alexander the subject of several paintings. Plutarch is much more positive about this painting in his *On the Fortune or Virtue of Alexander* II.2 (*Moralia* 335a); see also *Demetrius* 22 and *Aratus* 13.

by heat: pleasant smells could be associated with the divine: see Plutarch, *On the Obsolescence of Oracles* 21 and 50 (*Moralia* 421b and 437c), in the second of which passages Plutarch also suggests that heat may be responsible. Aristoxenus of Tarentum was a pupil of Aristotle, best known for his extensive writing on music. The philosopher Theophrastus succeeded Aristotle as head of the Peripatetic school; among his many writings was a lost treatise *On Smells*.

11 *pankration*: for Alexander's dismissive attitude to athletics, see D. Kyle, *Sport and Spectacle in the Ancient World* (Oxford, 2007), 236–7, and references there. For Philip's interest in the violent pankration, see *Eumenes* 1 with note.

tutor: a tutor (*paidagōgos*) was normally of low status, but as a relative of Olympias Leonidas clearly was not. Several times in the life Alexander recalls lessons Leonidas taught him: chapters 22 and 25.

12 *Phoenix . . . Peleus*: Phoenix was the teacher and mentor of Achilles, Peleus was Achilles' father. For Alexander's identification of himself with Achilles, see chapter 15. See also A. Erskine, *Troy between Greece and Rome: Local Tradition and Imperial Power* (Oxford, 2001), 228–9.

Bucephalas: Thessalian horses were celebrated, although at 13 talents Bucephalas seems not a little over-priced. Diodorus 17.76 reports a different story, that the horse was a gift from Demaratus of Corinth (see chapter 9). Bucephalas' name meant 'head of an ox', which was variously explained: either he was marked with the head of an ox to identify him or he had a white patch on his head that resembled one (Arrian, *Anabasis* 5.19.5).

13 *rudders too*: from a lost play by the 5th-C. Athenian tragedian Sophocles.

13 *resettled the town*: Stagira had been destroyed in 349 during Philip's conquest of the Chalcidic peninsula, a region that bordered on Macedon. When Aristotle joined the Macedonian court in 343/2, he already had connections with the royal household as his father had been court doctor to Amyntas III, Philip's father. At the time Alexander would have been about thirteen.

used to frequent: Mieza was situated in the foothills some 40 km from Pella in the area of modern Naoussa. The sanctuary where Aristotle taught has been identified with the remains of an architectural complex that links a set of three caves.

14 *Onesicritus*: chief helmsman of Alexander's fleet, who wrote a lost work on the education of Alexander, modelled on Xenophon's *Cyropaedia* (*Education of Cyrus*). The '*Iliad* of the casket' took its name from a casket of Darius: see chapter 26.

Harpalus: a boyhood friend of Alexander, Harpalus was left in charge of Babylon during the India campaign; see further chapters 10, 35, and 41.

Philistus' works: in the first half of the 4th C. Philistus of Syracuse wrote a history of Sicily, a curious work for someone campaigning in India to read, but perhaps meant to indicate that Alexander's ambitions lay in the West as well as the East.

Telestes and Philoxenus: two celebrated dithyrambic poets from Sicily, both living in the late 5th and early 4th C.

Anaxarchus . . . Calanus: Anaxarchus, a philosopher from Abdera who accompanied Alexander (see chapter 28), was the author of a work on kingship, an unusual theme for a philosopher at the time but one that would become increasingly popular in the Hellenistic period. Xenocrates was head of the Academy and Alexander's attitude to him can be contrasted with that of Antipater (*Phocion* 27). Dandamis and Calanus were two Indian philosophers: chapters 65 and 69.

Maedians: a tribe located in the area of the upper Strymon valley. The site of Alexandropolis (its name recalling his father's Philippopolis) is not known.

Macedonian dead: at the battle of Chaeronea, fought in 338, Philip defeated the combined forces of Athens and Thebes and thus acquired effective control of Greece: see *Demosthenes* 19–21. The Theban Sacred Band was an elite force of 300. Plutarch draws on his own knowledge of the battlefield as a native of the region. The communal grave of the Macedonians has been found along with another for the Sacred Band: see J. Ma, 'Chaironeia 338: Topographies of Commemoration', *Journal of Hellenic Studies*, 128 (2008), 72–91.

15 *Philip and Cleopatra*: his new bride was from a Macedonian noble family, thus her prospective children might be considered more Macedonian than Alexander, whose mother Olympias was a Molossian. The marriage took

place in 337. Philip continued to be married to Olympias, but her influence must have suffered.

Europe to Asia: a reference to Philip's plan to attack Persia; at the time of his assassination in 336 advance forces had already crossed to Asia, but it was to be Alexander who launched the attack.

Demaratus of Corinth: a prominent pro-Macedonian in Corinth, he would later join Alexander on his campaign (chapters 37 and 56) even though he was in his sixties by the time of Alexander's accession.

satrap of Caria: Pixodarus thus ruled Caria for the Persian king; his approach to Philip may have been in anticipation of Philip's invasion of Asia. There is disagreement over the date, but it is most likely 336, after Philip's marriage.

Arrhidaeus: Philip's eldest son, by Philinna of Larisa. As Philip III Arrhidaeus he would eventually succeed Alexander in name at least, although power would be held by others: see chapter 77; *Eumenes* 13; *Phocion* 32–3.

16 *Philotas*: son of Philip's general Parmenio; it may have been he who told the king about Alexander's approach to Pixodarus. He would later be executed by Alexander in a crackdown on dissent (chapters 48–9).

highest honour by him: Harpalus became treasurer, Nearchus admiral of the fleet, Erigyius cavalry commander, and Ptolemy a Companion and Bodyguard (and later king of Egypt). In contrast to the others, Erigyius was not Macedonian by birth and was probably older (born *c.*380). It is usually suggested that they were punished for bad advice, but it may be that Philip was concerned that Alexander was building up what was in effect his own personal court.

spotless either: Philip was assassinated in Macedon in 336 by Pausanias, one of his bodyguards, who was killed while fleeing. One explanation was that this was a personal grudge due to the assault, but as with all assassinations, conspiracy theories multiplied and some implicated Olympias and Alexander (see also Justin, *Epitome* 9.7).

bride too: Euripides, *Medea* 288, where Creon, ruler of Thebes, tells Medea that he is aware that she is threatening himself (the giver of the bride), his daughter (the bride), and Jason (the groom and Medea's former lover). In the context of Plutarch this seems to refer respectively to Attalus, his niece Cleopatra, and Philip, whose marriage is mentioned in the previous chapter. The quote could also be taken more loosely, since Philip died at the celebration of his daughter's marriage (but Plutarch does not tell us that).

brutal way: according to Justin (*Epitome* 9.7.7), Olympias forced Cleopatra to hang herself after making her witness the murder of her infant daughter. Pausanias (8.7.7), on the other hand, has both mother and child (wrongly said to be a son) roasted to death in a large bronze pot. Alexander did, nonetheless, execute Cleopatra's uncle Attalus. For the insult, see in particular Diodorus 16.93–4.

17 *major engagement*: in mid-335 Alexander attacked both the Triballians, a powerful Thracian tribe from the lower Danube, and the Illyrians; for a narrative, see Arrian, *Anabasis* 1.4–6.

he was a man: the Thebans revolted around September 335, many believing Alexander to have been killed in battle against the Illyrians (Arrian, *Anabasis* 1.7.2). The Athenians, after initially promising support, backed down, leaving the Thebans to resist alone (*Demosthenes* 23); for Phocion's scornful remarks about Demosthenes' provocation of Alexander, see *Phocion* 17.

Philotas and Antipater: in response to Alexander's ultimatum demanding the leaders of the revolt, the Thebans themselves demanded two leading Macedonians. On Antipater, see Biographies of Prominent Figures. Arrian, *Anabasis* 1.7 presents a more restrained Alexander, concerned to reach a negotiated settlement.

Cadmeia: the fortified acropolis of Thebes.

rest into slavery: Pindar was a celebrated poet of the early 5th C., many of whose poems survive. Thebes was re-founded by Cassander in 315, although it was never to regain its former status. It should not be forgotten when reading this account that Plutarch was a Boeotian.

18 *freedom and leave*: Plutarch tells the story at greater length in *Concerning the Virtues of Women* 24 (*Moralia* 259d–60d), his source apparently being Aristobulus (*Moralia* 1093c).

safety in Athens: for the reaction in Athens, *Phocion* 17, *Demosthenes* 23. On the Eleusinian Mysteries, see note to p. 185.

rulers of Greece: the anecdote is repeated at *Phocion* 17.

anger of Dionysus: the god was the son of Semele, daughter of Cadmus of Thebes, hence his supposed sympathy for Thebes. Alexander blamed Dionysus for the drunken murder of Cleitus (chapters 50–1), because he was the god of wine; the refusal of Alexander's troops to march into India (chapter 62) was a blow to a king who sought to march further east than Dionysus (see Arrian, *Anabasis* 5.1–2).

19 *put in charge*: this was a meeting of the League of Corinth that had been established by his father in the aftermath of Chaeronea to unite the Greeks under his leadership for a war against Persia. Plutarch has his chronology wrong here; the meeting occurred in 336 before his campaigns in the north and the revolt of Thebes (Arrian, *Anabasis* 1.1).

I would be Diogenes: Diogenes of Sinope was the founder of Cynicism, a philosophy that rejected the norms of society. The anecdote of a meeting between a young king who sought to rule the world and a philosopher who needed nothing was much repeated in antiquity, and captured the imagination of artists right into the modern era, to the extent that it was parodied by Landseer with a pair of dogs. The story may have come from Onesicritus (chapter 8), who was a pupil of the Cynic Diogenes.

Leibethra: a town in southern Macedonia near Mt Olympus, reputed to be the burial-place of Orpheus.

5,000 horse: in *On the Fortune or Virtue of Alexander* 3 (*Moralia* 327d–e) Plutarch gives some of his authorities for these figures. Aristobulus put the size of Alexander's army at 30,000 infantry and 4,000 cavalry, Ptolemy 30,000 infantry and 5,000 cavalry (the figure used by Arrian, *Anabasis* 1.11.3), and Anaximenes offered the higher figure of 43,000 infantry and 5,500 cavalry. Also at the high end was the expedition's ill-fated historian Callisthenes, who gave the infantry as 40,000 and the cavalry as 4,500 according to Polybius (12.19). Figures for Alexander's army are also recorded by other writers, but all lie within this range. The discrepancy between the high and the low figures is sometimes explained by assuming that the high figure included Philip's advance force (on which see note to p. 15).

20 *debt as well*: Aristobulus of Cassandreia and Onesicritus (see note to p. 14) both accompanied the expedition, while Duris of Samos (*c*.330–*c*.260 BCE) wrote a history of Macedon in at least 23 books.

Companions: the Companions (*Hetairoi*) were an elite group of nobles who surrounded and advised the king, to be equated with the Friends (*Philoi*) of the Successor kings; indeed Plutarch occasionally calls them 'Friends', as later in this chapter. The term 'Companions' also referred to the Macedonian cavalry.

Perdiccas: one of Alexander's seven Bodyguards (on whom see note to p. 46); see also Biographies of Prominent Figures.

Hellespont: dividing Europe from Asia; Alexander crossed in spring 334.

after his death: the herald was Homer, whose epic poem the *Iliad* had Alexander's ancestor Achilles as its central character. Achilles' friend was Patroclus, whose death at the hands of the Trojans was a turning-point in the *Iliad*. Alexander's identification with Achilles is often matched by pairing his friend Hephaestion with Patroclus. Arrian (*Anabasis* 1.12), for instance, has Hephaestion lay a wreath at the tomb of Patroclus while Alexander does the same at that of Achilles. By visiting Troy, Alexander both evokes the age of heroes and reminds a wider audience of earlier conflicts between East and West.

Alexander's lyre: Alexander was an alternative name for Paris, son of Priam, whose abduction of Helen had prompted the Trojan War.

Artemisios: the Macedonian months of Artemisios and Daisios are approximately the same as April and May.

21 *cavalry squadrons*: first of several occasions on which Alexander ignores Parmenio's advice (see also chapters 19, 29, 31, 32, 38); this is part of a tradition to be found in other accounts of the campaign and leads up to Parmenio's eventual execution (chapter 49). The description of the battle here can be compared with Arrian, *Anabasis* 1. 13–16. At Diodorus 17.19, in contrast, Alexander, in keeping with Parmenio's advice, crosses at dawn.

21 *Rhoesaces and Spithridates*: two brothers from a very distinguished Persian family; Spithridates was satrap of Lydia and Ionia (Diodorus 17.20; Arrian, *Anabasis* 1.12).

Cleitus the Black: Cleitus, son of Dropidas, was commander of the royal squadron of the Companion cavalry. The epithet 'Black' distinguished him from his namesake, the infantry commander Cleitus the White. Despite saving Alexander's life Cleitus would later be killed by him in a drunken quarrel (chapters 50–1).

22 *Lysippus sculpted*: according to Arrian, *Anabasis* 1.16, who gives the dead as more than 60 cavalry and about 30 infantry, the sculptures represent the twenty-five Companions who died in the first assault of the battle. Originally displayed in Dium in Macedonia, the group was brought to Rome in the 140s BCE.

barbarians who live in Asia: Alexander presents himself here as leader of the Greeks with a pointed reference to Sparta's refusal to participate in the League of Corinth. Note the sharp polarity here between Greeks and barbarians. Demosthenes may have accused the Macedonians of being barbarians but this dedication aligns them firmly with the Greeks.

territory around them: although Halicarnassus (modern Bodrum) was captured in late 334, its Persian garrison retreated to a citadel, where they held out for some time (Arrian, *Anabasis* 1.20–3, 2.5).

23 *open up for me*: from an unknown play by the Athenian dramatist Menander (*c*.342–*c*.291), a leading figure in New Comedy. The historian Callisthenes in particular was said to have offered this kind of fanciful account of the campaign.

Aristotle and philosophy: Theodectes was a 4th-C. rhetorician and poet from Phaselis in Lycia, whose writings on rhetoric are known to have been discussed by Aristotle. Valerius Maximus (8.14. ext. 3) even suggests that Aristotle complained that Theodectes had passed off his ideas as his own, although Alexander's admiration for the Lycian writer suggests otherwise.

Phrygia: spring 333.

Memnon: a native of Rhodes, Memnon was a high-ranking commander in the Persian armed forces. At the time of his death (from illness) in summer 333 he was leading a naval campaign to win over the Aegean, presumably with a view to taking the war to the Greek mainland. He had already captured Chios and was besieging Mytilene. For his wife Barsine, see chapter 21.

600,000 men under him: surely an exaggeration, but one reproduced also by Arrian, *Anabasis* 2.8.8.

24 *Philip of Acarnania*: he had been attached to Philip's court and had known Alexander since the latter was a boy (Q. Curtius Rufus 3.6.1). The story demonstrates the importance of mutual loyalty for Alexander. Arrian's telling is far more restrained, with no emotional outburst from Philip (*Anabasis* 2.4.7–11). Note again how Parmenio's advice is ignored.

25 *loss of use of his senses*: it is not impossible that the illness Alexander contracted in Cilicia was malaria, and that it was this that would eventually kill him: see D. Engels, 'A Note on Alexander's Death', *Classical Philology*, 73 (1978), 224–8.

Amyntas: Amyntas, son of Antiochus, had fled Macedon after the death of Philip for reasons that are unclear: Arrian, *Anabasis* 1.17.9.

26 *Chares*: a Greek from Mytilene, he was a member of Alexander's court and author of a lost history of Alexander, much cited by Plutarch; see chapters 24, 46, 54, 55, and 70.

outstanding victory: the battle of Issus, the second of Alexander's three great victories over the Persians, was probably fought in early November 333.

Leonnatus: Macedonian aristocrat and one of Alexander's Bodyguards (on which see note to p. 46) who would become (for a short while at least) an important figure in the years immediately after Alexander's death (see *Eumenes* 3).

27 *Barsine*: daughter of Artabazus, satrap of Hellespontine Phrygia, she bore Alexander a son Heracles in the mid-320s. The last member of the Argead line, albeit illegitimate, Heracles was murdered by Polyperchon on the orders of Cassander *c.*308 (Diodorus 20.28).

torment to the eyes: this recalls and inverts Herodotus 5.18–20, where Persian ambassadors to Macedon are struck by the beauty of the Macedonian royal women, whom they describe as torment to their eyes. But whereas the Macedonian Alexander, when faced with Persian royal women, exercised restraint, the Persian ambassadors instead sexually assault the Macedonian women (and are killed in consequence).

28 *Hagnon*: an influential Greek from Teos in Asia Minor with a reputation for extravagance and flattery; see also chapters 40 and 55. In the years immediately after Alexander's death he is linked first with Craterus and then Antigonus. He was the subject of an honorific inscription from Ephesus in 322/1.

queen of Caria: Ada was sister of Mausolus of Halicarnassus. She had ruled Caria briefly from 344 to 340 before being overthrown by her younger brother Pixodarus (on whom see chapter 10). She was reinstated by Alexander.

plenty of time: this questionable explanation of Alexander's reputation for heavy drinking stems from Aristobulus: see Arrian, *Anabasis* 7.29.4. Despite this, the king's drinking is a recurring feature of the Life: chapters 4, 50, 67, 75.

29 *Royal Diary*: see further chapter 76.

children, and wives: after the digression on Alexander's self-control, Plutarch returns to the aftermath of his victory at Issus in November 333.

30 *Tyre*: the Phoenician island city of Tyre was an important Persian naval

base with a reputation for being impregnable. Nebuchadnezzar's siege of the city in the 6th C. BCE was said to have lasted thirteen years. Alexander's siege was rather shorter and was over by August 332. That he could take a city such as Tyre sent a strong message to any other cities thinking of resisting him.

30 *spoke his name*: the Greeks identified Heracles with Melqart, the protecting deity of the city of Tyre. Alexander's request that he be allowed into the city to sacrifice to the god was turned down by the Tyrians: Arrian, *Anabasis* 2.16.7

'Tyre will be yours': splitting the Greek word for satyr, '*sa-tyros*', 'your Tyre'. Satyrs were half-man and half-goat and often associated with sources of water, such as fountains, springs, and wells.

Phoenix: for comparison between Lysimachus and Phoenix, see chapter 5. Phoenix was a warrior himself, and although old went with Achilles to Troy.

31 *Gaza*: an important mercantile city that lay at the head of the route followed by the incense caravans from Arabia. The siege lasted from September to October 332.

Cleopatra: Alexander's sister, daughter of Philip and Olympias.

32 *safe keeping*: see chapter 8.

name men give it: Homer, *Odyssey* 4.354–5. The city that Alexander founded here was Alexandria. It was developed by the Ptolemies as their capital city and royal residence, continuing as one of the most important cities in the Mediterranean until late antiquity. For the varying stories about its foundation, see A. Erskine, 'Alexandria in the Alexandrian Imagination', in S. Ager and R. Faber (eds.), *Belonging and Isolation in the Hellenistic World* (Toronto, 2013), 169–83.

Ammon: the oracle of Ammon (the Egyptian Amun-Re) was south-west of Alexandria at the Siwa oasis in the Libyan Desert in western Egypt. The oracle was long known to the Greeks, who identified Ammon with Zeus. According to Arrian (*Anabasis* 3.3) Alexander was imitating his ancestors Heracles and Perseus. Alexander's journey there covered some 550 km (340 miles).

33 *killed them*: the story of the Persian king Cambyses' failed attempt to destroy the sanctuary in the late 6th C. BCE is told by Herodotus (3.25–6).

its journey: for Callisthenes of Olynthus, see chapters 52–5. Aristobulus apparently had the expedition guided by crows, while Ptolemy claimed that snakes showed the way: Arrian, *Anabasis* 3.3.5–6.

god was his father: traditionally the pharaoh, the ruler of Egypt, was considered to be the son of Amun-Re. The identification between Ammon and Zeus certainly would have enabled Alexander's claim that he was son of Zeus, although some scholars argue that he was already making this claim before he went to Siwa.

34 *Psammon*: nothing is known of him, although his name is suspiciously like Ammon.

blessed gods: Homer, *Iliad* 5.340, when Aphrodite is wounded by Diomedes at Troy.

Hephaestion: one of Alexander's closest friends, whose death affected him deeply (chapter 72). He was also one of the seven Bodyguards (on whom see note to p. 46).

35 *pleasure or satisfaction*: Anaxarchus was a philosopher from Abdera who accompanied Alexander and is said to have become very wealthy as a result. This story is attributed to Satyrus by Athenaeus (6.250 f.). Another version of the story has only a single satrap's head; after falling out with Nicocreon of Cyprus, Anaxarchus told Alexander that the only thing lacking at his banquet was a satrap's head, by which he meant the head of Nicocreon (Diogenes Laertius, *Lives of the Philosophers* 9.58). For his response to the murder of Cleitus, see chapter 52.

from Egypt: spring 331.

alliance with him: this delegation most likely took place in the previous year, when Alexander was at Tyre, as Arrian (*Anabasis* 2.25) reports. The next chapter opens with the death of Darius' wife Stateira in childbirth, which, assuming Darius was the father, would have occurred in 332.

marching against him: this is the conclusion to a letter in which Alexander says that anything that Darius could offer him (money, land, daughter) already belongs to him (Arrian, *Anabasis* 25).

36 *Lord Oromazes*: Plutarch's way of referring to Ahuramazda, the protecting god of the Persian king; see also *Artaxerxes* 29. Thus in the 5th-C. Bisitun inscription Darius I wrote: 'By the favour of Ahuramazda I am king; Ahuramazda bestowed the kingdom upon me.'

37 *Cyrus*: Cyrus the Great founded the Persian empire and ruled it from 559 to 530.

a million men: Darius' army was larger than Alexander's, but not on this scale. Its actual size is hard to estimate. Arrian, *Anabasis* 3.8.6 broadly agrees with Plutarch, but Q. Curtius Rufus (4.12.13) is more restrained, with 200,000 infantry and 45,000 cavalry.

Persian clothing: thus foreshadowing the real Alexander's adoption of Persian dress (chapter 45).

38 *its upkeep*: Strabo 16.1.3 says the king was Darius I.

eclipse: since this took place on 20 September 331, the battle of Gaugamela should be dated to 1 October. It was fought in what is now northern Iraq.

40 *wear into battle*: the description of his armour helps to set the heroic character of the battle; it can be compared to Homer's description of the arming of Achilles in *Iliad* 18 and vase paintings that show Achilles and Hector as they prepare to depart for battle.

where Darius was: this scene in which Alexander and Darius are eye to eye in the midst of the battle recalls the Alexander mosaic found in the House of the Faun at Pompeii, although it is not known whether that mosaic represents Issus or Gaugamela.

41 *given birth*: these horses may have been considered faster as they were keen to get back to their offspring; compare Herodotus 3.105 on female camels.

Plataean territory: the site of the battle of Plataea fought in 479, the decisive land battle of the Second Persian War. Alexander is presenting his campaign as revenge for the Persian Wars, a justification already voiced by his father Philip when he established the League of Corinth (Diodorus 16.89); see S. Wallace, 'The Significance of Plataia for Greek *Eleutheria* in the Early Hellenistic Period', in A. Erskine and L. Llewellyn-Jones (eds.), *Creating a Hellenistic World* (Swansea, 2011), 147–76. Plataea had been destroyed by the Thebans in 373 (Pausanias 9.1.5–8, Diodorus 15.46.6), following an earlier destruction at the same hands during the Peloponnesian War.

his part in the battle: although only briefly mentioned by Herodotus (8.47), Phayllus' reputation continued in antiquity. Pausanias records a statue of him at Delphi and summarizes his achievements (10.9.1–2).

42 *Adiabene*: the reading in the manuscripts is Ecbatana, but that is in Media, not Babylonia, and Alexander did not reach it until the following year. For the presence of naphtha in Babylonia, see Strabo 16.1.15–16, citing Posidonius. The extended discussion of naphtha here and Alexander's fascination with it may be intended to reflect Alexander's own fiery, impulsive, and destructive nature; see also chapter 4 and in chapter 63 the comparison of Alexander in battle to 'a flash of flame'; see further D. Sansome, 'Plutarch, Alexander and the Discovery of Naphtha', *Greek, Roman, and Byzantine Studies*, 21 (1980), 63–74.

in the tragedy: reported graphically in the messenger's speech of Euripides, *Medea* 1136–1230.

43 *took control of Susa*: Alexander entered the administrative centre of the Persian empire in December 331.

purple cloth from Hermione: purple dye was produced from several kinds of marine molluscs: see A. Marzano, *Harvesting the Sea: The Exploitation of Marine Resources in the Roman Mediterranean* (Oxford, 2013), ch. 5. There were a number of important centres of production in the Peloponnese, including the small coastal city of Hermione in the Argolid. Five thousand talents of cloth was an enormous amount, estimated at 130 metric tonnes or 143 tons.

Dinon: author of a Persian history, *Persica*, cited a number of times by Plutarch in his *Artaxerxes*. He is often dated to the early 330s, but evidence that his son Cleitarchus was tutor to Ptolemy IV Philopator (*c.*244–204) suggests a later date.

refuge there: Persis, roughly equivalent to the modern province of Fars in Iran, was the heartland of the Achaemenid dynasty.

44 *the palace*: of Persepolis, located in Persis to the north-east of modern Shiraz; extensive remains survive today. For an impressive reconstruction of some of the buildings visit <http://www.persepolis3d.com>. Plutarch does not actually mention the palace by name, but it is clear from the story of Thais and the burning of the palace that follows that it is the Persepolis palace that he has in mind. Alexander spent the early months of 330 there. He also sacked the nearby treasury city of Pasargadae: Arrian, *Anabasis* 3.18.

became king: Ptolemy (see chapter 10) became king of Egypt; according to Athenaeus 13.576de, Thais married Ptolemy and had three children by him.

destroyed Athens by fire: in 480 during the Persian Wars (Herodotus 8.50–5).

45 *a premeditated act*: Arrian (*Anabasis* 3.18.11–12), who used Ptolemy as a source, gives a much less dramatic account of the destruction of Persepolis with no mention of Thais. Here is another of those cases where Parmenio and Alexander disagree about what to do (see note to p. 21). Parmenio is against burning it (Why destroy what is yours? Destroying it would give the impression to the people of Asia that you are not intending to stay), but Alexander saw it as means of punishing the Persians (see note to p. 41).

fire extinguished: the story parallels the digression on naphtha, in which on impulse a boy is set on fire and then hurriedly put out.

very generous: the next four chapters focus on Alexander's generosity and concern for others.

show it off to him: Ariston was commander of the Paeonian cavalry; according to Q. Curtius Rufus 4.9.24–5 the head belonged to the Persian Satropates, whom Ariston had killed in battle.

rejected his gifts: see further *Phocion* 18.

Proteas: he had quite a reputation as drinking-partner of Alexander's (see Athenaeus 4.129a) and one story even attributes Alexander's death to a drinking contest with Proteas (Athenaeus 10.434a–b). He was a nephew of Cleitus the Black, whom Alexander murdered at a drinking-party: chapters 50–1.

46 *Friends and Bodyguards*: on Friends, see note to p. 20; the Bodyguards (*sōmatophylakes*) were an elite group of seven nobles who were given this title by the king. Arrian, *Anabasis* 6.28.4, lists the seven in 325 when their number was increased to eight.

Mazaeus: one of Darius' satraps, he played an important role in the resistance to Alexander, commanding the cavalry at Gaugamela. Subsequently he surrendered Babylon to Alexander and was then appointed by Alexander as satrap of Babylon, a step that marked a new approach to the government of the empire. Mazaeus held the position until his death in 428. His son Antibelus joined Alexander after the overthrow of Darius by Bessus in 330 (Arrian, *Anabasis* 3.21.1), two other sons later enrolled in the Companion cavalry (Arrian, *Anabasis* 7.6.4).

46 *Bagoas' residence*: Bagoas had been a powerful eunuch at the Persian court.

Antipater: see Biographies of Prominent Figures.

gently and reasonably: for Hagnon see chapter 22, Leonnatus chapter 21, and Philotas chapter 10 with their respective notes. A hunting net of 100 stades would have been around 18 km (11 miles).

47 *coming to help*: Alexander's killing of the lion evoked the lion-slaying activities of his ancestor Heracles, who famously wore a lion-scalp headdress. The base of Craterus' monument at Delphi survives, accompanied by a verse inscription. In contrast to Plutarch, the verse presents Craterus as saving Alexander's life by killing the lion himself. Lion-killing was not restricted to Alexander and Craterus: see also the boasts of Lysimachus at *Demetrius* 27, with the note. For Craterus, see Biographies of Prominent Figures; for Lysippus' sculptures of Alexander, chapter 4; Leochares of Athens was responsible for the statues of Philip II and his family in the Philippeum at Olympia (Pausanias 5.20.10).

Peucestas: a Macedonian noble, probably born in the early 350s. For a while, as satrap of Persis, a moderately influential figure after Alexander's death (*Eumenes* 13–16).

48 *hellebore*: in the wrong dose it could kill.

Harpalus into trouble: in 324, fearing Alexander would punish him for abuse of power, Harpalus fled to Athens (*Demosthenes* 25). Alexander's unwillingness to believe the messengers may suggest that the anecdote refers to Harpalus' first desertion in 333 (Arrian, *Anabasis* 3.6.7).

free-born family: for the same anecdote but with a different protagonist, see Plutarch, *Sayings of Kings and Commanders* 27.21 (*Moralia* 181a) and *On the Fortune or Virtue of Alexander* II.7 (*Moralia* 339c–d).

Seleucus: infantry commander and one of Alexander's Companions, he later founded the Seleucid dynasty. See Biographies of Prominent Figures.

in the sanctuary: the famous sanctuary of Artemis at Ephesus; Megabyzus was the hereditary name of the priests of the sanctuary.

At the time in question: probably May 330. Plutarch here returns to where he broke off the narrative in chapter 38. Bessus was satrap of Bactria and a relative of Darius, thus in the best position of those around Darius to claim the throne for himself, which he did, taking the royal name Artaxerxes: see Arrian, *Anabasis* 3.25.3.

49 *shortage of water*: 3,300 stades was roughly 600 km (365 miles); for a fuller account of the pursuit and its difficulties, see Arrian, *Anabasis* 3.21.

50 *attached to it*: Bessus was probably captured in 329 and executed the following year. Arrian, *Anabasis* 4.7.3–4 reports that his nose and ears were

cut off (making clear his disapproval of Alexander's adoption of a barbarian practice), but has nothing to say about the mode of execution. The treatment of Bessus emphasized his disloyalty to Darius and the illegitimacy of his self-proclaimed kingship, while at the same time presenting Alexander as the true successor, evident both in his actions as Darius' avenger and the respect he showed the body of the king. That Darius himself obtained the throne by dubious means is overlooked, even though it was allegedly one of the charges that Alexander made against Darius earlier in the campaign (Arrian, *Anabasis* 2.14.5).

Exathres: also known as Oxyathres; according to some accounts Alexander handed Bessus over to him for punishment. His daughter married Craterus in the mass wedding at Susa.

Caspian Sea: the Greeks conceived the inhabited world to be surrounded by an outer sea known as the Ocean. Whether individual seas were part of this outer sea or separate inland seas was a matter of debate. Herodotus (1.202–3) had held (in contrast to Hecataeus of Miletus) the Caspian Sea to be an inland sea. Alexander never carried out his plan to explore the Caspian Sea: Arrian, *Anabasis* 7.16.1–4. Lake Maeotis is the Sea of Azov. The four gulfs of the outer sea referred to here are the Caspian Sea, the Mediterranean, the Persian Gulf, and the Red Sea. On the impact of Alexander's campaigns on geographical knowledge, see K. Geus, 'Space and Geography', in A. Erskine (ed.), *A Companion to the Hellenistic World* (Oxford, 2003), 232–45.

doing obeisance before him: the issue of obeisance (*proskynēsis*) would cause considerable resentment among both Macedonians and Greeks, see further chapter 54; the practice was a way of displaying deference to a superior, in this case the king, and the gesture adopted depended on the status of those performing it, a small bow and a blown kiss for those of high rank and prostration for those of low rank. The ritual was viewed very negatively by Greeks, both because Greek envoys would have had to prostrate themselves before the Persian king and because for Greeks prostration was something that was done before a god (Herodotus 7.136, see also Chilonis doing obeisance before an altar at *Agis and Cleomenes* 18). The whole historiographical tradition about the introduction of *proskynēsis* at Alexander's court is subjected to a searching and sceptical analysis by H. Bowden, 'On Kissing and Making Up: Court Protocol and Historiography in Alexander the Great's "Experiment with Proskynesis"', *Bulletin of the Institute of Classical Studies*, 56 (2013), 55–77.

than the former: a *kandys* was a Median or Persian coat with long hanging sleeves; a *tiara* was a high conical headdress. Alexander's adoption of elements of Persian dress together with his use of *proskynēsis* may have been prompted by the need to demonstrate to his non-Greek subjects that he was the successor to Darius.

51 *queen of the Amazons*: Alexander's encounter with the Amazon queen, who was keen to have his child, is related by Q. Curtius Rufus 6.5.24–32 and

Diodorus 17.77.1–3; see further E. Baynham, 'Alexander and the Amazons', *Classical Quarterly*, 51 (2001), 115–26.

51 *Lysimachus*: he accompanied Alexander on campaign and was later an important successor king ruling Thrace and various nearby territories; see Biographies of Prominent Figures. He was one of Alexander's seven Bodyguards (on whom see note to p. 46).

Hyrcania: Plutarch is not overly concerned with keeping to Alexander's itinerary and here returns to Hyrcania, which Alexander entered 'with the pick of his fighting force' in chapter 44.

52 *oversee this project*: for the completion of their military education and the resentment they caused among the Macedonian troops, see chapter 71.

policy he was pursuing: Alexander married Rhoxane, daughter of the Bactrian noble Oxyartes, in 427. The marriage is introduced here in the context of blending cultures well before it actually happened, but Plutarch displays little interest in Alexander's prolonged campaigning in the region of Bactria.

53 *companions*: in this case 'companions' refers to the Companion Cavalry that Philotas commanded: see note to p. 20.

54 *third of these sons*: the executions of Philotas and Parmenio occurred in autumn 330 and marked a significant shift in Alexander's relationship with his high command. Scholars debate the guilt of Philotas, but Parmenio's execution would have been a necessary consequence of executing the son, regardless of whether he was implicated in any conspiracy (see also note to p. 21). By 330 Parmenio must have been in his late sixties. Of his two other sons, Nicanor had fallen ill and died during the pursuit of Bessus earlier the same year, while Hector, probably the youngest, had drowned in the Nile a year or so before.

55 *Cleitus too*: not as soon after as Plutarch implies. The execution of Philotas was in 330, while the killing of Cleitus the Black took place in 328, in Maracanda (Samarkand), the main city of Sogdiana. Cleitus had previously saved Alexander's life at the battle of the Granicus (chapter 16), and was promoted to joint commander of the Companion Cavalry with Hephaestion after the death of Philotas.

spirit: spirits (*daimones*) could be associated with individuals and influence their actions for good or ill.

Dioscuri: the twins Castor and Pollux, who play a much larger role in Arrian's account (*Anabasis* 8.4). There Alexander omits to sacrifice to Dionysus and sacrifices to the Dioscuri instead, another reason for Dionysus' anger. Then in the drinking-session that follows comparisons are made between the achievements of the Dioscuri and those of Alexander.

barbarians and enemies: Cleitus' negative representation of those Persians who had joined Alexander's court.

56 *Xenodochus of Cardia and Artemius of Colophon*: nothing further is known of these two Greeks.

Aristonous: the manuscript reading is Aristophanes, but no such Bodyguard is known. Aristonous is known to have been one of Alexander's seven Bodyguards: note to p. 46.

Macedonian: there has been much debate whether this was a dialect of Greek or a distinct language, with scholarly opinion now inclining to the former. Whichever it was, its use by Alexander would have been one of the ways in which he showed his Macedonian soldiers that he was one of them; see also *Eumenes* 14.

What evil customs rule in Greece: from Euripides, *Andromache* 693, where Peleus goes on to complain that, although many fight, the honour of victory goes only to the commander.

57 *three blankets on top of you*: in other words, Anaxarchus had abandoned the thin cloak, that marked out philosophical asceticism, for the indulgence of several blankets.

58 *country of his birth*: Callisthenes' home city Olynthus had been destroyed by Philip II in 348. In contrast to others, therefore, his motives for participating in Alexander's expedition were selfless.

intelligence to himself: quoting a lost play of Euripides.

one's speech: this time the play survives: Euripides, *Bacchae* 267, supposedly written in Macedon.

criminals become respectable: a hexameter verse of unknown origin quoted elsewhere by Plutarch (*Nicias* 11; *Sulla* 39).

braver man than you: Homer, *Iliad* 21.107, spoken by Achilles to Hector, shortly before he kills him, thus implicitly comparing Alexander to the ill-fated Hector rather than his role model Achilles.

59 *act of obeisance*: see note to p. 50.

conspiracy of Hermolaus: known as the Pages' Conspiracy; in 327 a group of young Macedonian nobles who acted as attendants on Alexander were accused of conspiring to kill him, led by Hermolaus, who was said to have a grudge against Alexander for ordering his flogging when he speared a boar ahead of the king (Arrian, *Anabasis* 4.13).

Craterus, Attalus, and Alcetas: at the time they were campaigning together under Craterus' command (see Arrian, *Anabasis* 4.22), a point that might be used to argue for the authenticity of the letter; Alcetas was the brother of Perdiccas.

60 *before the congress*: the general assembly of the League of Corinth, founded by Philip II in 337 as a way of unifying the Greeks under the command of the Macedonian king.

a rare treat: Plutarch has already related Demaratus' comment in chapter 37, in the context of the capture of Persepolis. Here, however, he is contrasted with Callisthenes; both men 'travel up country to Alexander' (for Callisthenes see chapter 53), but their reactions to Alexander taking the place of the Persian king are very different, and so in consequence is

Alexander's treatment of them, one meeting a shabby and louse-ridden death, the other honoured by a magnificent funeral. Eighty cubits was about 120 feet or 35 metres.

60 *into India*: late spring 327; Q. Curtius Rufus 6.6.14–16 places the booty-burning incident a few years earlier, in 330.

61 *refused to stay*: a symptom perhaps of a broader unhappiness about being stationed so far from Macedon and Greece, as shown, for example, by the refusal of Alexander's soldiers to march on into India (chapter 62; Arrian, *Anabasis* 5.27.5–6) and by the revolt after Alexander's death of the Greek mercenaries settled in Bactria (Diodorus 18.7). Neither Menander nor Orsodates are otherwise known.

impotent man: Alexander was succeeded by his half-brother Arrhidaeus who was considered incapable and, once he was born, by his infant son Alexander IV; see further the note to *Eumenes* 3.

relief of their weariness: for the phrase see Plato, *Menexenus* 238a, and Dionysius of Halicarnassus, *On the Style of Demosthenes* 29, on Athena's gift of the olive.

62 *insecure at the top*: Sisimithres is to be identified with the Chorienes of Arrian, *Anabasis* 4.21, where there is a full account of the capture of the 'Rock of Chorienes' in 327. Chorienes is perhaps the chieftain's official title. According to Arrian, he surrenders, overawed by the scale and effectiveness of Alexander's assault on this seemingly impregnable position. Far from thinking him a coward, however, Alexander reinstates him as commander of the stronghold.

Alexander: killed during the assault on Aornus on the Indus river in the winter of 327/6, his death is the subject of a highly stylized account in Q. Curtius Rufus (8.11.15–16) that draws on Virgil.

Nysa: an Indian city captured in 327, said to have been founded by Dionysus: Arrian, *Anabasis* 5.1–2.

Taxiles' kingdom in India: Taxiles was the ruler of Taxila, a city situated some 30 km (or 20 miles) north-west of the Pakistani capital of Islamabad. For the excavations, see J. Marshall, *Taxila: An Illustrated Account of Archaeological Excavation* (Cambridge, 1951). Alexander crossed the Indus in early 326.

63 *annihilated them all*: during the siege of Massaga in the Swat Valley in 327: see also Diodorus 17.84. Arrian (*Anabasis* 4.27.3–4) is a dissenting voice in excusing Alexander's behaviour here and blaming the mercenaries.

great many of them too: these were the Brahmans who acted as advisers to Indian rulers; see also Arrian, *Anabasis* 1.17.1–2 on the revolt of Musicanus. In Indian culture Brahmans had a special status and were exempt from capital punishment, making Alexander's execution of them particularly shocking to Indians.

battle against Porus: fought in summer 326 against Porus, Indian ruler of the region to the east of the river Hydaspes (Jhelum) in north-west

Pakistan. Although Plutarch cites Alexander's letters for his account of the battle, their authenticity has often been questioned by scholars.

65 *Potamon of Lesbos*: a rhetorician from Mytilene (late 1st C. BCE/early 1st C. CE) who wrote a lost work on Alexander.

Ganges as well: the refusal of Alexander's men to continue is often known as the mutiny at the Hyphasis, after the river where this took place (the modern Beas). Other sources report that Alexander was twelve days' march from the Ganges (Diodorus 17.93.1–2; Q. Curtius Rufus 9.2.1–3). In reality the Ganges river itself is about 400 km (250 miles) from the Beas.

Sandrocottus: as the Mauryan ruler Chandragupta was known to the Greeks. Between the late 320s and the end of the century he created an Indian empire for himself. His agreement with Seleucus occurred in 305.

altars to the gods: if our other sources are to believed, these were also on a grand scale, twelve altars around 22.5 metres (75 ft) high: Arrian, *Anabasis* 5.29.1, Diodorus 17.95.

66 *iniquity and low birth*: this report of Chandragupta's views may come from the *Indica* of Megasthenes, a Greek who spent time at his court.

outer sea: Alexander set off down the Indus to the Indian Ocean in November 326. For the outer sea, see note to p. 50.

flash of flame: see note to p. 42.

67 *pulled through*: removing an arrow without leaving the head was not a simple task, as the example of Alexander shows; see C. F. Salazar, *The Treatment of War Wounds in Graeco-Roman Antiquity* (Leiden, 2000).

gymnosophists: as the name implies, these were philosophers or wise men who went around naked. It is of Greek coinage, and it may be a mistake to try to match the term up with a particular group of Indian wise men. Certainly there seems no precision in Plutarch's use of it. The exchange between Alexander and the gymnosophists can be located within a tradition of stories that place kings and wise men in dialogue with each other (although in this case ten wise men), for example, Alexander's meeting with Diogenes in chapter 14 or Solon's with Croesus. See R. Stoneman, 'Naked Philosophers: The Brahmans in the Alexander Historians and the Alexander Romance', *Journal of Hellenic Studies*, 115 (1995), 99–114.

Sabbas' rebellion: Sabbas (also known as Sambus) was an Indian ruler whom Alexander had appointed as a satrap; for the rebellion, see Arrian, *Anabasis* 6.16.

68 *in too much awe of convention*: here the gymnosophists come across as more Cynic than the Cynics, both in their rejection of convention and in their ascetic lifestyle, a characterization that surely owes much to the Cynic Onesicritus himself.

seven months: arriving at the Indian Ocean in July 325.

Nearchus: Nearchus' account of the voyage formed the basis of the second half of Arrian's *Indica*.

68 *gone worse for him*: the crossing of the Gedrosian desert (the modern Makran) took place in roughly October 325; Plutarch's casualty figures are exaggerated and the march through it, while certainly challenging, may not have been the disaster that the sources present (thus A. B. Bosworth, *Alexander and the East* (Cambridge, 1996), 166–85). Alexander may have been motivated by a desire to do what the Persian king Cyrus the Great had failed to do: Arrian, *Anabasis* 6.24.3.

69 *revel*: the story of this Bacchic procession in emulation of Dionysus' return after his conquest of India is rejected by Arrian, *Anabasis* 6.28.1–3.

palace of Gedrosia: this surely should be the palace of Carmania.

70 *Thapsacus*: a city on the Euphrates; for Alexander's naval preparations, see further Arrian, *Anabasis* 6.19.

ruled by a woman: Epirus had in fact been ruled by Olympias since her brother died in 331.

Ochus: Artaxerxes III Ochus ruled for about twenty years, until his death in 338, when he was succeeded by Darius III.

Poulomachus: Cyrus' tomb was in Pasargadae, a city he had founded. The looting of the tomb was also attributed to the local satrap Orxines (Q. Curtius Rufus 10.1.30–5; Strabo 15.3.7).

71 *seeing the king in Babylon*: Calanus thus predicts Alexander's death, but unlike Arrian (*Anabasis* 7.18.6), Plutarch leaves it up to the reader to see this.

'*The Tomb of the Indian*': this holy man's self-immolation is also told by Strabo 15.1.73 (who records the inscription on the tomb) and Dio 54.9. It occurred during an embassy to Augustus while the latter was in Greece in 20 BCE, and appears to have taken place in front of him.

before dying: Promachus' death after drinking 13 litres of undiluted wine contrasts with that of Calanus immediately before. Greeks (but not necessarily Macedonians) usually drank wine diluted. For Macedonian drinking culture, see E. Borza, 'The Symposium at Alexander's Court', *Ancient Macedonia*, 3 (1983), 45–55.

mass marriage of his Companions: in April 324; around ninety marriages took place: see Arrian, *Anabasis* 7.4, and Chares cited in Athenaeus 12.538b. The most significant of these in the long term was probably that of Seleucus to Apama, which formed the basis of the Seleucid dynasty and meant that the dynasty joined both traditions (*Demetrius* 31). They also included Artonis, the wife of Eumenes (*Eumenes* 1).

72 *siege of Perinthus*: in 340/39; see *Demosthenes* 17.

trained and educated: see chapter 47.

73 *speaking kindly to them*: this mutiny occurred at Opis in 324 and was followed by a huge reconciliation feast. As at the Hyphasis two years before, Alexander secluded himself in his tent, this time with more success. Plutarch omits to mention that Alexander executed thirteen men who were at the forefront of the discontent (Arrian, *Anabasis* 7.8).

Ecbatana in Media: in early autumn 324.

grief at his death: Alexander's grief may be intended to evoke that of Achilles over Patroclus in Homer's *Iliad*, book 23. For Alexander's identification with Achilles, see chapter 15.

sacrificial rituals in his honour: hero cult could give a dead mortal an almost divine status, especially if backed by the authority of an oracle. Cult tended to be local and focused around a tomb.

Cossaeans: a tribe in the Zagros Mountains, whose reputation for brigandage may have been used as a justification for Alexander's brutal treatment of them: see Arrian, *Anabasis* 7.15.

Stasicrates: the architect of the proposed Athos sculpture is variously named elsewhere as Deinocrates, Diocles, and Cheirocrates.

74 *set out for Babylon*: early 323. From this point on Plutarch builds up to Alexander's death with mounting portents. The Chaldaeans were priests of Bel at Babylon, with a reputation for prophecy.

without saying a word: his name, Dionysius, hints at the influence of the god Dionysus, whose enduring anger against Alexander over the destruction of Thebes was noted in chapter 13. If there is any truth to the story, it may have its origins in a 'substitute king' ritual by which portents are defused by putting a substitute king in place and then executing him, a practice for which prisoners were very useful.

Antipater and his sons: Craterus had recently been sent to Macedon to take Antipater's place as governor of Macedon, but Alexander's death meant that the change of governor never occurred.

75 *for him to recover*: some might feel that Cassander's anxiety was prompted by the knowledge that he had directly or indirectly killed so many of Alexander's relatives, including his mother Olympias, his wife Rhoxane, and his children Alexander and Heracles, in an effort to ensure the security of his position as ruler of Macedon. See Biographies of Prominent Figures.

76 *great drama*: Medeius was a Thessalian from Larisa. Plutarch here rejects the story that Alexander died after downing a huge goblet of undiluted wine (thus Diodorus 17.117).

thirtieth of Daisios: the month of Daisios equates to May/June. Disagreement about Alexander's death, however, extends even to the date, with the Royal Diary in the next chapter giving it as 28 Daisios. The date is usually taken to be 10/11 June 323 on the basis of Babylonian astronomical records.

Royal Diary: the authenticity of the Royal Diary has been questioned. Apart from a banal reference to Alexander's hunting (chapter 23), which might well have been from the days leading up to his illness, it is cited only for his death, both by Plutarch and Arrian (*Anabasis* 7.25–6). This has led some to argue that it was concocted by Alexander's officers after his death to prevent conspiracy theories circulating.

Peithon: one of Alexander's Bodyguards (on whom see note to p. 46).

76 *sanctuary of Sarapis*: both Plutarch and Arrian mention the sanctuary of Sarapis, which would be consistent with the god's earlier role in supposedly releasing Dionysius to sit on the king's throne. The passage, however, presents a problem, because it places Sarapis in Babylon some years before the accepted date for the initial establishment of his cult in Egypt by Ptolemy I. As a result it has been suggested that the Babylonian sanctuary was that of Oserapis/Osiris-Apis, an earlier native Egyptian version of Sarapis.

77 *administered the poison*: as royal cupbearer, son of Antipater and lover of Medeius, the host of Alexander's final drinking-party, Iolas was triply implicated in any suspected poisoning. Cassander would get his revenge by orchestrating Olympias' execution.

through everything else: Nonacris was an Arcadian town in the Peloponnese where the waters of the Styx, the river of the Underworld, were said to drip from a rock; hence the association of its waters with death. Plutarch may dismiss the story, but for him its appeal would lie in the contrast between the fiery Alexander and the icy coldness of the water that would kill him.

quarrelling among themselves: see *Eumenes* 3, with note.

without showing any signs of decay: Q. Curtius Rufus (10.10.9–13) reports that it lay for seven days in the heat without decaying. The Egyptian and Chaldaean embalmers 'at first did not dare to touch him, almost as if he were still breathing. Then, after they had prayed that it might be right and proper for mortals to handle a god, they treated the body.' See further A. Erskine, 'Life after Death: Alexandria and the Body of Alexander', *Greece and Rome*, 49 (2002), 163–79.

poisoned by Olympias: this rather abrupt end has led some to think that the Life is incomplete. Rhoxane's pregnancy and the brief account of Arrhidaeus suggest that Plutarch is moving in the direction of the succession and the joint kingship of Alexander IV and Philip Arrhidaeus, but then the Life stops without Alexander IV even being born.

DEMOSTHENES

82 *Sosius Senecio*: Q. Sosius Senecio, Roman consul of 99 and 107 CE, is also addressed in the opening sentences of *Dion* and *Theseus*, and so is usually taken to be the dedicatee of the *Parallel Lives* as a whole.

eyesore afflicting Piraeus: so said Pericles at a time of war with Aegina in the mid-5th C., as Plutarch himself recorded at *Pericles* 8.

the city where I live is small: Plutarch came from the Boeotian city of Chaeronea.

83 *fifth book of parallel Lives*: only occasionally does Plutarch indicate the order in which he wrote the Lives; elsewhere he tells us that the Pericles/Fabius pairing was the tenth book (*Pericles* 2) and Dion/Brutus the twelfth (*Dion* 2).

Ion says: Ion of Chios, a very versatile Greek writer of the 5th C. BCE, whose work ranged from tragedies to philosophy.

the ever-excessive Caecilius: Caecilius of Caleacte was a Greek literary critic of the late 1st C. BCE whose views were attacked in Longinus' *On the Sublime*.

'*Know thyself*': this was included among several sayings inscribed on the temple of Apollo at Delphi. Plutarch elsewhere sees it as having a major influence on Socrates' thinking (*Against Colotes* 20).

84 *Theopompus*: a 4th-C. Greek historian from Chios, author of the now-lost *Philippic History*, the fifty-eight books of which, despite its title, ranged far more widely than Philip II of Macedon.

deny it as a slur: in his *Against Ctesiphon* (171–2) the contemporary orator Aeschines claimed that Demosthenes' maternal grandfather Gylon of Cerameis had gone into exile after betraying Nymphaeum, an Athenian-held city in the Crimea. In exile, said Aeschines, he had married a Scythian woman. Such an accusation would have called into question not only Demosthenes' Athenianness but also, by virtue of a barbarian grandmother, his Greekness. For Aeschines, see the introduction to this Life.

guardians: Demosthenes had three guardians, Aphobus, Demophon, and Therippides.

'*Batalus*': Aeschines has two versions of the origin of this nickname—that it was given to Demosthenes as an infant by his nurse (*Against Timarchus* 126), and that he was called it by other boys while growing up (*On the False Embassy* 99). Demosthenes, however, attributes it to Aeschines (*On the Crown* 180).

Antiphanes: a 4th-C. comic poet, who mocks Demosthenes in chapter 9.

Oropus: Callistratus of Aphidna, a prominent Athenian politician of the first half of the 4th C., was somehow implicated in the loss of Oropus, a town on the border between Attica and Boeotia, which was occupied by the Thebans in 366/5. Later he spent time in exile, but he was executed in the mid-350s after returning to Athens.

got his way: the scholarly consensus is that Demosthenes was born in 384, although this story would suggest that he still had not reached eighteen by the time of the trial, which must have been later than 366/5.

85 *Isaeus as his rhetoric teacher*: Isaeus was an Athenian speech-writer of the first half of the 4th C., whose eleven surviving speeches all deal with issues of inheritance, a topic of particular interest to Demosthenes as he set about prosecuting his guardians.

Isocrates: an influential teacher of rhetoric (436–338), many of whose works survive today.

Hermippus: a 3rd-C. BCE biographer from Smyrna, cited several times in *Demosthenes* (13, 28, and 30). The sources Hermippus is said to have referred to are obscure. Ctesibius wrote a work *On Philosophy* (pseudo-Plutarch, *Lives of the Ten Orators*, *Moralia* 844c); he is perhaps to be identified with the cynic philosopher Ctesibius of Chalcis, known to have spent time at the court of Antigonus Gonatas; less plausibly with the Alexandrian inventor or the famously long-lived historian. This Callias of Syracuse is surely too early to be identical with the historian of the Syracusan tyrant Agathocles at the end of the 4th C.

85 *Alcidamas*: a 4th-C. rhetorician and writer from Asia Minor, who taught in Athens.

to prosecute them: Demosthenes brought the first prosecution in 364/3. Five of these prosecution speeches survive, Orations 27–9 against his guardian Aphobus and 30–1 against Aphobus' brother-in-law Onetor. For these speeches, see D. M. MacDowell, *Demosthenes: Speeches 27–38* (Austin, Tex., 2004).

failure would bring real danger: alluding to Thucydides 1.18.3.

champion dolikhos-runner: the *dolikhos* was a long-distance running race. Laomedon is otherwise unknown.

86 *struggles ahead*: Plutarch tells a variant of this story in *Whether an Old Man Should Engage in Public Affairs* 23 (*Moralia* 795d). For a Periclean influence on Demosthenes, see chapter 9 of this Life. Eunomus has been identified with various men of the same name, a general, an ambassador, and a pupil of Isocrates, who may all be a single person, but there is no certainty.

Satyrus the actor: several actors of this name are known in the 4th C.

train his voice: for further techniques allegedly used by Demosthenes, see chapter 11 and the pseudo-Plutarchan *Lives of the Ten Orators* (*Moralia* 844c–f).

87 *Pytheas*: one of those who prosecuted Demosthenes in 324 for taking bribes from Harpalus: *Lives of the Ten Orators* (*Moralia* 846c); see also *Phocion* 21.

Demades: see Biographies of Prominent Figures. For Demades' skill at impromptu speaking, see chapter 10. For a negative portrayal of Demades, see *Phocion*.

making speeches: Aeschines, *Against Ctesiphon* 152, contrasting Demosthenes' cowardice in action with his boldness in delivering the funeral eulogy for those who died at the battle of Chaeronea in 338, despite having been responsible for their deaths.

anti-Athenian invective: this speech is usually placed in 343, when Python is said to have come to Athens as a representative of Philip II, although an altercation between the two men is also reported before Chaeronea at a meeting of the Boeotian assembly (Diodorus 16.85); the speech is referred to by Demosthenes himself in *On the Crown* 136.

Lamachus of Smyrna: this encounter may have taken place at the Olympic

Games of 324, the occasion of the announcement of Alexander's decree for the return of exiles. Philip had destroyed Olynthus in 348 and Alexander destroyed Thebes in 335.

88 *Eratosthenes*: Eratosthenes of Cyrene (276–194 BCE) was an Alexandrian scholar and polymath.

Demetrius of Phalerum: Athenian politician who went into exile in Alexandria after being overthrown in 307: see further *Phocion* 35 and 38 with notes. His extensive writings (around fifty-five titles are known) included works on rhetoric, Athenian politics, and Fortune. The oath mentioned here was also mocked by the comic poets: *Lives of the Ten Orators* (*Moralia* 845b). Also cited in chapter 14.

take over: also quoted in Athenaeus 6.223d–e, who gives the preceding line.

on Halonnesos: Demosthenes' speech was about the Athenian recovery of the north Aegean island of Halonnesos, which had been occupied by Philip; his wording about 'taking the island' was picked up by Aeschines, *Against Ctesiphon* 83. A speech entitled *On Halonnesos* does survive among the works of Demosthenes, but is usually now attributed to his contemporary Hegesippus; the misattribution was perhaps caused by the use of similar phrasing to this in section 5 of the speech.

Ariston of Chios: Ariston was a 3rd-C. Stoic philosopher; Theophrastus was a leading Peripatetic philosopher (*c.*370–288), now known especially for his work on botany, but his extensive writings also covered rhetoric.

Polyeuctus of Sphettus: one of the anti-Macedonian politicians demanded by Alexander after the destruction of Thebes (chapter 23); mocked by Phocion for being overweight (*Phocion* 9).

89 *many a fine phrase*: these two comparisons with Phocion also appear in that Life, chapter 5.

Aesion: a contemporary of Demosthenes, said to have been a fellow student with him in literary studies (*Suda*, s.v. Demosthenes); this passage is often taken as evidence that copies of Demosthenes' speeches were circulated in his lifetime.

90 *the sow teaching Athena*: Festus' Lexicon explains that 'this is a proverb where one person teaches another about a subject of which he [the teacher] is ignorant'.

the war: the Phocian War, more commonly known as the Third Sacred War, began in 356 and ended in 346. Athens backed Phocis while its opponents Thebes and Thessaly won the support of Philip of Macedon, hence Demosthenes' *First Philippic* delivered in 351, following Philip's decisive victory at the battle of the Crocus Field in 352.

prosecution of Meidias: Demosthenes' speech prosecuting Meidias for assaulting him in the Dionysia in 348 survives, although it may never have been delivered. In it (§154) he gives his age as thirty-two, most likely an understatement if the usually accepted date of birth of 384 is correct.

90 *kind of heart*: Homer, *Iliad* 20.467, said of Achilles.

91 *Melanopus*: on one occasion (Aristotle, *Rhetoric* 1.14, 1374b) he was prosecuted by Callistratus (on whom see chapter 5), on another, in 371, he went to Sparta on an embassy backed by Callistratus (Xenophon, *Hellenica* 6.3.2).

Nicodemus of Messene: hardly anything is known of this man. His change of allegiance from the Macedonian ruler Cassander to Demetrius the Besieger is likely to have taken place around the time when Demetrius set up the Hellenic League in 302 (*Demetrius* 25).

Panaetius: a 2nd-C. BCE Stoic philosopher from Rhodes.

On the Exemptions: speech 20, *Against Leptines*. This speech opposed Leptines' law preventing hereditary honours, which would have benefited Ctesippus as the son of the great general Chabrias; see *Phocion* 7.

Moerocles, Polyeuctus, and Hypereides: all anti-Macedonian politicians who appear in various lists of those demanded by Alexander: see chapter 23 and Arrian, *Anabasis* 1.10.

Cimon, Thucydides, and Pericles: 5th-C. Athenian politicians; Cimon and Pericles were the subjects of Lives by Plutarch (included in Oxford World's Classics *Greek Lives*). Thucydides was the son of Melesias, and is to be distinguished from the historian.

Ephialtes, Aristeides, and Cimon: 5th-C. Athenian politicians, the latter two being subjects of Lives by Plutarch; their incorruptibility is mentioned in *Cimon* 10; Ephialtes, a radical democrat and much less well known, was not otherwise admired by Plutarch (*Pericles* 7, 10).

Susa and Ecbatana: Persian cities; on the gold, see further chapter 20.

92 *Antiphon affair*: the incident is referred to in Demosthenes, *On the Crown* 132–3. The Areopagus Council tried a limited range of offences including deliberate murder and arson.

Theoris: the trial of a Lemnian sorceress of this name is mentioned in Demosthenes, *Against Aristogeiton* 79–80.

Apollodorus: the son of the banker Pasion, an ex-slave. His prosecution of Timotheus for debts to his father occurred in the late 360s. His father's bank was again the subject of his litigation against Phormio and subsequently Stephanus about a decade later. Plutarch treats all these speeches as written by Demosthenes and they appear among the Demosthenic corpus (nos. 45, 46, 49), but scholars have attributed some or all of them to Apollodorus himself.

cutlery shop: perhaps an allusion to the knife-making business of Demosthenes' father (chapter 4).

twenty-seven or twenty-eight years old: one manuscript gives his age as thirty-two or thirty-three years old.

On the Exemptions: see note to p. 91.

93 *Demetrius of Magnesia*: writer in the 1st C. BCE, who dedicated his *On Concord* to Cicero's friend Atticus.

Idomeneus: Idomeneus of Lampsacus was a late 4th/early 3rd-C. biographer and politician; he wrote a book on Athenian demagogues, the fragments of which suggest a work devoted to gathering anything bad that could be said about politicians.

came to trial: this dispute between Aeschines and Demosthenes was over their respective roles in the negotiations with Philip that led to the Peace of Philocrates in 346. The speeches on the embassy are Demosthenes 19 and Aeschines 2, dating from 343. The speeches *On the Crown* were delivered in 330 (see chapter 24).

ambassadorial commission: this was the second of two Athenian embassies in 346 (see previous note).

Philocrates: Athenian politician after whom the peace of 346 was named.

drove out the Macedonians: the large island of Euboea stretched down the east coast of the Greek mainland. In 341, in alliance with Callias, tyrant of the Euboean city of Chalcis, the Athenians overthrew the Macedonian-backed tyrannies of his neighbours Philistides of Oreus and Cleitarchus of Eretria.

Byzantium and Perinthus: strategically important cities on the Sea of Marmara, the former at the mouth of the Bosporus, the latter about halfway along its northern shore. An Athenian expedition went to defend them from Philip in 340. Both cities had originally broken away from Athens as a result of the Social War of 357–355, fought by Athens against disaffected allies at the time of the Second Athenian Confederacy.

94 *Crobylus*: according to the lexicographer Harpocration this was a nickname (meaning 'Topknot', a hairstyle) of the orator Hegesippus.

Phocian War: see note to p. 90.

took possession of Phocis: the capture of the Phocian city of Elatea in 339 gave Philip access to a key route into Boeotia; the stunned reaction in Athens and the address by Demosthenes that followed is described by him in his *On the Crown* 169–80.

as Marsyas informs us: this embassy consisted of members of prominent Macedonian families, including Cassander, son of Antipater, who would later become ruler of Macedon. Two Macedonian historians named Marsyas are known, one from Pella, who may have been a half-brother of Antigonus Monophthalmus, and another later historian from Philippi (consequently known as Marsyas the Younger).

honourable course of action: the alliance between Athens and Thebes took place in 339.

95 *sue for peace*: it is likely to have been in this context that Phocion recommended accepting Philip's peace offer (*Phocion* 16).

Pythia: title of the priestess of the oracle of Apollo at Delphi.

95 *Sibylline Books*: prophetic writings, supposedly the pronouncements of a prophetess known as the Sibyl.

new name as a result: Plutarch is here writing as an inhabitant of Chaeronea, the site of the battle in which Philip defeated the combined Greek forces in 338. He has surprisingly little to say about the battle itself. Plutarch here derives the name of the river Haemon from the Greek for blood, *haima*.

Duris: on Duris see note to p. 20. He was also tyrant of Samos.

96 *reason their touchstone*: Epaminondas, the subject of a lost Life by Plutarch, was a Theban general, who was one of the key figures behind the rise of Thebes earlier in the 4th C. He is said to have ignored omens before his decisive victory over Sparta at Leuctra in 371 (Diodorus 15.52). According to Plutarch (*Pericles* 6), Pericles, influenced by the rationalist approach of philosophers such as Anaxagoras, was sceptical about omens, but there is no obvious case of his ignoring oracles or omens in a military context. Thucydides (1.118) does report that the Spartans received a favourable oracle from Delphi before the Peloponnesian War at the time of Pericles' leadership.

how much money he had received: the Persian king's support for Demosthenes is likely to have been a response to Philip's designs on Asia Minor. Sardis was captured by Alexander in 334.

97 *Pausanias*: this was the bodyguard of Philip who assassinated the king at the Macedonian city of Aegae in 336: see *Alexander* 10.

hating his own child: see Aeschines, *Against Ctesiphon* 77–8.

98 *the king's generals in Asia*: Plutarch does not say which king this is, but it is most likely to be an attempt to foment revolt among Macedonians ill-disposed to Alexander. Diodorus 17.3 and 17.5 tells of secret Athenian negotiations, including correspondence from Demosthenes, with the Macedonian general Attalus, who had been sent as part of an advance party into Asia by Philip. It is also possible that 'the king' here is the Persian king.

Margites: Margites, a man of singular stupidity, was the hero of a comic epic poem attributed to Homer.

lost their city: Thebes was destroyed by Alexander in 335 (*Alexander* 11).

Demosthenes . . . Charidemus: at *Phocion* 17 Hypereides is also included among those demanded by Alexander. For Idomeneus and Duris, see notes to pp. 93 and 20 respectively.

Aristobulus of Cassandreia: he accompanied Alexander's expedition, and his account was an important source for Arrian's history of Alexander.

99 *Phocion*: an alternative manuscript tradition gives Demades' name in this last sentence. The reading 'Phocion', however, fits better with Plutarch's account at *Phocion* 17, and there is no obvious reason why a scribe should introduce Phocion's name into the text in error.

Spartans were crushed: the rebellion of Agis, with support from Persia, took place in 331, three years after Alexander crossed into Asia.

came to trial: in 336 (Plutarch dates it too early) Ctesiphon had proposed giving a gold crown to Demosthenes for services to the city. Aeschines then began a prosecution against Ctesiphon on the grounds that this was illegal, but the prosecution did not take place until 330. Although it was Ctesiphon who was being prosecuted, the target was Demosthenes, whose celebrated speech *On the Crown* was a defence of his whole career. Both Aeschines' and Demosthenes' speeches survive.

twenty per cent of the votes: prosecutors who failed to get a fifth of the votes were fined 1,000 drachmas and banned from pursuing the same kind of prosecution in the future.

Harpalus: a boyhood friend of Alexander who had served as the king's treasurer in Ecbatana and Babylon. On Alexander's return from the East in 324 Harpalus, fearing punishment for embezzlement and general abuse of his position, fled with a substantial sum of money and 6,000 mercenaries. He had earlier been made a citizen of Athens after making gifts of grain to the city.

100 *man with the cup*: it was customary at a symposium for the man who held the cup to have the right to speak.

Callicles: very likely Callicles the banker, to whom Phocion owed money: *Phocion* 9.

he says: in a letter to the Athenian Council and Assembly (*Letter* 2.17).

101 *the owl, the snake*: both creatures often appearing in representations of Athena. The owl famously appeared on the coinage of Athens (and much later on the Greek 1 euro coin).

Alexander died: in June 323.

Antipater: see Biographies of Prominent Figures.

Callimedon 'the Crab': see *Phocion* 27, with the note there.

throw them out of Greece: for Leosthenes and the Lamian War (323–322), see also *Phocion* 23–6.

Phylarchus: a 3rd-C. BCE historian whose work was used elsewhere by Plutarch, especially in his *Agis and Cleomenes*, but also in the *Pyrrhus* and *Aratus*.

Demon of Paeania: presumably to be identified with the Demon in chapter 23 who was among the Athenians demanded by Alexander.

102 *take him back*: Alcibiades' return to Athens was in *c*.407, during the Peloponnesian War, having been in exile since 415.

Metageitnion . . . Pyanepsion: successive months in roughly late summer and autumn 322. At Crannon in Thessaly the Macedonians under Antipater and Craterus (see Biographies of Prominent Figures) defeated the combined Greek forces. Munychia was a hill overlooking the Piraeus; see further *Phocion* 27 with note.

102 *Lacritus*: a teacher of rhetoric from Phaselis in Asia Minor, the subject of Demosthenes' speech, *Against Lacritus*.

Anaximenes' lectures: a rhetorician and historian from Lampsacus who had spent time at the Macedonian court.

while he was still alive: according to another account reported in *The Lives of the Ten Orators* (*Moralia* 849b), Hypereides bit his tongue off during torture rather than reveal any secrets.

Calauria: the modern island of Poros in the Saronic Gulf.

103 *unburied*: in Sophocles' play *Antigone*, Creon, ruler of Thebes, issues an order that the corpse of Polyneices, Antigone's brother, should be left unburied.

104 *Demochares*: Demosthenes' nephew, who was himself an important Athenian politician (see *Demetrius* 24). He was the proposer of a decree honouring Demosthenes in 280/79 and the author of an extensive history of the period.

Thesmophoria: an annual festival in honour of Demeter that was celebrated by women. The fasting took place on the second day.

Prytaneum: this was a central feature of the Greek city, home to the sacred hearth of Hestia and the meeting- and dining-place of the *prytaneis*, those who chaired the Council and the Assembly. It was a major honour to be given the right to dine here.

105 *Perdiccas*: for an alternative version in which the letter is written to Antigonus Monophthalmus, see *Phocion* 30. In the aftermath of Alexander's death Perdiccas was briefly one of the most powerful men in the empire, until he died during an unsuccessful invasion of Ptolemy's Egypt in 320.

Deinarchus of Corinth: see *Phocion* 33 with note.

PHOCION

109 *tongue and belly*: as an orator with an allegedly insatiable appetite for gifts and luxury (a point made by Antipater himself at *Phocion* 30), Demades is aptly represented by the tongue and belly. The anecdote recurs in Plutarch's *On Love of Wealth* 5 (*Moralia* 525c), again in a contrast with Phocion, and on this occasion the connection with greed is made explicitly. For more on Demades and Antipater see Biographies of Prominent Figures.

It takes its leave: spoken by Ismene to Creon at *Antigone* 563–4.

sign of disdain: with hindsight we can see these opening remarks as the first of several allusions to Socrates, who was tried and executed in 399 in the aftermath of the Peloponnesian War. The Life of Phocion ends with an explicit comparison between Phocion and Socrates.

wounded or injured: honey was commonly used to treat wounds, but it did sting, so like truth and good sense its purpose was beneficial.

110 *'heart-easing'*: The Greek word is *menoeikēs*, which Homer tends to use when things are plentiful, often food and drink: see *Iliad* 9.90, 23.29, *Odyssey* 5.166.

material necessity: this reflects Plutarch's adherence to and interpretation of Platonic philosophy; this conception of God as the supreme being owes much to Plato's *Timaeus* (note especially 48a), a work by which Plutarch was greatly influenced.

Cato the Younger: Phocion's Life was paired with that of the 1st-C. BCE Roman politician Marcus Porcius Cato, who committed suicide in 46 rather than submit to Julius Caesar: see further the introduction to this Life.

dregs of Romulus: in *Letters to Atticus* 2.1.8 Cicero writes that Cato gives his opinion as if he is in the *Republic* of Plato rather than the dregs of Romulus, but he does not relate this to Cato's failure to gain the consulship.

111 *Idomeneus*: such slurs were typical of Idomeneus' writing: see note to p. 93 (*Demosthenes* 23).

Glaucippus: this orator was the son of the leading Athenian politician Hypereides, who is also reported to have delivered a speech against Phocion (*Lives of the Ten Orators* (*Moralia* 848d)). There may be some confusion in the tradition here. Little else is known of Glaucippus (Athenaeus 13.590c; *Suda*, s.v. Hypereides).

Xenocrates: Xenocrates of Chalcedon was Plato's successor as head of the Academy from 339 to 314. Phocion was also linked with the Cynic Diogenes of Sinope (Diogenes Laertius, *Lives of the Philosophers* 6.76).

112 *hand outside of his cloak*: keeping the hand within the cloak was a sign of self-control, the Greek virtue of *sōphrosynē*, particularly among orators, though less common in Phocion's day: Aeschines, *Against Timarchus* 1.25–6. For Duris, see *Demosthenes* 19.

wearing a cloak: going without shoes and cloak and the general ascetic tenor of this passage recalls Socrates: Xenophon, *Memorabilia* 1.6.2; Plato, *Symposium* 220b. In the parallel life (chapter 6) the philosophical Cato too is represented in this way.

Chares: Athenian general (*c*.400–*c*.325), to be distinguished from the Alexander historian, Chares of Mytilene.

Zeno: the philosopher Zeno of Citium (335–263) was the founder of Stoicism.

arguments and phrases: some of the anecdotes about Phocion's speaking style also appear from a different perspective in *Demosthenes* 10; see the note there (p. 88) for Polyeuctus of Sphettus.

Chabrias: Athenian general (*c*.420–357); for his heroic death at Chios during the Social War (357–355), Athens' war against disaffected allies at the time of the Second Athenian Confederacy, see Cornelius Nepos, *Chabrias*.

113 *Naxos*: fought at sea off Naxos in 376, this was an Athenian victory over

the Spartans. There is no mention of Phocion's role in Diodorus' account of the battle (15.34.5), where Cedon commands the left wing.

113 *Great Mysteries*: the autumn celebration of the Eleusinian Mysteries, lasting for about ten days in the month of Boedromion (September/October); 16 Boedromion would have been the second day.

contributions: the 'charter' of the Second Athenian Confederacy in 377 had explicitly ruled out 'tribute' (*phoroi*), with its echoes of the earlier Athenian empire; see P. J. Rhodes and R. Osborne, *Greek Historical Inscriptions 404–323 BC* (Oxford, 2003), no. 22. Instead there were 'contributions' (*syntaxeis*) approved by the *synhedrion* of the confederacy, but this, says Plutarch elsewhere (*Solon* 15), was merely a more attractive term for the same thing.

Ctesippus: his extravagance was notorious, and he was even reputed to have sold the stones of his father's tomb to finance his lifestyle: Athenaeus 4.165e–66b. Demosthenes wrote *Against Leptines* for him.

114 *Eubulus . . . Hypereides*: all five were well-known 4th-C. orators. Demosthenes, Lycurgus, and Hypereides appeared in the Alexandrian canon of ten Attic orators, with the result that at least some of their works survive today.

Diopeithes . . . Chares: all 4th-C. generals, with Chares the most prominent: see chapter 5. Leosthenes was a key figure in the Lamian War against Macedon: chapter 23.

Pericles, Aristeides, and Solon: all subjects of Lives by Plutarch (*Pericles* and *Solon* are included in Oxford World's Classics *Greek Lives*).

the lovely Muses: Archilochus of Paros (7th C.) was both a poet and a soldier, hence the references to the Muses (which inspired his poetry) and Enyalius (god of war, often identified with Ares). The lines are also quoted by Athenaeus (14.627c), where the first line is slightly different, making Archilochus very clearly the subject.

addressed as such: Athena was worshipped both as Athena Polias (of the city) and Athena Promachos (first in battle).

115 *disapproved of everything they did*: like Socrates, Phocion is thus the subject of an oracle from Delphi; in Socrates' case it was that no one was wiser than Socrates (Plato *Apology* 21a).

Callicles: see *Demosthenes* 25.

a taste of me: the story is also included among Aesop's Fables, no. 47 in the edition of E. Chambry.

dispute with the Boeotians: most likely to be the disagreement over Oropus in 366; see *Demosthenes* 5.

116 *ten Athenian citizens*: after the sack of Thebes in 335; see further chapter 17 and *Demosthenes* 23. Lycurgus was one of the ten.

Laconistes: Demosthenes (*Against Conon* 34) includes Archibiades among a number of Athenians who sought to imitate Spartan behaviour and appearance, hence the nickname.

sycophant Aristogeiton: several speeches *Against Aristogeiton* survive, one by Deinarchus and two attributed to Demosthenes. The negative view presented here is typical: see *Suda*, s.v. Aristogeiton (two entries). For 'sycophant', see the Glossary.

117 *Macedonian hands*: Plutarch of Eretria approached Athens in 348 (although alternative dates have been proposed). Contemporary sources place much less stress on Macedon at this point and date Philip's installation of tyrants to some years later (Demosthenes, *Third Philippic* 57–8; Aeschines, *Against Ctesiphon* 3.86–7). Nonetheless, Philip may have tried to stir up some trouble to distract the Athenians from his activities at Olynthus.

118 *elite troops*: the battle of Tamynae is the first occasion in which these elite Athenian troops, the *epilektoi*, are known to have been used. They are attested through to the 2nd C. BCE. Among their number at Tamynae was the orator Aeschines, as he himself reports in his *On the Embassy* 169. See further L. Tritle, '*Epilektoi* at Athens', *Ancient History Bulletin*, 4 (1990), 54–9.

119 *taken alive by the enemy*: not only Molossus but also his troops were captured, forcing the Athenians to pay out a ransom of 50 talents and bringing an end to Athenian influence on the island (with the exception of Carystus).

Byzantium: Philip's drive to the Hellespont took place in 340 and involved unsuccessful sieges of both Perinthus and Byzantium: see *Demosthenes* 17. One of Chares' goals was to protect the grain-ships sailing from the Black Sea. This he failed to do, allowing Philip to capture some 230 ships while he was away at a meeting with Persian officials.

send a force first: the context of this appeal is obscure. Demosthenes, *On the False Embassy* (87, 204, 295), delivered in 343, represents certain elements in Megara as prepared to hand their city over to Philip, and this is the context in which Phocion's relief mission is usually placed, thus a few years before the events of the preceding chapters.

120 *all the way down to it*: like the Long Walls of Athens. This was not the first time that Megara had had such walls, but the earlier set was destroyed in 424 (Thucydides 4.109).

peace terms Philip was offering: for Philip's peace proposals, see *Demosthenes* 18.

After the defeat: at the battle of Chaeronea in Boeotia in Sept. 338, when Philip defeated the combined armies of Athens and Thebes; see *Demosthenes* 17–21 for the battle and the build-up to it.

Charidemus: a Euboean mercenary leader who had been granted Athenian citizenship in 357 (see Demosthenes, *Against Aristocrates*, delivered in the late 350s). Strongly anti-Macedonian, he was one of those whose extradition Alexander demanded (chapter 17), and he subsequently fled to the Persian court, where his outspoken criticism of Darius' inner circle before Issus led to his execution.

120 *conference*: held in Corinth to establish an alliance under the leadership of Philip and known as the League of Corinth in modern scholarship. Demades had been taken prisoner by Philip at Chaeronea.

121 *one man*: Philip was assassinated in 336; on hearing the news, Demosthenes celebrated, despite the recent death of his daughter (*Demosthenes* 22).

savage man: quoting Homer, *Odyssey* 9.494, said to Odysseus by his comrades as they try to restrain him from taunting the Cyclops Polyphemus during their escape.

destruction of Thebes: Alexander destroyed Thebes in 335 shortly after his accession (see *Alexander* 11); the Athenians listed were among at least eight whose surrender was demanded by Alexander; see *Demosthenes* 23, where, however, Hypereides is not mentioned. A rather different image of this assembly appears at Diodorus 17.15, where there is uproar when Phocion suggests that these men should willingly sacrifice themselves for the state.

Nicocles: on Nicocles' loyalty in death, chapter 36.

122 *Chares of Mytilene*: one of Alexander's courtiers, whose often lively history was frequently used by Plutarch in his Life of Alexander.

100 talents: such a sum would have made Phocion one of the richest men in Athens.

offering it: perhaps recalling Xenophon, *Oeconomicus* 2, where Socrates argues that he is rich enough and has no need of money.

Echecratidas . . . Demaratus and Sparton: Echecratidas was a Peripatetic philosopher from Methymna on Lesbos; Athenodorus was a mercenary leader, perhaps from the Athenian cleruchy on Imbros, who was captured fighting for Darius. Nothing else is known of Sparton, but his brother Demaratus later commanded the Rhodian navy.

123 *four cities in Asia*: Alexander sent Craterus back to Macedon to take Antipater's place, but died while Craterus was still on his way. The gift of a city recalls the Persian king's gift of three cities to Themistocles (Plutarch, *Themistocles* 29). For more on Craterus, see Biographies of Prominent Figures.

Melite: a quarter of Athens near the agora.

Cephisodotus the sculptor: perhaps the father of Praxiteles, he was famous for a sculptural group in which Peace was represented carrying an infant Wealth: Pliny, *Natural History* 34.50.

Dismount: this race involved a fully armed contestant jumping out of a moving chariot, racing alongside it on foot, and then jumping back in again. The history of the contest is said to have gone back to the very first Panathenaic festival, where it was introduced by Erichthonius, the inventor of the four-horsed chariot. See P. Schultz, 'The Iconography of the Athenian *Apobates* Race: Origins, Meanings, Transformations', in O. Palagia and A. Choremi (eds.), *The Panathenaic Games* (Oxford, 2007), 59–72.

124 *the famous 'regime'*: this was the Spartan system for training their young men, known as the *agōgē*, that lasted from the age of seven through to twenty-nine. With its stress on obedience and endurance, it prepared them for military service. Xenophon is the only other foreigner known to have enrolled his sons in the *agōgē* in this period, but he was living in the Peloponnese. Given its exceptional character, Phocion's decision to send his son to finish his education in Sparta can hardly have been viewed as anything other than a political statement by his fellow Athenians. Since it follows the victory in the Panathenaic Games, Phocus would have been relatively old when he entered the *agōgē*.

messing together: the legendary Spartan lawgiver Lycurgus (subject of another of Plutarch's Lives, included in Oxford World's Classics *Greek Lives*) established Sparta's *agōgē* and military system, according to which all male citizens ate together in dining clubs or messes known as *phiditia*, each composed of a group of about fifteen.

triremes: Alexander would make this demand in his capacity as leader of the League of Corinth; the ships would have been for his campaign against Persia.

just a slave: perhaps a jibe at Pytheas' background as the son of a miller: *Suda*, s.v. Pytheas. He features several times in *Demosthenes*: see chapters 8, 20, 27.

Harpalus: renegade treasurer of Alexander, who fled amid various scandals to Athens in 324. Demosthenes was one of those who fell victim to accusations that he had benefited from Harpalus' generosity: *Demosthenes* 25–6 with note there.

125 *monument to her memory*: Pythonice (also Pythionice), who had died while Harpalus was still in Babylon, was one of the most celebrated courtesans of the time. Her memorial may not have been quite as unimpressive as Plutarch suggests, and certainly Pausanias spoke highly of it (1.37.5, see also Athenaeus 13.594e–595c). For the various controversies around her life and memory, see D. Ogden, 'How to Marry a Courtesan in the Macedonian Courts', in A. Erskine and L. Llewellyn-Jones (eds.), *Creating a Hellenistic World* (Swansea, 2011), 221–46, esp. 224–7.

Alexander really was dead: Alexander died in Babylon in June 323, see *Alexander* 75–7.

the War for Greece: news of Alexander's death sparked a widespread rebellion (323–322) against Macedonian rule in Greece, with Boeotia and Euboea almost the only regions to remain loyal to Macedon. It is also known as the Lamian War, after the town of Lamia in Thessaly, where the Macedonian general Antipater was besieged by Leosthenes. The latter's death in battle there changed the direction of the war, with the result that the coalition led by Athens was soon defeated at Crannon by the combined forces of Antipater and Craterus. See also *Demosthenes* 27–8.

Hypereides got to his feet: Hypereides would later give Leosthenes' Funeral Oration, much of which still survives.

125 *army put together by Leosthenes*: the core of Leosthenes' army was a body of 8,000 mercenaries that had been disbanded by Alexander and repatriated back to Greece.

126 *Antiphilus*: knowledge of this man is largely limited to this Life, although Diodorus (18.13.6) does praise his military ability.

127 *ravaging the countryside*: Rhamnous is on the north-east coast of Attica, facing Euboea. It has been conjectured that Micion was commander of Antipater's fleet, but nothing more is known of him.

Leonnatus fell: a Macedonian nobleman related to the mother of Philip II, who served with Alexander throughout the campaign and distinguished himself in India (see *Alexander* 21 and 40); after Alexander's death he was assigned the satrapy of Hellespontine Phrygia. He crossed from Asia in response to an appeal by Antipater (*Eumenes* 3, Diodorus 18.14.5). It was while relieving Antipater, who was besieged in Lamia, that Leonnatus was killed.

Menon of Thessaly: an aristocrat from Pharsalus, later killed fighting against Polyperchon (Diodorus 18.38.5–6). His daughter Phthia married into the Molossian royal house (*Pyrrhus* 1).

Crannon: fought in August 322. Diodorus (18.17.5) also suggests that loss of life was moderate, reporting 130 on the Macedonian side and over 500 on the Greek. According to him, Greek morale and discipline were already deteriorating before the battle.

Demosthenes and Hypereides fled: at this point the Athenian people condemned Demosthenes to death on the motion of Demades (*Demosthenes* 28).

128 *preparing to invade Attica*: the Cadmeia is the acropolis of Thebes in Boeotia. Diodorus 18.18.1–2 emphasizes the role of Demades in the embassy rather than Phocion.

the philosopher Xenocrates: on Xenocrates, see note to p. 111. His biography appears in Diogenes Laertius, *Lives of the Philosophers* 4.9, where this encounter with Antipater is presented rather differently: Antipater is so appreciative of the philosopher's wit that he releases the Athenian prisoners.

property-based ancestral constitution: an appeal to an 'ancestral' constitution was commonly used to justify change, and would be used again a few years later in order to reverse these changes: see chapter 32. This was effectively an anti-democratic revolution with Macedonian backing that would have recalled the oligarchic governments of 411 and 404–3. Diodorus 18.18.4 places the property qualification for political participation at 2,000 drachmas.

Munychia: a hill overlooking the Piraeus, where a Macedonian garrison would be placed for much of the next century until its removal in 229. Its strategic position gave those who held it control over both Athens and the Piraeus.

129 *Callimedon, nicknamed 'the Crab'*: although an Athenian, Callimedon had put the Macedonian case to the Greek states at the time of the Lamian War (*Demosthenes* 27). His nickname, which can also be translated as 'Beetle', was probably given to him by the comic poets, who enjoyed making fun of him (Athenaeus 3.100c–e, 104c–d).

Menyllus: known almost entirely from this Life.

dismay on the part of their enemies: Plutarch may have been thinking of the combatants at Salamis, who saw bright lights from Eleusis and heard what sounded like a procession escorting Iacchus (*Themistocles* 15). See also the coincidence of Athenian success and the Mysteries at the battle of Naxos in chapter 6, with the note there.

heights of Artemis: Munychia was the site of a shrine of Artemis. Dodona in Epirus was home to a prestigious oracle of Zeus.

washing his piglet: initiates to the Mysteries would purify both themselves and their piglets in the sea. Whether the piglet was immediately sacrificed or accompanied the initiate on the procession to Eleusis is disputed. A similar shark attack is recorded for 339 BCE (Aeschines 3.130 with scholia), the story of one perhaps influencing the other. Cantharus was the Great Harbour of the Piraeus.

too poor for citizenship: Diodorus 18.18.4–5 gives a figure of 22,000 disenfranchised, which some scholars correct to 12,000, whereas those who met the property qualification come to 9,000.

130 *deaths of Demosthenes and Hypereides*: see *Demosthenes* 28–30.

looking for Antigonus: Antigonus Monophthalmus (the One-Eyed) was killed in battle at Ipsus by a coalition of Cassander, Lysimachus, and Seleucus: see *Demetrius* 28–30.

Hagnonides: an anti-Macedonian politician, among those accused of taking money from Harpalus. Later he would be one of those responsible for Phocion's death: chapters 33 and 35.

banished: since the Ceraunian mountains were in Epirus and Cape Taenarum was in the very south of the Peloponnese, banishment beyond them would have meant exclusion from Greece.

moderate and lawful: note Plutarch's approval of this form of oligarchic government.

131 *a flatterer at the same time*: Plutarch was particularly fond of this rejoinder of Phocion, quoting it on five other occasions (at *Agis* 2, for example).

Cassander had assumed control: in 319. For Cassander, Antipater's son, see Biographies of Prominent Figures.

Antigonus Monophthalmus: Plutarch himself elsewhere (*Demosthenes* 31) says that Demades' letter was written to Perdiccas, a version which would seem to be confirmed by Diodorus 18.48.1–4.

132 *second-in-command*: Antipater died in 319 in his late seventies. Antipater's decision to give the regency to Polyperchon, a Macedonian commander

in his sixties who had campaigned with Alexander, rather than to his son Cassander, led to a decade of conflict for Macedon and Greece.

132 *Nicanor*: it is not clear who this man is. Some have suggested the commander of Alexander's disbanded Greek fleet, others Nicanor of Stagira, a friend of Aristotle.

the king in his care: as successor to Antipater, Polyperchon had taken over the guardianship of the kings, Philip III Arrhidaeus and Alexander IV. Philip, a half-brother of Alexander III, was in his late thirties, but due to some obscure mental impairment could not rule in his own right (see *Alexander* 77); Alexander IV was only an infant. The king mentioned here would be Philip Arrhidaeus, who was murdered by Olympias in 317.

their ancestral constitution: Polyperchon sought to win over the Greek states from Cassander by offering a return to the status quo before the Lamian War, thus restoring democracy to all those cities that had suffered at Antipater's hands (Diodorus 18.55–7). This time an appeal to the ancestral constitution justifies a return to democracy (contrast chapter 27).

133 *untrue and unreliable*: Diodorus 18.64 describes how Nicanor kept his intentions secret and gradually built up his garrison to withstand a siege; see also Cornelius Nepos, *Phocion* 2. Nothing more is known of Philomelus of Lamptrae.

Alexander arrived with an army: a fuller narrative of Alexander's actions is to be found in Diodorus 18.65–6. Alexander was a relatively minor player in the wars of the Successors, active largely in the Peloponnese where he was murdered in 314. His wife Cratesipolis was a famous beauty, who attracted the attention of Demetrius Poliorcetes (*Demetrius* 9).

fled the city in terror: for Hagnonides, see chapter 29; for Callimedon, see chapter 28; and for Phocion's son-in-law Charicles, see chapters 21–2.

Deinarchus of Corinth: pro-Macedonian politician, numbered by Demosthenes among those Greeks who had betrayed their city to Philip (Demosthenes, *On the Crown* 295). Not to be confused with orator and Athenian metic Deinarchus, who was originally from Corinth.

134 *the king and his Friends beneath it*: the golden canopy and the throne recall Alexander's appropriation of Darius' throne (*Alexander* 37). All this is deliberate construction on Polyperchon's part to reinforce his own authority as regent. The Friends (*Philoi*) were the king's inner council and would become typical of the Hellenistic court.

Hegemon: Demosthenes, *On the Crown* 285, presents him as a pro-Macedonian politician.

with a spear: Philip has been interpreted as imitating Alexander, who had punished inappropriate speech in front of the king in a similar way when he killed 'Black' Cleitus with the thrust of a spear (*Alexander* 51).

Cleitus: 'White' Cleitus was a veteran of Alexander's Persian campaign, who had variously served Craterus, Perdiccas, and Antipater before joining Polyperchon.

Cerameicus: a north-western suburb of Athens, associated particularly with pottery workshops.

every man and woman: the whole tone of this is very hostile to democracy. It was not an uncommon claim among those opposed to democracy to allege that it wished to enfranchise slaves: see, for instance, Theramenes at Xenophon, *Hellenica* 2.3.48. Women, of course, were not allowed at assemblies either.

135 *death*: by having Phocion very explicitly propose his own penalty (as sometimes happened in Athenian trials), Plutarch again evokes the memory of Socrates.

Demetrius of Phalerum: Demetrius, a pupil of Aristotle, would return to lead an oligarchic government in Athens between 317 and 307, and probably presented his late friend as some kind of oligarchic martyr. See L. O'Sullivan, *The Regime of Demetrius of Phalerum in Athens, 317–307 BCE: A Philosopher in Politics* (Leiden, 2009).

136 *cost of the dose*: this passage is sometimes used as evidence that the condemned had to pay for their own poison, but it may simply be that if the allocation proved inadequate it was the gaoler who paid. For modes of execution, see S. C. Todd, 'How to Execute People in Fourth-century Athens', in V. Hunter and J. Edmondson (eds.), *Law and Social Status in Classical Athens* (Oxford, 2000), 31–51. Again Socrates is recalled in the manner of Phocion's execution, poisoned by hemlock and surrounded by friends, although in Phocion's case his friends die too.

19 Munychion: May 318.

public bloodshed during a festival: there is a festival too at the time of Socrates' execution, but in his case the execution is delayed until the festival is over.

137 *state funeral*: the rehabilitation of Phocion would have taken place at the time of Demetrius of Phalerum, whose oligarchic government was backed by Cassander.

did not turn out well at all: Athenaeus (4.168e–f) presents a damning picture of Phocus, a man with a drink problem who was hated by everyone in Athens and who spent his entire inheritance.

reminded the Greeks of Socrates: here for the first time the link with Socrates is made explicit—see the Introduction and notes to chapters 2, 4, 8, 18, 34, 36, and 37.

EUMENES

142 *Duris*: see note to p. 20.

pankration: a violent combat sport in which almost everything was permitted except biting and gouging, even strangulation. The object was to make the opponent acknowledge defeat.

142 *advanced by Philip*: Nepos, *Eumenes* 1, says that Eumenes held the office of secretary for seven years under Philip, until the king's assassination in 336.

force on his own: in 326, after the revolt of the Indian city of Sangala was put down, he was sent with a force of 300 cavalry to two other cities that had joined the revolt to assure them that Alexander would treat them well: Arrian, *Anabasis* 5.24.

Cavalry Commander: Hephaestion died in 324: see *Alexander* 72. On Perdiccas, see Biographies of Prominent Figures. The position of Cavalry Commander (Hipparch) was an important one and may imply that Eumenes' role in the campaign had been more active than the sources suggest.

Neoptolemus: probably a member of the Molossian royal house of Epirus; the hostility between the two men would eventually end with Eumenes killing Neoptolemus on the battlefield (chapter 7).

mass wedding: this took place at Susa in 324; see *Alexander* 70.

Artonis: reading here the emendation 'Artonis', the name given by Arrian, *Anabasis* 7.4, rather than the unlikely 'Barsine' that appears in the manuscripts of Plutarch. The other sister is given by Arrian as Artacama.

Heracles: born some time in the mid-320s, he was murdered by Cassander and Polyperchon in 310/9. For his mother Barsine, see *Alexander* 21.

pipes or acting: Euius from Chalcis on Euboea played the pipes at the mass wedding at Susa; of Mentor nothing is known.

143 *the outer sea*: see *Alexander* 68, with note.

tomb: for Hephaestion's tomb, see *Alexander* 72.

as a foreigner: as a citizen of Cardia Eumenes was Greek rather than Macedonian.

compromise: Alexander died in Babylon in June 323 (*Alexander* 75–7). On his death the infantry supported Alexander's half-brother Philip Arrhidaeus for the throne, a man who is presented as being mentally incapable in some way. The Companions preferred to champion Alexander's unborn child by Rhoxane. It was agreed that if the child were a boy he would share power with Arrhidaeus, hence the joint kingship of Philip Arrhidaeus and Alexander IV. Both would be under the supervision of a guardian, who would therefore be able to exercise power on their behalf, as Perdiccas did in the early years after Alexander's death.

144 *Ariarathes*: Ariarathes I of Cappadocia (*c.*404/3–322), after ruling the region on behalf of the Persian king, was left in place by Alexander.

Leonnatus and Antigonus: for Leonnatus see notes to pp. 26 and 127; for Antigonus Monophthalmus (the One-Eyed), see Biographies of Prominent Figures.

Lamia: Alexander's death had prompted a rebellion against Macedon under the leadership of Athens and Aetolia, known as the Lamian War (323–322): see further *Phocion* 23–6. Antipater (see Biographies of

Prominent Figures) had governed Macedon and Greece during Alexander's absence in Asia.

marry her: marriage to Cleopatra, sister of Alexander the Great, would add weight to Leonnatus' claim to the Macedonian throne. Any hopes came to nothing, as he was killed in battle while lifting the siege of Lamia: *Phocion* 25.

taken prisoner: and then impaled along with his relatives, according to Diodorus 18.16.

145 *kings*: Perdiccas had custody of the two kings, Alexander IV and Philip III Arrhidaeus.

Craterus: one of the most senior of Alexander's officers, he was on his way to replace Antipater as regent of Macedon when Alexander died. In the end he joined forces with Antipater to put down the Greek rebellion and married the latter's daughter Phila. See also Biographies of Prominent Figures.

campaigning against Ptolemy: according to the chronology adopted in these notes, these events (i.e. Craterus and Antipater's invasion of Asia and Perdiccas' invasion of Egypt) occurred in spring 320. An alternative chronology would place them in the previous year: see further p. xviii with n. 4.

Alcetas: Perdiccas' younger brother, himself a veteran of Alexander's campaigns.

146 *At the time in question*: 320, but see note to p. 145.

147 *Pigres*: otherwise unknown.

'*Athena and Alexander*': contrast this with Demetrius' dream of Alexander before Ipsus, *Demetrius* 29.

Pharnabazus, the son of Artabazus: Eumenes' brother-in-law (see chapter 1), albeit one of many, as Artabazus was reported to have had twenty-one children, including eleven sons.

149 *kill or be killed*: this emotional death scene is completely lacking in Diodorus 18.30, where Craterus is trampled to death unrecognized after falling from his horse. Nor does Diodorus make mention of Eumenes' stratagem of keeping Craterus' identity secret before the battle, although it is recorded in Arrian, *Successors* 1.27.

mutiny in Egypt: Perdiccas was murdered in 320 in his tent by a group of officers after a failed attempt to cross the Nile had left some 2,000 of his men dead.

war against Eumenes: the broader political context is of only secondary importance in Plutarch's account; thus he has nothing to say about the meeting at Triparadeisus in the late summer of 320, at which Antipater established a new settlement for Alexander's empire, one which had no place for Eumenes or any other adherents of Perdiccas. It was here that Antigonus was assigned the command against Eumenes (Diodorus 18.39).

149 *list to the managers*: thus demonstrating his continued loyalty to the kings; Mt Ida was in the Troad in north-west Asia Minor.

Cleopatra: Alexander's sister had been sent by her mother Olympias to Sardis, where she fended off various marriage proposals—including one from Perdiccas, delivered by Eumenes, not mentioned by Plutarch but recorded by Arrian (*Successors* 1.26, 25.2–6).

150 *prerogative of the king*: Eumenes had been in the service of Perdiccas, regent for the kings. His actions here suggest that he continued to present himself as acting on behalf of the kings, even though Perdiccas was dead and the kings were now in enemy hands.

setbacks and failures: for the sentiment, see also Polybius 6.2.

Orcynia: Eumenes' defeat here is to be identified with the heavy defeat in Cappadocia narrated by Diodorus (18.40) in which some 8,000 of his men died. There are, however, some scholars who believe these to be two separate battles, and argue that Plutarch simply omitted the latter.

151 *too large to hide*: defeated and with Antigonus in pursuit, the men probably did not need much persuasion; Diodorus' picture (18.41) of mass desertion is more plausible.

153 *chaos*: before Antipater died in 319 he had chosen the veteran general Polyperchon to take over the position of regent for the kings rather than his own son Cassander, who was designated as Polyperchon's deputy. Cassander soon broke from Polyperchon and looked instead to Antigonus for assistance in the ensuing conflict.

Hieronymus: Hieronymus of Cardia wrote an important, now lost, history that covered the years from the death of Alexander to the death of Pyrrhus in 272 and perhaps beyond: see J. Hornblower, *Hieronymus of Cardia* (Oxford, 1981). His history lies behind the narrative of the Successors in Diodorus, books 18–20. Hieronymus was intimately connected with the leading figures, serving in turn Eumenes, Antigonus Monophthalmus, Demetrius, and Antigonus Gonatas. See also Introduction to *Eumenes*.

154 *Olympias*: the mother of Alexander the Great had retired to her native Epirus during the latter part of her son's reign. Protective of her grandson Alexander IV, she subsequently joined forces with Polyperchon. See Biographies of Prominent Figures.

Cyinda: this Cilician fortress held huge quantities of Macedonian treasure, much of it transferred from the Persian city of Susa; see also *Demetrius* 32.

Silver Shields: these were an elite Macedonian infantry unit, numbering around 3,000. Antigenes, who was probably with Alexander's campaign from the beginning, had achieved some measure of power in his own right as the largely absent satrap of Susiana. He was awarded the province by Antipater in recognition of the prominent role he had played in the assassination of Perdiccas. Much less is known about the less important Teutamus.

dream: Eumenes' ruse is reported by a number of sources, with Diodorus 18.60–1 providing the fullest account.

joined forces: Eumenes marched eastwards towards the centre of the old Persian empire, where Peucestas, the influential satrap of Persis since 324, was leading a coalition of satraps that sought to curb the expansionist plans of Peithon, satrap of Media (see Diodorus 19.14).

155 *Pasitigris*: lies to the east of Susa and flows into the Persian Gulf.

splendid banquet: Diodorus 19.22 describes the lavish feast put on by Peucestas in Persepolis, part of his bid for the loyalty of the troops.

156 *Macedonian*: on this see *Alexander* 51.

made camp: Plutarch devotes much space to this battle that did not in the end take place, an incident which serves to demonstrate both the soldiers' belief in Eumenes as their general and Antigonus' high opinion of him as a rival general. It was followed shortly afterwards by the inconclusive battle of Paraetacene in the latter part of 317, about which Plutarch has nothing to say at all (for the battle and its aftermath see Diodorus 19.26–34). Instead he skips straight to the battle of Gabene. Plutarch also avoids mentioning that the reason for Eumenes' illness was said to have been an over-consumption of alcohol (Diodorus 19.24).

158 *battle*: the battle of Gabene was fought in the winter of 317/16, although an alternative chronology would place it in the following winter (see also Diodorus 18.39–43).

159 *baggage*: this hardly conveys why the baggage was such an important issue; it would have included not only the booty from their years of campaigning with Alexander but also their wives and families, as is evident in the response in the next chapter.

160 *arguing for his death*: Demetrius is the subject of the next Life in the volume; Nearchus was Alexander's admiral. Despite their defence of him, Eumenes had been condemned to death some five years before by an army assembly in Egypt following the death of Perdiccas: see chapter 8.

161 *wife and children*: compare the way Seleucus returned the ashes of Demetrius to his son Antigonus Gonatas, *Demetrius* 53. The execution of Eumenes took place in early 316, by strangulation on his gaolers' own initiative, according to Nepos, *Eumenes*.

Arachosia: one of the most easterly satrapies in what is now southern Afghanistan.

DEMETRIUS

167 *Ismenias of Thebes*: a celebrated pipe-player. Several stories associate him with Alexander, including one in the *Alexander Romance* that presents him begging the king not to destroy Thebes.

168 *Antigeneidas*: another famous Theban pipe-player, also contemporary with Alexander.

168 *as great as their virtues*: see Plato, *Republic* 6.491e, 495a–b.

Antigonus Monophthalmus: see Biographies of Prominent Figures. His son Philip died in 306; see R. Billows, *Antigonos the One-Eyed and the Creation of the Hellenistic State* (Berkeley, 1990), 419–21, and chapter 23.

Dionysus: for this dual character of Dionysus, see e.g. Diodorus 4.4.4. Whether in practice Demetrius modelled himself on Dionysus is disputed; his coins show him with bull's horns, interpreted by some scholars as those of Dionysus, by others as those of Poseidon. For further comparison with Dionysus, see chapter 12.

169 *killed a son*: Philip V (ruled 221–179) executed his son Demetrius in 180: see *Aratus* 54.

Mithradates: known as Mithradates Ctistes (the Founder), due to his role as founder of the kingdom of Pontus. Lived *c*.349–266, so despite what Plutarch says probably a dozen or so years older than Demetrius. The passage is discussed in detail by A. B. Bosworth and P. V. Wheatley, 'The Origins of the Pontic House', *Journal of Hellenic Studies*, 118 (1998), 155–64 (esp. 161–3).

170 *in its eighth generation*: Mithradates VI Eupator was defeated by the Roman general Pompey in the Third Mithradatic War in 63 BCE.

contact with one another: Empedocles was a 5th-C. philosopher from Sicily, whose theory was laid out in his largely lost work *On Nature*. Change in the natural world is to be explained by the interaction between the elements (earth, fire, water, and air) on the one hand, and the forces of Love and Strife on the other. Plutarch was particularly interested in Empedocles, and wrote a substantial, but now lost, work on him: J. P. Hershbell, 'Plutarch as a Source for Empedocles Re-Examined', *American Journal of Philology*, 92 (1971), 156–84.

Ptolemy: satrap of Egypt, later Ptolemy I Soter of Egypt; see Biographies of Prominent Figures.

twenty-two years old: winter of 314/13 (see also Diodorus 19.69; Appian, *Syriaca* 54.274), an important date in establishing the chronology of Demetrius' life: see P. Wheatley, 'The Lifespan of Demetrius Poliorcetes', *Historia*, 46 (1997), 19–27, who argues that Demetrius was born in 336 and died in early 282 rather than 283, as often thought.

5,000 dead: the battle at Gaza was in late 312; for an account of the battle, see Diodorus 19.80–5.

171 *eager to see his son*: Antigonus was campaigning in Asia Minor (where the Phrygian town of Celaenae was located) while his son was in the south; in Diodorus' account (19.93) it is the arrival of Antigonus that prompts Ptolemy to leave Syria.

Nabataean Arabs: this people from northern Arabia had earlier inflicted a heavy defeat on Antigonus' general Athenaeus (Diodorus 19.94–5). Prior to this incident the Nabataeans are unknown to history.

recovered it: Seleucus (see Biographies of Prominent Figures) had been expelled from Babylon in 316 and recovered the satrapy in winter 312/11, assisted by a small body of troops provided by Ptolemy, with whom he had taken refuge.

172 *enslaved by Cassander and Ptolemy*: their campaign to 'liberate' Greece began in 307. Cassander (see Biographies of Prominent Figures) had had Athens subject to him since 317, while Ptolemy (but only since 308) had a garrison on the Acrocorinth, a key strategic location in the Peloponnese. Antigonus had first put himself forward as defender of Greek freedom in 315 during his lengthy siege of Tyre.

Demetrius of Phalerum: oversaw an oligarchic government in Athens on behalf of Cassander from 317 to 307. After his expulsion he joined the court of Ptolemy I in Alexandria, where he is said to have helped establish the Library. He was also a Peripatetic philosopher. He died in the 280s. See also *Phocion* 35, with note.

Munychia: a hill overlooking the Piraeus; see further *Phocion* 27, with note.

26 Thargelion: June 307.

Ptolemy's ships: Ptolemy had been allied to Cassander since the previous year.

expel the garrison, and restore their laws and their ancestral constitution: these three elements were all components of freedom. The 'ancestral constitution' could be a very flexible notion, appealed to by both democrats and oligarchs; see *Phocion* 27, with note.

173 *Aristodemus of Miletus*: one of Antigonus' most trusted associates, who stands out for his diplomatic skills.

Cratesipolis: for her husband Alexander, see *Phocion* 33. After he died in 314, Cratesipolis continued to exercise power over Sicyon and Corinth until she yielded them to Ptolemy in 308. Pagae, an emendation for the manuscript reading Patrae, was a harbour town of Megara on the Corinthian Gulf. Patrae, on the other hand, was some 150 km west of Megara. Some of the problems of this passage are explored by P. Wheatley, 'Poliorcetes and Cratesipolis: A Note on Plutarch, Demetr. 9.5–7', *Antichthon*, 38 (2004), 1–9, who defends the manuscript reading but suggests that the episode might be moved to a later more suitable context, favouring Demetrius' invasion of the Peloponnese in 303.

Stilpo: a celebrated philosopher, head of the Megarian school, who numbered Zeno, the founder of Stoicism, among his pupils. There is an echo here of the exchanges between Alexander and Diogenes at *Alexander* 14.

174 *actually a monarchy*: the Lamian War followed the news of the death of Alexander in 323 and lasted until the battle of Crannon the following year. Plutarch's comments refer not only to the government of Demetrius of Phalerum ('the Phalerean') but also to the intervening oligarchy of Phocion (322–318): see *Phocion* 27–33. There was a very brief democratic revival after the fall of Phocion.

decrees and contracts: this is an early example of the use of the term

'Saviour' in Hellenistic ruler cult. Although Demetrius and Antigonus do appear as 'Saviours' in inscriptions, the phrase 'Saviour Gods' is otherwise not attested for them, nor is there any epigraphic evidence that Athens did use the priest's name on official documents. For another account of their honours, see Diodorus 20.46. In general see J. Mikalson, *Religion in Hellenistic Athens* (Berkeley, 1998), ch. 3.

174 *the robe of Athena*: this was the decorated robe (*peplos*) that was woven anew each year and presented to the goddess Athena Polias at the Panathenaic festival.

Stratocles: son of Euthydemus, prominent in Athens until Demetrius' and Antigonus' defeat at Ipsus in 301. He is found proposing an honorific decree in 293/2, which suggests that he made something of a comeback after Demetrius' recovery of Athens in 294.

Cleon: a popular 5th-C. politician, portrayed very negatively by Thucydides and lampooned by the comic poet Aristophanes in the *Knights*.

battle of Amorgos: naval battle in the Lamian War, 322 BCE.

175 *hotter even than fire*: line 382 of Aristophanes' *Knights*, spoken by the chorus to describe the vanquishing of Cleon by another, even more demagogic politician.

Demetrias: 'the old and new' day was the last day of the month; thus the last day of Munychion, for instance, would become the Demetrias of Demetrion. There is no evidence other than this for the renaming of Munychion, which continues to be epigraphically attested in this period.

Demetria: this festival appears to date from after Demetrius' return to Athens in 294, suggesting that Plutarch is bringing together honours from different periods. Despite Plutarch, inscriptions indicate that the Dionysia continued to be celebrated.

comedies: see also the verses of Philippides quoted at the end of chapter 26.

176 *benefactions to Athens*: Philippides' benefactions and his relationship with Lysimachus are well conveyed in an important Athenian decree of 283/2 in his honour; for the text, M. Austin, *The Hellenistic World from Alexander to the Roman Conquest* (2nd edn., Cambridge, 2006), no. 54. For Lysimachus, see Biographies of Prominent Figures.

at Delphi: probably in the late 290s; this may refer to the shields dedicated by the Athenians at Delphi after the battle of Plataea (479 BCE), which the Aetolians in control of Delphi at the time either had removed or were threatening to remove.

returned to Athens: elsewhere she is named as Euthydice (Diodorus 20.40); for her son with Demetrius, see chapter 53. Miltiades was a distinguished early 5th-C. Athenian general and politician who commanded the forces at Marathon. Ophellas was murdered in 308.

Alexander's Successors: for Antipater and Craterus, see Biographies of

Prominent Figures. For the Successors in general, see R. Waterfield, *Dividing the Spoils: The War for Alexander the Great's Empire* (Oxford, 2011).

older: the marriage occurred *c.*320 when Demetrius would have been fifteen or sixteen years old. Phila, already married twice, may have been about thirty at the time.

177 *you're servile*: from Euripides, *Phoenician Women* 395.

Cleonides: named as Leonidas in the *Suda*, s.v. Demetrius.

overall supremacy: the battle, fought in early 306, took place just off Salamis in Cyprus (not to be confused with the island of Salamis near Athens); for a fuller account, see Diodorus 20.49–52. Occupation of Cyprus had allowed Ptolemy to raid Antigonid possessions along the coast of Asia Minor and Syria.

178 *Lamia*: an Athenian, of whom more is told by Athenaeus, *Deipnosophists* 6.253a–b, 13.577c–f. See P. Wheatley, 'Lamia and the Besieger: An Athenian Hetaera and a Macedonian King', in O. Palagia and S. V. Tracy (eds.), *The Macedonians in Athens, 322–229 BC* (Oxford, 2003), 30–6.

We met Ptolemy: the manuscripts of Plutarch read 'King Ptolemy', which is usually amended as here. A case for keeping the manuscript reading has been made by A. B. Bosworth, 'Ptolemy and the Will of Alexander', in A. B. Bosworth and E. Baynham (eds.), *Alexander the Great in Fact and Fiction* (Oxford, 2000), 207–41, at 229–30. He suggests that Ptolemy had already been informally using the title king, so the point being made by Aristodemus is that Antigonus and Demetrius, being victorious over Ptolemy, were truly kings.

179 *diadem*: this was a cloth headband that came to signify kingship, most noticeable now in Hellenistic ruler portraits. Its origins are uncertain.

styled himself in his letters: Cassander's reluctance to take the title king is not borne out by other evidence: see Diodorus 20.53 and the legends on Macedonian bronze coinage and inscriptions on statue bases where he appears as King Cassander.

in a dream: Medeius of Larisa was a Thessalian aristocrat who accompanied Alexander on his campaign. He is said to have hosted Alexander's final banquet, at which the king became ill. He was a man of considerable status and served the Antigonids as admiral; a decree of 303/2 honouring him is known from Athens and another, probably of 294–287, from Gonnoi in Thessaly.

180 *Thasian or Chian 'flux'*: the wines of Thasos and Chios were famous. The Greek *rheuma*, translated here by the archaic medical term 'flux', could refer both to an unhealthy discharge from the body and the flowing of liquid more generally; hence the joke about wine.

181 *Aeropus of Macedon*: short-lived king of Macedon in the early 4th C.

Attalus Philometor: Attalus III of Pergamum (*c.*170–133, reigned 138–133), whose scientific writings on botany and agriculture were cited in antiquity by such as Pliny the Elder.

181 *'sixteens' and 'fifteens'*: impressively large warships; see further chapter 43.

city-takers: elaborate siege-engines; see the description in the next chapter.

war with the Rhodians: a year-long siege in 305/4; see also Diodorus 20. 81–8, 91–100.

at the base: roughly 21 metres at the base and 30 metres in height; for a more detailed description with different measurements, Diodorus 20.91.

182 *forty mnas*: about 17 kg. Nothing else is known about Zoïlus.

weighed just one: a talent was approximately 26 kgs. Alcimus was killed during an unsuccessful night attack on the city (Diodorus 20.98); it is most likely this man who is honoured in a fragmentary Athenian inscription of 306/5.

seal unbroken: correspondence between Philip II of Macedon and his wife Olympias, the mother of Alexander. Athenian probity in this matter is remarked upon again at *Precepts of Statecraft* 3 (*Moralia* 799e).

An astonishing painting: Ialysus was the eponymous founder of Ialysus, one of the three cities of Rhodes before the synoecims of the late 5th C. Apelles of Colophon was one of the most celebrated painters in antiquity and a contemporary of Protogenes: see *Alexander* 4.

consumed in the fire: the painting was still on Rhodes when Cicero visited in the 1st C. BCE; later it was kept in the temple of Peace dedicated by Vespasian in 75 CE, but the date of its destruction by fire, and what fire that might have been, are unknown.

183 *city under siege*: Demetrius returned to Athens in 304.

Thermopylae: site of the famous battle against the Persians in 480 and entrance to central and southern Greece.

184 *Demochares of Leuconoe*: Athenian politician and orator, nephew of Demosthenes (see *Demosthenes* 30), initially favourable to Demetrius' restoration of democracy, but around 303 he was exiled and did not return until 286/5. His often polemical history of Athens in this period had considerable influence.

in the Peloponnese: Demetrius invaded in early 303.

sister of Pyrrhus: see *Pyrrhus* 4.

185 *Philip and Alexander*: the establishment of the short-lived Hellenic League in 302 could be represented as a revival of Philip's League of Corinth (see *Alexander* 14). A fragmentary inscription recording the charter of the new league survives; for the text see M. Austin, *The Hellenistic World from Alexander to the Roman Conquest* (2nd edn., Cambridge, 2006), no. 50.

island governor: all titles that would make them subordinate to a king. Agathocles was ruler of Syracuse and much of Sicily until his assassination in 289/8.

Lysimachus' Penelope: Penelope was the famously chaste wife of Odysseus who waited for him for the duration of the ten-year war and beyond. The wife here is most likely Lysimachus' third, Arsinoe, daughter of Ptolemy I of Egypt, whom he married *c.*299. Demetrius' jibe would have gained added force from the age gap of some forty years between Lysimachus and his wife.

final revelation: full initiation into the Eleusinian Mysteries in honour of Demeter and Kore should take well over a year. After taking part in the Lesser Mysteries in the early spring (at Agra, a suburb of Athens), the candidate would be initiated at the Great Mysteries in September/October (at Eleusis), before returning to the main festival for the final revelation a year later.

Pythodorus: the Torch-bearer was a priest of Demeter and Kore, so could speak with authority on the matter.

Munychion: Demetrius' return to Athens would thus have been roughly in April 302, although a case can be made for April 303: A. G. Woodhead, 'The Calendar of the Year 304/3 B.C. in Athens', *Hesperia*, 58 (1989), 297–301.

186 *Lynceus of Samos*: comic poet and writer of letters with a particular fondness for describing royal banquets; he was the brother of the historian Duris—on whom see note to p. 20.

Lamia: in myth a monstrous woman with removable eyes who stole and ate little children, hence used as bogey to instil discipline in children. Demochares of Soli is otherwise unknown and may be an error for the Athenian Demochares.

Alexander, his king: there are various versions of Lysimachus' encounter with a lion, not all of which hold Alexander responsible. Q. Curtius Rufus 8.14–16 knows the story but attributes his injuries to a successful struggle with a huge lion during a lion hunt in Syria and also tells another story of how he had attempted to save Alexander from a charging lion only for the king to kill the lion himself. Craterus too is said to have saved Alexander from a lion, see *Alexander* 40, with note. Such lion-slaying prowess evoked Alexander's ancestor Heracles and helped Craterus and Lysimachus assert their superiority in the struggle that followed Alexander's death.

187 *Bocchoris*: the Greek version of Bakenrenef, an 8th-C. Egyptian pharaoh who was noted among Greeks for his wisdom and his ability as a lawgiver (Diodorus 1.65 and 79).

188 *welcome*: contrast *Eumenes* 6, where both sides use 'Alexander' in their watchwords.

the two sides engaged: the battle of Ipsus was fought in Phrygia in Asia Minor in late 301.The coalition against Antigonus consisted of Seleucus, Lysimachus, Ptolemy, and Cassander, although only Seleucus and Lysimachus were present at the battle. Cassander's troops were commanded by his brother Pleistarchus.

Antiochus, the son of Seleucus: Antiochus I Soter, who succeeded his father, ruling from 281 to 261; see further chapter 38.

189 *sanctuary*: the celebrated sanctuary of Artemis.

190 *Pyrrhus' hands*: the eighteen-year-old Pyrrhus, whose sister Deidameia was married to Demetrius, fought on the Antigonid side at Ipsus; see further *Pyrrhus* 4.

Apama: Seleucus had married her at the mass wedding at Susa in 324 (*Alexander* 70).

Agathocles: Lysimachus married Arsinoe, who would later marry first her half-brother Ptolemy Ceraunus, and then her full brother Ptolemy II; Agathocles married Lysandra.

191 *Sidon and Tyre*: two Phoenician cities on the coast of modern Lebanon; for Alexander's siege of Tyre, see *Alexander* 24–5.

never free of poverty or want: Plato, *Laws* 5.736e.

Lachares: an Athenian commander who used his mercenary troops to seize power with the backing of Cassander *c.*300. After his overthrow he fled to Boeotia.

192 *Epicurus*: founder of Epicureanism, he had taught in Athens since 306; his philosophical school took the form of a community of friends who lived together.

most agreeable to the people: the city surrendered in *c.*295; despite its democratic pretensions, the new regime is usually considered to be oligarchic in character.

surrendered to King Demetrius: contrast Demetrius' 'liberation' of the city in 307 (chapters 7 ff.), when no garrison was put in place

Archidamus: Archidamus IV, king of Sparta from *c.*305 to 275, grandfather of Agis IV, whose life is included in this volume.

193 *ashes*: from a lost play of the 5th-C. Athenian tragedian Aeschylus.

fire in the other: from a lost poem by 7th-C. Greek poet Archilochus of Paros.

before dying: Cassander died in 297; his son Philip IV, aged about eighteen, outlived him by only four months before succumbing to a wasting disease, according to Pausanias (9.7.3). The middle brother, Antipater, was probably sixteen at the time.

from the Peloponnese: Thessalonice was daughter of Philip II and half-sister of Alexander the Great. She appears to have favoured the younger son, Alexander, and arranged that the two boys should rule jointly, before her murder at the hands of the elder in 294.

Alexander's borders: on Pyrrhus' intervention, see *Pyrrhus* 6.

194 *king of Macedon*: in 294, probably in the autumn.

after his death: in 310 or shortly after, Cassander executed Alexander's son and heir, Alexander IV, together with the boy's mother Rhoxane. He had earlier put Alexander's own mother Olympias to death and was said to have been behind the murder of Heracles, Alexander's son by Barsine.

195 *his heir*: Antigonus Gonatas, who would rule Macedon from 277 to 239; see Biographies of Prominent Figures.

children and mother: captured on Cyprus (chapter 35).

queen of the barbarian eastern satrapies: that Antiochus should marry his father's wife is best explained in terms of dynastic politics and the need for a smooth succession. At roughly the same time Antiochus also became co-ruler with his father. As Plutarch's story shows, many found love a more satisfactory explanation than practical politics. Antiochus was put in charge of the eastern satrapies, the region to the east of the Euphrates.

Erasistratus: fictitious though the story may be, the doctor is often identified with the celebrated physician Erasistratus of Ceos (*c*.315–240).

Sappho: late-7th-C. female poet from Lesbos; this poem survives in part—for text and translation see Fragment 31 in D. Campbell's *Greek Lyric*, vol. 1, in the Loeb Classical Library series.

196 *Antiochus and Stratonice*: the story of Antiochus' lovesickness was the subject of paintings by Jacques-Louis David (1774) and Jean-Auguste-Dominique Ingres (1840), as well as an opera by Étienne-Nicholas Méhul (1792).

Cleonymus the Spartan: see further *Pyrrhus* 26.

Hieronymus: Hieronymus of Cardia; see the introduction to *Eumenes* and note to p. 153.

197 *Dromichaetes*: king of the Getae, north of the Danube, who captured Lysimachus in 292.

repopulated: Alexander had destroyed Thebes in 335 (see *Alexander* 11). In 315 Cassander re-founded it (Diodorus 19.53–4), well over twenty years before Demetrius first captured the city, so it is unclear why Plutarch gives the figure of ten years.

the god . . . founder of their line: the Pythian Games were held every four years in honour of Apollo. There was a cult of Apollo Patroos (Ancestral Apollo) in Athens and a tradition that Ion, founder of the Ionians, was a son of Apollo and the Athenian Creusa; thus Euripides' play, *Ion*. Demetrius' celebration of the festival in Athens took place in 290.

198 *wounded each other*: for a vivid description of this combat, see *Pyrrhus* 7.

could be detected: elaborated on at *Pyrrhus* 8.

199 *Axius bridge*: the Axius was a river near the Macedonian capital Pella.

Timotheus: the poet Timotheus of Miletus (*c*.450–360); for the rest of the verse, see Plutarch's *Agesilaus* 14.

'*Law is king of all*': from a lost poem by the 5th-C. Boeotian poet Pindar; also quoted by Plato (*Gorgias* 484b) and Herodotus 3.38.

dispensing justice: Plutarch's remarks on Zeus combine two passages of Homer, *Iliad* 1.238–9 and *Odyssey* 19.178–9.

200 *their size*: on these ships, W. M. Murray, *The Age of Titans: The Rise and Fall of the Great Hellenistic Navies* (Oxford, 2012). Athenaeus 5.203d–204e

gives a fuller description of the huge ship of Ptolemy IV Philopator (ruler of Egypt, 221–205).

200 *united against Demetrius*: in 288, see also *Pyrrhus* 10–12.

201 *seven years*: his Macedonian reign ended in 287, though some prefer 288.

Cassandreia: Cassander had re-founded the city of Potidaea on the Chalcidice peninsula as Cassandreia *c.*316.

202 *waste away to nothing*: this tragedy is now lost.

Ismenus' streams: Euripides' *Bacchae* 4–5, where the god Dionysus describes his arrival in Thebes in human form. Plutarch changes the verse from first person to third.

choosing archons: see chapter 10 and note. The Athenian revolt occurred in 287 or 286.

negotiate with him: this was most likely the Athenian Crates, son of Antigenes, who would later be head of the Academy. Demetrius may have lifted the siege but he continued to maintain garrisons in Piraeus and on the Munychia hill: see chapter 34.

203 *giving her away*: for the betrothal, see chapter 32.

To which we've come: from the play by Sophocles, in which the lines are addressed by the blind Oedipus to his daughter Antigone. It takes only a slight change to the spelling of Antigone to transform the meaning of the sentence, which originally translated as 'O child of an aged, blind man, Antigone, what lands are these to which we've come?' Demetrius' father Antigonus was famously one-eyed.

204 *Patrocles*: he already had some experience of Demetrius, having been Seleucus' man in charge of Babylon *c.*311, when Demetrius captured the city (Diodorus 19.100; see also chapter 7).

205 *Cyrrhestica*: a region of northern Syria.

the coast there: thus heading west into Caria.

207 *Syrian Chersonese*: likely to be the city of Apamea on the Orontes river: G. Cohen, *The Hellenistic Settlements in Syria, the Red Sea Basin, and North Africa* (Berkeley, 2006), 97–8. Demetrius' captivity would have begun in 285.

Stratonice: Demetrius' daughter, married first to Seleucus, then to his son and heir Antiochus (chapter 38).

killed Demetrius: for Lysimachus' hostility to Demetrius, see chapter 25.

208 *after his capture*: for Dromichaetes and Lysimachus, chapter 39 and note.

Xenophantus: from Thebes, known also from an honorific inscription on Delos.

Demetrias: a city in northern Thessaly founded by Demetrius *c.*290.

209 *Romans conquered Macedon*: the last king, Perseus, was defeated by the

Romans at the battle of Pydna in 168 and was taken to Rome as a prisoner, where he graced the triumph of Aemilius Paullus before eventually dying under house arrest in an Italian town. See R. Waterfield, *Taken at the Flood: The Roman Conquest of Greece* (Oxford, 2014).

Roman counterpart: the Life of Antony.

PYRRHUS

216 *Thesprotians and Molossians*: together with the Chaonians (see chapters 18 and 28) these were the leading peoples of Epirus.

Pelasgus: eponymous ancestor of the mythical pre-Greek Pelasgians.

Deucalion and Pyrrha: survivors of Zeus' great flood, one the son of Prometheus, the other the daughter of Epimetheus. The sanctuary of Zeus at Dodona was said to have been the oldest oracle in the Greek world. Pyrrhus was a very active supporter, in particular through extensive building work.

Hyllus: son of Heracles.

civilized code of laws: ruling in the latter part of the 5th C. Tharrypas (also named as Tharyps, Tharybas, and Arrybas) is said to have been influenced by Athens when making these reforms: see Justin, *Epitome* 17.3.10 and 12. In general, the early history of the dynasty is obscure.

Menon of Thessaly: from Pharsalus, his family appears to have had longstanding links with the Molossian royal family (see Xenophon, *Anabasis* 2.6.28). For his service in the Lamian War (323–322), see *Phocion* 25, with chapters 23–5 and accompanying notes for the war itself.

to power instead: the Molossians turned against Aeacides after he went to help Olympias against Cassander in 317 or 316 (Diodorus 19.36). For most of the next ten years or so the rulers of Epirus were backed by Cassander, but the details of who ruled when are hard to recover. Plutarch's enigmatic phrase 'the sons of Neoptolemus' presumably refers to the side of the family descended from Aeacides' uncle Neoptolemus I: see the family tree, p. 215.

217 *Glaucias*: king of the western Illyrian tribe, the Taulantians. The choice of Glaucias was not chance; his wife Beroa was also from the Aeacidae, the Molossian ruling family (Justin, *Epitome* 17.3.19).

218 *set him on the throne*: in 307 or 306.

right big toe: this might be compared to the Royal Touch of kings of France and England, by which they were said to be able to cure diseases such as scrofula: see M. Bloch, *The Royal Touch* (London, 1973).

seventeen years old: in 302.

Neoptolemus' hands: it is very likely, but not certain, that this is the same Neoptolemus who is believed to have ruled after the expulsion of Pyrrhus' father Aeacides.

218 *his wife*: one of Demetrius' several wives. For the marriage in 303 see *Demetrius* 25; for her death only a few years later see *Demetrius* 32. Her earlier betrothal to Alexander IV would have taken place when her father Aeacides was providing military assistance to Alexander's grandmother Olympias before the capture of the young king by Cassander in *c*.316 (Diodorus 19.11, 19.35). Alexander was murdered on the instructions of Cassander in 310 or 309.

Ipsus: fought in 301: see *Demetrius* 28–30.

left in his care: see *Demetrius* 31.

hostage: this was a common practice in such diplomatic agreements; as the marriage to Antigone suggests, it did not preclude his being a respected figure at court. The deal between Demetrius and Ptolemy was brokered by Seleucus (*Demetrius* 32).

Berenice: Berenice I was a Macedonian noblewoman who came to Egypt when her cousin Eurydice, daughter of Antipater, married Ptolemy. At what point she herself became a wife of Ptolemy is unclear, but it is a sign of her influence that it was her son, Ptolemy II Philadelphus, who succeeded to the throne in 282. Nothing is known of her first husband, Philip.

219 *recover the throne*: in 297, most likely killing Neoptolemus later that year.

220 *invited Pyrrhus to come*: Cassander had died in 297 and was succeeded very briefly by his eldest son, Philip. On his death Antipater and Alexander ruled jointly until their mother's murder in 294. See also *Demetrius* 36.

Stymphaea . . . Amphilochia: Stymphaea (= Tymphaea) and Parauaea had been seized by Philip II of Macedon some fifty years earlier; possession of Ambracia, Acarnania, and Amphilochia extended Pyrrhus' kingdom southwards around the Ambracian Gulf. Ambracia (modern Arta) was developed by Pyrrhus as his capital.

Lysimachus: see Biographies of Prominent Figures.

221 *proclaimed king of Macedon*: the story of mutual suspicion and assassination, both successful and unsuccessful, is told in *Demetrius* 36.

Deidameia's death: Plutarch presents this as if Deidameia's death occurred around this time, but his narrative in the *Demetrius* (32) clearly dates it to Demetrius' time in Cilicia, *c*.299. For Pyrrhus' incursions into Thessaly, see *Demetrius* 40.

brought him to battle: told more briefly in *Demetrius* 41.

glorious name of Achilles: Pyrrhus not only traced his ancestry back to Achilles (chapter 1), he also bore the name of Achilles' son. In engaging in single combat he was conducting himself like a Homeric hero and, since Alexander too had placed considerable emphasis on Achilles, imitation of Achilles also became imitation of Alexander, an appropriate model for a man aspiring to be king of Macedon (see next chapter). The helmeted head on his coins is also believed to be that of Achilles.

222 *inclined their heads*: see *Alexander* 4.

military treatises he wrote: now lost, but mentioned in Aelian (*Tactica* 1), Cicero (*Letters to Friends* 9.25), and Athenaeus Mechanicus (*On Siege-engines*).

Life of Scipio: this Life of Scipio Africanus, who defeated Hannibal in the Second Punic War, is now lost. In *Flamininus* 21 a different list is attributed to Hannibal (Alexander, Pyrrhus, and himself); see also Livy 35.14 and Appian, *Syrian Wars* 10.

Polyperchon: Macedonian general and key figure in the early wars of the successors: see in particular *Phocion* 31–3, *Eumenes* 12–13.

223 *let them go*: also told in Plutarch, *On the Sayings of Kings and Commanders* 37 (*Moralia* 184d) and Valerius Maximus 5.1 ext. 3.

Autoleon of Paeonia . . . Agathocles of Syracuse: the Paeonians were a tribe to the north of Macedonia while the Illyrians were directly north of Epirus. Agathocles was the expansionist ruler of Syracuse in Sicily from 316 until his assassination in 289/8.

Corcyra: modern Corfu.

sharpened steel: Euripides, *Phoenician Women* 68; this is the first of two quotations from this play, on which see D. Braund, 'Plutarch's *Pyrrhus* and Euripides' *Phoenician Women*: Biography and Tragedy on Pleonectic Parenting', *Histos*, 1 (1997), 113–27.

After this battle: Plutarch returns here to the victory over Pantauchus, described in chapter 7. Much of the material in chapter 10 (Pyrrhus' plundering expedition into Macedon, Demetrius' grandiose plans) is also covered in *Demetrius* 44.

224 *the other kings became afraid*: Lysimachus, Seleucus, and Ptolemy; see *Demetrius* 44.

married her: in 291/90; nonetheless Lanassa does not get a mention in *Demetrius*.

225 *Nesaean stallion*: a highly esteemed horse, used by the Persian aristocracy, named from the Nesaean plain in Media: see Herodotus 7.40; Arrian, *Anabasis* 7.13. The Successors often seem to have dreams of Alexander: see *Eumenes* 6 and *Demetrius* 29.

226 *land between them*: in 287, see Justin, *Epitome* 16.2.1–4.

went to Athens: in 287 or 286 Athens revolted from Demetrius (see *Demetrius* 46), who had been in control of the city since 294. Note how Pyrrhus displays a respect for Athena not shown by Demetrius (*Demetrius* 23–4). An important inscription in honour of Callias, an Athenian in the service of Ptolemy, shows that support for Athens also came from Ptolemy: M. Austin, *The Hellenistic World from Alexander to the Roman Conquest* (2nd edn., Cambridge, 2006), no. 55.

Demetrius' final defeat in Syria: Demetrius reached Asia in 286, where he attacked Lysimachus' possessions; by the following year he was a captive of Seleucus and remained so until his death in 282; see *Demetrius* 49–52.

227 *driven back to Epirus*: in 285.

battle-cry and war: Homer, *Iliad* 1.491–2.

Rome and Tarentum: Tarentum, the leading Greek city in southern Italy, saw its influence over its Greek neighbours being eroded by the increasing power of Rome. Attempts to reassert their position led to war with Rome, with the result that in 280 Pyrrhus crossed to Italy. The Tarentines made a habit of asking for military assistance from mainland Greece. In the 4th C. first Archidamus III of Sparta, then Pyrrhus' great uncle Alexander the Molossian, went to the aid of Tarentum; both died there.

228 *Lucanians, Messapians, Samnites*: non-Greek peoples of southern Italy. The Samnites in particular had a long history of conflict with Rome.

Cineas: he also wrote an epitome of Aeneas Tacticus and a history of some sort: F. Jacoby, *Fragmente der griechischen Historiker/Brill's New Jacoby*, no. 603. The dialogue with Pyrrhus recalls other such alleged exchanges between wise men and monarchs, both Hellenistic and earlier, such as that between Solon and Croesus on the nature of happiness (Herodotus 1.30–3 with 1.86), Alexander's exchanges with both the Cynic Diogenes and the Indian wise men (*Alexander* 14 and 64), and Demetrius Poliorcetes and Stilpo (*Demetrius* 9).

won by speech: Euripides, *Phoenician Women* 517–18.

229 *dreams for the future*: through the interventions of Meton and Cineas respectively, both the Tarentines and Pyrrhus are warned to think about the consequences of their actions, but both carry on regardless. They also act as a way of introducing a new stage in the life of Pyrrhus as he embarks on a five-year adventure in the West.

231 *Laevinus*: Publius Valerius Laevinus, consul of 280, whom posterity knows only for this defeat.

these barbarians' discipline: Greeks lumped all non-Greeks together as barbarians and often viewed them negatively, in particular believing them to be very impulsive and lacking self-control; hence Pyrrhus' surprise at Roman discipline. The story is alluded to also at *Flamininus* 5. See further A. Erskine, 'Polybios and Barbarian Rome', *Mediterraneo Antico*, 3 (2000), 165–82.

232 *in good order*: the battle of Heraclea in 280.

233 *elephants*: the Romans had no previous experience of elephants in battle, so their horses were untrained to deal with them. The use of war-elephants was a relatively recent development in Greek warfare; indeed, the first time Greek forces faced elephants was at Gaugamela in 331, and the practice was subsequently adopted by the Successor generals (see *Eumenes* 14; *Demetrius* 28–9).

Dionysius: Dionysius of Halicarnassus wrote his *Roman Antiquities* in the late 1st C. BCE. This covered the history of Rome from its origins until the beginning of the First Punic War, in twenty books. The books on Pyrrhus only survive in fragments and excerpts (which do include a short section on this battle, 19.12).

Hieronymus: see note to p. 153.

Gaius Fabricius: Gaius Fabricius Luscinus, consul of 282, subsequently consul again in 278 and censor in 275.

234 *Appius Claudius*: Appius Claudius Caecus, a distinguished Roman senator, former holder of both the consulship (307 and 296) and censorship (312). Some version of Appius' speech was known to Cicero in the 1st C. BCE (Cicero, *Brutus* 61, *De Senectute* 16).

235 *Alexander's Bodyguards*: Appius' jibe is only loosely true, but the gist is clear, that Pyrrhus was dependent on and inferior to those who accompanied Alexander. The Bodyguards (*sōmatophulakes*) were an elite group of seven, then later eight, membership of which was a mark of the trust that Alexander had in them (Arrian, *Anabasis* 6.28), and included Ptolemy, at whose court Pyrrhus resided, and Lysimachus. It would be mistaken, however, to see their role as solely that of bodyguard; they were often commanders in their own right.

many kings: the Senate was in fact a council composed largely of former magistrates. Cineas is not the only Greek to note the puzzling character of the Roman constitution. Polybius devoted book 6 of his history to it and there compared the consuls to kings.

Lernaean Hydra of some kind: the Hydra was a mythical multi-headed snake that lived in the marshes of Lerna near Argos. Not only did it have a disturbing number of heads (some accounts give it fifty or 100), it also had the capacity to grow a new head or even two for any one that was cut off. Killing it was the second labour of Heracles.

236 *Epicurus*: founder of the Epicurean school, he was born in Samos to Athenian parents. He began teaching in Athens in about 306 and died in 270. If true, the story would be a sign of his influence, but it is likely to have been apocryphal. In chapter 14 Cineas resumes the theme of happiness begun in his dialogue with Pyrrhus.

Saturnalia: a Roman festival celebrated in December during the winter solstice.

Fabricius' consulship: Fabricius was actually consul in 278, so a year after the battle of Asculum, which follows rather than precedes it in Plutarch's account. Perhaps Plutarch's interest in Fabricius has led him to include this letter earlier in his narrative alongside the other stories of Fabricius' integrity.

237 *Asculum*: also known as Ausculum, a city in Daunia, to be distinguished from the more northerly Asculum Picenum. Another account of the battle, fought in 279, is to be found in Dionysius of Halicarnassus, *Roman Antiquities* 20.1–3.

238 *Royal Notebooks*: what exactly these were and even their existence has been

questioned; the only other citation of them is by Dionysius of Halicarnassus (*Roman Antiquities* 20.10.2); see F. Jacoby, *Fragmente der griechischen Historiker/Brill's New Jacoby*, no. 229.

238 *completely undone*: hence the phrase 'Pyrrhic victory'.

239 *free the island from tyrants*: the death of Agathocles of Syracuse in 289/8 had led to instability on the island, and by 279 the Carthaginians were besieging Syracuse. There had long been a Carthaginian presence on the island, but it was usually limited to the west. Pyrrhus' Sicilian connections should not be overlooked; Agathocles had been his father-in-law and was grandfather of Pyrrhus' son Alexander (chapter 9).

crying out for a king: events had moved fast while Pyrrhus was away. Seleucus defeated and killed Lysimachus at the battle of Corupedium in 281, only to be assassinated by Ptolemy Ceraunus later the same year. Ptolemy, a son of Ptolemy I of Egypt, went on to claim the Macedonian throne, which he held for only a short while before his own death in battle in 279 against the invading Celts (also called Gauls). The Celts would reach as far as Delphi before their final defeat.

Libya: used of North Africa, where Carthage was located.

Eryx: a precipitous mountain in western Sicily overlooking Drepana (modern Trapani), home to a cult of Astarte.

240 *divinely inspired madness*: see Homer, *Iliad* 5.185, 6.101, and 9.238; the description of Pyrrhus' assault on the wall is surely deliberately reminiscent of Alexander's attack on the Malli when he too was first to scale the city wall (*Alexander* 63).

many of their garrisons: the Mamertines were Campanian mercenaries, previously in the pay of Agathocles, who had seized the city of Messana. Their name derived from Mamers, the Oscan god of war, equivalent to the Roman Mars and the Greek Ares. The Mamertine problem continued after Pyrrhus, and it was a Mamertine appeal to the Romans that set in motion the First Punic War in 264, giving the Romans an opportunity to intervene in Sicily, for which see Polybius 1.7–11.

between themselves and the Greeks: just as the Persians had been seen as the threat to mainland Greece, so the Carthaginians were seen as the threat to the western Greeks. Historians even synchronized the Persian Wars with Carthaginian aggression in 5th-C. Sicily (Pindar, *Pythian* 1.71–80, Herodotus 7.166). Thus, just as Alexander had eliminated the barbarian threat in the East, Pyrrhus would do the same in the West.

241 *a few years later*: Pyrrhus left Sicily in 276; the First Punic War was largely fought in Sicily and lasted from 264 until 241.

242 *Curius*: Manius Curius Dentatus, a formidable Roman commander, who was now, in 275, holding his third consulship. He would go on to hold the censorship in 272 before his death in 270.

243 *not long afterwards*: after Curius' victory over Pyrrhus at Malventum

(renamed Beneventum, Livy 9.27) in Campania in 275, the Romans completed the conquest of Italy with the capture of Tarentum in 272. The conclusion of the First Punic War in 241 brought much of Sicily under their direct control as a Roman province, with the rest of it joining in 211.

Antigonus, the son of Demetrius: Antigonus II Gonatas, see Biographies of Prominent Figures. Pyrrhus invaded Macedon in 274.

244 *Athena Itonis*: a sanctuary in Thessaly.

brave spearmen: the epigram appears in the *Palatine Anthology* (6.130) under the name of Leonidas of Tarentum. The use of the name Aeacidae points to the heroic ancestry of Pyrrhus and his family, who traced their descent back to Aeacus, grandfather of Achilles: see chapter 1, although there they are called Pyrrhidae.

scattering the bones: Aegae (modern Vergina) was where the Macedonian kings were buried. Some evidence for the Celtic looting of the tombs has been found during archaeological excavations of the site.

leapt at the chance: Plutarch continues his theme of an impulsive Pyrrhus leaping at any opportunity that presents itself. Other evidence suggests that Cleonymus had been with Pyrrhus for some time and had commanded forces in the invasion of Macedon (Polyaenus 2.29.2). He was the uncle of Areus, the ruling Agiad king in Sparta (see *Agis and Cleomenes* 3) and had himself been overlooked for the kingship back in 309/8, after which he had led an earlier expedition to south Italy to help Tarentum (in 303).

245 *Spartan education*: known as the *agōgē*, it was famous for instilling discipline and endurance in those who undertook it: see *Phocion* 20 with note.

Archidamia: widow of the Spartan king Eudamidas I and grandmother of Agis, she is described elsewhere by Plutarch (*Agis and Cleomenes* 7) as one of the richest Spartans.

246 *Phylarchus*: author of a twenty-eight-book history that began with Pyrrhus' invasion of the Peloponnese in 272 and ended with the death of the Spartan king Cleomenes III in Alexandria in 220/19. He himself lived from 272 to 188. See further *Agis and Cleomenes*, with introduction. The emphasis on Spartan women no doubt comes from him; they also play a prominent role in *Agis and Cleomenes* (e.g. 6–7, 20, 43). According to his measurements, the Spartans' trench was about 9 feet wide (2.75 metres), about 6 feet deep (1.8 metres), and over 250 yards (230 metres) long.

247 *eagle*: Pyrrhus was known as 'the Eagle', chapter 10. Alluded to also in chapter 31.

'*one omen . . . defence of Pyrrhus*': a play on Homer, *Iliad* 12.243, where Hector says 'one omen is best of all, to fight in defence of one's country'. Both Hector and Pyrrhus ignored the signs and warnings and were killed shortly afterwards.

248 *Corinth*: one of the strongest of Antigonus' Peloponnesian garrisons was based on the Acrocorinth, which rose high above the city of Corinth.

248 *victims' livers had no lobes*: the entrails of a sacrificed animal were believed to be a source of omens; lack of lobes on the liver was particularly worrying: see *Alexander* 73 and Xenophon, *Hellenica* 3.4.15.

251 *Apollo Lyceius*: *lykos* in Greek meant 'wolf', and so the title Lyceius would mean Apollo of the Wolves. Danaus was a mythological figure who had fifty daughters, the Danaids, while his twin brother Aegyptus had fifty sons. In order to avoid having to marry his daughters to his brother's sons he had fled with them to Argos.

253 *Alcyoneus*: the son of Antigonus Gonatas.

barbarian: decapitation was often associated with barbarians.

Fortune: an important theme in Plutarch's Life of Demetrius.

ARATUS

258 *Polycrates*: relatively little is known of this man, but from the first chapter it is clear that he is from Sicyon and a descendant of Aratus. He is likely to be identical with or the son of Tiberius Claudius Polycrates, who is found in a contemporary honorific decree from Delphi.

Chrysippus: Chrysippus of Soli, an influential Stoic philosopher of the 3rd C. BCE, described as the second founder of the school.

Dionysodorus of Troezen: a Greek grammarian active in Alexandria, probably in the 2nd C. BCE. The proverb was known to Cicero, *Letters to Atticus* 1.19.10.

shines forth: *Pythian* 8.44–5, written by the 5th-C. Boeotian poet Pindar.

Dorian mode of aristocracy: it is unclear what period Plutarch has in mind here. The Dorians were one of the main ethnic groups of Greece, with a strong presence in the Peloponnese; Dorian cities there included Sparta, Argos, Corinth, and Sicyon. The undiluted Dorian character of Sicyon's aristocracy can hardly have survived the tyranny of the Orthagorid dynasty that took power in the mid-7th C. and ruled the city for about a hundred years. One member of the dynasty, Cleisthenes, even renamed the three Dorian civic tribes with offensive names such as Pigmen (Herodotus 5.68). But Plutarch may have had a more recent revolution in mind. For the harmonious character of the Dorian state as set up by Lycurgus in Sparta, see *Agis and Cleomenes* 37. See also Plato, *Republic* 399a and *Laches* 188d for praise of the Dorian mode. For the history of Sicyon, see A. Griffin, *Sikyon* (Oxford, 1982).

259 *Argos by night*: the history of Sicyon between Cleon and Abantidas is confusing. Pausanias (2.8) offers an even more concise and rather different reading of events. Both agree, however, that Aratus left Sicyon at the time of Abantidas' tyranny. The death of Aratus' father Cleinias is usually dated to 264.

win crowns: the ancient pentathlon consisted of five events: discus-throwing, the long jump, javelin-throwing, running, and wrestling. At the major panhellenic festivals the prize for victory was a crown, which at Olympia would be made of olive while at Delphi it was laurel.

His statues: Pausanias records a statue of Aratus in the theatre at Sicyon (2.7.5) and another at Olympia in honour of a victory in the chariot race (6.12.5–6).

mattock: digging could be part of the training for an athlete, especially a pentathlete.

Memoirs: see the introduction to this Life.

Deinias and Aristotle the logician: these men are not otherwise known, although there has been speculation that Deinias is the historian of the Argolid cited in chapter 29, and that Aristotle might be identified with the friend of Aratus in chapter 44. The representation of Abantidas and his successors as tyrants may reflect the hostile stance taken by Aratus in his *Memoirs*.

260 *similarity*: these similarities were presumably based on comparing statues. Periander was a tyrant of Corinth in the late 7th/early 6th C. Myrsilus, a 3rd-C. writer from Lesbos, may be Plutarch's source for all three comparisons.

Aetolian plot: the Aetolian League was increasingly influential in central Greece, but the reason for this intervention in Sicyon is unknown.

Antigonus: Antigonus Gonatas, ruler of Macedon from 277 to 239. See Biographies of Prominent Figures.

Ptolemy: Ptolemy II Philadelphus, ruler of Egypt from 282 to 246.

Ecdelus: at *Philopoemen* 1 Ecdelus is named as one of the mentors of Philopoemen (see also the accompanying note). Aristomachus is otherwise unknown.

Arcesilaus: from Pitane in Aeolia in Asia Minor, lived 316/15 to 242/1. He was head of the Academy from *c.*268 and was later considered to be the founder of the sceptical Middle Academy.

exiles: according to chapter 9, there were some eighty exiles as a result of Nicocles' recent tyranny and around 500 other exiles from earlier tyrannies.

261 *king's horses*: the presence of a royal Macedonian stud here in the territory of Sicyon suggests that relations between the tyrants and Macedon were reasonably good, though not so good that Nicocles was free from worry that Aratus might seek help from Macedon: chapter 4.

263 *visible in Corinth*: Corinth is around 15 miles/25 km to the east.

264 *internecine strife*: for Aratus' resolution of this problem, see chapter 14.

Achaean League: originally a confederacy of twelve Achaean cities, it had been active in the fifth and fourth centuries before coming to an end in circumstances that are obscure. It was subsequently revived in a new form in the 280s and 270s. Polybius 2.41–3 gives a brief history of the league before Aratus. For the history and nature of the league, see E. Mackil, *Creating a Common Polity: Religion, Economy, and Politics in the Making of the Greek Koinon* (Berkeley, 2013).

264 *what he did*: Sicyon was liberated in 251 and joined the Achaean League very soon afterwards, perhaps even in the same year. Aratus was twenty at the time (Polybius 2.43).

being Dorians: see chapter 2, with note.

265 *cautious fingers*: Polybius 4.8 contrasts Aratus' brilliance and boldness in devising and carrying out various stratagems with his hesitancy and lack of courage in more orthodox warfare. Plutarch would have been familiar with the passage: see C. Pelling, 'Aspects of Plutarch's Characterisation', *Illinois Classical Studies*, 13 (1988), 257–74, at 264–8.

the king: whether this refers to Antigonus or Ptolemy must be a matter for conjecture. Antigonus has been favoured since M. Holleaux, 'Sur un Passage de la vie d'Aratos par Plutarque', *Hermes*, 41 (1906), 475–8. But a case can be made for Ptolemy, given the positive depiction of their relationship in chapter 12 and the reference there to Ptolemy's generosity. Antigonus, on the other hand, is earlier (9) described as begrudging Sicyon its restored freedom, and then in chapter 12 it is he who is the enemy when Aratus lands on Hydrea.

266 *Timanthes*: perhaps the painter; see chapter 32.

Roman ship: Rome was by this stage a powerful city in Italy, contending with Carthage for control of Sicily, but evidence for a Roman presence of any sort in the East is surprisingly scanty, making this incidental reference particularly interesting. It is possible that it was an Italian merchant ship rather than a Roman one.

Pamphilus or Melanthus: two 4th-C. painters, both leading figures in the so-called Sicyonian school of painting. Melanthus (also Melanthius) was a pupil of Pamphilus.

Apelles: a famous 4th-C. painter, whose paintings included one of Alexander: see *Alexander* 4 and also *Demetrius* 22.

267 *Polemon*: a 2nd-C. BCE geographer from Ilium in the Troad, whose works included one on the paintings of Sicyon (Athenaeus 13.577b–c).

safe and secure: the problem that Aratus needed to solve was the exiles' claim on their former property, which in some cases dated back fifty years (see chapter 9). For praise of Aratus' handling of this situation, see Cicero, *On Duties* 2.81–3.

268 *play-acting and trumpery*: see further the introduction to *Demetrius*.

first Generalship of the Achaean League: in 245. Locris and Calydon were located on the other side of the Gulf of Corinth.

Boeotarch, Abaeocritus: the seven Boeotarchs were the chief magistrates of the Boeotian League. Boeotian military action against Aetolia took place with the encouragement of the Achaeans: see Polybius 20.4 on the general decline of Boeotia.

269 *for the second time*: this must in fact have been two years later in 243, since the Generalship could not be held in successive years (chapter 24).

Acrocorinth: towering over Corinth was this fortified mountain, 575 m. high, from which not only Corinth could be controlled but also the surrounding region and movement into and out of the Peloponnese across the Isthmus. Its strategic value meant that it was home to a series of garrisons installed by occupying powers, even in more recent times when it was held by the Ottomans.

'sister to Marathon': Chares was a leading 4th-C. Athenian general. His victory came while assisting the rebellious Persian satrap Artabazus against the Persian king in 355/4: see the scholion to Demosthenes 4.19 (translated in P. Harding, *From the Peloponnesian War to the Battle of Ipsus* (Cambridge, 1985), no. 72) and Diodorus 16.22.

their rule from outside: Pelopidas was a prominent Theban general, who in 379 had played a major role in expelling the Spartan garrison from the Cadmeia, the acropolis of Thebes. He was the subject of another of Plutarch's Lives, where the comparison also occurs (*Pelopidas* 13). Thrasybulus fought against the rule of the Thirty Tyrants in Athens in the late 5th C. Note the way that the Macedonians are contrasted with Greeks as foreigners, although the Greek does not go so far as to label them 'barbarians' (unlike chapter 38); for a different representation, see *Alexander* 16, with note.

fetters of Greece: the Acrocorinth was one of the fetters, along with Chalcis in Euboea and Demetrias in Thessaly: Polybius 18.11. Philip V was king of Macedon from 221 to 179: see further chapters 46–52.

Alexander: son of Craterus, the half-brother of Antigonus Gonatas, he had been governor of Corinth and commander of the garrison for his uncle until 249 (or, less probably, 252), when he rebelled and went into alliance with the Achaean League. He died in 245.

Demetrius: Antigonus Gonatas' successor Demetrius II ruled Macedon from 239 until his death in 229. He was the father of Philip V.

270 *Amoebeus*: famous lyre-player.

old man: Antigonus would have been about seventy-five when he seized the Acrocorinth in 245.

Persaeus: a Stoic philosopher, pupil of Zeno of Citium the founder of the school; see further chapter 23.

This is what happened: Plutarch offers the fullest account of Aratus' capture of the Acrocorinth in 243, but see also Polyaenus, *Stratagems* 6.5 and Pausanias 2.8.4.

271 *Phocion and Epaminondas*: Phocion repeatedly turns down large sums in *Phocion* 18, 21, and 30). The 4th-C. Theban general Epaminondas was the subject of a lost life by Plutarch; for his 'indifference to money', see *Philopoemen* 3.

275 *Cenchreae*: there are several accounts of Persaeus' role in the fall of the

Acrocorinth, but very little agreement between them. Even his survival is disputed: according to Pausanias (2.8.4, 7.8.3) he was killed in the attack. Cenchreae was Corinth's port on the Saronic Gulf about 4 miles (7 km) away, so if he did survive he did not go very far. For Persaeus' place at the Macedonian court, see A. Erskine, 'Between Philosophy and the Court: The Life of Persaios of Kition', in A. Erskine and L. Llewellyn-Jones (eds.), *Creating a Hellenistic World* (Swansea, 2011), 171–94.

275 *Zeno's teaching*: the Stoic wise man was an ideal and in practice no Stoic claimed to be one: see R. Brouwer, *The Stoic Sage: The Early Stoics on Wisdom, Sagehood and Socrates* (Cambridge, 2014), ch. 3.

sanctuary of Hera: this would have been the sanctuary of Hera Akraia on the strategically important Perachora promontory, not the sanctuary of Hera by one of the city-gates of Corinth, since that was already in his possession (chapters 21 and 22).

Lechaeum: the port of Corinth on the Corinthian Gulf, hence the capture of the king's ships.

'the last of the Greeks': see *Philopoemen* 1.

plundered it: Aratus' objective was to drive out the Macedonian garrisons in Attica and near by (see Pausanias 2.8.6) and generally foment rebellion against Macedon.

Ptolemy: Ptolemy II Philadelphus had died in 246 and was succeeded by his son Ptolemy III Euergetes, who ruled until 221.

276 *could be done*: the assassination took place in 240. Aristomachus appears to be one of a family of Argive tyrants, whose two successors Aristippus and Aristomachus were also his sons. His father is very likely to have been the Aristippus who supported Antigonus against Pyrrhus in the late 270s (*Pyrrhus* 30) and who may have begun this tyrant dynasty: see F. Walbank, *A Historical Commentary on Polybius*, vol. 1 (Oxford, 1957), 265. For the reinstatement of their statues by Antigonus Doson, see chapter 45.

277 *thirty mnas*: this is a relatively small sum (half a talent), and the Mantineans as arbitrators may have been trying to have it both ways, finding for Argos while only issuing the Achaean League a nominal fine. Shortly afterwards Mantinea joined the Achaean League. See S. Ager, *Interstate Arbitrations in the Greek World, 337–90 B.C.* (Berkeley, 1997), no. 39.

278 *successful*: although Plutarch writes at length about Aratus' dealings with Argos, he gives little indication of chronology. The events that follow, however, must fall between Aristippus' accession in 240 and his death in 235.

freedom was the prize: the Argive reluctance to help Aratus might suggest that Aristippus was not as unpopular as he is made out to be here. The Nemean Games were a panhellenic festival that took place every two years, overseen by Argos, although that role had once been played by Cleonae, hence Aratus' hosting of a rival Nemean festival there.

279 *Deinias*: 3rd-C. Argive historian, author of a work on Argos.

took control: the king would have been Demetrius II, who had succeeded Antigonus Gonatas in 239 (see note to p. 269) and continued his father's policy of supporting this dynasty of Argive tyrants (see note to p. 276).

280 *as tyrant*: Lydiadas had been ruler of Megalopolis since around 245.

elected him their General: Lydiadas brought Megalopolis into the Achaean League in 235 and held the Generalship for the first time in 234/3.

third Generalship: his second Generalship was 232/1 and his third 230/29.

281 *turn into a hawk*: one of many fables attributed to Aesop. The cuckoo presumably was once a hawk, just as Lydiadas was once a tyrant. That certainly is the implication of Aristotle's *Enquiry into Animals* 6.7.563b, which argues in detail against the view that the hawk transforms itself into a cuckoo.

war against the Aetolians either: after tracing Aratus' and Achaea's relationship with the tyrants of Argos and Megalopolis, Plutarch returns to the 240s and Achaea's relationship with Aetolia.

Pellene: an Achaean city.

he had readily available: between the seizure of the Acrocorinth in 243 and the Aetolian incursion into the Peloponnese in 241, Achaea had made an alliance with the revolutionary Spartan king Agis IV. The reasons for the Aetolian attack are obscure; it has variously been interpreted as a raid and as a more substantial attempt, backed by Macedon, to undermine the growing Achaean League. The story is told in more detail in *Agis and Cleomenes* 13–15, although neither account satisfactorily explains why Aratus avoided battle.

sanctuary of Artemis: see Pausanias 7.27.

282 *to defend himself*: a variation on this is told by Polyaenus, *Stratagems* 8.59, in which a priestess, dressed up as the goddess in armour and helmet and leading a procession, terrifies the Aetolians. In Polyaenus, however, the goddess is Athena.

depiction of the battle: Timanthes may be identical with the friend of the same name mentioned in chapter 12. The expulsion of the Aetolians from Pellene is picked out by Polybius (4.8) as one of Aratus' great achievements.

against the Achaeans: presumably Plutarch has in mind the Aetolians, Macedon, and the various Peloponnesian tyrants, such as Lydiadas of Megalopolis (who had not yet in 239 joined the Achaean League) and Aristippus of Argos.

between the two leagues: the alliance was most likely agreed in 239–238: see J. Scholten, *The Politics of Plunder: Aitolians and their Koinon in the Early Hellenistic Era, 279–217 BC* (Berkeley, 2000), 131–44. Pantoleon of Pleuron was a leading Aetolian politician who held the Generalship of the league five times.

282 *with the Acrocorinth*: for Erginus, see chapter 18.

283 *over and over again*: for his first attack, see chapter 24.

Thriasian plain: a plain to the west of Athens.

accession to the throne: Demetrius II succeeded in 239 and ruled for ten years.

Demetrius' general Bithys: no more is known about this battle. It is likely that it was fought in the Peloponnese somewhere between Tegea and Sparta in the later 230s, perhaps a consequence of Lydiadas' abandoning Macedon for Achaea. Bithys is otherwise unknown, unless he is the man of the same name honoured in an Athenian inscription.

turned to for help: the Athenian revolt must have happened in the first half of 229, before Aratus took over the Generalship from Lydiadas.

against their neighbours: the new Macedonian king was having to deal with a rebellion in Thessaly in the south and an invasion by the Dardanians in the north.

284 *pay off his troops*: according to Polybius 2.44, in the aftermath of the death of Demetrius Aratus launched a campaign to win over the various Macedonian-backed tyrants in the Peloponnese, on the one hand offering inducements such as bribes and promises of political office in the league, on the other threatening military action.

Phlious: ruled by the tyrant Cleonymus (Polybius 2.44).

their General: Aristomachus was General for 228/7.

Cleomenes: Cleomenes III, king of Sparta from about 235 to 222. In general, this account by Plutarch of the conflict with Cleomenes in the 220s needs to be read alongside his Life of the king in *Agis and Cleomenes* (chapter 22 onwards). They are not always consistent with each other, the differences probably to be explained by Plutarch's prioritizing different sources in each Life—Aratus' *Memoirs* in *Aratus* and Phylarchus in *Agis and Cleomenes*. A further account, also indebted to Aratus' *Memoirs*, is to be found in Polybius 2.47–70.

Pallantium: see *Agis and Cleomenes* 25.

for the twelfth time: 227/6, but this must be a slip for 'tenth time'.

Mount Lycaeum: the modern Diaforti, lying in the border area between Elis, Messenia, and Arcadia. For the monument to those who died in the battle, Pausanias 8.28. The battle occurred in spring 227.

285 *the resident aliens*: see also Polybius 2.57–8, who says that Aratus later installed a garrison of 200 mercenaries and a body of 300 settlers; it is possible that the resident aliens and settlers are to be identified with each other. Mantinea had only been acquired by Cleomenes from the Aetolians two years before.

reined in: Aratus would have been about forty-four years old in 227 while Cleomenes was a little over thirty.

286 *Aegium*: meeting-place of the Achaean league, home to its sanctuary of

Zeus Homarius. The hostility to Aratus hints that Lydiadas (who was a Megalopolitan) may not have been as unpopular as Plutarch suggested.

for the time being: knowledge of what Aratus thought of doing but did not in the end do very likely comes from his *Memoirs*.

Megistonous: the husband of Cleomenes' mother Cratesicleia is mentioned several times in *Agis and Cleomenes* (chapters 28, 32, 40, and 42), where he is an early supporter of Cleomenes' revolutionary actions, including the killing of the ephors. There is, however, no reference to this battle in that Life. How Megistonous came to be released after his capture is not said, but it was clearly not long before he was back in Sparta.

elected General: for 225/4, the first of several occasions on which Timoxenus would hold the Generalship. For Aratus' refusal of the office, see also *Agis and Cleomenes* 36. Plutarch is moving ahead here. The defeats at Mantinea and Hecatombaeum (chapter 39) fall in 226/5 and in *Agis and Cleomenes* 36 are held responsible for Aratus' decision not to stand.

absolute power: the revolution of Cleomenes took place in 227: see *Agis and Cleomenes* 29–34.

barbarian stronghold: anti-Macedonian rhetoric going back to Demosthenes tended to represent them as barbarians; see also chapter 16 (Greeks vs. foreign imperialists) and the note there.

Heraclid: the two Spartan royal families, the Agiads and the Eurypontids, traced their ancestry back to Heracles.

287 *Antigonus*: Antigonus Doson, who ruled Macedon from 229 until his death in 221.

Aesop's hunter: there are several versions of this fable (see Aristotle, *Rhetoric* 2.1393b and Phaedrus 4.4). Essentially, a horse is angry with a boar or stag and so turns to a hunter to get his revenge, but the hunter's condition is that the horse must take the bit between his teeth, and as a result the horse finds that it has voluntarily enslaved itself.

to call in Antigonus: this volte-face was the most controversial act in Aratus' career, and Plutarch brushes over the complicated and secretive diplomatic overtures that Aratus made to Antigonus, for which see Polybius 2.47–51. The results are treated in chapters 41–2. For a very negative view of Aratus' actions in inviting Antigonus in the Peloponnese, see *Agis and Cleomenes* 37, an interpretation that may be influenced by Phylarchus.

Hecatombaeum: for these defeats see *Agis and Cleomenes* 35.

offered him hostages: according to *Agis and Cleomenes* 38 Aratus' actions here were influenced by his knowledge that the agreement with Antigonus was virtually settled. Aratus' conditions are slightly different in *Agis and Cleomenes*, a discrepancy that is perhaps to be explained by careless reading of his source.

288 *agitators in the cities*: people variously hoped or feared that the Spartan social reforms (land redistribution and cancellation of debts) would be exported to their cities: see *Agis and Cleomenes* 38.

288 *absolute authority*: see the beginning of chapter 41 for his election as 'General with unrestricted powers'; it is likely, but not certain, that these were the powers he used to carry out the executions.

no worries or suspicions: Aratus' flight from Corinth is told differently at *Agis and Cleomenes* 40; there, for instance, it is Aratus who summons the Corinthians to a meeting rather than the other way around.

289 *their towns to him*: Troezen, Epidaurus, and Hermione: see *Agis and Cleomenes* 40. On the Headland, see also *Demetrius* 25. While the order of events is relatively secure, the exact chronology is less certain, but 225 seems the most probable date for the capture of Corinth and the neighbouring towns.

thirty-three years: Plutarch is mistaken here. Aratus' liberation of Sicyon occurred in 251 and this election took place in 224 at the latest, thus not even thirty years apart.

Eurycleides and Micion: two brothers who were leading politicians in Athens and were influential in the liberation of the city from Macedonian control in 229. Achaean frustration at their subsequent policy of neutrality is evident in Polybius 5.106.6–8. See C. Habicht, *Athens from Alexander to Antony* (Cambridge, Mass., 1997), 173–8.

Tripylus . . . Megistonous: the details here differ from those at *Agis and Cleomenes* 40, where the ambassadors are named as Megistonous and Tritymallus of Messene, with the embassy of Megistonous coming first.

six talents a year: at some point, probably winter 226/5, Ptolemy had stopped his subsidy to Aratus and the Achaeans and transferred it to Cleomenes (thus Polybius 2.51).

the other way around: this was reported by Aratus in his *Memoirs*: see *Agis and Cleomenes* 40.

290 *his son*: also called Aratus, see chapter 49 ('the younger Aratus').

several hostages: the meeting which agreed to the alliance most likely took place in spring 224.

Ministers: the senior magistrates of the league, known as the *dēmiourgoi* and, in the early 2nd C., ten in number.

the former Antigonus: i.e. Antigonus Gonatas, as opposed to the current king of Macedon, Antigonus Doson.

despite being young: rather surprising given that Antigonus was in his late thirties and the age-difference between himself and Aratus was less than ten years.

291 *stiff resistance*: see further *Agis and Cleomenes* 41.

Aristotle: possibly to be identified with the murderer of Abantidas (chapter 3).

retreated to Mantinea: see further *Agis and Cleomenes* 41–2.

292 *without the due process of law*: after Aristomachus had laid down his tyranny and brought Argos into the Achaean League, he had held the Generalship

(chapter 35), but his execution suggests that he had been involved in the Argive decision to switch sides to Sparta (chapter 39). Regardless of criticism of the manner of his death, which is found as early as Phylarchus, Polybius (2.59) thought Aristomachus' punishment well deserved.

in honour of Antigonus: thus Antigonus was the recipient of cult honours from the Achaean states. As with the honours to Antigonus Monophthalmus and Demetrius Poliorcetes in Athens (*Demetrius* 10–13, 23–4) these were not uncontroversial, but in this case Plutarch refrains from the kind of moral judgement he made there, though the restraint is not so evident at *Agis and Cleomenes* 37. Polybius 2.70.5 notes that Antigonus was granted every honour and it is evident that the festival of the Antigoneia was still being celebrated fifty years later (Polybius 30.29.2).

pulled down: the Argive tyrants (see chapter 25 with note) had been supported by Macedon.

law of reprisal: Polybius (2.56–8) makes a strong defence of the Achaeans, justifying their actions on the basis that when the Mantineans went over to Sparta they massacred the Achaean garrison that they themselves had requested. But at the same time he also rejects the more extreme elements of Phylarchus' account, which is presumably the basis of the negative picture presented by Plutarch here.

Simonides: a much-quoted poet of the late 6th and early 5th C. from the island of Ceos.

293 *'lovely Mantinea'*: from Homer's catalogue of ships in the second book of the *Iliad* (line 607). The settlement continued under the name of Antigoneia until the 2nd C. CE, when the emperor Hadrian changed it back (Pausanias 8.8).

Sellasia: in summer 222; see *Agis and Cleomenes* 48–50.

with his health already failing: Antigonus is thought to have been suffering from tuberculosis.

Antigonus' death: in 221, see *Agis and Cleomenes* 51.

Caphyae: in 220, treated in detail by a highly critical Polybius (4.9–12). The battle was fought at the time of Aratus' thirteenth Generalship.

intervene in Greek affairs: this marked the beginning of the Social War (220–217) between Macedon, Achaea, and their allies on the one side and the Aetolians on the other.

294 *Apelles and Megaleas*: these men had been appointed to their positions in Antigonus' will, Apelles to be guardian of Philip and Megaleas to be chief secretary and so responsible for the king's correspondence (Polybius 4.76, 4.87). By 218 both had fallen from favour and had little choice but to end their lives (Polybius 5.28).

Eperatus: General in 218–217, see the very negative portrayal of him in Polybius (5.1.7, 5.30).

against the Aetolians: the three instances given here are all treated in more detail in Polybius: Philip's restoration of order in Sparta in 220 (4.22–4); Crete became an extension of the Social War (4.53–5, summed up at 7.11.9); the Social War against Aetolia (5.102–3).

294 *had them executed*: the fine and the events leading up to the executions (as well as the suicides of Apelles and Megaleas) are treated in much more detail by Polybius (5.15, 25–9).

his true nature: both Plutarch and Polybius (4.77, 7.11, 7.13.7, and 10.26) draw attention to the change in Philip's character, but their explanations are almost the opposite of each other. Polybius sees Philip as a good king corrupted, whereas for Plutarch Philip's fundamental badness gradually became apparent. On Philip, see F. W. Walbank, *Philip V of Macedon* (Cambridge, 1940).

affair with his wife: the wife was Polycrateia, who may subsequently have married Philip (Livy 27.31); some scholars have even conjectured that she was the mother of Philip's successor, Perseus: see E. Carney, *Women and Monarchy in Macedonia* (Norman, Okla., 2000), 193–4. This was not the only such affair, although the only one to end in marriage. According to Polybius (10.26), he made a habit of seducing widows and married women but, as his character deteriorated, he took whatever women he wanted (like a traditional tyrant).

295 *treatment of Messene*: in 215 or 214.

Demetrius of Pharos: a supporter of Rome in the First Illyrian War (229–8), he had been rewarded with considerable power in Illyris, only to fall out with Rome ten years later. Defeated in the Second Illyrian War of 219, he fled to the Macedonian court.

296 *Messene was not to be his*: this account of events at Messene is probably derived from Polybius, to judge by what survives of this portion of his work (7.12–14).

ignominious manner possible: in 215 during the Second Punic War Philip had made an alliance with Hannibal against Rome, an alliance that led to the First Macedonian War. Philip turned his attention to the Adriatic, where he launched a new fleet of 120 ships, only to find it trapped by the Romans in the mouth of the river Aous, with the result that he was forced to burn many of them himself (Livy 24.40).

297 *friendship with a king*: Polybius (8.12.1–5) gives a slightly fuller account of the poisoning of Aratus; there Taurion is said to have had particular responsibility for the Peloponnese. Philip had quite a reputation for getting rid of people, so much so that Flamininus was said to have taunted him about it when they met (Polybius 18.7.6; *Flamininus* 17). It is quite likely, however, that Aratus died of natural causes, probably tuberculosis.

seventeenth Generalship: his death probably occurred in 213, possibly during his sixteenth rather than seventeenth Generalship.

Founder and Saviour of the City: the people of Sicyon are honouring Aratus after death by taking the exceptional step of elevating him to heroic status, which effectively exempts him from the usual Greek bar on burial within a city's walls. He was not, however, the first to be buried there; in the 4th C. Euphron had been buried in the agora and honoured as a founder (Xenophon, *Hellenica* 7.3.12). The Arateium would have been a heroön or hero sanctuary, the location of the cult of the hero. The annual sacrifices allow the hero to be remembered by the community. For heroic honours for Aratus, see also Polybius 8.12.7–8 and Pausanias 2.8.1, 2.9.4, 2.10.3 (where he is a son of the healer god Asclepius).

Soteria: the festival of Salvation, with the sacrifices carried out appropriately by the priest of Zeus the Saviour.

298 *Guild of Dionysus*: groups of travelling professional actors, musicians, and stage technicians.

from suffering: the date of his mysterious death is unknown, perhaps the last decade of the century. He held the Generalship in 219/18.

His defeat: for Philip's defeat at the battle of Cynoscephalae in 197 and its aftermath, see *Flamininus* 7–12.

exceptional son: Demetrius, who went as hostage to Rome: see *Flamininus* 9, with note.

Gnathaenion, a seamstress: elsewhere Plutarch adds that she was from Argos (*Aemilius Paullus* 8). It is not certain who the mother of Perseus was: see also note to p. 294.

ended with him: in 168 Perseus was defeated by the Roman commander Aemilius Paullus at the battle of Pydna in the Third Macedonian War. For the triumph, see Plutarch's detailed description at *Aemilius Paullus* 32–4.

AGIS AND CLEOMENES

303 *Ixion myth*: Ixion was a mythical king of Thessaly, who, when he lusted after Zeus' wife Hera, was tricked into raping a cloud in the form of the goddess instead. As punishment he was nailed to a revolving wheel for eternity. Aeschylus and Euripides both composed lost tragedies on aspects of the Ixion myth. An early version of it survives in Pindar, *Pythian* 2.21–48.

about their sheep: from a lost tragedy, perhaps *The Shepherds*.

Theophrastus: the philosopher Theophrastus of Eresus on the island of Lesbos (late 370s to early 280s) was Aristotle's successor as head of the Peripatetic school.

at the same time: see *Phocion* 30. For Antipater see Biographies of Prominent Figures.

304 *always following its head*: one of Aesop's Fables, also told by Babrius (no. 134).

Tiberius and Gaius Gracchus: Agis and Cleomenes were paired with these two Roman brothers, who held the tribunate in 133 and 123–122 respectively (included in the Oxford World's Classics *Roman Lives*).

305 *things changed*: it is clear from the beginning of chapter 5 that Plutarch has in mind the period that followed Sparta's victory over Athens in the Peloponnesian War (431–404).

Eurypontid: one of the two Spartan royal houses; the other was the Agiad. Between them they supplied the two kings of Sparta.

man in Greece: Agesilaus II (*c*.445–359), king from 400 until his death, was also the subject of one of Plutarch's Lives (included in the Oxford World's Classics *Greek Lives*).

Manduria in Italy: Archidamus III (*c*.400–338), king from 360/59 until his death. Like Pyrrhus later, he had accepted an appeal for help from the South Italian city of Tarentum.

leaving no heir: Agis III (reigned 338–331) raised a rebellion against Macedon in the late 330s (see also *Demosthenes* 24), while Alexander was campaigning against Persia. Antipater had been left in charge of Macedon during Alexander's absence. Agis' brother Eudamidas reigned from 331 to around 305.

battle of Plataea: in 479, the decisive land battle of the Persian Wars, in which the Greek forces defeated the Persians commanded by Mardonius (Herodotus, book 9). Pausanias was a member of the Agiad royal family and acted as regent for his nephew Pleistarchus, whose father Leonidas I had died at Thermopylae. His victory at Plataea brought him considerable fame, but arrogance and accusations of medism (collaboration with the Persian enemy) brought about his downfall and death, probably in the early 460s. His son Pleistoanax succeeded to the Agiad throne in 458.

Sparta to Tegea: Pausanias was king twice, first as a minor during his father's exile from 445 to 426, when his father returned; then as an adult from 408 to 395. Blamed for the death of the Spartan general Lysander, he went into exile at nearby Tegea, where he died in 380 (Xenophon, *Hellenica* 3.5.6–7, 17–25).

succeeded him: the dates of their reigns are as follows: Cleombrotus I (380–371), Agesipolis II (371–370), Cleomenes II (370–309), and Areus I (309–265). Cleomenes II's reign was distinguished only by its length.

Cleonymus: for the story of Cleonymus and his jealous rivalry with Acrotatus (reigned 265–262), see *Pyrrhus* 25–9.

306 *Seleucus*: presumably Seleucus I Nicator, since Seleucus II Callinicus did not come to the throne until 246, after Leonidas had become king of Sparta in the later 250s. Seleucus Nicator died some years before this in 281, but Pausanias 3.6.7 describes Leonidas as an old man at the time of his accession. He is also said to have married a satrap's daughter and had children by her: see chapters 10 and 11.

ancestral constitution and training regime: in other words, the institutions attributed to the legendary Spartan lawgiver Lycurgus. What this ancestral constitution consisted of changed with time, although emphasis was always laid on the Spartan education system, the *agōgē* (see also *Phocion*

20). For a sense of how the traditional Spartan system was understood in the 4th C. BCE, see Xenophon's *Constitution of the Lacedaemonians*; in contrast, Plutarch's *Lycurgus* (included in the Oxford World's Classics *Greek Lives*) presents a much later view and one that begins with the disclaimer that almost nothing can be said about Lycurgus which is not disputed.

gold and silver: Lycurgus was said to have banned gold and silver currency in favour of iron (Plutarch, *Lycurgus* 9).

their allotted farms on to their sons: there were said to have been 9,000 allotments for Spartan citizens (Plutarch, *Lycurgus* 8).

Epitadeus: this is the only reference to this man, and many now believe he was invented to explain the supposed abandonment of the Lycurgan property system. Those who believe he is a historical figure would usually locate him at the beginning of the 4th C.

just a few hands: the decline in the number of Spartan citizens by the 4th C. is observed by Aristotle (*Politics* 2.1270a).

307 *seasoned with daring*: Lysander was a descendant of Lysander, the great Spartan general of the Peloponnesian War (Pausanias 3.6.7), about whom Plutarch wrote a Life. Mandrocleidas is perhaps to be identified with the ambassador of *Pyrrhus* 26.

308 *most of the wealth*: Aristotle, *Politics* 2.1270a, puts the women in control of almost 40 per cent of the whole country.

not citizens for Sparta: cancellation of debts and redistribution of land were common slogans of the aspiring tyrant, and the acquisition of a bodyguard an important first step: see e.g. Diodorus 19.9 on Agathocles of Syracuse, and Plato, *Republic* 8.566d–e on the tyrant in general.

ephorate: Lysander was elected for the year running from autumn 243 to autumn 242.

Council of Elders: the Gerousia, the governing body of the Spartan state, made up of twenty-eight elders and the two kings.

4,500 lots, and the outer territory 15,000: the loss of Messenia had halved Spartan territory, so it is interesting to see that these figures are exactly half those given by Plutarch for Lycurgus' original reform (*Lycurgus* 8). This coincidence is perhaps a sign that the revolutionaries of 3rd-C. Sparta were rewriting the past and so shaping subsequent interpretations of Lycurgus. See chapter 32 for the role of the Stoic Sphaerus in Cleomenes' revolution.

309 *400 or 200 men*: the size of these communal dining messes, to which its members contributed, contrasts with the much smaller sizes given for the original messes attributed to Lycurgus—fifteen, according to *Lycurgus* 12.

love of money: Lycurgus was said to have received an oracle to this effect from Delphi (Diodorus 7.12.5).

venerable oracle: Thalamae lay near the border with Messenia; Spartan leaders are reported to have spent the night there and received the oracle in their dreams; thus Cicero, *On Divination* 1.96, and chapter 28.

309 *Pasiphaë*: this explanation derives the name Pasiphaë from the Greek *pasi phainein*, 'reveal to all'. Cassandra, daughter of the Trojan king, famously had prophetic powers, but thanks to Apollo was destined never to be believed. After the Trojan War she was brought home by Agamemnon only to be murdered by his wife Clytemnestra, hence this and other cults associated with her in the Peloponnese. Another interpretation of the oracle is found at Pausanias 3.26.1, where the oracle is in fact that of Ino.

seercraft: Amyclas was a legendary king of Sparta. Phylarchus was a contemporary Greek historian, who was a major source for Plutarch's Lives of Agis and Cleomenes (see the introduction to the Life).

almost 300 years: this is puzzling. In chapter 4 he is compared with Agesilaus, the early 4th-C. king who took a Spartan army into Asia Minor, but that is well short of 300 years. It may be an error, or perhaps Plutarch is looking back further, maybe to Leonidas at Thermopylae in the Persian Wars of the early 5th C. (see chapter 14 for a comparison to him).

310 *expelling foreigners*: a very similar explanation is given in Plutarch's *Lycurgus* 27; the practice, known as *xenēlasia*, was commented on negatively in Pericles' funeral speech (Thucydides 2.39.1).

high honour in Sparta: Terpander was a 7th-C. poet and musician from Antissa on Lesbos, Thaletas of Gortyn on Crete (also known as Thales) was an early-6th-C. poet, and Pherecydes of Syros was a 6th-C. writer on the gods and cosmogony. All had associations with Sparta in various stories: Terpander was the first winner of the citharodic competition at the Carneia (Athenaeus 14.635e); Thaletas was invited there by Lycurgus (Plutarch, *Lycurgus* 4); and, in an example less convincing in terms of respect for foreigners, Pherecydes was killed and skinned by the Spartans (Plutarch, *Pelopidas* 21).

Timotheus' case: Phrynis and Timotheus were both celebrated musicians and innovators of the 5th C. Spartan disapproval may have been more to do with their broader musical innovation and rejection of tradition than the number of strings; see M. Maas, 'Timotheus at Sparta: The Nature of the Crime', in N. K. Baker and B. R. Hanning (eds.), *Musical Humanism and Its Legacy: Essays in Honour of Claude V. Palisca* (New York, 1992), 37–52.

Heraclid: the two Spartan royal families traced their ancestry back to Heracles.

311 *exonerate them*: no other example of this procedure is known.

joined him there: Leonidas was not the first leading Spartan to take refuge in this sanctuary on the Spartan acropolis; Pausanias, the victor of Plataea, had done so in 470s, but far from being saved, he starved to death there (Thucydides 1.134). The early Spartan king Charillus had also taken refuge there, though with less fatal results (Plutarch, *Lycurgus* 5 and chapter 30).

the kings: referring to Agis and Cleombrotus. The ephors object to Agis and his associates' proposals but do not question the deposition of Leonidas.

should not intrude: there is no known precedent for this, and it may be that this interpretation is a product of revolutionary Sparta. Significantly, Cleomenes III would later say the ephors had originally been the king's assistants (chapter 31), a position consistent with the argument of Lysander and Mandrocleidas.

312 *did not happen*: the Aetolian invasion was in the summer of 241; Aratus was the chief magistrate of the Achaean League (see also *Aratus* 31).

313 *Baton of Sinope*: from Sinope on the Black Sea, Baton most probably lived in the late 3rd and early 2nd C. BCE. A number of titles of his works are known, including several on tyranny, but it is not clear in what context this remark would have been made. This is the only occasion on which Plutarch cites Baton.

Aratus wrote: in his *Memoirs*, which Plutarch makes extensive use of in his Life of Aratus.

314 *a second term as ephor*: the ephorate could only be held for a single year.

sanctuary of Poseidon: it is not clear which sanctuary is intended here; there was a famous sanctuary on Cape Taenarum where refuge could be taken (see Thucydides 1.133).

316 *Agesistrata*: the mother of Agis, see chapter 4.

a proper trial: kings were tried before the Council of Elders and ephors together, Pausanias 3.5.2.

318 *since the Dorians first settled in the Peloponnese*: in other words, in the whole history of Sparta, given that the Spartans were a Dorian people.

Leuctra: this momentous Spartan defeat at the hands of the Thebans in 371 marked the end of the Spartan army's reputation for invincibility. After this point the death of a Spartan king in battle would therefore be less surprising (e.g. Agis III, Areus I, and Acrotatus, the deaths of all of whom were reported in chapter 3). It is Greek respect for the Spartan king that Plutarch has in mind, and so Leonidas I, who was killed in battle at Thermopylae against the Persians, would be excluded from the reckoning.

not killed: Theopompus is credited with the conquest of Messenia. Pausanias (4.6.4–5) too argues that Theopompus was not killed, and cites verses of the Spartan poet Tyrtaeus (on whom see chapter 23) in support of this. Aristomenes was a legendary figure in the Messenian resistance to Sparta.

Leonidas' life: see chapter 12.

newborn baby: Pausanias (2.9.1, 3.10.5) names the boy as Eurydamidas, a name usually amended to Eudamidas. He died while still a child, allegedly poisoned by Cleomenes.

too young for marriage: he was probably nineteen or twenty.

graceful woman in Greece: what Plutarch does not say is that by marrying the mother of heir to the Eurypontid throne the Agiad Cleomenes became his guardian, thus effectively merging both kingships into one when he succeeded to the throne in 235. Given her alleged influence on Cleomenes, she is surprisingly absent from the Life of Agis.

319 *Sphaerus of Borysthenes*: Sphaerus came from a town in the northern Pontus but studied in Athens under Zeno, the founder of Stoicism, and his successor Cleanthes. This visit to Sparta will have fallen before Cleomenes became king and may have been in the early 230s. See the brief biography at Diogenes Laertius, *Lives of the Philosophers* 7.177–8 (who says he comes from Bosporus). Sphaerus returned to Sparta when Cleomenes was king: see chapter 32.

count the cost: Tyrtaeus was a 7th-C. poet with a particular penchant for martial poems and songs, some of which survive. Leonidas was the king who led the Spartan army at Thermopylae.

potentially harmful: Plutarch was frequently critical of Stoicism; his works include *On Stoic Self-contradictions* and *Against the Stoics on Common Conceptions.*

Leonidas' death: around 235.

training regime: the *agōgē*, which Agis had wanted to revive; see chapter 4 with note. See P. Cartledge, *Spartan Reflections* (London, 2001), ch. 7.

320 *as the Spartans call it*: this is peculiarly Spartan vocabulary of homosexual love: see also Xenophon, *Symposium* 4.15; Aelian, *Varia Historia* 3.12. As the older man, Xenares would have been the 'inspirer'. See further P. Cartledge, 'The Politics of Spartan Pederasty', *Spartan Reflections* (London, 2001), ch. 8.

single political unit: for Aratus and his political ambitions, see *Aratus.*

callow youth: *Aratus* 35, in contrast, presents Aratus as wary of conflict with Cléomenes.

the Spartans and the Megalopolitans: this was Spartan territory which Philip II had assigned to Megalopolis at the time of his invasion of the Peloponnese in 338: see S. Ager, *Interstate Arbitrations in the Greek World 337–90 BC* (Berkeley, 1996), no. 45. Cleomenes' occupation of the territory occurred in 229–228; see also Polybius 2.46.

321 *withdrew his forces*: see *Aratus* 35. Aristomachus had been tyrant of Argos before joining the Achaean League. He was General of the League for 228/7.

earlier Spartan king: Agis II, who ruled from 427 to 400; see Plutarch, *Spartan Sayings* (*Moralia* 215d).

with a garrison: for the events at Mount Lycaeum and Mantinea, see also *Aratus* 36.

Archidamus: fled Sparta after his brother's execution. His recall presumably followed the death of Agis' son: see chapter 22, with note.

322 *on Cleomenes*: Polybius (5.37) had no doubt that Cleomenes was responsible.

Leuctra: in 227, to be distinguished from Leuctra in Boeotia, site of the famous Spartan defeat.

Lydiadas of Megalopolis: for his career, see *Aratus* 30, 35, and 37.

Tarentines and Cretans: these were mercenary troops, light cavalry and archers respectively. For Achaean use of Tarentines, see *Philopoemen* 10.

purple robes and a crown: here the emphasis is on the magnanimity of Cleomenes, whereas in the version of the battle told at *Aratus* 36–7 it is on the culpability of Aratus.

Megistonous: around this time (see *Aratus* 38) he was captured in battle against Aratus, but returned to Sparta in circumstances that are obscure.

323 *sanctuary of Pasiphaë*: see chapter 9, with notes.

mothakes: these were boys below the status of full Spartans who were brought up alongside a full Spartan, to whom they would therefore have a particular loyalty: see Phylarchus in Athenaeus 6.217e–f.

stabbed them: the killing of the ephors took place in 227.

324 *penalties for disobedience*: this is not said in any surviving work of Aristotle's; it perhaps occurred in his lost work on the Spartan constitution.

hand in hand: from the *Cypria* of Stasinus of Cyprus, quoted at greater length in Plato's *Euthyphro* (12a–b).

fear of their leaders: Homer, *Iliad* 3.172 (Helen addressing Priam) and 4.431 (of the Achaean battle-line) respectively.

war against the Messenians: Messenia was said to have been conquered over the course of two wars, one in the 8th C., the other in the 7th C.

an office of their own: see also the interpretation of the ephorate under Agis, chapter 12. Note how the removal of the ephors is justified by the non-Lycurgan nature of the office, and so is in harmony with Cleomenes' aim of reviving the Lycurgan constitution.

325 *Asteropus*: despite his supposed influence, he is not otherwise known.

refuge at an altar: see Plutarch, *Lycurgus* 5; the altar was that of Athena of the Bronze House.

no one to defend it: see chapter 39.

326 *rather than a handle*: the Spartans thus adopted the equipment of the Macedonian phalanx; see also the later Achaean army reforms (*Philopoemen* 9).

famous 'regime': this was the Spartan system for training boys and young men known as the *agōgē*; see also Agis' attempted revival in chapter 4, with note. The *agōgē* was abolished by the Achaean Philopoemen in 188 (see *Philopoemen* 16 with note), but later revived. See N. Kennell, *The Gymnasium of Virtue: Education and Culture in Ancient Sparta* (Chapel Hill, NC, 1995).

to help him: Sphaerus is known to have written two books on Sparta, *On the Spartan Constitution* and *On Lycurgus and Socrates*, which suggests that his help with the reorganization involved at the least historical research and perhaps significantly more. See A. Erskine, *The Hellenistic Stoa: Political Thought and Action* (London, 1990), ch. 6.

326 *same house*: Cleomenes was of the Agiad house. The Eurypontid throne was without an heir after the killing of Archidamus, the brother of Agis, on his return from exile (see chapter 26). Eucleidas died at Sellasia (chapter 49).

widespread damage to the farmland: early 226.

Guild of Dionysus: see note to p. 298.

327 *Life of Lycurgus*: see Plutarch, *Lycurgus* 12.

true descendant of Heracles: see chapter 11; the remark calls into question other dynasties that made such claims, notably the Ptolemies (see e.g. Theocritus, *Idyll* 17) and the Antigonids.

black broth: supposedly the favourite dish of the Spartans (Plutarch, *Lycurgus* 12), but positively disgusting to others. Its unappetizing character gave rise to a number of anecdotes that served to emphasize the traditional image of the hardy Spartan. Thus, a man from Sybaris, a city synonymous with self-indulgence, said, on tasting the broth, 'Now I know why the Spartans do not fear death' (Athenaeus 4.138d). Or there was the Spartan cook who claimed that to appreciate it you had to have trained the Spartan way and bathed in the Eurotas, the river that flowed by Sparta (Plutarch, *Spartan Customs* 2 (*Moralia* 236f); *Lycurgus* 12).

messes: see chapter 8 with note.

two kotylae: a little over half a litre (about 1 pint).

328 *character and conversation*: this description of Cleomenes' dining practices is drawn from Phylarchus, as is clear from Athenaeus 4.141f–142f, where an extended passage of Phylarchus is quoted. Comparison of the two passages shows how Plutarch has made it his own.

that year: Hyperbatas was General from roughly May 226 to May 225. The events in this chapter are treated very briefly at *Aratus* 39.

every other year: see *Aratus* 24.

as it were: for Aratus' refusal of the Generalship in 225, with the same metaphor, see *Aratus* 38.

329 *thirty-three years*: see note to p. 289, where the same error appears.

liberation of the Acrocorinth: Aratus expelled the Macedonian garrison from the Acrocorinth in 243: see *Aratus* 18–24.

Memoirs: for Aratus' *Memoirs* see introduction to *Aratus*.

removed from Athens: for the liberation of Athens in 229, see *Aratus* 34.

women's quarters of his home: Philip V was said to have abused his position as a family guest by having an affair with the wife of Aratus' son: see *Aratus* 49.

330 *consumption*: for cult honours to Antigonus Doson, see *Aratus* 45 with note.

tainted by imperfection: for a less critical view of Aratus' actions, see *Aratus* 38 and 41–2, and Polybius 2.47–51.

Cylarabis gymnasium: 300 paces from the city, according to Livy 34.26; see also *Pyrrhus* 32. For Aratus' conditions, see also *Aratus* 39.

vilifying him: *Aratus* 39 expands on the abuse.

Aegium: the main meeting place of the Achaean League.

331 *Nemean festival*: July 225; for the festival see *Aratus* 27 with note.

the Shield: see also *Pyrrhus* 32.

many of his men: for Pyrrhus' death at Argos in 272, see *Pyrrhus* 32–4.

Solon: famous lawgiver of the early 6th C., supposedly responsible for a cancellation of debts at Athens; subject of one of Plutarch's Lives (included in the Oxford World's Classics *Greek Lives*).

lightening its load: it is not clear when this was, but it may have been in 241 or 240, shortly after the death of Agis IV.

332 *Tritymallus of Messene*: *Aratus* 41 gives the name Tripylus, who may be the same man, but the order of the embassies would then be reversed.

from King Ptolemy: Aratus had been receiving 6 talents a year from Ptolemy III Euergetes (*Aratus* 41), but it was the Achaean policy of opposition to Macedon that justified the subsidy. Once Ptolemy heard rumours that the Achaean had been negotiating with Macedon, he stopped funding him (probably winter 226/5) and directed his resources to Cleomenes instead (Polybius 2.51).

Sicyon's farmland: *Aratus* 41 offers a different order of events. Cleomenes is already encamped outside Sicyon when the Achaean assembly meets to decide on the alliance with Antigonus, and according to Polybius 2.52.5 it is only while there that he learns about the alliance.

Geraneia mountains: Antigonus would have crossed these mountains in the Megarid as he approached the Isthmus.

Oneia mountains: to the south of the entrance of the Peloponnese.

333 *Aristotle*: a friend of Aratus, according to *Aratus* 44.

away from Corinth: the revolt of Argos, which most likely took place in 424, was thus a crucial moment in the war.

the Shield: a manoeuvre similar to the one he had used in his initial capture of Argos (see chapter 17). It is possible that these 'vaults' are to be identified with the many Bronze Age chamber graves to be found at the foot of the Aspis (Shield) hill.

Cretans: see chapter 27, with note.

334 *promising his support*: Ptolemy III Euergetes (see chapter 40, with note). The date at which Ptolemaic funding began is not clear. Polybius 2.51 suggests that it was around 225 or even earlier, but in Plutarch Cleomenes' family do not go to Egypt as hostages until after Antigonus' advance into the Peloponnese. Possibly their detention there should be dated earlier

(despite Plutarch's claim that they comforted Cleomenes in his grief), or alternatively Cleomenes may have requested additional assistance from Egypt and they were the price. Ptolemy may even have been celebrated in sculpture in Sparta, if a marble head found there has been correctly identified: O. Palagia, 'Aspects of the Diffusion of Ptolemaic Sculpture Overseas', in K. Buraselis *et al.* (eds.), *The Ptolemies, the Sea and the Nile: Studies in Waterborne Power* (Cambridge, 2013), 160–71.

335 *the gift of the gods*: this sentiment recalls the Stoic distinction between our response to circumstances, which is in our power, and the circumstances themselves, which are fated.

reduced to Laconia itself: in 223; for other accounts of this stage of Antigonus' campaign in the Peloponnese, see Polybius 2.54–5 and *Aratus* 45.

500 talents: therefore 6,000 helots bought their freedom in this way.

White Shields: an elite Macedonian force.

on its flanks: far from being in the vicinity, Antigonus was away at Aegium, three days from Megalopolis (Polybius 2.51), a point made by Plutarch himself in chapter 46.

Megalopolitans' insistence: Polybius (2.48 and 50) stresses the role of the Megalopolitans in the appeal to Antigonus.

337 *in his Life*: see *Philopoemen* 5.

as Polybius says: Polybius 2.64; Plutarch's account of Cleomenes' attempt on the Argolid follows this chapter of Polybius closely.

338 *Cylarabis*: for the gymnasium see chapter 38, with note.

Heraeum: a well-known sanctuary of Hera near Argos.

Demades: a late 4th-C. Athenian politician, negatively depicted in *Phocion*. See Biographies of Prominent Figures.

Archidamus: the Eurypontid king (*c.*469–427) at the beginning of the Peloponnesian War, the first stage of which (431–421) was named the Archidamian War after him.

339 *financial difficulties*: Polybius 2.63 reports Phylarchus as writing that ten days before the defeat at Sellasia an ambassador came from Ptolemy terminating his financial assistance and telling him to make peace with Antigonus (see also the reference to negotiations at Ptolemy's court in chapter 43).

from Polybius: Polybius 2.65 gives the breakdown of Antigonus' forces, which were made up of 28,000 infantry and 1,200 cavalry. The comments on Fortune echo Polybius 2.70.

Cleomenes' defeat: the generally accepted date for the battle of Sellasia is summer 222. Sellasia lay on Laconia's northern frontier, some 13 km (8 miles) along the main road from Sparta. For a different perspective on the battle, see *Philopoemen* 6 and Polybius 2.65–9. For modern attempts to reconstruct the battle see W. K. Pritchett, *Studies in Ancient Greek Topography*, vol. 1 (Berkeley, 1965), 59–70, and J. D. Morgan, 'Sellasia Revisited', *American Journal of Archaeology*, 85 (1981), 328–30.

krypteia: Plutarch, *Lycurgus* 28 explains the *krypteia*: some of the more able young Spartans would be dispersed across the region. After keeping themselves concealed during the day, they would emerge to kill helots on the road at night. They were also known to enter the fields in the daytime and kill some of the stronger ones labouring there. It is not clear how this would work in the context of Sellasia. Perhaps they were a special unit who had been trained in this way and therefore were themselves adept at carrying out and spotting subterfuge in battle.

340 *five stades*: about 1 km or just over half a mile.

Gythium: the port of Sparta, some 45 km (28 miles) away.

customs and constitution: what this involved is unclear. Certainly the ephorate was reintroduced.

341 *schools*: presumably the schools of philosophy, where the fate of Antigonus would nicely illustrate in a positive way the saying that no man should be judged happy until he is dead (Herodotus 1.32.7–9).

Therycion: one of Cleomenes' two foster-brothers who carried out the murder of the ephors (chapter 29).

342 *we want to*: the arguments used by Cleomenes in his response to Therycion show signs of Stoic influence, that there is a right time for suicide (Diogenes Laertius, *Lives of the Philosophers* 7.28), and that it should be done for the sake of others, not oneself (Diogenes Laertius 7.130).

343 *into the hands of women*: Ptolemy III Euergetes died in 221 and was succeeded by his son, Ptolemy IV Philopator (born *c*.244, reigned 221–204). Polybius 5.34 offers a damning portrait of Philopator as a king who neglected his kingdom to concentrate instead on women, partying, and drinking.

begging for the gods: such behaviour was associated with the priests of the ecstatic cult of Cybele. The theme is continued in chapter 57.

their mother: Berenice II, wife of Ptolemy III Euergetes, who would be murdered along with her son Magas (Polybius 5.36).

armed and ready: the story of Cleomenes' boast is told in quite a different way in Polybius (5.36). There, so far from opposing the murder of Magas and Berenice, he supports it after Sosibius the chief minister offers to help him in the future. Realizing that Sosibius is worried that the mercenaries might in some way upset their plans, Cleomenes assures him that the majority would be loyal to himself not Magas. Sosibius then proceeds with the murders.

344 *had died*: Antigonus Doson died in 221; for the manner of his death see chapter 51. He was succeeded by Philip V, the son of Doson's predecessor, Demetrius II. For Philip, see Biographies of Prominent Figures.

Aetolian War: see *Aratus* 47; this was the beginning of the Social War (220–217), which found the Aetolians fighting both the Macedonians and their Achaean allies.

344 *Apis bull*: the cult of this sacred bull took place at the traditional Egyptian capital of Memphis and dated back to Old Kingdom Egypt, centuries before the coming of the Greeks and Macedonians. It was, however, already known to Herodotus (2.153, 3.28) in the 5th C. BCE. On its death the bull was embalmed and interred with great ritual. The cult continued until the mid-4th C. CE.

battle-cry and war: Homer, *Iliad* 1.491–2.

reason for his hatred: the reason given by Polybius (5.37) is quite different and reflects a more negative tradition about Cleomenes: it was Nicagoras, he reported, who had arranged the supposedly safe return of Agis' brother Archidamus from exile to take up the vacant Eurypontid throne, only to find that Cleomenes double-crossed him and murdered Archidamus. In chapter 26, however, Plutarch exempts Cleomenes from any blame in the murder.

sambuca-girls: the sambuca was a stringed instrument, probably triangular in shape.

living on handouts: if chapter 53 is to be believed, the handouts were substantial, but his 24-talent allowance may have stopped or been reduced with the death of Ptolemy III Euergetes.

345 *beggar-priest*: see chapter 54, with note.

Canopus: a town in the Nile delta about 25 km (16 miles) east of Alexandria.

347 *capture of Megalopolis*: see chapter 44.

as I have described: Cleomenes died in 219. The circumstances of his death are also related by Polybius 5.37–9, who, despite being unsympathetic to him politically, is generous in his assessment of the king in death: 'a man who not only had a way with people, but also had a natural aptitude for the conduct of affairs. In short, he was naturally endowed with the qualities of a commander and a king' (translation by Robin Waterfield, *Polybius: The Histories* (Oxford, 2010)).

348 *familiar of heroes*: for the association of snakes with heroes, see D. Ogden, *Drakon: Dragon Myth and Serpent Cult in the Greek and Roman Worlds* (Oxford, 2013), 249–54. For the idea that bone-marrow could produce snakes, see also Pliny, *Natural History* 10.188.

PHILOPOEMEN AND FLAMININUS

PHILOPOEMEN

355 *Cleander of Mantinea*: known only from accounts of Philopoemen's life; see also Polybius 10.22.1 and Pausanias 8.49.

Achilles was brought up by Phoenix: a slightly forced comparison, but one that gives Philopoemen a nicely heroic start. Phoenix, like Cleander, was an exile from his own home. He found refuge in the house of Peleus, father of Achilles, who entrusted him with the task of acting as Achilles' mentor on the campaign against Troy (Homer, *Iliad* 9.438–44).

Ecdelus and Demophanes of Megalopolis: there is some uncertainty as to their names, alternatives being Ecdemus and Megalophanes (F. W. Walbank, *A Historical Commentary on Polybius*, vol. 2 (Oxford, 1967), 223–4; see also Polybius 10.22 and Pausanias 8.49). Little more is known about them, although Ecdelus' activity in Sicyon is expanded on in *Aratus* 5 and 7.

Arcesilaus: head of the Academy in the mid-3rd C.; see further *Aratus* 5, with note.

Aristodemus . . . Nicocles: Aristodemus ruled Megalopolis from roughly the mid-260s until his assassination in the late 250s, while Nicocles was tyrant of Sicyon for a mere four months before his overthrow by Aratus in 251; see further *Aratus* 3–9.

best possible lines: Cyrene was an old Greek colony in north Africa to the west of Egypt. Their intervention probably took place not long after the death in 253 of Magas, the ruler of Cyrene, and certainly before Ptolemy III seized control of it in 247.

last of the Greeks: it is not known which Roman said this; see also Pausanias' statement (8.52) that Philopoemen was the last benefactor of Greece. Plutarch makes reference to it again at *Aratus* 24. Later Brutus would call his co-conspirator Cassius 'the last of the Romans': Plutarch, *Brutus* 44.

survives at Delphi: Plutarch bases this remark on his own observation, although we might have less faith than he in the verisimilitude of an honorific statue. Pausanias (8.49), perhaps drawing on Polybius, reports Philopoemen's ugliness without comment.

356 *Doric accent*: a dialect of Greek, found in the Peloponnese.

schools: presumably discussions in philosophical schools; see also *Aratus* 29 and *Agis and Cleomenes* 51.

Epaminondas: Theban general who defeated Sparta at Leuctra in 371 and was instrumental in the foundation of Philopoemen's home city of Megalopolis. Comparison is made again with Epaminondas in chapter 14. Plutarch wrote a Life of Epaminondas that is now lost.

shun and scorn athletics himself: Alexander also had a dismissive attitude to athletics: *Alexander* 4. As a Platonist, Plutarch would have been familiar with Plato's critical view of athletic training (*Republic* 3.403c–404b). See also Z. Papaconstantinou, 'Athletic Critics of Greek Sport', in P. Christesen and D. G. Kyle (eds.), *A Companion to Sport and Spectacle in Greek and Roman Antiquity* (Chichester, 2013), 320–31.

357 *conducive to courage*: Homer's *Iliad* and *Odyssey* were central works in Greek culture and education; Philopoemen's selective reading serves to highlight his preoccupation with military matters. Alexander called the *Iliad* 'a handbook of warfare' and kept his copy under his pillow (*Alexander* 8).

357 *Evangelus' Tactics*: this work, probably written in the 3rd C. BCE, is now lost; Plutarch's text suggests that it contained diagrams, making it the earliest known treatise on tactics to be illustrated, a feature of later treatises such as those by Asclepiodotus and Aelian Tacticus.

Alexander historians: see the introduction to *Alexander*.

358 *King Cleomenes of Sparta*: for the career of Cleomenes, see *Agis and Cleomenes*. The attack on Megalopolis took place in autumn 223, recounted in *Agis and Cleomenes* 44–5 and Polybius 2.55, 2.61–2.

laden with booty: there was disagreement over the amount of booty; Polybius (2.62) rejects Phylarchus' figure of 6,000-talents' worth in favour of a much more cautious 300 talents.

against Cleomenes: in 225/4 pressure from Cleomenes had forced the Achaeans to make an alliance with the Macedonian king Antigonus III Doson: see *Aratus* 42 (with 38). The battle of Sellasia was fought in 222 some 13 km (8 miles) north of Sparta; see also *Agis and Cleomenes* 48–9 for a different perspective on it.

Eucleidas, Cleomenes' brother: joint king with Cleomenes since 227, he was killed in the battle (*Agis and Cleomenes* 32 and 49).

359 *thonged javelin*: Greek javelins had a leather thong near their centre of gravity which was wrapped around the javelin. As it unwound it increased the javelin's speed and (by spinning it around) its stability.

youngster from Megalopolis: Philopoemen was actually around thirty when he fought at Sellasia. The story is also told by Polybius (2.68).

on service there: Philopoemen served as a mercenary commander on Crete for some ten years, from *c.*220 to 210. Very little is known about his activity there.

360 *Cavalry Commander*: in 210–209; the Cavalry Commander or Hipparch was the second-in-command of the Achaean League.

Larissus river: this acted as the border between Achaea and Elis; the battle, which took place in 209, was part of the wider conflict of the First Macedonian War (214–205), with Achaea allied to Macedon on the one side and the Aetolian League and Rome on the other. Rome reinforced Elis within days of this battle (Livy 27.31–2).

humane form of government: Aratus had brought his home state of Sicyon into the Achaean League in 251, thus inaugurating a period of expansion for the league, much of it under his leadership; for a similar very positive evaluation of the league see Polybius 2.37–8.

361 *Ptolemy*: Ptolemy III Euergetes, who ruled Egypt from 246 to 221, a Macedonian because the Ptolemaic dynasty was founded by the Macedonian Ptolemy, son of Lagus, who had campaigned with Alexander: see Biographies of Prominent Figures. For his support for Aratus, see *Aratus* 12–13, 15, 24, and 41.

Antigonus and Philip: Antigonus Doson and Philip V ruled Macedon from 229 to 221, and from 221 to 179 respectively. See further *Aratus* 38 ff.

leading man in the state: Philopoemen held the highest position in the state, the office of General (*stratēgos*), for the first time in 208–207, for the second time in 206–205, and on six subsequent occasions. It was not permitted to hold the office in consecutive years (*Aratus* 24).

as I have said in his Life: these themes are scattered through the Life (e.g. *Aratus* 10, 14–15, 28), but nowhere in quite the same form as here.

battle formation and weaponry: the general sense of the army reforms is clear enough. Philopoemen changed the army from being relatively lightly armed to being heavy-armed infantry operating in a Macedonian-style phalanx. The detail of this paragraph, however, is not always easy to follow, and Plutarch himself may not have understood the reforms properly. Other surviving accounts are Pausanias 8.50.1 and Polyaenus 6.4.3, which agree with the general tenor of Plutarch's account while disagreeing on detail.

broken up: the first part of this sentence is obscure. It may be that underpinning it is an unspoken opposition between Roman-style fighting in small, flexible tactical units (maniples) and the greater solidity of the Macedonian phalanx. The old Achaean system thus fell halfway between the two and could have developed in either direction. For some of the issues posed by the reforms, see J. K. Anderson, 'Philopoemen's Reform of the Achaean Army', *Classical Philology*, 62 (1967), 104–6.

362 *dinners and tableware*: for this lifestyle competition among the Achaeans, see Polybius 11.8.4–7. Purple was a very expensive dye: see note to p. 43.

Thericlean vases: Thericles was a famous 5th-C. Corinthian potter who gave his name to a style of highly prized vase: see Athenaeus 11.470e–472e.

put them to use: Homer, *Iliad* 19.15–23.

Machanidas, the tyrant of Sparta: the career of Machanidas is poorly documented. He led Spartan expansion between 209 and his death at Philopoemen's hands in 207, but his career prior to that is conjectural; he may have come to power initially as a regent *c.*211.

363 *Tarentines*: light cavalry that would have been made up of mercenaries. Polybius (11.12.7) tells us there were also Tarentines fighting on the Spartan side. The term 'Tarentines' could refer to a style of cavalry fighting rather than to native Tarentines, and many prefer the former interpretation here, but the fall of Tarentum to Rome two years earlier in 209 may have forced many Tarentines to serve overseas as mercenary horsemen. See G. R. Bugh, 'The Tarantine Cavalry in the Hellenistic Period: Ethnic or Technic?', in J.-C. Couvenhes *et al.* (eds.), *Pratiques et identités culturelles des armées hellénistiques du monde méditerranéen* (Bordeaux, 2011), 283–92.

shield-fellows: outside the context of this battle these two men are unknown. As 'shield-fellows' they would have provided Philopoemen with protection in battle.

364 *generalship that day*: for a fuller account of the battle, see Polybius 11.11–18. Although the bronze statue of Philopoemen is long lost, the inscription on the base survives: 'The confederation of the Achaeans honours Philopoemen of Megalopolis, son of Craugis, for his courage and the goodwill he has shown towards them.'

for the second time: Philopoemen held the Generalship for the second time in 206/5. The Nemean festival took place every two years in the sanctuary of Zeus at Nemea in the Argolid in the north-eastern Peloponnese.

Timotheus' Persians: written by Timotheus of Miletus in the late 5th C., the poem told the story of the battle of Salamis in the Persian Wars. The last 250 lines or so survive from a papyrus roll found in Egypt in 1902. The line quoted here most probably referred to Themistocles. Since Pylades was himself from Megalopolis (Pausanias 8.50), the choice of verse may not have been a coincidence.

assassins to Argos: the attempted assassination is also reported by Pausanias (8.50) and Justin, *Epitome* 29.4; if it has any basis, it is presumably to be dated to some time between 206 and Philopoemen's second departure for Crete in 200. Philip had quite a reputation for political assassinations: see also *Aratus* 52.

365 *city walls*: this closely follows Polybius 20.6.11–12, who mentions the incident in the context of Megara rejoining the Achaean League in 192/1, but the date of the incident itself is uncertain. It could fall before or after Philopoemen's second absence in Crete (200–194).

regained its freedom: the relief of Messene occurred in 201 at a time when Philopoemen did not hold any official position in the League. Nabis ruled Sparta from 207 until his assassination in 192.

war at home: not only did Philopoemen's lengthy absence in Crete (200–194) mean that he was absent for the war against Nabis, it also meant that he was away for the duration of the Second Macedonian War between Rome and Macedon (200–196). By the time he returned in 194 the political landscape of Greece had changed significantly. For events in his absence, see *Flamininus* 3–12, and for a modern narrative of them, R. Waterfield, *Taken at the Flood: The Roman Conquest of Greece* (Oxford, 2014), esp. chs. 4–6.

366 *Aristaenus*: a leading figure in the Achaean League in the early 2nd C., holder of the Generalship several times between 199 and 185. The evidence for his native city is mixed, but he most likely comes from Dyme, despite chapter 17, where he is said to be from Megalopolis.

outlying villages to secede: expanded on in chapter 1 of the Comparison: 'out of anger Philopoemen denied his native city the contributions it received from its outlying dependencies'.

cunning and crooked tactics: the Cretans were famously dishonest: see, for example, Paul's Epistle to Titus 1: 12; 'Cretans are always liars, evil brutes, lazy gluttons' (a line attributed to the 7th-C. Cretan Epimenides); and

Polybius 8.18 for a negative and stereotypical view of the Cretan mentality as duplicitous and self-interested.

defeated by Flamininus: for Flamininus' victory over Philip V in the Second Macedonian War, see *Flamininus* 8–10. It is unlikely that Philopoemen was as isolated from news of events in mainland Greece as Plutarch seems to imply. Crete is about just over 100 km or 60 miles from the Peloponnese.

at war with Nabis: fought in 195 to liberate Argos from Spartan control despite Nabis' having been a Roman ally in the recent war against Macedon. Achaea fought alongside Rome, having switched its allegiance from Macedon to Rome during the course of the Second Macedonian War (see *Flamininus* 5).

were corrupted: on the various reports of Epaminondas' naval expedition of 364, see J. Buckler and H. Beck, *Central Greece and the Politics of Power in the Fourth Century BC* (Cambridge, 2008), 174–5. Plato is quoted from *Laws* 4.706c. Philopoemen was General for 193/2.

367 *crew's lives in danger*: Livy 35.26 is even less respectful of Philopoemen's naval skills, reporting that the veteran ship had been captured some eighty years previously and fell apart at the first knock against an enemy vessel.

siege of Gythium: Gythium had been Sparta's main port on the Laconian coast until lost to Rome and its allies in 195 (Livy 34.29–30). At the time of Nabis' siege in 193 it was garrisoned by the Achaeans.

enslaved to Philip and the Macedonians: at the Isthmian Games in 196 Flamininus had declared the Greeks free, to great applause from the crowd: see *Flamininus* 10. Plutarch has already noted how on a previous occasion Philopoemen was acclaimed in the theatre (chapter 11).

368 *assassinated by the Aetolians*: in 192 Nabis had requested help from his Aetolian allies; instead of help they sent a force of just over a thousand to initiate a coup, perhaps with a view to establishing a more satisfactory ally in power in Sparta as the likelihood of war between them and Rome intensified, perhaps thinking that without the provocative presence of Nabis Achaea would stay neutral.

brought it into the league: this was the beginning of a turbulent relationship, in which influential Spartans repeatedly sought Roman help to break away from the league. Ultimately the failure to incorporate Sparta satisfactorily into the league was a crucial factor in the Achaean War and the demise of the league in the 140s.

Timolaus: as a guest-friend he would have had family links to Philopoemen dating back generations. Plutarch here closely follows Polybius 20.12. The episode is probably to be dated to 191, and reflects the tension in Sparta that would soon lead to the expulsion of those put in power by Philopoemen (see next chapter).

369 *King Antiochus and the Romans were in Greece*: in 192 Antiochus III (the Great) accepted an Aetolian invitation to cross over to mainland Greece. He arrived with a relatively small force, presenting himself as

the champion of Greek freedom. The Romans who had withdrawn their forces in 194 returned and defeated Antiochus at Thermopylae in 191 before pursuing him into Asia Minor. Initially the commander was the consul Manius Acilius Glabrio, but Flamininus was also attached to the expedition as a legate. See further *Flamininus* 15–17.

369 *troubles started*: these events took place in 191. Philopoemen's reluctance to allow Diophanes and Flamininus to take military action would have been partly to avoid attracting Roman attention to Achaean expansionism and partly to protect his own settlement in Sparta. The continuing internal conflict in Sparta and the resulting groups of exiles are hard to disentangle and have thus inspired various competing scholarly reconstructions.

says 350: this massacre (at Compasium) occurred during Philopoemen's Generalship in 189–188, prompted by a Spartan attempt to capture the town of Las on the Laconian coast. The lower figure reflects Polybius' Achaean background, while the higher stems from the Spartan Aristocrates, who wrote a work on Sparta, probably in the 1st C. BCE, which was also used by Plutarch in his *Lycurgus* (4 and 31). Plutarch omits to mention that the eighty who died went to the Achaean camp under promise of safe conduct (Livy 38.33). The intervention provided the opportunity to get rid of any vestige that was left of the revolutionary Sparta of the previous half-century and at the same time assert Achaean dominance in the Peloponnese.

stoa in Megalopolis: according to Livy 38.34 the original stoa had been destroyed by the Spartans.

Lycurgan way: Lycurgus was the legendary Spartan lawgiver, subject of Plutarch's *Lycurgus* (translated in Oxford World's Classics *Greek Lives*), whose name had been invoked by the revolutionary rulers who had caused such problems for Achaea: see *Agis and Cleomenes*, esp. chapters 9–10, 31–2. In particular, Philopoemen brought an end, albeit temporary, to the Spartan training regime, the *agōgē*, the revival of which had been such an important part of Cleomenes' reforms.

trouble and destruction: some time after the Roman defeat of the Achaean League in 146.

370 *Romans and Antiochus*: in 192: see note to p. 369.

Chalcis: the main city of Euboea.

no sign of their officers: this interpretation of Antiochus' actions, both in terms of his marriage and the idleness of his army, runs throughout the sources: *Flamininus* 16, Polybius 20.8, Appian, *Syrian Wars* 16, and Livy 36.11. Renaming his new bride Euboea (as Polybius reports), however, suggests that the marriage may have been more political than the sources allow, as does his use of Chalcis as his base (*Flamininus* 16).

close at hand: Plutarch is looking ahead here. For Polybius, Rome attained worldwide power with the defeat of Macedon at Pydna in 168 (3.1.9–10), but Plutarch, writing much later, may have taken a longer view.

doom of Greece: the views of Aristaenus and Philopoemen are compared in greater detail by Polybius (24.11–13).

his defeat of Antiochus: Glabrio defeated Antiochus at Thermopylae in 191: see also *Flamininus* 15.

371 *eighth time*: in 183–182.

taken alive by the enemy: as would shortly happen to Philopoemen himself, the work, Plutarch implies, of a vengeful deity (Nemesis). Philopoemen's remark is no anomaly; it is in keeping with the character Plutarch has presented throughout the Life: competitive, contentious, and proud (especially chapters 3 and 17).

Deinocrates of Messene: a talented soldier who had campaigned with Flamininus and was on close terms with him, but also, if the rather cutting character-sketch by Polybius (23.5) is any guide, something of a schemer and pleasure-seeker. See also *Flamininus* 17.

to save Colonides: Livy 39.49.1 gives the name of the town as Corona, which neighbours Colonides (Pausanias 4.34). Polybius' account is now lost, and it may be that he mentioned both towns. Livy's account suggests that Philopoemen was accompanied not only by the young Achaean nobles but also by Cretan and Thracian mercenaries.

372 *Nabis from their city*: see chapter 12.

the dungeon: this is perhaps to be identified with an underground chamber found by Petros Themelis in 2006 to the south of the temple of the local heroine Messene.

373 *Lycortas*: father of the historian Polybius and a supporter of Philopoemen. By this stage he had already held the Generalship once and would be chosen General to complete Philopoemen's year. Bringing Messene and Sparta back into the League, he continued Philopoemen's policy in the face of opposition from others in the League, notably Callicrates of Leontium, who favoured closer alignment with Rome.

straight to retaliation: this united Achaean response is not confirmed by an important new inscription, which suggests instead that, while the Megalopolitans were pushing for action against Messene, other parts of the league were more restrained: N. Luraghi and A. Magnetto, 'The Controversy between Megalopolis and Messene in a New Inscription from Messene', *Chiron*, 42 (2012), 509–50. This article also contains an excellent summary of the background to the dispute and Philopoemen's death.

Polybius: the historian, who also wrote a life of Philopoemen (see introduction to this Life). On the assumption that he was born in 200, he would have been about eighteen at this time. See also P. Kató, 'The Funeral of Philopoemen in the Historiographical Tradition', in E. Stavrianopoulou (ed.), *Ritual and Communication in the Graeco-Roman World* (Liège, 2006), 239–50.

374 *stoned to death*: this act of vengeance against the Messenian prisoners

recalls Achilles' killing of twelve Trojans at the funeral pyre of Patroclus (Homer, *Iliad* 23.175–83).

374 *in other ways as well*: Plutarch refrains from saying that Megalopolis granted Philopoemen cult honours after his death, but it is clear from Diodorus 29.18 that it did, including an altar and annual sacrifice. There are parallels here with the treatment of Aratus, and an inscription shows that Philopoemen too was linked with Zeus Soter: C. P. Jones, *New Heroes in Antiquity: From Achilles to Antinoos* (Cambridge, Mass., 2010), 33–4.

destruction of Corinth: Lucius Mummius destroyed the great city of Corinth in 146 BCE, at the end of the Achaean War, although the degree of destruction may not have been as emphatic as the ancient sources suggest: see E. Gebhard and M. Dickie, 'The View from the Isthmus, ca 200 to 44 BC', in C. K. Williams and N. Bookidis (eds.), *Corinth, the Centenary, 1896–1996* (Athens, 2003), 261–78.

such an illustrious man: for Polybius' role in the defence of these statues, see Polybius 39.3. The legates are the Commission of Ten who had arrived to arrange the post-war settlement. On statues of Philopoemen, see chapters 2 and 10 with accompanying notes.

FLAMININUS

Greek inscription: the use of Greek in a Roman public inscription at this early date is striking and may be intended to reflect Flamininus' achievement in Greece. The hippodrome is most likely the Circus Flaminius, and the statue of Apollo would have been part of the booty from the capture of Carthage in 146. Although many statues of Flamininus were set up in his lifetime, none is known to have survived even as a copy, but his portrait does appear on a gold coin (J. M. C. Toynbee, *Roman Historical Portraits* (London, 1978), 19–20), a good image of which can be found on the British Museum website, <www.britishmuseum.org>.

375 *Hannibalic War*: named after the Carthaginian general Hannibal, who invaded Italy; also known as the Second Punic War (218–202). Flamininus was military tribune in 208 under M. Claudius Marcellus (*c.*270–208). Plutarch also wrote a Life of Marcellus.

for the second time: Tarentum had been captured by the Romans in 272 after the withdrawal of Pyrrhus. During the Second Punic War it was captured by Hannibal in 213, then recaptured by the Romans under Q. Fabius Maximus in 207. Flamininus held Tarentum from 205 with praetorian powers (see Livy 29.13).

colonies: Narnia was in Umbria, Cosa in Etruria. Plutarch is inconsistent with Livy, who makes no mention of Flamininus in connection with these two colonies (32.2), but instead makes him one of those responsible for the settlement of Scipio Africanus' veterans in 201 and for the augmentation of the colony of Venusia in southern Italy the following year (31.4, 31.49). Livy is usually preferred here.

tribunate of the people: this magistracy was restricted to plebeians, so Flamininus as a patrician would not have been able to hold it anyway.

force his way illegally: there is no suggestion of illegality in Livy's recounting of the tribunes' arguments (32.7). It was only during the first quarter of the second century that the order in which magistracies were held (the *cursus honorum*) became more formalized. The praetorship became a prerequisite for the consulship in 196 and the *lex Villia annalis* of 180 stipulated minimum ages for each magistracy. It was nonetheless unusual at this period, but not unprecedented, for a man as young as Flamininus to be elected to the consulship. Scipio Africanus was thirty when elected to the consulship of 205.

war against Philip and the Macedonians: the Second Macedonian War, which had begun in 200. Flamininus was the consul for 198. Assigning public duties by lot was a common practice in Rome, not limited to the allocation of provinces, here referring to the region in which a military command will be exercised rather than a territory already subject to Rome.

376 *little to do with Rome*: Plutarch has in mind the Greeks of mainland Greece rather than those of South Italy or Sicily, who had long been familiar with Rome. Even in Greece it is a little exaggerated. The Greeks of the west coast of the Balkans had been familiar with Rome since the time of the First Illyrian War (229–228). The First Macedonian War (214–205) had brought Rome into contact with even more Greek states, but in contrast to the Second Macedonian War, Rome did not have a significant military presence.

Sulpicius Galba and Publius Villius: Publius Sulpicius Galba Maximus and Publius Villius Tappulus, consuls of 200 and 199 respectively.

commander of the fleet: Lucius Quinctius Flamininus went on to obtain the consulship in 192 before scandal (and Cato) forced him out of the Senate in 184 (chapters 18–19). He died in 170.

Hannibal: in the Second Punic War, Publius Scipio Africanus defeated Hannibal's younger brother Hasdrubal at Baecula in Spain in 208, before going on to defeat Hannibal himself at Zama in North Africa in 202.

Apsus river: an Illyrian river now called the Semeni, but Livy is surely right to place Philip's resistance at the Aous gorge (32.5.8–11), which is located a little further south. Both lie in modern Albania. For a vivid description of the landscape of this part of the campaign, see N. G. L. Hammond, 'The Opening Campaigns and the Battle of the Aoi Stena in the Second Macedonian War', *Journal of Roman Studies*, 56 (1966), 39–54.

Tempe: the Vale of Tempe is a gorge 8 km/5 miles long through which the river Peneus flows into the plains of Thessaly.

377 *fear of Philip*: Livy (31.11) also has a shepherd (but only one) revealing the little-known route that would circumvent Philip's position, but there are several differences between the two accounts. Crucially, Livy

has the initiative coming from Charops (as does Polybius 27.15), and it is he who sends the shepherd. Flamininus then contacts Charops to ask if the shepherd can be trusted; the reply is that he could trust him so long as everything was under Flamininus' control rather than the shepherd's, a reply that explains why in both versions the shepherds are put in bonds. Charops' grandson of the same name would later become a notorious pro-Roman politician in Epirus (Polybius 30.12, 32.6).

378 *side with the Romans against him*: on the initiative of Aristaenus the Achaeans had switched their allegiance to Rome in 198 (Livy 32.19–23). Plutarch exaggerates the enthusiasm of the Greek cities: see Livy 32.15 on Thessaly and 32.19–23 on division within the Achaean League.

allies of the Romans: the Aetolians had allied with Rome during the First Macedonian War, but their decision to make peace with Philip in 206 without consulting Rome had not been well received there.

Opus to his protection: Opus was the main city of eastern Locris in central Greece. In Livy's telling of this incident (32.32) the city is divided into two parties, both in agreement that they want to rid themselves of Philip, but the wealthier group preferring to turn to the Romans while the other looked to the Aetolians.

379 *this barbarian formation*: see *Pyrrhus* 16, with note.

champion their freedom: Plutarch is already looking forward to the freedom declaration at the Isthmian Games of 196 (chapter 10). For the observation of Greek qualities in the Romans, see also Plutarch, *Marcellus* 20.

at their meeting: in 198; for a detailed account of these negotiations, which took place at Nicaea, see Polybius 18.1–12. Plutarch's account is misleading, because the negotiations only broke down after the key points had been referred to the Senate, hence the ambassadors mentioned in chapter 7.

Brachyllas: shortly after the end of the war he would be assassinated with, it was said, the approval of Flamininus: Polybius 18.43.

he died: Attalus I of Pergamum had supported Rome since the First Macedonian War, beginning what would be a long-standing relationship between Rome and Pergamum. He was seventy-two when he died and had ruled for some forty-four years. He was succeeded by Eumenes II.

380 *confront Philip*: the battle of Cynoscephalae, as it is usually known, was fought in Thessaly in spring 197. Polybius' description of the battle survives (18.18–27), see also Livy 33.1–18. On the battle see N. G. L. Hammond and F. W. Walbank, *A History of Macedonia*, vol. 3: *336–167 BC* (Oxford, 1988), 429–43, and N. G. L. Hammond, 'The Campaign and the Battle of Cynoscephalae in 197 BC', *Journal of Hellenic Studies*, 108 (1988), 60–82.

outside his camp: this bad omen is not mentioned in other accounts of the battle.

381 *mutually supportive whole*: for a contemporary analysis of the inflexibility

of the Macedonian phalanx in contrast to the Roman legion, see Polybius 18.27–32.

taken prisoner: the bones of the Macedonian dead were said to have been still lying on the battlefield six years later in 191, when Antiochus III arrived in Greece (chapter 15) and very deliberately prepared an impressive funeral for them (Livy 36.8, Appian, *Syrian Wars* 16). Roman losses were low in comparison, in the region of 700 men according to Polybius 18.27.

382 *more than Philip*: Alcaeus was a contemporary poet from Messene in the Peloponnese, who wrote a number of epigrams attacking Philip. Emathia was the region of Macedon where the royal city of Aegae was located.

first to enslave: under Philip II and Alexander the Great in the 4th C. BCE.

ten ships: according to Polybius 18.44, he was allowed to keep six ships.

hostage: Demetrius was released early (see chapter 14), but his years as a hostage and intimate of the Roman aristocracy left him well disposed to Rome, with the result that he was said to have fallen victim to court intrigue, initiated by his elder brother Perseus, and was murdered in 180 on his father's instructions: Livy 40.5–24 and *Aratus* 54.

already resident in Antiochus' court: in fact Hannibal did not go to Antiochus' court until 195: see Livy 33.45–9.

383 *giving to Greece*: in more detail, Polybius 18.44–5. On the fetters of Greece, see *Aratus* 16, with note.

At the Isthmian festival: one of the four panhellenic festivals, held every two years in June/July on the Isthmus of Corinth. Plutarch's account of Flamininus' proclamation largely follows Polybius 18.46. The choice of Corinth as the venue for the announcement may have been deliberate. It cannot have escaped the audience that the end of Macedonian power in Greece occurred at the very place where Philip II had first established it through his alliance of Greek states, known to modern scholars as the League of Corinth.

and Perrhaebians: claims to be fighting on behalf of the freedom of the Greeks were not new in Greek politics (see *Demetrius* 8, with notes), but, while using a familiar language, Flamininus' announcement was unusually specific. By marking out for freedom Macedon's allies and subject territories, it effectively broke Macedonian power in Greece. These included Corinth, Thessaly, and Euboea, each home to one of the fetters of Greece. On the announcement and its implications, see R. Waterfield, *Taken at the Flood: The Roman Conquest of Greece* (Oxford, 2014), 98.

384 *fell down into the stadium*: this is mentioned in neither Polybius' nor Livy's accounts, but does occur in Valerius Maximus 4.8.5. A shout from a Roman assembly also causes a bird to fall out of the sky in Plutarch's Life of Pompey, where the explanations offered are similar (*Pompey* 25). The coast, where Plutarch says the shout could be heard, was about 8 miles (5 km) distant.

384 *Agesilaus, Lysander, Nicias, and Alcibiades*: for his selection of military leaders Plutarch goes right back to the 5th and 4th centuries; the first two are Spartan, the second two Athenian; all were the subjects of Lives by Plutarch; *Agesilaus*, *Nicias*, and *Alcibiades* can be found in the Oxford World's Classics *Greek Lives*.

385 *Marathon . . . on Cyprus*: all these battles were fought against the Persians, the first four were the key battles of the Persian Wars themselves, while the Athenian general Cimon (also subject of a Plutarchan Life, translated in Oxford World's Classics *Greek Lives*) gained success at Eurymedon, a river in southern Asia Minor, in the mid-460s and at Cyprus in the late 450s.

little in common with them: very few gave the Romans significant Greek ancestry, although the Arcadian Evander sometimes finds a role in the prehistory of Rome (see Polybius 6.11a, Virgil, *Aeneid* 8.333–5); an exception would be Dionysius of Halicarnassus, who argues in the first book of his *Roman Antiquities* that the Romans were really Greek in origin. More widespread was belief in the Romans' Trojan ancestry, which gave them a worthy past in the Greek heroic age without making them Greeks; see the verses in chapter 12 and A. Erskine, *Troy between Greece and Rome: Local Tradition and Imperial Power* (Oxford, 2001).

Philip's garrisons: Publius Cornelius Lentulus, who had been praetor in 203, went to Bargylia in Caria in south-west Asia Minor; little is known of Lucius Stertinius (and he only appears here due to a manuscript emendation). For these campaigns see Polybius 18.48, Livy 33.35, 33.39.

within his empire: Publius Villius Tappulus was one of the commissioners who met Antiochus at Lysimacheia (although Plutarch names Antioch): Polybius 18.50; see also chapter 3 for Villius.

at Argos: on the festival see *Philopoemen* 11 with note. On this occasion (in 195) the festival had been delayed by the war with Nabis (Livy 34.41). It is a reflection of the changing politics of the time that in 209 it had been Flamininus' adversary Philip who had been celebrating the Nemean Games (Polybius 10.26).

resident-alien tax: foreigners resident in Athens (metics) paid an annual poll-tax of 12 drachmas in the classical period. For the philosopher Xenocrates, see *Phocion* 4 (with note) and 27. Later Xenocrates would refuse to allow Phocion to make him a citizen to free him from the burden of the tax (*Phocion* 29). According to another story, when he was unable to pay the tax, the Athenians put him up for sale and he was bought by Demetrius of Phalerum, who then freed him (Diogenes Laertius, *Lives of the Philosophers* 4.14). The unusual number of tax stories associated with Xenocrates suggests that there was an original incident that prompted them all.

386 *born of Aeneas*: Aeneas was a Trojan hero, who, after surviving the fall of Troy, wandered the Mediterranean until he landed in Italy where his descendants founded Rome. For Rome's supposed Trojan ancestry, see

note to p. 385. The Tyndaridae were Castor and Pollux, also known as the Dioscuri. These two Greek heroes had been revered in Rome since the early 5th C., when their contribution to the Roman victory at the battle of Regillus was said to have earned them a temple in the Forum. At the time of the Second Macedonian War, when Flamininus made this dedication, their image was featured on Roman coins.

general populace: Nero's speech, delivered in November 67 CE, survives as an inscription; for the text, see R. K. Sherk, *The Roman Empire: Augustus to Hadrian* (Cambridge, 1988), no. 71.

war against Nabis: in 195 (see *Philopoemen* 14–15).

387 *the cause of Greece*: for Flamininus' jealousy of the Achaean General, see *Philopoemen* 15.

388 *'Philips'*: these were Macedonian gold coins. The triumph lasted three days (Livy 34.52). The suggested reading 'Tuditanus', if correct, may refer to Gaius Sempronius Tuditanus, consul of 129, whose writings are poorly known through scanty later citation.

holding hostage: Philip's younger son Demetrius: see chapter 9. Despite this reference to Philip as an ally, it is unlikely that he had a formal alliance with Rome: see E. Gruen, 'The Supposed Alliance between Rome and Philip V of Macedon', *California Studies in Classical Antiquity*, 6 (1973), 123–36.

invaded Greece: in 192, see *Philopoemen* 16 with note. Contrary to what Plutarch says, Antiochus' force was striking for not being sizeable, a point made by Livy (35.43); there were only 10,000 infantry and 500 cavalry. This has led to considerable scholarly debate about his intentions.

stance towards Rome: see chapters 9–10.

Glabrio: Manius Acilius Glabrio, consul of 191.

Thermopylae: this battle of Thermopylae took place in 191 (Livy 36.15–19). The Romans, under the leadership of the Scipio brothers, then pursued Antiochus to Asia where he was defeated at the battle of Magnesia in late 190. In the settlement of Apamea in 188 he lost virtually all his possessions in Asia Minor.

389 *favourable terms*: for a fuller account of the events in this paragraph, see Livy 36.22–35.

headquarters for the war: for Antiochus' marriage, see *Philopoemen* 17 with note; his use of Chalcis as base adds a further weight to the argument that the marriage was political.

O Titus, saviour!: the base of a statue of Flamininus dedicated by two gymnasiarchs survives today and in the inscription he is described as 'Titus, saviour and benefactor': see R. K. Sherk, *Rome and the Greek East to the Death of Augustus* (Cambridge, 1984), no. 6a. In the examples that Plutarch gives it is evident that Flamininus is being given divine honours: he even has his own priest. There is a marked contrast between Plutarch's neutral presentation of these honours for a Roman and his judgmental approach to the honours for the Macedonian kings Demetrius Poliorcetes (*Demetrius* 10–13) and Antigonus Doson (*Agis and Cleomenes* 37).

389 *honours are empty*: R. K. Sherk, *Rome and the Greek East to the Death of Augustus* (Cambridge, 1984), no. 6, collects several examples, some from the immediate aftermath of the proclamation of 196, some from this later visit to Greece.

390 *out of the Peloponnese*: see Livy 36.32.

friends and relatives: see Polybius 18.7, but Polybius refers only to 'friends' and makes no mention of 'relatives'; Plutarch may have been thinking of Philip's murder of his son Demetrius, even though that did not happen until 180. The alleged poisoning of Aratus would be an example of the murder of a friend (*Aratus* 52). Flamininus' humour is edited out of Livy's Roman version (32.34).

under way: the story is told at *Philopoemen* 18 and Polybius 23.5.

consul Marcellus: Flamininus held the censorship in 189 with M. Claudius Marcellus, consul of 196. He had served under his colleague's father early in his career: see chapter 1.

391 *had been free*: Livy (38.28) makes no mention of this law in his account of Flamininus' censorship. The tribune is presumably Quintus Terentius Culleo, who would go on to be praetor in 187.

Leader of the House: the Princeps Senatus, who would be called upon to speak first in any debate. This was the third time that P. Scipio Africanus, the conqueror of Hannibal, had been honoured in this way (Livy 38.28).

Marcus Cato: M. Porcius Cato, known as Cato the Elder (234–149), had been consul in 195; he was beaten to the censorship of 189 by Flamininus in a particularly acrimonious election campaign (Livy 37.57–8), but succeeded on the next occasion, five years later. He was the subject of another of Plutarch's Lives (included in Oxford World's Classics *Roman Lives*).

Lucius: see chapter 3.

Valerius Antias: 1st-C. BCE historian, author of a lost history of Rome.

Cato himself: see Livy 39.42 and Cicero, *On Old Age* 12.42, in which Cato expounds his views on old age (hence its alternative title, *Cato the Elder* or *Cato Maior*). Plutarch himself also tells the story at *Cato the Elder* 17. The incident had occurred during Lucius' consulship of 192, so Lucius had gone through his brother's censorship unscathed.

became censor: in 184 BCE.

392 *on serious charges*: one of the responsibilities of the censors was to let out public contracts; on this occasion the bids accepted for public works were so low and those accepted for revenue-producing contracts so high that the successful bidders pressed to have the contracts revised. Flamininus championed their cause with substantial support in the Senate. See also

Plutarch, *Cato* 19, and Livy 39.44, and on the main issues surrounding Cato's censorship, A. Astin, *Cato the Censor* (Oxford, 1978), ch. 5.

no need for him to do so: for the first occasion, see chapter 1; the date of the second tribunate is unknown.

the battle in Phrygia: the battle of Magnesia in 190 in which the Romans defeated Antiochus III. In fact the battle took place in Lydia, not Phrygia. For Hannibal's presence at Antiochus' court, see chapter 9, with note.

Hannibal fled again: it was a requirement of Antiochus' peace treaty with Rome that he give up Hannibal (Polybius 21.43.11).

393 *Flamininus was unmoved*: Livy's presentation of these events is rather different (39.51). Far from Flamininus acting on his own initiative, Hannibal is one of the main reasons that he was sent (the other is Prusias' war with Eumenes); and Livy's Prusias is only too happy to give Hannibal up to further his own interest. Hannibal would have been in his mid-sixties at the time (183 or 182 BCE).

poisoning attempt: the Roman consul Gaius Fabricius wrote to Pyrrhus warning him of an attempt on his life (*Pyrrhus* 21).

394 *but first*: a different list is attributed to Hannibal at *Pyrrhus* 8 (Pyrrhus, Scipio, himself). If there is any basis to the story, then we might follow Livy (35.14) in dating the meeting in Ephesus to 193.

Aristonicus: laid claim to the Attalid throne after the death of Attalus III in 133, perhaps with reason (he may have been the illegitimate son of an earlier king, Eumenes II), but any claim he had was not accepted by Rome. He led a sustained campaign against Rome until his final defeat in 130.

Mithradates: in the First Mithradatic War (89–85) the king of Pontus won over most of the cities in Asia Minor and invaded mainland Greece, exposing the fragility of Roman rule in the East. Despite being defeated in the first war he continued to cause problems for Rome until Pompey led a successful campaign that resulted in Mithradates' suicide in 63.

slaughtered and scourged: Gaius Marius was a very successful Roman general celebrated for his defeat of invading northern tribes and Jugurtha in North Africa. He held the consulship seven times, including five years in succession. Forced to flee Rome by Sulla, his return several years later led to a notorious bloodbath, vividly described in Plutarch's *Marius* 43–5 (included in Oxford World's Classics *Roman Lives*).

395 *did not die on the battlefield*: his death in 174 was, however, marked by an impressive funeral put on by his son. The whole affair lasted four days and included seventy-four gladiators fighting over three days (Livy 41.28). He would have been in his mid-fifties when he died.

COMPARISON OF PHILOPOEMEN AND FLAMININUS

396 *Archedemus*: one of the Aetolian commanders at Cynoscephalae (Polybius 18.21.5).

TEXTUAL NOTES

ALEXANDER

4.3: Reading τὸν κεραυνοφόρον with the MSS and recent editors, without Coraes's emendation.
7.2: Reading κατάρτυσιν with Hamilton.
7.9: Retaining μετὰ with the MSS.
10.3: A lacuna in the text should presumably be filled with something like this, and τὸν 'Αλέξανδρον changed to τοῦ 'Αλεξάνδρου.
15.3: Punctuating with a comma after στήλην, with Hamilton.
16.1: Reading τῆς εἰσόδου τῆς ἀρχῆς with Ziegler.
16.11: Reading <πρὸς> ἑτέραν δὲ with Hamilton.
17.6: Reading προσεχεῖς . . . πάτους with an anonymous editor and Ziegler.
20.13: Reading <καὶ> ἠσκημένα with Sintenis.
21.9: Reading κατὰ τὸ κάλλος with Stephanus, and keeping the words in their original place in the text.
26.6: Reading ἀνῆπται with Powell.
26.14: Retaining the MSS text without a lacuna.
32.1: Reading ἐπελθόντας with the Aldine edition.
33.8: Reading ἀποπτυρόμενοι with Held.
34.3: Retaining τι μεθέξων with the MSS.
35.1: Reading 'Αδιαβηνοῖς with Kramer.
35.13: The word 'naphtha' and at least one theory have dropped out of the transmitted text.
37.2: There is almost certainly a lacuna in the text, which would have contained a mention of the capture of Persepolis, which is then referred to simply as 'there' in the rest of the paragraph.
39.7: Retaining ἐνδόξως ἄγε with the MSS.
42.6: Retaining ἀνυδρίαν with the MSS.
47.1: Reading προσέλαβε and omitting <πεῖραν> with an anonymous editor.
47.1: Reading ἐνώπιον with Ziegler. But it seems to me that more is wrong with this sentence. The sense we want is something like: '. . . at the moment, as long as the barbarians could see them face to face, <they regarded them as true men>, but that if all they did . . .'.
47.2: Reading ἀφιέναι γε τοὺς βουλομένους ἐφῆκε μαρτυράμενος, without, therefore, a lacuna in the next line, with Coraes.
49.3: Reading Δίμνος here and below, with Ziegler, following Curtius and Diodorus.
51.4: Omitting Ziegler's added ἐὰν.
51.6: Reading 'Αριστόνου with Palmer.
51.8: There is no need to posit a lacuna here.
58.6: Hamilton points out that there is no need to read a lacuna here, as the Teubner does.

60.1: Reading ἀντιπόρους with one MS and recent editors.
60.15: Retaining τοὺς αὐτονόμους with the MSS.
62.4: Reading Σανδρόκοττος with Ziegler, here and below.
68.6: Reading πόλεων with Reiske.
75.2: There is a short lacuna in the text.
77.4: The text is corrupt, but the sense is secure.

DEMOSTHENES

3.2: A word or two—perhaps just the word for 'a saying'—have dropped out of the text.
14.4: Reading Θεόπομπος with some MSS. See B. L. Cook, 'Theopompus, Not Theophrastus: Correcting an Attribution in Plutarch, *Demosthenes* 14.4', *American Journal of Philology*, 121 (2000), 537–47. Plutarch wrote 'Theophrastus' again for 'Theopompus' in ch. 25 below.
19.3: Retaining ἐπὶ δὲ τούτῳ with the MSS.
22.5: I have supplied a few words (from 'just as . . .') to fill a lacuna in the text.
23.6: Retaining ἐν with the MSS.
25.8: see note to §14.4 above.

PHOCION

2.6: Retaining περιελιττομένην with the MSS.
29.3: Reading τ<οι>οῦτο (Waterfield).
30.1: Retaining the MSS καί.

EUMENES

5.8: The last two clauses contain gaps, but they can be filled with a reasonable degree of certainty.

DEMETRIUS

4.2: Reading ἐπανελθὼν with some MSS.
5.4: Reading ἐπειπὼν with Emperius.
9.5: Reading Παγαῖς (Kaltwasser) or Πηγαῖς (see *Aratus* 43.1).
9.9: Reading πάντως with Campe.
12.3: Reading ᾧπερ ... προσενυφῆναι with P.
19.2: Reading Μήδειος with Wilamowitz.
36.10: The text is a little corrupt, but the sense is plain enough.

PYRRHUS

3.3: Reading ἐχόμενος with K and Flacelière.
16.11: Reading τῆς δόξης ... τὴν ἀρετὴν with Madvig.
21.7: Retaining ὑλώδη with the MSS.

29.1: Reading αὐτὸν with P.
30.1: Reading φιλονεικία for the incomprehensible (and much emended) ἀλκὴ (Waterfield).

ARATUS

3.3: Reading γεγονέναι κομψότερον <εἰκὸς > with Henry ap. Porter.
6.2: Reading ἐξ ὀλίγου (Waterfield).
8.5: Reading ἐπῆλθεν with the majority of the MSS.
12.2: Retaining Μοθώνης with the MSS. Since this place on Cape Malea is otherwise unknown, and is not the famous Methone in the south-west Peloponnese (though that too could also be spelled 'Mothone'), we might as well preserve the received text.
12.2: Reading Ὑδρέας with Bergk.
13.5: Reading διήλειψεν with an anonymous editor and Flacelière.
14.4: Reading στάλαις (line 2; anon.) and δασμὸν (line 5; Orsi).
16.1: Reading Ἀβαιοκρίτου with Wilamowitz.
18.5: Retaining just ἄγουσαν with the MSS.
19.3: Reading προ<ελ>έσθαι (Waterfield).
23.2: Reading κατακρατεῖσθαι with the MSS.
25.3: Reading <ἀνάξιον> ἄνθρωπον with Kronenberg.
35.5: Reading περὶ <τῶν> αὐτῶν with Manfredini.
38.4: Reading (cf. *Cleomenes* 11.3) περιοίκων instead of μετοίκων ('resident aliens'), though the mistake may have been Plutarch's or his amanuensis's.
38.8: Retaining the MSS καίτοι.
40.1: Reading οὐδεὶς with Flacelière.
41.1: Reading οὐ πολλοί with PR.
41.4: Retaining the MSS ποιεῖν.
45.1: Retaining the MSS ὅτι.
49.1: Reading ἀναλύουσα with Mittelhaus.
52.3: Retaining the MSS φθορὰν.
53.5: Deleting τοῦ μηνὸς with Porter.

AGIS AND CLEOMENES

18.3: Reading τοῦ θεοῦ with Bryan. But possibly Plutarch forgot that it was Agis, not Cleombrotus, at Athena's altar.
18.4: Reading τοὺς πρὸ τοῦ ἐφόρους with Schneider.
25.10: Deleting μάτην with Richards. The word, meaning 'in vain', is out of place here, but it is hard to explain its presence. It has perhaps become detached from its proper context, but quite where it might belong is unclear to me.
44.3: Reading διασπάσαι with Harrison.
48.2: Conjecturing τοῦ ἀρτοποιῆσαι (Waterfield).
52.8: Reading this sentence as a question; the omission of the question-mark at line 13 is probably a misprint in the Teubner.

56.1: Reading δι' ἀπορίαν ὡς οἶμαι with some combination of the MSS.
56.4: Reading <οὐ> μετρίως with Reiske.

PHILOPOEMEN

1.5: Reading ἀπεργασόμενοι with AK.
9.9: Reading κάδων with Erbse.
9.9: Transposing this last clause from a couple of lines later, with Schaefer.
18.10: Retaining ἀφιστάμενος with the MSS.
21.8: A word or two appears to have dropped out of the text; I have added 'as they marched'.

FLAMININUS

12.12: Reading ἔοικε with Hecker.
14.2: Reading Τουδιτανὸν with Flacelière.

GLOSSARY

aedile Roman magistrate, elected annually with particular responsibility for the maintenance of the city of Rome, an optional early stage in a Roman political career.

archon the term for public officials in many Greek states. In Athens from the 5th C. BCE archons were usually chosen by lot and held the post for only a year; thus they were concerned more with routine administration than the exercise of political power. The chief archon, the eponymous archon, gave his name to the year. In many states one of the archons was called the **polemarch**, literally 'war-leader'.

Assembly (Athenian) known as the *ekklēsia*, this was the main decision-making body of the city of Athens; attended by adult male citizens. Its usual meeting-place was the Pnyx but it also met in the Theatre of Dionysus.

Attica the immediate territory (*khōra*) of Athens, largely rural and covering about 2550 km² (roughly 1,000 mi²).

Boeotarch the seven Boeotarchs were the chief officials of the federal Boeotian League.

Cavalry Commander (Hipparch) in the Achaean League this was a senior post, filled by election. In general, for instance in the Macedonian army, it was an important military position.

censor one of the most prestigious positions in the Roman state; two censors were elected for eighteen months every four or five years, with responsibility for overseeing the citizen lists, organizing state contracts, and general supervision of morals, in which latter role they might review the membership of the Senate. The post was usually restricted to ex-consuls.

city-taker (*helepolis*) elaborate, towered siege-engine used by Demetrius in his siege of Rhodes. It helped give him his epithet Poliorcetes (the Besieger).

Companion (*Hetairos*) one of an elite group of nobles who surrounded and advised the Macedonian king. The term 'Companions' also referred to the Macedonian cavalry.

consul along with his colleague in the office, the consul was the chief magistrate of the Roman state. He was elected annually and had both civil and military responsibilities.

cubit *see* **stade**

Council (Athenian) known as the *boulē*, this was a body of 500 (600 after 307/6) male citizens over the age of thirty that prepared business for the Assembly and carried out routine civic administration. Membership was for a year and selection was by lot.

diadem cloth band signifying kingship that was wrapped around the head, with the ends loose. Its origins are uncertain.

dithyramb choral hymn in honour of Dionysus.

ephebes young men undertaking various forms of training (military, physical, and intellectual) usually centred on the gymnasium. In 4th-C. Athens this involved two years of compulsory military training around the age of eighteen, but by the early 3rd C. training was no longer compulsory and lasted only a year.

ephor one of a board of five civil magistrates in Sparta, elected annually with extensive powers.

Forum the main public space in Rome, situated beneath the Capitoline and Palatine hills.

Friend (of a Hellenistic king) formal title designating those closest to the king in a Hellenistic court (Greek: *philos*).

greave leg-protectors, worn especially by hoplite soldiers.

guest-friendship a relationship between families of different communities that may go back generations. It imposed on them obligations of reciprocal hospitality.

gymnasiarch civic official responsible for overseeing the gymnasium.

helots serf-like population in Laconia and neighbouring Messenia.

hippodrome stadium for horse- and chariot-racing.

hoplite Greek heavy infantry soldier; *see* **phalanx**.

Hypaspist member of elite infantry unit in the Macedonian army.

legate Roman senators assigned to serve a provincial governor or general abroad.

legion largest Roman infantry unit, composed of between 4,200 and 5,000 men, divided into thirty units known as maniples.

libation ritual pouring of a liquid such as wine onto the ground as a way of honouring gods, heroes, or the dead.

medimnus a Greek measurement of capacity for dry commodities, roughly 52 litres (11 gallons).

mna *see* **talent**

Ocean, the sea that surrounds the inhabited world (*oikoumenē*) so that the latter forms a huge island that could in theory be circumnavigated.

oligarchy literally 'rule of the few', characterized by restrictions on political rights and eligibility for office, and sometimes emphasis on the council rather than the assembly. In Greek political theory it was opposed to democracy; in practice, especially in the Hellenistic period, the dividing-line was much hazier.

paean a song addressed to the divine, commonly in thanks or making a request.

perioeci literally 'those who live around', especially used of the free non-Spartiate population of Laconia that could live in perioecic cities such as Gythium.

phalanx, phalangites the massed body of heavy infantry, whether in traditional Greek hoplite formation armed with short spear and shield, or the

Macedonian phalanx with its long pike (*sarissa*), as developed by Philip II and Alexander.

praetor Roman magistrate below the level of consul, annually elected, with judicial responsibilities in Rome and military duties outside it. There were six praetors each year in the 2nd C. BCE.

proconsul an ex-magistrate given the power to act as if he held the office of consul ('pro-' meaning 'in place of'). This was especially useful when a commander on campaign needed his term of office extended.

Pythia priestess of Apollo at Delphi, famous for her prophetic utterances.

rhapsode a performer trained in the recitation of epic poetry, especially that of Homer.

satrap regional governor of the Persian empire.

Senate an aristocratic council of 300 ex-magistrates (senators), effectively the governing body of the Roman state, even though in theory its role was advisory.

Silver Shields an elite Macedonian infantry unit.

Spartiate a full Spartan citizen.

stade 600 Greek feet or 400 cubits. Ancient writers are not consistent in their use of the stade as a unit of measurement, but 8 stades are roughly equivalent to 1 mile and 5 stades close to a kilometre.

stoa a covered colonnade, walled to the rear and open at the front, often along the side of a public space.

sycophant individuals who habitually brought private prosecutions against fellow citizens for personal gain.

symposium aristocratic male drinking-party.

talent a very large sum of money, equivalent to 26 kg or 57 lbs of silver or 60 mnas.

tribune of the people one of ten (elected annually by the plebeian assembly), whose traditional duty was to protect plebeians, that is to say, the bulk of the Roman citizen body. They had the right to propose laws and to veto the acts of other magistrates or even a decree of the Senate. To be distinguished from military tribunes, who were senior officers within a legion.

trireme a long Greek warship, powered by three banks of rowers, although with mast and sails for long voyages. In various forms this was the standard warship for most of antiquity.

triumph a Roman procession celebrating military victory.

trophy dedication of enemy arms on the battlefield after a victory.

tyrant a military dictator, ruling a Greek city, often backed by mercenaries and an outside power such as Macedon.

BIOGRAPHIES OF PROMINENT FIGURES

Antigonus I Monophthalmus (the One-Eyed) (*c*.382–301 BCE) was a Macedonian noble who became one of the most powerful generals in the wars of the Successors. He served first Philip II, then Alexander, who in 333 appointed him satrap of Greater Phrygia in Asia Minor. In his late fifties at the time of Alexander's death, he aligned himself with Antipater against Perdiccas and Eumenes. He was as skilled a political operator as he was a general, something very necessary in the complex mix of warfare and ever-changing alliances that characterized the years immediately after Alexander's death. By the winter of 317/16, when he defeated Eumenes at Gabene in the heart of the old Persian empire, he had control of a territory that extended from the Aegean to the furthest edges of Iran. His unconcealed ambition provoked his rivals to form a coalition against him, which led to a short-lived peace in 311 and ultimately to Antigonus' death at the battle of Ipsus ten years later. In the meantime, Antigonus showed himself adept at manipulating public opinion and his own self-image. In 315 at Tyre he declared himself the champion of Greek freedom, in 306 he and his son Demetrius Poliorcetes were the first to take the title of king, and a year or so before his death they together revived Philip's League of Corinth.

Antigonus II Gonatas (*c*.320–239 BCE) was the son of Demetrius Poliorcetes and Phila, a daughter of Antipater, and grandson of Antigonus Monophthalmus. He was the ruler of Macedon from around 277 until his death. He inherited from his father the title of king and his military bases in Greece, but he did not have a kingdom until victory over the Celts who had invaded and destabilized Macedon gave him the chance to claim the Macedonian throne. Antigonus' reign was considerably longer than that of his father a decade earlier and brought Macedon much-needed stability. He led a recovery in Macedonian fortunes both at home and abroad, winning back control of Thessaly and re-establishing Macedonian hegemony in the rest of Greece. In contrast to his grandfather's support for Greek freedom, however, Antigonus wielded his influence through garrisons and tyrannies. As a result he also had to deal with challenges to Macedonian authority, such as the Chremonidean War of the 260s, when several Greek states including Athens allied with Ptolemy II of Egypt against him. This resistance may have been broken, but he was unable to stop the rise of the Achaean League in the 240s and with it Aratus' seizure of his main Peloponnesian stronghold, the Acrocorinth, in 243, a few years before his death. He was succeeded by his son Demetrius II, who ruled for ten years.

ANTIPATER (*c.*397–319 BCE) was an influential figure in Macedonian politics over many decades. He was close to Philip II, acting as his ambassador to Athens in 346 and again in 338 after Chaeronea. During Alexander's campaigns in the East he stayed behind as governor of Macedonia with responsibility for maintaining Macedonian authority in Greece and the surrounding areas, crushing Spartan resistance under Agis III. Alexander's death in 323 sparked a vigorous Greek revolt, led by Athens and the Aetolians, known as the Lamian War. Victorious, he installed an oligarchy in Athens, overseen by a Macedonian garrison. More significantly, he sought to bring stability to a vast Macedonian empire that was struggling in the face of many competing interests, but the effectiveness of his settlement at Triparadeisus in 320 was undermined by his death shortly afterwards. At that settlement Antipater took on the role of regent for the two kings, a move that would lead to conflict between Polyperchon, who inherited the regency, and his son Cassander, who did not.

CASSANDER (died 297 BCE) was the eldest son of Antipater and ruler of Macedon from 316 until his death. His date of birth is uncertain, but he may have been in his mid-thirties or older at the time of his father's death in 319. He had remained in Macedon during Alexander's campaign, which means that little is known about his life during those years. At Triparadeisus in 320 Antipater became regent for the two kings, but on his death he bequeathed this role not to Cassander but to an older general, Polyperchon, who had recently returned from Asia with Craterus. Cassander was made deputy but, unhappy with this, he allied himself to Antigonus Monophthalmus. By 316 he had gained control of Macedon and soon was a leading figure in the coalition against his erstwhile ally and mentor. In the last decade of the third century his control of mainland Greece was seriously undermined by the campaigns of Demetrius Poliorcetes, but was re-established after the victory at Ipsus in 301. Shortly before this, in *c.*304, Cassander took the title of king and began minting coins in his own name. He may have gained a certain legitimacy by marrying Alexander's half-sister by Philip II, Thessalonice (after whom he named a city), but he did a thorough job of eliminating the more immediate members of Alexander's family, being responsible for the executions of his mother Olympias, his wife Rhoxane, his son Alexander IV, and indirectly his illegitimate son Heracles.

CRATERUS (died 320 BCE) was one of Alexander's most reliable and trusted generals, extremely popular with the soldiers. He accompanied Alexander throughout the campaign, until in 324 he was sent back to

Macedon to replace Antipater as governor of Macedonia. He only reached as far as Cilicia when news came that Alexander had died. He then continued to Greece, where he assisted Antipater in the suppression of the Greek rebellion against Macedon (the Lamian War). Far from replacing Antipater, he formed an alliance with him and married his daughter Phila. But advancing into Asia Minor to tackle the forces of Perdiccas, he was defeated and killed in battle against Eumenes. His widow would go on to marry Demetrius Poliorcetes and become the mother of the Macedonian king Antigonus Gonatas.

DEMADES (*c.*380–319 BCE) was an Athenian politician and orator who became particularly influential after the Athenians' defeat at Chaeronea in 338, but little is known of his life before then. Captured in the battle, he subsequently played an important role in the negotiations that led to the peace settlement between Philip and Athens. In the next two decades he cautioned restraint in dealing with Macedon (advising against involvement in the revolts of Thebes and Agis) and interceded with Macedon where necessary (dissuading Alexander from pursuing the extradition of various anti-Macedonian politicians, including Demosthenes). In 324/3 he proposed that Alexander be given divine honours, only to be prosecuted for this after Alexander's death, but his services were required again for the negotiations with Antipater that brought the Lamian War to a conclusion. But in 319 Cassander unexpectedly executed him for allegedly intriguing with Perdiccas against Antipater.

LYSIMACHUS (*c.*350s–281 BCE) became one of Alexander's seven Bodyguards in 328, an elite group close to the king. After Alexander's death he was allocated Thrace as his satrapy, which would eventually become the basis of his kingdom. Much of his early years here were spent consolidating his rule in the region. His first wife was Antipater's daughter Nicaea. He was part of the coalition that sought to put a check on Antigonus' ambitions (see *Antigonus I Monophthalmus* above). In *c.*305 he followed Antigonus in adopting the title of king. It was the defeat of Antigonus and Demetrius at Ipsus that really changed his fortunes. As a result he acquired large swathes of territory in Asia Minor, including Ephesus, where his fortifications are still visible. After the death of Cassander in 297 he also directed his attention towards Macedon. In the late 290s he suffered the ignominy of being captured by Dromichaetes, a chief of the Getae, and then being released in exchange for renouncing possessions beyond the Danube. A dynastic dispute, supposedly engineered by his young wife Arsinoe, a daughter of Ptolemy I, led to the death of Agathocles, his son by his first wife, and prompted the intervention of Seleucus, who defeated and killed Lysimachus in the ensuing battle of Corupedium in 281.

PERDICCAS (died 321 BCE), son of Orontes, was a Macedonian noble, roughly the same age as Alexander. He was one of the seven elite Bodyguards and an able military commander (despite the negative coverage he received in Ptolemy's memoirs). It was a sign of his status that he was the recipient of the dying Alexander's signet ring in 323. Perdiccas then used the settlement at Babylon to reinforce his position, obtaining control over the main contingents of the army. Antipater and Craterus, however, were suspicious of his intentions and invaded Asia Minor to curb his growing power. In the meantime Perdiccas attempted to launch an assault on Ptolemy in Egypt, but the campaign went so badly wrong that he ended up being killed by his own soldiers.

PHILIP II (382–336 BCE) was king of Macedon between 359 and his assassination in 336. When he came to the throne Macedon was a weak and unstable kingdom at the mercy of outside powers, whether marauding Illyrian tribes or interventionist Greek states. He transformed the kingdom into one that dominated Greece, first making major reforms to the army, then establishing Macedonian authority over Thessaly, and afterwards gradually extending Macedon's influence southwards. How to respond to Philip was something that divided cities, as the speeches of Demosthenes and Aeschines testify at Athens. Greek resistance to Philip was broken at the battle of Chaeronea in 338, when he defeated the combined forces of Athens and Thebes. The following year he established the League of Corinth (as it is now known), that gathered all Greek states together under his leadership, although Sparta was a notable exception. Here he announced his intention to conduct a war of revenge against Persia, a campaign that was just beginning when he was assassinated.

PHILIP V (238–179 BCE) was an Antigonid king of Macedon, the son of Demetrius II, who had died in 229. Too young to rule in his own right, Philip was adopted by Antigonus Doson, whom he succeeded in 221. Philip's reign began with the kind of conflict to which Macedonian kings would have been accustomed, the Social War between the Aetolians and their allies and Macedon's Hellenic alliance, which had been established by Doson at the time of his agreement with Aratus' Achaean League. But soon Philip was having to deal with a new and unfamiliar state, Rome. Roman intervention in Illyris in the early 220s would have made Macedon aware of their power and the challenge it posed to Macedonian interests in the western Balkans. In 215 Philip made a treaty with the Carthaginian Hannibal, who was at that time in Italy inflicting a series of devastating defeats on Rome. The Romans responded, albeit not immediately, by making an alliance with Macedon's enemy, the Aetolians, in what has become known as the First Macedonian War (214–205), a name that reflects the way the historical focus is increasingly on Rome. Peace allowed the Romans to concentrate on defeating Carthage, but the conflict resumed in 200, and this time its impact on Philip was far more serious. Defeat at Cynoscephalae in Thessaly in 197 forced him to come to terms and relinquish most of his possessions outside Macedon. Now an ally of Rome, he cooperated with them in their campaign against Nabis, and in the one against Antiochus III and the Aetolians. As Philip took steps to revive Macedon, his relations with Rome deteriorated and Roman interference in the succession led Philip to execute his pro-Roman son Demetrius, leaving the way open for his eldest son Perseus to succeed unopposed.

PTOLEMY I SOTER (SAVIOUR) (*c*.367–282 BCE), son of Lagus, was the founder of the Ptolemaic dynasty in Egypt. A Macedonian noble, he served on Alexander's campaign, and from 330 was one of his elite Bodyguards. In the settlement of Babylon that followed Alexander's death he received the satrapy of Egypt. Although making Egypt his base, he was keen to expand his territory, something that often brought him into conflict with Antigonus and Demetrius. Early targets were the neighbouring regions of Cyrene and Coele-Syria, and the island of Cyprus that he lost to Demetrius in 306 (and won back in 295). Later his naval influence extended right into the Aegean, where he took control of or perhaps even founded the League of Islanders. He adopted the title of king in 305, shortly after Antigonus and Demetrius. Alexander was especially important in the Ptolemaic self-image: Ptolemy kidnapped Alexander's body from Perdiccas, made Alexandria the seat of his royal residence, and wrote his own account of Alexander's campaigns. The dynastic succession was relatively smooth, with his son by Berenice sharing the throne with him for the last three years of his life.

SELEUCUS I NICATOR (CONQUEROR) (*c*.358–281 BCE), son of Antiochus, was the founder of the Seleucid dynasty, whose empire at its height covered much of the old Persian empire. He was a senior officer in Alexander's army, and after his death took over the command of the Companion cavalry. In 320, at Triparadeisus, he was awarded the satrapy of Babylonia, which he held until forced out by Antigonus in 316. After this he took refuge with Ptolemy, who helped him reclaim his satrapy in 312. A leading member of the anti-Antigonid coalition, he played an important role in the victory at Ipsus in 301, which enabled him to add northern Syria to his empire. Relations with Ptolemy deteriorated after Ipsus over competing claims to Coele-Syria, an issue that would continue to cause problems between the two kingdoms into the second century. This change is reflected in his marriage in 298 to Stratonice, the daughter of the recently defeated Demetrius. Even at the end of his life Seleucus was still aiming to expand his territories. Taking advantage of Lysimachus' succession problems, he invaded Asia Minor and defeated the king at Corupedium in 281. Advancing towards Macedon for his first sight of home in some fifty years, he was assassinated by Ptolemy Ceraunus, the eldest son of Ptolemy I, who, on being overlooked for the Egyptian throne, had taken refuge first with Lysimachus then with Seleucus. Again the Seleucid succession was smooth. Antiochus I had been co-ruler with his father since 294.

INDEX OF LITERARY AND HISTORICAL SOURCES CITED BY PLUTARCH

An asterisk identifies authors at least some of whose work is preserved in its entirety; the rest are known only through fragments, such as those quoted by Plutarch. See the *Oxford Classical Dictionary* (4th edn., 2012) for longer entries. Dates are BCE unless otherwise stated. A = *Alexander*, Ag = *Agis/Cleomenes*, Ar = *Aratus*, D = *Demosthenes*, Dm = *Demetrius*, E = *Eumenes*, F = *Flamininus*, P = *Philopoemen*, Ph = *Phocion*, Py = *Pyrrhus*.

Ister, third-century antiquarian, lived and worked in Alexandria: A46
Lamachus of Smyrna, author of a panegyric of Philip and Alexander, perhaps delivered at the Olympics of 324: D9
Letters, directly quoted: A7, 22, 28, 41, 47, 55 (Alexander); A39 (Olympias); Ag25 (Cleomenes III); Py21 (Gaius Fabricius)
*Livius, Titus (Livy), Roman historian of Rome, 59 BCE–17 CE: F18, 20
Lynceus of Samos, fourth-century comic poet, brother of Duris: Dm27
Marsyas, historian of Macedon: D18
*Menander of Athens, late-fourth-century poet of New Comedy: A17
Myrsilus of Methymna, third-century historian, especially of Lesbos: Ar3
Onesicritus of Astypalaea, encomiastic Alexander historian, accompanied eastern expedition as chief helmsman: A8, 15, 46, 60, 61, 65
Oracles: Ag9 (Pasiphaë); Ar53, Ph8 (Delphi); D19 (Sibylline verses, twice)
Panaetius of Rhodes, second-century Stoic philosopher: D13
Pappus, otherwise unknown source for Hermippus: D30
Philip of Chalcis, otherwise unknown author: A46
Philip of Theangela, otherwise unknown author: A46
*Philip V, king of Macedon 221–179, wrote epigram in response to Alcaeus: P9
Philippides, Athenian poet of New Comedy, late fourth/early third centuries: Dm12, 26
Philon of Thebes, otherwise unknown author: A46
Phylarchus of Naucratis (?), historian, covered period from death of Pyrrhus in 272 to death of Cleomenes III in 220: Ag9, 26, 49, 51, Ar38, D27, Py27
*Pindar of Cyncoscephalae in Boeotia, fifth-century praise-poet: Ar1, Dm42
*Plato, fourth-century Athenian philosopher: Dm1, 32, P14
Polemon of Ilion, geographer, early second century: Ar13
*Polybius of Megalopolis, second-century historian of Rome's rise to world empire: Ag46, 48, Ar38, P16
Polyclitus of Larisa, Alexander historian with a strong interest in geography: A46
Potamon of Mytilene, first-century rhetorician and historian: A61
Ptolemy I of Egypt, Alexander historian, died 283: A46
Pytheas, fourth-century Athenian politician, opponent of Demosthenes: D20
Royal Diary (Alexander III): A23, 76
Royal Notebooks (Pyrrhus): Py21
*Sappho, seventh/sixth-century poetess from Lesbos: Dm38
Sempronius Tuditanus, Gaius, consul 129, historian: F14
*Simonides of Ceos, lyric poet and epigrammatist, late sixth century to early fifth century: Ar45
*Sophocles, fifth-century Athenian tragic poet: A7, Ag1, D29, Dm45, 46, Ph1
Sotion, first-century CE Peripatetic author of miscellanies: A61
*Theophrastus of Eresus, philosopher and polymath, succeeded Aristotle as head of Lyceum, fourth to early third centuries: A4, Ag2, D14, 17, 25

INDEX OF PROPER NAMES

Authors are collected and more fully identified in the Index of Sources. Names which are mere patronymics or identifying birthplaces have been omitted, as have god names that occur in oaths. A = *Alexander*, Ag = *Agis/Cleomenes*, Ar = *Aratus*, D = *Demosthenes*, Dm = *Demetrius*, E = *Eumenes*, F = *Flamininus*, FcompP = *Comparison of Philopoemen and Flamininus* (at the end of these two Lives), P = *Philopoemen*, Ph = *Phocion*, Py = *Pyrrhus*.

MORE ABOUT **OXFORD WORLD'S CLASSICS**

American Literature

British and Irish Literature

Children's Literature

Classics and Ancient Literature

Colonial Literature

Eastern Literature

European Literature

Gothic Literature

History

Medieval Literature

Oxford English Drama

Philosophy

Poetry

Politics

Religion

The Oxford Shakespeare

A complete list of Oxford World's Classics, including Authors in Context, Oxford English Drama, and the Oxford Shakespeare, is available in the UK from the Marketing Services Department, Oxford University Press, Great Clarendon Street, Oxford OX2 6DP, or visit the website at www.oup.com/uk/worldsclassics.

In the USA, visit www.oup.com/us/owc for a complete title list.

Oxford World's Classics are available from all good bookshops. In case of difficulty, customers in the UK should contact Oxford University Press Bookshop, 116 High Street, Oxford OX1 4BR.

A SELECTION OF **OXFORD WORLD'S CLASSICS**

	Classical Literary Criticism
	The First Philosophers: The Presocratics and the Sophists
	Greek Lyric Poetry
	Myths from Mesopotamia
APOLLODORUS	The Library of Greek Mythology
APOLLONIUS OF RHODES	Jason and the Golden Fleece
APULEIUS	The Golden Ass
ARISTOPHANES	Birds and Other Plays
ARISTOTLE	The Nicomachean Ethics Politics
ARRIAN	Alexander the Great
BOETHIUS	The Consolation of Philosophy
CAESAR	The Civil War The Gallic War
CATULLUS	The Poems of Catullus
CICERO	Defence Speeches The Nature of the Gods On Obligations Political Speeches The Republic and The Laws
EURIPIDES	Bacchae and Other Plays Heracles and Other Plays Medea and Other Plays Orestes and Other Plays The Trojan Women and Other Plays
HERODOTUS	The Histories
HOMER	The Iliad The Odyssey

A SELECTION OF **OXFORD WORLD'S CLASSICS**

HORACE	The Complete Odes and Epodes
JUVENAL	The Satires
LIVY	The Dawn of the Roman Empire Hannibal's War The Rise of Rome
MARCUS AURELIUS	The Meditations
OVID	The Love Poems Metamorphoses
PETRONIUS	The Satyricon
PLATO	Defence of Socrates, Euthyphro, and Crito Gorgias Meno and Other Dialogues Phaedo Republic Symposium
PLAUTUS	Four Comedies
PLUTARCH	Greek Lives Roman Lives Selected Essays and Dialogues
PROPERTIUS	The Poems
SOPHOCLES	Antigone, Oedipus the King, and Electra
SUETONIUS	Lives of the Caesars
TACITUS	The Annals The Histories
THUCYDIDES	The Peloponnesian War
VIRGIL	The Aeneid The Eclogues and Georgics
XENOPHON	The Expedition of Cyrus

A SELECTION OF **OXFORD WORLD'S CLASSICS**

Thomas Aquinas	**Selected Philosophical Writings**
Francis Bacon	**The Major Works**
Walter Bagehot	**The English Constitution**
George Berkeley	**Principles of Human Knowledge and Three Dialogues**
Edmund Burke	**A Philosophical Enquiry into the Sublime and Beautiful** **Reflections on the Revolution in France**
Confucius	**The Analects**
René Descartes	**A Discourse on the Method** **Meditations on First Philosophy**
Émile Durkheim	**The Elementary Forms of Religious Life**
Friedrich Engels	**The Condition of the Working Class in England**
James George Frazer	**The Golden Bough**
Sigmund Freud	**The Interpretation of Dreams**
G. W. E. Hegel	**Outlines of the Philosophy of Right**
Thomas Hobbes	**Human Nature and De Corpore Politico** **Leviathan**
David Hume	**An Enquiry concerning Human Understanding** **Selected Essays**
Immanuel Kant	**Critique of Judgement**
Søren Kierkegaard	**Repetition and Philosophical Crumbs**
John Locke	**An Essay concerning Human Understanding**

A SELECTION OF **OXFORD WORLD'S CLASSICS**

NICCOLÒ MACHIAVELLI	**The Prince**
THOMAS MALTHUS	**An Essay on the Principle of Population**
KARL MARX	**Capital** **The Communist Manifesto**
J. S. MILL	**On Liberty and Other Essays** **Principles of Political Economy and Chapters on Socialism**
FRIEDRICH NIETZSCHE	**Beyond Good and Evil** **The Birth of Tragedy** **On the Genealogy of Morals** **Thus Spoke Zarathustra** **Twilight of the Idols**
THOMAS PAINE	**Rights of Man, Common Sense, and Other Political Writings**
JEAN-JACQUES ROUSSEAU	**The Social Contract** **Discourse on the Origin of Inequality**
ARTHUR SCHOPENHAUER	**The Two Fundamental Problems of Ethics**
ADAM SMITH	**An Inquiry into the Nature and Causes of the Wealth of Nations**
MARY WOLLSTONECRAFT	**A Vindication of the Rights of Woman**

A SELECTION OF **OXFORD WORLD'S CLASSICS**

	The Anglo-Saxon World
	Beowulf
	Lancelot of the Lake
	The Paston Letters
	Sir Gawain and the Green Knight
	The Poetic Edda
	The Mabinogion
	Tales of the Elders of Ireland
	York Mystery Plays
Geoffrey Chaucer	**The Canterbury Tales** **Troilus and Criseyde**
Guillaume de Lorris and Jean de Meun	**The Romance of the Rose**
Henry of Huntingdon	**The History of the English People 1000–1154**
Jocelin of Brakelond	**Chronicle of the Abbey of Bury St Edmunds**
William Langland	**Piers Plowman**
Sir John Mandeville	**The Book of Marvels and Travels**
Sir Thomas Malory	**Le Morte Darthur**

A SELECTION OF **OXFORD WORLD'S CLASSICS**

	An Anthology of Elizabethan Prose Fiction
	Early Modern Women's Writing
	Three Early Modern Utopias (Utopia; New Atlantis; The Isle of Pines)
FRANCIS BACON	**Essays** **The Major Works**
APHRA BEHN	**Oroonoko and Other Writings** **The Rover and Other Plays**
JOHN BUNYAN	**Grace Abounding** **The Pilgrim's Progress**
JOHN DONNE	**The Major Works** **Selected Poetry**
JOHN FOXE	**Book of Martyrs**
BEN JONSON	**The Alchemist and Other Plays** **The Devil is an Ass and Other Plays** **Five Plays**
JOHN MILTON	**The Major Works** **Paradise Lost** **Selected Poetry**
EARL OF ROCHESTER	**Selected Poems**
SIR PHILIP SIDNEY	**The Old Arcadia** **The Major Works**
SIR PHILIP and MARY SIDNEY	**The Sidney Psalter**
IZAAK WALTON	**The Compleat Angler**

A SELECTION OF **OXFORD WORLD'S CLASSICS**

	Travel Writing 1700–1830
	Women's Writing 1778–1838
William Beckford	**Vathek**
James Boswell	**Life of Johnson**
Frances Burney	**Camilla** **Cecilia** **Evelina**
Robert Burns	**Selected Poems and Songs**
Lord Chesterfield	**Lord Chesterfield's Letters**
John Cleland	**Memoirs of a Woman of Pleasure**
Daniel Defoe	**A Journal of the Plague Year** **Moll Flanders** **Robinson Crusoe** **Roxana**
Henry Fielding	**Jonathan Wild** **Joseph Andrews and Shamela** **Tom Jones**
John Gay	**The Beggar's Opera and Polly**
William Godwin	**Caleb Williams**
Oliver Goldsmith	**The Vicar of Wakefield**
Mary Hays	**Memoirs of Emma Courtney**
Elizabeth Inchbald	**A Simple Story**
Samuel Johnson	**The History of Rasselas** **Lives of the Poets** **The Major Works**
Charlotte Lennox	**The Female Quixote**
Matthew Lewis	**The Monk**

A SELECTION OF **OXFORD WORLD'S CLASSICS**

Henry Mackenzie	**The Man of Feeling**
Alexander Pope	**Selected Poetry**
Ann Radcliffe	**The Italian** **The Mysteries of Udolpho** **The Romance of the Forest** **A Sicilian Romance**
Clara Reeve	**The Old English Baron**
Samuel Richardson	**Pamela**
Richard Brinsley Sheridan	**The School for Scandal and Other Plays**
Tobias Smollett	**The Adventures of Roderick Random** **The Expedition of Humphry Clinker**
Laurence Sterne	**The Life and Opinions of Tristram Shandy, Gentleman** **A Sentimental Journey**
Jonathan Swift	**Gulliver's Travels** **Major Works** **A Tale of a Tub and Other Works**
John Vanbrugh	**The Relapse and Other Plays**
Horace Walpole	**The Castle of Otranto**
Mary Wollstonecraft	**Letters written in Sweden, Norway, and Denmark** **Mary and The Wrongs of Woman** **A Vindication of the Rights of Woman**

A SELECTION OF **OXFORD WORLD'S CLASSICS**

Ludovico Ariosto	**Orlando Furioso**
Giovanni Boccaccio	**The Decameron**
Luís Vaz de Camões	**The Lusíads**
Miguel de Cervantes	**Don Quixote de la Mancha** **Exemplary Stories**
Carlo Collodi	**The Adventures of Pinocchio**
Dante Alighieri	**The Divine Comedy** **Vita Nuova**
Galileo	**Selected Writings**
J. W. von Goethe	**Faust: Part One and Part Two**
Franz Kafka	**The Metamorphosis and Other Stories** **The Trial**
Leonardo da Vinci	**Selections from the Notebooks**
Lope de Vega	**Three Major Plays**
Federico Garcia Lorca	**Four Major Plays** **Selected Poems**
Niccolò Machiavelli	**Discourses on Livy** **The Prince**
Michelangelo	**Life, Letters, and Poetry**
Petrarch	**Selections from the Canzoniere and Other Works**
Luigi Pirandello	**Three Plays**
Rainer Maria Rilke	**Selected Poems**
Giorgio Vasari	**The Lives of the Artists**